LIBRARY OF HEBREW BIBLE/ OLD TESTAMENT STUDIES

458

Formerly Journal for the Study of the Old Testament Supplement Series

Editors
Claudia V. Camp, Texas Christian University
Andrew Mein, Westcott House, Cambridge

WOMEN IN THE SEX TEXTS OF LEVITICUS AND DEUTERONOMY

A Comparative Conceptual Analysis

Deborah L. Ellens

t&t clark

NEW YORK • LONDON

For my parents
Mary Jo Lewis Ellens
and
Jay Harold Ellens

With all my love

T & T Clark International, 80 Maiden Lane, New York, NY 10038

T & T Clark International, The Tower Building, 11 York Road, London SE1 7NX

T & T Clark International is a Continuum imprint.

The NewJerusalemU font used to print this work are available
from Linguist's Software, Inc., PO Box 580, Edmonds, WA 98020-0580 USA.
Tel (425) 775-1130. www.linguistsoftware.com

Library of Congress Cataloging-in-Publication Data
Ellens, Deborah L.
  Women in the sex texts of Leviticus and Deuteronomy : a comparative conceptual analysis
/ Deborah L. Ellens.
    p. cm. -- (The library of Hebrew Bible/Old Testament studies ; 458)
  Includes bibliographical references and index.
  ISBN-13: 978-0-567-02942-3 (hardcover : alk. paper)
  ISBN-10: 0-567-02942-5 (hardcover : alk. paper)
  1. Bible. O.T. Leviticus--Criticism, interpretation, etc. 2. Bible. O.T.
Deuteronomy--Criticism, interpretation, etc. 3. Women in the Bible. 4. Sex in the Bible. 5.
Women--Legal status, laws, etc. (Jewish law) 6. Jewish law. I. Title. II. Series.

  BS1255.6.W7E45 2007
  222'.1306082--dc22

                              2006038803

  06 07 08 09 10   10 9 8 7 6 5 4 3 2 1

Printed in the United Kingdom by Biddles Ltd, King's Lynn, Norfolk

CONTENTS

Part III
EXEGESIS 2—DEUTERONOMY TEXTS

ACKNOWLEDGMENTS

I am indebted to many individuals without whose help this study would have remained unpublished.

The Claremont School of Theology library staff went beyond the call of duty to facilitate my research. Koala Jones, Elaine Walker and Betty Clements: I am so grateful for your help with securing difficult-to-find books, checkout limits and interlibrary loan privileges. I do not exaggerate when I say that without your help, the task would have been impossible. From the bottom of my heart I thank you.

The conscientious and incisive editorial work of Duncan Burns was a significant factor in the preparation of my original manuscript for publication. Thank you, Duncan, for hard work and insightful advice.

I am grateful to Marvin Sweeney and Karen Torjesen for serving on the dissertation committee at the origination of this work. And I am grateful to Kristen de Troyer for friendship and encouragement. I owe more than can be described to Dr. Rolf P. Knierim, the chair of my dissertation committee. For all that he taught me and for his lasting support and encouragement I am truly thankful.

For friendship and extraordinary conversation, intellectual stimulation and professional encouragement, I thank you Mignon Jacobs.

My parents have supported me throughout every phase of this project. Their steadfast love has been a source of enduring strength. My husband's love and support has been unwavering. Thank you.

Above all, I am grateful to that One who has created me, given me breath and sustained me. You are All in all.

ABBREVIATIONS

ABD	*The Anchor Bible Dictionary*. Edited by D. N. Freedman. 6 vols. New York: Doubleday, 1992
AnOr	Analecta Orientalia
BAR	*Biblical Archaeology Review*
BASOR	*Bulletin of the American Schools of Oriental Research*
BBR	*Bulletin for Biblical Research*
BDB	*Hebrew and English Lexicon of the Old Testament*. Edited by Francis Brown, S. R. Driver and C. A. Briggs. Translated by Edward Robinson. Oxford: Clarendon, 1979
BHS	*Biblia Hebraica Stuttgartensia*. Edited by K. Elliger, W. Ruldolph et al. Rev. ed. Stuttgart: Deutsche Bibelstiftung, 1967/77
BTB	*Biblical Theology Bulletin*
BZAW	Beihefte zur Zeitschrift für die alttestamentliche Wissenschaft
CBQ	*Catholic Biblical Quarterly*
CD	Cairo Damascus Document
CH	Codex Hammurabi
D	Deuteronomic/Deuteronomistic Writings
DST	Deuteronomy Sex Texts
ExpTim	*Expository Times*
FCB	The Feminist Companion to the Bible
FOTL	Forms of the Old Testament Literature
HAR	*Hebrew Annual Review*
H	Holiness Code
HL	Hittite Laws
HS	Hebrew Studies
HTR	*Harvard Theological Review*
HUCA	Hebrew Union College Annual
HWJ	*History Workshop Journal*
IDB	*Interpreter's Dictionary of the Bible*. Edited by G. A. Buttrick. 4 vols. Nashville: Abingdon, 1962
IDBSup	*Interpreter's Dictionary of the Bible: Supplement Volume*. Edited by K. Crim. Nashville: Abingdon, 1976
IEJ	*Israel Exploration Journal*
Int	*Interpretation*
JAOS	*Journal of the American Oriental Society*
JASO	*Journal of the Anthropological Society of Oxford*
JBL	*Journal of Biblical Literature*
JBQ	*Jewish Bible Quarterly*
JBR	*Journal of Bible and Religion*
JETS	*Journal of the Evangelical Theological Society*
JHS	*Journal of the History of Sexuality*

JJS	*Journal of Jewish Studies*
JNSL	*Journal of Northwest Semitic Languages*
JQR	*Jewish Quarterly Review*
JSOT	*Journal for the Study of the Old Testament*
JSOTSup	Journal for the Study of the Old Testament: Supplement Series
JR	*Juridical Review*
JTS	*Journal of Theological Studies*
LH	Laws of Hammurabi
LST	Leviticus Sex Texts
LXX	Septuagint
MAL	Middle Assyrian Laws
MT	Masoretic Text
OT	Old Testament
P	Priestly Writings
PJ	Targum Pseudo Jonathan
Q	Qumran
RB	*Revue biblique*
RIDA	*Revue internationale des droits de l'antiquité*
RQ	*Restoration Quarterly*
SJOT	*Scandinavian Journal of the Old Testament*
TDOT	*Theological Dictionary of the Old Testament.* Edited by G. J. Botterweck, H. Ringgren and H. J. Fabry. Translated by J. T. Willis, G. W. Bromiley and D. E. Green. Grand Rapids: Eerdmans, 1974–
THAT	*Theologische Handwörterbuch zum Alten Testament.* Edited by E. Jenni and C. Westermann. 2 vols. Munich: Kaiser, 1971
ThWAT	*Theologisches Wörterbuch zum Alten Testament.* Edited by G. J. Botterweck, H. Ringgren, and H. J. Fabry. Stuttgart: W. Kohlhammer, 1970–95
UF	*Ugarit-Forschungen*
VT	*Vetus Testamentum*
ZAW	*Zeitschrift für die alttestamentliche Wissenschaft*

Part I

INTRODUCTION

Chapter 1

INTRODUCTION

A. *The Problem*

1. *Thesis of This Study*
a. *General Statement.* The writers of the biblical laws, like the writers of other legal corpora throughout history, considered the regulation of sex to be of some importance. Throughout history such regulation has been part of the total jurisprudential effort to preserve peace and order in any society. James A. Brundage states that "every human society attempts to control sexual behavior, since sex represents a rich source of conflicts that can disrupt orderly social processes."[1] Tikva Frymer-Kensky's observations with respect to sex in the Bible coincide with Brundage's remarks. She asserts that sexuality in the Bible has to do with "social control and behavior."[2] Its concern is "who with whom and when."[3]

A study and comparison of two groups of sex laws in the Bible, those in Leviticus and Deuteronomy, reveal that factors even more narrowly focused than the general desire to control social behavior shape the texts. These factors, comprised of the writer's motivations, intentions, and concerns, as reflected in the text, are responsible for differing conceptual matrices within Leviticus and Deuteronomy. Thus, while Leviticus and Deuteronomy share much in their worldviews regarding sexual intercourse, their overriding interests in this matter are different. Whereas the interest of the Leviticus sex texts (LST) is *ontology*,[4]

---

1. James A. Brundage, *Law, Sex, and Christian Society in Medieval Europe* (Chicago: University of Chicago Press, 1987), 1.
2. Tikva Frymer-Kensky, "Sex in the Bible," in *In the Wake of the Goddesses* (New York: Fawcett Columbine, 1992), 197.
3. Ibid., 197.
4. Deborah F. Sawyer, *God, Gender and the Bible* (London: Routledge, 2002), 9. J. Butler, *Gender Trouble: Feminism and the Subversion of Identity* (London: Routledge, 1990), ix. Deborah Sawyer, commenting on Judith's Butler's ideas about the status of identity-categories, aptly states the following: "Instead of understanding identity categories ontologically (primarily, as binary masculine and feminine gender underpinned with compulsory heterosexuality) and as informing and formulating particular socio-political contexts, they are, in fact, the products of those contexts. Clearly, the Bible, in both religious and cultural terms, can be understood as such a discourse par excellence that has *effected*—constructed—identity categories. But, as Butler points out, the institutions, practices and discourses that construct identity are themselves multiple and diffuse with their own histories." I agree, of course, with these statements. While my attribution of "ontology" to LST, in contradistinction to the attribution of "property" to DST, is a description of the *sort of exercise* in

that is, the classification or order of kinds and their relationships;⁵ the interest of
the Deuteronomy sex texts (DST) is *property*, that is, the man's ownership of

which the authors of LST and DST engage, it is *not* a description of the "meta-status" of the
categories which LST delineate or presume. That is, it is not a statement about their status as
necessary or contingent, essential or constructed. The categories which LST delineate explicitly, as
well as the implicit identity-categories which LST presume, are, indeed, both constructions, as
Sawyer states, following Butler. The quantum which LST "defend" or "argue for" is, however, an
ontology-quantum. It is that type of exercise. On the other hand, the quantum which DST "defend"
is a property-quantum. These are two different types of exercise. On the meta-level, DST's exercise
may be a sub-set of LST's exercise. However, it is an exercise with different aims and consequences.
The "meta-status" of delineated and presumed categories of either LST or DST is outside the bounds
of this study. See below. E. J. Lowe, *A Survey of Metaphysics* (Oxford: Oxford University Press,
2002), 13–14, defines "ontology" as follows: "...[Aristotle's] view was that metaphysics is the
science of being qua being, and for that reason conceptually prior to any special science with a more
limited subject matter. This view places *ontology*—the study of what categories of entities there are
and how they are related to one another—at the heart of metaphysics...metaphysics is concerned
with the fundamental structure of reality as a whole." Obviously, LST do not delineate a category of
entities which can be divided, for example, into universals and particulars. Nor are LST, a limited
selection of texts, concerned with "reality as a whole." I use the word "ontology" to mean only that
LST assume, as well as delineate, categories of kinds or entities and their relations, which are
significant for the world, which belongs to LST. Protection of that delineation is its primary concern.
The enterprise of the *sex texts in Leviticus* might be described more specifically as moral ontology, a
subset of a broader ontology. William Schweiker, "Power and the Agency of God," *Theology Today*
52 (July 1995): 205, describes moral ontology as follows: "...at the root of all cultures and communities is some moral ontology, some construal of the moral space in which human life takes place
and how persons and communities are to live in that space... I can isolate two features of a moral
ontology, that is, two features of critical reflection on the moral space of life aimed at providing
direction for how to live. First, a moral ontology presents a picture of the moral space of life, that is,
it provides a generalized description of how a community or society understands the domain of
human life and how to orient life within it. This feature of a moral ontology is, properly speaking, an
act of metaphysical reflection. The purpose is to provide an account of reality and the place of human
beings and moral values in reality... Second, a moral ontology is also the analysis of the basic
structure of the moral space of life." LST's aim is the moral space pertaining to sexual intercourse.
Charles Taylor, *Sources of the Self* (Cambridge, Mass.: Harvard University Press, 1989), 28, in his
discussion of moral ontology, elaborates on this moral space: "What this brings to light is the
essential link between identity and a kind of orientation. To know who you are is to be oriented in
moral space, a space in which questions arise about what is good or bad, what is worth doing and
what not, what has meaning and importance for you and what is trivial and secondary." LST protect
a kind of moral space for a particular orientation. DST do not. DST protect *one element* of a
particular orientation within a presumed moral space.

Thus, application of the term "ontology" (coined in the seventeenth century of the common era)
to LST's interest is heuristically useful, not for the sake of anachronistically anchoring LST within
the discipline of metaphysics; nor for attributing a certain status to the categories it delineates, but
rather for the sake of distinguishing LST's concerns from DST's concerns. Protection of "the
structure" or "the orientation" or "the moral space" is LST's primary concern. By contrast, protection of a particular type of owned-property, woman's sexuality, is the concern of DST.

5.   This attribution to the Priestly Writings (P) is, of course, nothing new. See Howard Eilberg-
Schwartz, *The Savage in Judaism: An Anthropology of Israelite Religion and Ancient Judaism*
(Bloomington: Indiana University Press, 1990), 218–21, and his comments on the attribution of
"ontology" to the priestly work of Leviticus. He suggests that this orientation in Leviticus is a direct
result of a priestly cosmogony, which can be found, incidentally, in Gen. 1:1–2:4. He states (p. 221):
"The two characteristics of the priestly taxonomy are precisely those that one might expect to find in

the woman's sexuality and its protection.[6] These differing interests influence subtle corresponding differences in the conceptualization of women in the two groups of texts.

b. *Specific Statement.* Three features reveal woman's conceptualization: (1) her marginalization, (2) her objectification and (3) her focalization.[7] A variety of textual components manifest these three features.

The primary component manifesting woman's marginalization is point-of-view. "Point-of-view," as I use it throughout this study, refers to the author's relationship to the audience which he addresses in the text. The author(s)/final-redactor(s) of both Leviticus and Deuteronomy has chosen an external narrator[8] to tell the larger story in which the sex laws are embedded.[9] This external narrator, in turn, describes a character such as Moses or Aaron as giving the laws to a human community, often at the explicit direction of Yhwh. Discernment of the redactional level, which is the source of the "voice" of the laws in their immediate context, is outside the parameters of this study. Nevertheless, I make a presumption that the author/redactor, whoever he was, would have accepted, as his own, the ideological stance of the laws *as he perceived it*, including the conceptualization of women. Since the parameters of this study exclude the larger contexts in which the sex laws are embedded, and presuming this ideological identification of author/redactor and "character lawgiver"; I refer throughout to the *author* as the one who addresses the community that receives the laws, leaving aside references to and questions concerning levels of narration derived from the larger context.

---

a system that links its classification scheme to God's activity at creation. In creating the world, God implanted distinct physical traits in objects so that Israel would be able to discriminate between them in the way that God wished. The physical characteristics are important, therefore, because they are concrete manifestations of divine will. In addition, the link between classification and creation may also explain the rigidity of the priestly scheme. Since the criteria of classification are fixed by God, no one has the power or right to tamper with them." Daniel Boyarin, "Are There Any Jews in 'The History of Sexuality'?," *JHS* 5 (1995): 343, writes: "What we must think of, in order to understand the levitical system, is the 'metaphysics' underlying it. These prohibitions belong to the Priestly Torah that emphasizes over and over in its account of the Creation in Genesis 1 that God has created from the beginning the separate kinds of creatures." See also Walter J. Houston, "Towards an Integrated Reading of the Dietary Laws of Leviticus," in *The Book of Leviticus: Composition and Reception* (ed. Rolf Rendtorff and Robert A. Kugler; Leiden: Brill, 2003), 158–60; idem, *Purity and Monotheism: Clean and Unclean Animals in Biblical Law* (JSOTSup 140; Sheffield: JSOT Press, 1993), 221–25.

6. This attribution to the Deuteronomic/Deuteronomistic Writings (D) and the distinction between LST and DST as an attribution to P and D is, of course, nothing new. See below under "Preliminary Clarifications."

7. See Chart 6 in the Appendix.

8. Mieke Bal, *Narratology: Introduction to the Theory of Narrative* (2d ed.; Toronto: University of Toronto Press, 1997), 22: "When in a text the narrator never refers explicitly to itself as a character, we may, again, speak of an external narrator (EN)."

9. By "larger story" I am referring simply to the narrative signals within the books themselves, such as, for example, Lev 1:1 where the narrator states: "And Yhwh called to Moses and spoke to him from the tent of meeting, saying…"

Thus, point-of-view, as I define it and use it, is indicated by such signals as the author's explicit reference to the addressee who receives the laws, his use of second and third person and his application of the taboos of the laws. Throughout all laws of LST and DST, point-of-view reveals gender asymmetry in the author's relationship to his audience. Woman's marginalization, as revealed by point-of-view, is always present. However, it may be complete or slightly mitigated.

The primary component manifesting the second feature, woman's objectification in the text, is the language-depicting-the-sex-act. "Language-depicting-the-sex-act" refers to that language which the author uses to describe or represent the act of sexual intercourse.[10] Within all laws of LST and DST, it reveals gender asymmetry. It is indicated by such signals as the grammar and syntax of the laws. Woman's objectification, as revealed by language-depicting-the-sex-act, is always present. In one rare instance, woman is the subject of a sexual gesture preceding the act of coitus.[11] Within some of the same laws she is the subject of acts unrelated to sexual activity. However, while these signals might be thought of as slightly mitigating the gender-polarizing effect of language-depicting-the-sex-act, they cannot nullify the fact that wherever the sex act is depicted, the woman is object and the man is subject.

The primary component manifesting the third feature, woman's focalization,[12] is the expectation the text harbors for the man and the woman with respect to the ideal which it "prescribes" for the community through the laws it

---

10. Athalya Brenner, *The Intercourse of Knowledge: On Gendering Desire and "Sexuality" in the Hebrew Bible* (Leiden: Brill, 1997). See Brenner's discussion, "Explicit Terms for Sexual Intercourse" on pp. 21–28.

11. Lev 20:17. In this law the sister "sees" her brother's nakedness, as he "sees" hers.

12. Bal, *Narratology*, 142–60. I have appropriated Bal's term "focalization," which she applies to narrative, for application to "law." While the legal materials of this study are embedded in narrative, and while casuistic law might be said to utilize some level or permutation of narrative, the legal materials of LST and DST belong to a genre recognizably distinct from narrative. My use of the term is therefore different from Bal's. I do not use "focalization" to represent what has generally been referred to by "point of view" with respect to narrative. Rather I use the term, narrowly and with specific emphasis, to refer to the way the "author" envisions the woman in relationship to the text's primary concern. This might be thought of as a kind of point of view but not the point of view which Ball describes for narrative texts. It refers to a distinction in the text different from the one she describes. In her study of narrative, Bal discards the use of "point of view" and replaces it with "focalization" for the following reasons (pp. 142–43): "I shall refer to the relations between the elements presented and the vision through which they are presented with the term *focalization*. Focalization is, then, the relation between the vision and that which is 'seen,' perceived... The theory of narration, as it has been developed in the course of this century, offers various labels for the concept here referred to. The most current one is *point of view* or *narrative perspective*. Narrative situation, narrative viewpoint, narrative manner are also employed... They are all, however, unclear on one point... They do not make a distinction between *those who see* and *those who speak*." Three elements are constitutive for my use of the term "focalization" with respect to the legal materials: (1) the primary concern of the text; (2) the woman character; and (3) the relationship of the woman character to that primary concern. The significant distinction is, therefore, the placement of the woman character vis-à-vis the primary concern of each law. That distinction is of value because it reveals differing conceptualities pertaining to woman's agency.

articulates.[13] Throughout the laws of LST and DST, this component reveals, to varying degrees and in various ways, depending on the law, either gender symmetry or gender asymmetry in the relationship of the woman and the man to the primary concern or intent of the law.

Women appear as characters in the text in one of three ways: (1) as agent, (2) as property, (3) as both agent and property. She is focalized, however, in one of four ways: (1) as agent, (2) as property, (3) as "forgotten" or (4) as "valued." In Lev 18:20, 19:20–22, 19:29, 20:10 and 21:9, woman's status as property is *a necessary element of the infraction*, but that *aspect* (property) of the infraction does not constitute the primary concern. These women have the "property" status of daughters or wives. While the daughter of Lev 19:29 does not act as an agent anywhere in the text, her status as "daughter-property" is not of concern to the law. That is to say, the security of that property vis-à-vis other male interests is irrelevant. Purity is the concern and the father's agency is limited for the sake of that concern. I call her focalization "valued" because she is not protected for the sake of any man's claims to or usurpation of her as "sexual-commodity." In Lev 19:29, the "daughter-property" is pictured as an agent with the power to harm her father. She is able to harm *because* she is his daughter; however, her "daughter-property" status is not the concern of the law per se. In Lev 18:20 and 20:10, the women are the "wife-property" of a man. This status is essential to the commission of the infraction; however, as will be shown below, the interest in that "wife-property" is not an interest to protect it vis-à-vis other male intrusions per se. In Lev 19:20–22, the woman's property status, a *legal* status, is the most polarized status among all women in LST. However, she is not *focalized* as property. She is focalized as "forgotten." With respect to the primary concern of the text, she is left aside. Some of the incest laws concern affines, but they are drawn into the list for blood considerations. As such, their "property-status" is incidental. Thus, a woman's status as property can be essential to commission of the infraction, even though that *aspect* of the infraction does not finally constitute the primary concern. Or her status as property can constitute the primary concern. Or she can be forgotten entirely with respect to the primary concern. Or, in one rare instance, she can be valued by the primary concern, such that a limitation is placed on the powers of her "male-owner."

The *focalization* of woman is indicated by a variety of textual features including the identification-of-women, the selection-of-laws, the reiteration-of-the-man-to-whom-the-woman-belongs and the structure-of-the-text.[14]

Where woman is not addressed or is addressed implicitly, she is marginalized. Where she is placed in the object slot of the grammar of the language-depicting-the-sex-act, she is objectified. Where the author's primary concern is to protect her sexuality as property, she is focalized as property. Where the author's primary concern is to protect an entity separate from her own body she is focalized as agent.

---

13. See n. 123 below.
14. These features are explained below in the exegesis of the texts.

Whereas woman's objectification is fairly straightforward and independent of her marginalization and her focalization; the latter two, by contrast, influence one another. For example, if the author explicitly addresses both men and women, chances are that he expects both of them to protect his primary interest or concern. If, on the other hand, the author explicitly addresses only the man, but a variety of features constituting woman's focalization indicates that he expects her to protect his primary interest as well, then we can surmise that he addresses her also, implicitly.

Throughout LST and DST, woman's marginalization and objectification remain relatively constant.[15] Her focalization, however, varies significantly. It is different in LST and DST.[16] In LST, for the most part, her focalization demonstrates a significant accrual of agency. She, as well as the man, must follow the laws in order to safeguard the classificatory principles which comprise the purity system of ancient Israel. LST protect this system from disorder and confusion or impurity. Thus, woman is focalized as an agent responsible for protecting a system beyond both herself and the man: a classificatory order. Where her status as property is essential to the scenario, that status serves the classificatory concern. By contrast, in DST the woman is focalized as the sexual property of the man, which can be stolen, damaged or surreptitiously misused. DST protect this property from other men. Thus, in DST woman appears in the text at times as agent but she is focalized as property. Her appearance as agent makes her responsible for protecting that property, which happens to be coterminous with herself: her sexuality. No larger concern than guarding her own sexuality, for the sake of the production of progeny, an enterprise devoted to the man's interest and welfare, belongs to her.

In this way the difference between the classificatory and the proprietary concerns of LST and DST respectively gives rise to different nuances in the conceptualization of women.[17]

2. *Preliminary Clarifications*

A more detailed, preliminary explanation of the terms "classificatory concern" and "proprietary concern" and their theoretical relationship, as well as their possible relationship in the "mind of the writers" of the laws, is essential for the exegetical and comparative study which follows.

I must emphasize that the point of this preliminary explanation is not to inform biblical scholars that Leviticus is concerned with classification or purity and Deuteronomy is concerned with property. These are, of course, well-known

---

15.   The conceptuality which generates their presence in the text may therefore be referred to by Knierim's term "*supratextual.*" See Rolf P. Knierim, *Text and Concept in Leviticus 1:1–9* (Tübingen: J. C. B. Mohr, 1992), 3.

16.   The conceptualities which generate woman's separate focalizations in LST and DST may, therefore, be referred to by Knierim's term "*intertextual.*" See ibid., 3.

17.   The focus of this study is the *effect* of the classificatory concern and the proprietary concern, which themselves are reflected as conceptual elements of the text. The focus of this study is not the ontology and the sociology per se, which have generated the text.

distinctions and alignments. Rather, the point is to lay the ground work which supports the assertion that these alignments lead to a significant difference in the conceptualization of women. Even though the purity/property distinction for the Priestly Writings (P) and the Deuteronomic/Deuteronomistic Writings (D) is common parlance among biblical scholars, the way in which it plays out with respect to the conceptualities inherent in the regulation of sex, including the conceptualization of women, has remained unrecognized.

a. *Classificatory Concern.* Jenson has proposed a model which he calls the "Holiness Spectrum,"[18] which serves as a tool for exploring "issues of classification, structure and grading" and "provides a framework for treating the various theories of holiness and purity" in P.[19] As a result of his overview, synthesis and critique of the various theories which have been proposed to explain purity,[20] he concludes that two in particular are most useful. He describes them as follows:

> Two theories stand out by virtue of their comprehensive scope and explanatory power. One is idealist, focusing on the human ability to classify the world, and to fuse together cultural, social and theological meanings. From this perspective holiness is wholeness and freedom from imperfection and anomaly, while impurity is defect and mixture. The other theory is realist, concentrating on the inescapable realities of death and life, and impurity points to death and expresses the negative side of the Priestly concern with life before the living God.
>
> The first theory is more suited to a structuralist approach, since it assumes stable, fixed structures or processes in terms of which deviations are significant. The second has a clearer referential content, and is concerned with irreversible events, events less amenable to a static structural analysis. However, these two approaches are often found to complement one another, and both may be related to the idea of order. Anomaly is as much an offence against an ordered world as is the destructive power of death. The Holiness Spectrum is one way to integrate the two theories through their common polar structure: normality–anomaly for one, and death–life for the other. Both are required to make sense of the full range of the Priestly world-view.[21]

---

18. Philip Peter Jenson, *Graded Holiness* (JSOTSup 106; Sheffield: JSOT Press, 1992), 36–38. See also Jacob Milgrom, "The Dynamics of Purity in the Priestly System," in *Purity and Holiness: The Heritage of Leviticus* (ed. M. J. H. M. Poorthuis and J. Schwartz; Leiden: Brill, 2000), 29–32; idem, *Leviticus 1–16* (New York: Doubleday, 1991), 253–58; David P. Wright, "The Spectrum of Priestly Impurity," in *Priesthood and Cult in Ancient Israel* (ed. Gary A. Anderson and Saul M. Olyan; JSOTSup 125; Sheffield: Sheffield Academic Press, 1991), 150–81.

19. Jenson, *Graded Holiness*, 88.

20. Ibid., 40–88.

21. Ibid., 88. Mary Douglas, *Purity and Danger* (London: Routledge & Kegan, 1966); idem, "The Abominations of Leviticus," in *Anthropological Approaches to the Old Testament* (ed. Bernhard Lang; Philadelphia: Fortress, 1985), 100–16. Douglas' theory as related in *Purity and Danger* is an example of the first kind of theory. See Jenson's discussion of her theory in *Graded Holiness*, 88. Feldman's theory is an example of the second kind of theory; see Emanuel Feldman, *Biblical and Post-Biblical Defilement and Mourning: Law as Theology* (New York: Ktav, 1977), 49. See also the following: Michael P. Carroll, "One More Time: Leviticus Revisited," in Lang, ed., *Anthropological Approaches to the Old Testament*, 117–26; L. William Countryman, *Dirt, Greed and Sex* (Philadelphia: Fortress, 1988), 24–27.

Jenson's statement that the two approaches "may be related to the idea of order" suggests that ultimately a concern for purity is a concern for classification or protection of boundaries, even if that concern manifests as a symbolic outworking of the death–life polarity.[22] In other words, whether "normality–anomaly" or "death–life" is the issue, a polarity is operative. The polarity itself is a classificatory structure. The following exegesis of LST and DST concurs with this assessment.[23]

My use of the term "classificatory concern" is, thus, interchangeable with other terms such as "purity concern," "protection of boundaries," "concern for classification" and "concern for order." However, understanding "purity concern" as a classificatory concern, and understanding "classificatory concern" as the protection of boundaries is useful for the sake of the comparison of LST and DST, because these particular correspondences reveal a common ground between the two groups of texts.

This common ground, in turn, leads to a fruitful comparison between LST and DST. Just as the purity concern of LST is a concern for protection of boundaries, so also is the proprietary concern of DST. In fact, theoretically speaking, the proprietary concern is a subset of the classificatory concern.[24] However, even

22. See also Houston, "Integrated," 159–61.
23. Jenson, *Graded Holiness*, 144. Jenson writes the following concerning Lev 18:6–23 and 20:10–21: "They list a number of sexual offences, including incest, adultery, bestiality and homosexuality. From a structural point of view, many of these can be understood as an illegitimate confusion of classes which should be kept distinct… But sexual integrity had a fundamental social and religious dimension. At the heart of the Priestly view of man and woman was a belief that the order of the world and society was based on marriage and the extended family. Any deviation from the norm threatened the stability and structure of Israel's existence as a holy people and was subject to severe legal sanctions (in most cases death)." However, as might be inferred from Jenson's earlier comments, even such "deviation from the norm" can be generalized as a concern for order; that is, a classificatory concern.
24. This assertion does not preclude the possibility that the entire "system" is subject to some kind of overarching moral principle. Hyam Maccoby, *Ritual and Morality: The Ritual Purity System and Its Place in Judaism* (Cambridge: Cambridge University Press, 1999), viii, states: "The proliferation of ritual rules in Judaism, especially in the area of ritual purity, tends to obscure the fact that ritual in Judaism is ultimately subordinate to morality, or, more accurately, exists as the self-identifying code of a dedicated group whose main purpose is ethical." The precise details of the purity system in ancient Israel, reflected especially but not exclusively in Leviticus, as well as the question whether or not a fundamental ethical principle ultimately governs the entire classificatory system, including ritual and moral impurity, is beside the point for this present study and out of its bounds. However, this study stands, along with Milgrom, Wright and others, on the premise that "ritual" and "moral" impurities are subject to a systemic whole and are, therefore, in some way "systematically interconnected." Wright, "The Spectrum," 151–52, states: "This paper…proposes and describes, in the first half, two main categories of impurities: tolerated and prohibited. The former are those usually called 'ritual' impurities and are the focus of the priestly (specifically P's) treatment of impurity. The latter are impurities arising from sinful situations. The paper argues that the two types are systematically interconnected and illustrates this by formulating a spectrum of impurity, ranging from least to most severe. Realizing that the two kinds of impurity are parts of a whole system becomes important for understanding the individual function and character of the different types of impurities. The second half of the paper discusses how the two types related to one another and shows, in particular, how the tolerated impurities may serve as means of supporting the larger moral

as a theoretical subset, the proprietary concern within DST differs from the classificatory concern within LST in two ways. First, it focuses on only one type of boundary—the boundary that protects a man's sexual property; whereas the classificatory concern focuses on many types of boundaries.

Second, in DST a shift with respect to the boundary and the primary concern of the law is apparent when compared with the same features in LST. Whereas the focus in LST is on boundaries and protection of their integrity per se, in DST the focus is exclusively on what the boundaries demarcate: property. DST are consumed with the idea that the property may be stolen or misused by another man. That is, DST are concerned primarily with the damage done to the male victim who is the owner of the property. The same kind of concern for the item which the boundaries demarcate is absent from LST. Rather, the concern in LST is that boundaries per se are crossed at all.

b. *Proprietary Concern*. The concern for property in the sex texts of Deuteronomy is a concern to guard and protect the sexuality of the woman. Other qualifications, as well, apply to the use of the word "property" in this study. Wegner,

---

order of society. In regard to this last point, it should be kept in mind that a lack of evidence makes explanation difficult. I have therefore used anthropological and sociological models to 'see behind' the priestly evidence. We should observe, moreover, that the priestly system of impurity and its larger system (or systems) of religion are prescriptive rather than descriptive, which means there may be a certain amount of idealization in the laws. Furthermore, priestly legislation as it stands may not describe a system of religion that was actually practiced, in and of itself, in history. It is perhaps to be considered a 'potential' system much like that of Ezekiel 40–48." See also the following: Jacob Milgrom, "Rationale for Cultic Law: The Case of Impurity," in *Thinking Biblical Law* (ed. Dale Patrick; Semeia 45; Atlanta: Scholars Press, 1989), 106: "Finally, it should be noted that the holiness of God is associated with His moral attributes (cf. Exod 34:6–7). It therefore follows that the commandments, Israel's ladder to holiness, must contain moral rungs. It is then no wonder that the quintessential program for achieving holiness, Leviticus chapter 19, is a combination of moral as well as ritual injunctions. Conversely, impurity, the opposing doctrine to holiness, cannot be expected to consist solely of physical characteristics. It must *ipso facto* impinge on the moral realm. This amalgam is achieved by the prescriptions for the חַטָּאת, the purification offering." Again from David P. Wright, "Two Types of Impurity in the Priestly Writings of the Bible," *Koroth* 9 (1988): 191: "But leaving open the absorbing issue of whether the permitted impurities are to be considered sinful, the spectrum of impurity offered here helps us see the interrelation of what are for us diverse kinds of evil. It comprehends all adverse conditions or actions, unintended or intended, that are deleterious to what is holy, be that God, his sanctuary, his people's land, or particular individuals among his people. If all these conditions or actions are not sins, they all are at least a threat to what is holy and hence must either be, when serious, avoided, or when less grave, controlled. For the Priestly writer, *all the defilement-creating conditions were of the same conceptual family*." From LST only one pericope belongs to the "ritual impurity" texts: Lev 15. The rest belong to the "moral impurity" texts. Jonathan Klawans has offered a brief and excellent overview of the issue in his "The Impurity of Immorality in Ancient Judaism," *JJS* 48 (1997): 1–16. See the following additional works for a thorough discussion of the subject: N. Kiuchi, *The Purification Offering in the Priestly Literature* (JSOTSup 56; Sheffield: JSOT Press, 1987); Jonathan Klawans, *Impurity and Sin in Ancient Judaism* (Oxford: Oxford University Press, 2000); Maccoby, *Ritual*; Jacob Neusner, *The Idea of Purity in Ancient Judaism* (Leiden: Brill, 1973); idem, "Uncleanness: A Moral or an Ontological Category in the Early Centuries AD?," *BBR* 1 (1991): 63–88; David P. Wright, *The Disposal of Impurity* (Atlanta: Scholars Press, 1987).

exploring the subject of women in the Mishnah, has offered a useful distinction defining property and personhood in her study. Since her discussion reveals several important subtleties which are applicable to the biblical text, she is worth quoting at some length:

> What distinguishes a legal *person* from a legal *chattel*? *Personhood* means the legal status defined by the complex of an individual's powers, rights, and duties in society. An entity possessing no powers, rights or duties is no person at all but merely an object or *chattel*. For instance, some slaveholding societies prescribe neither rights nor duties for slaves. If the law mandates no food ration and sets no limit to the work load, owners may treat slaves as they wish, even starve them or work them to death. The slave is a mere beast of burden, an animate chattel. Other cultures may legislate rights and duties for slaves, *pro tanto* recognizing their personhood. All societies have rules, whether customary or written, that define the relative status of men, women, and children as well as various subgroups within society. The ratio of an individual's entitlements to his or her obligations defines the level of personhood. So in order to assess the level of an individual's personhood in the mishnaic system, we must know the extent of his or her powers, rights and duties—and above all how his or her personal status sets legal bounds to them.[25]

Wegner explains that even though the ratio of powers and rights to duties determines an individual's level of personhood,[26] duties as well as powers and rights are a "mark of personhood."[27] She writes:

> The possession of legal duties as much as the enjoyment of legal rights is a mark of personhood, because the imposition of duties implies that the bearer possesses the intelligence and morality to carry out such duties without physical compulsion. Suppose a man's household includes wives, slaves, and cattle. If the system assigns duties to the wives but not to the slaves or the oxen, then even though all three are set to work, only the wives count as persons. Slaves, like oxen, are chattels in that system—not because they lack morality and intelligence, but because the system chooses to ignore their possession of those faculties.[28]

These powers, rights and duties, as Wegner suggests, are determined by gender as well as by the legal limitations of an individual's "personal status."[29]

Discernment of the limits set by personal status is thus as essential as discernment of the ratio of powers, rights and duties for the purpose of identifying an individual's level of personhood. An understanding of the significance of the limits set by personal status requires a comparison of the powers, rights and duties comprising the statuses of the various "characters" in the text; since, as Wegner states, "those who possess more claims on others than others have on them enjoy higher status than those who owe many duties to others and have few claims against them."[30] Thus, as Wegner states, such comparisons necessarily

25.   Judith Romney Wegner, *Chattel or Person?* (New York: Oxford University Press, 1988), 10–11.

26.   Ibid., 12.

27.   Ibid., 12.

28.   Ibid., 11.

29.   Ibid., 11–12.

30.   Ibid., 12.

reveal that "the level of woman's personhood is governed not only by her gender, it depends also on her legal relationships to specified men or on the lack of such relationships."[31]

Hence, fathers have rights to disposal of and remuneration from their daughter's sexuality while mothers do not have the same rights with respect to either their sons' or daughters' sexuality. Husbands and fiancés have rights to exclusive use of their wives' sexuality while wives do not have such rights to their husband's sexuality. The status of mothers and wives limits their powers and rights as compared to the powers and rights afforded to fathers and husbands by their status.

However, the powers and rights of the average mother and wife become apparent when her status is compared to the status of women such as the war bride and the שִׁפְחָה. Thistlethwaite, agreeing with Wegner, states the following:

> There are degrees of sexual property within Israel, and these degrees come in to play particularly with the treatment of concubines and slaves, i.e., those women sold into servitude or captured in war.[32]

Only two of the sex laws of LST and DST treat women who are either "servant/slave" or "captured in war": Lev 19:20–22 and Deut 21:10–14. The war bride of Deut 21:10–14 becomes the sexual property of a man in a manner different from the average Israelite woman. So also, the שִׁפְחָה of Lev 19:20–22 is bound to and exchanged by a man in a manner different from the average Israelite woman. Westbrook makes this distinction obvious in the following comments:

> …The rules that governed the condition of female slaves are of particular jurisprudential interest because they arose from a conflict between family law, which applied to slaves as persons, and property law, which applied to slaves as chattels. Sometimes the one institution prevailed, sometimes the other, and sometimes the rules represented a compromise between the two. The legal framework for sexual relations between free persons was either concubinage or marriage. Both applied to female slaves, but in differing measure. Since a female slave was property her owner could exploit or dispose of her sexuality like any other beneficial aspect of property. She could thus be made her owner's concubine or could be given in concubinage to another at her owner's behest. Where concubinage resulted in motherhood, however, the slave might be accorded some qualified protection from the consequences of her status as property.[33]

The average Israelite woman, as represented in sex texts other than Lev 19:20–22 and Deut 21:10–14, is sexual property because of the way the powers, rights

---

31. Ibid., 12.

32. Susan Brooks Thistlethwaite, "'You May Enjoy the Spoil of Your Enemies': Rape as a Biblical Metaphor for War," *Semeia* 61 (1993): 64. Countryman, *Dirt*, 153, states: "Not all property was governed by the same rules; human property could not be disposed of in exactly the same ways as animals or land. The Torah prescribed that slaves, for example, were not to be treated in the same way as cattle: one might deal with one's cattle as one wished, but one must not deliberately kill one's slave (Exod. 21: 20–21)."

33. Raymond Westbrook, "The Female Slave," in *Gender and Law in the Hebrew Bible and the Ancient Near East* (ed. Victor H. Matthews, Bernard M. Levinson and Tikva Frymer-Kensky; JSOTSup 262; Sheffield: Sheffield Academic Press, 1998), 214–15.

and duties of fathers, husbands and fiancés are configured with respect to marriage or the process of arranging marriage, in contradistinction to the powers, rights and duties of women. The women in these laws are sexual property because they are the daughter of someone and will someday become the wife of someone; or because they are the wife of someone; or because they are in the process of becoming the wife of someone. However, although they are property *in this respect*, they have certain rights, even if these rights are a function of their relationship to the men to whom they belong. They cannot be "taken" in the way a war bride is taken. And they cannot be "sold" in the way a שִׁפְחָה is sold.[34]

Wegner's model, which tracks powers, rights and duties, examines the treatment of women with respect to legal categories. My model, which tracks marginalization, objectification and focalization, examines the treatment of women with respect to literary[35] categories. However, the legal categories are present within my model as well.

For example, the slight amelioration of woman's marginalization and woman's focalization as agent imply her legal *duty* to uphold the law. Furthermore, they imply that her *duty* to uphold the law in LST is similar to the man's duty, whereas in DST it is different from the man's duty. Accordingly, this *duty* itself implies that both she and the man have the *right* to non-contamination in LST, even if the categories constituting contamination are configured differently for men and women. In DST, as the man has the *right* to protection of his property; so also she, as that property, has the *right* to be protected, even if her protection as property is a function of gender asymmetry. Her focalization both as agent and as property in DST implies her *duty* to the man to whom she belongs. Furthermore, it reveals that the man does not have the same *duty* to her with respect to his own sexuality. In addition, she is never protected from the man who owns her. That conceptuality is non-existent in both LST and DST. Accordingly, her focalization as the sexual property of the man implies his *right* to exclusive use of her sexuality and her lack of such *right*. In addition, this feature reveals the man's *power* to acquire, exchange and use her, as well as her lack of reciprocal *power*. Finally, the presence of property components in LST, which

---

34. Ibid., 223. While "ownership implied the exclusive right to exploit the sexuality of a female slave" in ways that were not possible with wives, those legal rights could also be curtailed, as Westbrook observes (p. 215): "Where concubinage resulted in motherhood, however, the slave might be accorded some qualified protection from the consequences of her status as property." And again (p. 217): "The contract protects the concubine from exploitation by the patron or from sale by the patron, his heirs, or his client, the immediate owner." Westbrook's discussion applies to the "legal framework of sexual relations between free persons" in the ancient Near East. That legal framework consisted of either concubinage or marriage (p. 214). Property law dealt with the former for the most part; family law with the latter (p. 214). However, Westbrook observes the following (pp. 237–38): "Finally, mention should be made of the special legal mechanism employed to regulate the status of a female slave. Where the property and family interests in her person were located in different persons, the law employed a subtle jurisprudential device: her legal personality was split between them, the two parts being governed by property and family law respectively. No better symbol could have been devised for the conflicting attitudes of the law towards the female slave."

35. I mean "literary" in the sense of "rhetorical" rather than "source-critical."

do not constitute its primary concern, indicate that, with respect to marriage, even in LST men have *rights* which women lack and women have *duties* which men lack.

One more difference between Wegner's methodology and my own must be noted. Wegner finds that the sages who wrote the Mishnah "vacillate" between treating women as chattel and as person, as if woman were some kind of "taxonomic conundrum" like the "*koy*."[36] Wegner has no problem discerning which texts deal with "proprietary interests" since they are the texts in which a man has a claim on a woman's sexuality.[37] My study, within its respective field, is narrower than hers. While her study is open to a treatment of all the texts of the Mishnah concerning women, I treat only the texts dealing with sexual intercourse in the Hebrew Bible. Such proprietary interest is not the concern of every biblical text treating sexual intercourse, even if it is often apparent that the female sexuality under discussion in some respect "belongs" to a particular man. Texts which do not have property as their primary interest focalize women differently than those that do.

Although Wegner's model is not actively used throughout this study, her qualifications and definitions are worth remembering, since her distinction between chattel and personhood is operative in this study.

c. *Intersection of Classificatory and Proprietary Concerns.* As stated above, if classificatory concerns are a concern for order and preservation of boundaries, then proprietary concerns are a subset of classificatory concerns. However, a decision by the author to regulate classificatory issues is different from a decision by the author to regulate property issues. These two issues, while theoretically related, constitute different foci as primary concerns with consequences for the treatment of women.

Nevertheless, wherever in LST a law occurs, regulating sexual intercourse with respect to the marriage bond, property issues, at least partially, constitute the classificatory concern even though the focus of the law is not on property per se. Conversely, in the rare instances in DST where laws regulating incest or bestiality occur, classificatory issues partially constitute the proprietary concern even though the focus of the law is not on classification per se. While the metaphysics of sex tells us that both property and purity components in varying ratios constitute most but no all sexual infractions, the primary concern of the text, rather than the metaphysics of the sex infraction, dictates whether property or purity issues are at stake in the laws.

That is to say, LST know, understand and sympathize with the proprietary concerns which are prominent in DST. In the same way, DST know, understand and sympathize with the classificatory concerns which are prominent in LST. The classificatory concerns, however, are not the interest of DST. Nor are the proprietary concerns the interest of LST. The property component, implicit in

36. Wegner, *Chattel*, 7.
37. Ibid., 19.

some LST, serves the classificatory interest just as the classification component implicit in some DST serves the proprietary interest.

Thus, the property and purity *components* of the *infractions* which the laws regulate must be distinguished from the property and purity *concerns* of the *texts* within which the laws stand.

3. *History of Research*

A brief discussion of two topics situates this present study within the history of research. The two topics are: (1) the purity/property distribution in the sex texts and (2) the construction of gender.

a. *Purity/Property Distribution.* Prior to 1990, only a handful of studies focused on "sex in the Bible." Among these works, both popular[38] and scholarly,[39] a

---

38. These discussions, written for the layperson, are general and are structured topically. Either they cite biblical texts in the course of their discussion, mostly by footnote or endnote, or they collate and summarize relevant texts under their chosen topics. Their aim is to inform and advise the reader concerning standards of conduct regarding his or her own twentieth-century sexual affairs. Thus, their final concern is hermeneutical or apologetic. They include such works as the following: William Graham Cole, *Sex and Love in the Bible* (New York: Association, 1959); Michael R. Cosby, *Sex in the Bible* (Englewood Cliffs: Prentice–Hall, 1984); Kevin Harris, *Sex, Ideology and Religion: The Representation of Women in the Bible* (Brighton, UK: Wheatsheaf; Totowa, N.J.: Barnes & Noble, 1984); Tom Horner, *Sex in the Bible* (Rutland: Charles E. Tuttle, 1974); Gerald Larue, *Sex and the Bible* (Buffalo: Prometheus, 1983); Frank L. Perry, Jr., *Sex and the Bible* (Atlanta: Christian Education Research Institute, 1982). David Carr's 2003 publication, *The Erotic Word: Sexuality, Spirituality and the Bible* (Oxford: Oxford University Press, 2003), is a valuable improvement on this kind of approach to sex in the Bible.

39. These studies are more focused in their treatment of the text than the popular literature. Often, but not always, they leave aside the explicit agenda of helping the contemporary individual with standards governing his or her own sexual practice. Prior to 1990, only a handful of scholarly studies made "sex in the Hebrew Bible" their primary focus. These include the following: Countryman, *Dirt*; Tikva Frymer-Kensky, "Law and Philosophy: The Case of Sex in the Bible," *Semeia* 45 (1989): 89–102; O. J. Baab, "Sex," *IDB*, 817–20; C. R. Taber, "Sex, Sexual Behaviour," *IDBSup* 297–301; Raphael Patai, *Sex and Family in the Bible and the Middle East* (Garden City, N.Y.: Doubleday, 1959). Out of this group Patai's and Countryman's works offer valuable hermeneutical insights. Patai's work builds a hermeneutic by way of comparative study. Countryman's work builds a hermeneutic by way of a systematic exegesis. Discussions concerning sex in the Bible also occur in the context of numerous studies of the more general topic "women in the Bible": Johs. Pedersen, *Israel: Its Life and Culture* (London: Oxford University Press, 1926), 60–81; Leonard Swidler, *Biblical Affirmations of Woman* (Philadelphia: Westminster, 1979), 139–57. Several works appeared prior to 1990 treating the subject of women and sex in the context of Judaism: Rachel Biale, *Women and Jewish Law* (New York: Schocken, 1984); Louis M. Epstein, *Marriage Laws in the Bible and the Talmud* (Cambridge, Mass.: Harvard University Press, 1942); idem, *Sex Laws and Customs in Judaism* (New York: Ktav, 1968); Leonard Swidler, *Women in Judaism* (Metuchen: Scarecrow, 1976), 126–66; Wegner, *Chattel*, especially pp. 12–14. This list, of course, does not include citations from copious material extant in the Mishnah. In addition to these treatments, many occasional scholarly articles treating specific exegetical problems with bearing on some individual sex texts appeared prior to 1990. These are too numerous and wide-ranging to cite. One example of this sort of work is Wenham's article on בתולה, which appeared in 1972: Gordon J. Wenham, *"Bᵉtûlāh 'A Girl of Marriageable Age,'"* *VT* 22 (1972): 326–48. A second example is the collection of articles concerning Num 5:11–31, previously published and gathered together in Alice Bach, ed., *Women*

systematic comparative study of women in the sex texts of Deuteronomy and Leviticus is lacking.[40] Since 1990, the number of studies devoted to "sex in the legal texts of the Hebrew Bible" has increased dramatically.[41] However, a systematic comparative study remains to be done of these two groups of texts.

---

in the Hebrew Bible (New York: Routledge, 1999), 461–522. A third example is the scholarly discussion on levirate law, which took place in the 1970s and earlier, continuing, of course, to this day. See the exegesis of Deut 25:5–10 below. Relevant citations for these kinds of works can be found in the footnotes of the discussion of each text which follows.

40. Studies comparing the Holiness Code or Priestly Writings with the Deuteronomic/Deuteronomistic Writings treat the sex texts minimally. If they explore them at all, they do so without specific interest in the women of these texts. Cholewinski, for example, makes a few comparative remarks concerning the treatment of women in the course of his discussion of the Holiness Code and Deuteronomy. But they are brief and peripheral to the main concerns of his study. See Alfred Cholewinski, *Heiligkeitsgesetz un Deuteronomium* (Rome: Biblical Institute Press, 1976), 289, 297, 298.

41. The following works are examples of treatments of the general topic of sexuality in the Hebrew Bible: Carr, *The Erotic Word*; Frymer-Kensky, "Sex in the Bible"; idem, "Sex and Sexuality," *ABD* 5:1144–46; Alice A. Keefe, "Women, Sex and Society," in *Woman's Body and the Social Body in Hosea*, Gender, Culture, Theory 10; Sheffield: Sheffield Academic Press, 2001); Daniel Seth Kunin, *The Logic of Incest: A Structuralist Analysis of Hebrew Mythology* (JSOTSup 185; Sheffield: Sheffield Academic Press, 1995); Meir Malul, *Knowledge, Control and Sex: Studies in Biblical Thought, Culture and Worldview* (Tel Aviv–Jaffa: Archaeological Center, 2002); Ken Stone, *Sex, Honor and Power in the Deuteronomistic History* (JSOTSup 234; Sheffield: Sheffield Academic Press, 1996). Other works which treat the specific topic of law and sexuality in the Hebrew Bible include the following: Calum M. Carmichael, *Law, Legend, and Incest in the Bible: Leviticus 18–20* (Ithaca, N.Y.: Cornell University Press, 1997); Danna Nolan Fewell and David M. Gunn, "The Subject of the Law," in *Gender, Power, and Promise: The Subject of the Bible's First Story* (Nashville: Abingdon, 1993); Ilona Rashkow, *Taboo or Not Taboo: Sexuality and Family in the Hebrew Bible* (Minneapolis: Augsburg Press, 2000). The following have the subject of "family law and women" or "law and women" in Deuteronomy and/or Leviticus as their main focus: Cheryl B. Anderson, *Women, Ideology, and Violence: Critical Theory and the Construction of Gender in the Book of the Covenant and the Deuteronomic Law* (London: T&T Clark International, 2004); Sarah J. Melcher, "The Holiness Code and Human Sexuality," in *Biblical Ethics and Homosexuality: Listening to Scripture* (ed. Robert L. Brawly; Louisville, Ky.: Westminster John Knox, 1996), 87–102; Carolyn Pressler, *The View of Women Found in the Deuteronomic Family Laws* (Berlin: de Gruyter, 1993). Engelken's work is an example of a study which does not treat the legal material with systematic focus but does treat elements of the text that have a direct bearing on the subject of women in the legal material; see Karen Engelken, *Frauen im alten Israel* (Stuttgart: Kohlhammer, 1990). Discussions which address themselves to sex and women in the context of Judaism have continued to appear since 1990. They include: Leonie J. Archer, *Her Price is Beyond Rubies: The Jewish Woman in Graeco-Roman Palestine* (JSOTSup 60; Sheffield: JSOT Press, 1990); Jeanne Becher, ed. *Women, Religion and Sexuality* (Philadelphia: Trinity, 1990); Daniel Boyarin, *Carnal Israel: Reading Sex in Talmudic Culture* (Los Angeles: University of California Press, 1993); Judith Plaskow, *Standing Again at Sinai* (San Francisco: Harper, 1990). The number of works, books and occasional articles treating the subject of homosexuality in the Hebrew Bible since 1994 is a manifold increase over studies treating the subject prior to that year. The current discussion now compels a wider relevance to more general subjects concerning gender: Boyarin, "'The History of Sexuality'?"; Bernadette J. Brooten, *Love Between Women: Early Christian Responses to Female Homoeroticism* (Chicago: University of Chicago Press, 1996); James B. DeYoung, *Homosexuality: Contemporary Claims Examined in Light of the Bible and Other Ancient Literature and Law* (Grand Rapids: Kregel, 2000); Robert A. J. Gagnon, *The Bible and Homosexual Practice: Texts and Hermeneutics* (Nashville: Abingdon, 2001); David M. Halperin, *How to Do the History of*

Nevertheless, occasional or implicative and sometimes substantive remarks by scholars about laws from LST and DST demonstrate one of two tendencies relevant to the comparative enterprise.

1) *Adultery Debate*. The first tendency is apparent, most prominently but not exclusively, in its association with the scholarly debate concerning adultery in Deuteronomy. That debate has centered primarily on the contrast between "criminal" and "tortuous" as qualifications of the biblical adultery laws.[42] Thus, one of the primary questions is whether the laws of adultery mediate individual property concerns, community concerns, religious concerns, or a combination of the latter two. As a result of this discussion, a contingent of scholars, with some variation, has posited that the adultery laws of Deuteronomy are crimes, not torts. In short, they are not laws which mediate property issues.[43] When scholars

Homosexuality (Chicago: University of Chicago Press, 2002); idem, *One Hundred Years of Homosexuality and Other Essays* (New York: Routledge, 1990); Martti Nissinen, *Homoeroticism in the Biblical World: A Historical Perspective* (trans. Kirsi Stjerna; Minneapolis: Fortress, 1998); Ken Stone, ed., *Queer Commentary and the Hebrew Bible* (JSOTSup 334; Sheffield: Sheffield Academic Press, 2001); Saul M. Olyan, " 'And with a Male You Shall Not Lie the Lying Down of a Woman': On the Meaning and Significance of Leviticus 18:22 and 20:13," *JHS* 5 (1994): 179–206; Michael L. Satlow, " 'They Abused Him Like a Woman': Homoeroticism, Gender Blurring, and the Rabbis in Late Antiquity," *JHS* 5 (1994): 1–25; Ken Stone, "Gender and Homosexuality in Judges 19: Subject–Honor, Object–Shame?," *JSOT* 67 (1995): 87–107. In addition to the above-cited works, two commentaries are excellent resources for some aspects of "sex and women in the Hebrew Bible": Athalya Brenner and Carol Fontaine, eds. *A Feminist Companion to Reading the Bible: Approaches, Methods and Strategies* (FCB; Sheffield: Sheffield Academic Press, 1997); Carol A. Newsom and Sharon H. Ringe, eds., *Women's Bible Commentary: Expanded Edition with Apocrypha* (Louisville, Ky.: Westminster John Knox, 1998).

42. Raymond Westbrook, "Punishments and Crimes," *ADB* 5:548. Westbrook explains the difference between crimes and torts as follows: "A tort is conceived of purely as a personal wrong against the victim. The initiative for proceeding against the tort-feasor (guilty party) is solely in the hands of the victim, and the purpose of the court's intervention is to *compensate* the victim for any harm caused him. A crime, by contrast, is conceived of as a wrong to society, in which the harm to the particular victim is incidental—indeed, there may be no specific victim at all. The initiative is in the hands of the state, which may proceed irrespective of the victim's wishes; and the purpose is to *punish* the offender." See also Martin J. Buss, "The Distinction Between Civil and Criminal Law in Ancient Israel," in *Proceedings of the Sixth World Congress of Jewish Studies* (ed. Avigdor Shinan; Jerusalem: Jerusalem Academic Press, 1977), 51–62.

43. For a brief summary of this debate and its development, see Raymond Westbrook, "Adultery in Ancient Near Eastern Law," *RB* 97 (1990): 542–80. See also Pressler, *View of Women*, 34–35 n. 41. This discussion originated with observations comparing the nature of adultery in the biblical texts with the nature of adultery in other ancient Near Eastern texts. See the following: Epstein, *Sex, Laws and Customs*, 199; Moshe Greenberg, "Some Postulates of Biblical Criminal Law," in *Yehezkel Kaufmann Jubilee Volume* (ed. M. Haran; Jerusalem: Magnes, 1960), 5–28; Walter Kornfeld, "*L'adultere dans l'orient antique*," *RB* 57 (1950): 92–109; E. Neufeld, *Ancient Hebrew Marriage Laws* (New York: Longmans, Green & Co., 1944), 169.

These comparisons generated the qualifications "private offence against the husband" and "sin against God" to describe the infraction of adultery referred to in these laws. Scholars applied the former to ancient Near Eastern adultery law and the latter to biblical adultery law. A subsequent development in the discussion compared Deuteronomy adultery laws with "earlier biblical adultery laws." See the following: David Daube, "Biblical Landmarks in the Struggle for Women's Rights,"

make such an assertion, the implication is that women themselves as property or their sexuality as property is not an issue in these laws.[44] I contend to the contrary that in DST property is precisely the issue, whereas in LST it is not.

Westbrook has noted that although torts are generally less serious infractions than crimes, "the same act may be both a tort and a crime."[45] Furthermore, he states that the crime/tort distinction derives from the modern legal system and that ancient Near Eastern legal systems worked differently.[46] He suggests three overlapping categories as a more pertinent description. The first category consists of infractions of low moral culpability which are equivalent to torts in modern legal systems. The initiative for righting the wrong is in the hands of the victim and the role of the court is to award compensation. The second category consists of infractions of high moral culpability. The effect of these infractions is intangible pollution. Society takes the initiative of righting the wrong by killing or exiling the offender. The third category of infractions is equivalent to crimes in

---

JR 23 (1978): 177–79; Henry McKeating, "Sanctions against Adultery in Ancient Israelite Society, with Some Reflections on Methodology in the Study of Old Testament Ethics," *JSOT* 11 (1979): 64; Anthony Phillips, *Ancient Israel's Criminal Law* (New York: Schocken, 1970), 14–16, 110–17; idem, "The Decalogue—Ancient Israel's Criminal Law," *JJS* 34 (1983): 1–20; idem, "Another Look at Adultery," *JSOT* 20 (1981): 3, 14–15; idem, "Some Aspects of Family Law in Pre-Exilic Israel," *VT* 23 (1973): 349–61; Louis Stulman, "Sex and Familial Crimes in the D Code: A Witness to Mores in Transition," *JSOT* 53 (1992): 47–63; Moshe Weinfeld *Deuteronomy and the Deuteronomic School* (Winona Lake, Ind.: Eisenbrauns, 1992), 283–85, 291; idem, "Deuteronomy: The Present State of Inquiry," in *A Song of Power and the Power of a Song* (ed. Duane L. Christensen; Winona Lake, Ind.: Eisenbrauns, 1993), 34.

These latter comparisons used a similar distinction, attributing "criminal" to the adulterous infractions of Deuteronomy's laws and "tortuous" to the adulterous infractions of "earlier biblical law." Thus, the primary observation in the case of both forms of the discussion, with some variation, is that, in biblical law or in Deuteronomy, adultery is a crime or a sin against the community or God rather than a tort against the husband. A number of scholars have challenged this view in both its original form and in its subsequent developments. See the following: Arnold A. Anderson, "Law in Old Israel: Laws Concerning Adultery," in *Law and Religion* (ed. Barnabas Lindars; Cambridge: James Clarke & Co., 1988), 13–19; Robert Gordis, "On Adultery in Biblical and Babylonian Law—A Note," *Judaism* 33 (1989): 210–11; Bernard S. Jackson, *Essays in Jewish and Comparative Legal History* (Leiden: Brill, 1975), 54; Samuel E. Loewenstamm, "The Laws of Adultery and Murder in Biblical and Mesopotamian Law," in *Comparative Studies in Biblical and Ancient Oriental Literatures* (Neukirchen–Vluyn: Neukirchener, 1980), 146–53; Pressler, *View of Women*, 108–11; A. Rofé, "Family and Sex Laws in Deuteronomy and the Book of Covenant," *Henoch* 9 (1987): 146; Westbrook, "Adultery," 542–80; idem, *Studies in Biblical and Cuneiform Law* (Paris: J. Gabalda et Cie, 1988), 108–9.

Counter critiques have ensued. See the following: Moshe Greenberg, "More Reflections on Biblical Criminal Law," in *Scripta Hierosolymitana* (ed. Sarah Japhet; Jerusalem: Magnes, 1986), 1–17; Henry McKeating, "A Response to Dr. Phillips by Henry McKeating," *JSOT* 20 (1981): 25–26; Phillips, "Another Look at Adultery"; idem, "A Response to Dr. McKeating," *JSOT* 22 (1982): 142–43.

44. Phillips, *Ancient Israel's Criminal Law*, 110–29 (117). See also M. Weinfeld, "The Origin of the Humanism in Deuteronomy," *JBL* 80 (1961): 243. He writes: "In Deuteronomy the author's primary concern is the protection of *man*, and primarily the man whose means of protection are limited; he is not concerned with offenses relating to property."

45. Westbrook, "Punishments," 548.

46. Ibid., 548. See also idem, *Studies*, 108–9.

modern systems. Initiative for righting the wrong is in the hands of the victim and the role of the court is to limit the level of revenge or ransom.[47] Westbrook places rape and adultery in the last category and incest in the second category. Presumably, seduction or rape of a virgin would fall into the first category.

Aside from the comments made by Westbrook, the exegetical implications of the crime/tort debate with respect to women are best answered by the exegesis which follows, in particular the exegesis of Deut 22:13–23:1, upon which crime/tort proponents rely heavily for support of their arguments. In addition, Pressler's study of family law in Deuteronomy establishes the idea that, in Deuteronomy, woman's sexuality is the property of the man, even if the laws accord her some degree of personhood with respect to other areas of her life.[48]

The results of the following exegesis demonstrate that in DST, even when incest for example is discussed, woman is focalized as property,[49] whereas the reverse is true in LST. And in LST, even when adultery for example is discussed, woman is not focalized as property, whereas the reverse is true in DST. The precise implications of this state of affairs, for the legal systematization of the sex laws of Leviticus and Deuteronomy, or for the reconstruction of the judicial system of ancient Israel, are outside the parameters of this study. It might be said briefly, however, that this state of affairs does not mean that the adultery infraction of LST, for example, falls into a different legal category than the adultery infraction of DST.

2) *First Tendency*. Several scholars have noted differences between the adultery laws of Deuteronomy and "earlier biblical adultery laws."[50] More than a few scholars have posited sweeping claims concerning the status of women on the basis of these differences. However, few scholars have made such observations and claims concerning differences with respect to women, between the adultery laws of Deuteronomy and the adultery laws of P, including the Holiness Code (H). For the most part, within this discussion a congruence of Deuteronomy and H or P with respect to women is assumed.[51]

---

47.   Westbrook, "Punishments," 548.

48.   Pressler, *View of Women*, 91.

49.   Ibid., 91. Pressler writes concerning texts in Deuteronomy: "The sexual offense laws, therefore, must be understood in the first place as protecting the rights of the husband...the woman's sexuality is her husband's property, not her own. Sexual violation of a married woman is a grave violation of her husband's claim."

50.   "Earlier laws" may refer to the Book of the Covenant or to other biblical texts perceived to be earlier such as Prov 6:27–35; Hos 2:4; Jer 3:8. Or, "earlier laws" may refer to layers within the book of Deuteronomy itself. See the following: Daube, "Biblical Landmarks," 177–79; Grace I. Emmerson, "Women in Ancient Israel," in *The World of Ancient Israel* (ed. R. E. Clements; Cambridge: Cambridge University Press, 1989), 380: Frymer-Kensky, "Sex in the Bible," 192–93; McKeating, "Sanctions," 63–65; Phillips, *Ancient Israel's Criminal Law*, 14–16, 110–17; idem, "Another Look at Adultery," 14; idem, "Some Aspects," 353–54; Rofé, "Family and Sex Laws," 148; Stulman, "Sex and Familial Crimes," 64–63; Weinfeld *Deuteronomy*, 283–85, 291.

51.   McKeating, "Sanctions," 64. For example, McKeating writes: "Effectively, what the legislators of D and H are doing is to make adultery into a sacral crime, by attaching penal sanctions to a divine prohibition which had been there for a very long time."

For example, Phillips posits an evolution in ancient Israel's law that is exemplified by differences between the Book of the Covenant and Deuteronomy and between Deuteronomy and Leviticus. In his discussion of the adultery laws, he contends that woman was first subject to Israel's criminal law with the Deuteronomic reform. Thus, in Deuteronomy woman is first treated as an equal member of the covenant community.[52] However, when Phillips notes the subsequent shift from Deuteronomy to Leviticus, which occurred because "the priestly legislation extended the crime of adultery to include all unnatural sexual offences," he fails to note a corresponding shift in the treatment of women.[53] Although he notices, among other things, that in Leviticus execution is replaced ultimately by excommunication,[54] that "the ancient custom of levirate marriage" is rendered illegal[55] and that sexual prohibitions now include relations with any relative regardless of marriage status,[56] he is virtually silent about any significant shift that may have occurred with respect to the treatment of women. Thus, Phillips and others characterize women in Deuteronomy and Leviticus monolithically.[57]

Archer's work is an example of a slightly different stance. She characterizes the sex texts in Leviticus and Deuteronomy monolithically in contradistinction to later texts. Citing Lev 20:10, Deut 22:22 and Exod 20:14, she posits that "originally" adultery was an "infringement of a husband's property rights."[58] She states:

> Gradually, however, and in keeping with a general evolution in ideas concerning sexual purity, the act came to be viewed as an evil in itself, as an offence against the moral sensibilities (and structural concerns) of the society at large.[59]

Archer's subsequent citation of Ben Sira indicates that the shift which she is noting is between the biblical texts and later texts.[60] This shift, as Archer perceives it, has consequences for the treatment of women. Whether or not Archer's

---

52. Phillips, *Ancient Israel's Criminal Law*, 110. Pressler, *View of Women*, 5, 33–35, 105–13. Pressler has exposed the inadequacies concerning Phillips' view and similar views that espouse Deuteronomy's innovative, positive treatment of women.

53. Phillips, *Ancient Israel's Criminal Law*, 121, 123.

54. Ibid., 125.

55. Ibid., 125.

56. Ibid., 126.

57. Weinfeld, *Deuteronomy*, 187–88, 291. Weinfeld, who shares the view with Phillips and others, that women are more positively treated in Deuteronomy, is, nevertheless, one exception to those who tend to view the treatment of women in Leviticus and Deuteronomy monolithically. Weinfeld contends that the divergence between Deuteronomy and the "Priestly document" stems "from a difference in their sociological background rather than from a difference in their chronological setting" (p. 180). He notes a sacral vs. secular distinction between the "Priestly document" and Deuteronomy as exemplified by the difference between the treatment of incest in the Priestly document (p. 187) and the "marked absence" in the Priestly document "of civil ordinances and regulations pertaining to conjugal life, which occupy so great a place in the book of Deuteronomy" (p. 187). See Pressler's critique in *View of Women*, 5, 33–35, 105–13.

58. Archer, *Her Price is Beyond Rubies*, 26.

59. Ibid., 26.

60. Ibid., 27.

perceptions concerning this shift are correct, her implied, monolithic characterization of Leviticus and Deuteronomy with respect to women is incorrect.

3) *Second Tendency.* The second tendency exhibited by scholarly remarks concerning the treatment of women in Deuteronomy and Leviticus characterizes sexual infractions in ancient Israel or the Hebrew Bible as having to do with both purity and property. Countryman's "biblical theology," a thorough study concerning sex in the Bible, is an example of this tendency.[61]

Many of these scholarly remarks can be construed as a description of the sociology of sex in ancient Israel rather than as a description of sex in the biblical text.[62] As such, their generalizations can be forgiven. Nevertheless, scholars are not always clear, when making these remarks, whether they are representing a sociology or an exegesis. If the generalization that "sexual infractions in ancient Israel have to do with both purity and property" represents an exegesis of the text, then that generalization, at the very least, misses significant nuances in the text and, at the very most, is misleading or erroneous.

a) *Occasional and Implicative Remarks.* Van der Toorn states that "adultery was viewed both as a property offence and as an infringement on a taboo."[63] Goodfriend states, concerning adultery, that "the economic aspect of the crime, i.e. as a simple violation of the husband's property, seems to have played a minor role compared with the social and religious dimensions of the crime."[64] Wegner characterizes the infractions of Lev 18:6–20 and 20:10–21 as having to do primarily with women who are the property of other men.[65] Matthews states the following concerning the legal codes of the Bible:

> When the Book of Deuteronomy (Deut 12–26) and other legal codes in the Bible refer to women and deal with women's issues, they are seldom interested simply in regulating physical relationships between men and women. Rather, these codes are concerned with more sweeping issues of social justice and the equitable distribution of goods and services through the maintenance of a strong subsistence economy. In addition, the legal vocabulary used when dealing with women and with sexuality is concerned far more with property than with gender and sexual contact. For traditional societies, such as the one that is portrayed in the Bible, social justice and sexual conduct are the basis of morality. Consequently, teachings dealing with virginity, marriage, divorce, infidelity, adultery, promiscuity, and rape are not only concerned with the sexual relationships of individuals or couples, but also with the social and economic relationships between the households in the village as a whole.[66]

61.   Countryman, *Dirt.*

62.   Victor H. Matthews and Don C. Benjamin, *Social World of Ancient Israel: 1250–587 BCE* (Peabody, Mass.: Hendrickson, 1993). The study by Matthews and Benjamin is an example of an admitted sociological study which examines the problem of sex in ancient Israel.

63.   K. Van der Toorn, *Sin and Sanction in Israel and Mesopotamia* (Assen: Van Gorcum, 1985), 17.

64.   Elaine Adler Goodfriend, "Adultery," *ADB* 1:82.

65.   Wegner, *Chattel,* 13.

66.   Victor H. Matthews, "Honor and Shame in Gender-Related Legal Situations in the Hebrew Bible," in Matthews, Levinson and Frymer-Kensky, eds., *Gender and Law in the Hebrew Bible,* 97.

Frymer-Kensky, in her discussion of the power of sex "to dissolve categories" demarcated by the animal–human boundary, states that "every legal collection strongly forbids bestiality (Exod 22:28, Lev 18:23, 20:15–16, Deut 17:21 [*sic*[67]]); Lev 18:23 explains that bestiality is תֶּבֶל '(improper) mixing.'"[68]

These statements fail to render a precise configuration of property and purity components constituting sexual infractions within the biblical text. While the statements of Van der Toorn and Goodfriend may accurately represent a sociology of sex in Israel; as exegesis, their remarks, like Wegner's remarks, ignore the fact that in Leviticus adultery is primarily a purity concern and not a property concern, whereas in Deuteronomy it is primarily a property concern and not a purity concern. While the latter alignment is unsurprising, the exclusivity of the alignment in each group of sex texts is what has gone unnoticed. Matthews' above remarks are an excellent description of what goes on in Deuteronomy. However, the application to Leviticus of the idea that "sexuality is concerned far more with property than with gender and sexual contact" is a conflation that misses important features of the text. This does not jeopardize the value of Matthews' ensuing discussion, however, because he aims at a sociology rather than an exegesis. Frymer-Kensky's remarks also miss or ignore nuances in the text. The orientation and emphasis of Deut 27:21 is different from that of Lev 18:23 and 20:15–16. While the author of Deut 27:21 undoubtedly knows that bestiality is "improper mixing" (תבל), this classificatory component serves the interests of his primary concern for property.

Thistlethwaite's and Niditch's remarks posit the property component of adultery and apply the purity component at the social level. They characterize sexual infractions with betrothed and married women as property offences which confuse the categories of society. While their statements are not inaccurate, they do miss nuances suggested by the text.

Thistlethwaite, commenting on adultery in a discussion on rape, states:

> This property violation strikes at the heart of the way the community is organized and maintained, and so is also pollution of that value system. This crime is so serious a disruptive evil that "you shall purge the evil from Israel" (Deut 22:22b) by killing the evil doers; the language of purging is a clear indication that the purity of Israel is at stake in this violation.[69]

Similarly, Niditch writes:

> Death is also the penalty for adultery; Lev 20:10 is of special interest: "If a man commits adultery with the wife of...his neighbor, he will surely die..." The wording is significant; the man is not killed because he is married but because the woman, his partner is married. The male adulterer is polluting another man's seed, destroying the neat socio-structural categories whereby each patriarchal line is kept pure (see also Deut 22:24). Any damage to the social structure through the confusion or blurring of categories which order and define it must be avoided or repaired.[70]

67. The citation should read Deut 27:21.
68. Frymer-Kensky, "Law and Philosophy," 96.
69. Thistlethwaite, "'You May Enjoy,'" 63.
70. Susan Niditch, "The Wrong Woman Righted: An Analysis of Genesis 38," *HTR* 72 (1979): 146.

Thistlethwaite's and Niditch's remarks support the idea that "pollution" is a component of adultery not only because it causes social confusion, but also because the property concerns of adultery are a subset of classificatory concerns. However, while a social *effect* of adultery may be pollution, the primary concern for regulation of adultery in Deut 22:22 is protection of property, the purge formula notwithstanding,[71] whereas in Leviticus the primary concern is protection of classificatory boundaries, including boundaries prior to the social effect. Furthermore, "pollution" per se of "the man's seed" is not the concern of Deut 22:24; whereas it is the concern of Lev 20:10. The concern in Deut 22:24 is, rather, the exclusive *right* a man has to the sexuality of his betrothed. This is a property concern. While the purity and property concerns are obviously related, as primary concerns, they are different issues.

These distinctions are significant because they affect the focalization of women in the text.

b) *Countryman.*

(1) *Introduction.* Countryman's study *Dirt, Greed and Sex* is an excellent and thorough assessment of the sex texts of the Bible, including those of Leviticus and Deuteronomy. His work is especially valuable for its hermeneutical insights, clarifying important distinctions in the sex texts. He describes his work as a "biblical theology" which "begins with the biblical texts themselves" in order "to understand how the biblical authors expressed themselves in terms of the ongoing religious tradition in which they lived and worked."[72] Thus, Countryman admittedly intends to represent the text by careful exegetical study. His assessment is a thoughtful approach to the problem of the purity and property components. He states the following, concerning the regulation of sex in the Bible:

> The picture that emerged was of a twofold sexual ethic inherited and transformed by the New Testament authors. One part of it was a property ethic; its cardinal sin was greed, leading one to trespass on one's neighbor's property. The other part was a purity ethic, against which the fundamental offense was—well, it is difficult to say in modern English. We are accustomed to refer to it in academic language as "impurity" or "uncleanness."[73]

Countryman's study of the New Testament convinced him "that all the significant texts dealing with sexual morality are expressions of these two principles."[74] This includes the texts of the Old Testament. These two principles—the principle of purity and the principle of property—are responsible for both the purity and the property ethics in the sex texts. He writes:

> In matters of sexual ethics, then, one cannot assume that an act treated in the purity code is simply and solely a purity concern. I shall show that adultery, prostitution, and incest had about them an element of property law as well. Since sexual acts are an area

71.   See the exegesis below.
72.   Countryman, *Dirt*, 2.
73.   Ibid., ix.
74.   Ibid., 4.

of great concern to any purity system, all sexual offenses are likely to be felt to some degree as purity offenses, and we need to pay close attention in order to distinguish between those rules that are prompted entirely by purity considerations and those where other concerns are at work, too.[75]

Countryman defines ethics as a systematic presentation of morals which themselves are a set of rules.[76] Ethics "involve principles which explain why the rules are valid."[77] The purity ethic is a set of rules which depends upon the principle of purity. The property ethic is a set of rules which depends upon the principle of property.[78] He, thus, describes the relationship of ethics and morality so as to situate property and purity concerns in relationship to one another within the text.

My assessment differs from Countryman's because I understand the distribution of purity and property components in the text and their relationship to the author's concerns for purity and property differently. I understand property issues to be a subset of classificatory issues. Therefore, while purity is always in some way a component of the infractions of the property sex laws, property is sometimes absent as a component of the infractions of the purity sex laws.[79] Nevertheless, regardless of the purity/property components constituting the infractions of each law, each component may be used by the author of the text to establish his primary concern to regulate either purity or property.

For example, an adultery law within LST serves a purity concern even though it consists largely of the property component. So also a bestiality law or an incest law in DST serves a property concern even though the purity component largely explains bestiality and incest.[80] Only in this way can all *sex infractions* be "expressions" of the principles of both purity and property. Within the *laws or texts dealing with sexual morality*, these "expressions" serve either the primary concern for purity or the primary concern for property. Again, these distinctions are significant because they affect the way women are focalized in the text.

Two examples from Countryman's study illustrate the point. The first example is his analysis of incest in the biblical text. The second is his analysis of adultery as represented in Lev 19:20–22. These two examples may serve as models for similar assessments of his treatment of bestiality and prostitution.

75. Ibid., 28.
76. Ibid., 5–6.
77. Ibid., 6.
78. Ibid., 6.
79. Ibid., 11. Countryman alludes to the same thing when he states the following: "All regulations dealing with human sexual activity, then, are related to purity ethics, since they deal with the body's boundaries. Not all originate, however, from that source. As we shall see, some sexual rules are simply and solely purity rules while others, even if they are sometimes presented as purity rules, have other rationales as well. To take an example from our own culture, we are likely to feel revulsion toward rape as dirty, but our more serious objection to it is that it violates its victim's freedom."

80. The issue of *blood* incest necessarily consists of the classificatory component. However, incest, more broadly defined to include affines as well as consanguines, begins to encompass the property component. For incest more broadly defined see Stephen F. Bigger, "The Family Laws of Leviticus 18 in Their Setting," *JBL* 98 (1979): 193.

(2) *Incest.* While Countryman admits that incest implies "an intolerable mixture of roles," he suggests that "we can in fact best understand it as a 'property' offense."[81] He writes as follows:

> We have already seen that the concept of incest in ancient Israel was quite different from ours. Where we define it primarily in terms of shared genetic endowment, Torah defined it as violation of the intra-family hierarchy… This hierarchy was an expression of property relations, a way of exercising ownership over human property, whether slaves or concubines or children or wives, which could not merely be manipulated like real estate or domestic animals.[82]

Countryman suggests, with respect to the woman–mother infraction (Lev 20:14), that, since the women are themselves hierarchically related, property concerns are involved.[83] But precisely how hierarchy among such women constitutes a property concern is unclear.

The woman becomes the property of the man who marries her, but what property concern prohibits the man from marriage to and sex with her mother? If the mother is a widow, then she is the property of no man, yet she is still forbidden. Is the mother in some way the property of the woman, that is, her daughter, whom the man marries? While women did indeed own other women on occasion in ancient Israel,[84] a daughter probably never owned her mother. Countryman seems to suggest, however, that "precedence" is a form of property taken from the mother when the daughter is the first wife, as in Lev 20:14, for example.[85] But in Lev 18:17, the mother is the first wife since the women are called "woman" and "daughter" rather than "woman" and "mother." Perhaps, Countryman would argue, a daughter even as a second wife, removes precedence as a form of property, from the mother. But why are daughters nowhere in LST forbidden to their biological fathers if the mother's precedence is a form of property which is of concern to the author?

In short, property concerns are not at stake in these laws. Classificatory issues are the concern. Hierarchy, in and of itself, contrary to Countryman's assertions, does not constitute a property concern. The two-sisters prohibition (Lev 18:18), over which Countryman reasons in the same way,[86] is devoid of property concerns as well. Prohibition of the mother's sister, that is, the aunt (Lev 18:13), is also problematic for the theory that hierarchy constitutes a property concern.

---

81.   Countryman, *Dirt*, 35. Careful exegesis of Lev 18 suggests otherwise. Here is where the difficulty first arises with Countryman's schema. The property component appears in incest only where the marriage bond or perhaps the father–daughter bond is in place. Lev 18 regulates several incest infractions in which such bonds are entirely absent. Furthermore, in Deut 27:20–23 the purity component of incest serves a primary concern for property issues.

82.   Ibid., 159.

83.   Ibid., 163.

84.   Thistlethwaite, "'You May Enjoy,'" 64.

85.   Countryman, *Dirt*, 163, states: "Such a marriage would create grave problems of hierarchy, for the daughter, as first wife, would have precedence over her mother, but would still owe her, as daughter, a respect inconsistent with that position. For similar reasons, two sisters could not be co-wives (Lev 18:18)."

86.   Ibid., 163.

(3) *Leviticus 19:20–22*. Countryman cites Lev 19:20–22 as evidence that property concerns as well as purity concerns characterize the adultery laws of H.[87] However, although property components are present in the infraction of this law, since the woman legally "belongs" to at least two men and since the law does not establish the property rights of one man over the other, property issues are not the primary concern. Both the purity and the property components, as the exegesis below demonstrates, serve the author's primary concern for purity. Countryman, referring to H, states:

> …and, in fact, that Code did treat adultery as a violation of purity (Lev 20:10). On the whole, however, the Torah saw in adultery a property violation.[88]

However, the property component is inherent in adultery because the woman belongs to someone. Sometimes that property component comprises the concern of the law and sometimes not. In DST it does. In LST it does not.

While property and purity components may constitute many sexual acts within the text of the Hebrew Bible, those components as a primary concern distribute according to a regular pattern which does not in fact depend upon the nature of the sex act. Rather, it depends upon the interests of the "author/text."

(4) *Conclusion*. In short, we cannot understand fully the treatment of women in these texts without noting the distinctions between the metaphysics of sex and the primary concern of the text.

b. *Gender Construction*. Since 1990, many studies with explicit interest in the construction of gender in the Hebrew text have been published.[89] A brief discussion of two of these works situates this present study with respect to that discussion.

1) *The Difference*. Anderson defines gender as "the oppositional attributes ascribed to men and women."[90] Her text-base, drawn from the Book of the Covenant and from Deuteronomic law, includes but is not limited to the sex texts. Anderson's text-base divides into laws that treat men and women similarly (inclusive laws) and laws that treat men and women differently (exclusive laws). Inclusive laws which "prescribe or proscribe attributes and behavior for both

---

87. Ibid., 36–37.
88. Ibid., 158.
89. Works especially relevant for the subject of "gender, women and law in the Hebrew Bible" include, among many others, the following: Anderson, *Women, Ideology, and Violence*; Brenner, *The Intercourse of Knowledge*; Eilberg-Schwartz, *The Savage in Judaism*; Cheryl A. Kirk-Duggan, ed., *Pregnant Passion: Gender, Sex, and Violence in the Bible* (SBLSS 44; Atlanta: Society of Biblical Literature, 2003); Matthews, Levinson and Frymer-Kensky, eds., *Gender and Law in the Hebrew Bible*; Pressler, *View of Women*; Sawyer, *God, Gender and the Bible*; Harold Washington, "'Lest He Die in the Battle and Another Man Take Her': Violence and the Construction of Gender in the Laws of Deuteronomy 20–22," in Matthews, Levinson and Frymer-Kensky, eds., *Gender and Law in the Hebrew Bible*, 185–213.
90. Anderson, *Women, Ideology, and Violence*, 2.

males and females" divide into those that do so implicitly and those that do so explicitly. Exclusive laws divide three ways: (1) those that apply only to women, (2) those that exclude women and (3) those that regulate based on a woman's relationship to a man.[91] Among other things, Anderson concludes that a "woman may be treated in both interdependent and subordinate ways under the same laws, depending on whether she is slave or free, foreign or Hebrew, married or single."[92] Most pertinent for this present study is the following conclusion:

> (1)...the inclusive laws create national, generational and class identities that apply to both men and women; and (2)...the exclusive laws, which treat women differently, present subordination to men as the gender role for women.[93]

In the third chapter of her study, Anderson reiterates as follows: "More precisely, this chapter will show that the inclusive laws construct the identities of class, generation, and nationality, whereas the exclusive laws construct gender."[94] A corollary, *for the texts which Anderson studies*, might be stated as follows: Where class, generation and nationality are the concern of the text, gender is not constructed; where these are not the concern of the text, gender is constructed.

Anderson's text-base is broader than the text-base of this study. I explore gender alignments with respect to a narrow set of relationships found in only those texts regulating sexual intercourse in Leviticus and Deuteronomy. Furthermore, the "polarized traits"[95] that this study examines are *not only* a function of the proscription or prescription of "behavior and attributes."[96] Rather, the *difference* is found in the relationship of the woman character to the text's primary concern. What the text proscribes or prescribes specifically may point to the primary concern, but it might not be coterminous with it. The primary concern is only one of the conceptualities operative in the text and may be signaled by a variety of factors *including* that which is specifically proscribed or prescribed. The *focalization difference* that this study looks at constructs agency as one aspect of the conceptuality concerning women. That agency, as a function of focalization, can be said to be patent in LST in all but two cases, and latent in DST in all but one case. However, the conceptuality is complex. For women, the accrual to *symmetry* of agency in LST has the seed of asymmetry in it, and the reverse is also true. The failure to accrue to *symmetry* of agency in DST has the seed of that accrual in it.

Despite the differences in our approach to the text, my finding is of similar typology to Anderson's finding in the following way. When the primary concern is "distracted" from "the woman's sexuality as property" to "her sexuality as ontology," she accrues a quality of agency which is otherwise absent.[97] Using

91. Ibid., 21.
92. Ibid., 49.
93. Ibid., 2.
94. Ibid., 51.
95. Ibid., 21.
96. Ibid., 21.
97. Other scholars have noted this typology in the treatment of women in the text. Usually the divide on the side of asymmetry, however it may be constituted, is posited as a function of sexuality

Anderson's definition of "gender," the finding might be stated as follows: A concern for ontology constructs symmetry, or a tendency to symmetry; a concern for reproduction constructs gender. If "ontology" is a supra-textual concept, like the concepts of nationality, class and race (not in a sociological sense but in the textual-conceptual sense), then the typologies of our findings are similar.

2) *The Category*. "Woman" in the conceptuality of the text is a rigid, protected category. It must not be violated, as is the case with other protected categories. The fact that it *must* be protected means that it can be violated.[98] The fact that it can be violated defies its presentation, on the surface, as essential rather than constructed or natural. I am not talking about the violation of *women* in the text. I am talking about violation of the *category* "women/woman" in the text. Questions such as these are outside the boundaries of this study, which does not examine the conceptualization of the *category* per se.

These fundamental questions are the subject of Brenner's study *Intercourse of Knowledge*, whose text-base intersects a variety of genres and whose methodology is mixed.[99] The issues which drive her study are the following:

> ...how, by what means and to what extent human love, desire and sex, possibly even "sexuality" (the sexual characteristics or impulse, as experienced by an individual or group of either gender), are gendered in the Hebrew Bible (HB). In other words, how are sex (biological, anatomical, physical) differences and similarities conceived of, and converted into, gender (social, functional) differences and similarities between women and men in HB language and various literary genres.[100]

Brenner's study reaches for the roots of the conceptual underpinnings of the very *categories* of "man and woman"/"male and female" in the text.[101] Much work remains to be done.

---

or reproductive issues, as is the case in this present study: see Pressler, *View of Women*, 91; Frymer-Kensky, "Deuteronomy," 59a. Wegner, *Chattel*, 19, notes the same divide in the Mishnah: "First, the key to differential treatment of women in the Mishnah lies specifically in the sexuality factor."

98.   Two such obvious violations are cross-dressing and lying with a man as with a woman. See Brenner, *The Intercourse of Knowledge*, 31–32.

99.   Ibid., 3.

100.   Ibid., 1–2.

101.   See ibid., 31–32. Brenner's comments are cogent: "A male sexual body may be primarily recognizable by its penis and ability to produce semen; a woman's sexual body is primarily defined by virginity (or its lack) and then menstruation. But penis and semen, virginity and menstruation and other sex-specific bodily attributes are not immediately apparent. They can be disguised or obliterated by clothing. 'There should not be a man's outfit on a woman, and a man should not wear a woman's garment, for all this is an abomination for Yhwh your god' (Deut 22.5). This short passage betrays a concern, perhaps an anxiety, about visible differences between the clothed male and female bodies: they should be clear-cut. The insistence on easily recognizable boundaries often signifies uncertainty about those same boundaries. In the present case, *visible* difference appears to be a stake. But, as usual, the visual is an aspect of the social. In other words, the instruction that sex (anatomy-biology) should correspond in appearance to gender (the social), and that the boundaries in both cases be unequivocal at all times, suggests uncertainties on the social as well as the corporeal level. This uncertainty about the clothed body, together with the insistence that the body be clothed (thus

However, this present study does not examine these precise questions, important and intriguing as they are. It does not engage the problem of gender construction at the level of the sexual dyad *as category*.[102] Rather, it asks questions about attributions that accrue to the dyad, which is itself "argued"[103] on the surface of the biblical text. This study presumes without investigation or apology the categorical sexual *divide* which the text presumes and presents on the surface.[104] The investigation and critique of that divide is essential for a full understanding of gender. However, it is simply not the task of this study. Nevertheless, this study does *point* to the more fundamental level of the dyad *as category* in the following way.[105] If, within the narrow confines of the regulation

more gendered than sexed), apparently promotes physical difference, hence gender difference. However, and paradoxically, biblical language is not consistent in this respect: the naked body is not similarly and unequivocally differentiated into female and male."

102. For examples of exegetical work which engage the gender question at this level, see the scholarly discussions of Lev 18:22 and 20:13 in: Boyarin, "'The History of Sexuality'?"; Olyan, "'And with a Male You Shall Not Lie'"; Satlow, "'They Abused Him Like a Woman'"; Jerome T. Walsh, "Leviticus 18:22 and 20:13: Who is Doing What to Whom?," *JBL* 120 (2001): 201–9.

103. Gina Hens-Piazza, "Terrorization, Sexualization, Maternalization: Women's Bodies on Trial," in Kirk-Duggan, ed., *Pregnant Passion*, 164: "Laws governing society and even regulatory statutes of religious organizations are not objective templates committed to maintaining moral order. Rather, they disclose themselves to be sites of power—power determined to control matters of sex, gender, and meaning as well as power willing to resort to violence to maintain this control."

104. See also Anderson, *Women, Ideology, and Violence*, 7: "In other words, the terms 'male' and 'female' are biological descriptions but the terms 'man' and 'woman,' which connote the appropriate behavior attributed to each sex, are sociologically defined terms... Most importantly, 'gender' is defined as the 'mutually exclusive scripts for being male and female.' Consequently, gender refers only to polarized attributes assigned to men and women respectively... Thus a discussion of gender does not include necessarily any and all laws that mention women because different treatment for men and women is not described in each and every law. As a corollary, then, not all laws concerning women construct gender."

105. I use "gender" in this paragraph, as Judith Butler defines it, to include within it the notion of the constructed status of sex as well as the constructed status of other attributions; see Butler, *Gender Trouble*, 11. "It would make no sense, then, to define gender as the cultural interpretation of sex, if sex itself is a gendered category. Gender ought not to be conceived merely as the cultural inscription of meaning on a pregiven sex (a juridical conception); gender must also designate the very apparatus of production whereby the sexes themselves are established. As a result, gender is not to culture as sex is to nature; gender is also the discursive/cultural means by which 'sexed nature' or 'a natural sex' is produced and established as 'prediscursive,' prior to culture, a politically neutral surface *on which* culture acts...it is already clear that one way the internal stability and binary frame for sex is effectively secured is by casting the duality of sex in a prediscursive domain. This production of sex as the prediscursive ought to be understood as the effect of the apparatus of cultural construction designated by *gender*. How, then, does gender need to be reformulated to encompass the power relations that produce the effect of a prediscursive sex and so conceal that very operation of discursive production?" See also Anderson, *Women, Ideology, and Violence*, 67–69. Anderson states: "Under these circumstances, the body becomes 'the direct locus of social control' or a text that can be analyzed for ideological content. In other words, even our sense of the human body is socially constructed, and variations in a culture's definition of the male versus the female body becomes discernible and significant... An analysis using postmodern feminist legal theory, therefore, looks for images of the female body that the laws create as forms of legal discourse. The recognition that legal discourse is 'a site of political struggle over sex differences,' according to Mary Jo Frug,

of sexual intercourse, a kind of gendered-agency attribute, for example, is taken to be essential to the dyad, then what of the implicit accrual of that agency to the "wrong" pole of the dyad, namely, to the woman, which this study discovers in LST? That accrual *begins* to explode the *notion* of agency as a gendered essential for the dyad, argued on the surface of the Hebrew text, even if that notion is restricted only to regulation of sexual intercourse, an arena in which the grammar of the text in nearly every case places the woman in object position. At the very least that *notion* is significantly altered. Eilberg-Schwartz states:

> The fact that the physical attributes of objects often serve as criteria for classification generates the second distinctive feature of the priestly taxonomy, namely, the fixed and unalterable character of its categories. By this I mean that all objects which share a specified set of physical traits fall into the same classification.[106]

This study presumes the state of affairs that Eilberg-Schwartz aptly describes. However, that one set of sex texts would attribute agency to one pole of the dyad only and another set of sex texts, juxtaposed canonically to the first set,[107] would cause even limited agency to accrue to the opposite pole as well, with respect to the same issue; says something about the fundamental conceptuality of "the fixed and unalterable character" of the categories of both sets of texts. It speaks to the construction of the categories of "man and woman"/"male and female" in the Hebrew text. *In this respect*, this study in *gender attribution* is a study in *gender construction*, pointing to the more fundamental level of dyad *as category* per se.

Thus, although this study might be considered an exploration in the discursive production of gender,[108] the more fundamental, categorical implications of such an exploration are not the express focus of this study, which sticks to its task.

c. *Summary*. Finally, among the studies of "sex and women in the Hebrew Bible," including studies of gender construction, a systematic comparison of the treatment of women in LST and DST remains to be done.

4. *Relevance of the Study*
Leaving aside the problems and assumptions of scholarly research regarding the distribution of purity and property, as described above, the text itself begs for a comparative study with respect to women. Two factors support this assertion. The first factor is obvious and uncontroversial, but nevertheless important. DST and LST are elements of canonically discreet constituents within the larger canonical unit called the "Pentateuch." The canonical juxtaposition of these elements itself prompts the *comparative* question.

results from the postmodern emphasis on language as constitutive of human experience. From this perspective, laws can provide information on aspects of the assigned female identity" (p. 69).
    106.   See Eilberg-Schwartz, *The Savage in Judaism*, 220.
    107.   See below under "Relevance of the Study."
    108.   Washington, "'Lest He Die,'" 186, 193–94.

Furthermore, within the context of modern scholarship, Deuteronomy and Leviticus are the most important representatives of P and D. Study of their sex texts serves as a test case for the more general comparison of the treatment of women in P and D. This type of question with respect to P and D is an old familiar within scholarly biblical research and is no less intriguing when narrowed to the subject of women and sex.

The second factor concerns the surface content of the texts. Although scholars have viewed these texts monolithically with respect to women, the average reader is immediately able to see that different interests and concerns shape these two groups of sex texts and that the implications for women are provocative. Scholars themselves have noted the differences without asking what such differences mean with respect to women. For example, whereas LST explore the subject of incest at great length, outside the curses of Deut 27 the subject of incest is treated in DST with respect to only one kind of incestuous infraction and in only one verse: Deut 23:1. Whereas DST contain laws on "rape" and illicit sex with respect to the subject of virginity, *no such laws* exist in LST. In fact, LST are entirely unconcerned with virginity except in the context of association with a priest. DST, on the other hand, devote an entire section of laws to the subject of virginity. These are intriguing differences and by no means the only ones that exist between these two groups of texts. Easily recognizable differences such as these underscore the relevance of a comparative exploration of these texts.

B. *Methodology*

As the above introduction to the "Problem" implies, this is first of all an exegetical study. The exegetical results are the foundation of the ensuing comparative analysis. Both the exegetical study and the comparative analysis are subject-oriented. Their orientation is defined by the question, What are the factors shaping the conceptualization of women in the two groups of sex texts and how do they compare? This question limits the text-base and the interest in the text-base. The limits, assumptions and some of the tools which have structured this study support the exploration of this question. As such, their explanation or definition is necessarily an explanation or definition of the boundaries of the study as a whole.

1. *Limits*
The text-base of this study is limited to pericopes in Leviticus and Deuteronomy in which women *are present* and which intend to regulate the act of sexual intercourse. The view of women in LST and DST is, therefore, a selective view and this must always be kept in mind. For example, while the absence of women from Lev 20:1–5, a Molek text, raises intriguing questions, that absence also excludes this law from the text-base as I have defined it.[109] This limitation,

---

109.   Although at least two recent studies have determined that the Molek texts refer to child sacrifice, both Lev 18:21 and 20:1–5 have sexual associations. See John Day, *Molech* (Cambridge:

however, does not deny that "absence" may, in fact, constitute significant "commentary." A selective view is helpful and perhaps necessary, even if, in the long run, our understanding of "women and sexuality" is altered by the larger picture.[110] Selective exploration reveals nuances that would otherwise go unnoticed, as indeed they have.[111] Furthermore, this delimitation serves the interests of manageability.[112]

One additional factor delimits the text-base. Texts such as Lev 18 and Deut 22:13–23:1 intend to regulate sexual intercourse itself. A text such as Lev 15:18, 24, 33 intends primarily to regulate something other than sexual intercourse, but regulation of sexual intercourse is explicitly integral to what it primarily intends to regulate.[113] Other texts, such as Deut 20:5–7, 23:19 and 24:5 do not intend to

Cambridge University Press, 1989); George C. Heider, *The Cult of Molek* (JSOTSup 43; Sheffield: JSOT Press, 1985). Lev 20:1–5 is excluded from this study, while Lev 18:21 is included, because Lev 18:21 is integral to the sex-law series of Lev 18; whereas Lev 20:1–5 is a discrete unit separate from the series of Lev 20:10–21.

110. Knierim, *Text and Concept*, 3–4, states: "Last but not least, discernible individual pericopes exist in their own right. In the biblical literature they are usually parts of compositions or works, and the influence of context on them must not be ignored. Nevertheless, they are units in their own right, and sometimes reveal their individuality even in tension with their context. While it is certainly legitimate to start the exegetical process of a larger literary work with the explanation of its macro-structure or -composition and subsequently to move to the explanation of its parts, it is equally legitimate to reverse that exegetical process because either process will ultimately control the results of the other. Specifically, however, an individual pericope in principle may, and often does, have a distinct focus which sets it apart even from such pericopes to which it belongs generically. And its distinctive individuality includes the relationship between its text and its concept or conceptual aspects. For this reason alone, exegetical work needs to inquire into the relationship of text and concept in individual pericopes as well as in larger works. It is, after all, not impossible that an outside concept controlling the interpretation of a pericope may obscure or even destroy its individuality."

111. However, I quote Boyarin, "'The History of Sexuality'?," 353, at this point as a cautionary note: "Neither the Bible nor...the Talmud knows of such a typology—of that entity called by us 'sexuality,' whose 'chief conceptual function,' according to Halperin, 'is to distinguish, once and for all, sexual identity from matters of gender—to decouple, as it were, kinds of sexual predilection from degrees of masculinity and femininity.' ...Precisely because there is no separate realm of sexuality with all its definitional fraughtness for self-identification and that of others, there is also no separate realm of the sexually forbidden. Of course, I do not mean that forbidden genital practices do not form distinct corpora within either biblical or Talmudic law codes. Where a man put his penis was categorized as a separate area of experience than what he put in his stomach, for instance. What I mean is that it does not have a separate ontological, axiological, or even moral status."

112. The legal texts explicitly regulating sexual intercourse in the Pentateuch outside of Leviticus and Deuteronomy are: Exod 20:14; 22:15–16, 18; Num 5:11–31.

113. This study, in its original form, included Deut 23:18–19 as part of the text-base; see my "A Comparison of the Conceptualization of the Women in the Sex Laws of Leviticus and in the Sex Laws of Deuteronomy" (Ph.D. diss. Claremont Graduate University, 1998), 39, 353–63. At that time, my understanding of v. 18, which followed Van der Toorn's reading of קְדֵשָׁה/קָדֵשׁ, compelled me to include vv. 18–19, so as to remain consistent with my text-base parameters; even though v. 18 posed a single anomaly among all the DST. See Karel Van der Toorn, "Female Prostitution in Payment of Vows in Ancient Israel," *JBL* 108 (1989): 193–205. Deut 23:18–19 was the *only* sex text which did not focus on the woman's sexuality as the property of concern. Rather, it focused on property that *came from* her sexuality, namely, funds from "prostitution" for payment of vows,

regulate sexual intercourse, nor is regulation of sexual intercourse integral to what they primarily intend to regulate. Nevertheless, their regulations imply something about sexual intercourse. What they imply may be inferred from their discussion of other matters such as marriage, for example, or it might be inferred from their relationship to the larger literary context. In the interests of manageability, this study excludes all texts from the last group, although I may refer to them for support or as an example or by way of illustration.

On occasion, however, discernment of the texts which fall into this last group presents a problem. Restrictions concerning sex often necessarily entail restrictions concerning marriage. For this reason, scholars have sometimes discussed a text regulating sex as if it were regulating marriage. In so far as sex restrictions entail marriage restrictions, this is legitimate. However, intercourse and marriage were not conceptually coterminous in ancient Israel even if intercourse was one part of the marriage process.[114] Stories such as the rape of Dinah and the rape of

property which presumably belonged, not to the man, but to herself. Bird's argument concerning the male cult prostitute dispels this puzzling anomaly; see Phyllis Bird, "The End of the Male Cult Prostitute: A Literary-Historical and Sociological Analysis of Hebrew QĀDĒŠ-QĔDĔŠÎM," in *Congress Volume: Cambridge 1996* (ed. J. A. Emerton; VTSup 66; Leiden: Brill, 1997), 42. Bird's statement alludes to the problem (p. 42): "It seems unlikely that any Israelite man would allow his wife or daughter to have intercourse with a stranger, even a 'sacred man,' at a sanctuary. The notion of analogous function fails to recognize the characteristic asymmetry of sexual roles, rights, and expectations that is the mark of patriarchal societies." Verse 19 does not regulate sexuality, implicitly or explicitly. It regulates wages from sexual activity. By itself, it falls outside the parameters of this study, both in its present and its original form. Verse 18, however, as I originally read it, fell, along with the Lev 15 texts, into that group of texts which "primarily intend to regulate something other than sexual intercourse, but *regulation of sexual intercourse* is explicitly integral to what they primarily do intend to regulate." However, following Bird's reading, Deut 23:18–19 falls within that group of texts which "do not intend to regulate sexual intercourse; nor is *regulation of sexual intercourse* integral to what they primarily do intend to regulate." It is, therefore, expelled from this study. Needless to say, I found Bird's argument convincing. She states that no linguistic evidence exists for the linkage of cultic service and prostitution in the cultures for which it is posited. See also Oden, whom she cites: Robert A. Oden, *The Bible without Theology: The Theological Tradition and Alternatives to It* (New York: Harper & Row, 1987), 131–53. She reads the parallel alignment of זונה with קדשה as polemic against the cultic functionary קדשה. This means that a קדשה is "as good as" a זונה, not that the two words refer to the same functionary. In other words, the two nouns are "an evaluative judgment and cannot be taken as role definition." See also Oden, *Bible without Theology*, 132. Oden suggests that the idea of sacred prostitution should be "investigated as an *accusation* rather than as a *reality*," based on the contrast between passionate denunciation and ambiguous evidence. His position supports Bird's position. In addition, Bird observes that the verses are not parallel. My original study supports this observation with respect to grammar and syntax. However, a conceptual parallelism does exist and that conceptual parallelism is necessary for her "evaluative judgment" explanation to work. See Ellens, "A Comparison," 259–60. According to Bird, קדש is a literary construction contributing to what I call the conceptual parallelism. She states that it is introduced for "comprehensiveness and balance"; see Bird, "The End of the Male Cult Prostitute," 50. I am willing to accept this latter explanation tentatively. Jacob Milgrom, *Leviticus 17–22: A New Translation with Introduction and Commentary* (New York: Abingdon, 2000), 1807, says the following in relation to cult prostitution in ancient Israel: "Cultic prostitution, meaning intercourse with strangers as a sacred rite to increase fertility, is nonexistent in the ancient Near East."

114. Neufeld, *Ancient Hebrew Marriage Laws*, 89. Referring to *"Biāh,"* he writes: "This form of marriage was most widely practiced from the very early stages of Hebrew civilization, and was

Tamar, the laws on "rape" and "seduction," references to prostitution, descriptions of the "unfaithful wife" and other signifiers make this point self-evident. Furthermore, a text can regulate sex issues without regulating marriage issues, even if it entails regulations for marriage, and even if part of the motivation in writing the sex text was ultimately to manage confusions concerning marriage.[115] Thus, to conclude that a text such as Lev 18 regulates marriage, as scholars have suggested, is incorrect.[116] Such a text may entail regulating principles concerning marriage, but it regulates sex.

Nevertheless, the tendency by scholars—quite legitimately—to use Lev 18 as an indicator of marriage rules demonstrates the close relationship between sex and marriage in the text. In fact, this relationship is such that the same word—לקח—is used on occasion to signify either and perhaps both in some instances. Thus, the text itself treats marriage and sex as overlapping vectors.[117] This is a function, perhaps of the fact that sexual intercourse played a part in the completion of the marriage process, as Driver, Miles and Landsberger conclude from Babylonian laws.[118] In fact, its use in conjunction with other words denoting

---

marriage in its simplest form, the essentials being (*a*) an intention of the parties to enter into a binding marital union and (*b*) actual consummation. Neither the mere intention nor the sexual act was in itself sufficient. Intention would be indicated by conduct such as courtship or by promises or other expressions aiming at an immediate union... But that an expressed intention was essential must be obvious; apart from such, cohabitation would simply have been illicit intercourse without involving the status of wedded spouses." Neufeld cites Gen 29:21 and Deut 21:13 as two examples of this type of marriage arrangement. See also Wegner, *Chattel*, 227 n. 84.

115. Mark G. Brett, "Motives and Intentions in Genesis I," *JTS* 42 (1991): 5, 9; Quentin Skinner, "Motives, Intentions and the Interpretation of Texts," *New Literary History* 3 (1972): 400–401. Brett's and Skinner's comments on the difference between *motive* and *intention* and on the possibility of discerning such in a work are helpful. Skinner's comments on the former are especially relevant at this point: "To speak of a writer's motives seems invariably to be to speak of a condition antecedent to, and contingently connected with, the appearance of his works. But to speak of a writer's intentions may be either to refer to his plan or design to create a certain type of work (his intention to do x) or to refer to and describe an actual work in a certain way (as embodying a particular intention in x-ing). In the former type of case we seem (as in talking about motives) to be alluding to a contingent antecedent condition of the appearance of the work. In the latter type of case, however, we seem to be alluding to a feature of the work itself, and to be characterizing it, in terms of its embodiment of a particular aim or intention, and thus in terms of its having a particular point."

116. Compare the following scholars: S. R. Driver, *The Book of Leviticus* (London: James Clarke & Co., 1898), 87–89; Martin Noth, *Leviticus* (Philadelphia: Westminster, 1977), 136; Pedersen, *Israel*, 64–66; J. R. Porter, *The Extended Family in the Old Testament* (London: Edutext, 1967), 9. Susan Rattray, "Marriage Rules, Kinship Terms and Family Structure in the Bible," in *SBL 1987 Seminar Papers* (SPLSP 26; Missoula, Mont.: Society of Biblical Literature, 1987), 537–44. Rattray uses this text to discuss kinship and marriage rules in ancient Israel. Her study is a legitimate use of the text since restrictions concerning sex entail restrictions concerning marriage in ancient Israel. However, this does not change the fact that the text itself regulates with respect to sex not marriage. See Gordon J. Wenham, *Leviticus* (Grand Rapids: Eerdmans, 1979), 253–58. See also the exegesis of Lev 18 below for a discussion of this issue.

117. Although Seebass fails explicitly to describe the distinction between these two vectors, that distinction is nevertheless clearly present in his discussion of לקח. H. Seebass, "לקח," *TDOT* 8:17.

118. G. R. Driver and John C. Miles, *The Babylonian Laws* (Oxford: Clarendon, 1952; repr., Oxford: Oxford University Press, 1960), 322. Benno Landsberger, "Jungfräulichkeit: Ein Beitrag

sexual intercourse in Lev 18:17–18; 20:14; Deut 21:11–12; 22:13; 23:1 indicates that this is so also in the Hebrew laws.

The overlaps occur as follows. In some texts לקח denotes both marriage and intercourse. In some texts it denotes one and connotes the other. In other texts it only denotes one. Those texts which denote marriage and in which sexual intercourse plays only an implied part have been left out of this study.

For example, both Deut 20:5–7 and 24:5 are excluded. These texts concern marriage issues. In the first, the man is *betrothed* and has not yet "taken her." The use of ארש signifies that the law is explicitly concerned with marriage status rather than sexual status, whether or not the two may have gone together. In the latter, the man is *newly married* and is commanded to rejoice in his wife whom he "has taken." The explicit issue in this text, as in the former text, is "the brink of marriage." In the first text, the man has yet to cross that brink (betrothed) or is in the process of crossing it; in the latter, he has just crossed (newly married). לקח in these texts may or may not mean sexual intercourse, but it most certainly means marriage. Even if לקח connotes intercourse as well as marriage, the issue of sex is incidental for understanding the intent of these two laws. Marriage, on the other hand, is constitutive for understanding that intent.

On these grounds it might be argued that Deut 21:10–14 and 25:5–10, both texts which intend to regulate with respect to marriage, ought also to be left aside. However, in Deut 25:5–10 the regulation of sex is essential to the regulation of marriage, the main concern of the law. The issues which motivate that marriage are explicit in the text and concern matters of sexual intercourse for the sake of producing progeny. For this reason I have included Deut 25:5–10. In the case of Deut 21:10–14, sexual intercourse is explicitly prescribed as part of the process of finalizing the marriage. Therefore, it is also included.

In the case of Deut 24:1–4, which also treats matters related to marriage, the sexuality factors are controversial. For this reason, the results of a more thorough exegesis, presented below, justifies its exclusion from the text-base. In addition, while Lev 21:9 is included, significant texts within its immediate context are not. Leviticus 21:7 and 13–15 are excluded because they do not regulate the act of sexual intercourse per se. Rather, they regulate marriage on the basis of sexual history. Undeniably, they are relevant to the topic of the treatment of women in Leviticus and Deuteronomy with respect to sexual intercourse, and their exegesis would most certainly reveal intriguing and significant details.[119] Nevertheless, because they do not regulate the sex act they are excluded.

At least one other text, which potentially carries significant import for the treatment of women and sexual intercourse, is also left aside by this study. Deuteronomy 15, especially in comparison with such texts as Exod 21, Lev

zum Thema 'Beilager und Eheschliessung,' " in *Symbolae Juridicae et Historicae* (ed. J. A. Ankum, R. Feenstra and W. F. Leemans; 2 vols.; Leiden: Brill, 1968), 2:42.

119.   For example, as Bird and Goodfriend have stated, we can infer from Lev 27:7, 14 that the ordinary non-priestly Israelite male could marry a prostitute without impunity. See Phyllis A. Bird, "The Harlot as Heroine: Narrative Art and Social Presupposition in Three Old Testament Texts," *Semeia* 46 (1989): 137 n. 39; Elain Adler Goodfriend, "Prostitution (Old Testament)," *ABD* 5:506.

19:20–22, 25:39–55 and Deut 21:10–14, raises intriguing questions concerning the treatment of women in the context of sexual intercourse.[120] This text is excluded, however, because it, as well, does not regulate sexual intercourse.

On the basis of these criteria, this study consists of an examination of the following texts:[121]

LST: Lev 15:18, 24, 33; 18; 19:20–22, 29; 20:10–21; 21:9
DST: Deut 5:18; 21:10–14; 22:13–23:1; 24:1–4; 25:5–10; 27:20–23; 28:30

As can be surmised from the above discussion, three factors signal the "coherence"[122] of this group of texts: (1) the boundaries known as "Pentateuch," "Deuteronomy" and "Leviticus"; (2) the distinctions shaped by the topic "regulation of the sex act with respect to women"; and (3) the boundaries defined by the genre of "law."[123] As a result of these boundaries and distinctions, the text-base of this study cuts across several conventional scholarly boundaries. For example, it cuts across the boundaries of "family law," irrespective of the definition of family law one uses. It cuts across the boundaries defined as the "Holiness Code." And its cuts across the "Deuteronomic/Deuteronomistic" boundaries.

2. *Tools*

a. *Exegesis.*

1) *General Considerations.* While my exploration of the above texts has relied upon the conventional methods of exegesis, my overriding interest in the women

---

120.   Dr. Marvin Sweeney pointed this out to me in conversation.

121.   Keeping track of some of the arguments of this study may be facilitated by the list of texts and their "summary titles" in Chart 1 of the Appendix.

122.   By "coherence" I do not mean lexical, grammatical, syntactical or structural coherence, although these may exist. I use coherence to signify only that these texts can sensibly and with profitability be taken as a group for serious study. Canonical, generic and topical boundaries constitute the sensibility of the undertaking. The fact that the study of such a group can raise and answer certain questions with respect to the treatment of women in the text constitutes the profitability of the undertaking.

123.   Throughout this study I refer to the legal materials of LST and DST as "law," without making finer distinctions such as those represented by the following list: (1) the legal report of the actual cases, that is, *"reports of* decisions" (Rolf P. Knierim, "The Problem of Ancient Israel's Prescriptive Legal Traditions," *Semeia* 45 [1989]: 14) (2) the legal prescription which looks to the future on the basis of past cases, that is, *"prescriptions for* decisions" (Knierim, "Problem," 14; idem, "Customs, Judges, and Legislators in Ancient Israel," in *Early Jewish and Christian Exegesis: Studies in Memory of William Hugh Brownlee* [ed. C. A. Evans and W. F. Stinespring; Atlanta: Scholars Press, 1987], 9) and (3) the legal instruction which aims to prescribe in advance the consequences of a future, imagined or potential event (Knierim, "Problem," 10; idem, "Customs," 13). See Knierim for an analysis of the problem represented by this list of distinctions: Knierim, "Customs," 3–15; idem, "Problem," 7–25. The extant texts within these three legal categories all in some way intend their promulgations to be binding. The same qualification may be made of the category of ethical instruction even if the latter is intended to be binding only by way of instructional force without the threat of legal consequences. See Dale Patrick, *Old Testament Law* (Atlanta: John Knox, 1984), 198. For this study, the shared qualification is *the* significant factor concerning these distinctions. It is significant, in particular, with respect to the focalization of the characters as I have defined it. Thus, since the categories share this qualification, their distinction is largely inconsequential for the purposes of this study.

in the text has necessarily prompted gender-oriented questions as part of the total process. In addition to the conventional methodologies, I have found useful the methodology concerning the conceptuality of the text that Rolf P. Knierim delineates and uses in *Text and Concept in Leviticus 1:1–9.*[124]

2) *Conceptual Analysis.*

a) *Fundamentals.* Conceptual analysis, an exegetical approach pioneered by Knierim, targets the subsurface of the text to discern the conceptualities that control and shape the surface.[125] A number of dissertations, under Knierim, during the last decade have used this method and delineated its fundamentals.[126] Several of them have been published.[127] This study, a revision of my dissertation, was also written under the guidance of Rolf P. Knierim and is an exemplar of that methodology.[128]

---

124.   Knierim, *Text and Concept*, 1–3, writes: "It has always been observed in biblical exegesis that the texts contain not only statements but also presuppositions. The surface level of a text communicates to the reader explicit information, but it also points to aspects beneath itself which are, nevertheless, implicitly operative in it and which generate and control its form and content. Texts are linguistic semantic entities in which explicit statements and their presuppositions interact. Exegesis must, therefore, do more than paraphrase what a text says. It must also, however, hypothetically, reconstruct a text's assumptions which lie underneath its surface. It must explain its system, its *Gestalt*, if for no other reason than to help us achieve a better understanding of the text's statements. In doing so, it must distinguish between the critical paraphrase of the text's message and the reconstruction of its assumptions, and attempt to explain the relationship of both and their mutual convertibility" (p. 1).

125.   Rolf Knierim, "Old Testament Form Criticism Reconsidered," *Int* 27 (1973): 435–68; idem, "Criticism of Literary Features, Form, Tradition, and Reaction," in *The Hebrew Bible and Its Modern Interpreters* (ed. Douglas A. Knight and Gene M. Tucker; Philadelphia: Fortress, 1985), 123–65; idem, *Text and Concept*, 1–4; idem, *The Task of Old Testament Theology: Substance, Method, and Cases* (Grand Rapids: Eerdmans, 1995).

126.   Tim Fearer, "Wars in the Wilderness: Textual Cohesion and Conceptual Coherence in Pentateuchal Battle Traditions" (Ph.D. diss., Claremont Graduate University, 1993); Randy Haney, "'And All Nations Shall Serve Him': Text and Concept Analysis in Royal Psalms" (Ph.D. diss., Claremont Graduate University, 1999); Mignon Jacobs, "Conceptual Coherence of the Book of Micah" (Ph.D. diss., Claremont Graduate University, 1998); Hyun Chul Paul Kim, "Salvation of Israel and the Nations in Isaiah 40–55: A Study in Texts and Concepts" (Ph.D. diss., Claremont Graduate University, 1998); Wonil Kim, "Toward a Substance-Critical Task of Old Testament Theology" (Ph.D. diss., Claremont Graduate University, 1996); Won W. Lee, "Punishment and Forgiveness in Israel's Migratory Campaign: The Macrostructure of Numbers 10:11–36:13" (Ph.D. diss., Claremont Graduate University, 1998); David B. Palmer, "Text and Concept in Exodus 1:1–2:25: A Case Study in Exegetical Method" (Ph.D. diss., Claremont Graduate University, 1998).

127.   Randy Haney, *Text and Concept Analysis in Royal Psalms* (Studies in Biblical Literature; New York: Peter Lang, 2002); Mignon Jacobs, *The Conceptual Coherence of the Book of Micah* (JSOTSup 332; Sheffield: Sheffield Academic Press, 2001); Hyun Chul Paul Kim, *Ambiguity, Tension, and Multiplicity in Deutero-Isaiah* (New York: Peter Lang, 2003); Won W. Lee, *Punishment and Forgiveness in Israel's Migratory Campaign* (Grand Rapids: Eerdmans, 2003).

128.   The above dissertations came out of the Knierim seminars which explicitly developed this methodology. The seminars that I attended immediately preceded them. However, the fundamental ideas giving shape to the method were already present in the seminars that I attended.

Among the above studies, David B. Palmer's dissertation, which delineates the method most clearly and systematically, is a good entry point for the method. All of these studies, however, following Knierim's lead, emphasize or assume the following points. First, the coherence of a text, as opposed to its cohesion, is conceptual and controls the structure and other surface elements. Second, conceptualities, which are of varied typology, may be immanent in a genre, a style, a situation, a theme, a plot, a concern, or an intention, and are accessed through surface elements such as structure, content, rhetoric, grammar and syntax.[129] Third, a concept may be specific to a single pericope or may extend to a larger context.[130] It may be intratextual, contextual, intertextual, or supratextual.[131]

A good conceptual analysis will insist on flexibility of expectation in terms of what might actually constitute a conceptuality or where a governing conceptuality might reside in the text. That flexibility is the function of a stance which gives ear to the text's voice, allowing the text to speak for itself, eschewing a stance which conjures a preconceived construct and forces it upon the text. However, in an effort to reconstruct an underlying conceptuality, a construct might be hypothetically "tried out" on a text. The power and confirmation of that construct is its capacity to explain otherwise disparate textual elements with consistency and without denying or "violating" any surface elements.[132] Such a hypothetical construct must be prompted by the surface elements.[133] Knierim has said the following:

> A *caveat* needs to be kept in mind, namely, the danger of circular argumentation in the determination of the relationship between text and concept. This danger always exists. But the possibility or danger of circular argumentation invalidates neither the basic necessity for determining the relationship between text and concept nor the legitimacy of hypothetically reconstructing a concept from a text. While reconstruction necessary for understanding is inevitably hypothetical, a hypothesis is better than none at all. Our option consists of the alternative between more or less substantiated hypotheses, not between a hypothesis or no hypothesis. The danger of circular argumentation is at any rate alleviated by the fact that the reconstruction, to whatever extent it can facilitate a better understanding of the text, is controlled by what the text permits.[134]

When discussing conceptuality, one must distinguish between construction of a text and exegesis of a text. In the exegesis of a text, surface is prior to

---

129. Knierim, *Text and Concept*; Palmer, "Text and Concept," 173–74.

130. Knierim, *Text and Concept*, 3.

131. Ibid., 3; Palmer, "Text and Concept," 179–80; Kim, "Salvation," 52–64.

132. Palmer, "Text and Concept," 174, states: "The task of exegetical method is to provide a reconstruction of the underlying concepts that successfully, or at least best, explains *all* the signals in the surface text."

133. Palmer, "Text and Concept," 173, states: "The only avenue available to the sub-surface of a text is reconstructed by analyzing the surface text, penetrating beneath this surface to those inexplicit elements which must be postulated in order to explain the explicit aspects. The analysis then returns again to the surface of the text in order to test, confirm, or modify, the reconstruction of the text's concepts in the light of its explicit aspects. This heuristic process may be described as coming to understand the text."

134. Knierim, *Text and Concept*, 2.

conceptuality. We begin with grammar, syntax and structure to discover the conceptuality that has motivated the selection of these elements and shaped them. In the generation of a text, however, conceptuality is prior. While conceptuality and structure, grammar or syntax may eventually, in the process of the construction of the text, exercise a "give and take," the "give" on the side of conceptuality is more fundamental than on the side of the surface elements.[135] It drives the manifestation of the text, not only in terms of sequence in construction, but also in terms of selection and use of surface elements. Conceptuality is the reason the text exists.[136]

If conceptuality is the source of the coherence of a text, then structure analysis may be the single most powerful tool available for accessing a particular kind of conceptuality: that is, the conceptuality of intent or interest or primary concern,[137] even if structure is unable to offer that conceptuality easily, and even if it is not the *only* element to deliver that conceptuality. Sometimes other features reveal the primary concern, which in turn suggests aspects of the structure. The primary concern, intention or interest of the text, whether we believe we can discover it or not, is not only fundamental to the text's existence, it provides the text's focus. Structure demonstrates that focus.[138] For nearly all the texts of this study, structure is significant.

---

135.   While a conceptuality may force the selection of a particular text-type, or structure, for example, during construction of the text, that structure (motivated to be selected by the conceptuality) may generate or reveal aspects concerning that conceptuality. That is to say, a surface form may function as a tool of extended discovery for the conceptuality that is responsible for its selection in the first place. However, whatever the dynamics involved in the process of the textual construction, whatever the *originating source* of the conceptuality, the end result is that in the text we have a conceptuality that uses the surface as a vehicle of communication.

136.   Palmer, "Text and Concept," 169, states: "That which is foundationally constitutive of a text, in which all aspects related to its generation and expression cohere, is its infratextual conceptuality or underlying thought system… This foundational role of conceptuality or thought in texts is grounded in the cognitive functions of the human mind discussed above, and becomes evident through the exegetical engagement of texts themselves."

137.   Ibid., 178, states: "The terms *macro-structure, micro-structure, unit(s)*, and *sub-unit(s)* are also used to refer to the relationship of the surface of a text to its conceptual sub-surface in terms of *structure*. In this regard conceptual analysis distinguishes between composition which refers to the cohesion of the surface text, and structure. Structure refers to the combination in the text of its underlying conceptual coherence and its compositional cohesion. A text's structure is that element of its surface which most directly reflects its underlying thought system. The structure analysis of a text expresses in schematic form the structural relationships of the text's content in terms of the relationships of its generic and literary elements. This structure analysis is to be distinguished from topical outlines that are imposed upon texts, or which summarize texts. The relationships that are schematically indicated in a structure analysis are those that are generated by the underlying thought system of the text."

138.   Ibid., 181–82, states: "The infratextual conceptuality of a text is not the same as the intentionality of its postulated author(s), redactor(s), or composer(s). This is the case although the two aspects of text-immanent infratextual conceptuality and antecedent intentionality interface given the nature of human thought, expression, and textuality. The reconstruction of infratextual concepts or underlying presuppositions is not an attempt to describe or reconstruct the postulated author's or redactor's psychology or psychological state(s) that were in effect when he/she/they composed the text. Instead, the focus is upon the text and not primarily upon the author(s). Infratextual conceptual

b) *Particulars*. Since this study is concerned primarily with the conceptualities which shape the ancient writer's understanding of women *as reflected in the sex texts*, I do not claim to treat all conceptual elements in the text. Because of my governing interest, I focus on a particular set of conceptualities: those that apply to women and sex.

Furthermore, I do not claim to treat those conceptual elements which have a larger *contextual* bearing on the treatment of women in the sex texts.[139] For example, since only the sex texts are examined, I do not claim in this study that the conceptualization of women in the sex texts is equivalent to the conceptualization of women which becomes apparent when looking at all texts concerning women in either Leviticus or Deuteronomy. In fact, as stated above, studies such as Pressler's suggest otherwise. Pressler concludes that in the family laws of Deuteronomy, woman is not the property of her husband.[140] At the very least, by law she has certain rights and responsibilities as a dependent family member.[141] While I do not contest the assertion that in family law women have certain rights and responsibilities which constitute personhood, however circumscribed by men, I do contend that in the sex laws of Deuteronomy she is conceptualized as property.[142]

---

analysis proposes the reconstruction and description of text immanent infratextual conceptualties, not the description of intentions or psychological states that may be located or resident in the author's(s') mind(s) as antecedent to but separate from the text in some way. Though conceptualized texts along with their concepts have been sourced by virtue of production in the mind(s) of some conceptualizer(s), once textual expression has eventuated, the conceptuality has become text immanent as an inherent infratextual aspect of that text as such. The object of inquiry in conceptual analysis concerns nothing other than what is an inherent aspect of the text. The antecedent conceptualizer(s) is (are) not directly the object of inquiry in conceptual analysis. Nevertheless one may also speak of the conceptualizers, be they authors, redactors, etc. as being present in this way within their conceptualized texts. That is to say, texts as conceptualized entities have a relationship to setting and also to intention as conceived in form-critical analysis." Palmer's point is that conceptual analysis reads the "text" and not the "author." However, the intentionality or concern *of the text* is text immanent and, as such, a legitimate target of conceptual analysis. Indeed, it may constitute the governing conceptuality of a text. This does not gainsay Palmer's point.

139. Knierim, *Text and Concept*, 2, states: "While the 'ideas' or 'concepts' or 'patterns' of worldview systems play a role in the so-called deep structure of texts, they neither self-evidently, nor necessarily, represent the concepts or assumptions (or assumed concepts and conceptual assumptions) that belong to the immediate reason for and meaning of an individual text, or of a coherent group of texts, or of a larger literary work. The conceptualities that are operative in the immediacy of a text are directly important for exegetical work."

140. Pressler, *View of Women*, 91.

141. Ibid., 7, 15, 83–86, 94, 96, 102–12.

142. Ibid., 90–92. Since Pressler examines the larger context, she speaks of the woman's *sexuality* as the property of the husband. Pressler, thus, implies a distinction between person and sexuality. See also the following pages: 31, 42, 86, 90–92, 94, 97–99. Wegner, *Chattel*, 6–12, 15–17, makes the same distinction concerning women in the Mishnah, observing that woman is treated as person in all respects except one. With respect to her sexuality, she is treated as chattel. While I would disagree with her characterization of the laws in Leviticus, the distinction that she, as well as Pressler, draws between chattel and person, and the relationship she establishes between these two factors and the sexuality factor, are helpful.

Therefore, this study examines, with respect to women, the conceptual underpinnings of the individual sex texts of Leviticus and Deuteronomy. Furthermore, this study is carried out with full awareness that the conceptual mix with respect to women may be different when the texts are read in their full context. While this study takes account of the immediate context of the individual texts, the larger *conceptual* context with respect to women is left aside.

b. *Comparison*. The comparison of the above texts is a process which goes beyond the exegesis of the texts. Many comparisons between these two groups of texts can be made. However, for this study, only comparisons related to the treatment of women are relevant.

Comparison of the texts proceeds in stages which I will call levels. The first level of comparisons takes place separately within the books of Leviticus and Deuteronomy. This level is a comparison of any two or more texts that fall within a particular rubric. The rubrics may differ typologically. For example, all texts having to do with "menstruation" are compared. Texts "which occur in series" are compared. Woman's marginalization, objectification and focalization in the texts are compared. The act of comparing itself is discernment of what is similar and dissimilar among texts with respect to significant gender factors or with respect to factors which have some bearing on the gender question. The first level is the discernment of the individual threads of the conceptual weave of the cloth that is the text.

The second-level comparison takes place, as well, within the separate books of Leviticus and Deuteronomy. Whereas the first-level comparison is analytic, this second-level comparison is synthetic. It is, in short, an assessment—a synthesis—of the first-level results. It involves looking for *patterns* in the texts shaped by the confluence of the results of comparisons of texts according to typologically different factors or rubrics. Thus, finding what is similar and dissimilar is only part of the task at the second level.

In order to discern *patterns*, modalities in addition to the modality of "similar/dissimilar" are significant. For example, modalities such as translatability or equivalence and intersection are important as well. In other words, since we are comparing the results under *dissimilar* rubrics, whether or not the results under one rubric signify on a deeper level of the text something that can or cannot be translated into what is signified under another rubric at the deeper level, is what is important. All of this is done with respect to the question concerning women. Thus, looking for patterns involves discernment of the larger matrix resulting from the relationships of significant factors belonging to typologically different rubrics. In other words, the shape of the conceptual matrix of all sex texts in Leviticus or all sex texts in Deuteronomy is examined. This second-level is a discernment of the weave of the cloth.

The third level of comparisons, like the first level, is analytic. The task at this level is to discern the similarities and differences between DST and LST with respect to the second-level results. Thus, the third-level comparison is an analysis of the results of the second level, relying for particular support on first-level information. The aim is to discover where the contours of the conceptual matrices of Deuteronomy and Leviticus overlap and where they deviate from one another. This level is a discernment of the larger pattern which the weave of the cloth constructs.

The fourth level is synthetic, like the second level. The exploration at this level examines the results of level three and discerns *patterns* which reach across both books. This is the point at which knowing that proprietary concerns are a subset of classificatory concerns is particularly helpful. The thesis of this work is established by the results at this level.

Although the investigation proceeds in stages according to the four described levels, minor adjustments to preceding level-results occur as the larger picture appears. The different levels of results inform one another.

3. *Caveats*

At this point, a few caveats concerning the negative limits of this study are in order. First, it does not seek to establish the historical provenance of the texts. Second, it does not seek to establish genetic relationships among the texts, or bodies of texts. Third, it does not seek to establish differences and similarities in the actual practices and ideology of groups, movements, or individuals in ancient Israel. Its scope is limited to the conceptual world of the text itself.[143]

Fourth, as stated above, the thesis which will be proven is proven for the sex texts alone. I do not claim that the thesis is true for those texts outside the sex-text group. Nor do I claim the thesis is true for the sex texts as read and seen in their larger context. Thus, I do not claim in this study that the conceptualization of women in the sex texts is equivalent to the conceptualization of women which becomes apparent when looking at all the texts concerning women in Leviticus and Deuteronomy. Nor do I claim that outside the sex texts property is the exclusive primary concern of Deuteronomy and purity is the exclusive primary concern of Leviticus. Furthermore, this study is not a description of sex in the Hebrew Bible in general.

Fifth, I am concerned primarily with discernment and comparison of the conceptuality, with respect to women, of the extant form of the individual texts. Often two or more redacted parts pose little problem conceptually with respect to women, even if they pose thematic, symbolic, grammatical or structural problems, or other problems related to topics other than women. I have, therefore, left redactional issues aside unless their exploration is essential for understanding that conceptuality.

---

143. As such, this study is, in effect, an analysis of the morphology of the text. This study nevertheless rests on historical-critical assumptions, in particular, the assumptions which distinguish between P and D with respect to their historical time, as discussed in studies pertaining to that subject. Moreover, the ensuing comparison within this study of the morphology of LST and DST has implications for historical-critical analysis of the extant redaction of P and D, as well as for the sociological or historical analysis of the redactors themselves.

Finally, this study is based on the text of Codex Leningradensis as represented in the *Biblia Hebraica Stuttgartensia* (*BHS*) edition. Since this is not a text-critical study, textual problems will be discussed only when confusion within the *BHS* edition of the Leningrad Codex suggests that text-critical analysis might help to dispel that confusion.

Part II

EXEGESIS 1—LEVITICUS TEXTS

Chapter 2

LEVITICUS 15:18, 24, 33B*

A. *Introduction*

Most, if not all, Hebrew Bible scholars would agree that property issues are not the primary concern of Lev 15. In fact, property issues, with respect to women or irrespective of women, in the sex verses (vv. 18, 24 and 33b), or in other verses, are of no concern whatsoever. The primary concern of Lev 15 is mediation of the impurity of genital discharge. The author is interested in intercourse only with respect to this primary concern. Furthermore, with respect to this concern, the author treats the woman and the man equally. Symmetry of focalization, with respect to gender, characterizes the sex verses as well as the chapter as a whole.

Although the woman's focalization is equal to the man's, point-of-view reveals her marginalization in the text, and language-depicting-the-sex-act reveals her objectification. Her marginalization is somewhat ameliorated, but her objectification is not. The structure, one indicator of her focalization, supports and extends the ameliorating impulses of point-of-view, rather than the objectifying impulses of language-depicting-the-sex-act. Thus, with respect to the author's primary concern, vv. 18, 24 and 33b as well as the chapter as a whole demonstrate remarkable gender symmetry. For this reason, statements such as the following by Thislethwaite cannot describe Lev 15:

> Pollution concepts are essential to understanding women's "otherness" in the biblical worldviews… The reproductive secretions of women are dirty because this particular cultural system has set off the reproductive capacity of women in a particular way.[1]

---

*   The present chapter is a revised version of the original second chapter of my Ph.D. dissertation, which, in earlier revised forms, was published elsewhere as: "Menstrual Impurity and Innovation in Leviticus 15," in *Wholly Woman Holy Blood: A Feminist Critique of Purity and Impurity* (ed. Kristin De Troyer et al.; New York: Trinity, 2003), 29–43; ibid, "Leviticus 15: Contrasting Conceptual Associations Regarding Women," in *Reading the Hebrew Bible for a New Millennium: Form, Concept, and Theological Perspective*. Vol. 2, *Exegetical and Theological Studies* (ed. Wonil Kim et al.; Harrisburg: Trinity, 2000), 124–51. The former is a more thorough revision emphasizing the contrast in conceptuality between the vocabulary used for menstruation and the structure of the text. Note that Fig. 2 of the present chapter corrects a misprint of the same figure in the 2003 essay.

1.   Thistlethwaite, "'You May Enjoy,'" 63.

To the contrary, her reproductive secretions are dirty because, like the man's secretions, they are genital discharges.

Thus, woman's focalization, despite her marginalization and objectification, is equal to the focalization of the man.

B. *Discussion*

1. *Point-of-View and Language-Depicting-the-Sex-Act*

The point-of-view is apparent in the first verse of the chapter. Yhwh instructs Moses and Aaron to address the בְּנֵי יִשְׂרָאֵל, a male community. Thus, the first two groups of laws begin respectively with אִישׁ אִישׁ (v. 2b) and וְאִישׁ (v. 16). However, the next two groups of laws begin with וְאִשָּׁה (vv. 19 and 25). These latter two groups of laws pertain to the uncleanness derived from the bodily emissions of the woman. Explicit reference to the man in these two groups of laws occurs only in v. 24. The emphasis on the man, created by his appearance as the initial character in that verse, is mitigated by two factors: (1) his explicit appearance elsewhere in the two units is non-existent, and (2) v. 24 is merely the final rule in a section emphasizing and pertaining to women.

The content of these latter two groups of laws in vv. 19–30 and the absence in the chapter as a whole of a male character who relays the information of vv. 19–30 to the woman suggests that בְּנֵי יִשְׂרָאֵל addresses a male community in the midst of which stand women who are also listening to Moses and Aaron.

While the author inserts no explicit male character between Moses and the woman in order to mediate her instruction, mediation is apparent in the instructions for offerings. Men go before Yhwh. Women go to the door. Wegner emphasizes that not only does the text fail to bring the woman into the presence of the Lord, but it also pictures the man *giving* his offering to the priest in the presence of the Lord and the woman *bringing* her offering to the priest at the door.[2] Wegner states that this asymmetry "deliberately highlights the contrast between the *legal capacity* of a male and the *legal incapacity* of a female to play an active cultic role."[3] Despite this asymmetry, men and women bring the same offering,

---

2.   Judith Romney Wegner, " 'Coming Before the Lord': The Exclusion of Women from the Public Domain of the Israelite Priestly Cult," in Rendtorff and Kugler, eds., *The Book of Leviticus*, 451–58. She states: "Whatever the topographical niceties here, it is clear that the text contemplates the man as symbolically bringing his offering '*into the presence of YHWH*' in a manner consciously denied to the woman" (pp. 457–58).

3.   Wegner, *Chattel*, 147. Wegner noted this gender alignment as early as 1988. For a fuller discussion see her more recent article, " 'Coming Before the Lord.' " Wegner critiques Milgrom's use of the principle of "condensation" to explain the absence of "before the Lord" in the woman's case as follows (p. 457): "It is equally surprising that a scholar of Milgrom's caliber, in today's climate of raised consciousness to gender issues, seems to have overlooked the fact that the omission of a phrase as significant as לִפְנֵי יהוה in the woman's case can hardly be due to 'condensation' or even mere inadvertence, but undoubtedly *reflects* the priestly view of women's ineligibility to enter, still more participate in, the public domain of the cult." Even having read, years ago, Wegner's original observations concerning this asymmetry (underlined and starred in pencil in my copy of her book), tucked away in her larger discussion of the Mishnah; I too did not take sufficient notice of the full import of this detail until her 2003 independent essay on the subject. She is absolutely right.

both go to the "door of the tent of meeting," and the priest propitiates לִפְנֵי יְהוָה on behalf of both of them. Thus, a mix of gender alignments manifests.

Language-depicting-the-sex-act, on the other hand, knows nothing of mixtures. It consistently places the man in the dominant position as subject. The woman is always object. In vv. 18 and 24 she is the direct object. In v. 33b she is the object of a preposition. In addition, the description of the sex act is designated by a function which occurs with respect to the male body (שִׁכְבַת־זָרַע) and not with respect to anything specific to the female body. In v. 18, this subject/object polarity is mitigated somewhat, perhaps by the emphasis of the proleptic referent. Nevertheless, the objectification of woman created by language-depicting-the-sex-act is pronounced.

Thus, the language-depicting-the-sex-act underscores woman's objectification. Point-of-view, as revealed by the content treating female bodily discharge and by the absence of a male character mediating woman's instruction, slightly ameliorates the marginalization created by the use of בְּנֵי יִשְׂרָאֵל and the presentation of offerings.

2. *Structure*

The structure extends the ameliorating impulses of point-of-view with remarkable deliberation. This deliberation is all the more stunning in the context of woman's objectification created by the language-depicting-the-sex-act and her marginalization signaled by the בְּנֵי יִשְׂרָאֵל address and the presentation of offerings.

a. *Macro- and Microstructures.*

1) *Macrostructure.* The structure of Lev 15 is as follows:

I.[4]	Introduction to a Yhwh Speech to Moses	15:1
II.	Speech	15:2–33
	A. Introduction	2a
	B. Main Body of Speech	2b–31
	1. specific stipulations: cases	2b–30
	a. regarding men	2b–18
	1) anomalous flow	2b–15
	a) unclean	2b–12
	b) clean	13–15
	2) non-anomalous flow	16–18
	a) general case: emission of semen	16–17
	b) special case: intercourse	18
	b. regarding women	19–30
	1) non-anomalous flow	19–24
	a) protasis	19a–19bα
	b) apodosis	19bβ–24
	(1) direct contact	19bβ–20
	(a) person	19bβ
	(b) objects	20

---

4. The organizing structural signals used throughout this study follow the precedent set by the FOTL commentary series.

The conditionals introducing each of the four major sections of the "Main Body of Speech," which contains the bulk of the author's discussion are as follows:

1.   A man: if his flow is flowing from his flesh...
2.   A man: if an emission of semen goes out from him...
3.   A woman: if she is flowing, blood is her flow from her flesh...
4.   A woman: if a flow of her blood is flowing...

Each conditional identifies the topic of its respective section, one of four kinds of genital flow. Each section treats the mediation of the impurity of its particular flow. The "Summary," underscoring the same concern, begins with an adjuration to separate the Israelites from their uncleanness and then states: "This is the law of one flowing..." Thus, Lev 15, structured according to a taxonomy of genital flows, instructs the reader in the science of the mediation of the impurity of these flows. In each case, the intent is to "map" the way from the impurity of the genital flow to purity for the sake of the individual and the community.

Two of the four major sections conclude with one of the three sex verses in the chapter. Verse 18, a conditional signaled by אֲשֶׁר, and v. 24, a conditional signaled by אִם, conclude the men's and women's non-anomalous sections, respectively. The third verse, v. 33b, concludes the summary of the entire chapter. The placement of vv. 18 and 24, each at the conclusion of the non-anomalous sections, supports the chapter's structural symmetry. Even the placement of v. 33b, in the summary rather than in the main body of the speech, may be an attempt by the author/redactor to protect the symmetry (gender or structure) of the chapter.[5] The four major sections fall into two larger divisions which constitute the main body of the Yhwh speech. These larger divisions divide according to gender. Thus, structural symmetry constitutes gender symmetry.

The first larger division concerns male genital discharge and the second, female genital discharge.[6] The two divisions each consist of an anomalous and a non-anomalous subunit. Altogether, these are the "four major sections." Each anomalous section divides into two units: one concerning purity, the other impurity. The anomalous/non-anomalous subunits of the divisions are reversed from one another, producing a chiasm of the form ABBA.

These two divisions are, thus, schematic reverse-images. These structural correspondences between the male and female sections are the most apparent indication of gender symmetry with respect to purity. They suggest that the concerns and categories addressed for both sections and therefore both genders are the same.[7] Differences that do occur between the two divisions are a function of non-gender factors.[8] Analysis of the structure of the three sex verses supports these assertions.

2) *Microstructure.*
a) *Verse 18.* The structure of v. 18 can be understood in at least one of two ways. The first possibility is that אֲשֶׁר is a conjunction translated "if"[9] and אִשָּׁה is a *casus pendens* construction as well as the proleptic referent to the accusative pronominal suffix. The second option is that אֲשֶׁר is a relative and אִשָּׁה is again the proleptic referent to the accusative pronominal suffix. In this case, all of v. 18a is the *casus pendens* construction.[10] Either way, the verse is a conditional.

---

5. A failure to understand the nature and placement of v. 33b gives rise to statements such as the following from Wegner, *Chattel*, 165: "Scripture applies the rules of contamination to '*anyone, male or female, who has a discharge, and* also the man who lies with a cultically unclean woman' (Lev 15:33, emphasis added). A woman who has intercourse with a cultically unclean man is not mentioned because the only pollution that matters is contamination of male by female. Mishnah, following Scripture, worries about women's cultic purity only as it affects their male contacts. The woman is a polluting *object*, the man is a *person*." In fact, this comment shows a misunderstanding of the nature of v. 33b, its place in the structure and the structure as a whole. See the discussion below.

6. Karl Elliger, *Leviticus* (Tübingen: J. C. B. Mohr, 1966), 192–93; Walter Kornfeld, *Levitikus* (Würzberg: Echter, 1983), 59–62; Baruch A. Levine, *Leviticus* (Philadelphia: Jewish Publication Society of America, 1989), 93–98; Milgrom, *Leviticus 1–16*, 904; A. Noordtzij, *Leviticus* (Grand Rapids: Zondervan, 1982), 152–57; Noth, *Leviticus*, 113; Porter, *Leviticus*, 117–22; Wenham, *Leviticus*, 216.

7. The following scholars make similar statements: Eilberg-Schwartz, *The Savage in Judaism in Judaism*, 181; Lawrence A. Hoffman, *Covenant of Blood* (Chicago: University of Chicago Press, 1996), 148; Shaye J. D. Cohen, "Menstruants and the Sacred, in Judaism and Christianity," in *Women's History and Ancient History* (ed. Sarah B. Pomeroy; Chapel Hill: University of North Carolina Press, 1991), 276; see also p. 291.

8. See the discussion below.

9. Richard Whitekettle, "Leviticus 15:18: Reconstructed Chiasm, Spatial Structure and the Body," *JSOT* 49 (1991): 35.

10. אִשָּׁה might be understood as a *casus pendens* within a *casus pendens*. See Bruce K. Waltke and M. O'Conner, *Biblical Hebrew Syntax* (Winona Lake, Ind.: Eisenbrauns, 1990), 76–77 #5, for the function of a relative in connection with a *casus pendens* construction.

With neither of these two possibilities is the woman, as Milgrom suggests, the grammatical subject of the verse.[11] In v. 18a the subject is the man not the woman. In v. 18b the verbs designate the plural subject. Undeniably, as a proleptic referent, the woman receives special emphasis. But she is not the subject of v. 18a and *she alone* is not the subject of 18b. Both the man and the woman become unclean during intercourse. Both are unclean only until evening. And both must cleanse. The content and syntax as well as the structure of the verse demonstrate that, with respect to purity issues related to sexual intercourse, the author treats the man and woman equally.[12]

b) *Verse 24*. Verse 24 is also a conditional, signaled by אִם. The protasis consists of two situations which must be true for the circumstances of the apodosis to take place. First, the man must lie with the woman. Second, "her impurity" must be upon him.[13] The apodosis which begins at 24aγ,[14] describes the extent of the

---

11.   Milgrom, *Leviticus*, 930. Whitekettle, "Leviticus," 35, states: "The word *'ašer* is of course most commonly read as a relative pronoun. This reading, however, would indicate that the subject of the verse is the woman, a reading ruled out by the plural subject of the verse's apodosis." While Whitekettle is correct when he says woman is not the subject, his latter description is inaccurate. אִשָּׁה is a *casus pendens* construction related to a resumptive pronoun in the accusative case whether or not אֲשֶׁר is a relative or a conjunction. See Waltke and O'Connor, *Biblical Hebrew*, 76–77 #5.

12.   Several scholars have posited that the menstrual taboo exemplified in the Bible is ultimately responsible for the subsequent isolation of women and their exclusion from religious practice in Judaism. See Léonie J. Archer, "Bound by Blood: Circumcision and Menstrual Taboo in Post-Exilic Judaism," in *After Eve: Women, Theology and the Christian Traditions* (ed. Janet Martin Soskice; London: Marshall Pickering, 1990), 45; idem, "The Role of Jewish Women in the Religion, Ritual and Cult of Graeco-Roman Palestine," in *Images of Women in Antiquity* (ed. Averil Cameron and Amélie Kuhrt; Detroit: Wayne State University Press, 1983), 275; Cohen, "Menstruants," 273–99; Eilberg-Schwartz, *The Savage in Judaism*, 171, 177–94. Hoffman, *Covenant*, 146–54, 171–72, 190–91; Wegner, *Chattel*, 162–66. Such developments in connection with the menstrual taboo are outside the bounds of this study. This development, as well as the broader implications of fluid symbolism as described by, among others, Eilberg-Schwartz and Hoffman, does not define the conceptuality of Lev 15. Lev 15, in fact, does not exhibit this isolation and exclusion. Rather, it demonstrates considerable equity in the treatment of men and women with respect to the purity issues of concern, as even Eilberg-Schwartz and Hoffman recognize. See Eilberg-Schwartz, *The Savage in Judaism*, 147; Hoffman, *Covenant*, 181–82.

13.   Milgrom, *Leviticus*, 940. See Milgrom's discussion of the possibilities for deciding whether v. 24 refers to the deliberate act of copulating with a menstruant or whether it refers to a situation of happenstance.

14.   Ibid., 940–41. Milgrom maintains that clause 24aβ is also part of the apodosis. He writes concerning 24aβ (p. 941): "But as part of the protasis this clause should begin *wĕhāyĕtâ*; MT's *ûtĕhî* rather indicates a consequence, hence it belongs with the apodosis…" In addition, Milgrom states that since the antecedent of אֹתָהּ is the menstruating woman, the blood flow is not something that happened accidentally during intercourse. Intercourse, in the context of menstruation, is intentional. Thus, "her impurity upon him" is not one of the contingencies of the protasis. Rather, it is one of the sure results of the case. Therefore it is a consequence. Thus, 24aβ is part of the apodosis. Milgrom's error is in assuming that the protasis of such a conditional will not have within it one situation (i.e. her impurity is upon him) that is a certain and sure consequence of a prior situation described in the same protasis (i.e. "a man lies with a menstruant"). Such a "consequence," according to Milgrom, can only be in the apodosis. But, in fact, the author might include such a consequence in the protasis

impurity and also consists of two parts. The first part states the duration of the man's impurity. The second part describes the contagious effects of his impurity. Like v. 18, the man is the subject and the woman is the object. Unlike v. 18, the woman appears only in the pronominal suffix. While mediation of her impurity is noticeably absent in v. 24, vv. 19–23 address that issue in detail.[15] Since the impurity of menstruation is more severe than the impurity of simple intercourse, the stipulations of vv. 19–23 are more than adequate to cover the woman's impurity for the situation of v. 24. Both the man and the woman are unclean for seven days. Stipulations for ablutions are absent for both. Both transfer their impurity to objects around them. Again, with respect to purity issues related to sexual intercourse, the author treats the man and woman equally.

c) *Verse 33b.* The complete sentence to which v. 33b belongs consists of vv. 32–33, the summary to the Yhwh speech. This unit begins with "this is the law of" followed by a taxonomy of flow cases. The taxonomy makes sense until the reader comes to v. 33b, which initially looks like a reference to v. 24.[16] However, such referencing in the summary, which includes v. 24 and excludes v. 18, is problematic in a text which otherwise pays close attention to thematic and structural balance. Furthermore, the structure of vv. 33aγ–33b seems to suggest that the category implicit in v. 33b is typologically the same as the categories implicit in v. 33aγ. If v. 33b refers to v. 24, then the structure belies the content.

The structure itself is the key to this dilemma. Verses 32–33 divide according to the components of a single, non-verbal clause.[17] הַזָּב in v. 32a refers to all flows treated in ch. 15.[18] The *waw* at the beginning of v. 32b is an epexegetical *waw*,[19] and vv. 32b–33b are a delineation of this הַזָּב. The first half of the delineation, vv. 32b–33aα, refers to non-anomalous flow.[20] The topic of the second half, v. 33aβ–33b, is more ambiguously expressed and its reference, therefore, difficult to identify. Either it refers to all flows and הַזָּב means the

---

for the sake of emphasis. Such a reading would translate as follows: "If a man lies with her so that her impurity is upon him, then he shall be unclean…" Milgrom's final point is: "Finally, the structure of the pericope—v 24 is a collapsed version of vv 19b–20a; because v 24b parallels v 20a, v 24a must correspond to v 19b—shows that this clause deals with the *consequence* of intercourse with a menstruant. The conclusion is therefore inescapable: (2) this clause is part of the apodosis…" The same critique applies to this statement. In addition, I would simply disagree that v. 24 is a collapsed version of vv. 19b–20a.

15.   This is a reversal of the exegetical principle described by Milgrom, *Leviticus*, 914: "The exegetical principle to be borne in mind is that the law presents the minimal act that will generate a specified penalty-purification, and leaves the more severe acts to be derived a fortiori."

16.   Ibid., 948.

17.   See the structure above.

18.   See Milgrom, *Leviticus*, 905, 945–48, for an excellent discussion of the difficulties of this unit and for a solution different from my own.

19.   Waltke and O'Connor, *Biblical Hebrew*, 652–53.

20.   שְׁכְבַת־זֶרַע indicates v. 32b refers to the non-anomalous issue from the man's body. The time designations associated with נִדָּתָהּ in vv. 19 and 25, as well as the comparisons made in vv. 25–26 to the non-anomalous sections, demonstrate that the flow which comes during the monthly cycle is what is meant unambiguously by נִדָּתָהּ.

same thing as הַזָּב in v. 32a; or it refers only to anomalous flow and, thus, means something different from the initial הַזָּב. The categories of vv. 32b–33b are as follows:

1. man with issue of semen (32b)
2. menstruant (33aα)
3. הַזָּב (33aβ–33b)
   a. male (33aγ₁)
   b. female (33aγ₂)
   c. man who lies with impure woman (33b)

The *lamed*s indicate that the writer perceived a–c to be equally weighted and on the same level. If הַזָּב of v. 33aβ refers to all flows, then #3 recapitulates the categories of the chapter including the ones listed in #1–#2. However, such recapitulation is incomplete and somewhat half-hearted in an otherwise highly systematized chapter. On the other hand, if הַזָּב of v. 33aβ refers only to anomalous flow, then vv. 32b–33aα refers to non-anomalous flow and v. 33aβ–33b to anomalous flows. The taxonomy of the summary is then concise and complete.

This latter solution is stymied, however, by the fact that v. 33b seems to refer to v. 24 which concerns *non-anomalous* flow.[21] Perhaps this latter assumption is mistaken. All three categories of vv. 33aγ–33b involve individuals who are flowing. Technically, a–b could cover the situation of c. Even though this is the case, the author includes c. He must have a reason.

If v. 33aβ–33b has to do with only anomalous flow, then v. 33b refers to the only situation of double flow involving intercourse not delineated in the main body of the speech: intercourse of a woman-with-anomalous-flow with a man-with- or without-anomalous-flow.[22] Verse 25bβ, concerning anomalous flow, underscores this connection: "she is טְמֵאָה." Verse 33b states that the man lies "with a טְמֵאָה." Thus the writer of the summary wants this particularly noxious situation emphasized. The question remains: Why does the author reference it in the summary and not in the main body of the text? Redaction is one plausible explanation. Another and perhaps complementary explanation is that the author/ redactor wants to preserve the symmetry of the chapter.

If the same situation occurred in the main body of the text, it would be in the woman's anomalous section. However, the corresponding situation (intercourse of a woman-without-flow with a man-with-anomalous-flow) is absent in the men's anomalous section. The most we can say about this latter exclusion is that the writer considered the impurity that obtained and the stipulations that prevailed in such a situation to be evident from other portions of the text.[23] Furthermore, since it did not involve *double* flow, the author was not concerned

---

21.　Milgrom, *Leviticus*, 948.

22.　The woman's anomalous flow qualifies this situation as anomalous whether or not the man's flow is anomalous.

23.　Perhaps they are evident in vv. 7 and 18. The situation of lesser or equal impurity can be understood to be the least that would apply to the situation of equal or greater impurity. See Milgrom, *Leviticus*, 914.

to emphasize it in the summary.[24] Double-flow intercourse always involves blood. The impurity of blood was of special concern.[25] Since such a stipulation concerning woman-without-flow with a man-with-anomalous-flow was not included in the men's anomalous section, a corresponding stipulation included in the woman's anomalous section would have upset the schematic, structural symmetry of the chapter. Thus, the author/redactor left it out of the main body of the text. However, he could not release the summary and the chapter until he named outright this one situation of intercourse involving double flow and thus blood, which was up to that point unnamed.[26]

If this scenario concerning v. 33b is accurate, then the author made a special effort to preserve the schematic, structural symmetry of the chapter.[27] In Lev 15, which divides into male and female sections, this amounts to an effort to preserve gender symmetry with respect to purity issues related to genital flow, in general, and sexual intercourse, in particular. However, the nomenclature used to designate the man and woman in v. 33b seems diametrically opposed to this effort.

Within Lev 15, the two terms used to designate the flowing woman or her flow have a necessary connection to the pejorative word field of impurity (טמא). The male nomenclature lacks such a necessary connection. As explained above, טְמֵאָה in v. 33b is a reference to the טְמֵאָה in v. 25. While v. 33b is unbalanced in its gender designations, the same is not true for the anomalous sections from which טְמֵאָה comes. Just as טְמֵאָה הוא occurs in the woman's section, so also טָמֵא הוא occurs in v. 2 of the men's section. Thus, within the chapter the author refers to both man and woman by nomenclature with a necessary connection to the pejorative word field of impurity. He highlights only the female nomenclature in v. 33b because only "intercourse in the context of double flow" is his concern and the impurity nomenclature of the woman in conjunction with יִשְׁכַּב is sufficient to identify that situation. The impurity nomenclature of the man is insufficient because it leaves out the blood factor. Furthermore, the אִישׁ of v. 33b refers to a man with or without anomalous flow. טָמֵא would have said less than

---

24. Wright, *Disposal of Impurity*, 195, states: "A question in regard to the *zāb* may be brought up at this point. If it seems logical to apply the pollution that sexual intercourse with a menstruant causes to the case of the *zābâ*, is it not logical to apply it also to the case of the *zāb*? I do not think this question can be decided. On the one hand, the pollution effect of all three cases otherwise is very similar. This may suggest that intercourse with a *zāb* brings pollution as in the case of the menstruant. On the other hand we noticed earlier…that the pollution of the *zāb* may be considered slightly less severe (in some way) than that of the menstruant and *zābâ*. If this is so, then perhaps the prescriptions may not intend that a *zāb* can pollute like a menstruant by sexual intercourse."

25. Evidently blood is of greater impurity than men's anomalous or non-anomalous flow. Wright, *Disposal of Impurity*, 187, states: "It may be that the editor perceived the impurity of an abnormal discharge in a male to be less severe in some way than that of a blood flow—normal or irregular—in a woman…"

26. The typological kinship of the components of v. 33aγ–33b derives from the anomalous-flow qualification present in each. This is enough to warrant the *lameds* even though 33b, unlike 33aγ2, names a *situation* involving individuals rather than naming simply individuals.

27. Contrary to Wegner, "'Coming Before the Lord,'" 459.

the author wanted. Thus, the factor governing the nomenclature of v. 33b is the gender-neutral blood factor.[28]

Again, with respect to purity issues, the author treats the man and woman equally.

b. *The Challenge*

1) *Introverted Structure.* The most significant challenge to the above interpretation is the structural solution which Milgrom and Whitekettle propose for the perceived syntactic and conceptual problems of v. 18. This solution posits an introverted structure[29] for Lev 15. Verse 18 is the center of the structure, belonging to neither the male nor female sections. While this structure demonstrates gender symmetry with respect to genital flow,[30] gender symmetry with respect to sexual intercourse is at least potentially compromised.[31] The male non-anomalous section lacks a verse corresponding to v. 24 in the female section. One might assert that v. 18, even as an independent unit, provides the balance. But v. 18 as an independent unit carries a different message than v. 18 as an integral part of vv. 16–18.[32] The chapter, then, structurally and thematically appears to be biased, protecting the man against the impurity of the woman.

These comments, however, only beg the question if they are used to discredit the chiastic structure. Such discredit must stand on more solid ground.

a) *Syntactic Difficulties: Milgrom.* One of the major syntactic puzzles of v. 18 is the initial placement of אִשָּׁה, which emphasizes the woman where one would expect emphasis to remain with the man.[33] Milgrom's solution to this puzzle suggests that v. 18 is an inverted hinge, an independent connecting unit between two texts (see Fig. 1).

A preceding word (אִשָּׁה), within the hinge, echoes the text following, and a following word (אִישׁ) echoes the text preceding.[34] This inverted hinge is the

---

28. See below for discussion of the gender of blood.

29. See Isaac M. Kikawada, "The Shape of Genesis 11:1–9," in *Rhetorical Criticism* (ed. Jared J. Jackson and Martin Kessler; Pittsburg: Pickwick, 1974), 23, for the use of this term.

30. Hoffman, *Covenant*, 147–50. Hoffman uses this structure to demonstrate that the taxonomy of genital impurity is not gender based. Rather, it is based on the normal/abnormal polarity.

31. Hoffman fails to notice this structural asymmetry in Lev 15. Ibid., 149.

32. Whitekettle, "Leviticus," 31–45. In fact, Whitekettle argues for the distinctive import of v. 18 as an independent center, which leads him finally to conclude that the primary concern of the chapter is "ideal physiological functioning of the reproductive system." At the very least, the chiastic structure fails to account for the deliberate placement of a sex verse as the conclusion of each non-anomalous section. Such placement underscores the fact that no special danger comes from intercourse because of the *gender* of the flow.

33. The פְתוּחָא preceding v. 18 indicates that the Masoretes also puzzled over this placement. See Milgrom, *Leviticus*, 930. Milgrom observes that the woman is the subject of the verse. As I have stated above, woman is not the subject. However, the question remains concerning the pronounced emphasis given to her within the men's section.

34. Ibid., 905, 930–31. See also H. Van Dyke Parunak, "Transitional Techniques in the Bible," *JBL* 102 (1983): 541.

foundation of Milgrom's introverted structure.[35] Milgrom cites Parunak as the source of his "hinge" model.[36] Of the several literary connectors Parunak describes, the inverted hinge is certainly the closest approximation to what we have in the text.[37] However, Parunak does not claim, nor can we assume, that he has described every type of linking structure that is either possible or that ever occurs. If v. 18 functions as a hinge, it follows a pattern which Parunak has not addressed.

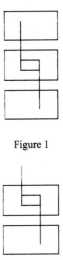

Figure 1

Figure 2

That v. 18 contains reverse echoes of preceding and following text is undeniable. However, as a hinge it is asymmetrically placed, embedded in one side of the structure. Call it an "inverted hanging hinge": Aba/B (see Fig. 2).

This placement accounts for two features of the text which Milgrom's structure ignores: the similar subject matter—semen—of v. 18 and vv. 16–17, and the symmetry created by the conclusion of each non-anomalous section with a verse on intercourse. Thus, while v. 18 may indeed function as an inverted hinge, such a function does not necessarily designate it as a separate case, as Milgrom suggests. Nor does it entail chiasm as the fundamental structure of the chapter.[38] The fact that Milgrom offers two structures even while calling the introverted structure a "more meaningful division" supports this observation.[39]

35.   Milgrom, *Leviticus*, 905.

36.   Ibid., 930–31.

37.   Parunak, "Transitional Techniques," 541, writes: "The inverted hinge, on the other hand, offers the pattern A/ba/B and reverses the order of the joining elements from that of the larger blocks of text."

38.   Milgrom, *Leviticus*, 930–31. Milgrom also refers to Lev 4:1–35 and Gen 11:5 as examples in which אשר is used "as both a pivot and a marker to indicate the transition to a new category within the same unit." While I have no quarrel with the idea that אשר might be used as a pivot and a

b) *Conceptual Difficulties: Whitekettle.* The conceptual difficulty in v. 18 has to do with the following question: Why does emission of semen or sexual intercourse, which is necessary to obtain something so highly valued as progeny, cause impurity?[40] Whitekettle's study ultimately attempts to answer this question. As part of his argument, which concludes that the functional ambiguity of the penis is the source of impurity,[41] he posits the structural and thematic independence of v. 18 and, thus, the "interlocking pivotal structure"[42] for the chapter. A related conclusion is that the primary concern of Lev 15 is the "ideal physiological functioning of the reproductive system" rather than mediation of impurity caused by genital discharge.[43]

Whitekettle posits structural independence based on two prior suppositions: (1) אִשָּׁר in v. 18 necessarily demarcates a distinct legal unit,[44] and (2) the non-contagious impurity of v. 18 indicates that it is not a subcase and is, therefore, independent of vv. 16–17.[45] These suppositions are erroneous.

Whitekettle has failed to notice the use of the אֲשֶׁר construction throughout the chapter. It occurs similarly in other clauses (vv. 4a, 4b, 9, 11, 12a, 20a, 20b), which Whitekettle himself would not identify as distinct legal units. The difference between them and v. 18 is that they can be read more easily as relatives than v. 18 since the subjects and verbs of their protases and apodoses agree in number. Nevertheless, like v. 18, they can also be read as conditionals with *casus pendens.*[46] The similarity is not accidental.

Whitekettle's conclusion that v. 18 is the independent center of the chapter because it is not a subcase of vv. 16–17 is also misguided. However, the literary phenomenon, on which he bases his conclusion, is real. The law on sexual intercourse concluding the men's non-anomalous section is a separate case, whereas in the women's non-anomalous section that concluding law is a subcase of the case which begins the section.[47] In fact, this construction, two separate but related cases, in the men's section is unique in the chapter.

Whitekettle, however, suggests more than this. Not only is v. 18 not a subcase, but it is also an independent unit. He bases this assumption on the

marker, I do quarrel with the idea that this usage in Lev 15 is at the center of a chiasm. Milgrom also cites Kikawada's analysis of Gen 11. See Kikawada, "Shape of Genesis," 18–32. Interestingly, Kikawada finds at least two "pivots" in his text: v. 5 and v. 8. However, only one of these, v. 5, functions as the center of a chiasm.

39. Milgrom, *Leviticus*, 904–5.

40. Whitekettle, "Leviticus," 31. Wenham, "Why Does Sexual Intercourse Defile (Lev 15:18)?," *ZAW* 95 (1983): 432. See also Eilberg-Schwartz, *The Savage in Judaism*, 186; Milgrom, *Leviticus*, 933–34.

41. Whitekettle, "Leviticus," 43–44.

42. Ibid., 37. This is his name for the introverted structure.

43. Ibid., 36–37.

44. Ibid., 35.

45. Ibid., 35–36.

46. Waltke and O'Connor, *Biblical Hebrew*, 77 #5. See their example of a relative, very similar to the ones used in Lev 15, under their discussion on the nominative absolute (i.e. *casus pendens*).

47. See the structure above, and also Whitekettle, "Leviticus," 35.

conclusion that whereas the impurity of the other sections is contagion, the impurity of v. 18 is not. Whitekettle notes that the subject of v. 18 is not singular, that a phrase analogous to "and her monthly flow touches him" (from v. 24) is absent, and that the man is explicitly mentioned even though we know already from vv. 16–17 that he is unclean during intercourse. Since these three factors occur, he concludes that the impurity of v. 18 is not contagion.[48]

However, the plural subject and explicit mention of the man are present for emphasis: *both* man and woman become impure during the desirable act of intercourse. Verse 24 lacks the same emphasis because vv. 19–23 unambiguously describe the woman's impurity already. Verse 24 emphasizes the fact that the man contracts the same level of impurity as the woman. The lack of the "analogous phrase" in v. 18 is a function of the number of discharges involved. In v. 18, only one discharge is involved. Thus, the reader knows without a doubt that the prescription applies to seminal discharge. In v. 24, two discharges of differing severity are involved: semen and blood. The author wants unambiguously to state that in v. 24 *blood* is the cause of the impurity. Thus, וּתְהִי נִדָּתָהּ עָלָיו occurs in v. 24 and no such phrase occurs in v. 18.

In fact, contrary to Whitekettle's contention, v. 18b indicates that contagion is at work: וְטָמְאוּ עַד־הָעָרֶב. Nothing could be plainer. Even Whitekettle's final answer concerning the source of impurity of v. 18 must admit contagion because of v. 18b.[49] Thus, the men's non-anomalous section is unique not because contagion is lacking, but because the "physiology" of that section in connection with impurity is open to confusion and misunderstanding.

The writer foresaw that if he allowed vv. 16–17 to encompass the situation of v. 18, analogously to the woman's non-anomalous section, or if he framed v. 18 as he framed v. 24, confusion would arise. Who can believe that sexual intercourse, necessary for the production of progeny, defiles? Not even twentieth-first-century scholars believe that the author of this ancient text believed it. The fact that they have taken the impurity caused by emission of semen during intercourse to be such a puzzle demonstrates this writer's remarkable foresight. The "desirability" and "normalcy" of intercourse creates the potential for misunderstanding and confusion. Thus, the writer includes explicit stipulation to dispel the potential confusion. He wants it understood that, contrary to what we might consider to be common sense, emission of semen causes impurity to both man and woman under *any* circumstance, even the desirable circumstance necessary for the production of progeny—sexual intercourse.

Whitekettle's argument for the *thematic* independence of v. 18 is from another direction. He bases it on the supposition that the following do not cause the impurity of v. 18:[50] loss of life liquids (i.e. the crossing of boundaries), emission of semen per se, and sexual intercourse per se.[51]

48. Ibid., 36.
49. Ibid., 44.
50. Whitekettle does not explicitly state the basis for his assertion concerning thematic independence. The summary given here is my interpretation of the inferences he seems to be drawing.
51. Whitekettle, "Leviticus," 33, 36.

Indeed, sexual intercourse per se is not the source of impurity. Emission of semen is.[52] Whether or not the power of the impurity of semen draws on a conceptuality concerning loss of life liquids or crossing boundaries is open to question.[53] The author mentions שִׁכְבַת־זֶרַע, a seeming repetition, because he wants no confusion to arise over the fact that specifically this genital discharge causes impurity.

Thus, Whitekettle's suppositions concerning structural and thematic independence cannot be sustained. Furthermore, genital discharge, not the woman, not the man, not intercourse, not the functional ambiguity of the penis, is the source of the impurity of v. 18.[54] The construction of v. 18 is a result of the writer's concern to emphasize the fact that during the "desirable" act of intercourse, which every married couple was expected to perform, impurity necessarily occurs to both individuals.

The logic of the impurity of genital discharge rules the chapter without exception, not even the exception of intercourse. The operative question is not: Why does semen or intercourse defile? It is, rather: Why does genital discharge defile? And this is a question which we must put to the entire chapter, not to just v. 18.

c) *Conclusion*. The arguments which support the introverted structure put forward by both Milgrom and Whitekettle are unfounded. While awkwardness and idiosyncrasies may characterize v. 18, far simpler solutions than that of the introverted structure explain them. The two-part structure, which demonstrates gender symmetry, with respect to purity issues related to genital discharge in general as well as to sexual intercourse in particular, is a more accurate rendering.

2) *Asymmetries*. In addition to the structural symmetries demonstrated by the anomalous/non-anomalous and pure/impure divisions, as well as the placement of vv. 18 and 24, other kinds of symmetries as well as asymmetries, gender-neutral as well as gender-specific, exist between the men's and women's sections. For the sake of brevity and focus, those demonstrated by the sex verses will be emphasized. In fact, the sex verses exhibit the most serious gender asymmetry that occurs in Lev 15. Nevertheless, they also demonstrate the author's equal treatment of the woman and the man with respect to his primary concern.

a) *Shorthand Technique*. Many of the most noticeable asymmetries that occur in the chapter and several that occur in the sex verses are the result of a shorthand literary technique.[55] This technique, described by Milgrom, is a gender-

---

52. For the practice of sexual intercourse without emission of semen, see Mantak Chia, *Taoist Secrets of Love: Cultivating Male Sexual Energy* (Santa Fe: Aurora Press, 1984), 113–39.

53. Whitekettle's argument that the boundaries of "one flesh" are constitutive during intercourse rather than the boundaries of the individual body is speculative regardless of Gen 2:24. See Whitekettle, "Leviticus," 33.

54. Milgrom, *Leviticus*, 44, states: "It is the discharge that contaminates, not the person. Hence, objects that are underneath him—bed, seat, saddle—but no others are considered impure."

55. It is called "condensation" by Wegner, " 'Coming Before the Lord,' " 457.

neutral feature of the text.[56] For example, mediation of the woman's impurity is noticeably absent from v. 24. Some prescriptions for ablutions for the man are lacking as well. In fact, ablutions are absent from the entire women's section but present in the men's section. This is a pronounced asymmetry.

Milgrom suggests that this asymmetry is a function of what I call the "short-hand technique." In Lev 15, this technique works in at least two ways. First, the author allows one section of text to rely upon another section for completion of its prescriptions.[57] Second, the author allows one phrase to signify more than it denotes at face value.[58] The absence of ablutions in vv. 19–30 is a function of both forms of this technique.[59] So also is absence of mediation of the woman's impurity in v. 24.[60] Other similar asymmetries in the chapter are due to this technique as well.

Wegner, however, argues that the ablutions are absent because a woman is ineligible to come into the presence of the Lord.[61] The ablutions are irrelevant for the woman because their performance is mandated only with respect to cultic acts, those acts in which the performer enters the presence of the Lord.[62] While Wegner's observations regarding presentation of the offerings are supported by an actual articulation in the text ("bring them to the priest in the presence of the Lord" rather than "give them to the priest at the door"), in addition to an "ellipsis," her observations regarding ablutions are supported by ellipsis alone. Furthermore, the ellipses, in fact, are distributed unevenly throughout the chapter, with respect to gender. In addition, the *woman*, as well as the man, is, in fact, required to bathe in the one prescription where she appears in the men's section: v. 18.

Milgrom presents an extensive discussion of many of these ellipses, some of which depend upon the "shorthand technique" and some of which depend upon

---

56. It might be argued that beginning the text with the men's section was a decision based on gender. This may be so. But that choice, having been made, the shorthand literary technique by which the woman's section depends on the prior men's section for completion is gender-neutral. The same dynamic is at work internally to the woman's section.

57. Milgrom, *Leviticus*. See the following pages for specific instances of the application of this technique: 905, 914, 919, 923–24, 934–37, 939–41. He writes (p. 924): "It should be noted, however, that these latter three, ostensibly, do not require ablutions at all (12:2; 15:19, 28)! Surely, this cannot be true. The problem resolves itself once it is realized that the *zāb* stands first in the list of genital discharges in chap. 15. The cases that follow, the menstruant and the *zābâ*..., abbreviate their contamination rules because they are derivable from the *zāb*." See also Levine, *Leviticus*, 97; Wright, *Disposal of Impurity*, 191.

58. Milgrom, *Leviticus*, 919. Milgrom has argued concerning *yiṭmā' 'ad-hā'āreb* that: "Bathing is always assumed by this expression, for it is a basic requisite for all purifications."

59. Ibid., 934–35, states: "There is no mention of ablutions for the menstruant or for the woman with chronic discharges (v 28). Still, all the statements regarding the duration of impurity automatically imply that it is terminated by ablutions... Besides, if a minor impurity such as a seminal discharge requires ablutions (15:16), all the more so the major genital discharges."

60. This is so since v. 24 relies on vv. 19–23 for completion of instructions regarding the woman's impurity.

61. As the topological gender discrepancies with respect to presentation of offerings suggests.

62. Wegner, "'Coming Before the Lord,'" 458–59. She notes the same absence of ablutions in Lev 12.

the science of the degree of impurity. The latter, of course, are not true ellipses.[63] In v. 18, which occurs in the first half of the chapter,[64] neither the man nor the woman is required to wash their clothes, perhaps presuming their nakedness. Nor is laundering of bedding mentioned; but as Milgrom observes, if soiled with semen, it would be required, as can be surmised from other verses in the chapter.[65] With v. 19 we move into the second half of the chapter.[66] This verse, which involves the woman's non-anomalous flow, mentions no ablutions at all for her, as Wegner correctly observes.[67] Nor, however, are ablutions mentioned for *the man* who touches her. Milgrom states: "As with the menstruant herself, ablutions are assumed here and in all of the following cases (vv 20–27; cf. the Note on 11:24)."[68] No ablutions, whatsoever, are prescribed for *the man or the woman* in v. 24 in connection with the most severe impurity involving both semen and blood.[69] In v. 28, as Wegner has observed, no ablutions are prescribed for the woman with anomalous flow.[70] Unless Wegner can explain *all* of the ellipses, including the ones connected to men, her criticism of Milgrom cannot stand and her theory that ellipses are a function of woman's obstruction from the cult also cannot stand. In view of the "condensations" in this chapter and the same kinds of "condensations" in other chapters, as detailed by Milgrom, the contention that the ablution-prescriptions, which occur in the men's section, serve the woman's section as well is plausible.[71]

b) *Blood*. The difference in duration of the woman's and man's impurity is one asymmetry, however, which is not due to this technique. Several scholars have

63. Milgrom, *Leviticus*, 905–41. The absence in v. 9 of washing, bathing and "he shall be unclean until evening" is because v. 10 refers to the chariot of v. 9 in addition to other kinds of seats (p. 917). The washing and bathing statement is absent in v. 10 because the phrase *yiṭmāʾ ʿad-hāʿāreb*, using an imperfect form, according to Milgrom implies temporary impurity, which by his understanding of the degrees of impurity is all that is required here (p. 910). He refers us to Lev 11, stating (p. 667): "That the impure person must undergo ablutions is implied, not only here but throughout the chapter. Ablutions are explicitly called for in Lev 11 only in the case of impure vessels: if ablutions are required for vessels contaminated by touch, all the more so for persons. Furthermore, one who eats the carcass of a pure animal ostensibly is only "impure until evening" (v. 40), but other texts inform us that he also requires ablutions (17:15; 22:6)." In v. 23, ablutions are missing for the man because the impurity is temporary (p. 910).

64. See the structure above.

65. Milgrom, *Leviticus*, 934.

66. See the structure above.

67. Milgrom, *Leviticus*, 934, states: "There is no mention of ablutions for the menstruant or for the woman with chronic discharges (v. 28). Still, all statements regarding the duration of impurity automatically imply that it is terminated by ablutions…"

68. Ibid., 935. See Jonathan Magonet, "'But if it is a Girl She is Unclean for Twice Seven Days…': The Riddle of Leviticus 12.5," in *Reading Leviticus: A Conversation with Mary Douglas* (ed. John F. Sawyer; JSOTSup 227; Sheffield: Sheffield Academic Press, 1996), 148–51. Magonet's observations concerning the "truncation" of the woman's section, which improve slightly on Milgrom's solution, lend even greater support to the symmetry of the male and female sections.

69. Only the man is declared unclean because the woman has already been declared unclean in v. 19.

70. Milgrom, *Leviticus*, 944. Of course, Milgrom takes the ablution prescription to be implicit.

71. See n. 57 above.

suggested that the blood of menstruation pollutes because of the *gender* of the blood.[72] In fact, this it not so. The blood of menstruation is a gender-neutral factor which pollutes for the same reason semen pollutes: its association with the potential or the capacity to create life. A review and critique of some of the salient points of Eilberg-Schwartz's theory of the pollution of bodily fluids[73] illustrates the major concerns in the discussion of such matters. It also serves as a springboard for my own explanatory preference concerning such pollution.

Eilberg-Schwartz suggests at least three polarities—each, to a greater or lesser degree, having the capacity to explain the pollution of bodily fluids. They are: the gender polarity,[74] the controllability/uncontrollability polarity[75] and the life/death polarity.[76] I will discuss each in the order I have listed them.

Eilberg-Schwartz himself provides the refutation of the gender polarity as an adequate explanation for the impurity of the blood in Lev 15. Speaking of Lev 15, he writes:

> The signification of women's bleeding thus depends upon the context in which it is viewed. When contrasted with the blood of circumcision, a contrast suggested by the proximity of circumcision to the bleeding associated with birth, female blood is a symbol of women's exclusion from the covenant. But this contrast disappears when menstrual blood is treated among other bodily emissions.[77]

In other words, even if the *gender* of the blood determines the impurity or purity of blood in the wider literary context, which includes texts on circumcision, or in the larger historical context, which includes the subsequent isolation of women, in the context of Lev 15 it does not. The gender polarity cannot explain the pollution of Lev 15.

Hoffman suggests even more strongly than Eilberg-Schwartz "that the key to body-fluid pollution should be sought in the issue of control."[78] Hoffman's

---

72. Eilberg-Schwartz, *The Savage in Judaism*, 174, 179–81, 186. "The difference between semen and menstrual blood might also be part of the symbolic domination of women. Although the loss of both fluids represents a missed opportunity for procreation, menstrual blood is more contaminating simply because of its gender" (p. 186). See also Hoffman, *Covenant*, 136–54; Archer, *Her Price is Beyond Rubies*, 37; idem, "Bound," 38–61. This conclusion is drawn by Eilberg-Schwartz and other scholars who compare the blood of menstruation with the blood of circumcision. They see circumcision and menstruation functioning as a polarity which ultimately has deleterious valuation for women. However, I am concerned, not with the larger context—literary or historical— but with Lev 15 in particular. Both Eilberg-Schwartz (*The Savage in Judaism*, 181) and Hoffman (*Covenant*, 147–48) themselves note that the gender polarity does not govern the fluid symbolism of Lev 15 asymmetrically. See also Mary Douglas, *Implicit Meanings* (London: Routledge & Kegan Paul, 175), 69.

73. Eilberg-Schwartz, *The Savage in Judaism*, 179–82.

74. Ibid., 182–86.

75. Ibid., 186–91.

76. Ibid., 182–86.

77. Ibid., 182.

78. Hoffman, *Covenant*, 154. See also Eilberg-Schwartz, *The Savage in Judaism*, 186–89. Archer ("Bound by Blood," 48) suggests something similar in connection with the nature/culture construct, and goes on to state (p. 51): "Within this scheme of thought, anything which cannot be controlled is labeled dangerous and marginal, particularly when society is working to preserve its

concern is less to explain the pollution of the biblical text than to explain subsequent rabbinic treatment of bodily fluids. His critique of Eilberg-Schwartz's version of the controllability theory is nevertheless relevant.

> Why should the Rabbis have overlooked the fact that at the moment prior to ejaculation a man has no more control over semen than a woman has over menstrual blood? Or that nocturnal emissions are even more unpredictable than the average woman's period, which at least is expected around a given time? Moreover, why should we believe that tears are controllable? Or breast milk? Or earwax or mucus that escapes in a "runny nose"? True, our own culture cleans up the human body in such a way that we like to imagine we have control over all such emissions. We cough involuntarily, and turn our faces away from an observer who pretends not to observe until we finish wiping our noses and mouths with a tissue. We keep our ears well-groomed. We "fight back tears," even though we know of times when "tears well up and overwhelm us," for which we may even dutifully apologize. Adults should not be "cry-babies." But all of that is our own cultural imagination at work, tidying up the untidy facts of bodily substances that defy our will more than they obey it.[79]

Thus, the uncontrollability/controllability polarity as an explanation of bodily-fluid pollution is limited. Hoffman offers a refinement of Eilberg-Schwartz's theory maintaining that the issue of control is less a "biological phenomenon" than a "social one":[80]

> The binary opposition obtains between men who are in control of their blood, so of themselves, and therefore of society; and women who, lacking control of blood and therefore of self, are thus denied control of society as well.[81]

While his refinement may account for the pollution of bodily fluid in the literature of rabbinic Judaism, it is more difficult to apply to Lev 15. Given the fact that Hoffman[82] himself, as well as Eilberg-Schwartz,[83] admits the lack of gender polarization as a structuring factor in the chapter, and given that Hoffman questions the nature of control over semen vs. menstrual blood, how then exactly does Lev 15 demonstrate the binary opposition he describes? In other words, Hoffman has discredited the controllability/uncontrollability polarity as presented by Eilberg-Schwartz, offering in its stead a refinement which suits the rabbinic literature but not Lev 15.

---

unity and to develop more sophisticated systems of self-definition, as was the case for the Jewish community in Palestine following the exile. The blood of childbirth and menstruation, which follows a passive and unstoppable cycle, can be construed (by the powers that be) to fall within this category, and so it is required that cultural regulation step in with restrictive legislation. That cultural regulation, as we have seen, is controlled by men, for (and this brings me to the third point) within this scheme of thought, woman herself is placed more fully within the realm of nature than man in consequence of the fact that more of her time and her body are seen to be taken up with the natural processes surrounding reproduction of the species."

79. Hoffman, *Covenant*, 154.
80. Ibid., 151–54.
81. Ibid., 154.
82. Ibid., 147–48.
83. Eilberg-Schwartz, *The Savage in Judaism*, 181.

The life/death polarity holds more promise, although Eilberg-Schwartz considers its explanatory power to be limited and Hoffman dismisses it on the basis of "anomalies" for which he believes it is unable to account.[84]

Before critiquing these "anomalies," however, I must respond to Eilberg-Schwartz's contention that since only some kinds of blood contaminate, "the prohibitions on the menstruous woman have nothing to do with the inherent quality of blood,"[85] contrary to the implications of the life/death polarity. Early in his argument, he dismisses the "horror of the blood" (Gen 9:4; Lev 17:11–14; Deut 12:23) as a factor explaining this severity.[86] He argues as follows:

> Indeed, there is warrant for arguing that the latter view in fact explains the menstrual taboo in Israelite religion, since Scripture states unequivocally that blood carries the essence of life (Gen 9:4; Lev 17:11–14; Deut 12:23… But the contrast between menstrual blood, which is contaminating, and the blood of circumcision or sacrifice, which is positively marked, indicates that only some kinds of blood are contaminating… Blood has different meanings depending upon how it originates and from whom it comes. Significantly, the familiar Israelite idea that "life is in the blood" appears only in contexts related to the slaughter of animals or murder, that is, acts in which a living being dies. Some blood is symbolic of life; other kinds of blood are not."[87]

In reply to Eilberg-Schwartz, it can be suggested that even if only some kinds of blood contaminate, it may still be the case that "life is in the blood" is true for all contexts. Life may be in all blood under all circumstances at the same time that "life" is at risk in only certain contexts or spillings, such as slaughter, murder and menses.[88] The factor constitutive for the risk of these situations is that life, manifested as a potential or actual living creature, is aborted by the spilling.[89]

In fact, two primary qualifications might be said to constitute the impurity of bodily fluids: (1) whatever kills life (blood spilled in murder), whatever represents a compromise in the process of making life, or whatever actually does compromise the process of making life;[90] (2) whatever is essential for life or for

84. Ibid., 185–86; see also Hoffman, *Covenant*, 151–52.

85. Eilberg-Schwartz, *The Savage in Judaism*, 179.

86. Ibid., 179.

87. Ibid., 179.

88. For example, life or life potential is not at risk when someone scrapes their knee. Richard Whitekettle, "Leviticus 12 and the Israelite Woman: Ritual Process Liminality and the Womb," *ZAW* 107 (1995): 394, writes the following regarding the opposite direction of blood loss: "Many possible situations in which there is potentially fatal bleeding, such as those involving wounds or accidents in the workplace, are not the subject of any legislative strictures." His point is that "blood" cannot be the factor aligned with the life/death polarity. It has to be something else. But blood that leads to death, such as severing an artery, is subsumed under the contamination of the corpse. Prior to the moment of death, it does not defile because of the contingency of such situations. If an artery in the arm is cut, the bleeding may be stopped by a tourniquet and the person may live. Such situations decide the contingency quickly. Upon that decision (death or life) the blood falls into the impure or pure category.

89. Wenham, "Why?," 434; Whitekettle, "Leviticus," 33. Frymer-Kensky, "Sex in the Bible," 189 n. 12, states: "Another element is present—blood and its associations with death—for contact with death also results in a week-long impurity."

90. For example, non-seminal discharge or anomalous female blood flow may indicate conditions which jeopardize the ability to conceive or to conceive a healthy, "whole" child.

creating life even if it is only part of the process of creating and does not ulti-mately become that life (semen, menstrual blood, lochial discharge).[91]

Objection to "horror of the blood" as a source of impurity is not the only problem Eilberg-Schwartz has with the life/death polarity as an explanation. He and Hoffman offer a list of anomalies for which they believe the polarity cannot account.[92] A critique of the three primary "anomalies" provides a model by which others might also be dismissed. These three "anomalies" can be posed in the form of the following questions.

1. Why does non-seminal discharge pollute more than seminal discharge if spilling of seminal discharge represents "life wasted" while non-seminal does not?
2. Why does the blood of birth pollute if that blood represents creation of new life?
3. Why does semen pollute during intercourse if this is the very act neces-sary for the creation of new life?

For the most part, discernment of what in the actual life of a community pollutes or cleanses is relatively simple.[93] This is one level of alignments in the purity system. A second level is the association of the life/death polarity, or some other construct, with the purity/impurity polarity. This second level of alignments is more difficult to discern. Its truth or value depends upon its capacity to explain all elements of the first level. The third level of alignments are even more diffi-cult to discern. This level has to do with *how* the second level explains the first level. My critique of Eilberg-Schwartz and Hoffman is a critique of their percep-tions of what is going on at this level. They believe that the life/death polarity cannot explain all the elements of the first level. I believe it can.

Examination of the three "anomalies" will demonstrate what I mean. The first "anomaly" suggested by Eilberg-Schwartz and Hoffman is, Why does non-seminal discharge pollute more than seminal discharge if spilling of seminal discharge represents life wasted or "abortion of life potential" while spilling of non-seminal discharge does not? Eilberg-Schwartz and Hoffman assume that since non-seminal discharge does not create life and since seminal discharge does, spilling of non-seminal discharge cannot be aligned with "life wasted" or "abortion of life potential." Therefore, it cannot be aligned with the pole oppo-site life, namely death, and therefore it cannot be aligned with impurity. But Lev 15 does align it with impurity. Thus, "life/death" cannot explain the pollution of non-seminal discharge.

91.   Kirsten Hastrup, "The Sexual Boundary-Danger: Transvestism and Homosexuality," *JASO* 6 (1975): 52: "It is not difficult to understand the danger of menstrual blood, since this is associated with 'a child not to become,' with death, and as both part of the woman and not so."

92.   Eilberg-Schwartz, *The Savage in Judaism*, 185–86; Hoffman, *Covenant*, 151–52.

93.   See Mary Douglas' essay, "Couvade and Menstruation," in *Implicit Meanings*, 60–72. On p. 60 Douglas states: "The same holds good for menstruation: in tribal society it is not universally hedged with ritual taboos. Each primitive culture makes its own selection of bodily functions which it emphasizes as dangerous or good. The problem then is to understand the principles of selection."

Their conclusion concerning the alignment of life/death and thus purity/impurity with non-seminal/seminal discharge is an assumption. This is important to notice. Perhaps the alignment works differently. What if, in the mind of the ancient writer, non-seminal discharge represents a distortion of seminal discharge so that it is not opposed to it but is rather a permutation of it? What if non-seminal discharge, an abnormal flow, is seen by the ancient writer to be something generically akin to semen, even though it does not result in life and does not even have the capacity to create life?[94]

Wenham suggests something like this in his explanation of the impurity of non-seminal discharge.[95] He seems to treat it as a protracted case of seminal emission. He writes: "Similarly too we presume that male semen was viewed as a 'life liquid.' Hence its loss whether long-term (15:1–15) or transient (15:16–18) was viewed as polluting."[96]

An examination of the nature of the flows and their relationships is helpful at this point. Non-anomalous male flow has different duration of impurity than anomalous male flow. Cycle is an insignificant factor with respect to the purity or impurity of male flow. Furthermore, the substance of the two flows differs. The first is called שִׁכְבַת־זֶרַע and the latter is called זוֹב. On the other hand, the non-anomalous female flow may or may not have the same duration as the anomalous female flow. Furthermore, the two flows are the same substance. Both are called דָּם. Thus, the *relationship* of anomalous to non-anomalous in the male and female sections is not entirely parallel when duration and substance are examined. Nevertheless, the placement of non-anomalous and anomalous flows in the structure of the text indicates that the writer, in fact, considered them to be typologically similar.

The qualification of "loss of life potential" is the most plausible explanation for typological similarity. Men's anomalous flow, although not the same as semen, like semen comes from the genitals. It is a sign of illness or infection which can potentially affect the life-giving capacity of the couple.[97] That the author perceived the potential of the life-giving semen itself to be somehow compromised is at least a possibility. He may have perceived male anomalous flow as effecting "diminished" capacity or as symbolic of it. This may be enough to account for its association with the "death pole" of the polarity. Thus, a

---

94. The question may then arise: Why does urine not have the same association? Urine is known to be a normal condition which occurs as a matter of regular practice in humans, before ejaculation becomes a matter of regular practice in the average person's life. Thus urination has a history of non-association with creation of life during the lifespan of the average male. Non-seminal discharge does not. It is an abnormal condition. Furthermore, some non-seminal discharges may affect the capacity to produce life or may be symptoms of an underlying condition which affects the capacity to produce life.

95. Wenham, "Why?," 434. See also Milgrom, *Leviticus*, 933–34; Eilberg-Schwartz, *The Savage in Judaism*, 183.

96. Wenham, "Why?," 434.

97. At the very least, a disease such as gonorrhea when passed to a woman may cause her sterility.

reworking of the alignments associated with the life/death polarity resolves this particular anomaly.

A second anomaly suggested by Eilberg-Schwartz and Hoffman is, Why does the blood of birth pollute if that blood represents creation of new life? But what if the correspondence that matters to the ancient mind is simply the *association with the capacity* to create life? In other words, the blood of birth is part of the blood that created life even though it has not become that life. It is part of the total process. Thus, the impurity is caused not so much by the fact that the blood is wasted as it is by the fact that the blood has/had an association and potential, a mantic power or capacity for creating life.[98] Whatever blood is seen as part of the process that actually creates life but has not become that life also pollutes, whether residual, left from a process completed, or whether an essential component of the life to be created. In fact, perhaps such blood pollutes to an even greater degree.[99]

---

98.   One might object that blood from a scraped knee is in the same way associated with the blood that sustains life in the injured person, even if, as a small amount, it is not essential to the life of that person. I can only surmise that the same *correspondences* do not hold for blood that is involved in the process of creating new life and blood that is involved in the process of sustaining an existing life. In other words, something about blood involved in the process of creating new life makes all of it pollute, while this same something is lacking in blood involved in the process of sustaining life such that all of it does not necessarily pollute. Perhaps the correspondence that matters is that all blood involved in the process of creating life is perceived as essential to that process, while blood spilled from a scraped knee is not essential to the process of sustaining the life of the injured party. He or she can afford to lose the little that is spilled.

99.   William A. R. Thomson, *Black's Medical Dictionary* (33rd ed.; Totowa: Barnes & Noble, 1981), 735: "Puerperium is the period which elapses after the birth of a child until the mother is again restored to her ordinary health. It is generally regarded as lasting for a month. One of the main changes that occurs is the enormous decrease in size that takes place in the muscular wall of the womb... There are often afterpains during the first day in women who have borne several children, less often after a first child... The discharge is blood-stained for the first two or three days, then clearer till the end of the first week, after which it becomes thicker and less in quantity, finally disappearing altogether, if the case goes well, at the end of two or three weeks." See David P. Wright and Richard N. Jones, "Discharge," *ABD* 2:205. Wright and Jones state that Lev 12 distinguishes at least two of the stages of lochial discharge that occur after birth. The first seven days after the birth of a male the woman is unclean כִּימֵי נִדַּת דְּוֹתָהּ. This is the time during which the *lochia cruenta* flows. This flow consists chiefly of blood. For the next two to three weeks the color of the flow becomes paler until it is a creamy color (*lochia alba*). Finally the flow disappears. This constitutes the seven days and thirty-three days of purification for a male baby. However, a male baby requires half the time of purification that a female baby requires. If that which has the potential to create life has the power to pollute, then, that a baby female, who eventually has the power to give birth to life, would cause greater pollution than the male baby, makes sense. Half of the purification period is for that pollution caused by the mother's flow and half is for the baby female's potential to duplicate her mother's pollution. Why this potential pollutes in this way at birth and not continuously throughout her life is another question, the answer to which can only be surmised. Proximity to the mother's pollution in conjunction with her own potential doubles the pollution of the situation requiring twice the period for cleansing. See also Kristen De Troyer, "Blood: A Threat to Holiness or Toward (Another Holiness)?," in De Troyer et al., eds., *Wholly Woman Holy Blood*, 56. De Troyer writes: "I fully agree with Levine's statement, 'It may have reflected apprehension and anticipation regarding the infant daughter's potential fertility, the expectation that she herself would someday become a new mother,' I prefer 'It reflects.'" See also Archer, *Her Price is Beyond Rubies*, 37–39. Archer

A related question is: If both semen and menstrual blood create new life, why does menstrual blood pollute more?[100] If the life/death polarity is constitutive, then more must be said than simply that "the life is in the blood." The life is also in the semen. Menstrual blood spilled is blood that would have created the life of a child. Semen spilled is semen that would have created the life of a child. However, semen in general manifests life only as potential, whereas blood in

writes: "Given this widely attested belief in the power of the fortieth day, why did the Hebrews see fit to add a further forty days consequent on the birth of a female child to the mother's period of impurity? The only possible explanation for this revision of the original superstition is that a daughter was regarded in some sense as inflicting 'double impurity' on her mother, first (as with a son) on account of the blood of her birth (the original taboo = forty days impurity) and secondly on account of her being female (additional taboo = extra forty days impurity)" (p. 38). Of course, the difference would be explained by proponents of the controllability/uncontrollability polarity by stating that the female is in some way invested with the quality of uncontrollability and thus requires the double time. Nevertheless, it must be noted that whichever polarity is chosen—life/death or controllability/uncontrollability—the same "stretch" must be made with respect to the female child. As the potential to create life is not yet fully developed in the female child, so also those qualifications (see Archer, "Bound by Blood," 51) which invest her with the uncontrollability that the male fears are not yet fully developed. Whitekettle, "Leviticus 12," 407, has proposed a structural solution for Lev 12 that is similar to his rendering for Lev 15. He states that the contamination of the puerperal period, forty days subsequent to parturition, is because the "puerperal reproductive system, though it acts typically or normally by discharging lochia, is nonetheless dysfunctional with regard to its systemic purpose." But that systemic dysfunction is known, identified, distinguished and categorized *because* of the discharge of blood and lochia, the static seven- and forty-day periods notwithstanding. That the time-period restriction be conterminous with the discharge is not necessary in order for the *genital flow* per se to be the source of the impurity. If the discharge is under or equal to the forty or seven days, the woman is pure at the end of that time period. If the discharge is more than the forty or seven days, stipulations in Lev 15:19–24 or in vv. 25–30 cover the anomaly, as Whitekettle himself suggests ("Levitical Thought and the Female Reproductive Cycle: Wombs, Wellsprings, and the Primeval World," *VT* 46 [1996]: 376–91 [382]). All situations, from a variety of possibilities, are therefore covered. Whitekettle offers an intriguing and plausible suggestion for the precise numbers "seven" and "forty," which are selected in Lev 15 and 12. However, I remain unconvinced that the systemic dysfunction is not due to discharge itself. In addition, Whitekettle's solution has no greater facility for addressing the double time for female children than other solutions that have been proposed, a problem which is not the subject of his essays. See also Hoffman, *Covenant*, 151–54, 164–65; Eilberg-Schwartz, *The Savage in Judaism*, 186–89. The most intriguing solution I have discovered in the secondary literature, so far, comes from Magonet, "The Riddle of Leviticus 12.5," 151: "There is a phenomenon that sometimes affects a new-born girl following the withdrawal of the maternal hormones—namely vaginal bleeding. I consulted a professor of Obstetrics and Gynaecology, the author of several textbooks on the subject, who confirmed that perhaps one in ten baby girls may bleed in this way, and even if no blood appears there may well be a discharge. He added that it is one of the first things told to midwives so that they do not become overly concerned when it happens. (Maternal hormones can also cause temporary breast development in babies of either sex and even lactation, leading to the superstition that this is 'witch's milk'). It is therefore altogether possible that with the birth of a baby girl we have the equivalent of two 'women,' each with an actual or potential vaginal discharge, to be accounted for. Since this uncleanness has to be ritually dealt with and the baby cannot do so, the mother with whom the child was formerly united and from whom she has emerged, symbolically bears the uncleanness so that the period is doubled. Thus we are dealing with simple mathematical logic, two generators of uncleanness require two periods of purification."

100. Eilberg-Schwartz, *The Savage in Judaism*, 186.

general manifests not only as potential when contributing to the birth of a child, but also as actual life. It is essential to the *actual*, continuing life of creatures. Perhaps this double qualification is the source of the difference in severity between menstrual blood and semen.

A third anomaly raised by Eilberg-Schwartz and Hoffman is: Why does semen pollute during intercourse if this is the very act necessary for the creation of new life? The same rationale can explain this anomaly as explained the blood-of-birth anomaly. Semen has the power to create life. It is this *association* which constitutes the impurity of intercourse, whether or not life results.

Thus, the blood itself, a gender-neutral factor, rather than the gender of the blood is responsible for the severity of the impurity of woman's genital discharge.[101]

c) *Menstruation as Illness*. One final gender asymmetry is the connection of menstruation with illness and the lack of such association with respect to seminal emission.[102] Both the cognate associations[103] of דָּוֶה and its metaphorical applications[104] in other parts of the Hebrew corpus support this connection. The

101.   Cohen, "Menstruants," 276. Cohen suggests that the difference in duration of separation on account of impurity between male and female non-anomalous flow is "probably because menstruation lasts longer than ejaculation." See also the explanations for the danger of menstruation among "ancient peoples" as suggested by William Phipps, "The Menstrual Taboo in the Judeo-Christian Tradition," *Journal of Religion and Health* 19 (Winter 1980): 299.

102.   Moshe Greenberg, "The Etymology of נִדָּה '(Menstrual) Impurity,' " in *Solving Riddles and Untying Knots: Biblical, Epigraphic, and Semitic Studies in Honor of Jonas C. Greenfield* (ed. Ziony Zevit, Seymon Gitin and Michael Sokoloff; Winona Lake, Ind.: Eisenbrauns, 1995). Greenberg's observations concerning נדד support the negative semantic connotations of דוה, even if נדה does not have the idea of illness wrapped in it. Greenberg states: "The morphology of *niddâ* immediately suggests an etymology from *ndd*. The semantic fields of Heb. and Syr. *ndd* indicate a basic meaning 'distance oneself' with negative connotation, as in flight or from disgust or abhorrence. Heb. *niddâ* appears to contain both ideas: distancing and separation due to abhorrence. The term has a specific abstract reference to menstrual impurity (as abhorrent [to males] and entailing separation of the sexes). It has a generic abstract reference to the state of 'impurity,' and a generic concrete reference to an 'impure thing/act' (what is to be kept apart, abhorred). The generic senses occur almost exclusively in biblical and Qumran nonlegal contexts; the specific abstract sense 'menstrual impurity' prevails in priestly legal texts. For the specific, concrete 'menstruant', Biblical Hebrew employs the euphemistic *dawâ*. In Mishnaic Hebrew *dawâ*, is replaced by *niddâ*, which no longer denotes a state but the menstruant herself (or, rarely, her blood). The first sign of this shift in usage occurs in Ezek 18:6—in accord with other evidence of the pivotal character of Ezekiel's language" (p. 76).

103.   Milgrom, *Leviticus*, 745–46, states: "An infinitive construct—not a plural noun—of the verb *dâwâ* (Lam 5:17; *Keter Torah*), which also appears as an adjective, *dâweh* (15:33; 20:18), *dawwây* (Isa 1:5; Jer 8:18) and as a noun, *děwây* (Ps 41:4), *dâwâ* (Isa 30:22), a menstruous garment (cf. *b. Nid.* 9a), and *madweh* (Deut 7:15; 28:60). The cognates, Akk. *Dawû* 'be sick, stagger' (*AHw*) and Ug. *Dwy* 'sickness' (*KTU* 1.16–*CTA* 16.6 [127] 35,51) conform to and confirm the contextual connotation of the biblical root 'be sick, infirm.' Interestingly, in Hittite, 'the linguistic form of the word for moon, *arma*– is not only associated with conception, pregnancy, and menstruation but also with weakness and sickness'… Thus philology confirms experience: menstruation is associated with sickness. Hence, *niddâ* and *dâwâ* are related."

104.   Deut 7:15; 28:60; Isa 1:5; 30:22; Jer 8:18; Ps 41:4; Job 6:7; Lam 1:13, 22; 5:17.

question with respect to the thesis of this study is: Does the impurity of menstruation derive from the illness connection or does it derive from the blood? The illness connection might be seen as gender-specific although not necessarily so. The blood connection, as established above, is gender-neutral.

Milgrom states uncategorically that "menstruation is associated with sickness."[105] However, he also states uncategorically that "Menstruation is a normal condition and is, therefore, not to be compared with abnormal genital discharges (vv. 13–5, 28–30)."[106] These two statements taken together may seem contradictory but in fact they are the truth of the text. The author uses nomenclature to discuss menstruation that reflects one set of conceptual associations related to menstruation. Perhaps these associations reflect the real experience of many women at menses.[107] Nevertheless, the structure of the text, which pairs seminal emission with menstrual flow, vis-à-vis the category of anomalous flow, makes a conceptual statement of its own. Seminal emission is a normal condition decidedly not associated with illness. So also is menstruation. Perhaps it is even as desirable as seminal emission. It is not associated with the illness or abnormality of anomalous flow.

Given the cognate associations and metaphorical applications of the word דָּוָה, which are perhaps clues to the world within which the author lives,[108] the statement which the author makes by means of the structure is truly remarkable. Milgrom underscores this point:

> Against this backdrop of Israel's immediate and remote contemporaries and what was probably the dominant practice within Israel itself…, the Priestly legislation on the menstruant is all the more remarkable. First and foremost, she is neither banished from the community nor even isolated within her home. The implicit assumption of the pericope on the menstruant is that she lives at home, communicating with her family and performing her household chores.[109]

Thus, although menstruation has association, even in the present text, with illness, the structure demonstrates that the author has made a conscious decision to treat menstruation as if it were a normal phenomenon. The association of menstruation with illness in the present text, indicated by vocabulary, may be a function of the implicit and unconscious assumptions of the writer's worldview and the culture from which he comes. His conscious decision, therefore, to treat menstruation as if normal is all the more stunning.

105. Milgrom, *Leviticus*, 746.

106. Ibid., 935. See also Levine, *Leviticus*, 92. Julius Preuss, *Biblical and Talmudic Medicine* (trans. and ed. Fred Rosner; New York: Sanhedrin, 1978), 375, states: "The *zaba*, or woman with a flux, is fundamentally different from the normal menstruating woman."

107. Penelope Shuttle and Peter Redgrove, *The Wise Wound* (New York: Grove, 1978), 41–42. Whether or not this experience is shaped by, derives from or is a function of gender bias inherent in and reaching across a variety of cultures, including that of ancient Israel, rather than hormonal changes, is a question outside the purview of this study. See also Hilary M. Lips, *Sex and Gender: An Introduction* (Mountain View: Mayfield, 1988), 174–84; Karen E. Paige, "Women Learn to Sing the Menstrual Blues," *Psychology Today* (September 1973): 41–46.

108. The gender asymmetries of the presentation of the offerings are also such clues.

109. Milgrom, *Leviticus*, 952–53.

3) *Summary.* While the introverted structure is asymmetrically gender qualified with respect to the sex verses, the two-part structure, conveying the primary concern of the writer, exhibits astonishing gender symmetry with respect to that primary concern.

Woman's focalization in the text is on par with man's focalization in the text. This symmetry is remarkable since the language-depicting-the-sex-act and, in part, point-of-view reveal the unsurprising fact that woman's position is highly circumscribed by man within the worldview of the writer, and that the writer takes such circumscription for granted.

C. *Conclusion*

All of this suggests an interesting conceptual movement with respect to woman in the text of Lev 15. The language-depicting-the-sex-act portrays woman as object and man as subject. Vocabulary referencing the female flow exhibits considerable gender asymmetry. The structure of the chapter, however, portrays them as equal with respect to purity issues. The evidence with respect to purity issues connected to intercourse demonstrates that women, like men, are subjects responsible for maintaining their own purity and the purity of the community. Furthermore, this concern for purity is not weighted as a greater concern for the welfare of the man than the welfare of the woman. Woman's action and state of being are as important as those of the man. The community's welfare depends equally upon the initiative, discernment and trustworthy action of men and women, with respect to their discharges. They are both agents responsible for management of matters pertaining to discharge.

In view of the fact that the author makes a statement of gender neutrality with the structure, the asymmetries would seem to be less a part of his programmatic, conscious agenda than part of the trappings of the world from which he comes. Clearly, we have before us in the text an interesting conceptual movement which understands woman to be circumscribed by man in a variety of ways and also sees her to be equal with respect to a particular issue.

This particular issue is a classificatory concern. Purity of the community is uppermost in the mind of the writer. The author's intention is not to forbid the flows or the sex acts described. Rather, his intention is to mediate impurity when it occurs. The author instructs the individual whose state of being and action affect this purity—men as well as women. Furthermore, he instructs them, with respect to this issue, with remarkable gender equity. The intent and concern of the author is not to legislate so as to protect, empower, favor or otherwise benefit one gender over the other with respect to this issue. Treatment of the woman's flow mirrors treatment of the man's flow.

Property issues, of course, are of no concern.

Chapter 3

LEVITICUS 18

A. *Introduction*

Wegner refers to Lev 18:6–20 as follows:

> Only *some* of these women are actual blood relatives of the man himself; but virtually *all* those listed are the sexual property of *other men*. The incest taboos thus protect private property as much as sexual propriety.[1]

On the other hand, Douglas has this to say about the same text:

> Incest and adultery (Lev XVIII, 6–20) are against holiness, in the simple sense of right order. Morality does not conflict with holiness, but holiness is more a matter of separating that which should be separated than of protecting the rights of husbands and brothers.[2]

The text itself is, to some degree, responsible for the opposing conclusions drawn by Wegner and Douglas concerning the intent of the bulk of the law series in Lev 18. In Lev 15, two sets of textual features point to opposing conceptual impulses with respect to women. A similar situation exists in Lev 18.

The point-of-view of Lev 18 and the language-depicting-the-sex-act are responsible for the most severe gender asymmetries of the chapter. They portray the woman as marginalized and objectified, circumscribed by and subordinate to the man. She is passive receiver. Man is subject, initiator and responsible agent. The author discusses the woman with his male audience and never the other way around. The male ego of the text mediates whatever instruction the author intends for the female Israelite. Her responsibilities under the law, with one exception, are only implied and all but entirely fade from the explicit text. The resulting, initial impression for the reader is that the law guards the sexual property of the man who is himself the sole guardian of sexual propriety.[3]

---

1. Wegner, *Chattel*, 13. See also Joanne M. Dupont, "Women and the Concept of Holiness in the 'Holiness Code' (Leviticus 17–26): Literary, Theological and Historical Context" (Ph.D. diss. Marquette University, 1989), 160.
2. Douglas, *Purity*, 53.
3. Biale, *Women and Jewish Law*, 179, states: "It should come as no surprise that the sexual prohibitions are addressed to men; most biblical legislation is. But in the case of sexual transgressions there is a further, more fundamental reason: men are presumed to be the active agents in sexual interactions. Men are the ones with greater physical power and the sanction of social conventions for initiating sex. In the case of incestuous relationships this is a particularly salient point: in the patriarchal family women rely on fathers, brothers, and husbands to be their protectors. The family is

However, while point-of-view and language-depicting-the-sex-act are responsible for this considerable gender asymmetry, they are also the source of evidence for a more complex conceptuality with respect to women than her marginalization and objectification imply. Moreover, other features of the text support this complexity.

While the point-of-view seems to indicate that the man is the guardian of sexual propriety, subtle contraindicators demonstrate an implicit expectation concerning the woman's responsibilities for such propriety as well. So also, subtle contraindicators related to language-depicting-the-sex-act suggest that the intent of the law is, in fact, not to protect woman or her sexuality as property. Rather, the intent is to restrict the actions of men and women for the sake of protecting certain boundaries in the way that Douglas describes. Furthermore, at least three other features of the text—selection-of-laws, the identification-of-women and the structure-of-the-text—confirm these contra-indicating impulses of point-of-view and language-depicting-the-sex-act, also revealing that the intent of the law is not to protect woman or her sexuality as property. These three features reveal that not only is woman *not* focalized as property, but, like her male counterpart, she is an agent responsible, however implicitly, for maintaining the purity of the social-sexual system to which she belongs.

Douglas' statement is, thus, closer to the truth than Wegner's. Furthermore, the truth of Douglas' statement applies to Lev 18:19–23 as well.

B. *Discussion*

1. *Point-of-View and Language-Depicting-the-Sex-Act*
a. *Point-of-View.* The point-of-view consists of a male author directing the instruction of his text to a mature, Israelite male ego and an implied female ego.[4] Although the woman is in the background of the text only, the instruction is meant for her as well as the man. Both are responsible for keeping the laws of Lev 18.

1) *The Bias.* God instructs Moses to speak to בְּנֵי יִשְׂרָאֵל. The first stipulation of the law series begins אִישׁ אִישׁ. Furthermore, throughout the chapter the second person masculine form of the verb occurs in addition to the second person masculine pronominal suffix. The author refers to the woman only by third person forms. He directs even the one law exclusively applicable to her, v. 23b, to the man. Furthermore, in vv. 6–20, the woman alone is taboo.[5] In vv. 21–23,

---

the structure protecting women from sexual exploitation by outsiders. If an 'insider'—father, brother, uncle, or brother-in-law—himself becomes a threat, seducing or even raping a woman within his own family, she has little protection."

4. Blu Greenberg, "Female Sexuality and Bodily Functions in the Jewish Tradition," in Becher, ed., *Women, Religion and Sexuality*, 32–33, asks: "Why is the language addressed to a man? Because it was understood that men were the initiators and aggressors in a sexual relationship. Moreover, in a patriarchal structure, men were heads of households and protectors of the women within them."

5. Neufeld, *Ancient Hebrew Marriage Laws*, 193.

others, outside the class of male Israelites, are taboo. The author never explicitly places the taboo on the male Israelite except with respect to another male.[6]

These three items—the named addressee, the use of second and third person, and the application of taboo—are the obvious results of the author's choice to address the male Israelite community. Perhaps, a less obvious result is the configuration of the prohibited boundaries.

The boundaries demarcated in Lev 18:6–18 are not "reciprocal and parallel"[7] for men and women. Biale, states, to the contrary, that whereas the laws of adultery do not apply equally to men and women, the laws of incest do.[8] However, before offering support for my argument, I must note that I believe Biale's instincts are on target. She is noticing something which is true about the text in her comparison of the two groups of sex laws. Her instinct seems to be targeting the accrual of agency to the woman in her focalization within the incest laws, as compared to the adultery laws. That is the observation of this study as well.

However, the most obvious evidence that the laws are not reciprocal and parallel for men and women is the absence of the uncle/niece prohibition and the presence of the aunt/nephew prohibitions. This is only one example, among several, of absences[9] characterized by gender asymmetry.[10] The origin and motivation of these asymmetries have been impossibly lost to time and we are left with only educated guesses to explain them. Such guesses point to a general pattern in which the "household" of a mature male is constitutive for the structure of the social world of the text.

While the text yields nothing, even for the sake of a guess concerning the motivation for the absence of the consanguinal niece/uncle prohibition, a guess, as partial explanation, might be surmised for the restriction on nephew/aunt relations. The male ego is second in the line of four generations and he is warned with respect to females one generation ascendent and two descendent.[11] The

6. This is the case with the law against homosexuality.
7. Biale, *Women and Jewish Law*, 183.
8. Ibid., 183.
9. Rattray, "Marriage Rules," 538, lists the following absences from the text: full sister, grandmother, a stepsister who is the daughter of one's stepfather, mother's brother's wife, niece and cousins. The mother-in-law, mother's sister's husband, father's sister's husband, mother's brother and father's brother can be added to her list. Her reading of v. 6 resolves the problem of the missing father/daughter prohibition. See below.
10. The absence of at least six relations demonstrates gender asymmetry: (1) consanguinal aunts are forbidden to nephews but consanguinal uncles are not forbidden to nieces; (2) patrilineal affinal aunts (father's brother's wife) are forbidden to nephews but patrilineal affinal uncles (father's sister's husband) are not forbidden to nieces; (3) grandfather/granddaughter relations are forbidden but grandmother/grandson relations are not; (4) wife of son is forbidden to father but husband of daughter is not forbidden to mother; (5) patrilineal affinal aunts (father's brother's wife) are forbidden to the male ego but matrilineal affinal aunts (mother's brother's wife) are not; (6) a stepsister who is the daughter of one's stepmother is forbidden but a stepsister who is the daughter of one's stepfather is not.
11. See Baruch Halpern's intriguing theory concerning this matter, in his "Jerusalem and the Lineages in the Seventh Century BCE: Kinship and the Rise of Individual Moral Liability," in *Law and Ideology in Monarchic Israel* (ed. Baruch Halpern and Deborah W. Hobson; JSOTSup 124; Sheffield: Sheffield Academic Press, 1991), 11–107 (57).

implied female ego, on the other hand is third in the line of four generations and she is warned, by implication, with respect to males two generations ascendent and one descendent. Thus, the male ego is older than the implied female ego. "Descendent," dependent, fertile females are paired with older males, who have the capacity to support dependents. That is, the male must be older than the female. Therefore, the nephew/aunt relation is forbidden. Furthermore, the male ego is old enough that his grandmother is perhaps no longer living, or, because of her age, is no longer deemed desirable. She can be presumed, perhaps, to have passed into menopause or beyond. Thus the grandmother/grandson prohibition is absent from the text.

Rattray is quite right when she says "that the list is not organized according to membership in a patrilineage or household constituency."[12] Nevertheless, while the list may not be so organized, prohibitions of certain relations may, in fact, owe their absence to such membership.[13] The daughter's husband is most likely not of the same household as the male ego whereas the son's wife is. So also the mother's brother's wife most likely belongs to another household, whereas the father's brother's wife does not. Prohibitions concerning at least most relatives belonging to another household are absent from the list. Since the mother's sister and the daughter's daughter, who also belong to other households, are present, perhaps consanguinal collaterals and descendents of consanguinal collaterals belonging to other households are always forbidden, whereas affines of other households are not. In addition, perhaps inheritance issues are responsible for the fact that the stepsister, who is the daughter of one's stepfather, is forbidden, and the stepsister, who is the daughter of one's stepmother, is not. That is, the male "step-household" absorbs a stepdaughter, who will marry into another household more thoroughly than a stepson, who has the capacity to compete in the inheritance.

These are only guesses. No single explanation derived from the text accounts for the gender asymmetries of the selected boundaries. Nevertheless, educated guesses suggest that the boundaries are a function of the fact that the male clan or family, in which the male is the authority and the female is subordinate, is constitutive for the social world of the text.

Boundary asymmetries occur in the second half of the law series as well as in the first half. In Lev 18:19–23, females are not warned against males with emission of semen, while males are warned against menstruants.[14] Lesbianism is

---

12.   Rattray, "Marriage Rules," 541, warns: "To return to the list of prohibited unions of Leviticus 18, it is clear that the list is not organized according to membership in a patrilineage of household constituency. That is, the list is not simply forbidding union between members of the same patrilineage, for brother's daughter and father's brother's daughter are apparently permitted. For the same reason one cannot assume that members of an extended household were forbidden to marry, and in any case neither hypothesis accounts for the prohibition of the mother's sister and the daughter's daughter (who might well be in a different patrilineage and who would certainly be living in a different household)." See also Frymer-Kensky, "Law and Philosophy," 94–95.

13.   See Halpern's theory concerning this matter, in his "Jerusalem."

14.   This asymmetry is due, of course, to the fact that emission of semen is an essential component of sexual intercourse which results in progeny.

not forbidden, while male homosexuality is.[15] And the Molek law is addressed only to the male.[16]

The asymmetry with respect to homoeroticism suggests that, in Lev 18,[17] penetration is the issue.[18] Insertion of the penis into a male body, as if it is a female body (anal intercourse), is the problem. This act is a crossing of the boundaries of categories which must be kept separate. The exegetical scholarly discussion since 1994 concerning Lev 18:22 and 20:13 has become increasingly astute.[19] Within the broader discussion pertaining to the ancient world, the following four categories are essential for understanding the problem: (1) penetrator/penetrated; (2) gender; (3) class or power; (4) honor/shame.[20] A construction lies behind the prohibitions, as Olyan states: receptivity is gendered as feminine.[21] The penetrator/penetrated dyad is aligned with the male/female dyad and, in Greece and Rome, with the younger/older or freeborn/slave dyad.[22]

Brooten rightly states that Olyan's work has "advanced our knowledge of these verses beyond the prior states of research."[23] On the basis of משכב זכר, "male vaginal penetration," in Num 31:17, 18 and 35 and Judg 21:11 and 12, he concludes that the meaning of משכבי אשה is "female vaginal receptivity."[24] This latter expression with respect to a sex act between men means, therefore, anal intercourse. Olyan argues that the law regulates no other homoerotic acts,[25] that the law is addressed to the penetrator rather than the penetrated man[26] and that,

15.   Brenner, *The Intercourse of Knowledge*, 139, rightly states that our concept of "homosexuality" has no equivalent in biblical literature.

16.   See below under the discussion of Lev 18:21.

17.   This is true for Lev 20 as well, where lesbianism is not prohibited either.

18.   Boyarin, "'The History of Sexuality'?," 344, states: "Were there a category of the homosexual whose activities are condemned per se, there is no reason that only the males would be included in it, nor any reason that only one male–male genital practice would be forbidden." Frymer-Kensky, "Law and Philosophy," 97, states that v. 22 lacks a corresponding stipulation for women because lesbianism does "not result in true physical 'union.'" See also idem, "Sex in the Bible," 196. However, Milgrom, *Leviticus 17–22*, 1786–87, argues that it has to do with spilling of seed, which corresponds with loss of life. With lesbianism there is no spilling of seed and therefore no prohibition. Furthermore, Milgrom suggests that the prohibition covers only male–male unions within the limited family circle. See also Countryman, *Dirt*, 34. For another proposal, see also Elizabeth Sarah, "Judaism and Lesbianism," in *Jewish Explorations of Sexuality* (ed. Jonathan Magonet; Providence, R.I.: Berghahn, 1995), 99. Brooten, *Love Between Women*, 62. Brooten, after stating that most explanations have unresolved problems, says the following: "In the end, the most plausible explanation may simply be that the lawmakers generally showed greater interest in males and their behavior."

19.   Satlow, "'They Abused Him Like a Woman,'" 1 n. 1. See Satlow for the inception of the ideas which have flourished in the exegetical discussion since 1994.

20.   Ibid., 1–4.

21.   Olyan, "'And with a Male You Shall Not Lie,'" 188.

22.   Ibid., 190–95; Satlow, "'They Abused Him Like a Woman,'" 1–4; Stone, "Gender and Homosexuality," 97–98, 100–101; Walsh, "Leviticus," 202–3.

23.   Brooten, *Love Between Women*, 61 n. 141.

24.   Olyan, "'And with a Male You Shall Not Lie,'" 185.

25.   Ibid., 184–86.

26.   Ibid., 186.

contrary to other places and times in the ancient world, in these two biblical laws, class and status played no part.[27] Furthermore, since only the insertive partner is addressed, the concern of this law is *not* that the male fails to conform to class.[28] As I have implied, in my introductory statements to "Point-of-View" and as I will argue below, I believe that the receptor (i.e. "female" character) is addressed implicitly.[29] Conformity to gender class is, therefore, not ruled out by my reading of the text. However, Olyan does not rule out ontology, even if he rules out conformity to gender-class as the explanatory key. He proposes that behind the law is the classificatory concern of mixing two bodily emissions: semen and excrement.[30]

Boyarin is articulate in his argument for the classificatory issue as the explanatory key to the law. Conformity to gender-class is the concern, according to his understanding. He writes:

> Male and female are among the kinds that were created at the very beginning (Gen 1:27). Now if we understand that it is the kinds that have to be kept separate, that is, the categories or types, because confusing their borders (*tebhel*) is an abomination—as opposed to a mere necessity to keep physically separate the tokens of the categories—then we can understand the specifics of the Torah's interdiction of male anal intercourse... The issue is gender (as the verse of the Bible explicitly suggests) and not "homosexuality," and gender is conceived around penetration and being penetrated.[31]

Boyarin concludes that status is not the issue.[32] In any case, for both Olyan and Boyarin, classificatory issues are the concern of the law.

By contrast, Walsh argues that status and honor/shame issues are at stake.[33] He states that the addressee is the receptor since, whereas ידע is used with שכב, משכב, זכר is used with משכבי אשה. He takes שכב to be "a cognate direct object construction," meaning that the man "lies the lying down of a woman" as in "to dream a dream" and "to sin a sin".[34] The addressee is a free male citizen who takes on the receptor role. Walsh states that "the male sexual role is to be the active penetrator; the passive role of being penetrated brings shame to a man (at least to a free adult male citizen) who engages in it and, in the later redactional stratum, also to the one who penetrates him."[35]

---

27. Ibid., 195.

28. Ibid., 199.

29. See the discussion below of vv. 23, 26 and 29.

30. Olyan, "'And with a Male You Shall Not Lie,'" 202–3.

31. Boyarin, "'The History of Sexuality'?," 343–44.

32. Ibid., 348.

33. Walsh, "Leviticus," 207.

34. Ibid., 205. Olyan, "'And with a Male You Shall Not Lie,'" 186. Olyan's reasoning for choosing the receptor is the fact that in the surrounding and other laws "the insertive partner" is addressed directly. However, perhaps "maleness" (as in "wearing a penis") is more constitutive than the "insertive" attribute for the addressee qualification; the number of male insertives and paucity of male receptors in the sum of laws notwithstanding.

35. Walsh, "Leviticus," 108. See Stone, "Gender and Homosexuality," for discussion of honor/shame and homosexuality in the biblical text.

Whether or not the addressee is the receptor or the penetrator, whether or not honor/shame is part of the socio-psycho matrix of Israelite life in the world of the text, whether or not mixture of fluids or conforming to class are the explanatory key to the law, the primary issue is *classificatory*. It is an ontological concern. Lesbianism does not violate that issue at stake in the text. Its prohibition is therefore absent and constitutes one of the many gender asymmetries of the text.

Thus, the author's point-of-view is gender-qualified. It influences his choice concerning the male direct-addressee, his use of second and third person, his application of the taboo and his construction of relationship boundaries. As a result, woman all but recedes from the explicit text as addressee. Nevertheless, she is implicitly present.

2) *Contraindicators*. Several features in the text, however, point to a more nuanced conceptuality than that suggested by the above description. At least two of these several features are aspects of the point-of-view itself. This more nuanced conceptuality suggests that, however circumscribed and dependent, women as well as men are responsible to the law of Lev 18.[36]

The first feature is the logic of the text. This feature *alone* cannot prove that woman is responsible to the law. However, in conjunction with other features, it lends credibility to the conclusion. Illicit sexual actions of women as well as men constitute a breach of the laws of Lev 18. In fact, in most cases described in Lev 6–23, the actions of both men and women are required for such a breach. While we cannot be sure that the woman is never forced under the prescriptions of this text, which has no concern for preventing the kind of scenario that we in the twenty-first century call rape; we can presume that she is often *not* forced and that the laws apply to consensual sex[37] as well as non-consensual.

The second feature is the conclusion of Lev 18 in conjunction with v. 23b. Verse 23b explicitly regulates the woman's behavior, even though it refers to her in third person and the regulation comes to her through the male, to whom it is addressed. The mechanics of bestiality differ for men and women.[38] Since this difference is significant for the author, he explicitly specifies and restricts the actions of each.

---

36. At least two scholars note that the laws of incest are addressed to the man and in the same breath state that these laws are nevertheless applied equally to men and women. Both scholars appeal to the penalties of Lev 20 as evidence. The evidence is available in Lev 18, however, without recourse to Lev 20. See Biale, *Women and Jewish Law*, 179; Greenberg, "Female Sexuality," 32.

37. This attribution of a form of agency to the woman does not mean that woman is "active" as opposed to "passive" in the act of sexual intercourse. That is another question. Brenner observes (*The Intercourse of Knowledge*, 142), on the basis of Lev 18:22 and 20:13, that women "do not possess an independent sexuality of their own."

38. Ibid., 146, states: "From the hierarchic and stereotypic point of view there is a role reversal inherent in the woman-animal situation. It is inconceivable that the animal—and a domesticated animal, a בהמה (whose status, despite its usefulness, is lower in the scheme of things than that of wild, often romanticized animals)—would be the initiator. In such a situation the 'woman' is an agent, she 'would stand' (תעמד, 18.24) in front of the animal or 'would come near' (תקרב, 20.16) it, thus departing from the properly passive receptive position which is conceived of as innately female."

The conclusion of Lev 18 specifies the parties responsible for keeping these laws. It begins with gender-specific nomenclature: the second person masculine plural address, specifying the community of male Israelites. In addition, it specifies הָאֶזְרָח וְהַגֵּר (v. 26b), which in no way neutralizes the gender specificity of the masculine address. But it continues by stating that כָּל who commit הַתּוֹעֵבוֹת הָאֵלֶּה (v. 29) will be cut off from the midst of their people. If הַתּוֹעֵבוֹת הָאֵלֶּה includes the infraction of v. 23b, then כָּל refers to women as well as men, regardless of the masculine nomenclature which precedes it. We have no reason to assume that v. 23b is excluded from הַתּוֹעֵבוֹת הָאֵלֶּה. Therefore, we have no reason to assume כָּל does not include women. The explicit regulation of v. 23b means that what the woman does is as important for the sake of purity as what the man does. In conjunction with v. 29, it suggests that, even if only by way of implication, the writer understands all the laws to regulate the woman as well as the man.[39] And this is so even though he frames the laws as if restriction of the male is the solution to the problem of illicit sex.

Furthermore, within the Hebrew corpus in general and within the book of Leviticus in particular, נפשׁ is used in gender-neutral[40] and even species-neutral[41] ways.

3) *Conclusion.* Thus, while the author explicitly addresses his text to men throughout, we cannot assume that he does not expect the law to govern the behavior of women as well. They are in some sense responsible.

b. *Language-Depicting-the-Sex-Act.*
1) *The Bias.* Just as the point-of-view portrays woman as marginalized, circum-scribed by and subordinate to man, the language-depicting-the-sex-act portrays woman as object and man as subject. The initial impression is that she is the man's property, which the law intends to protect.

In the bulk of the laws (vv. 6–19) גלה is the verb depicting the sex act. The man always uncovers the woman's nakedness and never the other way around.[42] In two instances (vv. 6 and 19) man is the subject of קרב which is used in conjunction with the prohibition against uncovering her nakedness.[43] In the

---

39.   Ibid., 146, states: "The insistence of Leviticus 20 that the responsibility and punishment for sexual transgression to be shared by female and male culprits is extreme, to the extent of including the poor animal in the punishment for bestiality; however, this inclusivity does *not* imply a recognition of either female or animal independent sexuality."

40.   Knierim, *Text and Concept*, 14.

41.   Indeed, even the responsibility of the animal cannot be ruled out *a priori*. However, the phrase וְנִכְרְתוּ...מִקֶּרֶב עַמָּם would seem to indicate that the author/redactor is concerned with responsibilities of humans—women as well as men—and the law. See the following: F. C. Fensham, "Liability of Animals in Biblical and Ancient Near Eastern Law," *JNSI* 14 (1988): 85–90; J. J. Finkelstein, *The Ox That Gored* (Transactions of the American Philosophical Society 71/2; Phila-delphia: The American Philosophical Society, 1981); A. Van Selms, "The Goring Ox in Babylonian and Biblical Law," *Archiv Orientální* 18 (1950): 321–30.

42.   However, see Ruth 3:7.

43.   קרב indicates that approach to the boundaries as well as the crossing itself is of concern in these instances. At v. 6, a Qumran document has the Hiphil form, תקריב, instead of the Qal form.

remainder of the laws of the first section (vv. 17 and 18), man is the subject of לקח, which is used in conjunction with לֹא תְגַלֶּה עֶרְוָה. In vv. 20, 21 and 23a he is the subject of נתן. Man is the subject of שׁכב only in the prohibition against homosexuality (v. 22). The one exception to this pattern supports the overall impression. It occurs in v. 23b where the woman is the subject in contradistinction to an animal. Thus, the syntax describing the sex act demonstrates unqualified gender asymmetry.

2) *Contraindicators*. However, as with the point-of-view, several features indicate a more nuanced conceptuality than woman's simple objectification by language-depicting-the-sex-act. In fact, the law does not protect woman or her sexuality as the property of the man.

a) *Verses 6–18*. In vv. 6–18, an examination of the use of עֶרְוָה and שְׁאֵר within the gender-polarized syntax demonstrates that the conceptuality regarding the sex act is more complex than that simple polarization would suggest.[44] While the man always uncovers the nakedness of the woman and she never uncovers his, her nakedness does not belong exclusively to him. In fact, even though the nakedness of a man never belongs to her, her nakedness "belongs" to herself and may even belong to other females.

"The nakedness of" denotes at least three, possibly four, different attributions.[45] Many scholars take the double attribution of nakedness in v. 7 to be the result of redaction.[46] A simpler explanation is that it is the conscious acknowledgment of the multivalence of this expression by the author. Verse 7 demonstrates two of the instances which the expression designates.[47] "To uncover the nakedness of the father" is to have intercourse with one's mother. "To uncover the nakedness of one's mother," again, is to have intercourse with one's mother.

This reading, of course, emphasizes the initiative and power of the male to an even greater degree, as Kornfeld notes; see Walter Kornfeld, "Ein unpublizierter Levitikustext," *ZAW* 87 (1975): 212.

44. See Levine's description of the relationship of these two terms in the text (*Leviticus*, 117, 119).

45. Melcher, "Holiness Code," 94, has described two of them well.

46. Bigger, "Family Laws," 196; Elliger, *Leviticus*, 231; Fred L. Horton, "Form and Structure in Laws Relating to Women: Leviticus 18:6–18," in *SBL 1973 Seminar Papers* (SBLSP 1; Cambridge, Mass.: Society of Biblical Literature, 1973), 29; Noth, *Leviticus*, 136; Porter, *Leviticus*, 145; Anthony Phillips, "Uncovering the Father's Skirt," *VT* 30 (1980): 39. Phillips' explanation, which takes v. 7a in its present form as "prohibiting sexual relations with either of one's parents," is unlikely. His assertion that it is "not the normal practice for legislation to say the same thing twice" is presumptive. Furthermore, the context of vv. 6–18 suggests that the text concerns women affines and consanguines as taboo. That one portion of v. 7 might legislate with respect to homosexual intercourse in the list of otherwise heterosexual consanguinal and affinal relations is unlikely, especially since the male's nakedness is used to refer to the female sexuality in other laws of the series of vv. 6–18. See Calum M. Carmichael, "Forbidden Mixtures," *VT* 32 (1982): 396 n. 7. For an interesting twist, see Frederick W. Bassett, "Short Notes—Noah's Nakedness and the Curse of Canaan: A Case of Incest?," *VT* 21 (1971): 323–37. See also discussions below under the exegesis of Deut 22:13–23:1 and 27:20–23.

47. Levine, *Leviticus*, 120. He calls 7aα₂ a circumstantial clause.

The woman in the first instance is the nakedness of the man. That is, her nakedness belongs to the man.[48] Nakedness of the woman in the second instance
belongs to the woman herself.[49] A third instance occurs in v. 10 where the granddaughter is considered to be the nakedness of the grandfather.[50] A fourth possible instance occurs in v. 17 where a granddaughter is the nakedness of the
grandmother.[51] That is, her sexuality belongs to the grandmother. No attribution
of a man's nakedness to a woman exists in the text.

These four attributions of "nakedness of" evidence two reasons for forbidding
intercourse in vv. 6–18: (1) her nakedness belongs to someone other than the
ego; (2) her nakedness belongs to the ego. The fact that a woman's nakedness
belongs to herself is never given as the reason she is forbidden to a man. A
mother's nakedness is forbidden to her son because that nakedness belongs by
marriage to a third party—the father. A granddaughter is forbidden to her grandfather because that nakedness belongs by blood to himself.[52] In the first case, the
"belonging" qualification means exclusive *right* to intercourse. In the latter case,
it means intercourse is *forbidden*. Thus, if the nakedness belongs to the male by
virtue of marriage and not by virtue of blood relation, then sexual access is
permitted. If the nakedness belongs to the male by virtue of blood relation and
not by virtue of marriage, then sexual access is forbidden. Since "nakedness of"
connotes absolute restriction from female sexuality as well as exclusive right to
female sexuality, it does not *necessarily* connote male ownership of women or
their sexuality.

Furthermore, the possibility that a woman's nakedness belongs to another
woman adds potentially to the multivalence of the phrase. This latter possibility
rests on an unconventional but conceivable reading of v. 17. The third feminine
singular suffix of עֶרְוָתָהּ is traditionally read as referring to the granddaughters.
However, referral to the grandmother instead is grammatically and syntactically
possible. עֶרְוָתָהּ would then designate the woman's granddaughters as her
nakedness, in the same way that women are designated as the nakedness of men
in other verses. For example, v. 7 states: "You shall not uncover your father's

48.   Melcher, "Holiness Code," 94. This, usage, as Melcher states, refers to the exclusive
jurisdiction a man has over his wife's sexuality.
49.   Ibid., 94–95. Melcher states that this usage refers to the woman's "sexual organs." In other
words, the legal jurisdiction of the first usage is absent. This usage is exampled throughout the text,
where nakedness is referred to as if it belongs to the woman herself: "nakedness of your mother,"
"nakedness of the wife of your father," "nakedness of your sister," "nakedness of the daughter of
your son or daughter," "nakedness of the daughter of the wife of your father," "nakedness of the
sister of your mother or father," "nakedness of your daughter-in-law," "nakedness of the wife of
your brother," "nakedness of a woman and her daughter." In fact, the nakedness of the half-sister,
stepsister, consanguinal maternal and paternal aunts, daughter-in-law and rival-sister is attributed to
no male at all, even though some of the women are described in other ways as "belonging" to a
male. No legal jurisdiction of a male is posited. See Bernard J. Bamberger, *Leviticus* (New York:
The Union of American Hebrew Congregations, 1979), 194 n. 6.
50.   Melcher, "Holiness Code," 94. This falls into the first example of Melcher's classification.
51.   See the discussion below.
52.   Horton, "Form and Structure," 24. Horton is noticing the same phenomenon when he says,
"ʿerwāh can be shared through genealogy or transmitted through sexual intercourse."

nakedness." That is, you shall not have intercourse with the woman belonging to him—your mother. The same concept occurs in v. 14, which states: "You shall not uncover your father's brother's nakedness." That is, you shall not have intercourse with the woman belonging to him—his wife. The unconventional reading of v. 17 states: "You shall not uncover a woman's nakedness." That is, you shall not have intercourse with the woman who belongs to her—her grand-daughter. In v. 17, unlike vv. 7 and 14, the "belonging" is consanguinal rather than affinal. Furthermore, the ego is not related by blood to the person who "owns" the nakedness under question. Nevertheless, the three verses share the following *conceptual* formula:

> Y (where Y is a woman) is forbidden in the following way: the nakedness of X (where X is the "owner" of the sexuality of Y) you shall not uncover.

Although, with the unconventional reading, the three verses share this concep-tual formula, they differ with respect to grammatical and syntactical form. Unlike the other two verses, v. 17 expresses the above concept by means of a purpose clause in conjunction with לקח. For this reason, one might question the significance of the shared conceptual formula. But failure of agreement in gram-matical and syntactical form is no argument against the unconventional reading. It means only that support for the unconventional reading must come from features other than grammar and syntax.

Another challenge to this reading is that the grammatical and syntactical form of v. 17 is similar to that of v. 18, where the pronominal suffix is traditionally read as referring to the sister rather than the woman. Moreover v. 18 has two purpose clauses in succession, the first of which undeniably refers to the sister rather than the woman. One might reasonably surmise, therefore, that לְגַלּוֹת עֶרְוָתָהּ, the second clause, also refers to the sister and not the woman. By anal-ogy, the reader might conclude that in v. 17 לְגַלּוֹת עֶרְוָתָהּ must also refer to the nakedness of the granddaughters rather than the woman.

However, we can easily turn the evidence of v. 18 on its head. The "victim" of the phrase לִצְרֹר is implied. It is the woman. The sister will be a rival to her. In agreement with the first phrase, לִצְרֹר, we might also read the second phrase לְגַלּוֹת עֶרְוָתָהּ as having a "victim," specified by the third person feminine singular suffix. Again it is the woman. By taking the sister, the woman's nakedness is uncovered. While the ego has a right to the woman's own nakedness, he does not have a right to her "extended" nakedness, that is, her blood relation. Either reading of v. 18 is plausible. Therefore, v. 18 cannot decide the issue in v. 17.[53]

In addition to the above challenges, v. 17 has text-critical problems, one of which concerns precisely the issue of the attribution of the woman's descendents to her nakedness. All witnesses except LXX, Syriac and Neofiti agree with the MT. LXX, Syriac and Neofiti attest to the third person plural pronominal suffix instead of the third person singular feminine. The pronominal suffix in this case refers to 17bα, the granddaughters. Taking the unconventional reading as valid,

---

53. The purpose clauses in vv. 21 and 23 are irrelevant because woman occupies an altogether different place in these verses. Furthermore, comparison is unhelpful since גלה does not occur.

the MT is the more difficult reading and least likely to be introduced. The LXX demonstrates a tendency to maintain consistency with respect to attribution of nakedness and a reluctance to attribute such to a woman.[54] Even though the three verses (vv. 7, 14 and 17) differ with respect to grammar and syntax, and despite the textual difficulties of v. 17, we can read all three as sharing the conceptual formula which attributes the affinal or consanguinal relation to the nakedness of the man or woman under question. If the suffix of עֶרְוָתָהּ thus refers to the woman, then the granddaughters are her nakedness.[55]

Furthermore, even if one rejects this unconventional reading, one must admit that the granddaughters are forbidden not because they belong to a man, but because they are the שְׁאֵר of a woman.[56] The same situation exists in v. 13 and possibly in vv. 18 and 19. Male ownership has nothing to do with this restricttion. Neither does any other mode of relationship with a male. Thus, kinship with a woman alone is grounds for forbidding sexual relations. Property concerns are irrelevant.

b) *Verses 19–23*. In vv. 19–23, as noted above, only three out of the six stipulations involve women. In one of those, v. 23b, woman is subject. Of the other two, v. 19 uses the "uncover nakedness" expression in conjunction with קרב. Verse 20, the remaining verse, uses נתן, implying reciprocity in the sexual act. Not only is woman absent from three out of the six laws, but in the other three "protection of her or her sexuality as property" is a possible issue in only one of them—v. 20.

3) *Conclusion*. The simple assertion that man is subject and woman is object cannot account for the conceptual complexity underlying the language-depicting-the-sex-act in Lev 18. While this polarization is certainly true, and while it is also true that a man's sexuality never belongs to a woman and a woman's "ownership" of her own sexuality is never grounds for forbidding a man access to her, a close examination demonstrates that assertions concerning male ownership of female sexuality or of the female herself fail to do justice to subtle nuances in the text.

---

54. Henry Sun, "An Investigation into the Compositional Integrity of the So-Called Holiness Code (Leviticus 17–26)" (Ph.D. diss., Claremont Graduate School, 1990), 119. The unconventional reading of v. 17 does not require the assumption that 17bα be a secondary insertion, as Sun's solution requires. Furthermore, either reading of שאר ה works with the unconventional reading. הֵנָּה refers to the daughter of her son and the daughter of her daughter.

55. The question is: Does this usage imply a legal jurisdiction? I think it is an open question.

56. Sun, "Investigation," 118–19. See Sun's notes on שְׁאֵר ה. Sun objects to the repointing of שַׁאֲרָה to שְׁאֵר ה on the grounds that the latter cannot account for the third person feminine plural הֵנָּה. He reads שַׁאֲרָה with Rashi and Ibn Ezra as "near kin." With Sun's reading, "the אשה and her בת are שארה." However, if הֵנָּה refers to both the "daughter of her son" and the "daughter of her daughter," then the third person feminine plural הֵנָּה poses no problem for the שַׁאֲרָה reading. Both readings are plausible. Neither reading is conclusively supported by the textual witnesses: LXX (οἰκεῖαι γάρ σοῦ εἰσιν); Vulgate (*quia caro illius sunt*); Samaritan Pentateuch (שארה הנה). Either reading supports my understanding of the text. I have, however, followed the reading that repoints שַׁאֲרָה to שְׁאֵר ה.

2. *Selection-of-Laws, Identification-of-Women, Structure-of-the-Text*

At least three other less subtle features of the text demonstrate that, rather than preservation of male property rights, the text's primary concern is simply the demarcation of certain boundaries, which I call genital boundaries. Furthermore, they indicate that woman, like the man, is an agent responsible to the laws. The three features of the text are as follows: (1) the selection-of-laws, (2) the identification-of-women and (3) the structure-of-the-text.

a. *Selection-of-Laws.* Scholars agree that the laws in Lev 18 divide into two parts. Although they vary in their opinions as to where the division occurs, most would agree that the first set of laws concerns sexual boundaries forbidding certain consanguines and affines as suitable partners.[57] The second set of laws (vv. 19–23[58]) concerns boundaries forbidding other things. The boundaries of the second set of laws guard categories more widely varied than the categories of the first set.

Discernment of the concern or intention of the text must account for the variety of categories in both sets of laws. The primary concern of a text is an idea, an interest or some other such construct which can explain the presence of all the elements of a text. If what the reader has discerned as the primary concern cannot explain all the elements of the text, then the reader has not yet found the primary concern.[59]

Within the second set of laws only v. 20 can be read as possibly protecting male property rights to a woman or her sexuality. Five[60] out of the six laws in the second set undeniably concern non-property issues with respect to women. From three[61] of those five, women are entirely absent. From one[62] of the remaining two, man is entirely absent. The final law[63] forbids the man to approach a

---

57. Levine, *Leviticus*, 117, states: "Two principles govern the definition of incest in the code of chapter 18 and throughout the rest of the Torah: (1) *she'er*, 'flesh relations,' sometimes known as consanguinal or blood relations and (2) *'ervah*, 'nakedness,' a euphemism for sexuality… The *she'er* relatives are in a different category from members of the family related by affinity, those who become a man's relatives by marriage… The basic principle regulating sexual union with affinal relatives is conveyed by the term *'ervah*… The interaction of these two principles, *she'er* relationship and *'ervah* (exclusive sexual access), account directly and by extension for all the prohibited sexual unions within the Israelite family."

58. See the structure below.

59. Adrian Schenker, "What Connects the Incest Prohibitions with the Other Prohibitions Listed in Leviticus 18 and 20?," in Rendtorff and Kugler, eds., *The Book of Leviticus*, 162–63, states: "The guiding hypothesis of the present examination is the supposition that the single precepts and their systematic order in Leviticus 18 and 20 are rationally transparent, because ancient oriental law in general and biblical law in particular follow rational principles, which means that they are logical and can be understood. Hence it is methodologically necessary for the interpretation to look in every case for an intelligible principle, although such seems at first sight to be lacking, and also for methodological reasons, to avoid such terms as 'archaic,' 'magic' and similar expressions in order to explain biblical commandments."

60. Verses 19, 21, 22, 23a, 23b.

61. Verses 21, 22, 23a.

62. Verse 23b.

63. Verse 19.

woman with menstrual impurity. Each of these laws except v. 19 has a concluding clause which specifically targets the purity issue.[64]

In v. 20 the woman "belongs" to the neighbor. Taken in isolation, this verse must be read as protecting the neighbor's property. In fact, the syntax of this verse is identical to the syntax of the verse on male bestiality (v. 23a) with the exception of לְזֶרַע, which is present in v. 20 but not in v. 23a.[65] The suggestion might be offered that just as an animal is property, so also is a neighbor's wife.

However, in v. 23a the owner of the animal (who may be the ego) as well as the owner's property rights are irrelevant. The owner is absent from the verse. The issue rather is breach of boundaries separating categories of species. The animal in question may be property or it may not. So also the "owner" of the woman is irrelevant. The issue is a breach of boundaries separating a woman who belongs to a particular sphere of marriage from all other men. She belongs, as it were, to another "species": that class of women who may not be approached sexually except by the one male to whose sphere she belongs. Property is not the issue. Demarcation of boundaries is.

Thus, an examination of the laws selected for inclusion in Lev 18 demonstrates the concern to demarcate and protect genital boundaries. All laws of both units have this primary concern in common.

b. *Identification-of-Women.* The second feature of the text which demonstrates that the preservation of male property is not the primary concern is the way in which the women are identified.

The first impression is that women are identified with respect to the males to whom they belong: "your father's wife," "daughter of your father," "daughter of your son," "daughter of the wife of your father," "born of your father," "sister of your father," "his wife," "your father's brother's wife," "wife of your son," "wife of your brother," "daughter of her son," "wife of your neighbor." Often, where a woman is not identified with respect to her relationship to a man other than the ego, another phrase occurs which attributes her nakedness to a man (v. 7). Thus, a large number of the women identified in Lev 18 are referenced with respect to men.

However, some are referenced with respect to women only: "daughter of your mother," "daughter of your daughter," "sister of your mother," "a woman and her daughter," "a woman and her sister." The text fails to mention males connected to these women because the point is irrelevant.

The text is not about women belonging to men.[66] Nor is it about the rights of men to women or to their sexuality.

---

64.   Verse 20, לְטָמְאָה־בָהּ; v. 21, ...תְחַלֵּל; v. 22, תּוֹעֵבָה הִוא; v. 23a, לְטָמְאָה־בָהּ; v. 23b, תֶּבֶל הוּא. In v. 19 such a clause is unnecessary because the information that impurity is the overriding concern with a menstruant is common knowledge.

65.   Perhaps the absence in v. 23a indicates the impossibility of conception in this situation.

66.   Jonathan R. Ziskind, "The Missing Daughter in Leviticus XVIII," *VT* 46 (1996): 127, states: "The purpose of this extensive use of this and other possessive forms was to impress upon the men to whom these laws were addressed a moral priority that went beyond an exhortation to stay

c. *Structure-of-the-Text.* The structure is the third feature of Lev 18 demonstrating that demarcation of genital boundaries rather than protection of male sexual property rights is the primary concern.

1) *Three Problems.* Three problems within the text affect decisions on structure. They occur in the following verses: 6, 9 and 11; 18; and 21.

a) *Verses 6, 9 and 11.* The first problem is the missing daughter. Closely related to this problem is the confusion in v. 9 concerning the meaning of the phrase מוֹלֶדֶת בַּיִת אוֹ מוֹלֶדֶת חוּץ and its relationship to בַּת־אָבִיךָ אוֹ בַת־אִמֶּךָ. More narrowly focused, the confusion concerns the meaning of מוֹלֶדֶת and, therefore, encompasses the phase מוֹלֶדֶת אָבִיךָ in v. 11 as well.[67]

Rattray has offered an elegant solution to these problems.[68] If her solution is correct, a coherent conceptual pattern becomes clear in Lev 18. This conceptual

away from these female relatives because they are the possessions of his close male relatives. If that were the only issue, then the rules forbidding rape and adultery would suffice."

67.   Several options have been proposed for resolving this confusion. Some scholars take v. 9 to mean full-sister or half-sister: Driver, *Leviticus*, 88; Elliger, *Leviticus*, 231–32; Levine, *Leviticus*, 120; Rattray, "Marriage Rules," 537 n. 1; N. A. Snaith, *Leviticus* (London: Thomas Nelson, 1967), 123; Wenham, *Leviticus*, 255. Some take it to refer to a full-sister or half-sister or legitimate or illegitimate birth: Driver, *Leviticus*, 88; Noth, *Leviticus*, 136; Rattray, "Marriage Rules," 537 n. 1. Others take it to mean full-sister or half-sister "brought up in the family or in another home": Bamberger, *Leviticus*, 194; Porter, *Leviticus*, 146; Wenham, *Leviticus*, 256. Verse 11 is usually taken to mean full- or half-sister: Levine, *Leviticus*, 120–21; Snaith, *Leviticus*, 123; Porter, *Leviticus*, 146.

68.   Rattray, "Marriage Rules," 537–44. See especially nn. 1–3 on p. 537. See Milgrom, *Leviticus 17–22*, 1527–31. Milgrom (p. 1749) states: "The major contribution of Rattray's list is that she has, in my opinion, satisfactorily accounted for the ostensible omission of the full sister and, especially, of the daughter from the list." I agree. The varied solutions to the missing daughter problem offered by scholars fall into at least four groups. The first relies on history of the transmission of the text, positing scribal error or some kind of redactional omission: Bamberger, *Leviticus*, 188–89; Driver, *Leviticus*, 88; Karl Elliger, "Das Gesetz Leviticus 18," *ZAW* 67 (1955): 2; Neufeld, *Ancient Hebrew Marriage Laws*, 198–99; Noordtzij, *Leviticus*, 185; Porter, *Leviticus*, 146. The second group relies on economics, positing loss of property on "loss of potential income that would tend to keep father/daughter incest from occurring": Sun, "Investigation," 151; Bassett, "Short Notes," 236; Wegner, *Chattel*, 27. The third group deals with the problem by relying on the "shorthand" exegetical principle, positing that "since a daughter is more closely related than a granddaughter, she would be forbidden *a fortiori*": Levine, *Leviticus*, 120. The fourth group posits the author's inability to interfere with the *patria potestas* of the *pater familias*: Frymer-Kensky, "Law and Philosophy," 94 n. 14; Ziskind, "Missing Daughter," 129. Ziskind offers a novel twist on this option. He suggests that the daughter is missing because the relation could not be articulated, as in the other prohibitions, with an intermediary relative. Ziskind seems to imply that, since such a prohibition was defending no "intermediary," it would be understood as undermining a father's authority, which the Priestly writer was afraid would discredit his program. In other words, only those prohibitions which mediated one individual's claim to someone's sexuality vis-à-vis a third persons' claim to that same sexuality (whether expressly articulated or not, I presume) were included in the list. Schenker ("What Connects the Incest Prohibitions?," 164–65) offers a fifth solution. Schenker states that the daughter is not missing because she shows up in v. 17. However, this verse refers to the *woman's* daughter. It does not cover, for example, the following scenarios: a husband and wife

pattern, which is not the subject of Rattray's essay and which she does not discuss, is the foundation of the structure I propose for the chapter.

Rattray reads מוֹלֶדֶת as a verbal noun meaning "family."[69] She suggests that מוֹלֶדֶת בַּיִת אוֹ מוֹלֶדֶת חוּץ modifies בַּת־אִמֶּךָ. The forbidden woman in v. 9 is thus a half-sister to the ego. The father of that daughter is either a male within the ego's father's family or a male outside that family. Three kinds of women are thus forbidden by v. 9: "his half-sister, whether the daughter of his father (and his stepmother) or the daughter of his mother (and her previous husband)."[70] The latter parenthetical phrase ("her previous husband") consists of two referential options: a man from the mother's second husband's family or a man outside that family.[71] Figure 3 illustrates the forbidden relationships of v. 9. Rattray applies the same reading of מוֹלֶדֶת to v. 11. Thus, the forbidden woman of v. 11 is a stepsister of the ego (they share the same mother), whose father is the same family as the ego's father. Figure 4 illustrates the forbidden relationships of v. 11.

In addition, Rattray reads שְׁאֵר בְּשָׂרוֹ of v. 6 as referring to a specific group of blood relations.[72] She bases her conclusion on the appositional clause following לִשְׁאֵרוֹ הַקָּרֹב אֵלָיו of Lev 21:2–3, which unfolds the meaning of שְׁאֵר. Rattray proposes that שְׁאֵר in Lev 18:6 designates the females listed in that appositional clause: mother, daughter and maiden sister. Thus, she asserts, the real question is not why the daughter is missing but why the mother is present in v. 7 since she is already represented by שְׁאֵר in v. 6. In response to this question she states that the mother prohibition establishes "the principle with the one case least likely to occur and most universally abhorred."[73] Interestingly, the only incest law in Deuteronomy, outside the curses of Deut 27, is the law in Deut 23:1 protecting the woman who belongs to the father. Perhaps, incest laws concerning women who are sexual partners to the father are in some way paradigmatic and are thus cited with special emphasis; exemplified in Lev 18 by the redundancy which Rattray's solution cannot avoid and in Deut 23:1 by singular inclusion.

---

have a daughter; the wife dies and the man remarries; he "takes" the daughter by the first wife (incest). Or a husband has two wives, one of whom has a daughter with him; the mother of the daughter dies; the father "takes" the daughter.

69.　Rattray, "Marriage Rules," 537 n. 1. Levine, *Leviticus*, 120. H. Haag, "מוֹלֶדֶת," *TDOT* 8:167. Haag states (p. 167): "We have found that the semantic spectrum of *môledet* revolves around the fundamental notion of birth (root *yld*) and expresses several relationships created through birth: place of birth, home, fatherland— descent, origin—race, descendents, family." He cites Gen 43:7 as one example in which מולדת must mean "family."

70.　Rattray, "Marriage Rules," 537.

71.　Ibid., 537 n. 1.

72.　Ibid., 542: Levine, *Leviticus*, 117, 120.

73.　Ibid., 542. Rattray notes that, in addition to being the rarest type, mother–son incest is also the incest act which is universally prohibited.

I. *Daughter of Father*

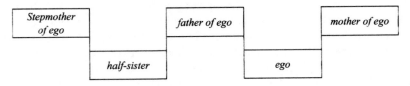

II. *Daughter of Mother*

a. *Born of father's kindred*

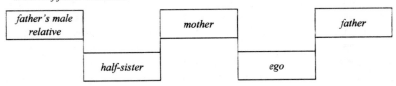

b. *born outside of father's kindred*

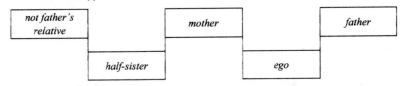

Figure 3. *Forbidden Women of Verse 9*

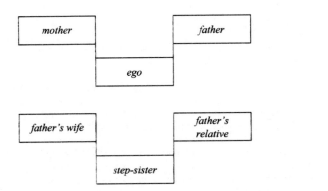

Figure 4. *Forbidden Women of Verse 11*

Sun has dismissed Rattray's explanation.[74] He states: "If the text intends to use the mother 'to establish the principle,' then why is the sister mentioned?"[75] Perhaps Sun has misunderstood Rattray's explanation of vv. 9 and 11.[76] The text beyond v. 6 does not mention the sister according to Rattray's reading. It mentions the half-sister and the stepsister. Second, Sun observes that Lev 21 and Lev 18 are addressed to different groups with different rules of conduct: the sons of Israel and the sons of Aaron. His implication is that שְׁאֵר probably does not designate the same thing in the two chapters.[77] However, the differences between the identity of the groups and their rules of conduct are irrelevant. The question is: Does Lev 21:2–3 represent a conceptuality with respect to blood relation that would have been generally understood as designated by שְׁאֵר? Nothing suggests that this is not the case unless one considers the "redundancy of v. 7," under Rattray's reading, to be such a suggestion. Given the coherence of Rattray's explanation, the force of that redundancy is insufficient to topple her solution.

Sun's final point is: "…the fact that Rattray's interpretation can (perhaps) account for Lev 18:6–18 in its present shape does not mean that it can account for the absence of the daughter at the earlier stage in which v. 6 was not yet attached to vv. 7ff (unless Rattray would view the prohibitions of vv. 6–18 as a literary critical unity, which she does not explicitly state)."[78] Sun's point is moot. The validity of a solution like Rattray's, concerned with the extant form, does not rest on its capacity to explain the omission at every proposed redactional stage in the history of the text.[79]

Sun's own solution to the missing-daughter problem relies on an economic explanation. The father whose daughter lost her virginity would himself lose "potential income."[80] The risk of this loss is sufficient to prevent father/daughter incest, which is why the daughter is absent from the text. As Sun states, "one does not have legislation concerned with one's personal use of one's personal property."[81] However, conceivably a man who desires to commit incest with his

74. Sun, "Investigation," 149–50.
75. Ibid., 149–50.
76. The explanations appear in her footnotes; Rattray, "Marriage Rules," 537 nn. 1–3.
77. Sun, "Investigation," 150.
78. Ibid., 150.
79. Different motivations and intentions impel redactors to make their changes along the way. The motivation to omit the daughter at one stage may be different from the motivation to maintain that omission at another stage. And an altogether different motivation may impel the redactor to reverse the omission. In any case, different and perhaps unrelated explanations for omissions or inclusions are required for each stage. The burden to discern the intent and explain the content of every stage does not rest on the person interested in the extant form. Furthermore, the plural form of קרב along with אִישׁ אִישׁ may be viewed as constituting one of Parunak's hinges, tying the plurals of the introduction to the singulars of the law series. See Parunak, "Transitional Techniques."
80. Sun, "Investigation," 151.
81. Ibid., 151. Wegner's explanation (*Chattel*, 27–28) is slightly different. She explains the absence of the daughter by the fact that she is the father's sexual chattel. Wegner states that the women listed in the incest series are the sexual property of the man as well (p. 28). She distinguishes the daughter from these other women as follows: "The daughter's absence from the list reflects the fact that her sexuality belongs to her father in the most literal sense" (p. 28). The question is what is the distinguishing mark of this "most literal sense" such that the daughter is left out and the others

daughter might be willing to pay for what he wants, that is, suffer the economic loss that loss of virginity incurs. This is the prerogative of the owner of private property. Certainly the author of the text would be aware that this is an option for the father, if Sun's scenario is correct. The question is: Does the author want or consider the force of his law to be as binding as only such economic loss?[82] The warnings concluding the chapter would seem to indicate the contrary.

Frymer-Kensky suggests a slightly different explanation. She states that "the idea of *pater familias* was still strong enough that the laws could not absolutely prohibit a father's access to his daughter."[83] Frymer-Kensky's solution is more plausible than the economic solution and cannot be ruled out as a possibility.[84] In any case, neither her explanation nor Sun's has the power to exclude Rattray's reading of the extant form of the text.

Rattray's solution, on the other hand, has the power to solve several difficult problems within Lev 18: a number of puzzles in vv. 9 and 11 and the alleged absence of the daughter. Furthermore, by means of it, a conceptual pattern ordering the structure of the text reveals itself.

Thus, following Rattray's lead, I have read v. 6 as one in a list of prohibitions concerning blood relations. If it is an introductory statement,[85] it functions only as Rattray suggests: "Hence mother, sister and daughter, as close kin, are automatically forbidden by Lev 18:6. The purpose of the list of Leviticus 18 is to indicate *who else* is forbidden by extension from these basic relationships."[86]

b) *Verse 18*. The second problem concerns sexual intercourse with and marriage to sisters.[87] Tosato has proposed that the women of v. 18 are "two women in

are included. Presumably it is the fact that "the minor daughter is mere chattel, but the adult daughter becomes *sui juris*, a person in her own right, for the father loses dominion over her at puberty" (p. 15). Wegner applies this latter description to women in the Mishnah. Nevertheless, the force of this description seems to be the source of her "most literal sense" applied to biblical law. But Wegner herself also states that the dominion lost by the father at puberty is taken up by the husband (p. 15): "A wife continues under male authority, for her father has transferred his dominion over her to the husband. This includes, in particular, the exclusive right to benefit from the bride's sexuality." But if the women listed in Lev 18 are the sexual property of their husbands, then the fact that the daughter is the sexual property of the father cannot be the reason why the daughter is missing.

82.   The same question can be asked concerning the risk of shame that loss of virginity may entail for the father. See Archer, *Her Price is Beyond Rubies*, 111–12. While Archer's discussion concerns the Graeco-Roman period, nevertheless the kinds of losses she describes in addition to economic loss are equally plausible in Lev 18: embarrassment, sullied reputation, marred purity of the father's household.

83.   Frymer-Kensky, "Law and Philosophy," 94 n. 14. If Frymer-Kensky is right, the grandfather is not *pater familias*, since his access to the granddaughter is prohibited. If he is *pater familias*, then Frymer-Kensky's solution fails.

84.   Nevertheless, as Sun, "Investigation," 159 n. 74, states, a "more thorough investigation of the structure of the clan and of the institution of the *pater familias*" is required.

85.   See the following for the contrary view: Levine, *Leviticus*, 120; Noth, *Leviticus*, 135; Snaith, *Leviticus*, 122; Sun, "Investigation," 127–28; Horton, "Form and Structure," 20–33.

86.   Rattray, "Marriage Rules," 542.

87.   לקח contextualizes the "uncover phrase" in vv. 17 and 18 just as קרב does in v. 19. Nevertheless, the primary concern in both cases is the crossing of genital boundaries. See Walter Kornfeld,

general" rather than two blood sisters.[88] The law thus guards against polygamy rather than "incest."[89]

Tosato conducts three "reexaminations": philological, literary and historical. Within his "literary re-examination," Tosato argues two points which have consequences for the structure and are the kernel of his case.[90] The first point concerns form and the second content. The aim of both arguments is to demonstrate that v. 18 goes with vv. 19–23, the "non-incest laws," rather than with vv. 7–17, the "incest laws."

He bases his division, with respect to form, on the following patterns: עָרוּת...לֹא תְגַלֶּה for vv. 7–17 and ו...לֹא for vv. 8–23.[91] He bases his division, with respect to content, on his reading of לִצְרֹר.[92] This phrase, he claims, captures the primary concern in v. 18: to prevent "'making an enemy, a rival' for the first wife."[93] Finally, Tosato adds that all cases of incest are implicitly perpetual while v. 18 is not, as בְּחַיֶּיהָ demonstrates. As a result of these assumptions, he concludes that v. 18 is "irreconcilable with the laws against incest, marking it instead as a law against a second marriage of the husband as long as the first wife is alive."[94]

Four points must be made in reply to Tosato. First, the occurrence of a permutation of עָרוּת...לֹא תְגַלֶּה in vv. 18 and 19 is one among several signals suggesting the possibility that the elements Tosato identifies as constitutive for the form of the individual prescriptions may not be constitutive for the structure of larger units in the text, including the chapter as a whole. Second, rather than reading לִצְרֹר as naming the primary concern of the law, one might read it as simply describing the additional trouble that this particular transgression of genital boundaries creates. In other words, לְגַלּוֹת עֶרְוָתָהּ might just as easily be read as naming the primary concern. Third, Tosato calls those laws which precede v. 18 incest prohibitions.[95] Thus, Tosato would agree that v. 16, a prohibition of intercourse with the brother's wife, is an incest prohibition. However, we know from the Hebrew corpus itself (Deut 25:5–10) that this is at least one

---

Studien zum Heiligkeitsgesetz (Vienna: Herder, 1952), 128. Although this law has to do with incest, as Kornfeld suggests, לקח and נלה ערוה are not synonymous, as he also suggests. In this verse and in v. 18, לקח denotes marriage as well as connoting sexual intercourse. On the other hand, נלה ערוה denotes intercourse alone. See Deut 22:13–23:1 below for a discussion of the marriage denotation and the sexual connotations of לקח. See also Lev 20:10–21 below.

88.   Angelo Tosato, "The Law of Leviticus 18:18: A Reexamination," *CBQ* 46 (1984): 201. He bases his interpretation on a reading of Lev 18:18 reflected in 11QTemple 57:17–19 and CD 4:12b–5:11a.

89.   See Bigger's broad definition of incest in "Family Laws," 193. Bigger seems to agree. Athalya Brenner, "On Incest," in *A Feminist Companion to Exodus to Deuteronomy* (ed. Athalya Brenner; FCB 6; Sheffield: Sheffield Academic Press, 1994), 124–29, provides a review of theories of incest.

90.   Tosato, "Law of Leviticus 18:18," 202–8.

91.   Ibid., 203–6.

92.   Ibid., 207–8.

93.   Ibid., 206. See also Bigger, "Family Laws," 201–2.

94.   Tosato, "Law of Leviticus 18:18," 207–8.

95.   Ibid., 204.

incest prohibition which has a tradition in ancient Israel of not being perpetual.[96] Tosato's point, however, may have less to do with the essential nature of incest than it has to do with the distinction created by בְּחַיֶּיהָ. But the *express* time limit in v. 18 is unique among *all* the laws.[97] Not only does the time qualification separate v. 18 from vv. 6–17, it also separates it from vv. 19–23.

Fourth, in every other case of both sections the primary concern is protecting boundaries, defined by consanguinal and affinal relations in vv. 6–17 and defined by other interests in vv. 19–23. If v. 18 is interpreted as preventing rivalry, as Tosato suggests, then it resembles neither vv. 6–17 nor vv. 19–23. However, if prohibition of intercourse with certain affines and consanguines is the primary concern, then v. 18 easily goes with vv. 6–17. This correspondence is also supported by others. For example, v. 18 mirrors v. 17 both with respect to the use of לקח and with respect to legislating against simultaneous marriage to and, therefore, intercourse with certain blood relations.[98] Thus, more confluence occurs if one sees v. 18 as maintaining the boundaries of blood relations rather than as preventing rivalry between "two women in general."

c) *Verse 21.* The third problem concerns the placement of the Molek verse in Lev 18.[99] Many scholars have considered this verse to be an insertion which is out of character with its present context.[100] I have read it, however, as an integral part of the second half of the law series. Regardless of its redactional history, it now forbids one of the five categories of sexual boundaries treated in vv. 19–23.

As part of his argument that the Molek passages refer to dedication, Weinfeld states that the present context of v. 21 "suggests its association with sexual transgressions."[101] His theory concerning dedication has drawn heavy criticism from Heider, Day and others[102] who have argued that such passages do indeed refer to child sacrifice. Nevertheless, Weinfeld's assertions concerning the "association with sexual transgressions" cannot be easily dismissed regardless of

96. That the tradition may or may not also belong to Lev 18 is beside the point. The point is that incest might not be *inherently* perpetual.

97. However, see the discussion of v. 19 below. The scenario of v. 19 is, indeed, contingent. This is the connection Tosato is making between v. 18 and the following unit. However, I take that connection to have the power of a linking device; not the power of a taxonomy which would group v. 18 with vv. 19–23.

98. Sun, "Investigation," 119.

99. Heider, *Molek*, 223–73. See Heider for a thorough summary and critique of the problem.

100. Dupont, "Women," 56; Elliger, *Leviticus*, 233; Heider, *Molek*, 247–48; Noth, *Leviticus*, 136.

101. M. Weinfeld, "The Worship of Molech and of the Queen of Heaven and Its Background," *UF* 4 (1972): 144: "In this connection the view of seed as semen is in fact not alien to the verses under discussion. The injunction in Lev 18.21, 'And you shall not give any of your seed (*wmzrʿk*) to pass to Molech,' follows the verse, 'And you shall not give the seed of your copulation (*škbtk lzrʿ*) to your neighbour's wife' (verse 20), and occurs before the verse, 'And you shall not give your copulation (seed) (*škbtk*) to any beast to defile yourself therewith' (verse 23). Even if the original meaning of seed in verse 21 was not semen but sons and daughters, the position of this verse in its present context suggests its association with sexual transgressions."

102. Day, *Molech*, 18–22; Heider, *Molek*, 66–81.

the way one reads phrases containing "some or all of the words *hᶜbyr ᵓt-bnw wᵓt-btw bᵓš lmlk*."[103]

Heider's explanation concerning v. 21 is unsatisfying. He has little to say about its meaning or rationale in the present context, beyond noting its "conflate nature" and its "loose relationship" to that context.[104] In fact, the "conflate nature" of the verse may evidence the intentional reconceptualization of material concerning child sacrifice and the Molek cult within a sexual context.

Day, on the other hand, has recently proposed an explanation that goes beyond the redactional explanation. On the basis of Lev 20:5, he suggests that v. 21 stands in its present "sexual context because the Molech cult is thought of metaphorically as an adulterous one vis-à-vis Yahweh."[105] He notes that the Old Testament "slips" easily from speaking of "literal adultery to spiritual adultery."[106] He writes:

> There is, therefore, every reason to believe that the law about Molech in Lev 18.21 is set in its present context because the cult is thought of as involving a spiritually adulterous relationship, just as in Lev 20.5. The only difference is that in Lev 18.21 the law is set more *in mediis rebus*, so to speak… Finally as other scholars have noted, the precise positioning of the Molech passage is conditioned by the use of the *Stichwörter lō ᵓtittēn* and *zeraᶜ* which it shares with the immediately preceding verse.[107]

If Day is right, then the author of Lev 18 has *recontextualized*[108] the sacrificial Molek material by using the "metaphor." On the basis of the metaphor, which was a common vehicle for describing idolatry with respect to Molek, the author has placed in an analogical context the prohibition against that idolatry, which is found in the metaphor. However, the author goes one step further. When he places the recontextualized Molek material, in the form of a metaphor, into Lev 18, he *reconceptualizes*[109] that Molek material. That is, the author "tweaks" the metaphor towards a realistic reading having to do with sexual transgression by placing it in the present context. Thus, the Molek material, in its present context has a sexual association, as Weinfeld states.[110] It refers to what only men (as opposed to men and women) do sexually in connection with Molek. Regardless of the fact that the originating reality behind the Molek passages may be child sacrifice, and regardless of the fact that child sacrifice has been placed in the vehicle of a sexual metaphor, in the present context the verse now guards one of the groups of five categories[111] of genital boundaries treated in vv. 19–23.

---

103. George C. Heider, "Molech," *ABD* 4:895.
104. Heider, *Molek*, 247–48.
105. Day, *Molech*, 23. Paul G. Mosca, "Child Sacrifice in Canaanite and Israelite Religion" (Ph.D. diss., Harvard University, 1975), 240, provides a different use of "metaphorical extension" as explanation of the sexual associations of the Molek verses.
106. Day, *Molech*, 23.
107. Ibid., 24.
108. Knierim, *Text and Concept*, 1 n. 1.
109. Ibid., 1 n. 1.
110. Weinfeld, "Worship of Molech," 143–44.
111. They are: menstruant, comrade's wife, Molek, male, animal.

2) *Structure*. With these decisions having been made concerning the structure, a conceptual pattern becomes clear in the text which demonstrates that the primary concern is protection of genital boundaries rather than protection of the woman as the sexual property of the man.

a) *Structure Proper*. The structure is as follows:

I.	Introduction	18:1
II.	Speech	18:2–30
	A. Command	2a
	1. speak: דבר	2aα
	2. say: אמר	2aβ
	B. Object of אמר: message to Israel from Yhwh	2b–30
	1. identification of speech source	2b
	2. ordinances: commands re: conduct	3–30
	a. general introductory prescriptions	3–5
	b. specific prescriptions re: sexual intercourse	6–23
	1) Re: consanguinity and affinity	6–18
	a) primary consanguinity	6–9
	(1) שאר בשרו	6
	(2) affines of father	7–9
	(a) mother of ego	7
	(b) wife of father	8
	(3) half-sister of ego	9
	b) secondary consanguinity	10–14
	(1) granddaughter of ego	10
	(2) daughter of wife of father	11
	(3) aunts	12–14
	(a) sister of father	12
	(b) sister of your mother	13
	(c) wife of brother of father	14
	c) primary consanguinity plus affinity	15–16
	(1) daughter-in-law	15
	(2) wife of brother	16
	d) affinity plus primary consanguinity	17–18
	(1) woman and daughter	17
	(2) woman and sister	18
	2) without respect to consanguinity and affinity	19–23
	a) menstruating woman	19
	b) wife of your comrade	20
	c) Molek	21
	d) male	22
	e) animal	23
	(1) command	23a–23bα
	(a) men	23a
	(b) women	23bα
	(2) grounds	23bβ
	c. general concluding commands	24–30

As noted above, the law series (vv. 6–23), surrounded by a parenetic framework, divides into two parts.[112] The first concerns laws which regulate the boundaries of sexual intercourse as defined by the relations of consanguinity and affinity. The laws of the second section regulate the boundaries of sexual intercourse as defined by other relations.

b) *First Section*. Part one of the law series, vv. 6–18, divides into four sections defined by various levels and combinations of consanguinity and affinity, which the women under discussion have with the ego.[113] Furthermore, it is arranged progressively with the closest relations placed first.[114]

The first four laws, vv. 6–9, guard against boundaries constituted by primary consanguinity.[115] The exception is the wife of the father in v. 8. She is related to the ego by primary consanguinity plus affinity. One would expect, therefore, to find this law with vv. 15–16 in the primary-consanguinity-plus-affinity category. However, this law and the subcase in v. 17 are the only disruptions in the pattern. The placement of v. 8 in the initial category of the law series can be explained by the paradigmatic nature of prohibitions related to women who are the sexual partners of the father.[116]

The second group, vv. 10–14, deals with relationships characterized by secondary consanguinity. Two members, vv. 11 and 14, of this group have secondary qualifications as well.[117] In this category of laws, the second qualification seems not to be constitutive for the structure. In v. 11, the forbidden woman's relation to the ego can be described in two ways since the ego is related to the forbidden

---

112.   Wenham, *Leviticus*, 249; Noth, *Leviticus*, 134–35, 136; Snaith, *Leviticus*, 121; Noordtzij, *Leviticus*, 182–89; Horton, "Form and Structure," 27, 31.

113.   See Chart 2 in Appendix. I have used the system of categorization described by Mace, *Hebrew Marriage*, 154–56. Primary consanguinity refers to an immediate collateral—brother or sister; an immediate ascendent—mother or father; or an immediate descendent—son or daughter. Secondary consanguinity refers to a collateral of any person who is of primary consanguinity—for example, mother's sister or father's sister; any person who is an ascendent or descendent of a collateral—for example sister's daughter, brother's daughter; or any person who is two or more generations ascendent from the ego—for example grandmother, grandfather, granddaughter, grandson. Mace starts with the following table and derives the "complete list of thirty relationships" of which a portion appears in the Holiness Code:

Consanguinity	*Consanguinity* + *Affinity*
mother	father's wife
daughter	son's wife
sister	brother's wife

114.   Schenker, "What Connects the Incest Prohibitions?," 163, divides the pericope into two sections: vv. 7–16 and vv. 17–18. I take the gradation of relations *throughout* vv. 6–18 to be constitutive and therefore divide the pericope into three sections on the same level.

115.   I do not take v. 6 as a general prohibition ruling the list of incest laws. Rather, I take it as a general prohibition ruling laws governing the primary consanguinity relations. Schenker, "What Connects the Incest Prohibitions?," 163, takes it as ruling vv. 7–16.

116.   See the discussion above. See also Rattray, "Marriage Rules," 542.

117.   See Chart 2, Appendix.

woman either through the father married to her mother, or through the father whose male relative was married to her mother. I have chosen the option which contains the most amount of information concerning her history as given in the text. This option fits the pattern.

The third category deals with women related by primary consanguinity plus affinity. The ego is related to the son and brother by primary consanguinity. The female is married to that blood relation.

The fourth category deals with women related by affinity plus consanguinity. Verse 17b, the subcase which disrupts the pattern, deals with affinity plus secondary consanguinity. No separate category exists for this particular combination and its inclusion here is a result of the connection of this blood relation to the woman of v. 17a.

Thus, the following factors are significant for the structure:

1. the first and second qualifications with respect to consanguinity and affinity in all categories except the secondary-consanguinity category;
2. only the first qualification with respect to consanguinity in the secondary-consanguinity category;
3. proximity to the father;
4. proximity to the ego.

The structure of the first section demonstrates that the author's primary concern is protection of genital boundaries constituted by consanguinal and affinal relations. Protection of women's sexuality, or woman herself, as property of the man, is not the intention of the text.

c) *Second Section.* The primary concern or intention of the second set of laws is also the protection of certain genital boundaries. These boundaries are not constituted by consanguinity and affinity. If the menstruating woman can be considered as incapable of conceiving,[118] or if the author perceived her as incapable, or even if the author perceived her as unlikely to conceive; then all five laws prohibit sexual interactions which fail to result in progeny for the male ego.

Furthermore, a pattern emerges even among these laws once this observation is made. Verses 20 and 21 refer to situations in which, if progeny results, that progeny is institutionally and legally separated from the ego. Verses 22 and 23 refer to situations which cannot result in conception at all. Verse 19, concerning the menstruating woman, would seem to belong to vv. 22 and 23. However, it has been placed by itself in initial position. The pattern just described looks like this:

---

118. Eilberg-Schwartz, *The Savage in Judaism*, 183, states: "Since a menstruating woman cannot conceive, sexual relations with her are unproductive... Since semen is perceived as being finite the prescriptions about sexual relations with menstruating women ensure that semen will not be 'wasted' on a woman at a time when she cannot conceive."

a) the contingent case: menstruant		19
b) the absolute cases		20–23
(1) progeny institutionally separated		20–21
(a) wife of comrade		20
(b) Molek		21
(2) no progeny at all		22–23
(a) male		22
(b) animal		23

Conceptual reasons exist for the placement of v. 19. Prohibition against intercourse with a menstruating woman is an impermanent boundary to sexual access with that woman. When her menses is complete the prohibition to sexual access is lifted. In this way, v. 19 differs from vv. 20–23. Furthermore, it shares this qualification with v. 18 of the previous section. This shared qualification is a link between the two sections.[119] In addition, the failure to produce progeny in the case of menstruating woman is not absolute. On occasion, menstruating women conceive.[120] This qualification, as well, separates v. 19 from what follows, since the failure of sexual intercourse to produce progeny *which would belong to the ego* is absolute in the situations of vv. 20–23.[121]

While failure to produce progeny is a qualification which all the situations of vv. 19–23 share, protection of progeny is not the intent of this section of laws. The most obvious situation which fails to produce progeny is missing from the list: intercourse with the barren woman. Thus, this section of laws does not prohibit all situations of unproductivity. In fact, it does not prohibit the most obvious situation. The author chooses to prohibit only situations which are qualified both by a blurring of the boundaries of unproductivity and by a blurring of the boundaries of a variety of other categories.

In the case of the menstruant, the ego enters the sphere of her personal impurity. In v. 20 the ego enters the sphere of another marriage. In v. 21 the ego enters into the sphere of another cult. In v. 22 the ego enters the sphere of another male. In v. 23 the male or female enters into the sphere of another species. The boundaries of v. 19 separate impurity. The boundaries of vv. 20 and 21 separate institutions. The boundaries of vv. 21 and 22 separate biotypes. Beyond her "unproductivity" the barren woman does not belong to a significant category— cultic, institutional or biological—which the male ego may not enter. She is therefore permitted, even though unproductive. We might surmise that just as

119.   This is what drew Tosato's eye.
120.   Eilberg-Schwartz, *The Savage in Judaism*, 183, also notes the unproductivity qualification of the stipulations of vv. 19–23. He states that "a menstruating woman cannot conceive," which, of course, is not true. Menstruating women have been known to become pregnant. Eilberg-Schwartz might argue that all that is necessary for his statement to hold for *this* text is that the author *believed* a menstruating woman cannot conceive. That is true.
121.   Schenker, "What Connects the Incest Prohibitions?," 168–69. Contrary to Schenker, I prefer to describe the unifying attribute to be prevention of those situations which fail to produce *progeny for the male ego* (i.e. progeny that continues within the community of Israel) rather than failure to produce progeny at all. The former leaves flexibility for at least two interpretations of the Molek law, while the latter does not.

section one cannot be said to protect boundaries of a patrilineage or household because certain household relation are permitted,[122] so also section two cannot be said to protect sexual intercourse for the sake of productivity because certain unproductive situations are permitted.

d) *Summary.* The structure demonstrates that protection of genital boundaries rather than protection of the woman or her sexuality, as the property of the man, is the primary concern of Lev 18.[123]

C. *Conclusion*

Thus, point-of-view and language-depicting-the-sex-act demonstrate considerable gender asymmetry. The asymmetry of point-of-view marginalizes woman, relegating her to the background of the text. The asymmetry of language-depicting-the-sex-act objectifies woman, leaving the impression that she or her sexuality is the property of the man, who is himself the guardian of sexual propriety. However, contraindicators related to point-of-view demonstrate that, even while her status is highly circumscribed by and dependent on the man, she too is responsible to the law. Contraindicators related to language-depicting-the-sex-act demonstrate that "ownership" of woman or her sexuality fails to name other nuances rendered by that language in the text.

Selection-of-laws, identification-of-women and structure-of-the-text reveal that neither woman as property nor her sexuality as property is the concern of the laws of Lev 18, which are "distracted" to the protection of a classificatory order, an ontology. With respect to this concern, woman is agent—circumscribed and subordinate though she may be. She is focalized like the man as one who must help to maintain the classificatory order.

This set of textual affairs illustrates the woman's overall dependence and subordination in Lev 18, but not her lack of responsibility. It illustrates that, rather than protecting the woman or her sexuality as property, the author intends simply to demarcate and protect genital boundaries, as Mary Douglas describes.[124]

Thus, woman is marginalized and objectified. But she is also focalized as agent. And she is not focalized as property.

---

122. Rattray, "Marriage Rules," 541.

123. Bigger, "The Family," 194, states: "The motives lying behind Hebrew incest prohibitions were not simple and it is no longer possible to determine the origin of incest beliefs in Hebrew history." In conclusion to his study, which attempts to discover the intent of various incest laws related by form, he states quite rightly (p. 203): "The family laws of Leviticus 18 thus demand order and purity in society which must begin from the local family group." See also Jenson, *Graded Holiness*, 145 n. 1.

124. Douglas, *Purity*, 53. See also Frymer-Kensky, "Sex in the Bible," 195–97, especially n. 58.

Chapter 4

LEVITICUS 19:20–22

A. *Introduction*

Leviticus 19:20–22 falls into the first of the two main types of sex texts described in the introduction.[1] It is a discrete unit of casuistic law which *intends* to regulate the *effects* of sexual intercourse. It is unique among all the sex texts because the woman it describes is legal property—no other woman in LST and DST is legal property.[2] She is a שִׁפְחָה.[3] Furthermore, two kinds of boundaries instead of one are relevant to the case. The first boundary guards the woman as the property of the master. The second boundary is similar to the boundaries of betrothal and marriage which guard a woman's sexuality for use by a single man. Although the woman is indisputably the legal property of one man—the master—and although her sexuality is "assigned"[4] to another man, the primary concern of the law is not the rights either of man to her or to her sexuality. Rather, the primary concern of the law is restoration of the male perpetrator to a state of purity.

B. *Discussion*

An understanding of the macrostructure is essential for determining the identity of the perpetrator. In addition, while an understanding of the macrostructure demonstrates that an essential component of Lev 19:20–22 is the use of personal property, the microstructure and the protected boundaries demonstrate that mediation of impurity caused by misuse of that property is the primary concern. Furthermore, the conceptualization of woman in this text is, at least partially, a function of this concern.

---

1. See the "Introduction" above.
2. Westbrook, "Female Slave." See p. 214 of Westbrook's study for a discussion of the way in which ancient Near Eastern Law splits the legal personality of slave-women.
3. Elliger, *Leviticus*, 259–60; Engelken, *Frauen im Alten Israel*, 127–69 (156–58); A. Jepsen, "Ama^H and Schiphcha^H," *VT* 8 (1958): 293; Jacob Milgrom, "The Betrothed Slave-girl, Lev 19:20–22," *ZAW* 89 (1977): 44–45; Baruch J. Schwartz, "A Literary Study of the Slave-girl Pericope—Leviticus 19:20–22," in Japhet, ed., *Scripta Hierosolymitana*, 244.
4. Schwartz, "Literary Study," 245–46. See Schwartz's suggestions concerning the distinction represented by נֶחֱרֶפֶת. He suggests (p. 246 n. 19) that "Even if there was no official act of betrothal, the 'assignation' of our passage is clearly of less finality than betrothal itself…" Elliger, *Leviticus*, 260, uses the word "*versprochen*" to describe the same idea.

1. *Property: Macrostructure*

a. *Structure Proper.* A collapsed version of the macrostructure is as follows:

I.	Introduction	19:1
II.	Speech	19:2–37
A.	Command: Introduction	2aα
B.	Object of Command: Message	2aβ–37
1.	general command	2aβ–2b
2.	specific commands	3–36
a.	man's relationship to others	3–18
1)	man's relationship to authority	3–8
a)	father and mother	3aα
b)	Yhwh	3aβ–8
(1)	Sabbath	3aβ–3b
(2)	other gods	4
(3)	זֶבַח שְׁלָמִים	5–8
2)	man's relationship to fellow man	9–18
a)	oppressed and sojourner	9–10
b)	your neighbor	11–18
(1)	oppression of neighbor	11–12
(2)	oppression of vulnerable	13–14
(3)	oppression in legal matters	15–16
(4)	oppression of your "brother"	17–18
b.	man's relationship to self	19–29
1)	introductory command	19aα
2)	specific commands	19aβ–29
a)	care of one's property	19aβ–25
(1)	crossbreeding cattle	19aβ
(2)	sowing two kinds of seed	19aγ
(3)	wearing fabric of two materials	19b
(4)	man with betrothed female slave	20–22
(a)	protasis: conditions	20a
α.	condition #1 שכבת	20aα
β.	condition #2 שפחה	20aβ
γ.	condition #3 נחרפת:	20aγ
δ.	condition #4 הפדה	20aδ
ε.	condition #5 לא חפשה	20aε
(b)	apodosis: consequence	20b–22
α.	introduction	20bα
β.	specification	20bβ–22
aa.	negative	20bβ
bb.	positive	21–22
α)	offering	21–22a
β)	result	22b
(5)	the land	23–25
b)	care of one's flesh and blood	26–29[5]
c.	man's relationship to others	30–36
1)	man's relationship to authority	30–32
a)	Sabbath and sanctuary	30
b)	clairvoyant practices	31
c)	elders	32

5.　See more detail on this portion of the structure below in the discussion of Lev 19:29.

	2) man's relationship to fellowman	33–36
	a) sojourner	33–34
	b) measures	35–36
3.	general command	37

This structure is based on suggestions by Magonet, who derives a five-part division of vv. 3–36 from a combination of formal and content features in the text.[6] He notes that his divisions form an ABCAB chiasm:[7]

1.   3–8:   man's relationship to God
2.   9–18:   man's relationship to fellow man
3.   19–29:   man's relationship to "self"
4.   30–31:   man's relationship to God
5.   32–36:   man's relationship to fellow man

Magonet fails, however, to examine the relationship of vv. 1–2 and 37 to this five-part division. However, the three-part division with which he begins his discussion incorporates these verses as follows: (1) 1–18; (2) 19–29; (3) 30–37.[8] Leaving aside vv. 1–2 and 37, both sets of Magonet's divisions, with minor exceptions, are apparent in my structure.

b. *Problems.* At least three problems exist with Magonet's five-part division.[9] The first concerns v. 3a. Magonet addresses this problem only obliquely. The second and third problems concern the sex texts of the chapter: vv. 20–22 and v. 29. Magonet fails to address these latter two problems even obliquely. All three problems, however, are surmountable. I will address the first two problems in the present discussion and the third problem in the exegesis of Lev 19:29.

The first problem is the seemingly anomalous appearance of the command "to fear one's mother and father" (v. 31) in the section Magonet labels "Man's Relationship to God." Magonet obliquely addresses the problem this classification poses for his divisions as follows:

> One might go further and note that the parallel between "revering" father and mother and "revering" My sanctuary (a parallel that is inevitably drawn by the reader given the six other similar instances in the chapter) leads to some sort of equation between the two spheres: reverence is demanded of the individual as he stands before his parents, the immediate source of his physical existence, and before the sanctuary, the symbol of God his Creator, in whose image he was created.[10]

---

6.   Jonathan Magonet, "The Structure and Meaning of Leviticus 19," *HAR* 7 (1983): 151–67.

7.   Magonet, "Structure and Meaning," 166.

8.   Ibid., 152.

9.   Ibid., 166. Magonet admits that his proposed scheme is an oversimplification "since within each of the three categories individual laws are found which specify a relationship with God."

10.   Ibid., 160. Gerald Blidstein, *Honor Thy Father and Mother* (New York: Ktav, 1975), 1–36. Blidstein's discussion of "Jewish reflection on filial responsibility" echoes the connection Magonet makes. See also Weinfeld's treatment of the relationship of honoring one's parents to honoring God in Moshe Weinfeld, "The Decalogue: Its Significance, Uniqueness, and Place in Israel's Tradition," in *Religion and Law* (ed. Edwin B. Firmage, Bernard G. Weiss and John W. Welch; Winona Lake, Ind.: Eisenbrauns, 1990), 17–18.

While this justification, for the sake of structure, is attractive and plausible, it is unnecessary. If we instead label the first (vv. 3–8) and fourth (vv. 30–31) sections "Man's Relationship to Authority" and move v. 32 from section five (vv. 32–36) to section four (vv. 30–31), the anomaly vanishes.[11]

The second problem concerns the slave-girl pericope in vv. 20–22. Magonet places this pericope in the "Man's Relationship to Self" section, vv. 19–29. He identifies the theme which ties the laws of this section together as follows:

> They seem to each pivot around two central but closely interrelated concepts: the limits imposed upon your freedom to use your property, expressed through prohibitions on making "unnatural" mixtures.[12]

As Magonet understands it, this then is the primary concern of the five laws in the third section (vv. 19–29) which he entitles "Man's Relationship to Self." However, if the master is not the perpetrator, as Milgrom and Schwartz argue, then the law does not concern the use of one's own property but rather the use of the property of another.[13] If, on the other hand, the master is the perpetrator, as Elliger suggests,[14] then the problem with Magonet's division vanishes. Magonet fails explicitly to discuss the identity of the perpetrator, referring us instead to Milgrom's discussion, thereby implying that he accepts Milgrom's assessment that the perpetrator is not the master.[15] This implication, however, conflicts with his divisions.

A review of the arguments of Milgrom and Schwartz clarifies the problem as well as the possibilities for a solution. Milgrom and Schwartz, in fact, follow Speiser's lead in their assessments.[16] Speiser presents a two-fold argument. First, he suggests that if the master were the perpetrator, שִׁפְחָה would have had the third masculine singular pronominal suffix attached. He writes:

> To be sure, the text is not specific on this point. Yet it implies a third party; one's own slave girl would be expressed as *šifḥāṭō*, not *šifḥā* [sic].[17]

Both Milgrom and Schwartz accept this part of his argument. However, to state that שִׁפְחָה, would have been שִׁפְחָתוֹ if the master were the perpetrator is to insist on the necessity of style to prove a point concerning content. The style which Speiser prefers is hardly as binding as required to dismiss an understanding such as the master–perpetrator correspondence. In fact, this correspondence is possible grammatically and syntactically even if it offends our aesthetic sensibilities.

Speiser bases the second half of his argument on his understanding of בִּקֹּרֶת which he translates as "indemnity" based on a derivation of בִּקֹּרֶת from Akkadian

---

11. The אֹבֹת and יִדְּעֹנִים, from whom one seeks direction in life, are forbidden sources of authority.

12. Magonet, "Structure and Meaning," 165.

13. Jacob Milgrom, *Cult and Conscience* (Leiden: Brill, 1976), 130 n. 46; idem, *Leviticus 17–22*, 1666. Schwartz, "Literary," 245. See also Levine, *Leviticus*, 131.

14. Elliger, *Leviticus*, 260.

15. Magonet, "Structure and Meaning," 163 n. 6; Milgrom, *Cult and Conscience*, 129–37.

16. Milgrom, *Cult and Conscience*, 130 n. 465; Schwartz, "Literary," 246 n. 20.

17. E. A. Speiser, "Leviticus and the Critics," in *Oriental and Biblical Studies* (ed. J. J. Finkelstein and Moshe Greenberg; Philadelphia: University of Pennsylvania Press, 1967), 129.

baqrum.[18] The assumption is that if any indemnity were paid, it would be paid to the master for economic loss. Thus, the master cannot be the perpetrator.[19] Both Milgrom and Schwartz discount this half of Speiser's argument, ruling out "indemnity" as a translation of בְּקֹרֶת.[20]

Milgrom and others, contrary to Speiser, assume בְּקֹרֶת derives from the Piel of בקר as used in Lev 13:36 and 27:33, meaning "to inquire, seek, investigate."[21] Schwartz, however, dismisses this reading as follows:

> The classical objection to this interpretation remains insurmountable: the precise circumstances of the case are stated explicitly in 20a and they are the sole *raison d'être* of the pericope. If the girl were fully betrothed or unassigned, no legal draftsman would have composed a law to deal with her case. In short, the ambiguity of the girl's status is a primary datum; it is not subject to verification.[22]

In other words, a law, with this reading, would apply only if it were known already that, while the slave girl could be ransomed, not only had she not been ransomed but she also had not been given her freedom. That is, the conditions for application of the law preclude the necessity of an investigation. Thus, בְּקֹרֶת is not "investigation."[23]

Schwartz suggests instead that "the primary meaning of the root בקר is 'split, divide.'"[24] He suggests that it means "differentiation" or "distinction" in the sense of "exception." The exception is that the death penalty is nullified. This suggestion by Schwartz is plausible. It means, however, that the second half of Speiser's argument that the master is not the perpetrator fails.

In fact, we do not know from the slave-girl pericope itself that the perpetrator is not the master or that he is the master. The surrounding laws, however, suggest a solution. Leaving aside the slave-girl pericope, the laws of vv. 19–29 cohere with respect to a single concern: the use of one's personal property. Furthermore, the units preceding and following vv. 19–29 do not demonstrate the same concern. Since this is so, and since other evidence concerning the slave-girl pericope is inconclusive, the immediately surrounding laws might serve as a pointer suggesting a correct reading. Just as the surrounding laws concern the use of one's personal property, so also does the slave-girl pericope. This means, however, that the master is the perpetrator.[25]

---

18.   Speiser, "Leviticus," 130–31. See also Phillips, "Another Look," 13.
19.   Speiser, "Leviticus," 130–31.
20.   Milgrom, *Cult and Conscience*, 129 n. 460, 130 n. 465; Schwartz, *"Literary,"* 250; Engel-ken, *Frauen im Alten Israel*, 158; Westbrook, *Studies*, 102–3; Countryman, *Dirt*, 36. Countryman's translation of בְּקֹרֶת as "damages" is the linch-pin for his understanding of the infraction of this law as a property offense. However, the property component of this law derives from the fact that the woman in some sense "belongs" to two men rather than from the use of בְּקֹרֶת.
21.   Milgrom, *Cult and Conscience*, 129 n. 460; idem, *Leviticus 17–22*, 1670–71.
22.   Schwartz, "Literary Study," 249.
23.   Milgrom, *Leviticus 17–22*, 1671, states that this meaning "flies in the face of all other attestations," three of which are from the Hebrew Bible (Lev 13:36; Prov 20:25b; Ezek 34:11–12).
24.   Schwartz, "Literary Study," 251.
25.   Westbrook, "Adultery," 565–66; idem, *Studies* 101–9. Westbrook also understands the "master" to be the perpetrator (*Studies*, 107–8). However, he pictures the scenario of the law

The first two problems concerning Magonet's divisions, which are the basis of my structure, thus resolve.

c. *Explanation of Structure.*

1) *Critique.* Sun has recently dismissed Magonet's suggestions as follows:

> But Magonet can only arrive at this conclusion by assuming that at one time, v. 37 originally closed the unit at v. 30 and was only secondarily moved to its present position in v. 37. But surely this implies that the unit which begins at v. 19 in the extant text reaches to v. 37. Thus, I cannot agree with his overall analysis in spite of his laudable attempt to interpret the various legislative blocks as larger units.[26]

However, Magonet never states that v. 37 originally closed the unit at v. 30. He states only that vv. 30–36 are an addition "placed at the end of the completed section 1–29 as appendices."[27] Magonet, in fact, fails to comment at all on the origin of v. 37. Furthermore, redactional history and redactional components do not necessarily determine the structure of a text. If v. 37 originally closed the

differently than I do. Westbrook understands the characters of the scenario to be שפחה, master and fiancé rather than שפחה, master and assignee. He reads (p. 107) אשה of v. 20 as "wife" rather than "woman." He repoints (p. 107) לאיש to לאיש. (See Milgrom, *Leviticus 17–22*, 1667.) Westbrook suggests (*Studies*, 106) that נחרפת refers to "pledge" rather than "assign" and that בקרת is best translated as "exception." As a result of these choices, Westbrook suggests ("Adultery," 566; *Studies*, 107) that this law refers to a situation in which the "husband has been forced to give his wife to a creditor in pledge and the creditor has slept with her." The pledge is thus cancelled and (*Studies*, 108) "the husband can claim back his wife, that is to say, cancel the pledge (and with it the debt). That is the role of the action *in rem: bqrt.*" Westbrook uses this understanding of the law in *Studies in Biblical and Cuneiform Law* to support his contention that adultery is a tort rather than a crime (p. 109) and that the husband's rights are the issue at stake in the law.

The plausibility of Westbrook's theory rests finally on the strength of his argument for נחרפת. He begins by asking why נחרפת is used instead of ארש if "some form of betrothal or assignment for marriage" is meant (*Studies*, 106). In reply, we might use similar logic to argue from a different direction. Since the infraction of Lev 19:20–22 does not require the death penalty, a plausible inference is that the arrangement referred to by נחרפת is akin but not identical to that referred to by ארש and therefore ארש is not used. The kinship of נחרפת and ארש is that both are bonds preceding marriage. The difference is that נחרפת is less binding than ארש. However, Westbrook peremptorily rejects the possibility that a variety of pre-marriage arrangements might have existed. He writes (p. 106): "This explanation is unsatisfactory, since this stage of betrothal in itself is sufficient to negate adultery: there is no death penalty for a stranger who has intercourse with a girl who is only promised. On this hypothesis, the reason given by Lev 19,10 [*sic*] for the absence of the death penalty—that the slave-girl has not yet been freed—would be otiose. We therefore, consider ourselves justified in looking in a different direction for the meaning of *nhrpt*." The otiosity, however, exists only if the distinctions among all stages or forms of pre-betrothal arrangements are such that penalties for intrusion upon any of them are always clear. In fact, we may surmise from the law itself that such penalties are not clear and that the law seeks to establish such clarity. In other words, the unusual circumstances of Lev 19:20–22 create enough confusion to necessitate the reason given in Lev 19:20 for the absence of the death penalty. Westbrook fails to offer evidence that compels the reader to reject such an understanding. Indeed, the fact that no change in the pointing of לאיש is required favors this latter understanding over Westbrook's own understanding ("Adultery," 565–66; *Studies*, 107–8).

26. Sun, "Investigation," 189 n. 55.

27. Magonet, "Structure and Meaning," 152.

unit 19–29 and was moved to the end of the supplemental unit 30–36, it does not follow that v. 37 necessarily closes the unit that begins with v. 19. Additions and other redactional alterations can change the intent and thus the relationships of the components of the original structure. Whether or not v. 37 closes the unit beginning with v. 19 depends on any number of features of signals in the text, the least among which may be the composition history.

In fact, based on the promptings of Magonet's analysis, I read v. 37 as closing the unit 2aβ–37. The law series begins with a general command to be holy (v. 2aβ–b) and ends with a general command to keep all Yhwh's statutes and ordinances and to do them (v. 37). Everything in between is a specification of these general statements, which are appositional to one another.

Furthermore, if v. 37 concludes vv. 2aβ–37, then the three major sections of the law series (vv. 3–18, 19–29, and 30–36) each have a שָׁמַר statement near or at their beginning and each is followed by a שָׁמַר statement. While the שָׁמַר statements beginning the sections serve different functions within each section, they all serve as "punctuation" supporting the three-part structure of vv. 2aβ–37, as well as the three-part structure of vv. 3–36.[28] In addition, if one reads v. 36b as a unit separate from v. 37, every subsection in the final unit vv. 30–36 has a concluding אֲנִי יְהוָה statement.[29] Formal features thus support the reading of v. 37 as a conclusion to the unit vv. 2aβ–37.

Thus, Magonet's five-part division is viable.

2) *Explanation.* The structure underscores the fact that the slave-girl pericope is a regulation dealing with property. The major divisions of the "Message" portion of my structure, based on Magonet's suggestions, are three: "General Command" (vv. 2aβ–2b), "Specific Commands" (vv. 3–36) and "General Command" (v. 37). The slave-girl pericope occurs in the "Man's Relationship to Self" section (vv. 19–29), the second of the three divisions which constitute the "Specific Commands" unit (vv. 19aβ–29).[30] The "Man's Relationship to Self"

---

28. In v. 3 the שָׁמַר statement follows the command to fear one's parents; see Magonet, "Structure and Meaning," 160. But, as Magonet suggests, this parent command is closely related to the Sabbath command. In vv. 3–8, the two commands occur together and in vv. 30–32 the Sabbath command occurs in close proximity to the command to revere elders. As one reveres one's parents or elders, so also one keeps the Sabbath. Thus, even though the Sabbath command is listed second in v. 3, it functions as part of the "frame" or "punctuation" which occurs throughout the chapter.

29. See Sun, "Investigation," 195. Sun groups v. 36b with v. 37 as the conclusion of vv. 19–37. But even Sun demonstrates an ambivalence concerning this understanding of the text. In a footnote he writes: "It remains possible that vv. 36b–37 serve a sort of double-duty function in closing both the unit vv. 19–37 and vv. 2–27; note the long self-identification formula in 2bβ, 36bα. Indeed, it might then also close the unit vv. 35–37!" (p. 195 n. 59).

30. Milgrom, *Leviticus 17–22*, 1665. Milgrom asks a question more fundamental than the question of placement. He asks why the law is present at all. He takes the אָשָׁם as the answer: "This case, therefore, falls into the same category as the other prohibitions in this chapter, whose violation prevents one from achieving the goal of the chapter—the attainment of holiness. Its wording, style and content are quintessential hallmarks of P. H has, therefore, incorporated this case into chap. 19 for two reasons: it completes H's comprehensive portfolio on P's *ʾāšām*, and, being a case of sacrilege, it belongs in chap. 19."

section consists of two parts: "Introductory Command" and "Specific Commands." The latter "Specific Commands" unit consists of two parts as well:
"Care of One's Property" (vv. 19aβ–25) and "Care of One's Flesh and Blood"
(vv. 26–29). The slave-girl pericope occurs in the first of these two sections:
"Care of One's Property."

2. *Purity: Microstructure and Boundaries*
Although the slave-girl pericope deals with property and understands the
infringement as an abrogation of sexual property boundaries, clues from the
microstructure, as well as clues from the boundaries themselves, demonstrate
that protection of rights to this sexual property are not the primary concern.
Rather, the primary concern is to mediate the impurity caused by the infraction.
The concern is classificatory. It pertains to crossing of boundaries per se.

a. חַטָּאת. However, טָמֵא is mentioned nowhere in Lev 19:20–22. חַטָּאת is
mentioned instead. The effects of this חַטָּאת are, in fact, what the אָשָׁם mediates.[31]
Kiuchi has suggested, however, that both חַטָּאת and טָמֵא are related to what is
designated as "uncleanness" in English. He writes:

> We shall point out below a possibility that the difference between חטאת (sin) and טמא
> (uncleanness) is essentially related to the dimension of uncleanness rather than to two
> mutually exclusive notions as their English equivalents suggests [*sic*]... All these
> observations lead to the inference that at least in the examined cases, חטאת (sin) is
> unlikely to be regarded as a notion essentially incompatible with 'uncleanness'; rather it
> is a kind of uncleanness, produced on a dimension different from that of a natural
> uncleanness...[32]

The concern in Lev 19:20–22 is for order and discreteness of categories regardless of the presence or absence of the words טָמֵא. Furthermore, in this passage
the general purity concern has not narrowed to a focus on property exchange or
loss or on reparation for such loss. Rather, the focus of this passage is on the
illicit crossing of boundaries, on the disruption of right order. This disruption or
impurity threatens the perpetrator[33] and presumably the community. The primary
concern is to mediate that *impurity*.

b. *Microstructure.* The microstructure underscores this point. The law consists
of a protasis and an apodosis. The protasis lists five conditions to be met in order
for the law to apply:
  1.   a man must lie with a woman;
  2.   she must be a שִׁפְחָה;[34]

---

31.   Rolf P. Knierim, "אשׁם," *THAT* 1:255.
32.   Kiuchi, *Purification*, 64–65. See also Jenson, *Graded Holiness*, 54, and my discussion
above in the "Introduction."
33.   Kiuchi, *Purification*, 37.
34.   Schwartz, "Literary Study," 244; Engelken, *Frauen im Alten Israel*, 127–84 (156–58);
Jepsen, "Ama^H," 293–97.

3. she must be "assigned";[35]
4. her status must be such that she is able to be redeemed but has not yet been redeemed;[36]
5. she must not have been *given* her freedom.[37]

If these five conditions hold, then the law applies. That is, the consequences of the apodosis go into effect. The consequences consist of two parts. First, the situation is an exception with respect to consequences normally applied in similar situations.[38] The perpetrators are not put to death. The reason, explicitly stated, is that the woman is not free. Second, the man is to bring an אָשָׁם, which the priest offers on his behalf. Subsequently, his חַטָּאת is forgiven him.

One individual is noticeably absent from the apodosis: the male "victim," that man to whom the woman is "assigned." And the woman is all but absent appearing only in 20bβ₂: "for she has not been given freedom." Such absences in a law which describes other consequences with detail are significant. They suggest that while minor focus is on the fate of the woman in conjunction with the male perpetrator, the major focus is on care for the male perpetrator. Not only is the male perpetrator the grammatical subject of the first portion of the protasis and a major portion of the apodosis, he is also the proleptic referent. Schwartz states the following:

> In light of the syntactical analysis, the legislative aim of the pericope may be defined as the obligation of the man who has had intercourse with an "assigned" slave-girl to offer an אָשָׁם, since the death penalty cannot be imposed. That the אָשָׁם-command, and it alone, is the central concern of the pericope is evident from the prominent place it holds, syntactically (it is the main clause), sequentially (it occurs last) and proportionally (it occupies a full twenty-six—precisely half—of the fifty-two words that make up the pericope).[39]

Schwartz's statement underscores the fact that the primary concern is not the wrong done to the male victim. Rather, it is the fact that forbidden boundaries have been crossed, creating a situation of impurity which must be rectified. Thus, the primary concern of the verse is "purity" of the male perpetrator rather than loss of sexual property by the male "assignee."

c. *Boundaries.*

1) *Assignee*/שִׁפְחָה. An examination of the boundaries relevant to this law also demonstrates that the primary concern is purity rather than property. Two sets of boundaries are important. The first is created by the master's ownership of the שִׁפְחָה. This is a property boundary. The second is created by the "assignment" or "pre-betrothal" of the שִׁפְחָה to another man.[40] This boundary does not protect

---

35. See n. 4 above.
36. Schwartz, "Literary Study," 246.
37. Ibid., 247.
38. See the discussion above on בִּקֹּרֶת.
39. Schwartz, "Literary Study," 244.
40. See n. 4 above.

property as the boundary created by the master/שִׁפְחָה relation does. The assignment boundary is instead similar to the boundary of marriage and betrothal. As
in marriage, the woman "belongs" to the man, such that the belonging affords
certain rights and responsibilities for both man and woman, and such that the
belonging is characterized by gender asymmetry to the man's advantage with
respect to power and authority. However, the boundary of "assignment" demarcates a weaker arrangement than that of marriage or betrothal.[41] Breach of the
latter requires the death penalty.

As Schwartz and others have noted, the peculiarities of the property boundary
and the assignment boundary and their conjunction create the ambiguity that
nullifies the death penalty and requires the אָשָׁם. The death penalty does not
apply because the woman is not free.[42] The master has simply made use of his
property as masters may do. The אָשָׁם is required because the שִׁפְחָה is "assigned."[43]
As any future arrangement reshapes the present, so also the assignment reshapes
the master's privilege to put his property to sexual use.

However, the primary concern of the law is the impurity incurred by the
perpetrator who committed the breach of the assignee/שִׁפְחָה boundary rather than
the protection of property rights or reparation for property damage or loss to the
assignee.[44] The primary concern is not to define one set of property rights over
against another. The concern is instead purity. The אָשָׁם rectifies the impurity
contracted by the perpetrator rather than the loss of damage to the assignee.[45]

2) אָשָׁם. An examination of recent discussion concerning אָשָׁם supports this
conclusion. Since, as Schwartz suggests, the "legislative aim" of the law is to
require the אָשָׁם, examination of the אָשָׁם also reveals the nature of the infraction
with which the law is concerned: mediation of impurity rather than mediation of
property loss.

Scholars agree that at least one component of the sin of *sancta*-trespass which
אָשָׁם addresses is some kind of epistemological ambiguity, which they typically
call "inadvertency."[46] As Schwartz indicates, only two textual instances match
the אָשָׁם with deliberate crimes: Lev 19:20–22 and Lev 5:20–26. He writes:

41. See n. 4 above.
42. Schwartz, "Literary Study," 248.
43. Ibid., 252.
44. Nor is reparation due to the master. Milgrom, *Leviticus 17–22*, 1665, states: "In this case,
surprisingly, the Bible does not compensate the owner at all. Herein is revealed the true marginality
of the case: on the one hand, because she is betrothed, the master, is in effect, only partial owner and
therefore not entitled to compensation; on the other hand, because she still is a slave, the laws of
adultery are not applicable and their penalties cannot be imposed on her paramour."
45. Knierim, "אָשָׁם," 252, characterizes the context of אָשָׁם in Lev 19:21b–22 as a situation in
which someone has an obligation resulting from guilt for which he gives something ("eine Situation
der Schuldverpflichtung, in der jemand etwas gibt"). If the perpetrator has an obligation in this law,
then it is an obligation to perform certain actions so that his sin can be forgiven by Yhwh. Accomplishment of these actions sets things right with Yhwh and lifts the effects of his sin from himself.
The obligation is thus also, ultimately, an obligation to himself.
46. This ambiguity is a component regardless of the view held concerning the consciousness of
the sinner. It is a component whether or not the scholar understands אָשָׁם to apply to the individual

> Only in two instances—the case of the slave-girl and the utterance of the false oath (Lev 5:20–26)—is an אשם prescribed for a crime committed with intent. In the latter case the reason seems to be that the two elements of repentance, contrition and confession of the guilty party, which are required by the law before the אשם can be offered, have the power of transforming "certain deliberate sins into inadvertencies, thereby qualifying them for sacrificial expiation." In the case of the slave-girl, there can be no doubt that the offense was committed willfully, and no mention is made of repentance. Here then is the only instance of an אשם prescribed for an intentional offense without prior contrition and repentance.[47]

Thus, the presence of אָשָׁם in this pericope presents a problem. Milgrom attempts to solve this problem by suggesting that the infraction of Lev 19:20–22, in effect a case of adultery, is a breach of the Sinaitic Covenant.[48] Thus, the infraction is a sin against God. "A collective oath against adultery" was made "when Israel became covenanted with its God."[49] This explanation fits Milgrom's scheme, which describes the אָשָׁם as applicable in three kinds of situations: (1) inadvertent and (2) suspected cases of *sancta*-trespass and (3) the "defrauding of a man in conjunction with a false oath to God."[50] The infraction by this explanation, then, fits the third situation). But Schwartz has rightly noted that the same "could be said of any violation of the Decalogue, as indeed of the entire Sinaitic law."[51]

Schwartz offers another solution. He suggests that while the assigned status of the woman nullifies the death penalty, the "great sin against God" which constitutes such an act must still be addressed.

> The reason follows from the nature of the case: the normal method of expiation in capital offenses—the death penalty—cannot be employed, and yet, the law would appear to assume, the fine legal distinction between "assigned" and "betrothed," while it suffices to render the offender unpunishable by the human court, does not cancel the "great sin against God" which adultery was considered and for which amends remain to be made. And so, since the חטאת is never applicable in other than deliberate sins, the אשם is prescribed. This is the meaning of בקרת תהיה: the situation is one of unprecedented fission: a capital crime which cannot be capitally punished; thus an אשם without the necessity of repentance.[52]

Schwartz seems to suggest that while the "adultery" itself, that is, the offense against the assignee, may be deliberate, the sin against God is not. Therefore, the אָשָׁם applies. However, surely a mature, male Israelite, "initiated" into the responsibilities of the adult community, would know that, as his deliberate

---

who sins and does not know it or who sins and later realizes it. It is a component whether or not the scholar understands the sin as involuntary, unpremeditated or unintentional. See the following: Gary A. Anderson, "Sacrifice and Sacrificial Offerings (Old Testament)," *ABD* 5:880-81; Kiuchi, *Purification*, 25–34; Rolf P. Knierim, "שגג," *THAT* 2:871–72; idem, "אשם," 252; Milgrom, *Cult and Conscience*, 7–12, 131; idem, "Sacrifices and Offerings (Old Testament)," *IDBSup*, 768; Schwartz, "Literary Study," 251–52.

47. Schwartz, "Literary Study," 251–52.
48. Milgrom, *Cult and Conscience*, 133–36; idem, *Leviticus 17–22*, 1676.
49. Milgrom, *Cult and Conscience*, 136.
50. Milgrom, "Sacrifices," 768–69. See Kiuchi's critique in *Purification*, 21–66 (31–34).
51. Schwartz, "Literary Study," 252 n. 49. See Milgrom's reply in *Leviticus 17–22*, 1675.
52. Schwartz, "Literary Study," 252. See Milgrom, *Leviticus 17–22*, 1672–74.

adultery is a sin against the assignee, so also it is a breach of the Sinaitic Covenant and thus a sin against God.

The question is: How does the epistemological ambiguity which אָשָׁם requires apply to the situation of the slave-girl pericope? Perhaps the above solutions are looking in the wrong place for that ambiguity. Perhaps the source of the ambiguity, in this case, has less to do with the consciousness of the perpetrator than with the nature of the boundary protecting the forbidden region.[53] As Schwartz explains, the assignee/שִׁפְחָה bond is weaker than the betrothal bond.[54] He calls it a "pre-betrothal" bond. We might call it a "virtual" bond. As such, it signals that it is not now real but what will be real in the future. Marriages are established, real and knowable. Betrothals are established, real and knowable. "Assignments" are virtual, unreal and "unknowable." The most they signify is the preliminary intention to establish what is real and knowable.

Just as an inadvertent infraction is characterized by an epistemological vacuum so also is the crossing of a "virtual bond" since it signifies what may become real in the future. This does not mean that the perpetrator did not know about the assignment. It means only that "assignment" does not compel the same degree of epistemological certainty as marriage or betrothal. For this reason, breach of the boundary protecting the assignment bond is similar to an inadvertent breach, requiring an אָשָׁם.

This explanation is perhaps the most that than be said about the epistemological conditions requiring the אָשָׁם in this passage. The least that can be said is that the breach of the "assignment" boundary is different from the breach of marriage or betrothal boundaries. The difference is constituted by the difference in strength of the boundaries or the degree to which they signify what is established in the present. The degree to which they signify what is established in the present itself corresponds to the difference between the death penalty and the אָשָׁם as consequences. Thus, the lesser degree of certainty characterizing the assignment boundary requires the אָשָׁם.

3. *Marginalization, Objectification and Focalization*
This text is part of a larger unit which begins with instruction from Yhwh to Moses, to address כָּל־עֲדַת בְּנֵי־יִשְׂרָאֵל. Furthermore, the law of vv. 20–22 places emphasis upon the man by beginning with "If a man lies with a woman…" (v. 20). Thus, a male community is explicitly addressed, and the woman is explicitly taboo to the man while the reverse scenario is only implied. Woman is, therefore, marginalized in the text. In addition, the language-depicting-the-sex-act pictures the man as subject and the woman as object.

Her focalization, however, is unique among the laws of LST and DST. Among the laws of LST she is the only woman who is the legal property of a master and whose sexuality, along with other aspects of herself, has been

---

53. Milgrom, *Leviticus 17–22*, 1675: "It falls into the gray area between a free person and a slave, in which the laws of adultery do not apply."
54. Schwartz, "Literary Study," 245–46, especially n. 19.

assigned to another man. The law recognizes the fact that her status as property changes when she is given her freedom or when she is redeemed.

Since the woman is focalized as property and since her status as property can change potentially to that of "free-woman-belonging-to-a–man," we might expect that the primary concern of the law would have to do with the rights of either the assignee or the master. However, the above exegesis suggests that this is not the case. Rather, the primary concern is to mediate the impurity of the male perpetrator. The focus of the law has less to do with the fact that a man's sexual property has been absconded or that a master has some limited leeway[55] to meddle with an assigned woman whom he owns, than it has to do with the fact that the male perpetrator is in need of restorative care because of his illicit actions. As a result, after a description of the situation of the law in the protasis, the male "victim" and the woman all but fade from view.

Thus, while her status as property is the source of the impurity which constitutes the author's primary concern, her relationship to that primary concern, that is, her focalization, is different from the focalization of women in DST. In both DST and Lev 19:20–22, breach of ownership of the woman by another man constitutes the infraction. However, in the present text the author is concerned for the perpetrator, whereas in DST the author is concerned for the male victim. The woman, by virtue of her property status, is an extension of the male victim in a way that is different from the extension in DST.

The author has been distracted from "the woman's relationship to the purity concern" towards another concern, namely, to "the male perpetrator's relationship to that primary concern for purity."[56] Her focalization is, therefore, also an exception among the laws of LST, shaped as it is by class and gender. She is a שׁפחה and she is "assigned. In this instance, the woman's agency does not "transcend" the property boundaries placed upon her, in connection with her sexuality, for the sake of protection of the system. Her "participation" in the infraction is not of concern to the law. Furthermore, neither her "impurity,"[57] nor her "actions" are conceived as something which must be remedied, as is the case with the man's actions. She is forgotten because of her status and her gender; the male victim is forgotten because of *her* status and because of the primary concern of the law.

Thus, her focalization is "forgotten."

C. *Conclusion*

Leviticus 19:20–22 is a law regulating use of property. The concern with respect to that use, however, is classificatory, a concern for purity rather than property

---

55. The leeway is the fact that the death penalty does not apply.

56. See Anderson's study of texts in the Book of the Covenant and in Deuteronomy (*Women, Ideology, and Violence*, 74), where she examines gender in relationship to class and nationality. She calls gender the "master status." In this law, class nullifies the agency factor that transpires in connection with other women in LST.

57. If, in fact, impurity is imputed to her.

rights, exchanges or losses. Thus, although the law regulates activity with respect to a woman who is, in fact, legal property, and although it never explicitly mentions the word for purity, it nevertheless supports the thesis that the primary concern of LST with respect to women and sexuality is purity rather than property. In this text, however, since she is "legal" property, woman does not appear either explicitly or implicitly as an agent with responsibilities for maintaining the purity of the system of which she is a part.

Woman is thus marginalized and objectified in Lev 19:20–22. Moreover, she is focalized as "forgotten." Her focalization, a function of gender and status, is singular among women of LST and DST. In Lev 19:20–22, her focalization as "forgotten" serves the author's primary concern for the purity of the perpetrator. Focalization to agent cannot break the bounds of class. This law highlights, *by contrast*, the presence of that agency which accrues to the other women in LST.

Chapter 5

LEVITICUS 19:29

A. *Introduction*

The law of Lev 19:29 concerns the sexuality of an unbetrothed, unmarried daughter. Pronounced gender asymmetries indicate that the daughter occupies a highly circumscribed position. Although her sexuality belongs to her father,[1] this law, far from protecting the father's rights concerning that sexuality, limits those rights in the interest of purity. The primary concern is thus preservation of the purity of the woman rather than protection of her sexuality as property. In this limited respect, the daughter is "valued," by the primary concern. That is her focalization.

B. *Discussion*

1. *Point-of-View and Language-Depicting-the-Sex-Act*
a. *Marginalization and Objectification.* The pronouns and verbs indicate that the father of the daughter is addressed. The law details his responsibilities, implying his control of female sexuality. The sex act per se is not depicted. Rather, the author refers to the "habitual" practice of harlotry in connection with the daughter. The daughter's objectification is revealed by her position as object of חלל. The father is subject. He takes the initiative. She lacks responsibilities and control as well as initiative. Although the law limits the father's control, that very limitation implies that her sexuality belongs to him.

Point-of-view and language-depicting-the-sex-act thus objectify the woman and relegate her to the background of the text.

b. *Contrasting Features.* However, two features—חלל and the macro-structure—contrast, at least partially, with this circumscription even if they do not neutralize it.

1) חלל. חלל occurs within the "Negative Command" section of v. 29, which divides into "Negative Command" and "Motivation."[2] It is one of two verbs

---

1. Archer, *Her Price is Beyond Rubies*, 46–53; Frymer-Kensky, "Law and Philosophy," 94 n. 14; idem, "Sex in the Bible," 192–93; Pressler, *View of Women*, 31; Wegner, *Chattel*, 13.
2. See the structure below.

used in this section. The other is זנה.[3] חלל expresses the basic command.[4] לְהַזְנוֹתָהּ is epexegetical.[5] The law states: "Do not profane your daughter by causing her

3.   See Bird's discussion of "*znh/zônâ*" in Phyllis Bird, "To Play the Harlot: An Inquiry into an Old Testament Metaphor," in *Gender and Difference* (ed. Peggy Day; Minneapolis: Fortress, 1989), 76–80; S. Erlandsson, "זנה," *TDOT* 4:99–101; Stephen A. Hooks, "Sacred Prostitution in Israel and the Ancient Near East" (Ph.D. diss., Hebrew Union College, 1985), 70–71; Moshe Greenberg, "The Decalogue Tradition Critically Examined," in *The Ten Commandments* (ed. Gershon Levi; English ed.; Jerusalem: Magnes, 1990), 104 n. 35. Bird, Erlandsson, Hooks and Greenberg agree that זנה refers to sex outside of marriage. Illicit sex within the context of a marriage bond, on the other hand, is represented by נעף. Scholars have also taken זנה to designate, among other things, sacred prostitution especially in the service of fertility rites. This explanation, however, has been called into question. See Milgrom, *Leviticus 17–22*, 1695–98; Léonie Archer, "The Virgin and the Harlot in the Writings of Formative Judaism," *HWJ* 24 (1987): 1–16; Bird, "To Play the Harlot"; Erlandsson, "זנה," 100; Eugene J. Fisher, "Cultic Prostitution in the Ancient Near East: A Reassessment," *BTB* 6 (1976): 231–35; Duane A. Garrett, "Votive Prostitution Again: A Comparison of Proverbs 7.13–14 and 21.28–29," *JBL* 109 (1990): 681–82; Goodfriend, "Prostitution (OT)", *ADB* 5:505–10; Kornfeld, *Levitikus*, 77; Van der Toorn, "Female Prostitution"; idem, "Prostitution (Cultic)," *ADB* 5:510–13. Van der Toorn has suggested that זנה refers to prostitution for the purpose of payment of vows.
      Within the scholarly discussion on prostitution in ancient Israel, Lev 19.29 is addressed peripherally, if at all. The act described in this verse cannot be an offense against the father (Bird, "To Play the Harlot," 77) since he initiates it. If it is payment for a vow (Van der Toorn, "Female Prostitution," 193), then we must presume that the father lacks the funds to pay for his daughter's vow, or he is unwilling to pay for it. Van der Toorn ("Prostitution," *ABD* 5:511–12) presumes that the reason a woman resorts to intercourse for payment of vows is because she lacks access to the funds of the husband or father. But in Lev 19:29, the father is the one who causes the daughter to harlot. Therefore, for this text, Van der Toorn's presumption fails. The question is: Why would a father urge his daughter into prostitution for payment of her vows? What father would approve his daughter's vow in the first place, if her prostitution was the only way to pay for it? Or does "cause to harlot" have some other meaning? See Milgrom, *Leviticus 17–22*, 1697. In addition, זנה in this law must represent something more than simple "sex outside the bond of marriage" (Bird, "To Play the Harlot," 77 n. 13) since, presumably, this alone would not be enough to motivate a father to cause his daughter to prostitute herself. See Hooks, "Sacred Prostitution," 103, 105. In addition, Hooks writes: "Finally, the suggestion that an Israelite father would be more likely to prostitute his daughter for religious than for other reasons is totally without foundation. This suggestion presumes a fully developed sex cult in Canaan which the available evidence simply does not sustain. For all the claims of women being dedicated by their parents to prostitution in the service of the gods, there is not a single account of such in all of the extant literature of the ancient Near East. Neither, therefore, should we understand this text from Leviticus to be a prohibition of such." Pressler suggests a likelihood that the prohibition attests to the practice of selling one's daughter into prostitution. Carolyn Pressler, "Wives and Daughters, Bond and Free: Views of Women in the Slave Laws of Exodus 21.2–11," in Matthews, Levinson and Frymer-Kensky, eds., *Gender and Law in the Hebrew Bible*, 158 n. 25. See also Jenson, *Graded Holiness*, 123 n. 3.
      Magonet, "Structure," 164, on the basis of the use of זמה here and in Lev 18:17 and 20:14, speculates about the possibility that this law may refer to incest. Interestingly, the incest interpretation seems to be the loci in Lev 21:9 for the divergence of some of its textual witnesses. See the discussion below. In short, more research is needed concerning the contribution this verse makes to our understanding of prostitution in ancient Israel.
4.   Milgrom, *Leviticus 17–22*, 1696. Milgrom takes the use of חלל to be figurative. He translates it as "degrade" rather than "desecrate."
5.   Waltke and O'Connor, *Biblical Hebrew Syntax*, 36.2.3e. See Waltke and O'Connor for the "gerundive, explanatory or epexegetical" use of *lamed* plus the infinitive.

to harlot."[6] Something can be profaned only if it is holy.[7] Thus, a daughter in Israel is holy. That is, she is consecrated or set aside. One component of her holiness is most certainly the fact that she is set aside for sexual access by one man, evidently in the context of marriage.[8] Just as Israel is consecrated to Yhwh, so also the woman is consecrated to one man. To profane her means that sexual access by more than one man takes place with respect to her. The text is unconcerned about the particular man to whom she is consecrated. Nor is it concerned with protection of her sexuality as the property of any one man. It is concerned only that her sexuality remain in reserve for one man. That is, it is concerned that only one man cross her genital boundaries.

However, one cannot rule out the possibility that another component of her holiness is that she, like her father, is consecrated to Yhwh. Concerning Lev 21:9, Elliger cites the daughter's share in the sacred offerings of her priest father as evidence of this fact.[9] He writes:

> Daß die Tochter in gewissem Sinne am dinglichen Heiligkeitscharakter des Vaters teilhat und infolgedessen auch sich selbst nicht nur moralisch, sondern auch kultisch „entweihen" kann, ist ein Gedanke, den vielleicht schon die Heiratsvorschriften für die Priester implizieren, der aber auch aus den Bestimmungen über die Beteiligung der Familienmitglieder am Genuß der heiligen Abgaben abgeleitet werden kann (vgl.22:1ff.).[10]

If the daughter of a priest shares in the holiness of her father, then certainly the daughter of an ordinary man shares in whatever holiness belongs to him in the "broader sense"[11] as a member of the community of Israel.[12]

---

6. Dupont, "Women," 215 n. 6, notes that Lev 21:15 and 19:29 "are the only two instances in the entire Hebrew Bible in which the writer speaks of 'profaning one's child/children.'"

7. See Wenham, *Leviticus*, 19, writes: "Everything that is not holy is common. Common things divide into two groups, the clean and the unclean. Clean things become holy, when they are sanctified. But unclean objects cannot be sanctified. Clean things can be made unclean, if they are polluted. Finally, holy items may be defiled and become common, even polluted, and therefore unclean." See Jenson, *Graded Holiness*, 46–48, 53–54, who critiques Wenham. His own explanation (p. 47) is as follows: "The holy-profane pair represents (positively and negatively) the divine sphere, and this may be distinguished from the human sphere (which is marked by the opposition between clean and unclean)." W. Dommershausen, "חלל," *TDOT* 4:416; H. Ringgren, "קדש," *ThWAT* 6:1190. See also Lev 10:10.

8. Julian Morgenstern, "The Decalogue of the Holiness Code," *HUCA* 26 (1955): 11, writes: "The verb in the *piˤel* means then, 'to set aside (as one's property); to make (something) one's own.' Accordingly in post-Biblical Hebrew the expression, *qaddeš ᵓiššah*, means 'to marry a woman,' literally, 'to make a woman one's own, and in consequence to make her forbidden, taboo to any other.'"

9. Jenson, *Graded Holiness*, 123 n. 3. However, regarding Lev 19:29, Jenson states: "The female members cannot be holy in the stricter sense, since they are not consecrated and are forbidden to enter the holy places." "Stricter sense" refers to the special requirements for holiness applied to priests as opposed to the general Israelite population. Nevertheless, Jenson admits (p. 123) that "the entire extended family of priests was affected by priestly status." He suggests that this state of affairs is a function of social and legal structures with which the laws of the cult must align.

10. Elliger, *Leviticus*, 289. See also Dommershausen, "חלל."

11. Jenson, *Graded Holiness*, 49: "The restriction of holiness to the priests and the sanctuary is in tension with other occurrences of the root where it has a much broader scope. Holiness can

The law limits the father's power to meddle with her holy status. Protection of her genitals serves the protection of her holiness. Protection of her holiness serves protection of the land, since disruption of her holiness by prostitution puts the land itself at risk for the spread of infamy.[13]

Thus the daughter herself, powerless as she may be, is an element whose activity is integral to the purity of the system to which she belongs, even if that activity is prompted by the initiative of one upon whom Israel bestows power— her father.[14] Use of חלל is thus double-edged. It implies an antonym which signals one of the most pronounced sexual gender asymmetries of ancient Israel: women are set aside for one man while the reverse is not so. Nevertheless, its prohibition stands in marked contrast to the circumscription represented by another asymmetry: the power and control of a father over his daughter's sexuality.

2) *Macrostructure.* The macrostructure provides an additional contrast. It demonstrates a revealing conceptual distinction qualifying the daughter.

Like Lev 19:20–22, this pericope falls within the "Specific Commands" section (vv. 19aβ–29) of the "Man's Relationship to Self" unit (vv. 19–29).[15] As stated above, Magonet suggests that "vv 19–29 all deal in some way with a man's relationship to his own possessions: his animals, crops and clothing (v. 19); his slaves (vv. 20–22); his land (vv. 23–25); his body (vv. 26–28); his offspring, his daughter (v. 29)."[16] However, a significant difference exists between the "possessions" of vv. 19–25 and vv. 26–29. The first section (vv. 19–25) treats possessions that can be inherited, bought, sold, exchanged, borrowed or stored. The second section (vv. 26–29) treats "possessions that are one's own flesh and blood." The structure is as follows:

b.[17] man's relationship to self		19–29
1) introductory command		19aα
2) specific commands		19aβ–29
a) care of one's property		19aβ–25
b) care of one's flesh and blood		26–29

describe God's demands on the whole of Israel, which is called to imitate God's own holiness (Lev 19:2). This meaning often occurs when the passage is referring to matters other than the cult in the narrower sense. Thus, holiness should characterize Israel in its distinctiveness in relation to the nations with regard to purity laws (Lev 11:44–45) or moral behaviour (Lev 19)."

12. Ze'ev W. Falk, "Spirituality and Jewish Law," in Firmage, Weiss and Welch, eds., *Religion and Law*, 132.

13. זמה refers to illicit sexual behavior. The same word describes lying with a woman and her daughter or granddaughter in Lev 18:17 and with a woman and her mother in Lev 20:14. In Judg 20:6 it describes, in conjunction with נבלה, the act which was committed against the concubine. Ezekiel (Ezek 22:9, 11) uses זמה to denote illicit sex. In addition, he uses it as a sexual metaphor to represent Israel's unfaithfulness and misdeeds. See especially Ezek 23.

14. Lev 19:2 addresses the כל־עדת בני־ישראל.

15. See structure above in discussion of Lev 19:20–22.

16. Magonet, "Structure," 165.

17. The enumeration reflects the larger structure from which I have taken this portion. See the discussion of Lev 19:20–22 above.

(1) eating blood		26a
(2) divination and conjuring		26b
(3) cutting hair		27
(4) tattooing body		28
(5) prostitution of daughter		29
(a) negative command		29a
(b) motivation		29b
c. man's relationship to others		30–36

This assessment of vv. 26–29 contains two problems. The first problem is the placement of the laws concerning eating blood (v. 26a) and divinatory practice (divination and conjuring, v. 26b) within the unit entitled "Care of One's Flesh and Blood" (vv. 26–29). This problem and its solution are similar to the problem in Magonet's schema of the placement of these same verses within the unit entitled "Care of One's Property" (vv. 19–29).[18] As mentioned above, Magonet suggests that the laws of vv. 19–29 impose limits on the use of personal property.[19] But laws prohibiting consumption of blood, divinatory practice, trimming hair and tattooing skin would seem to be out of place in such a unit. Magonet, however, suggests that the body itself is the "property" regulated by such laws. Prohibitions against eating blood, divinatory practice, trimming hair and tattooing skin limit bodily abuse. The connection is obvious with respect to eating blood, trimming hair and tattooing skin, which trespass on the body.[20]

However, the connection is less obvious with respect to divinatory practice. Magonet follows Wenham in his explanation. Since Joseph, in Gen 44:5, both divines (נחשׁ) and drinks from the stolen cup, Magonet and Wenham suggest that divinatory practice may involve drinking.[21] Thus, the law of v. 26b prohibits "abuse" of the body by drinking, just as v. 26a prohibits "abuse" of the body by eating.[22]

However, Magonet's and Wenham's explanation can, at most, account for the prohibition against נחשׁ. A prohibition against ענן follows it. If ענן refers to "telling the future," or a similar activity,[23] then an altered state of consciousness is required. Although such an altered state may be pronounced, more or less, or noticeable in individuals who have this ability, it is nevertheless required. Physiological changes often, if not always, accompany such an altered state. Furthermore, if the Poel of ענן means to "conjure spirits" or to "cause something to appear,"[24] then an altered state and the accompanying physiological changes

18. See the discussion above.
19. Magonet, "Structure," 165.
20. Ibid., 164. Magonet writes: "The first command concerns the food one takes into the body, and its position may have been influenced by the previous section on produce that may be eaten."
21. Wenham, *Leviticus*, 272; Magonet, "Structure," 164.
22. Magonet, "Structure," 164, states: "Though it is generally assumed that Joseph performs hydromancy, the juxtaposition in 44:5 of the fact that he both drinks and divines from this cup, may suggest that the drinking was a part of the divination process—in which case we might have a further aspect of the 'abuse' of the body through 'drinking' as well as 'eating.'"
23. "ענן," BDB, 778.
24. William L. Holladay, "ענן," in *A Concise Hebrew and Aramaic Lexicon of the Old Testament* (Grand Rapids: Eerdmans, 1971), 278.

are even more likely. The latter activity would require an extraordinary use of the energetic stores of the body. Similar alterations may be involved in divination (נחש). However, even if no physical harm and no significant change comes to the body during these divinatory practices, the issue which places the law at this point in the text is the fact that the body is used at all for whatever is signified by ענן and נחש. The body becomes the vehicle for the information which the esoteric practice yields.

Since we cannot know for sure to what esoteric practice words like נחש and ענן refer, our explanations can be only educated guesses. Turning the argument around, circular though such a move may be, we might surmise that the placement of these two prohibitions in the text lends credence to the explanation just given. In any case, my structure assumes that the phenomenon which concerns the author about נחש and ענן is the harm that comes to the body through such activity.

A legitimate objection to this assumption is that v. 31, which forbids similar esoteric practice, is in the "Man's Relationship to Others" section rather than in the "Man's Relationship to Self" section. However, the prohibition of v. 31 is against seeking the esoteric services of others, whereas the prohibitions of v. 26 are against one's own practice of such esoteric activity. A comparison of the three verses, Lev 19:31, 20:6 and 20:27, underscores the point. One can either *turn to* אבת and יִדְּעֹנִים (Lev 19:31; 20:6), or one can *have within oneself* אבת and יִדְּעֹנִים (Lev 20:27). The fact that the author of Lev 20 felt compelled to add v. 27 even though v. 6 preceded it suggests that the distinction just described identifies a significant difference in the mind of the writer. If this is so, then Lev 19:31, in all probability, refers to the act of seeking out such esoteric services from another individual rather than to the act of carrying out such esoteric practice with one's own body. This conclusion, in turn, supports the above structure.

A second problem with my assessment of vv. 26–29 concerns my placement of the prostitution prohibition in the unit entitled "Care of One's Flesh and Blood." The "property" of this section is one's digestive system, hair and skin. A daughter's sexuality would seem to be generically different from one's own digestive system, hair and skin. Furthermore, prostituting her would seem to be generically different from abusing one's own body.

However, while Magonet has characterized the laws of vv. 26–28 as limiting actions against *bodily abuse*, to say simply that they limit actions against one's "flesh and blood" or one's "self" is sufficient. A daughter who is one's שְׁאֵר is, at least by extension, one's "flesh and blood" or one's "self."[25]

In conclusion, the placement of the prostitution prohibition is revealing. It does not occur in the section treating property which can be bought, sold, borrowed, exchanged or stored. Rather, it occurs in the section treating "possessions"

25. While nowhere in Leviticus is it stated that a daughter is her father's nakedness, the fact that the loss of virginity or harlotry profanes the priest father in Lev 21 would suggest such is the case. Magonet, "Structure," 164, writes: "If the principle of Lev 21:9, that a daughter of a priest who becomes a prostitute thereby defiles him, is more generally operative, then her actions are also effectively an abuse of his person."

which belong to a man because they are his own flesh and blood. The daughter is like the father's own flesh and blood. The "property" managed by Lev 19:29 is thus man's very self.

2. *Primary Concern*

But management is prescribed only for the sake of purity. Both the microstructure and the proximal laws concerning "unnatural mixtures"[26] demonstrate that the primary concern with respect to regulation of sexual intercourse in this law is preservation of purity rather than the protection or even management itself of property.

The microstructure of Lev 19:29 consists of two parts: "Negative Command" and "Motivation." The "Motivation" consists of two parts as well. These latter parts name sequential consequences to the land if the command is unheeded. Thus the "Negative Command" serves the "Motivation." The law separates the daughter from harlotry and profanation. It separates the land from harlotry and infamy. It separates the daughter for the sake of separating the land. The primary concern of the law is preservation of the purity of the land.

The proximal unnatural-mixture laws also support the idea that purity is the primary concern of Lev 19:29. As stated above, Magonet has characterized the laws of vv. 19–29 as placing limits "upon your freedom to use your property, expressed through prohibitions on making 'unnatural' mixtures."[27] Since I divide vv. 19aβ–29 into two parts (vv. 19aβ–25 and vv. 26–29), Magonet's statement applies in my structure to the first part. A similar statement may be applied to the second part: the laws of 26–29 place limits upon your freedom to use your own flesh and blood (or self), expressed through prohibitions on making unnatural mixtures.

This means that the prohibition against prostituting a daughter, like the other prohibitions of vv. 19aβ–29, is a prohibition concerned to protect order or discreteness of categories. It is concerned with classificatory issues. In fact, this is its primary concern.

C. *Conclusion*

Thus woman is marginalized and objectified. She is not focalized as an agent responsible for upholding the law. Her status is "daughter-property." She belongs to her father, whose sexuality she is. Protection of her purity, despite her circumscribed and subordinate position, is essential to protection of the purity of the system as a whole. The law sets limits on his property rights for the sake of these larger concerns. She is one constituent of the classificatory system which the law protects. She is focalized as "valued." Her focalization serves the purity concern.

---

26.   Magonet, "Structure," 165.
27.   Ibid., 165.

Chapter 6

LEVITICUS 20:10–21

A. *Introduction*

Leviticus 20:10–21, like Lev 18, is a series of sex laws. Unlike the Lev 18 sex-law series, which is the sole content of a single Yhwh speech, the Lev 20 sex-law series is one of several items of content within a single Yhwh speech. Leviticus 20 is casuistic law, while Lev 18 is apodictic law. Accordingly, Lev 20 applies penalties while Lev 18 lacks penalties. In addition, more of the laws in Lev 20 than in Lev 18 contain what Schulz calls *Qualifikationsurteile, Bezichtigungsurteile* and *Schuldurteile*.[1] In Lev 18 the consanguinal/affinal laws are separate from laws protecting other kinds of boundaries, whereas in Lev 20 the two sets of laws are intermingled.

Despite these differences, the sex-law series of Lev 18 and Lev 20 share the gender asymmetries created by point-of-view and language-depicting-the-sex-act. Responsible for the most severe gender asymmetries of vv. 10–21, point-of-view and language-depicting-the-sex-act marginalize and objectify the woman. She is circumscribed by, dependent on and subordinate to the man, leaving the initial general impression that the law guards and regulates the woman as man's sexual property.

However, although point-of-view and language-depicting-the-sex-act are responsible for this gender asymmetry, they are also, as in Lev 18, the source of subtle contraindicators which suggest a more complex conceptuality with respect to women than the asymmetries suggest. Contraindicators connected to point-of-view alone demonstrate that woman, as well as man, is responsible to the law. Contraindicators connected to both point-of-view and language-depicting-the-sex-act favor the woman, ameliorating her circumscription. In addition, at least one contraindicator suggests that the primary concern of the series is classificatory- rather than property-oriented.

Furthermore, three additional features of the text—the selection-of-laws, the identification-of-women and the structure-of-the text—indicate that the intent of the laws is to protect sexual boundaries in general rather than woman's sexuality as man's property. In fact, woman is focalized, like man, as agent. Subordinate though she may be, she is responsible, as is the man, to protect the classificatory order which constitutes Israel's purity system.

---

1. Hermann Schulz, *Das Todesrecht im Alten Testament* (Berlin: A. Töpelmann, 1969), 140–41.

B. *Discussion*

1. *Point-of-View and Language-Depicting-the-Sex-Act*
a. *Point-of-View.*

1) *The Bias.* Four features within the sex laws of Lev 20, similar to those in the sex laws of Lev 18, are a function of point-of-view and support woman's marginalization in the text. They demonstrate her circumscription and subordination. These four features are: application-of-taboo, named-addressee, use-of-second-and-third-person, and boundary alignments.

a) *Application-of-Taboo and Named-Addressee.* Every sex law except the laws of vv. 16 and 19 begins with אִישׁ אֲשֶׁר. This initial focus on the man in the protasis centralizes his action. The woman is taboo to the man. The reverse is left undescribed in the text. This focus is consonant with the use, in v. 2, of בְּנֵי יִשְׂרָאֵל, the collective, male named-addressee of the Yhwh speech in which vv. 10–21 occur.[2] The application-of-taboo and the named-addressee thus evidence the marginalization of woman's representation in the text.

b) *Use-of-Second-and-Third-Person.* The use of the second and third masculine pronouns and verbs throughout the laws supports the gender bias of the application-of-taboo and the named-addressee.

The only feminine pronouns in the laws occur in vv. 14, 17 and 18. They refer respectively to the woman's relationship to her mother, to her own nakedness and to her blood flow. They never refer to her relationship to a man.

Three feminine verbs also occur. The first describes the woman drawing near to a beast in order to copulate with it (v. 16). The second describes the sister seeing her brother's nakedness (v. 17).[3] The third describes the menstruant uncovering the source of her blood flow (v. 18). In only the second example does the woman act vis-à-vis a man. In fact, this is the only instance in the entire text where woman acts vis-à-vis a man, sexually or otherwise.

Aside from these examples, every other verb and pronoun, including those that obviously refer to both genders, is masculine.

Furthermore, the masculine gender is represented by second person direct address in the verbs of three laws.[4] Verse 19 addresses the man directly by a second person singular verb in the protasis. The second masculine direct address also occurs in verbs within the apodoses of vv. 15 and 16. In addition, second masculine pronominal suffixes occur in vv. 14 and 19. The use of the second person masculine in verbs and pronouns marginalizes the woman to a greater

---

2.   Milgrom, *Leviticus 17–22*, 1766, states: "Although chap. 20, like chap. 18, concerns the father's house, it probably is addressed to the community, which has the responsibility for carrying out the punishment…"

3.   Melcher and Milgrom, following her, note the remarkable gender equity in the description of the violation of this verse; see Melcher, "Holiness," 94; Milgrom, *Leviticus 17–22*, 1753.

4.   Scholars consider v. 19 to be an insertion because of its deviation. See Elliger, *Leviticus*, 266–67; Noth, *Leviticus*, 151; Sun, "Investigation," 255.

degree than the use of third person, shifting the conversation to direct communication with the man and referring to her as if she is entirely absent. Even if the second person masculine is the result of redactional insertion or copyist error, it contextualizes the conversation as a whole. The impression left by these occasional intrusions of the second person masculine is that even where it is absent the conversation is between a male author and a collective male audience.

The use of second and third masculine pronouns and verbs, thus, reveals the marginalization of woman in the text.

c) *Boundaries Protected.* Several alignments with respect to the boundaries, which the sex laws of Lev 20 protect, also demonstrate gender asymmetry and reveal woman's circumscribed position.

The presence of a law prohibiting homosexuality and the corresponding absence of a law prohibiting lesbianism is one of these alignments.[5]

The remaining alignments concern the representation of (i.e. the presence or absence of) consanguinal and affinal boundaries in the prohibitions. The following list of relations permitted to one gender but forbidden to the other illustrates the gender asymmetry resulting from this representation:

1. husband of sister not forbidden to woman; wife of brother forbidden to man (v. 21);
2. mother's or father's brother not forbidden to woman; mother's or father's sister forbidden to man (v. 19);
3. father's sister's husband permitted to woman; father's brother's wife forbidden to man (v. 20);
4. daughter's husband not forbidden to woman; son's wife forbidden to man (v. 12);
5. mother's husband not forbidden to woman; father's wife forbidden to man (v. 11).

In addition to the above relations, grandparents and grandchildren are "not forbidden" for both men and women. Maternal, collateral affines—mother's sister's husband or mother's brother's wife—as well as the paternal collateral affine—father's sister's husband—are "not forbidden" for both men and women. Nevertheless, the obverse of the latter relation, father's brother's wife, is, in fact, forbidden (v. 21). In addition, the obverse of the law concerning a woman and her mother is absent from the text. Gender symmetry and asymmetry, thus, distribute unevenly throughout the relations.

Nevertheless, these gender alignments reveal two patterns. First, men sexually engage and marry younger women while women do not sexually engage and marry younger men.[6] That is, the male ego of the text is older than the implied female ego of the text. Three descendent relations are forbidden to the woman and only one ascendent, while three ascendent relations are forbidden to the man

5. See the discussion of Lev 18:22 above.
6. See the following counter-examples to this restriction at Gen 35:22; 38; 2 Sam 16.

and only one descendent. In other words, the mature male aligns with a young, fertile, dependent female while the reverse does not occur.

Second, as in Lev 18, relations such as the husband of the daughter, the husband of the sister and the mother of the wife may owe their absence to membership in other male households. Such absences may reveal the dominance of the male household even if "membership" fails to explain all absent and present relations in the series.[7]

The gender alignment created by the absence of the father–daughter prohibition is less certain. If the father's-wife prohibition of v. 11 does not cover the mother–son relationship,[8] then the absence of a father–daughter prohibition results in gender *symmetry*.[9] However, if the father–wife prohibition, in fact, covers the mother–son relationship,[10] then the absence of the father–daughter prohibition results in gender *asymmetry*.

Nevertheless, the representation of consanguinal and affinal boundaries in the text exhibits considerable gender asymmetry.

2) *Contraindicators*. The above description, however, is complicated by certain other features in the text, at least three of which have to do with point-of-view. The three features connected with point-of-view are: the logic-of-the-text, the generations-represented and the grammar-of-the-penalties.

The first feature, the logic-of-the-text, in conjunction with other features, lends credibility to the idea that despite the named-addressee, application-of-taboo, use-of-second-and-third-person and boundary-alignments, woman as well as man is responsible to the law. As in Lev 18, the actions of both men and women are necessary for most of the breaches that constitute illicit sexual activity.[11]

The second feature concerns generations. Three generations occur in Lev 20 rather than four, as in Lev 18. Furthermore, within these three generations the male and female egos occupy the *same level*, unlike Lev 18. Women one generation ascendent (father's brother's wife, father's wife, mother's or father's sister) and one generation descendent (son's wife) are forbidden to the male ego. Members of his own generation are also forbidden (the sister, daughter of mother or father, and the wife of brother). Men one generation ascendent (husband's

---

7. See the discussion of Lev 18.

8. See the discussion below of Deut 23:1 where the use of לקח rules out the possibility that the father's wife refers to the addressee's mother. Milgrom, *Leviticus 17–22*, 1749, states that the mother is assumed: "The implication of the missing mother needs to be underscored. It means that incest with one's mother is such an egregious crime that the death penalty is taken for granted."

9. Whether or not this gender symmetry means that the absence of the father–daughter prohibition is due to a reluctance, as stated by Frymer-Kensky, to curb the *patria potestas* with respect to the daughter, is still an open question. See Frymer-Kensky, "Law and Philosophy," 100–101 n. 14. Rattray's solution for Lev 18, of course, does not apply to Lev 20:10–21. See the proposed solutions for the missing daughter under the discussion of Lev 18 above, n. 68.

10. It may, in fact, cover the mother–son relationship regardless of the distinction made in Lev 18 between the "father's wife" and "your mother" (Lev 18:7 and 8).

11. See the discussion of Lev 18 above, concerning consensual and non-consensual factor.

father) and one generation descendent (husband's son, husband's brother's son, son of brother or sister) are forbidden by implication to the female ego. Members of her own generation are also forbidden by implication (husband's brother, brother, i.e. the son of mother or father). The male ego and the female ego of the text thus occupy the same generation.

The third feature concerns the formulations of at least portions of the penalties.[12] These formulations, which occur in the apodoses, relativize the gender asymmetry of the grammar of the protases. While the initial focus, in the protasis, is on the male, at least some portion of the consequence of every law refers to both men and women by way of the third masculine plural or singular verb in conjunction, often, with an additional reference, which reiterates that the law applies to both genders. In the two cases where singular verbs seem to apply to men only, an accompanying phrase belies that impression by explicitly including both men and women. Verse 10 has הַנֹּאֵף וְהַנֹּאָפֶת. Verse 17 has וְנִכְרְתוּ לְעֵינֵי בְּנֵי עַמָּם.[13] Thus, whereas point-of-view and language-depicting-the-sex-act demonstrate woman's circumscribed status, the penalties demonstrate that when punishments are distributed or blame apportioned, the woman shares equally with the man in that distribution.[14]

However, if we conclude from this relativizing in the penalties that woman is equally responsible as man to the laws, then we must be willing to at least

---

12. Schulz, *Todesrecht*, 141. Schulz's analysis of clauses occurring in the apodoses is heuristically helpful for understanding the nature of the penalties. He describes the occurrence of five *Urteilen* in the apodoses: "*1. Feststellungsurteile, 2. Qualifikationsurteile, 3. Bezichtigungsurteile, 4. Schuldurteile, 5. Todesdeklarationen.*" All five *Urteile*, according to Schulz, are "*deklaratorische Urteile*" and belong to a larger cultic, juridical process. However, although these *Urteile* may share these two qualifications, they nevertheless differ in their relationship to the infractions of the laws. The first three *Urteile*, regardless of the part they play in the juridical process, in some way *qualify* the infractions of the laws. The last two *Urteile*, on the other hand, *state* the cultic, juridical *consequences* of the infractions to the perpetrator. These latter, the *Schuldurteile* and the *Todesdeklarationen*, are the penalties. See Knierim's critique of Schulz. Rolf P. Knierim, "The Problem of Ancient Israel's Prescriptive Legal Traditions," *Semeia* 45 (1989): 9–11.

13. In each of these verses the third masculine singular is used in part of the penalty, referring exclusively to the male. In v. 10, an accompanying phrase distributes the penalty equally. In v. 17, an accompanying penalty distributes responsibility equally. In v. 10, הַנֹּאֵף וְהַנֹּאָפֶת immediately follows the penalty. This and the fact that the laws in vv. 11–13, 15 have the plural form of the same phrase, is perhaps why the textual witnesses diverge at מוֹת־יוּמָת. The fact that the penalty is followed by the explicit naming of the perpetrators makes the textual difficulty and the singular verb moot problems for our purposes. Both man and woman are to be executed. A similar but less clear exception exists in v. 17. The last phrase of the penalty states: עֲוֹנוֹ יִשָּׂא. This phrase follows the clause, "the nakedness of his sister he has uncovered." Immediately preceding that clause, however, is the first part of the penalty, which states: וְנִכְרְתוּ לְעֵינֵי בְּנֵי עַמָּם. In this first part the sister is clearly included. If being cut off is a more severe consequence than carrying one's sin, as I shall argue, then the singular forms of the final phrase are also a moot problem for our purposes. Both sister and brother are cut off.

14. Olyan, "'And with a Male You Shall Not Lie,'" 187, reads the penalty of 20:13, concerning homosexuality, as shifting the conceptuality of 18:22. In Lev 18, according to Olyan, the penetrator was addressed. In Lev 20, both the receptor and the penetrator are addressed. Both are guilty. I, of course, would argue that the receptor of Lev 18 is also addressed implicitly.

consider the same possibility for the animal.[15] Fensham states the following in his analysis of Lev 20:15–16: "In Leviticus the liability of the animal is accepted and this is punished by the death sentence."[16] To state that an animal is liable is to indicate that legal consequences may fall to that animal if certain circumstances transpire. It does not, however, delineate the precise nature of the animal's responsibility to the law. The problem of animal liability has been aired extensively within the goring-ox discussion.[17]

Van Selms and Jackson, participants in this discussion, both conclude that the goring-ox is killed in order to protect the community.[18] However, Jackson notes that the conclusion drawn for the goring-ox fails to explain the killing of the animal in the bestiality laws. Concerning Lev 20:15–16, he writes:

> The motive for its inclusion in Leviticus can hardly have been to safeguard the community against a reoccurrence of the offense, as in *Ex.* 21:28. The animal was here the victim, not the initiator. Nor is it described as an "abomination" (Cf. *Lev* 20:13) or the like, which might involve the danger of contagion, comparable to the destruction of Akhan's beasts (Josh 7:24–5) or the animal which touched the mountain (*Ex.* 19:13).[19]

15.　Some interesting gender correspondences arise in connection with the verbal vocabulary of the bestiality laws. These correspondences *prima facie* might seem to suggest that the female, like the animal, is classed as property. However, a careful reading belies this suggestion. In the male bestiality law, unlike any of the other laws of Lev 20, a separate penalty is given for each "perpetrator." The male shall "be put to death" (מוֹת יוּמָת). The verbal phrases, one of which is second masculine singular and the other of which is third masculine plural, are in apposition to one another. See Fensham, "Liability of Animals," 88. Fensham's reading is incorrect. הרג does not apply to only the woman and מות to only the animal. Both verbal phrases apply to both the woman and the animal. In addition, the phrase "their blood is upon them" is attributed to the female and the animal as well. Thus, the verb used to describe the disposal of the animal in the male-bestiality law is also used to describe the disposal of the *female and the animal* in the female-bestiality law: הרג. However, such equivalence cannot be used to equate the woman and the beast under the rubric of property or under some other rubric since the verb used to describe the disposal of the male in the male-bestiality law is also used to describe the disposal of the female and the animal in the female-bestiality law. Nor ought the grouping of the female with the animal in the penalty, in contradistinction to the division of penalties in the male bestiality law, be put to such use since women throughout the series are grouped with men as well in the penalties. The division of penalties in the male law and the grouping of penalties in the female law are due to point-of-view. Although the male is discussed in third person, he is one among the group to which the author explicitly addresses his text. The female and the beast are not within that group. This is the case even if the female is addressed by implication. Thus, she and the animal are grouped together in the penalties.

16.　Fensham, "Liability of Animals," 88.

17.　Ibid., 86–88; Finkelstein, "The Ox That Gored," 70–72; Jackson, *Essays*, 108–52; idem, "Travels and Travails of the Goring Ox," in *Studies in Bible and the Ancient Near East* (ed. Yitzhak Avishu and Joseph Blau; Jerusalem: E. Rubenstein's, 1978), 41–56; Van Selms, "Goring Ox," 329. See also Meir Malul, "The Laws of the Goring Ox in the Old Testament and the Ancient Near East," in *The Comparative Method in Ancient Near Eastern and Biblical Legal Studies* (Neukirchen–Vluyn: Neukirchener, 1990), 113–52.

18.　Van Selms, "Goring Ox," 329; Jackson, *Essays*, 120.

19.　Jackson, *Essays*, 118–19. Jackson's explanation for the killing of the ox in Lev 20 is diachronic. He posits that the concept of divine punishment of animals was established with the goring ox scenario as a means of community protection (pp. 108–19). The bestiality law is a late development in which the penal notion prompted by the goring-ox scenario is applied.

That the latter contagion, as well as the "reoccurrence possibility," is not responsible for the killing of the beast seems plausible. However, Finkelstein's explanation for that killing in Lev 20:15–16, utilizing purity/impurity constructs, is also plausible.[20] He writes:

> Bestiality offends against divine creation in two respects. First, it violates the hierarchical order of the universe, in which man occupies an exclusive and superior position vis-à-vis all other terrestrial life. Second, it aims directly at the very principle of Creation: the separation of species and even of such phenomena as day and night, the waters above the "firmament" and the waters below it, the seas and the dry land, and so on. Creation consists of separation, the marking off of borders. The blurring of these borders is a reversion to Chaos... No mercy can therefore be shown to the perpetrators. They must be promptly rooted out and executed. And the animals that served unwittingly in the perversion of bestiality and thereby became visible testimonies of human infamy similarly had to be destroyed.[21]

If Finkelstein is correct, then we have come full circle to the classificatory idea. The animal is liable for the same reason the humans are liable: the boundaries guarding the categories of creation are blurred.

Thus, three features—logic-of-the-text, generations-represented and grammar-of-the-penalties—demonstrate that the conceptuality concerning women is more complex than the gender asymmetries of the point-of-view. Furthermore, at least one contradindicator suggests that the primary concern of the series is classificatory- as opposed to property-oriented.

b. *Language-Depicting-the-Sex-Act.*

1) *The Bias.* Just as point-of-view marginalizes woman, so also language-depicting-the-sex-act objectifies her. It constructs her objectification by her consistent placement in the object slot and the man's consistent placement in the subject slot of the grammar of the text. Only three exceptions to this subject/object polarization occur. Two of these exceptions maintain the picture of her circumscription. In v. 16, woman is the subject in contradistinction to an animal. In the second, v. 18, she uncovers the source of her blood flow when a man lies with her. The third exception, however, in v. 17, is a contraindicator to her circumscription and will be discussed below. In every other instance of language-depicting-the-sex-act between man and woman, man is the subject and woman the object.

The following verbs depict the sex act, directly or obliquely, in Lev 20: נאף, ראה, גלה, רבע, קרב, נתן, לקח, שכב.

a) נאף. נאף occurs once in this series in the neighbor's-wife law (v. 10),[22] where man is the subject and woman the object. It is a technical term for illicit sex breaching the boundaries of marriage.[23]

20. Finkelstein, "The Ox That Gored," 70.
21. Ibid., 71–72.
22. This verse has a textual problem which leaves the general sense of the law unaffected. See Dominique Barthélemy et al., *Preliminary and Interim Report on the Hebrew Old Testament Text*

Since it denotes breach of marriage boundaries, property or "belonging" is a conceptual component of this word. Other occurrences of the word support this statement. It occurs three times in the Pentateuch in Exod 20:14, Lev 20:10 and Deut 5:18; and is represented once in each of the following: the Book of the Covenant, the Deuteronomic work and the Holiness Code. In the Book of the Covenant and in the Deuteronomic work it occurs in apodictic laws. In each instance, the apodictic law sandwiches between a law forbidding killing and a law forbidding stealing. Killing is the removal of the ultimate "property": one's life. Stealing is the removal of one's material goods. Adultery is the removal of something between one's life and one's material goods: one's wife.[24] Several occurrences of the word in the Wisdom Books[25] and in the Prophets[26] support this association as well.

Thus, the adultery law in Lev 20, which uses נאף, instead of תִּתֵּן שְׁכָבְתְּךָ, as in Lev 18, has clear associations with the conceptualization of and concern for woman as property.

b) שכב. שכב describes illicit sex with the father's wife, the daughter-in-law, another man, the menstruant and the father's brother's wife. In each case the woman is the object of a preposition. The man is subject of the verb. Since she is the object of a preposition, the שכב phrase seems to connote her cooperative participation.

However, an *Urteil*[27] concerning "uncovering nakedness" accompanies three of the שכב phrases (vv. 11, 18, 20). In these *Urteile*, which also refer to the sex act, woman is direct object and man is subject. All room for her cooperative

---

Project, vol. 1 (Stuttgart: United Bible Societies, 1976), 194. The Text Project describes this as a case of haplography. They propose that between the words in the phrase אֵשֶׁת אִישׁ was another word, אִישׁ. The divergence among the witnesses is an attempt to smooth the awkwardness caused by the haplography. They state: "The phrase in question is an ancient precision the purpose of which is to confine the precept to the single case of adultery committed with the wife of another Israelite." This sense is similar to the sense that Michael Fishbane (*Biblical Interpretation in Ancient Israel* [Oxford: Clarendon, 1985]) proposes, although Fishbane does not resort to reconstruction. Fishbane (pp. 169–70) states: "…the law in Lev 20:10 is prolix. The protasis is uncharacteristically repeated before the apodosis. This stylistic anomaly had led to various emendations of the passage, with either the one or the other protasis deleted as a dittography. However, such solutions totally miss the mark. The second protasis clause—'if a man commits adultery with his neighbour's wife'—is rather to be considered a legal explication of the first, so that adultery is not prohibited with any woman, but precisely with the wife of one's neighbour, i.e. another Israelite (cf. Lev 18:20)."

23. Bird, "To Play the Harlot," 77; Fishbane, *Biblical Interpretation*, 169; Goodfriend, "Prostitution," 5:509.

24. See the discussion of the structure of Deut 5 below.

25. Prov 6:32; 30:20; Ps 50:18; Job 24:15. For the use of Prov 6:32 as evidence that the death penalty was not applied in cases of adultery in ancient Israel, see the following: Frymer-Kensky, "Sex in the Bible," 193; Jackson, *Essays*, 60; McKeating, "Sanctions," 59; Phillips, "Another Look," 4.

26. See Jer 7:9; 9:1; Ezek 16:38; 23:37, 45; Hos 4:2.

27. Schulz, *Todesrecht*, 139–45. See p. 144 especially for a complete list of the occurrences of the *Urteile* in Lev 20.

participation has vanished. Furthermore, of the two unaccompanied שכב phrases, one concerns male homosexuality. This leaves only one law concerning women with an unaccompanied שכב phrase. That law concerns the daughter-in-law. This lone example is unable to withstand the weight of the three opposing examples to prove the idea that the שכב phrase connotes cooperative participation in its conceptualization of the sex act.

The object status of the woman is thus strengthened by the accompanying *Urteil* in at least three instances of the שכב phrase, suggesting that the latter phrase conceptualizes woman as sexual object upon which man acts.

c) לקח. Biblical scholars generally read לקח as signifying marriage.[28] Throughout Lev 20 man is the subject of this verb. He always "takes" the woman. The reverse never occurs. לקח is thus concerned with the establishment of boundaries which demarcate "ownership" by or "belonging" to a man.

d) יתן שכבתו and תקרב לרבעה. תקרב שְׁכָבְתוֹ. יִתֵּן שְׁכָבְה and תִּקְרַב לְרָבְעָה occur in the bestiality laws. The author includes separate bestiality laws for men and women, as in Lev 18. In both laws the human is subject and the animal is object. In the male bestiality laws of both Lev 20:15 and 18:23a, the phrase יִתֵּן שְׁכָבְתוֹ depicts the sex act. The female bestiality laws, however, use phrases that differ slightly between the two chapters. In 18:23b, the woman stands (עמד) before a beast to copulate (רבע) with it. In 20:16, she draws near (קרב) to copulate (רבע) with it.

Of the three verbs used in the female bestiality laws, one, עמד, occurs only in 18:23b as a description of the woman's position. One, קרב, occurs in 18:6, 14 and 19 and suggests the idea that not only is sexual intercourse forbidden but activity leading up to it is also forbidden.

The final verb, רבע, depicts the sex act in only three instances in the Hebrew corpus: Lev 20:16; 18:23 and 19:19.[29] In the first two instances, it designates sex between a woman and an animal. In the last instance it designates the copulation of two kinds of animals, suggesting that a constituent of the word field for רבע is "to breed," that is, to conceive, to be pregnant and to produce offspring. If this is so, then, the language of breeding describes the woman's actions while the language of depositing describes the man's action.[30]

The language of depositing in the male bestiality law consists of the phrase יִתֵּן שְׁכָבְתוֹ. It seems to imply reciprocity since nothing can be given without being received. However, this implication for reciprocity is meager and the focus of

---

28. Neufeld, *Ancient Hebrew Marriage Laws*, 91; Noth, *Leviticus*, 150; Porter, *Leviticus*, 165; Wegner, *Chattel*, 227 n. 84.

29. Abraham Even-Shoshan, "1רבע," in *A New Concordance of the Old Testament* (2d ed.; Jerusalem: Kiryat-Sefer, 1989), 1058, lists רבע meaning "to lie down" as a separate verb from רבע meaning "to copulate." Both BDB, 918, and Holladay, on the other hand, list the two meanings under the same verb. The use in Lev 18 where the woman stands (עמד) in order to copulate or breed (רבע) supports Even-Shoshan's distinction.

30. The fact that human–animal unions fail to produce offspring does not nullify this connotation.

the law is one-sided. An examination of יִתֵּן שְׁכָבְתּוֹ clarifies the point. In 18:20 the phrase describes sex with the neighbor's wife. In this latter scenario, the phrase connotes the idea of releasing one's seed to a place outside the sphere of one's own marriage and lineage and into the marriage and lineage of another.[31] It connotes a similar idea in the bestiality laws of Lev 18 and 20. One releases one's seed outside the sphere of one's marriage, lineage and species. The Molek law (18:21)[32] says: וּמִזַּרְעֲךָ לֹא־תִתֵּן לְהַעֲבִיר לַמֹּלֶךְ. The man releases his seed outside the sphere of his own marriage, lineage and cult.

The use of נתן in these sex laws, thus, follows a pattern. In Lev 18, laws using נתן occur only in section two of Lev 18:6–23.[33] They concern only the non-affinal/non-consanguinal boundaries. Interestingly, the lone non-affinal/non-consanguinal relationship lacking נתן occurs in the homosexuality law. Although the law forbids the male biotype to another male for purposes of "penetrating sex," it does so because that biotype is the *same* rather than different. Thus, נתן, in connection with a word representing seed, describes depositing the seed in "outside" spheres demarcated by different biotype and institutional boundaries: species, cult or marriage.

"Depositing" is thus a greater part of the conceptual matrix of יִתֵּן שְׁכָבְתּוֹ than "reciprocity." The difference in language between the male and female bestiality laws may be a function of the differing physiologies of the male and female. However, the contrast also undoubtedly reveals a difference in conceptualization of the relationship of man and woman to sex in general. Men deposit seed; women breed. The man's relationship to sex has to do with the immediate result of orgasm. The woman's relationship to sex has to do with the long-term result of conception. Men have orgasms, women produce offspring. This conceptualization, needless to say, is an objectification of women.

יִתֵּן שְׁכָבְתּוֹ and תִּקְרַב לְרִבְעָה thus demonstrate considerable gender asymmetry, revealing woman's circumscription.

e) נלה. Six laws within Lev 20:10–21 use some form of the following phrase: נלה ערוה. Leviticus 20 shares with Lev 18 three gender asymmetries connected to the use of this phrase. The first is that, while woman's nakedness belongs to a man in three instances in vv. 11, 20 and 21; a man's nakedness *never* belongs to a woman. The second is that, while man always uncovers woman's nakedness in vv. 11, 17, 18, 19 and 20, she never uncovers his. In both chapters, man is always the subject of נלה when the man is the object. Although the attribution of a woman's nakedness to herself occurs, such attribution does not occur in an *Urteil*. In other words, the fact that a woman's nakedness belongs to herself is never the grounds for a prohibition against a man uncovering her nakedness.

---

31.   The neighbor law of Lev 20:10, which, unlike 18:20, uses נאף instead of נתן, concentrates less on the idea of disposition of seed than it concentrates on the specific idea of intruding on another's marriage.

32.   See also Lev 20:2.

33.   See the structure of Lev 18 above.

Two slight differences between Lev 18 and Lev 20, significant with respect to gender, exist in connection with this phrase. First, in contrast to Lev 18:17, Lev 20 lacks the possibility that a woman's nakedness belongs to another woman. The second difference derives from the absence of the granddaughter law. Because of this absence, the attribution of "nakedness of a woman" to a man is not grounds for both absolute restriction from female sexuality as well as exclusive right to female sexuality, as it is in Lev 18.[34] In Lev 18, this double attribution proved that "nakedness of" does not *necessarily* connote male ownership of female sexuality. This "proof" is absent from Lev 20.

The use of נלה in Lev 20, as in Lev 18, thus demonstrates considerable gender asymmetry.

f) *Conclusion.* In conclusion, language-depicting-the-sex-act reveals woman's highly circumscribed position. The central focus is on man. Woman is referred to with respect to his actions. With rare exception she is object while he is subject.

2) *Contraindicators.* However, as in Lev 18, several features related to language-depicting-the-sex-act indicate that this subject/object polarization is, on occasion, broken. In addition, these features indicate a more nuanced conceptuality with respect to women than the polarization at first suggests. Furthermore, at least two of those contraindicators also suggest that the primary concern is classificatory rather than property-oriented.

The first feature is a general and somewhat vague contraindicator. It concerns the range of verbs chosen for depicting the sex act. While man is, with rare exception, the subject of language-depicting-the-sex-act and woman the object, from the range of verbs available to depict the act, words denoting finding, seizing, capturing, holding and humbling are absent from the text as they are absent from Lev 18. Thus, while the language-depicting-the-sex-act of Lev 20, without question, objectifies woman, it objectifies her by means of language which fails to attribute to man the widest possible range of discretion for disposing of her sexuality. Such a range might be expected if her sexuality were routinely focalized as property.

More concrete and specific contraindicators are available in connection with four of the verbs depicting the sex act: ראה and רבע, לקח, נלה.

a) נלה. In vv. 17, 18 and 19, the phrase "nakedness of" denotes a woman's nakedness without reference to a man, just as in v. 17 the "nakedness of" phrase denotes a man's own physical nakedness without reference to a woman.[35]

Moreover, in v. 18 woman as well as man is the subject of a נלה verb. The infraction described by this clause is not the sex act per se. Rather, it is the fact that the sex act necessarily involves exposure and, thus, proximity to or contact with her blood. Although the language-depicting-the-sex-act, of which she is

---

34. See the discussion of Lev 18 above.
35. The denotation concerning a man's own nakedness is absent from Lev 18.

subject, is thus oblique, it nevertheless portrays her, as well as the man, as responsible for the illicit sex act that transpires. Thus, while the woman is not the subject in contradistinction to the man, she, like him, bears responsibility in the breach of this law.

Finally, both Lev 20 and Lev 18 offer at least three reasons why a woman is forbidden. The three reasons, introduced into the text by the נלה phase, are as follows. First, woman is forbidden because she "belongs" to a man by virtue of the institution of marriage (v. 11, 20, 21). Second, she is forbidden because she is related to a man by blood (vv. 17, 19). Third, a woman is forbidden because she is related to someone to whom the man is married (v. 14). Thus, kinship alone may be grounds for forbidding sexual relations. Accordingly, property, ownership or belonging of female sexuality is not the primary concern. Rather, the concern is the breach of a system of boundaries defined by consanguinal, affinal and other relations.

The contraindicators of נלה reveal that woman's sexuality is occasionally attributed to herself, that woman is, in one instance, subject, and that the primary concern of the text is classificatory rather than property-oriented.

b) לקח. Although לקח connotes the demarcation of certain ownership or property boundaries, that connotation is contextualized in Lev 20 to include a broader valence than marriage alone. In fact, within vv. 14, 17 and 21, the prohibitions using לקח are primarily concerned with classificatory issues involving sexual combinations rather than marriage or property issues per se.

Two of the laws, vv. 17 and 21, contextualize לקח by use of the phrase עֶרְוַה x נִלָּה. This phrase iterates the prohibited deed and demonstrates that sexuality, not marriage, is at issue. In addition, לקח in each law is contextualized by what Schulz calls a *Qualifikationsurteil*. While חֶסֶד הוּא in v. 17 cannot be shown necessarily to target classificatory as opposed to property concerns, נִדָּה הוּא in v. 21 can be shown to target that concern. נִדָּה connotes the natural impurity of a menstruant.[36] It is synonymous with menstruation in Lev 15 and 18:19 and describes a woman who has given birth in Lev 12:2 and 5. Leviticus 20 draws on the connotations of natural impurity connoted by this word to qualify the act of לקח with respect to one's brother's wife. The qualification demonstrates that the primary concern is the impurity—that is, the improper combination or mixture of categories, resulting from "taking" and "uncovering nakedness." The remaining law, v. 14, which uses זִמָּה הוּא, demonstrates that the improper combination is, in fact, sexual, since זִמָּה is used throughout the Hebrew corpus to refer specifically to illicit sexual activity.[37] Thus, the act of *taking* a daughter and her mother is illicit *sexual* activity.

The question is why an author with classificatory concerns pertaining to sex selects לקח, connoting property concerns, out of the range of words available to him to regulate the sex act. A tentative two-fold explanation might be surmised

---

36. J. Milgrom, D. P. Wright and H. Fabry, "נִדָּה," *ThWAT* 5:252.
37. See זמה הוא in the above discussion of Lev 18 and 19:29.

accounting for its use in Lev 18 as well as in Lev 20. The occurrence of לקח in Lev 18 and Lev 20 is as follows:

Lev 18	*Lev 20*
1. in subcase of woman/daughter law forbidding *taking* grandchildren of woman one takes as wife (v. 17)	1. in woman/mother law forbidding *taking* a woman and her mother (v. 14)
2. in two-sister law forbidding *taking* two women who are sisters (v. 18)	2. in sister law forbidding *taking* one's own sister (v. 17)
	3. in brother's-wife law forbidding *taking* one's brother's wife (v. 21)

The above instances represent five different scenarios. Of these five scenarios, three are connected to important biblical literary traditions. These traditions concern *marriages* consisting of precisely those relationships forbidden in the laws of Leviticus which use לקח.

For example the levirate-law tradition is related to the brother's-wife law (Lev 20:21).[38] The story of Judah and Tamar[39] and the story of Ruth[40] are also related to this law. The assumption, in each case, is that marriage of a brother to his dead brother's wife is acceptable.

The tradition concerning Abraham and Sarah[41] is related to the sister laws (Lev 20:17 and 18). The story of Tamar and Amnon is related to these laws as well.[42] Tamar says to her brother Amnon: וְעַתָּה דַּבֶּר־נָא אֶל־הַמֶּלֶךְ כִּי לֹא יִמְנָעֵנִי מִמֶּךָ.[43] Again, the assumption underlying these traditions is that marriage between brother and sister is acceptable. These traditions involve half-sisters. Although Lev 20 lacks distinctions concerning half-, step- and full-sisters, quite possibly v. 17, in fact, covers all these relations.[44]

Finally the Leah/Rachel story is related to the two-sisters law of Lev 18:18.[45] Again, the assumption in this tradition is that marrying two sisters is acceptable.

Thus, three of the five laws using לקח are associated with traditions that presume the forbidden relation is acceptable for marriage. This presumption

38. Deut. 25:5–10. This connection holds whether or not one decides that the laws in Leviticus nullify levirate law, as Phillips does; see Phillips, *Ancient Israel's Criminal Law*, 125.

39. Gen 38.

40. Ruth 1–4. Although Boaz is not the brother of the dead husband, levirate law is the basis of marriage between Boaz and Ruth.

41. Gen 20:12.

42. 2 Sam 13.

43. 2 Sam 13:13b.

44. Milgrom, *Leviticus 17–22*, 1753, seems to read this verse as referencing a half-sister. He states: "Presumably, the addressee thought that marriage with a half sister was not a violation... Sexual congress with a full daughter or sister is missing, just as in chap. 18... Surely, incest with a full sister (same father and mother) or daughter (issue of his loins) should incur the death penalty. The only solution that occurs to me is that these two unions were not subject to *human* sanctions. A full sister and an unmarried daughter are under the complete control of the addressee. These unions would be conducted secretively. Even if they became known, who would or could prosecute him?" (p. 1753).

45. Gen 29.

motivates the use of לקח.[46] Existent literary traditions allow combinations which authors of Lev 18 and 20 wish to forbid. לקח addresses this allowance.[47]

However, the two remaining relations—grandchildren (Lev 18:17b) and the woman and her daughter (Lev 20:14)—lack association with an existent literary tradition. Of all the laws treating sexual relations with women, the laws of Lev 18:17 and 20:14 are the only ones which treat women, whom a man may marry and engage sexually, if conditions are right. A man can always "take" the grandchild of a woman as long as he has not taken the woman herself. A man can always "take" a woman's mother as long as he has not also taken the woman herself. In other words, the forbidden relations are contingent rather than necessary. Thus, as tradition validates the previous three cases, custom validates the cases in Lev 18:17bα and 20:14. The author tackles that validity by the use of לקח lest that validity itself be used to justify the sexual combination he is forbidding.

This theory comes up against one minor inconsistency in Lev 18:17a which concerns the woman/daughter relation. It lacks לקח. The theory that expects the presence of לקח here is unable to explain its absence. Perhaps in this one instance the author missed a step in his attention to tagging the normally valid marriage arrangements, by means of לקח, which are contrary to his prohibitions. In any case, the theory accounts for five out of six relevant scenarios in the laws of Lev 18 and 20. This score lends credence to the idea of a possible authorial "misstep."

If the above theory is acceptable, the use of a verb which connotes property concerns by an author who is interested in classificatory rather than property issues is explained. While woman is always the object of לקח, and לקח denotes marriage, in Lev 20 לקח is contextualized to connote prevention of certain sexual combinations rather than regulation of woman as sexual property.

c) רבע. Since woman is the subject of רבע in v. 16 vis-à-vis an animal and not vis-à-vis a man, her place as subject in this verse does not serve as a significant contraindicator to the circumscription indicated by language-depicting-the-sex-act. In fact, it supports that circumscription. Nevertheless she does act. Presumably she acts on her own initiative, although we cannot be sure. She is actor and initiator, albeit vis-à-vis an animal.

d) ראה. Woman is also the subject of the verb ראה in v. 17. This instance is a surprising exception to the circumscription which characterizes every other

---

46. The fact that this presumption motivates the author need not mean that Lev 20:21 necessarily nullifies levirate law or that the author was against the levirate arrangement. It need mean only that the author targets, with לקח, those situations in which the forbidden relation is under *certain* circumstances possible at all. Since in certain special circumstances (i.e. when the brother dies) marriage to the brother's wife is possible, the author uses לקח.

47. One need not assume some kind of literary dependence of Lev 18 and 20 on Genesis, Samuel and Ruth for this hypothesis to hold. One need only take the stories of Genesis, Samuel and Ruth as exemplary of existent practice, thought or custom with which the writer might have been familiar for the hypothesis to hold.

example of language-depicting-the-sex-act. In all DST and LST, this is the only instance where woman is the subject of such language in contradistinction to a man.[48] While "seeing someone's nakedness" may refer only obliquely to sexual intercourse, it most certainly refers to sexual activity in general. Woman is subject and man is object.

An obverse statement accompanies this reference indicating that the brother, as well, sees her nakedness. This latter symmetry is overshadowed, of course, by the fact that the initial verb introducing illicit sexual activity between sister and brother is לקח, of which the brother alone is the subject and the sister the object.

Nevertheless, woman is subject of language-depicting-the-sex-act vis-à-vis a man.

c. *Conclusion.* Point-of-view and language-depicting-the-sex-act picture woman as object, marginalized, circumscribed by, dependent on and subordinate to the man, leaving the impression that the law guards and regulates the woman as his sexual property. A closer look modifies this impression on two counts. First, the asymmetries of point-of-view and language-depicting-the-sex-act are qualified and sometimes ameliorated by other related features which reveal a more complex picture. Second, at least two of these features demonstrate that the primary concern of Lev 20 is to keep the categories of creation distinct by demarcating sexual boundaries rather than protecting woman's sexuality as male property.

2. Selection-of-Laws, Identification-of-Women, Structure-of-the-Text
In addition to the subtle contraindicators of point-of-view and language-depicting-the-sex-act, three overt features of the text demonstrate that the primary concern of Lev 20 is classificatory rather than property-oriented. They also demonstrate that the woman, like the man, is agent and responsible to the law. These features are: selection-of-laws, identification-of-women and the structure-of-the-text.

a. *Selection-of-Laws.* The first feature, selection-of-laws, reveals that the author has included laws which the reader clearly cannot construe as protecting man's sexual property.

For example, neither v. 13 nor v. 15, the homosexuality and male-bestiality laws, from which women are entirely absent, protect female sexuality as property. Likewise, the menstruant law, rather than protecting a man's rights to female sexuality, guards against the contagion of "natural" impurity caused by woman's blood. Finally, in the laws forbidding "the sister of your mother" (v. 19aα) and "both a woman and her mother" (v. 14), the women are not designated as belonging to any man. Their sexuality as the property of a man is irrelevant.

---

48. In Lev 21:9 she is the subject, in contradistinction to her father, but she is not the subject within language-depicting-the-sex-act. See the discussion below. In Lev 18:23b, 20:16, and 20:18 she is the subject of language-depicting-the-sex-act, but not in contradistinction to a man.

The mere presence of the above five laws within the sex-law series of Lev 20 demonstrates that something other than protection of woman's sexuality as property of the man is the primary concern.

b. *Identification-of-Women.* Three sets of identifications, the second feature indicating the primary concern, occur throughout the laws and demonstrate that classificatory issues are primary.

The first set occurs in the protases. It identifies the woman in one of two ways, either by reference to a man or by reference to a woman. Identification-of-women by reference to men occurs in seven laws. Five of those seven laws identify women exclusively by reference to men: vv. 10, 11, 12, 20 and 21. This referencing explicitly attributes their "belonging" to a man: neighbor's wife, father's wife, daughter-in-law, aunt (father's brother's wife) and brother's wife. However, two of the seven laws, vv. 17 and 19, identify women both by reference to men and by reference to women: daughter of father and sister of father as well as daughter of mother and sister of mother. Whatever "belonging" to men is implied in these two laws fades entirely in the context of the corresponding reference to women. Two additional laws identify women exclusively by reference either to other women or to only the implied female ego herself. They concern a woman and her mother (v. 14) and the menstruant (v. 18). The fact that in several laws the relationships women have to men are irrelevant indicates that women's sexuality as property is not the concern.

The second set of identifications, already mentioned above,[49] occur in the apodoses. These identifications are as follows: "the adulterer and the adulteress," "the two (of them)," "him and them." These outright identifications[50] of the woman and the man in the apodoses are equivalent in every case. From protasis to apodosis, the gender asymmetries of grammar level out by means of this equivalent outright-identification.

The third set of identifications reference the woman to the ego. They occur in both protases and apodoses. In vv. 17a and 17b, the relevant identification is "his sister." In v. 19b, the relevant identification is "his next of kin." In v. 20a, it is "his aunt." These three identifications emphasize the fact that the laws intend to protect boundaries defined by consanguinity. Property is a non-issue.

Thus, the identification-of-women in Lev 20 demonstrates that protection of boundaries for classificatory purposes is the primary concern rather than property. In addition, identifications in the apodoses indicate a leveling in the gender asymmetries of the grammar.

c. *Structure-of-the-Text.* The fourth feature which demonstrates that the primary concern of Lev 20:10–21 is classificatory- rather than property-oriented is the structure of the text.

---

49.   See the discussion under "Contraindicators" in "Point-of-View." See especially my cautionary footnote in that discussion.

50.   By "outright identification" I mean all identifications except those made by means of pronominal suffixes and verbal affixes.

1) *Structure Proper.* A partially collapsed structure of Lev 20 follows:

I.		Introduction	20:1
II.		Speech	20:2–27
	A.	Command: אמר	2aα
	B.	Object of Command: what to speak	2aβ–27
		1. foreign cult practice	2aβ–8
TRIGGER		2. cursing parents	9
		3. sexual improprieties	10–21
		a. community executes penalty	10–16
		1) marriage boundary	10–12
		a) one boundary: wife of neighbor	10
		(1) circumstance	10a
		(2) consequence	10bα–β
		(a) sentence	10bα
		(b) specification	10bβ
		b) more than one boundary	11–12
		(1) wife of father	11
		(a) circumstance	11a
		α. circumstance proper	11aα
		β. meaning of circumstance	11aβ
		(b) consequence	11b
		α. sentence	11bα
		β. responsibility	11bβ
		(2) זֶבַח שְׁלָמִם	12
		(a) circumstance	12aα
		(b) consequence	12aβ–b
		α. sentence	12aβ
		β. evaluation	12bα
		γ. responsibility	12bβ
		2) non-marriage boundary51	13–16
		a) human	13–14
TRIGGER		(1) gender boundaries: lie with a male	13
		(a) circumstance	13aα
		(b) consequence	13aβ–b
		α. sentence	13aβ
		β. evaluation	13bα
		γ. responsibility	13bβ
		(2) affinal-consanguinal boundary	14
		(a) circumstance	14aα
		(b) consequence	14aβ–bα
		α. evaluation	14aβ
		β. sentence	14bα
		(c) warning	14bβ
		b) animals	15–16

---

51.   The distinction between "marriage boundary" and "non-marriage boundary" has to do with the *boundary* that stands in the way. Marriage is the boundary in the "marriage boundary" section. Other boundaries obstruct in the "non-marriage boundary" section. For example, in v. 14 the woman and her mother are forbidden not because a marriage boundary obstructs, but because the blood relation between a woman and her mother exists. This law has to do with the construction of an affine relation in the context of a consanguine relation that itself obstructs the affine relation.

		(1) men	15
		(a) circumstance	15aα
		(b) consequence	15aβ
		(2) women	16
		(a) circumstance	16aα
		(b) consequence	16aβ–16b
		α. sentence	16aβ–bα
		β. responsibility	16bβ
	b.	community not the executor of penalty	17–21
		1) nuclear collateral: sister	17
		a) circumstance	17aα
		b) consequence	17aβ–17b
		(1) evaluation	17aβ
		(2) sentence #1	17aγ
		(3) sentence #3	17b
		(a) circumstance reiterated	17bα
		(b) sentence proper	17bβ
TRIGGER		2) menstruant	18
		a) circumstance	18a
		(1) basic statement	18aα
		(2) specifying statements	18aβ–γ
		b) consequence	18b
		3) ascendent and affinal collaterals	19–21
EXTENDED TRIGGER		a) sister of mother or father	19
		(1) command	19a–bα
		(a) prohibition	19a
		(b) grounds	19bα
		(2) sentence	19bβ
TRIGGER		b) father's brother's wife	20
		(1) circumstance	20a
		(a) circumstance proper	20aα
		(b) specification	20aβ
		(2) consequence	20b
		(a) responsibility for crime	20bα
		(b) sentence	20bβ
TRIGGER		c) brother's wife	21
		(1) circumstance	21aα
		(2) consequence	21aβ–b
		(a) evaluation	21aβ
		(b) circumstance reiterated	21bα
		(c) sentence	21bβ
	4.	separating from the nations	22–26
	5.	prophesying spirits	27

2) *Analysis of Structure.*

a) *Demarcation of Pericope.* The sex-law series is a discrete unit embedded in a Yhwh Speech to Moses. The unit immediately following the series concerns the separation of Israel from the nations. The unit immediately preceding the series is a prohibition against cursing one's parents. The fact that the cursing-parents law has the same penalty as the initial laws of the sex series is too little to override the thematic difference between that law and the initial laws of the sex series. Furthermore, if participation in the cult of Molek and conjuring spirits are direct acts of dishonor to God, if cursing one's parents is a direct act of dishonor to them, and if dishonoring one's parents is like dishonoring God,[52] then v. 9 is not only thematically different from vv. 10–21, it is also at least tenuously associated with the unit that precedes.[53] Thus, I have separated v. 9 from the sex series.[54] Nevertheless, the similarities of the penalties in v. 9 and vv. 10–13 are a linking device between the two sections. This linking device I call a "trigger."

Triggers occur throughout the series. They are similar to Parunak's "key-word"[55] and are the same type of phenomenon which Tigay has noticed structuring the laws of Deuteronomy.[56] The function of the triggers is two-fold. Within the static text they are transitional devices linking two sections. However, analysis of the structure demonstrates that they were also generative devices in the dynamic process of writing the text. Thus, they are responsible, at places, for the sequence as well as the linkage of the laws.

b) *The Sex-Law Series.*[57] The series itself lacks the neat division found in Lev 18 between consanguinal/affinal sex laws and other sex laws. In Lev 20, the other sex laws are dispersed throughout the consanginal/affinal sex laws so as to defy all recognition of a single ordering principle. In fact, no *single* feature organizes the unit. The elements which are constitutive for the structure are several and operate at different levels of the text.[58]

Discernment of a structure, constituted in such a fashion, is necessarily a circular enterprise. This circularity is what Tigay targets when he states: "Admittedly, a degree of subjectivity enters into such explanations. This is because in this kind of organization the compiler himself is making subjective

---

52. See the discussion of Lev 19 above.

53. Milgrom, *Leviticus 17–22*, 1744. Milgrom groups this law with the sex-law series. He states: "It reflects a patriarchal society that relates all familial relationships, by the twin principles of consanguinity and affinity, back to one's father and mother. It adverts to the unstated premise that dishonoring parents—that is, the breakdown of obligations to one's father or mother—is able to lead to the breakdown of relationships with the other members of the familial chain, including the sexual taboos." Actually, Milgrom's statements holds true by virtue of the parental law's immediate proximity to the series. However, the sex-law series is a discrete unit without the parental law.

54. Contrary to Sun, "Investigation," 241–43

55. Parunak, "Transitional Techniques," 529.

56. Jeffrey H. Tigay, "Some Principles of Arrangement in the Laws of Deuteronomy" (paper presented as part of Biblical Law Group at the Annual Society of Biblical Literature Meeting, November 20, 1994), 12; idem, *Deuteronomy* (Philadelphia: The Jewish Publication Society of America, 1996), 449–51. See also Shalom M. Paul, *Studies in the Book of the Covenant in the Light of Cuneiform and Biblical Law* (Leiden: Brill, 1970), 106. Paul calls this phenomenon "concatenation."

57. See Chart 3 in the Appendix.

58. Tigay, "Some Principles," 12, makes the same assertions concerning laws in Deuteronomy. He writes: "In what follows I argue that Deuteronomy is arranged by a mixture of intrinsic, subject-based links and extrinsic, associative ones." See also Tigay, *Deuteronomy*, 449–51. See Schenker, "What Connects the Incest Prohibitions?," 172, for an alternative structure.

links, and sometimes it is difficult to identify what was in his mind."[59] The "proof" of such a structure is, in the end, nothing more than a convergence of several patterns constituted by a variety of signals operating in the text.

(1) *Several Converging Patterns*. The first major division of vv. 10–21 in the above structure derives from the "nature of the penalties." Beyond this initial division, the "nature of the penalties" loses its constitutive power. The combinations of penalties that string leap-frog fashion through the second half of the text, vv. 17–21, evidences this fact. Nevertheless, four patterns converge in support of the initial division and the structure as a whole: the gradation of penalties, the first and last crime, the arrangement of the forbidden relationships, the "their-blood-is-upon-them" clause and the immediacy or eventuality of the penalties.

(a) *Gradation-of-the-Penalties Pattern*. Before exploring the first pattern, two cautionary notes must be considered. The first comes from Porter, who, on the basis of what he takes to be the composite nature of Lev 20, states the following:

> Thus it is hazardous to take all the material in chapter xx together, as Pedersen does, and to assume that some of the punishments are intended to be less harsh than others and that the degree of severity is determined by the closeness of relationships.[60]

In response to Porter, the following can be said. The extant form of the text is well worth considering, if only to explore the intent and conceptuality of the final redactor, however seam-filled his final work may be. Second, redaction is not an argument *prima facie* against gradation. Finally, whereas deducing "degree of severity" from "closeness of relationship" may be methodologically unsound, and if "degree of severity" and "closeness of relationship" form two patterns which converge in the text, then drawing conclusions from that convergence concerning their relationship, in fact, may not be methodologically unsound.

The second cautionary note is more useful and comes from Jackson who writes the following:

> Nor does the imposition of the same penalty for different offences necessarily imply the same value judgments of those offences. The variation possible in the range of penalties is far less than the gradations of value.[61]

We might extend this cautionary note to an even more general two-part statement: gradations of value concerning infractions cannot be successfully derived from penalties alone, nor can absolute gradations of value concerning penalties be derived from infractions. However, although values cannot necessarily be derived from penalties or infractions, converging patterns in the text, with respect to penalties and other factors including gradations, may, in fact, suggest something interesting about their relationships.

---

59.   Tigay, "Some Principles," 12; idem, *Deuteronomy*, 451.
60.   Porter, *Extended Family*, 5.
61.   Jackson, *Essays*, 35–36.

Discerning a gradation among penalties depends upon three factors: (1) what the penalty is, (2) what item of value the penalties take from the perpetrator and (3) how the value divested by one penalty compares to the value divested by other penalties.

Our discernment begins with two assumptions: first, that the order of the penalties in vv. 10–21 is deliberate and sensible; second, that this order possibly represents a gradation. Our discernment proceeds by developing a theory which seeks to validate these two assumptions. The argument that follows is such a theory.

If we select death as the penalty which deprives the perpetrator of the greatest value, then a pattern emerges, one which corresponds to other patterns in the text. This correspondence is the validation. The claim is not that some other penalty could not be selected as the one removing the greatest value. The claim is only that death, as a selection, manifests a pattern which then converges with other patterns in the text. For example, conceivably life without children might be a life not worth living. In that case, the penalty of childlessness would deprive the perpetrator of the greatest value. However, the selection of childlessness, as the harshest penalty, fails to manifest a pattern which converges with other patterns in the text. Additionally, it might be judged that the evaluative standard must be something other than "what takes the most or least from the perpetrator." Again the claim is not that some other evaluative standard cannot be chosen. The claim is only that the "depriving-value" standard manifests a pattern which converges with other sensible patterns in vv. 10–21.

Convergence aside, the plausibility of the pattern which manifests by selecting the death penalty as the harshest penalty is confirmed by a brief comparison of the penalties. Without his life, the perpetrator is unable to produce progeny. If the perpetrator dies childless,[62] at least he or she lives his or her life without premature end. Death takes away two things. Childlessness takes away only one of those two things. Death is the harsher penalty.

The cut-off penalty is less harsh than death and more harsh than childlessness.[63] Scholars have suggested a variety of interpretations for כרת.[64] Hutton, for example, on the basis of 1 Sam 28:9, claims that כרת does not end the perpetrator's life.[65] Rather, כרת divests a person "of his inheritance rights, his status, his rights to participate in the worshiping community."[66] Additionally, the perpetrator "is placed under the threat of divine wrath."[67] Without inheritance, status and worship rights the fulfillment that children represent in ancient Israel

---

62. Rodney R. Hutton, "Declaratory Formula: Forms of Authoritative Pronouncement in Ancient Israel" (Ph.D. diss., Claremont Graduate School, 1983), 147, states: "Thus to 'die childless' did not mean execution but rather was the invocation of a curse of life-long infertility."

63. For the non-executionary nature of v. 20bβ, see Hutton (ibid., 121–24) on the difference between Qal and Hophal in the death sentences.

64. See G. F. Hasel, "כָּרַת," *TDOT* 7:347–49.

65. Hutton, "Declaratory Formula," 138.

66. Ibid., 142.

67. Ibid., 142.

is empty. Thus, accepting Hutton's definition, כרת removes less than death and more than childlessness.

However, Wold, who has done an extensive study of כרת in the Pentateuch, offers another interpretation.[68] He claims that כרת indicates "a divine curse of extinction visited upon the sinner and his seed."[69] It is premature and childless death.[70] The terror of such a penalty is three-fold. First, one's death is contextualized in terms of the sin one has committed. Second, one's death may come sooner rather than later. Third, one's line is extinguished. Nevertheless, the perpetrator himself or herself is not executed. Furthermore, one's death and the extinction of one's line is not immediate. One might enjoy one's children until their *eventual* extinction. Thus, accepting Wold's definition, כרת removes less than immediate execution and more than childlessness.[71]

Wold, however, disagrees with this latter evaluation. He considers כרת to be the harshest of all penalties, including immediate execution.[72] He writes:

> ...the Priestly Writer invokes the *kareth* curse for deliberate trespasses [*sic*] against the rules of personal conduct which define and preserve the distinction between the sacred and the impure...[73]

כרת crimes, according to him, are the most "heinous variety" because their impurity lodges "in the adytum of P's Tabernacle."[74] His assessment thus seems to rest upon an assumption concerning the relationship between כרת and the crimes against which it is levied. However, while Wold argues convincingly about the nature of the crimes for which כרת is levied; his argument for the conclusion that כרת is a fate worse than death is unclear.[75] Furthermore, Jackson's cautionary note must at least lend pause to the reader who accepts Wold's assessment.[76]

Most importantly, however, Wold's assessment is unable to satisfactorily explain the differentiation of penalties in vv. 10–21. If the sister and menstruant infractions constitute an "intentional disregard for the Priestly distinction between the holy and the profane,"[77] which, as Wold contends, is the reason כרת is threatened,[78] do not all the other illicit sexual relationships exhibit the same disregard? Why, then, do the sister and menstruant laws both invoke כרת while the others do not? In short, beyond explaining the severity of the crimes for which כרת is given, Wold, has, in fact, offered no clear argument for the assertion that כרת is a penalty worse than death.

---

68.   Donald J. Wold, "The *Kareth* Penalty in P: Rationale and Cases," in *SBL 1979 Seminar Papers* (2 vols.; SBLSP 16–17; Missoula, Mont.: Scholars Press, 1979), 1:1–45.

69.   Ibid., 1:1–45 (24).

70.   Ibid., 1:19.

71.   See below.

72.   Wold, "*Kareth*," 2.

73.   Ibid., 2.

74.   Ibid., 7.

75.   Ibid., 7, 19, 20, 22.

76.   See above.

77.   Wold, "*Kareth*," 13.

78.   Ibid., 13, 16, 20, 22.

Although his assessment of the value which כרת divests is unhelpful, his definition of כרת is satisfactory. כרת prematurely takes one's own life and the life of one's descendents, *eventually*. Part of the onerous quality of this penalty is that the perpetrator must wait for the inevitable premature death and extinction. Final resolution is eventual. Childlessness, on the other hand, has no eventuality about it. Once childlessness is pronounced, the perpetrator has been divested of the value the penalty intends to remove. Under the כרת penalty, the perpetrator must wait to be fully divested. Since כרת prematurely takes the perpetrator's life and the life of his children and grandchildren, and since it must be awaited, it is a harsher penalty than both childlessness and "sin carry."

The penalty "sin carry" is characterized by a slightly different kind of eventuality—it deprives the individual of the luxury of propitiating the deity,[79] punishing the perpetrator with an unresolvable, bad conscience. A bad conscience is no trivial matter. In cases, it can debilitate and negatively alter one's life. The eventuality affects more than a bad conscience, however. Under this penalty, the perpetrator is unable to resolve the negative situation he or she has created. He or she is unable to cleanse the personal impurity the negative situation causes. He or she is unable, finally, to set things right. This penalty is less harsh than כרת because the perpetrator is not divested of his or her life immediately or eventually as a result of his or her sin. It is more harsh than childlessness because the life he or she lives is now burdened with the unresolvability of his or her sins. The childless penalty, on the other hand, is resolute. Moreover, it affects only one aspect of one's life. A bad conscience affects *every* aspect of one's life. Thus, "sin carry" is harsher than childlessness.

Two observations must be made before drawing a final conclusion regarding gradation of penalties. Where two or more penalties are attached to a single law, I have assumed that the harshest penalty among them is constitutive for the gradation. This fits the gradation pattern exhibited by the sequence of penalties in the text. Furthermore, among the death penalties, the constitutive factor for gradation is the execution factor. All forms, מות יומת, "burning" and "their blood is upon them," are executions.[80] The claim is not that the variation in these execution penalties is irrelevant. The claim is only that they are irrelevant for gradation.

Thus, a plausible gradation, correlating with the order of the penalties in the text, may exist.[81] Furthermore, this gradation supports the first major division

79. Robin Cover, "Sin, Sinners (Old Testament)," *ABD* 6:39b. To the contrary, Cover suggests that the sins to which "sin carry" applies are forgivable. If this is so, then the sinner carries his guilt until it is "removed through cultic rite and divine forgiveness." However, whether or not this possibility is part of the conceptual make-up of the "sin-carry" penalty is an open question.

80. Neufeld, *Ancient Hebrew Marriage Laws*, 203, takes burning to be more severe than simple death and "childless they shall die" more severe than "their sin they shall carry." He bases the latter on the fact that the direct aunt belongs to no male whereas the affinal aunt does. The latter, he concludes, is therefore more severe than the former.

81. Milgrom, *Leviticus 17–22*, 1742. See also p. 1767, where Milgrpm states: "The penalties are different and cannot be reconciled: in chap. 18, the miscreants are punished with *kārēt*, but in

between vv. 16 and 17. All penalties prior to v. 17 are the harshest penalty: immediate execution. All penalties after v. 16 are not.

(b) *First-and-Last-Crime Pattern.* Without drawing conclusions regarding the relationship between the above gradation and the nature of the crimes committed, in accordance with Jackson's cautionary note, one observation concerning the crimes can be made.

It just so happens that the very infraction associated with the established tradition of levirate law correlates with the least harsh penalty.[82] The law which concerns the marriage boundary outside the family, on the other hand, has the initial position among the laws correlated with the harshest penalty. This latter infraction causes social conflict not only in the family but within the larger community, a sphere outside the *patria potestas*. For this reason, it is a more serious matter. If these observations are accurate, then at least the infractions on the extreme ends of the series plausibly correlate to the penalty gradation.

(c) *Arrangement-of-Relationships Pattern.* The arrangement of relationships is a pattern which converges with the proposed gradation pattern. A major split in the relationships of the laws corresponds to the first main division of the penalties.

Among the consanguinal/affinal relations, only those which correspond to a direct line of ascendence or descendence incur the death penalty and occur in the first section. All other consanguinal/affinal relations are laterals. They do not incur the death penalty and they occur in the second section.[83] If direct-line ascendents and descendents, affinals or consanguinals, are indeed one's closest blood relatives, as Hutton suggests,[84] then these affinal/consanguinal relations constitute a pattern converging with the gradation of penalties.[85]

In addition, the non-consanguinal/non-affinal relations also form a converging pattern. The only non-consanguinal/non-affinal relation not receiving the death penalty and not occurring in section one is the menstruant relation.

---

chap. 20, the punishments are graded: *kārēt*, extirpation by God (vv. 17–18, possibly v. 19…), is preceded by severer (immediate) execution by judicial authorities (vv. 9–16) and followed by less stringent childlessness…"

82. Milgrom, *Leviticus 17–22*, 1758.

83. Hutton, "Declaratory Formula," 147–49, has noticed these same correspondences.

84. Ibid., 148. "The first half, vv. 9–16, concerns offenses of first-order abberant [*sic*] behavior, those committed with one's closest blood relatives: father or mother (v. 9), father's wife (v. 11), son's wife (v. 12), wife's mother (v. 14), along with three other forms of abberant [*sic*] sexual behavior such as male homosexuality (v. 13) and bestiality (vv. 15f.). Verse 17, however, begins a section concerning offenses of second order abberant [*sic*] behavior, those committed against members of the extended family who are at least once removed from a direct line of consanguinity: sister or half-sister (v. 17), maternal or paternal aunt (v. 19), uncle's wife (v. 20), brother's wife (v. 21)."

85. Jenson, *Graded Holiness*, 144, states: "The punishments for incest were graded in accord with the distance from the immediate family circle. Thus Lev 20 distinguishes between marriages where the partners are to be cut off (vv. 17–18), and those in which the couple will be childless."

This happens to be the only non-consanguinal/non-affinal relation which is contingent.[86] Thus, the contingent relation is the one that lacks the death penalty. This pattern, again, converges with the gradations.

(d) *Their-Blood-is-Upon-Them Pattern.* A more minor converging pattern is the "their-blood-is-upon-them" clause. This supplementing clause, which occurs in the first section along with the execution penalties, is completely absent from the second section.[87]

(e) *Immediacy-or-Eventuality-of-Penalties-Pattern.* If the above proposal for the penalties is correct, then a converging pattern also occurs with respect to the executor of the penalties. In section one, the executor is the collective addressee בְּנֵי יִשְׂרָאֵל. In the second section, the executor is God or fate.[88]

(f) *Conclusion.* These converging patterns can hardly be unintentional. They support the first major structural division of the text between vv. 16 and 17.

(2) *Structural Pattern.*[89] Additional converging patterns become apparent when the structural pattern is explored.

Four elements are constitutive for the structure of Lev 20:10–21: (1) the nature of the penalties; (2) the triggers within penalties; (3) the types of boundaries; and (4) the numbers of boundaries. These four elements reduce to two groups: those associated with penalties and those associated with protected boundaries. Thus, the structuring signals come from both the protases and the apodoses.

The proposal which follows includes both diachronic and synchronic explanations of the structure since both were operative in the formation of the text.

(a) *Section One.* Within the first section of the structure (vv. 10–16), the first division is between laws dealing with marriage boundaries (vv. 10–12) and laws dealing with other boundaries (vv. 13–16). This division comes between vv. 12 and 13. The two consanguinal/affinal laws (vv. 11 and 12) are grouped together with the paradigmatic[90] father law (v. 11) leading the pair. The neighbor's-wife

---

86. In other words, a woman who is a menstruant will sometimes be a non-menstruant. An animal will never not be an animal (vv. 15 and 16) and a man will never not be a man (v. 13). Obviously, in this day and age, one's sex is conceived as a contingency. In addition, a greater amount of ambiguity surrounds the idea of the sex of an individual. The point is that the author of the ancient text would have conceived, implicitly or explicitly, that one's sex was non-contingent, and more than likely non-ambiguous. At least, this seems to be the argument on the surface of the text.

87. Schulz, *Todesrecht*, 141. Schulz classes this phrase as a *Todesdeklaration*.

88. Wenham, *Leviticus*, 279, is noticing the same difference between the two sections when he describes the difference as that between capital crimes and crimes "for which no human penalty is laid down, but instead divine punishment is promised." See Hutton's comments on capital and non-capital offense ("Declaratory Formula," 121–24).

89. See the structure above.

90. See the discussion of Lev 18 above.

law (v. 10), however, begins the section. In addition to the fact that the neighbor's-wife law is not consanguinal/affinal, several other differences apply between it and the laws that follow.

First, the infraction of this law occurs within the context of the larger community while the infractions of the two following laws occur within the context of the family or clan.[91] Second, the neighbor's-wife law concerns only the following boundaries: the marriage boundary demarcating the relationship of the neighbor and his wife, and the "inside/outside-the-family" boundary demarcating the relationship of neighbor and wife to the ego. Among the laws of vv. 10–16, it forbids a relationship that has the least number of affinal/consanguinal connections to the ego. In fact, it has none. The two following laws (vv. 11 and 12) deal with the boundaries of marriage, affines/consanguines and generation. For this reason, a subdivision occurs between vv. 10 and 11.

The second part of the first section, laws dealing with non-marriage relationships (vv. 13–16), divides into laws dealing with only humans (vv. 13–14) and laws dealing with animals (vv. 15–16). A corresponding difference exists with respect to penalties. In the animal section (vv. 15–16), each law contains two statements of explicit death whereas the preceding laws contain only one.[92]

The homosexuality law (v. 13) leads the first division of this second part of the first section because its penalty is similar to the penalty of the law which concludes the immediately preceding section (v. 12). Thus, the two penalties act as a "trigger" for the ordering of the laws at this juncture as well as acting as a transitional link between the sections. The woman/mother law (v. 14) follows the homosexuality law (v. 13) because it belongs in the human section of this division. The animal section (vv. 15–16), then, follows the woman/mother law.

(b) *Section Two*. The second major section (vv. 17–21) lacks a joining trigger to the first major section (vv. 10–16). The law which deals with the least number of affinal/consanguinal boundaries (v. 17) again comes first in the second section, as it does in the first section. The single boundary of the sister law (v. 17) is the collateral consanguinal boundary.[93] This is a boundary of the *nuclear* family. As well as placing it in initial position, these qualifications separate it from the laws of vv. 19–21.

The laws of vv. 19–21 deal with more than one affinal/consanguinal boundary. The various boundaries of vv. 20–21 are easy to see. In addition to the affinal and consanguinal boundaries, the generational boundary also applies to v. 20. The same is the case for the law of v. 19.

The menstruant law is inserted between v. 17 and vv. 19–21 for the following reasons. The trigger "be cut off" in the menstruant law (v. 18) matches the same

91. Milgrom, *Leviticus 17–22*, 1747.
92. In the male-bestiality law the two penalties are split between the man and the animal. In the female-bestiality law the two penalties apply to both the woman and the animal.
93. The father–daughter and mother–daughter relations are consanguinal, as is the sister–brother relationship. Thus, one type of boundary is involved.

phrase in the sister law (v. 17). The prohibition against sister-of-mother-and-father relations (v. 19), one class of three contiguous collateral, consanguinal/affinal relations, follows the menstruant law (v. 18) because the trigger "their sins they shall carry" reaches back to the same phrase in v. 17. This law does not immediately follow the sister law (v. 17) because another law with "their sins they shall carry" (v. 20) must follow it (v. 19). Thus, the best place for the menstruant law (v. 18) is right after the sister law (v. 17) because it matches only the sister law. The sequence continues to the end with the same logic. The father's-brother's-wife law (v. 20) follows the sister-of-mother-or-father law (v. 19) because of the "sin shall carry" phrase and because another law (v. 21) which matches its "childless" lexeme must follow it. Thus, the last four laws are ordered by triggers.

Corresponding to this line-up in the second section is the fact that the strictly consanguinal relationships precede the affinal relationships, continuing Hutton's idea of the closest blood relations coming before other blood relations.[94]

Thus, several signals order the text and several features converge with that ordering.

3) *Summary.* The synchronic-boundary features which are constitutive for the structure of the text demonstrate that the primary concern is classificatory- as opposed to property-oriented. The author protects boundaries associated with natural impurity, species and biotype as well as marriage. Furthermore, consanguinal boundaries, as well as affinal boundaries, are constitutive for the structure. Their protection is thus also a component of the primary concern. The variety of boundaries which are constitutive for the structure and protected by the laws of vv. 10–21 demonstrates that the primary concern is protection of sexual boundaries in general rather than the protection of woman's sexuality as the property of man.

C. *Conclusion*

The above scheme, *if* it reflects the organizing principles of the author, demonstrates that factors other than property are at stake in this text even with regard to those relationships in which a woman clearly belongs to a man.

Although point-of-view and language-depicting-the-sex act marginalize and objectify the woman, they are also responsible for subtle contraindicators, which, in addition to the three factors—selection-of-laws, identification-of-women and structure-of-the-text—demonstrate that the concern is classificatory rather than property-oriented.

The woman is focalized, in the chapter as a whole, as agent. She is responsible to the laws. She, like the man, must protect the classificatory system which orders their world. She is not focalized as property.

---

94. Hutton, "Declaratory Formula," 148.

Chapter 7

LEVITICUS 21:9

A. *Introduction*

The instruction of Lev 21 is addressed to the male priests. Woman is, thus, marginalized in the text. However, the fact that *her* actions constitute the infraction suggests that she is also implicitly addressed. The sex act in the law of Lev 21:9 is not explicitly depicted. Furthermore, in this law, the woman is also not objectified.

Leviticus 21:9 regulates the sexuality of the daughter of an ordinary priest, specifically addressing the subject of her prostitution. She appears as character-agent by the language which refers to her sexual activity. She is focalized as agent by her relationship to the author's primary concern. Although the property component is necessarily present because of the father–daughter relationship, that property component is of no concern to the law. That is, although the daughter's sexuality "belongs" to the father, the primary concern is not the loss of control concerning power over or rights to progeny, brideprice, prestige or other property aspects related to the daughter's sexuality. The primary concern is exclusively to ensure that the daughter's behavior protects her father's sanctity.[1] The law guards against imperilment of the priest's consecrated status as a result of his daughter's actions. This is a classificatory rather than a property concern.

B. *Discussion*

Form and content are the two components informing the conclusion by most scholars that v. 9 is an insertion.[2] Although the laws of vv. 1–15, including v. 9, address the sons of Aaron, the daughter, rather than the priests themselves, is the subject in v. 9. The surrounding laws regulate death-matters or marriage-matters, whereas v. 9 regulates sexuality-matters. The law of v. 9 is casuistic. The surrounding laws are apodictic. Nevertheless, the relevance of v. 9 to the present context is clear. It, as well as the surrounding unit, pertains to issues concerning the priest's family.

---

1. Tikva Frymer-Kensky, "Virginity in the Bible," in Matthews, Levinson and Frymer-Kensky, eds., *Gender and Law in the Hebrew Bible*, 79–90. See Frymer-Kensky's interesting discussion on the possible motivations for valuation of female virginity.
2. Dupont, "Women," 62, 213–14; Elliger, *Leviticus*, 280–81.

The macrostructure, the microstructure and other features, including the holy/ profane and pure/impure domains as well as the father–daughter relationship, are essential for understanding the underlying conceptual matrix and the primary concern which it informs.

1. *Macrostructure*

The macrostructure reveals that the prostitution law of v. 9 occurs within a Yhwh Speech to Moses. It extends from v. 1 to v. 15. A collapsed version of the structure of this speech is as follows:

I.	Introduction to Yhwh Speech		21:1aα
II.	Speech		21:1aβ–15
	A.	Introduction	1aβ–ba
	B.	Main Body of Speech	1bβ–15
	1.	ordinary priests	1bβ–9
		a. specific laws: death	1bβ–5
		b. general law	6
		c. specific laws: marriage	7
		d. general law	8
		d. specific law: daughter	9
	2.	high priest	10–15
		a. basic identification	10a
		b. limiting commands	10b–15
		1) death	10b–12
		a) mourning	10b
		b) corpses	11
		c) sanctuary	12
		2) marriage	13–15
		a) commands	13–14
		b) grounds	15

Leviticus 21:1–15 is part of a unit encompassing all of Lev 21 and Lev 22. This unit consists of several Yhwh speeches instructing a segment of male Israelites: the priests. The law addresses women only by implication and, then, only by mediation through the priests.

Verses 1bβ–15 divide into two major sections.[3] The first, vv. 1–9, applies to ordinary priests. The second, vv. 10–15, applies to the high priest.[4] Both sections begin with death laws, followed by marriage laws. In addition, the first section concludes with the prostitution sex-law of v. 9.

The intended purpose in the treatments of death, marriage and prostitution is two-fold. First, the laws explicitly protect the ordinary priest and the high priest. Second, the laws explicitly protect the progeny of the high priest and, implicitly,[5] though less stringently, the progeny of the ordinary priest. The death laws explicitly protect the *purity* of the priest. The marriage laws explicitly protect the *sanctity* of the priest and his progeny. Finally, the prostitution sex-law

---

3. Christine E. Hayes, "Parallelism and Inversion in Lev 21:1b–15," in Milgrom, *Leviticus 17–22*, 1834–36. See Hayes for some other interesting patterns in the pericope.

4. Milgrom, *Leviticus 17–22*, 1834.

5. The allowance of the widow and the prohibition of the וחללה זנה are the source of this claim.

explicitly protects the sanctity of the ordinary priest and implicitly protects the sanctity of the high priest.[6]

A daughter who has turned to prostitution poses the same danger that the improper handling of death and marriage poses. Whereas the death and marriage laws provide guidelines for avoiding the danger, the prostitution sex-law provides instruction for eliminating the danger: she is burned.[7]

2. *Microstructure*

The microstructure reveals that v. 9 consists of a protasis and an apodosis preceded by a proleptic referent naming the subject. The *atnah* signals the division between the protasis and the apodosis. The grammatical possibility of dividing the verse between אָבִיהָ and הִיא seems to have bothered witnesses such as the LXX and the Vulgate, who have a plus, "the name of the father," before אָבִיהָ. The possibility that a daughter might play the harlot with her father has perhaps motivated this plus.[8] However, the fact that the punishment or purge concerns only the daughter demonstrates that the prohibition of incest is not, in fact, the aim of the law.[9]

The subject of the law named in the proleptic referent is the daughter. The daughter is the subject of the finite verb, the participle and the passive verb. The father is the object of the participle. He receives the effect of her action, taken on her own initiative. In all of LST and DST, this law is the only instance where the woman alone is the subject of the protasis at the same time that man alone is the object.[10] This is, accordingly, the only instance among those texts, in which the woman's power to harm the man is explicitly named, while the reverse is not true. Furthermore, this single instance of the woman's power to harm involves priests who operate at higher levels of sanctity than the ordinary man.

The gender alignments of this verse are, however, not an exception to the subject/object gender correspondences in the language-depicting-the-sex-act of other passages, since v. 9 does not depict the sex act. The daughter is the subject not of sexual actions but of the effects of sexual actions. The gender alignments are, nevertheless, an exception to the agent/receiver pattern of other passages. The daughter profanes her father. Accordingly, the law implies that the daughter

---

6. The law of v. 9 also applies to the high priest. See Milgrom, *Leviticus 1–16*, 914, for the exegetical principle undergirding this conclusion.

7. Wright, *Disposal of Impurity*, 91 n. 19, 288–90. See Gen 38:24; Lev 20:14.

8. Magonet, "Structure," 164, suggests the possibility that incest may be the concern of Lev 19:29 on the basis of the use of זמה both there and in Lev 18:17 and 20:14. See Milgrom, *Leviticus 17–22*, 1528, and also the discussion above of Lev 19.

9. Milgrom, *Leviticus 17–22*, 1528, states: "As for the assumption of 'sex rights' for the father, it has no basis either in the Bible or in the ancient Near East."

10. In Lev 20:17 both the man and the woman serve as both subject and object in the protasis. See the discussion above. In Lev 18:23b and 20:16, woman is the subject in contradistinction to an animal. In Lev 20:18, woman is subject in the apodosis in contradistinction to her own blood flow. In Deut 25:5–10, the woman is the subject in one portion of the apodosis where she removes her brother-in-law's sandal and spits on him, humiliating him as a result of his failure to establish the name of his brother.

has a responsibility to avoid such behavior. The father, however, has no responsibility, implied or otherwise, except, perhaps, as a member of the community, to carry out the penalty against his daughter.

Several gender asymmetries, contrasting to the subject/object gender correspondences are apparent. While the daughter jeopardizes her own holiness,[11] her loss of sanctity is a concern only in so far as it affects her father's status.[12] In addition, profanation of the mother, who is not a priest, is not an issue. The illicit sexual behavior of a son is also not an issue. Any woman is potentially a source of jeopardy to the sanctity of the priest, depending on her sexual activity. Priests, whose role women can never assume, are as a result of their sexual activity never potential sources of jeopardy to the sanctity of the woman. Thus, the power of the daughter, exhibited by the subject/object gender correspondences in this law, derives from her highly circumscribed position in the larger social configuration.

These are obvious correspondences, readily apparent without microscopic analysis. They are the seed-bed for the primary concern of this verse, which is also obvious: protection of the sanctity of the ordinary priest.

3. Conceptual Matrix

Less apparent, perhaps, is the relevance or lack of relevance of the father's "ownership" of his daughter's sexuality to the sanctity concerns of the prohibition. The relationship of holiness to impurity, as well as the conceptual matrix concerning the father–daughter relationship, demonstrates that something other than "ownership" of the daughter's sexuality, per se, is the primary concern.

a. *Holy/Profane and Pure/Impure.* The deeds compromising the daughter's sexuality fall into a class of pollutions which Frymer-Kensky calls "danger pollutions." These pollutions, according to Frymer-Kensky, while no danger to other individuals, are a danger to the community, "for if too many individuals commit these deeds, then the whole society might be considered polluted and might thus be in danger of a collective catastrophe."[13] Indeed, such communal danger is explicitly stated in the prostituting-daughter law of Lev 19:29, while the danger to the father (if it exists at all, it would exist whether or not he was the source of her illicit behavior) is ignored. But in Lev 21:9 the community is not the specific concern. Rather, the concern is the sanctity of the father, with respect to which the daughter's deeds are apparently not neutral.[14]

---

11. See the discussion of Lev 19:29 above.

12. Milgrom, *Leviticus 17–22*, 1810, compares the stringency placed upon the priestly daughter (lacking in Exod 22:15–16 and Deut 22:28–29) with some societies which place greater restriction upon royalty than on commoners. See also Jenson, *Graded Holiness*, 123.

13. Tikva Frymer-Kensky, "Pollution, Purification, and Purgation in Biblical Israel," in *The Word of the Lord Shall Go Forth* (ed. Carol L. Meyers and M. O'Connor; Winona Lake, Ind.: Eisenbrauns, 1983), 404.

14. Jenson, *Graded Holiness*, 123, states: "Sexual sins may have constituted an offence against the special holiness of the priestly line, since she is said to profane her father (את־אביה היא מחללת, Lev 21.9)."

The origin of the danger to the father is the relationship of the holy/ profane domain to the purity/impurity domain.[15] Purity is a requirement for sanctity.[16] Impurity has the power to desanctify.[17] The daughter is holy in a broad sense.[18] She has engaged in sexual activity which is impure and thus profaned herself. The priest is holy in a narrow sense.[19] The daughter's impure behavior is a danger to him just as it is a danger to herself.

b. *Father–Daughter Sphere.* Although the daughter's sexuality "belongs" to the father, and although compromise of that sexuality desanctifies the father, the "ownership" component of her desanctifying impurity—including usurpation of authority, control, "remuneration" in the form of brideprice or other rights, such as those connected to progeny—is peripherally relevant, if at all, to the author of the text. Rather, the violation of boundaries alone, the disruption of the categories and order of creation, is the concern.

That the daughter's sexuality "belongs" to the father is an essential component of the scenario, even if it is of peripheral concern to the author. The difference in treatment, within this text, between the harlot (וְנָה וְחַלְלָה) and the harloting daughter[20] is evidence of this fact. The daughter receives the death penalty for harloting. The harlot, however, carries on with her profession and life, such that she is a potential wife against whom a priest must be warned. The difference between them is the father. The daughter is circumscribed by a male, her father, while the harlot is circumscribed by no male.[21] The circumscription is the evidence that the daughter "belongs" to the father. Thus, "ownership" is one component of the conceptual matrix informing the negative qualification of the daughter's behavior.[22] However, while this "belonging" or "ownership" is an

15.   Ibid., 40–55. See Jenson for a discussion of the distinctions concerning the relationship of holy, profane, pure and impure to one another. See also Wenham, *Leviticus*, 18–25.

16.   Jenson, *Graded Holiness*, 53, 55.

17.   Ibid., 52, writes: "It is a serious cultic sin to bring the unclean into contact with the holy. Such an action produces a dangerous mismatch of levels in the Holiness Spectrum, since the holy and the unclean are at least two degrees removed and at opposite poles." The desanctification, according to Jenson and Amorin, may be negative or positive depending on the impurity (p. 51, citing N. D. Amorin, "Desecration and Defilement in the Old Testament" [Ph.D. diss., Andrews University, 1986]). In v. 9 it is negative. See Frymer-Kensky, "Pollution," 403–5 and Milgrom *Leviticus 17–22*, 1810, who states: "In this verse, the twice attested *ḥll* apparently takes on a metaphoric connotation, typical of H…"

18.   Jenson, *Graded Holiness*, 123 n. 3. See pp. 48–49 for Jenson's use of "broad" and "narrow."

19.   Ibid., 48–49, 123 n. 3.

20.   Bird, "To Play the Harlot," 78. See Bird's comments concerning the relationship between the verbal and nominal uses of זנה.

21.   Ibid., 77, states: "Whereas the promiscuity of a daughter or levirate-obligated widow offends the male to whom each is subject and is penalized accordingly, the harlot's activity violates no man's rights or honor, and consequently is free from the sanctions imposed on the casual fornicator."

22.   Niditch, "The Wrong Woman Righted," 147, writes: "Certainly the Old Testament discourages such illegal unions, as is indicated by a formal expression of the law at Lev 19:29; yet once a girl is not seen in the role of daughter, virgin, and nubile woman, she is, in effect, outside the rules. Prostitutes seem to have an accepted, outcast place in society. A priest may not marry a *zōnâ* (Lev

essential component, it is not the issue at stake in the law. Furthermore, "owner-ship" as an essential component does not derive from the father's capacity to establish that the progeny is his own.

The intersection of virginity and marriage in the text underscores the point. Only the high priest must marry only a virgin.[23] The text states the reason explicitly: וְלֹא־יְחַלֵּל זַרְעוֹ. Purity of descent is the issue.[24] At least three factors constitute this purity. If Levine is correct in his assumption that עַם of מֵעַמָּיו "refers specifically to the priestly clan,"[25] then the first factor is the guarantee that the progeny descend biologically, maternally and paternally, from the priestly line.[26] If, however, Levine is incorrect and עַם refers to Israel in general, then the first factor is the guarantee that the progeny descend biologically, maternally and paternally, from Israelite lineage. This first factor thus protects the capacity to know that the "genetics" of the child are either priestly or of Israelite descent, depending on how עַם is understood. The second factor is the guarantee that the progeny is from the priest's own seed. The fact that only a virgin qualifies is evidence of this factor. The third factor is the guarantee that the progeny comes through a woman whose sexual boundaries have never been crossed by a man. The fact that only a virgin and also "not-a-widow" qualify, the narrowest standard applied in the text, protects the capacity to know that the progeny enters the world through the purest of all possible channels. All three factors constitute purity of descent for the high-priestly progeny.

21:7, 14); she is a liminal character, outside the social order. By the same token, however, she belongs to a special class of women who can 'play the harlot' without being condemned. In effect, one could fall between the proper categories and survive, once that outside betwixt-and-between status was itself institutionalized and categorized."

23. Contrary to Snaith, *Leviticus*, 143. See Wenham, "*Bᵉtûlāh*," 336–38. Wenham's arguments against "virgin" as the denotation of בתולה in Lev 21 rests on the assumption that "redundancy" in lists like those in vv. 3, 7 and 13–14 do not, or should not, occur. He suggests that, if בתולה meant "virgin," the אשר clause would not occur in v. 3. Furthermore, if בתולה meant "virgin," v. 7, instead of listing the forbidden women would simply read (p. 336): "They shall marry a virgin." Finally, he states, concerning vv. 13 and 14: "If *betûlāh* means 'teenage girl' and not 'virgin,' the more detailed description of the high priest's bride is explicable… But unless *betûlîm* denotes a condition distin-guishable from virginity, the specifications for the high priest's wife seem somewhat redundant" (pp. 337–38). However, the author lists the women not because the items on the list are not coterminous with בתולה, but because the author wants to make sure his point is heard—emphatically. See the discussion above on Lev 18:7 for comments on the same technique present there. Even Wenham states (p. 338): "this passage does not add up to proof that *betûlāh* does not mean 'virgin,' for it is clear that one of the qualifications for priests' brides was virginity." See also Clemens Locher, *Die Ehre einer Frau in Israel* (Göttingen: Vandenhoeck & Ruprecht, 1986), 178, and also the discussion of Deut 22:13–23:1 below.

24. Dupont, "Women," 215 n. 6; Engelken, *Frauen im alten Israel*, 29. Sun, "Investigation," 273, notes that "Only here does one חלל one's זרע." See also Wenham, "*Bᵉtûlāh*," 339.

25. Levine, *Leviticus*, 145.

26. Ibid., 145. According to Levine et al., עם "refers specifically to the priestly clan." See also the following: Dommershausen, "חלל," 415; Judith Romney Wegner, "Leviticus," in *The Women's Bible Commentary* (ed. Carol A. Newsom and Sharon H. Ringe; Westminster: John Knox, 1992), 42; Wenham, *Leviticus*, 292; M. Zipor, "Restrictions on Marriage for Priests (Lev 21,7.13–14)," *Bib* 68 (1987): 259–67.

For the ordinary priest, however, purity of descent is constituted by the second factor only—מֵעַמָּיו is not a requirement. Nor is the narrowest standard for purity of the channel a requirement. If the ordinary priest does not marry a virgin, then he must marry a widow.[27] The allowance of the widow does not nullify the relevance of the second factor since the widow's genital boundaries are as secure as a virgin's. That is, those who have crossed her sexual boundaries are quantifiable: they are finite, legitimate and dead. The harlot and divorcee are forbidden because their genital boundaries are less secure.[28] Factors one, two and three thus protect the capacity to *know* three items of information: (1) that the "genetics" of the child is priestly or of Israelite lineage, depending on the reading of עַם, (2) that the "genetics" of the child is the man's own and (3) that the channel meets the narrowest standard of purity humanly possible in terms of boundaries crossed.

However, with respect to the daughter of the *ordinary* priest, all three factors are irrelevant. If the first factor is irrelevant for the potential wife of an ordinary priest, it must also be irrelevant for his daughter. Thus, the law of v. 9 does not intend to ensure that the ordinary priest's grandchildren come from the priestly line. In addition, since the grandfather-priest will always know that the progeny which the daughter bears are his own, having been delivered from her womb, the second factor is irrelevant as well. Thus, the law of v. 9 does not intend to ensure that the ordinary priest's grandchildren are his own. It intends to ensure something else. If the first and second factors are irrelevant, the narrowest standard for the purity of the channel is also irrelevant. Thus, the law of v. 9 does not intend to ensure that no man has *ever* crossed the woman's sexual boundaries. In

---

27.   Several scholars note that, on the basis of זנה וחללה, the ordinary priest is required to marry a virgin or a widow. See Noordtzij, *Leviticus*, 217; Noth, *Leviticus*, 156; Jenson, *Graded Holiness*, 130. Jenson suggests that an ordinary priest was allowed to marry a *priestly* widow only and that prostitutes were forbidden to him because, "like a divorcee or non-priestly widow, she would have had sexual relations with a non-priest." However, the text does not state the requirement that the widow be priestly. Furthermore, such a conclusion cannot be inferred from Lev 21, regardless of the requirements listed in Ezek 44:22. Levine, *Leviticus*, 143, reads זנה וחללה as hendiadys: "degraded by harlotry." Zipor, "Restrictions," 263, also regards the phrase as hendiadys. In v. 14, however, the two words are reversed and the conjunction is lacking. For this reason, he suggests that the two words in v. 14 refer to two kinds of women—harlot and hierodule—and that the author of vv. 10–15 misunderstood v. 7. However, the hendiadys construction is not essential for reading the two words as working together, denoting one kind of woman. זנה in v. 14 can be read as a participle serving as an adjectival modifier of the type which Waltke and O'Connor (*Biblical Hebrew Syntax*, 73–74) call "adverbial apposition": "one defiled by harlotry" or a "harloting defiled-one." The relationship of these two words in Lev 19:29 and 21:9 supports the conclusion that they work together in v. 14 as well as in v. 7. Thus, I take them as referring to one kind of woman in both v. 7 and v. 14. Nevertheless, more work is needed to determine the precise denotation of the joint use of זנה and חללה. See Milgrom's discussion (*Leviticus 17–22*, 1806–8). Milgrom also rejects hendiadys (p. 1808). Engelken, *Frauen im alten Israel*, 28, understands v. 14 as follows: "Jede andere Frau ist ihm als Ehefrau verboten, aufgezält werden die Witwe, die Geschiedene, die חללה, gemeint ist wohl die vergewaltigte Frau, und die Hure." See the discussion above on sacred prostitution for Zipor's suggestion concerning "hierodule."

28.   Jenson, *Graded Holiness*, 130; Wenham, *Leviticus*, 291; Zipor, "Restrictions," 259.

conclusion, the father/daughter boundaries do not protect progeny as the marriage boundaries do.

Furthermore, they do not protect the father's right to be the single enjoyer of the daughter's sexuality.

They do, however, in all probability, protect at least one property item, as suggested by other passages from the Hebrew corpus: brideprice. Deuteronomy 22:28 and Exod 22:16 demonstrate that recorders/composers of biblical laws were capable of articulating the protection of such an item. If protection of brideprice were the impurity component of concern to the author of v. 9, we would expect explicit mention of it. But such articulation is absent from Lev 21:9.

This process of elimination leads to one final concern as the aim of the law of v. 9. This final concern is a fourth factor. The boundaries of v. 9 demarcate the sphere to which the father and daughter belong just as the boundaries called "marriage" demarcate the sphere to which the husband and wife belong. As the fidelity of the wife is essential for protection of the boundaries of concern in Lev 18:20, so also the virginity of the daughter is essential for the protection of the boundaries of concern in Lev 21:9. The impurity of an adulterous woman derives from the fact that a strange man crosses the boundaries of the sphere defined by marriage. The impurity of the prostituting daughter derives from the fact that strange men have crossed the boundaries of the sphere defined by the father/daughter relationship, asexual as it may or may not be.

The primary concern of v. 9 is thus the breach itself of the boundaries demarcating the father/daughter sphere. In other words, the issue is classificatory, pertaining to order and crossing boundaries. While the boundaries protect a father's rights to his daughter's sexuality as marriage boundaries protect a husband's rights—even though a father's and husband's rights to utilization of that sexuality differ—the issue in v. 9 is not usurpation of rights. Rather, the issue is the compromise of a "category," the father/daughter sphere, which is just as essential to Israelite life and worldview as marriage. This alone constitutes the impurity of v. 9.

C. *Conclusion*

Although the daughter's sexuality "belongs" to the father, the primary concern of the law of v. 9 is the desanctification of the father. The impurity of his daughter's actions causes that desanctification. Disruption of order or blurring of categories rather than loss of property constitutes that impurity. The primary concern, desanctification of the sacred by intersection with the impure, is a classificatory issue rather than a property issue. Thus, while the woman is objectified and marginalized, and although she is also the property of the father, she is nevertheless focalized as agent responsible for her father's sanctity.

Part III

EXEGESIS 2—DEUTERONOMY TEXTS

Chapter 8

DEUTERONOMY 5:18

A. *Introduction*

Deuteronomy 5:18 is the seventh commandment in the unit known as the "Ten Commandments." This unit occurs within the second introductory framework to what scholars[1] generally consider to be the central law code of Deuteronomy (12:1–26:15). The crossing of boundaries per se, that is, classificatory considerations, is immaterial to the primary concern of this single sex law. The primary concern is protection of woman's sexuality as the property of the man.

B. *Discussion*

1. *Contrary Signals*

Two features in the text seem, at the least, to disqualify the above assertion as an expectation. At the most, they seem to belie its truth. The first feature is point-of-view. The second feature is the relationship of the clauses in v. 21.

a. *Point-of-View.* Although all verbs and pronominal suffixes are masculine, the point-of-view of the chapter demonstrates remarkable gender inclusiveness in its designation of the addressee. Two gender-neutral phrases, כָּל־יִשְׂרָאֵל (v. 1) and כָּל־קְהַלְכֶם (v. 22), refer to the individuals within the gathering before Moses. These phrases, different in their denotation from a phrase such as בְּנֵי יִשְׂרָאֵל, refer to a group of individuals consisting of both genders. Weinfeld writes the following:

> The author of Deuteronomy describes Moses as speaking before a vast audience comprising tribal leaders, officers, elders, men, women, and children, and even resident aliens (cf. 29:1, 9 and 31:12).[2]

---

1. For example, see the following: C. Brekelmans, "Deuteronomy 5: Its Place and Function," in *Das Deuteronomium* (ed. N. Lohfink; Leuven: Leuven University Press, 1985), 164–73; Ian Cairns, *Deuteronomy: Word and Presence* (Grand Rapids: Eerdmans, 1992), 14; A. D. H. Mayes, "Deuteronomy 5 and the Decalogue," *Proceedings of the Irish Biblical Association* 4 (1980): 68–83 (73); Tigay, *Deuteronomy*, xxiv–xxvi; Moshe Weinfeld, *Deuteronomy 1–11* (New York: Doubleday, 1991), 2–4.

2. Weinfeld, *Deuteronomy 1–11*, 126, 237. See also Tikva Frymer-Kensky, "Deuteronomy," in Newsom and Ringe, eds., *The Women's Bible Commentary*, 54.

If Weinfeld is right, then two more phrases, less gender-neutral in their denotation, are also implicitly gender inclusive in their connotation: אֲבֹתֵינוּ (v. 3) and הָאָדָם (v. 24).

Three additional phrases are explicitly inclusive, specifically referring to the man and the woman as if they are equal. The addressees must honor both father and mother (v. 16); must cause both sons and daughters to keep the Sabbath rest; and must cause maidservants and manservants to keep the same rest. Among these latter inclusions concerning the Sabbath-rest, the wife is noticeably absent. Frymer-Kensky's understanding of this absence nevertheless supports the inclusive representation of the gathering before Moses. She writes:

> The inclusion of the daughter and the female slave shows that women are to stop working on the Sabbath. Is the wife not mentioned because "a woman's work is never done" and the wife still has to work? But if the wife worked, so would the daughter and the maidservant. Quite the contrary, the omission of a phrase "and your wife" shows that the "you" that the law addresses includes both women and men, each treated as a separate moral agent.[3]

Frymer-Kensky asserts that the other commandments also include women, since women too were expected to refrain from such acts as murder, stealing and improper use of Yhwh's name.[4]

Thus, although all verbs and pronominal suffixes throughout the chapter, without exception, are masculine, they represent, for the most part, both genders. Woman's marginalization in the text is ameliorated, at least if compared with the sex laws of Leviticus just exegeted. Accordingly, point-of-view seems to belie the assertion that the primary concern of the sex law of v. 18 is to protect the woman's sexuality as the property of the man. At the least, it seems to disqualify the expectation that this is so.

b. *Arrangement of Clauses in Verse 21.* Just as point-of-view seems to belie the above assertion, so also does the arrangement of the clauses in v. 21. From this arrangement, Phillips has concluded that, whereas women are classed as property in Exod 20, they are not classed as property in Deut 5.[5] In fact, women are equal. Weinfeld's opinion, with respect to women, aligns with Phillip's opinion. He sees the arrangement of the clauses as a symptom of Deuteronomy's special attention to women's rights.[6]

---

3. Frymer-Kensky, "Deuteronomy," 54.

4. Ibid., 54.

5. Anthony Phillips, *Deuteronomy* (Cambridge: Cambridge University Press, 1973), 50. Referring to the difference between Exod 20:17 and Deut 5:21, Phillips writes: "The change in order is due to the deuteronomic law, which apparently for the first time brought women within the scope of the covenant community (cp. 7:3; 13:6; 15:12–17; 17:2–5; 22:22), and could therefore no longer be treated as simply another item of personal property." Pressler, *View of Women*, 108, critiques Phillip's assumption and those similar to his regarding the equality of women in Deuteronomy.

6. Weinfeld, *Deuteronomy 1–11*, 317–18, states: "The Deuteronomic version inverted the order of these two commandments. Unlike the Exodus version, which has 'house' before 'wife,' Deuteronomy puts first 'wife' then 'house' and devotes to the 'wife' a separate command, which suits the general tendencies of this book. Deuteronomy gives special attention to women's rights (cf. Deut

An exploration of the use of חמד is essential to understanding this arrange-ment, and the use of חמד has generated considerable scholarly discussion and creates at least two exegetical problems. The first problem concerns the meaning of חמד. The second problem concerns the separation of its direct object, woman, from the list of direct objects associated with אוה. The second problem also concerns the placement of its clause in initial position.

1) *First Exegetical Problem.* The first exegetical problem consists of two related parts.[7] The first part concerns the "plain" sense of the text. BDB defines חמד as "to desire" or "to take pleasure in."[8] It defines the Hithpael of אוה as "to desire," "to long for" or "to lust after."[9] These meanings designate moods, dispositions, emotions or mental inclinations. Such phenomena are difficult, if not impossible, to police or prosecute. Scholars who have presumed that Deut 5:7–21 consists of laws, the infractions of which were prosecutable, have concluded that חמד and אוה must mean something other than "desire"[10] or "covet"[11] or some other desig-nation which denotes mindset, emotion or feeling. As a result, such scholars have extended the meaning of חמד in one of several ways.[12] For example, many have included within the meaning some sort of developed intent which neces-sarily entails or includes the act of taking. However, such an explanation runs the risk of redundancy, either with v. 18 or v. 19.[13]

This potential redundancy is the second part of the first exegetical problem. In a list such as the Ten Commandments, a redundancy is indeed unexpected. Various scholars have gone through exegetical gymnastics, including the development of an extended meaning for גנב,[14] in order to circumvent this

---

15:12–18 with Exod 21:2–11; Deut 22:28–29 with Exod 22:15–16…) and therefore he gives preference to the wife and reserves for her a separate injunction. By the same token she does not join the slave, the animal, and so on, contrary to the arrangement in the Exodus version." See Pressler's critique (*View of Women*, 105–8).

7. See Greenberg, "Decalogue Tradition," 106–9, for an excellent summary of this problem.

8. "חמד," BDB, 326. See also G. Wallis, "חָמַד," *TDOT* 4:457–58.

9. "אוה," BDB, 116. See also Günter Mayer, "אָוָה," *TDOT* 1:135. "ʿavah is synonymous with chamadh, 'to desire'."

10. Alexander Rofé, "Tenth Commandment in the Light of Four Deuteronomic Laws," in Levi, ed., *The Ten Commandments*, 48–50.

11. Ibid., 45–48.

12. Albrecht Alt, *Kleine Schriften Zur Geschichte Des Volkes Israel*, vol. 1 (Munich: Beck, 1959), 333–34; Cairns, *Deuteronomy*, 78, 80; Peter C. Craigie, *The Book of Deuteronomy* (Grand Rapids: Eerdmans, 1976), 163; Greenberg, "Decalogue Tradition," 106; Jackson, *Essays*, 203; Patrick D. Miller, *Deuteronomy* (Louisville, Ky.: John Knox, 1990), 95; Eduard Nielsen, *The Ten Commandments in New Perspective* (London: SCM Press, 1968), 91; Phillips, *Ancient Israel's Criminal Law*, 149. See especially Rofé, "Tenth Commandment," 45–48, for a summary and analy-sis of the problem. See also J. J. Stamm and M.E. Andrew, *The Ten Commandments in Recent Research* (trans. M. E. Andrew; London: SCM Press, 1967), 102–3; Gerhard von Rad, *Deuteronomy* (Philadelphia: Westminster, 1966), 59.

13. Greenberg, "Decalogue Tradition," 108.

14. This extended meaning is based on the use of גנב in contexts such as Exod 21:16 and Deut 24:7. Alt, *Kleine Schriften*, 336. Greenberg, "Decalogue," 105–6. V. Hamp, "גָּנַב," *TDOT* 3:42; Nielsen, *Ten Commandments*, 91; Stamm and Andrew, *Ten Commandments*, 103–5.

redundancy. Jackson addresses the problem directly,[15] asserting that חמד does, in fact, denote a mental or emotional state of mind in Deut 5:18.[16] He states:

> Nowhere in the narrative immediately concerning the ten commandments do we find any allusion to a method of enforcement to be applied by man. This is not to say that the Decalogue is only ethics and that no means of enforcement was conceived to exist. The means of enforcement was the power of God to punish under the terms of the covenant by which Israel accepted the law. Indeed, in the Deuteronomic tradition the duty to observe the commandments is linked with the motive clause "that you may live."[17]

This understanding leaves the exegete free from the necessity to extend the meaning of חמד.

Nevertheless, Jackson examines the arguments of those bound by this necessity as a result of their assumptions. His examination is instructive. First, he states that deriving the meaning of "to take" for חמד from most instances where it occurs with the complementary verb לקח cannot be done. The "parallelism" posited for such a deduction is lacking.[18] Furthermore, in cases where such parallelism is actually present, the necessary connection cannot be made without confusion of context and meaning.[19] In response to the fact that two texts[20] actually exist which support a more "concrete" meaning for חמד, he states:

> The best that can be said of the interpretation of *hamad* as "to take" is that there is the possibility that the word can bear that meaning in some contexts. That this is the regular meaning of the verb completely fails to proof.[21]

Jackson also critiques the reconstruction of an extended meaning for גנב as represented by Alt.[22] Such a reconstruction becomes a necessity once the extended meaning for חמד is accepted, if redundancy is to be avoided.[23] The argument for

---

15. Jackson, *Essays*, 203. See Jackson also for a brief review of the history of the problem. See the following scholars whose positions align with Jackson: Craigie, *Deuteronomy*, 163; Greenberg, "Decalogue," 108; A. D. H. Mayes, *Deuteronomy*, (Greenwood: Attic, 1979), 172; Moshe Weinfeld, "The Uniqueness of the Decalogue and Its Place in Jewish Tradition," in Levi, ed., *The Ten Commandments*, notes (p. 9) that such a law cannot be enforced and states that "the Hebrew Bible itself does not call the Ten Commandments 'laws,' or even 'commandments'. It calls them 'words.'" He writes (p. 10): "In the light of all this we must conclude that the rules of the Decalogue were understood to be in a different class from the other commandments and statutes in the Torah, such as are subject to the judgments and sanctions of human courts." However, Weinfeld (*Deuteronomy 1–11*, 316) contradicts this statement in his commentary, in which he states that חמד means more than just intention. He writes: "One must admit, however, that in Hebrew and in other Semitic languages, the distinction between cause and effect is sometimes blurred (cf. *pĕʿulāh* 'work', as 'wages' in Lev 19:13 and *hata't* 'sin,' in the sense of product of sin—[golden calf in Deut 9:12], and therefore *hmd* might sometimes connote more than just intention."

16. Jackson, *Essays*, 211. See also Wallis, "חָמַד," 457–58.

17. Jackson, *Essays*, 212–13.

18. Ibid., 204–5.

19. Ibid., 204–5.

20. Ps 68:17 and Exod 24–34. Ibid., 205.

21. Ibid., 206.

22. Alt, *Kleine Schriften*, 335–39; Jackson, *Essays*, 207.

23. Jackson, *Essays*, 207.

the extended meaning rests on two assumptions.[24] The first is that since the sixth and seventh commandments are capital, so also must the eighth commandment be capital. Its capital nature is revealed by the presumed relationship between Exod 21:16 and Deut 5:19. This relationship is the grounds for the assertion that גנב means "kidnapping." Jackson gives a three-part reply to this argument.[25] First, some of the Ten Commandments are not capital. Second, the formal relationship presumed between Exod 21:16 and Deut 5:19 is more distant than is required for the solution to work. Third, no text where the verb גנב stands alone "can be understood to bear" the extended meaning.[26] If the original form of Deut 5:19 was shortened from a form explicitly specifying kidnapping, as Alt presumes, then, according to Jackson, "it must have been realized that a radical alteration in meaning was thereby being effected."[27] Jackson's implication is that such shortening would have been unlikely given the change in meaning that would have necessarily resulted. Jackson's argument is reasonable and convincing.

Furthermore, Weinfeld, citing Ibn Ezra, notes a pattern in the text which supports Jackson's assertion that חמד refers to a mental process:

> Ibn Ezra discerned a gradation in this set of injunctions: first comes murder, which entails destruction of body; second, adultery, which is violating another's body; then comes taking by force another's property; afterward, crime against another's property not by physical force, but by mouth; and finally comes coveting, which is neither by force nor by mouth but through mere intention… [T]here is gradual progress in the order of the last commandments: taking away property by force, causing the taking away of another's property by mouth (bearing witness), and mere coveting of another's property.[28]

This gradation is also reasonable and convincing. If indeed it exists, then the rhetoric of the passage confirms Jackson's understanding even if our sensibilities about the way the ten commandments ought to behave does not. That is, the rhetorical style of the passage "expects" a non-prosecutable infraction in the concluding law.[29]

24. Ibid., 208–9.
25. Ibid., 208–9.
26. Ibid., 208–9.
27. Ibid., 209.
28. Weinfeld, *Deuteronomy 1–11*, 313, 315. The gradation Weinfeld describes misses some important distinctions with respect to the adultery law. He characterizes this law (p. 313), in accordance with Ibn Ezra, as a law prohibiting that "which is violating another's body." However, the fact that נאף is used and the fact that married men are nevertheless free to engage unattached women while the reverse is not so, demonstrates that the law is best characterized as a law prohibiting that "which violates another man's sexual property" not that which violates another's body. Thus, Ibn Ezra's characterization in the gradation of the laws is inaccurate. The gradation works, however, even with his characterization.
29. This understanding, of course, aligns with the current consensus that such laws are in fact some form of legal instruction or "moral precept." See Patrick, *Old Testament Law*, 198–200. See also "Introduction," n. 123 above.

2) *Second Exegetical Problem.* The second exegetical problem concerning חמד
is the separation of the woman from the other properties of v. 21[30] and her
placement in initial position. This configuration has convinced Phillips that she
is equal to the man.[31] Weinfeld reads it as a symptom of Deuteronomy's tendency to protect her rights.[32]

A comparison of the "coveting" law in Exodus with the "coveting" law in
Deuteronomy reveals the source of Phillips' and Weinfeld's conclusions. In
Exod 20:17 חמד is used twice. In the first instance, "house" is the direct object of
חמד. In the second instance, "everything else" the neighbor owns is the direct
object of חמד. In this latter instance, a variety of living, breathing properties are
specifically listed as the direct object of חמד, including the wife. Thus, the wife
is listed as if she is one among several of the husband's properties. Deuteronomy 5, however, uses two different verbs: חמד and אוה. The wife is the single
direct object of חמד. "Everything else" which the neighbor owns is the direct
object of אוה. In this latter list, the following are explicitly specified: house,
field, manservant, maidservant, ox and ass. Phillips has concluded therefore that,
whereas the woman is classed as property in Exod 20, in Deut 5 she is not
classed as property.[33] In fact, she is equal.[34] Weinfeld has concluded that her
rights are being protected.[35]

However, at least one alternative understanding of the separation between
woman and the remaining properties is possible. The separation of the woman
and the use of the two words חמד and אוה may be a function of the sexual component of "desiring" a woman. An entire class of inner moods and mental inclinations accompanies the desire for a woman that does not accompany the desire

---

30.　The textual witnesses diverge both with respect to the placement of the wife and with
respect to the use of חמד and אוה. The MT separates the woman from the other possessions which are
the direct object of אוה. It makes her the direct object of חמד. The Samaritan Pentateuch, in contrast,
follows Exod 20:17, which uses the same verb twice and separates the house from the other
possessions, including the wife. The LXX follows the arrangement of MT but uses the same verb
twice: ἐπιθυμήσεις. The Vulgate places the woman at the top of the list of possessions without
separating her by a second verb. All possessions, including the woman, are governed by the verb
concupisces. Rofé, "Tenth Commandment," 50–51, noting that a manuscript of Deuteronomy from
Qumran Cave IV and two phylacteries from Qumran all use the same verb twice, addresses this
problem as follows (p. 51): "Even though the Masoretic reading has so little support on this point, it
is unlikely that scribes from the fifth century onward would have been so bold as to amend the Ten
Commandments by changing 'covet' to 'crave.' To the extent that they did make emendations, it is
more reasonable to suppose that they tried to bring the text of the Decalogue in Deuteronomy into
line with its primary formulation in Exodus 20. That is what was done in other passages in the
Qumran Cave IV document, and what was attempted in the Nash Papyrus. It may be concluded,
therefore that the Masoretic text of Deuteronomy 5.18, though unsupported by any other sources,
transmits an ancient reading from late pre-exilic or early postexilic times." The same argument
might be applied to the placement and separation of the wife. See Weinfeld, *Deuteronomy 1–11*,
283–84, for an excellent summary of the text-critical problem.

31.　Phillips, *Deuteronomy*, 50.

32.　Weinfeld, *Deuteronomy 1–11*, 317–18.

33.　Phillips, *Deuteronomy*, 50.

34.　Phillips, *Ancient Israel's Criminal Law*, 110; idem, *Deuteronomy*, 50.

35.　Weinfeld, *Deuteronomy 1–11*, 317–18.

for the remaining properties. The separation and the use of the two verbs is a result of this difference. A sexual denotation for חמד or even a sexual connotation in its regular usage is unnecessary for this explanation to hold. In fact, חמד need not have a sexual component in its conceptual matrix at all. The sexual component enters by means of the use of the two different words for "desire," one in connection with the woman and the other in connection with the remaining properties. In other words, the *context* of v. 21 introduces the sexual component. Thus, חמד, in contradistinction to אוה, represents the sexual component present in desiring another man's wife. This sexual component, however, does not nullify the status of the woman's sexuality as property. Her sexuality, as the man's property, has distinction, by way of difference, among his other properties. It may even be more valued than those other properties. But it is property nevertheless.

Furthermore, the initial placement of the woman in Deut 5 follows the order within the commandments themselves. Just as גנב follows נאף, so also do the "remaining properties" follow the wife. The sequence may, conceivably, reflect that her status as property is somewhere between the status of the man and the status of his other properties. This, however, is a status not equal to the status of the man.[36]

3) *Conclusion.* Thus, the meaning of חמד and the arrangement of the clauses in v. 21 do not, in fact, belie the thesis that the primary concern of the sex law is woman's sexuality as property. Nor do they disqualify that thesis as an expectation.

2. *Supporting Signals*

Contrary to the signals of point-of-view and the initial impressions concerning the use of חמד, the use of נאף and the structure of the text demonstrate with clarity that the primary concern of v. 18 is woman's sexuality as the property of the man.

a. נאף. Although several explicit references treat the man and woman equally, and although the masculine verbs and pronominal suffixes implicitly refer to both genders, such inclusive references are entirely lacking in the sex law of v. 18. This verse stands in marked contrast to the inclusiveness which otherwise characterizes the chapter. The conceptual matrix of נאף, of which man is subject and woman object, is responsible.

A consensus exists among scholars that נאף refers to sexual relations with another man's wife.[37] Its use within the Hebrew corpus confirms this consensus

---

36. Ibid., 316. In fact, Weinfeld notes that "the last two prohibitions in the Decalogue correspond to the two commandments of *P tn'p* and *tgnb.*" I accept this correspondence without accepting Weinfeld's extended meaning for חמד. Weinfeld himself presents conflicting statements concerning the extended meaning. See n. 15 above.

37. For example, see the following: Bird, "To Play the Harlot," 77; Cairns, *Deuteronomy*, 77; Fishbane, *Biblical Interpretation*, 169; D. N. Freedman and B. E. Willoughby, "נאף," *ThWAT* 5:124.

view.[38] Of the two other occurrences of נאף in the Pentateuch, Lev 20:10 explicitly forbids sex (נאף) with a neighbor's wife. The other occurrence, in Exod 20:14, a text similar to Deut 5:18, lacks the reference to marriage that is present in Lev 20:10. Nevertheless, occurrences within the Wisdom Books and the Prophets also support the association of נאף with marriage.[39] Since adultery is sex with another man's wife, נאף does not forbid sex between a married man and an unattached female. This means that while a woman must preserve herself exclusively for her husband, the man must simply avoid intrusion on another man's marriage.[40] The woman is the sexual property of the husband while the husband is not the sexual property of the woman.

Women and men are both forbidden from committing adultery (v. 18), whereas men alone are forbidden from coveting their neighbor's wife (v. 21). Nevertheless, just as forbidding a man from "coveting" (either חמד or אוה) protects *another man's property*,[41] so also forbidding a man or a woman from committing adultery protects *another man's property*. If the reader considers "What the law protects," then the two laws are equally non-inclusive. Just as only men are forbidden from coveting, so also only the sexual property of the man is protected.

The point is not trivial. As a result of this feature, in comparison to all the other laws of the chapter, the point-of-view of these two laws (vv. 18 and 21) dramatically shifts in favor of the man.[42] The shift itself demonstrates that the primary concern of the adultery law is protection of the woman's sexuality as property. Thus, Thistlethwaite is correct when she writes: "What is forbidden

---

Frymer-Kensky, "Sex in the Bible," 191; Goodfriend, "Prostitution," 509; Greenberg, "Decalogue," 104; Mayes, *Deuteronomy*, 170; Phillips, *Deuteronomy*, 49; Stamm and Andrew, *Ten Commandments*, 100; Weinfeld, *Deuteronomy 1–11*, 314. נאף is not used simply to prohibit "sexual relationships between two persons, one or both of whom are married to another party or parties," as Craigie (*Deuteronomy*, 160) suggests. The married man is not forbidden to have sexual relations with unattached women by prohibitions using נאף.

38. See the discussion of Lev 20 above.

39. See the discussion of Lev 20 above.

40. William Johnstone, "The 'Ten Commandments': Some Recent Interpretations," *ExpTim* 100 (1988/89): 456, writes: "In the Hebrew Bible, while, by adultery, the wife destroys her own marriage, the husband addressed here, destroys the marriage of his neighbour (polygyny is permitted)." Neufeld, *Ancient Hebrew Marriage Laws*, 163, states: "As in other Semitic legal systems, Hebrew law imposes no restraints on the husband in the sphere of extra-marital intercourse, which was not regarded as adulterous. A man cannot sin against his own wife, as his wife has no proprietary rights as against him which he can infringe. Accordingly the adulterous conduct of a Hebrew man must refer exclusively to the case of a man having intercourse with another man's wife or betrothed, the offence being thus interference with that man's property."

41. Woman is not included as responsible to the law of v. 21, on the other hand, because a woman coveting another woman is of no consequence that matters to the author. See the footnotes concerning lesbianism in discussions of Lev 18 and 20 above.

42. All other laws of the chapter require the man and woman to maintain behavioral standards that protect both man and woman in the same way. For example, presumably honoring parents will lengthen the days of both men and women, while "not committing adultery" and "not coveting a man's wife" protect the man's property exclusively.

in the Decalogue is the control of someone else's sexual property, i.e. adultery."[43]

Several scholars have stated that the primary concern of v. 18 is not only to protect the property of the man, but also to preserve the family and protect the progeny. However, while such values may *motivate* the law, they are not its express *intent*.[44] The intent is exclusively to protect male sexual property.

The sex law thus stands in stark contrast to the inclusiveness exhibited by significant features of point-of-view. Thus, objectification is unmitigated while woman's marginalization is comparatively ameliorated.

b. *Structure.* The structure of Deut 5 also supports the assertion that the primary concern of v. 18 is to protect the sexual property of the man. A highly collapsed version of the structure follows:

I. Introduction	5:1aα
II. Moses Speech to All Israel	5:1aβ–26:19
A. Adjuration and Theophany	1aβ–31
1. Adjuration Proper	1aβ–1b
2. History	2–31
a. basic statement: covenant	2–3
b. detailed statement: theophany	4–31
1) character positions	4–5bβ₁
a) Yhwh and Israel	4
b) Moses	5aα–5bβ₁
2) Yhwh speech to Israel's Assembly	5bβ₂–31
a) speech	5bβ₂–22
(1) introduction: לאמר	5bβ₂
(2) speech proper	6–21
(a) identification of speaker	6
(b) commands	7–21
α. honor God, Sabbath, parents	7–16
β. protection of property	17–21
1a. kill	17
2a. adultery	18
3a. steal	19
4a. false witness	20
5a. desire (חמד)	21a
6a. covet (אוה)	21b
(3) mode of delivery	22
(a) Yhwh spoke	22a
(b) Yhwh wrote	22b
b) Responses	23–31
(1) Israel's response	23–27
(2) Yhwh's response	28–31
A. Adjuration and Other Gods	5:32–11:7
B. Adjuration and Future Choices	11:8–26:19

---

43. Thistlethwaite, "You May Enjoy," 72.

44. See the distinction made between motivation and intention in the "Introduction" above.

Verse 18 is embedded in a "Yhwh Speech to Israel's Assembly." That speech is relayed by Moses in a "Moses Speech to 'All Israel.'" The "commands" of the Yhwh speech divide into two parts. The sex text occurs in the second part. Weinfeld describes some of the significant distinctions between the two parts:

> In contradistinction to the first pentad, where "YHWH (your God)" appears in each commandment, the second pentad does not contain the Tetragrammaton at all. In the second pentad one finds commandments of a moral nature that appeal to the human being as such (see the INTRODUCTION to the Decalogue) and not just to the Israelite people. The Deuteronomic version of the Decalogue enhances the uniformity of the second pentad by making it, as it were, one sentence: "You shall not murder *and* not commit adultery *and* not steal *and* not bear false witness...*and* not covet."[45]

The first section consists of a group of associations—honoring God, keeping the Sabbath and honoring parents—similar to those that occur in Lev 19 and 20.[46] The second section, on the other hand, guards against the removal of one's life, a man's wife, one's material possessions and one's reputation. These are all forms of property. As was noted previously, the adultery law sandwiches between the law on murder and stealing.[47] Murder takes the most important, most essential possession of a man: his life. Stealing takes less essential material possessions. Adultery takes something in between murder and stealing: a man's wife. Furthermore, the law takes so seriously the protection of wife and material possessions that it forbids the mental/emotional act which precedes their theft by adultery, stealing or other means.

The section within which v. 18 stands thus concerns protection of property. The placement of v. 18 supports the assertion that the primary concern of the adultery law is to protect the man's sexual property.

C. *Conclusion*

Classificatory concerns are left aside to maintain the single focus on protection of woman's sexuality as property.

Nevertheless, woman, who also stands before Moses as he speaks, is responsible to the law just as the man is responsible. She is moral agent. She is expected to protect the man's sexual property, which, in this case, happens to be coterminous with her body. The burden placed upon her agency is more stringent than upon the man, who need not guard his body with respect to unattached women.

---

45. Weinfeld, *Deuteronomy 1–11*, 313; idem, "Uniqueness," 11; Mayes, "Deuteronomy 5," 75–76.

46. See the discussions of Lev 19 and 20 above.

47. The textual witnesses diverge with respect to the order of these three commandments. While the textual problem is significant as far as text problems go, it is unimportant for our purposes, since the gradation does not depend upon that order. The gradation does, however, happen to coincide with the order of the MT, lending support to its status as the best reading. See the following for summaries and a variety of critiques of and solutions to the textual problems: Richard A. Freund, "Murder, Adultery and Theft," *SJOT* 2 (1989): 72–80; Goodfriend, "Adultery," 82b; Mayes, *Deuteronomy*, 170; Weinfeld, "Uniqueness," 7 n. 22; idem, *Deuteronomy 1–11*, 282–83, 313.

Thus, although woman's marginalization is mitigated, her objectification is not. She is an implicit addressee who accrues a semblance of agency from that feature of the text. But she is focalized, unquestionably, as property. The text's primary concern is protection of her sexuality as property of the man.

Chapter 9

DEUTERONOMY 21:10–14

A. *Introduction*

Deuteronomy 21:10–14 regulates special circumstances concerning marriage rather than sexual intercourse per se. Its primary concern is to facilitate the acquisition[1] as well as the subsequent contingent disposal of a woman as wife from the community of the enemy during wartime, for the express purpose of the use of that woman's sexuality in the production of progeny. Since the law stipulates sexual access to the woman as one component of the procedure which establishes her as wife, I have included it among the sex texts of Deuteronomy.

The law of Deut 21:10–14 assumes the man's right to the captive woman's sexuality and utilizes that right to complete her transformation from female enemy captive to Israelite wife. Once she becomes his wife, the law guarantees the man's right to dispose of her. The law's primary interest is to protect the male captor's right to acquire, marry and dispose of the female captive, for the purpose of the production of progeny. The law presumes, however, that the status of a wife-in-Israel can be lowered only so far. It therefore limits the manner of the captor-turned-husband's disposal. Although this limitation protects the status of the female-captive-turned-Israelite-wife, the law treats the female captive and the female-captive-turned-Israelite-wife, including their sexuality, as the exclusive property of the male captor. Furthermore, the law's interest in the woman's sexuality is a property interest. Her sexuality is an object of ownership. It is also an instrument which establishes ownership. As such, the woman is focalized as property.

B. *Discussion*

1. *The Signals*
a. *Point-of-View.* The author of the law establishes point-of-view by addressing the male Israelite warrior directly with second person verbal and pronominal forms. The conversation between the male author and the male Israelite community is overtly exclusive. The law refers to the woman by the exclusive use of

---

1. Frymer-Kensky, "Deuteronomy," 55.

third person forms.² Any regulation which applies to her is thus mediated through the male warrior. Although nearly the entire conversation between men concerns matters pertaining to her, she recedes to the background of the text. Point-of-view thus marginalizes the woman in the text. This marginalization is somewhat ameliorated by the fact that she has minimal responsibilities during the mourning ritual, which she is *forced* to exercise. More importantly, however, that amelioration is demonstrated by the fact that she has certain minimal rights once she has been "raped" and has been made an Israelite wife.

b. *Language-Depicting-the-Sex-Act.* While point-of-view marginalizes, language-depicting-the-sex-act objectifies. The language-depicting-the-sex-act occurs within a single clause, v. 13bβ₁: תָּבוֹא אֵלֶיהָ.³ The verbal root בוא depicts the sex act⁴ in one of two ways; either it directly signifies the physical entry of the man into the woman during the sex act, or, more likely, it signifies the sex act by metonymy or perhaps synecdoche, since one of the components either associated with or constituting the process of sexual intercourse is to "enter" the tent or room or space of the woman; and since, on occasion in the Hebrew corpus, the בוא phrase occurs in conjunction with a second phrase which less ambiguously denotes sexual intercourse.⁵

While the clause "you shall go into/to her" in Deut 21:13 may signify only the man's approach and not the sex act per se, a variety of signals indicate that, in fact, it signifies the sex act.⁶ 13bβ₁ precedes two additional clauses: "he lords over her" and "she becomes his wife." Sexual intercourse is an essential com-

---

2. Change of person is a function of point-of-view rather than redaction, as Merindino suggests. See Rosario Pius Merendino, *Das Deuteronomische Gesetz* (Bonn: Peter Hanstein, 1969), 243. See also Mayes, *Deuteronomy*, 301; Pressler, *View of Women*, 10.

3. Although sexual connotations are not entirely absent from its signification, the root בעל, in both nominal and verbal forms, denotes marriage rather than sex per se. See Gen 20:3; Exod 21:3, 22; Deut 22:22; 24:1, 4; 2 Sam 11:26; Isa 54:1; Esth 1:17, 20; Prov 12:4; 30:23; 31:11, 23, 28. See the following: Wegner, *Chattel*, 13; Roland de Vaux, *Ancient Israel*, vol. 1 (New York: McGraw-Hill, 1965), 26; Greenberg, "Female," 9; Neufeld, *Ancient Hebrew Marriage Laws*, 142, 232; David R. Mace, *Hebrew Marriage* (New York: Philosophical Library, 1953), 193–94; Pedersen, *Israel*, 62–63. For the use of לקח in this passage, see the discussion below under "structure."

4. Wenham, "*Bᵉtûlāh*," 331. Horst Dietrich Preuss, "בוא," *TDOT* 2:21. Landsberger, "Jungfraü-lichkeit," 41–42. Driver and Miles (*Babylonian Laws*, 322), commenting on Babylonian Law, state that marriage is not completed until sexual intercourse takes place. See Neufeld, *Ancient Hebrew Marriage Laws*, 89–93, especially p. 89 n. 1 and p. 90. Neufeld calls this *Biāh* marriage.

5. See Gen 39:14 and perhaps 2 Sam 12:24, for example. Three times in the Hebrew corpus the woman herself is the subject of בוא in conjunction with an ancillary clause depicting the sex act. In one of these ancillary clauses, man is the subject, and in the ancillary clauses of the other two examples, the woman is the subject; see 2 Sam 11:4; Gen 19:33 and 34, respectively. In all three cases the sex acts are illicit. For the most part, בוא is used alone, without accompanying clauses, to depict the sex act—as, for example, in Deut 21:10–14. As a metonymic representation, בוא is slightly more distant from the sex act than the metonymic of שכב or גלה ערוה, for example. That is, in the sequence of events which constitute the total process of sexual intercourse, its metonymy is more distant from the act of physical union than the other designations. As a literal representation, however, it is the closest, most graphic portrayal of the sex act.

6. Wenham, "*Bᵉtûlāh*," 331.

ponent of the relationships which both latter clauses represent. Moreover, the warrior has selected this woman because she is "fair of form," not because she cooks, cleans or weaves well. The sexual undercurrent of the text is established already within the protasis. Because of these signals, we are compelled to read בוא as signifying the sex act.

Woman is the object of בוא and man is the subject. This same alignment continues throughout the law's description of the interaction, sexual or otherwise, between the man and woman. Only when the woman is by herself, performing actions pertaining to herself, is she the subject.[7]

Language-depicting-the-sex-act thus objectifies the woman.

c. *Structure.* The gender biases of the structure coincide with the biases of language-depicting-the-sex-act and point-of-view. The structure demonstrates that the woman is at the disposal of the man, even to the extent of legitimizing an act which according to our twenty-first-century, Western understanding is called rape. The structure focalizes the woman and her sexuality as property of the man.

1) *The Context.* Women are the focus of at least two laws in ch. 21. Verses 10–14 deal with the captive-woman-turned-Israelite-wife. Verses 15–17 treat issues concerning the inheritance of the sons of two wives. They occur within a series of laws generated by means of key words and topics as described by Tigay.[8] Braulik has suggested that Deut 21:1–23 "assembles some rather different laws under the theme of premature death."[9] From the topic of war, in ch. 20, in which men kill without an accounting of who kills whom, the author moves to the topic of a single death, for which an accounting is also lacking. From the subject of the spilling of blood in these two scenarios, the author moves to the subject of the acquisition of a woman who no longer belongs to any man, because the blood of the men to whom she did belong has been spilled. From acquisition of the female captive as wife, the author moves to the subject of wives. From the subject of the inheritance of the sons of two wives, he moves to the subject of sons. From the subject of the son who commits a crime punishable by death, he moves to the subject of crimes punishable by death.

Because it operates consistently throughout the two chapters, generation of the text by means of key words and topics provides a more satisfying accounting

---

7. Pressler, *View of Women*, 15. The LXX, however, seems to present the man as loosening her hair, pairing her nails and removing her mantel, since three of the verbs in the preliminary and mourning rites are second person singular: ξυρήσεις, περιονυχιεῖς, περιελεῖς. 11QTemple 63, 12–13 unequivocally places the man in subject position. It has second person masculine, singular verbs: והסירותה, ועשיתה, וגלחתה. See Yigael Yadin, ed., *The Temple Scroll* (3 vols.; Jerusalem: Israel Exploration Society, 1983), 1:364, 2:286, 3:plate 78.

8. See the comments above in the discussion of Lev 20. See also Tigay, "Some Principles," 12; idem, *Deuteronomy*, 449–51.

9. Georg Braulik, "The Sequence of the Laws in Deuteronomy 12–26 and in the Decalogue," in Christensen, ed., *A Song of Power*, 328.

of the separation of vv. 10–14 from ch. 20 than redaction.[10] Thus, the author has intentionally[11] placed the law of the captive bride between laws concerning war and laws concerning wives.

2) *The Structure Proper.* Deuteronomy 21:10–14 is one of several casuistic laws within the context of ch. 21. It consists of a protasis and an apodosis as follows:

I.	Protasis	21:10–11
A.	General Scenario	10
1.	go to battle	10a
2.	win	10b
a.	Yhwh gives	10bα
b.	take captives	10bβ
B.	Specific Scenario	11
1.	see	11a
2.	desire	11bα
3.	take	11bβ
II.	Apodosis	12–14
A.	Acquisition Procedure	12–13
1.	preparation	12–13a
a.	what the man does	12a
b.	what the woman does	12b–13a
2.	completion	13b
a.	time	13bα
b.	action	$13b\beta_{1-3}$
1)	you go	$13b\beta_1$
2)	you master	$13b\beta_2$
3)	she becomes	$13b\beta_3$
B.	Negative Contingency	14
1.	protasis	14aα
2.	apodosis	14aβ–b
a.	stated positively	14aβ
b.	stated negatively	14aγ–b
1)	specific	14aγ
2)	general	14b

The protasis, vv. 10–11, describes a scenario in which a man goes to battle, sees a beautiful woman and selects (לקח)[12] her from among the captives with the purpose of making her his wife. The apodosis consists of vv. 12–14.

a) *Pressler.* Pressler has stated that dividing the protasis and the apodosis between vv. 11 and 12 is unacceptable, since such a division makes it appear that the man marries the woman twice:[13] "If a man...marries (לקח), then a

---

10. The following scholars suggest redaction: Cairns, *Deuteronomy*, 189; S. R. Driver, *Deuteronomy* (New York: Charles Scribner's Sons, 1906), 244; Mayes, *Deuteronomy*, 301; von Rad, *Deuteronomy*, 137.

11. G. J. Wenham and J. G. McConville, "Drafting Techniques in Some Deuteronomic Laws," *VT* 30 (1979): 251, have discovered a chiastic pattern in the text which underscores the deliberate nature of the arrangement.

12. Wegner, *Chattel*, 227 n. 84.

13. Pressler, *View of Women*, 10.

man…shall marry (בעל).” Furthermore, she takes the change in person at v. 12b to be structurally significant.[14] Pressler's conclusions depend upon her understanding of v. 11bβ (וּלְקַחְתָּ לְךָ לְאִשָּׁה) and upon her understanding of the significance of the change in person.[15] A reconsideration of both features, however, leads to a different conclusion.

If the apodosis begins with v. 12, v. 11bβ does not, as Pressler suggests, necessarily describe the immediate consummation of the procedure by which the woman becomes a wife.[16] Verse 11bβ may be read as describing the general act of removing or selecting a woman from among the captives for the intended purpose of making her a wife. The apodosis, extending from v. 12 through v. 14, then describes the procedure that must transpire for the fulfillment of the intended purpose. Pressler's understanding of v. 11bβ is thus not necessary.

Furthermore, the first specification in the description of the procedure for making a captive a wife supports the division between v. 11 and v. 12 as follows. The specification states that the man is to take the woman to his house, a specific locale. This locale is removed from the battlefield. It is within the community of Israel, removed from the public sphere of that community. It is an arena of privacy—namely, the home of the man who desires the woman. It is the place where the woman transforms from captive to wife. The specification of locale is not, as Pressler suggests, part of the conditions of the protasis.[17] Rather, it is part of the instructions for the transformation procedure, as the Masoretes understood it to be. This specification thus belongs with the apodosis.

While Pressler's conclusion is correct that "the switch from direct address to third person may indicate that the warrior addressed is responsible for seeing that the woman's actions are carried out,"[18] her understanding of the significance of this switch for the structure is incorrect. The transformation procedure is not contingent upon the man's bringing the woman to his house in addition to other actions listed in the protasis. Rather, it is contingent upon only his desire for and selection of the woman from among the captives with the intention of making her his wife. The switch in person is a function of point-of-view and is not a constitutive signal for the structure.

b) *Verse 13bβ*. The clause depicting the sex act is thus one among several acts within a transformation procedure that makes the woman a wife.[19] The man brings her to his house. She prepares her body and she mourns. The man completes the process with a sexual act by which he becomes her husband and she his wife.

The three clauses 13bβ$_{1,2 \text{ and } 3}$ read one of two ways. The sexual act might be seen as the final component in the final phase of the procedure. Clauses 13bβ$_2$

14. Ibid., 10.
15. Ibid., 10.
16. Ibid., 10.
17. Ibid., 10.
18. Ibid., 10.
19. Washington, "Lest He Die," 205.

and 13bβ₃ are then appositional to one another. They describe the new status that transpires because of the act described in 13bβ₁. Alternatively, the clauses might be read as describing two additional steps, instead of one, in the procedure: (1) you shall go into her and (2) you shall marry her and she shall be for you as a wife. In the latter instance, 13bβ₂ and 13bβ₃ qualify one another.[20] With either reading, the woman is transformed with respect to status, with respect to nationality, and with respect to familial association by a sexual act within a well-defined and limited context.[21] The transformation is effected upon her.

Washington suggests that waiting a full month, one complete menstrual cycle, assures the man that the progeny is his own.[22] The guiding principle of this procedure, then, is not to effect a helpful adjustment for the woman. Rather it is the production of *legitimate* progeny.[23] The entire procedure prepares for the scenario in which progeny might be produced and fostered properly, so that the child might serve a legitimate and fitting purpose in Israel. The woman moves from the property status of a war-captive/slave and enters the status of a wife,[24] whose sexuality serves her husband's need for *legitimate* progeny.

The structure thus focalizes the woman and her sexuality as property.

2. *The Concern of the Law*

We, in the twenty-first-century Western world, call the instrumentation of sex, in 13bβ₁, serving the woman's transformation, rape. The category of rape, however, is absent from the law of Deut 21:10–14. In fact, the law has no concern for sex per se, beyond the function of sex as a source of motivation for the woman's selection and as instrumentation for her transformation for the sake of the production of *legitimate* progeny. The instance of the instrumented sex of the law may or may not yield that progeny, but it will most certainly yield the transformation—and *that* is the primary interest of the law. The law assumes, without reflection, that such instrumentation is legitimate.

Nevertheless, some scholars understand this law as placing restraints on male sexual activity in consideration of the female captive. A few scholars have even suggested that the law intends to prohibit rape. Niditch, whose position falls outside these two groups, nevertheless, shares their contention that restraints placed by the law pertain to sexual activity.[25] While the two previous groups contend that the law limits, to varying degrees, sexual activity with the female captive, Niditch contends that the law in some way judges the sexual activity of 13bβ₁.

20. Neufeld, *Ancient Hebrew Marriage Laws*, 90.

21. Ibid., 91.

22. Washington, ' "Lest He Die," ' 206, asks: "And why the unusual designation for the period, ירח ימים, rather than the expected יום שלשים? An obvious solution is that by waiting a 'full month,' that is long enough for the woman's menstrual cycle to be completed, the man is assured his paternity of any children resulting from intercourse with her."

23. Westbrook, "Female Slave," 221–22. See Westbrook's interesting observations on legitimate/illegitimate children in cuneiform law.

24. Ibid., 235, states: "There is no question of slave concubinage here; the text explicitly refers to the formation of marriage and to its termination by divorce."

25. Susan Niditch, "War, Woman, and Defilement in Numbers 31," *Semeia* 61 (1993): 50.

a. *Contrary Opinion: Sex Is the Concern.*
1) *Placement of Restraints.* Those scholars who see the law as placing restraints on the male warrior, in favorable consideration of the woman, imply that the ritual that leads to the consummation of marriage, or that the marriage itself, in some way protects or serves her welfare.[26] Pressler explicitly raises the question as follows:

> It is not possible to say whether Deut 21:10–13 had yet a third purpose, that is, to protect the captive woman by providing her with marital status. Presumably male and female captives were brought back to serve as slaves.[27]

Otto takes a more extreme position:

> This provision surely did not present the right opportunity to overthrow the patriarchal features of society, since it was intended to protect the most vulnerable women. But compared with the average and usual treatment of captive women in antiquity this provision in Deut 21.10–14 was a moral revolution on the long road towards equal dignity and rights of men and women.[28]

Otto's point is that, w*ithin the ancient context,* this law may have been an improvement. If Westbrook's observations on cuneiform slave laws can be taken to suggest a range of possible social configurations implicit in the world that generated the Hebrew text, then we might say that this female captive of war is, oddly enough, given the highest status out of the range of statuses available, and that Otto is, in some sense, right.[29] The question is: Why is the woman given this highest possible status? The answer is that the procedure, ending in marriage to a war captive, serves the production of *legitimate* progeny for the male captor.

Israelite men cannot produce *legitimate* progeny willy-nilly by sexually forcing foreign women taken in war.[30] Legitimate progeny require something

---

26.   Cairns, *Deuteronomy*, 189; Calum M. Carmichael, *Women, Law and the Genesis Tradition* (Edinburgh: Edinburgh University Press, 1979), 23; Driver, *Deuteronomy*, 244; Miller, *Deuteronomy*, 159; Tigay, *Deuteronomy*, 194; von Rad, *Deuteronomy*, 137; Michael Walzer, *Just and Unjust Wars* (New York: Basic, 1977), 135; Weinfeld, *Deuteronomy*, 239. See also Richard Clifford, *Deuteronomy* (Wilmington, Del.: Michael Glazier, 1982), 112–13, who suggests that while the case of the law is that of the male, the perspective is that of the woman. However, a more accurate description is that the point-of-view is a male's point-of-view, and that limited consideration, subject to narrow constraints, is given to the woman.

27.   Pressler, *View of Women*, 13.

28.   Eckart Otto, "False Weights in the Scales of Biblical Justice? Different Views of Women from Patriarchal Hierarchy to Religious Equality in the Book of Deuteronomy," in Matthews, Levinson and Frymer-Kensky, eds., *Gender and Law in the Hebrew Bible*, 145.

29.   Westbrook, "Female Slave," 214–38. Otto's observation ("False Weights?"), of course, while it may not be the kind of discourse that "liberates," does not dispute the horror that is worked upon the captive by the slaughter of her kin, including the men to whom she belongs, by appropriation and disposal of her body at the whim of her captor, and by the utilization of her sexuality for the production of progeny.

30.   Ibid., 220–23. See Westbrook's discussion of the status of offspring, with respect to concubinage and marriage in ancient Near Eastern law. That the status of "wife" is essential to the legitimation of offspring is evident by Westbrook's remark concerning HL 31 (p. 228): "It is neces-

more. The procedure of the law manufactures the setting which delivers that "something more." Westbrook states the following:

> ...I consider that in ancient Near Eastern law a man could not be master and husband at the same time because of the conflicting logic of the two institutions. The purpose of marriage is to produce legitimate offspring who can inherit from their father, if there is anything to inherit. Children begotten upon a slave are the fruits of their father's property. As such, they are not capable of inheriting from him; rather, they are part of his estate, to be inherited by his legitimate heirs. Even if it were conceded that by a special rule the children were free while their mother was not, the logic of the law would still produce absurd consequences: on the father's death, the children would inherit their own mother as a slave.[31]

If this law, *within the ancient setting*, in any way "improves" upon the condition of a woman-captive of war, that improvement is only an *effect* ancillary to the main purpose of the entire procedure, namely, the production and legitimization of progeny, which the woman is undeniably forced to render to her captor.[32] If this is in "favor" of the woman, then it is in favor only because it enables her to give the male captor what he wants and needs. The favor is aimed at progeny.

It might be suggested that the entire arrangement enables her to achieve the destiny which "necessarily" belongs to a woman in the ancient Near East: production of progeny. She is already a captive of war. It makes the best of a bad situation. It might even be said that the empathy of the law for the woman shows up in the use of the word וּבְכְתָה. She is allowed to weep for her mother and father. The procedure recognizes her loss. Furthermore, it cannot be denied that under the contingency of rejection, the law protects the woman from slavery.[33] In these ways the law might be said to show consideration for her.

A twenty-first-century critique is, of course, unknown to the law. The law presumes the legitimacy of the killing of the males of her family;[34] it presumes that her life belongs to the male warrior regardless of her own desires or predilections;[35] it denies her capacity to control her own sexuality;[36] and it provides for her disposal.[37] Nevertheless, any favorable consideration for the woman in

---

sary that the slave achieve the status of wife and not merely concubine, because the purpose is to provide legitimate offspring, primarily for the husband and secondarily for the first wife."

31. Ibid., 234.

32. See Washington, ' "Lest He Die," ' 206; Westbrook, "Female Slave," 220–23. Washington's observations concerning the waiting period and Westbrook's observations concerning the status of offspring support this conclusion.

33. See Cairns, *Deuteronomy*, 190. Phillips, *Deuteronomy*, 140–41, takes this as an example of the "deuteronomic humanitarian outlook." See Pressler's critique of these kinds of statements from Phillips and others (*View of Women*, 105–11).

34. Certainly the ancient context would have understood this as a "lack of consideration," even if it couldn't be helped.

35. This critique may not have been understood in the ancient context as a "lack of consideration."

36. This critique most certainly would not have been understood in the ancient setting as "lack of consideration."

37. The provisions of the law demonstrate that the ancient setting understood this as "lack of consideration."

the law is contextualized by the "violence of war," and that conceptuality, with its horrors *for the Israelite woman* as well as for the Israelite man, is in all likelihood known to the world of the text. For this reason and from *this* place, the law can be critiqued on its own grounds.

For example, Deut 28:30 applies the scenario of plunder, conjuring in its literary context the horrors of war. The betrothed Israelite woman is violently taken, as the result of a curse against the Israelite man who disobeys Yhwh.[38] The text is addressed to the Israelite man. The plunder of his wife is a horror for him. To surmise, however, that the constructor of the text could not have imagined the horror of such a scenario for the *Israelite woman* reaches in the direction of implausibility. Even with its gender biases, the text implicitly evokes the horror *for the Israelite woman who is plundered*, as well as for the Israelite man who is the victim of the plundering. If the conceptual category of "plunder" can evoke the experience of horror *for their own women*, even with that conceptual category's gender biases, then surely Israelite men, specifically the constructors of the discourse, can imagine the existence of such a conceptuality and experience for the captive foreign woman.[39] If they/he can imagine this, then, on some level, the text can be critiqued *within its own world*, despite the obvious dismissal of "woman's horror" as a category of significance for male discourse.[40]

38. See the discussion of Deut 28:30 below.

39. Contrary to Clifford, *Deuteronomy*, 112–13; Miller, *Deuteronomy*, 159; Tigay, *Deuteronomy*, 194. The *ancient context* itself would have recognized production of progeny for the enemy to be an eclipse of the woman's "welfare," or at least an eclipse of her happiness, even if this law does not attest to that recognition, and even if her cultural subjugation as a form of abuse remains unrecognized. The ancient context would have configured her identity, integrity and personhood differently from twenty-first-century configurations. Nevertheless, the captors of the text would have recognized the woman's situation as signifying the capstone of violence against the community from which she comes, in particular against the men, now dead, through whom her welfare, duty and destiny would have transpired. They would have considered her plight irrelevant, but they would have understood it. The warrior takes her sexuality, which admittedly never belonged to her in the first place, and uses it to take something from "her" men: their potential progeny. See Brenner, *The Intercourse of Knowledge*, 138, who states: " 'Rape' of females and males in the HB, each in its own way, signifies an attempt to enforce or regulate social hierarchy among males by means of sexual activity." See also Sandie Gravett, "Reading 'Rape' in the Hebrew Bible: A Consideration of Language," *JSOT* 28 (2004): 280; Carolyn Pressler, "Sexual Violence and Deuteronomic Law," in Brenner, ed., *A Feminist Companion to Exodus to Deuteronomy*, 103; F. Rachel Magdalene, "Ancient Near Eastern Treaty-Curses and the Ultimate Texts of Terror: A Study of the Language of Divine Sexual Abuse in the Prophetic Corpus," in *A Feminist Companion to the Latter Prophets* (ed. Athalya Brenner; FCB 8; Sheffield: Sheffield Academic Press, 1995), 338. The ancient context with respect to this scenario, of course, would have understood the violence to be "fair" or just. After all, the Israelite warrior won the war with the help of Yhwh no less. However, in this qualified respect, the *ancient world of the text and its author* would have understood the woman's agony and the acts against her as agonizing, precisely because she came from the defeated community where she and her sexuality belonged to *other* men, and precisely because the victors could imagine the same thing happening to themselves and to the women they themselves owned, as per Deut 28:30. On these grounds, which are its own, the *ancient context* can be critiqued, "prior" to a critical stance from our own world.

40. At this point, an entire conceptual matrix, supporting the production of identity, "insider" and "outsider," and the moral agglutinations subsumed within it, suggests itself.

The procedure of the law, including the mourning period *in that ancient context*, is not prescribed in favorable consideration of her. Rather, it is a necessary step in the process of the assimilation of someone stripped of her identity and expected to function eventually as an Israelite wife.[41] It is an astute facilitation of her transformation, recognizing that the transformation cannot be complete without her physical and heart-felt release of the place from which she comes. Legitimate, wholesome progeny require it. The procedure expects her *to get over it*, in one month's time, according to the cycle of the moon. It preserves, first of all, the welfare of the Israelite warrior and the progeny he will beget on the woman. She may be "fair of form," but she is, first of all, for breeding, not pleasure. The law prepares for that breeding. The captor may have selected her because of sexual desire, but he marries her for the legitimation of progeny. He makes her sexuality his own. Her welfare beyond that purpose is incidental to this law.

Any restraints upon the male captor serve that purpose.

2) *Prohibition of Rape.* Some commentators identify the concern of the law more narrowly than the preceding group. They explicitly state that the law actually prohibits rape.[42]

Although the error of this position is so obvious as to make a critique seem trivial, their position, perhaps, contains a kernel of truth. The warrior, in fact, rapes the woman.[43] Provision for consent or dissent is lacking. The law does not prohibit rape.[44] However, while this is true, neither does the law "self con-

---

41. Pressler, *View of Women*, 12–13. Since the three bodily rituals are separated from and precede the mourning period in the text, Pressler concludes that they pertain to something other than mourning. She suggests that removal of the garment of captivity is symbolic of the removal of the status of captivity. The use of נלה for "to shave" indicates that this is a purification rather than a mourning ritual. Niditch, "War," 50, calls it a "rite of passage." Most certainly, the three rituals as well as the mourning period are transformative instruments which facilitate assimilation of the female enemy captive to her new community, elevation of her status to Israelite wife, and integration into a new familial setting. See also the following: Cairns, *Deuteronomy*, 189; Craigie, *Deuteronomy*, 281; Earl S. Kalland, "Deuteronomy," in *The Expositor's Bible Commentary*, vol. 3 (ed. Frank E. Gaebelein et al.; Grand Rapids: Zondervan, 1992), 132; Mayes, *Deuteronomy*, 303; Phillips, *Deuteronomy*, 140; Tigay, *Deuteronomy*. 194.

42. See Richard Elliott Friedman, *Who Wrote the Bible?* (New York: Harper & Row, 1987), 30; Kalland, "Deuteronomy," 132; Miller, *Deuteronomy*, 159; Alexander Rofé, "The Laws of Warfare in the Book of Deuteronomy: Their Origins, Intent and Positivity," *JSOT* 32 (1985): 30.

43. Washington, ' "Lest He Die,' " 205, states: "The provision for treatment of the war-captive woman can be viewed as a prohibition of rape only under the premise that women possess no personhood or bodily integrity apart from the determination of men. The fact that the man must wait for a month before penetrating the woman (ואחר כן תבוא אליה, 21.13) does not make the sexual relationship something other than rape, unless one assumes that by the end of the period the woman has consented. Commentators sometimes entertain this notion, perhaps evoking the familiar psychological phenomenon of a captive's identification with her captor. But to assume the consent of the woman is to erase her personhood. Only in the most masculinist of readings does the month-long waiting period give a satisfactory veneer of peaceful domesticity to a sequence of defeat, bereavement, and rape."

44. Pressler, *View of Women*, 11, states: "Commentators frequently understand the purpose of this law as a prohibition against rape in the battlefield. It is unlikely that this was the aim of the law.

sciously" legitimize rape.[45] While the law legitimizes the sex act as instrumentation for transformation, the law does not understand that the woman has been raped.[46] We call it rape. The law does not. Simply put, the law is not "self-aware" at all with respect to the category of rape.[47]

We have argued that the law should not be translated to read: 'If you desire her, then you shall marry her.' Rather, the man's desire to marry the woman is part of the protasis. The law has to do with a case where a man wishes to marry a foreign captive; it then provides a means for him to do so. Moreover, the law is concerned with what happens within the household, not what happens on the battlefield. All of the actions commanded by the law take place within the household. Finally, such a prohibition would not be in keeping with the tenor of Deut 20:14 which instructs the soldiers to plunder the wives and children of their enemies: 'Devour the spoil of your enemies.'" Pressler ties her interpretation to her understanding of the structure in which the protasis and apodosis separate between v. 12a and v. 12b. However, the same conclusion concerning the intent of the law is possible with the division occurring between vv. 11 and 12, as described above.

45.   Washington, '"Lest He Die,'" 187, states: "I propose that the laws are productive of violence: they render warfare and rape intelligible and acceptable, providing a means for people both to justify and endure violence." That the law lacks the "modern" conceptual matrix constituted by the concepts of force, consent, and a female's right to disposal of her own sexuality, among other concepts does not gainsay Washington's contention (ibid., 213) that this law and others like it are a "discourse of male power," which "far from ameliorating male domination...install it and circulate its force"—a contention with which I fully agree.

46.   For a discussion of עָנָה, see below.

47.   This concept is now well understood in scholarly circles and need not be overly argued here. See, for example, the following small sample of scholarly comments. Pressler, "Sexual Violence," 103, states: "Indeed, in the Deuteronomic law, the offense is not against the woman at all. As is widely recognized, Deuteronomic law (in common with most biblical and ancient Near Eastern texts) views female sexuality and reproductive capacity as a male possession. A woman's sexuality belongs first to her father, then later, to her husband. Violation of her sexuality is in the first place an offense against her father or husband's claims. The nature and gravity of the offense are determined by which male's claims are being violated. The offense is not 'rape' according to the modern definitions of that term... An examination of the Deuteronomic laws treating forcible violation of women leads to a sobering conclusion: these texts do what rape does. They eliminate women's will from consideration and erase women's right to sexual integrity." Brenner, *The Intercourse of Knowledge*, 136, states: "The [modern] concept of 'rape,' as defined in western legal systems, is non-existent in biblical language as we have it... Biblical literature, be it narrative or prescriptive, lacks not only a specific term for 'rape' but also a conceptual reference to it. Some of the terms employed are gender-specific and others are not. At any rate, none of them corresponds fully to the western category of 'rape.'" Alice A. Keefe, "Rapes of Women/Wars of Men," in *Women, War, and Metaphor: Language and Society in the Study of the Hebrew Bible* (ed. Claudia V. Camp and Carole F. Fontaine; Semeia 61; Atlanta: Society of Biblical Literature, 1993), 79, states: "But while the ideologies which undergird rape's permissibility in our own time must be continually resisted, cultural meanings surrounding rape in a pre-modern agrarian culture such as ancient Israel cannot be automatically collapsed into our own. Between ancient Israel and the modern West is an arena where differences may be encountered, particularly here in different modalities of meaning, regarding such basic elements in human experience as the female body, sexuality and violence." Gravett, "Reading 'Rape,'" 279, states: "A number of biblical translators and commentators now use the word 'rape' in their renderings and discussions of texts, even though many scholars consider this terminology problematic because no Hebrew verb or phrase precisely corresponds to contemporary understandings of rape." Further, on pp. 280 and 298, Gravett states: "Such cultural differences certainly influence renderings from Hebrew to English and translators must determine whether the word 'rape' as presently understood can accurately depict events described in some biblical accounts. In drawing such

The law is concerned to facilitate marriage to a female captive by an Israelite warrior. Sex with such a woman is one component of the process by which that occurs. The law considers such sex to be licit. If either prohibition or legitimization of rape were an agenda, we might expect the law to address a broader range of scenarios. The law leaves unaddressed such scenarios as the one in which a man forces sexual intercourse with a female captive without intending or desiring to take her as a wife.[48]

The law thus neither prohibits nor legitimizes rape.

3) *Niditch.* Niditch, of course, has no trouble identifying this scenario as an instance of rape.[49] However, she sees the law as concerned with sexual purity. Thus, even though she diverges from the previous scholars with respect to the rape issue, she nevertheless shares their assumption that the law is in some way concerned about the sex that transpires in the scenario.

Niditch states that the law forbids the man to sell the woman *because* he has had sex with her. She writes:

> There is an assumption that a virgin woman can be altered like clothing. Once she has sex, however, she becomes unalterable, marked or branded by her husband's "personness." Thus Deut 21:14 insists that the Israelite husband is in some way responsible for the female captive he has raped. She cannot be sold like a slave. His person and hers have become interwoven through sexual contact. The woman, moreover, can transmit the man's essence to another man who lies with her, while for his part, he absorbs her essence. It is not lightly that the tradition in Genesis 2 describes man and woman as becoming one flesh, nor surprising that men become unclean by having intercourse with a woman who is unclean (Lev 15:24). It is understandable in this system of symbols that a priest must marry a virgin who is to be filled with his holiness alone (Lev 21:7).[50]

In response to Niditch, it must first be noted that the woman in this passage is, in fact, not designated a virgin.[51] The absence of this specification is consistent

---

conclusions, translators must balance the fundamental cultural differences between the ancient and modern communities with the need to communicate effectively scenes of and laws about sexual violence in the Hebrew Bible… Bridging the ancient and contemporary communities by reading 'rape' does not alter the events various texts describe, but rather captures horrifying moments with clarity for an English reader." Washington, "Lest He Die," 208–9, states: "The lack of a legal category or even a word for rape as such in the Hebrew Bible illustrates the fact that the cultural meaning of sexual violence against women is a complex social production that is inextricably tied up, in experience and in representation, with exchanges of power. Sexual experiences of pleasure or distress, of mutuality or coercion, are available to individuals only as discursive products, contingent upon the cultural forms through which they are realized. There is no unmediated experience of sexuality or of violence apart from the channels of meaning and power constructed in a particular culture."

48. Pressler, *View of Women*, 13–14.

49. Niditch, "War," 50.

50. Ibid., 50–51.

51. Ibid., 50–51, states: "While Deut 21:10–14 does not mention virginity directly, the captured woman is pictured as a virgin bride who weeps leaving father and mother… While Deut 21:10 allows that the captive be a mature virgin woman—she is called 'woman' and not 'child'—Numbers

with the absence of the same specification in Deut 20. Deuteronomy 20 and 21 contrast dramatically, in this respect, with such texts as Num 31 and Judg 21. In addition, Niditch's assumption that the conceptuality of the Leviticus passages applies to the Deuteronomy passage is questionable. Such applicability is less than self-evident.[52] For example, a study of LST and DST suggests that virginity, as an issue of sexual purity, is a concern in Leviticus *only* in connection with priests. It is a concern in DST *only* in connection with the liminal scenarios of transfer from father to husband/future-husband, with special but not exclusive emphasis on the harm done to the father by loss of the daughter's virginity.[53] Presumably, DST would recognize the legitimacy of marrying a widow, for example, or even a divorced woman, both of whom are not virgins.[54] Thus, the concerns with respect to virginity in LST and DST are not coterminus. Therefore, to apply the conceptuality of one set of texts to the other without consideration of their differences is hasty.

The real source of Niditch's reading seems to be her understanding of עִנָּה, however, rather than her comparisons with Lev 15 and 21. The motive clause in which עִנָּה appears is part of the subcase embedded within the law. The subcase covers the contingency under which the man decides, presumably after the assimilation procedure and the marriage,[55] that he does not want the woman as a wife. This subcase is a second component of the second part of the apodosis of the law which begins in v. 10. The contingency is subject to the circumstances of the protasis in vv. 10–11, as are the statements of vv. 12–13. The motive clause states that the man cannot sell the woman or treat her as merchandise[56] because עִנִּיתָהּ. Since Niditch reads עִנָּה as "rape,"[57] she perceives the concern of

---

31 puts her age further back to make the fence around her purity stronger and I believe to have her 'unmarked,' blank-state quality all the clearer." Washington, "'Lest He Die,'" 204, states: "…it is important to notice that the woman might also have had a husband and children before her capture. The woman whom the victorious Israelite will marry is identified only as an adult female whom the man finds attractive (אֵשֶׁת יְפַת־תֹּאַר, v. 11). It is not necessary that she be a virgin (בְתוּלה) or an unbetrothed young woman (נַעֲרָה אֲשֶׁר לֹא־אֹרָשָׂה). The law respects such distinctions only within the Israelite community (as in the Deuteronomic laws of adultery and sexual assault, Deut 22.13–30), where a woman's status as the wife of a husband, or a marriageable (unbetrothed) young woman, determines the degree of a man's offense in having unauthorized sexual intercourse with her."

52.   For instance, men become unclean, as well, in Lev 15 by having intercourse with a healthy woman who is not menstruating. Furthermore, their semen seems to be the source of that uncleanness. This latter scenario necessarily informs the scenario in which a man has intercourse with a menstruant. Niditch's citation of Lev 15 is, thus, a skewed application of the passage.

53.   See Chapter 15, "Comparative Analysis," below.

54.   See the discussion of Deut 24:14 below.

55.   See the discussion below on pp. 184–85.

56.   A. Alt, "Zu *hit̠ʿammēr*," *VT* 2 (1952): 153–59; Craigie, *Deuteronomy*, 282; M. David, "*hit̠ʿāmēr* (Deut xxi 14; xxiv 7)," *VT* 1 (1951): 219–21; A. R. Hulst, *Old Testament Translation Problems* (Leiden: Brill, 1960), 16; Kalland, "Deuteronomy," 133 n. 14; Mayes, *Deuteronomy*, 303–4; Phillips, *Deuteronomy*, 141; Pressler, *View of Women*, 14 n. 16; Tigay, *Deuteronomy*, 195 n. 35.

57.   Niditch, "War," 50, states: "Thus Deut 21:14 insists that the Israelite husband is in some way responsible for the female captive he has raped." Mayes, *Deuteronomy*, 304, also reads עִנָּה as "rape." See also Neufeld, *Ancient Hebrew Marriage Laws*, 81 n. 1.

the subcase to be the fact that the woman has been accessed sexually. Sexual access to the female captive is then, at least, a sub-concern of the law.

Even Thistlethwaite, who recognizes that the scenario of the passage does not fit into the category of "rape in ancient Israel," nevertheless feels compelled to read עָנָה as narrowly signifying "rape." Thistlethwaite rightly defines "rape" in ancient Israel as theft of sexual property.[58] However, the men to whom she belonged are dead so that even by the conceptuality of that world the issue cannot be "rape," except in some extended sense of the concept. She writes:

> Since this forced marriage of a captive woman is regarded as a humiliation of her (21:14), she may not be sold if subsequently she fails to please her husband. The humiliation of her condition is acknowledged and the term for rape, עָנָה, is employed. In the case of a captive it would appear that there is no sexual property holder to be offended, yet the use of עָנָה, translated either "humiliated" or "dishonored," indicates that there was some recognition of her liminal status, not only captive foreigner, but wife in Israel... Rape in war does not fall into this system. It is completely outside the boundaries of Israelite definitions of sexual conduct and only requires regulation when sexual contact with a captive woman might begin to impinge on legitimacy.[59]

Thistlethwaite's reading of עָנָה, therefore, also assumes that sex, beyond mere motivation and instrumentation, is a concern of the law. She presumes that the source of its use is the woman's liminal status, as captive/ wife. She admits that the captive, by definition cannot be raped. The use of עָנָה must, therefore, derive from the "wife" component of the liminal status. But by Thistlethwaite's own definition, rape of one's wife is an oxymoron. Her reading, therefore, makes little sense in the context of her definition of "rape in ancient Israel," a definition I contend is correct.

b. *Supporting Opinion: Sex Is Not the Concern.* An examination of the use of Frymer-Kensky's suggestions clarifies the issue. עָנָה is used within the Hebrew corpus to signify sexual acts which "are in some way improper and which debase the woman."[60] In fact, it can signify rape.[61] However, Frymer-Kensky, as well as

---

58. Thistlethwaite, "You May Enjoy," 63–65, 69, states: "Sexual crimes relate to the female as sexual property... In the Hebrew Bible the offended party is the one who is the sexual property holder: in the case of the betrothed woman, her husband; in the case of the unmarried virgin, her father... There are degrees of sexual property within Israel, and these degrees come in to play particularly with the treatment of concubines and slaves, i.e. those women sold into servitude or captured in war. Their status is even less protected and there seems to be no definition of rape that can apply to their situation... Those women allowed to live are booty; they are no one's sexual property since their males have been killed. They therefore do not fall into the category of people who can be violated by rape. There is no party to offend... On one level, because the biblical definition of women is as the sexual property of designated males, biblical writers did not recognize rape in war under their own designations of rape as theft of sexual property. It was not rape by their lights, since no sexual property holder was left alive to be offended. The terminology employed is 'enjoyment of the spoils.' It is possible to say, in these terms, that no, rape in war is not the conduct of 'Holy War' simply because no 'rape' is actually occurring."

59. Thistlethwaite, "You May Enjoy," 65.

60. For the use of עָנָה in the Hebrew corpus, see the following works: Frymer-Kensky, "Deuteronomy," 55; idem, "Law and Philosophy," 93 and 100 n. 9; idem, "Sex in the Bible," 192; Keefe,

Pressler, contends that it can also "signify sexual intercourse with a consenting woman."[62] In addition, Frymer-Kensky asserts that it can signify non-sexual abusive behavior.[63]

If ענה "rarely corresponds to forcible rape,"[64] then the function of the motive clause, in which ענה stands, must be re-evaluated. Frymer-Kensky's reading is suggestive. She takes the use of ענה in Deut 21:14 to signify the fact that the man has abused the woman by raising her expectations and then dashing them to pieces. She writes:

> In this law of the captive bride the man has put his captive in a position in which she expected to become a wife, and then he has not carried through. Does this law apply only if he has sexual intercourse with her and then does not want to keep her as his wife? Taking her home and letting her go through this ritual of separation may mislead her even if he lets her go after the month without having intercourse with her. He cannot be allowed to gain by such behavior and instead must emancipate her.[65]

"Rapes of Women," 81, esp. nn. 1 and 2; Pressler, *View of Women*, 11 n. 6; Weinfeld, *Deuteronomy*, 286. Although Weinfeld's conclusions concerning the use of ענה in the Hebrew Bible are correct, he has reached those conclusions by at least one intriguing inference concerning Deut 21:14. He writes: "Nor is the same phrase (תחת אשר עניתה) in Deut 21:14 to be understood as referring to rape, for the woman was taken sexually only after her marriage to the Israelite and after she had dwelled in this household for a month." If Weinfeld means that married women cannot be raped by their husbands, then the inference is, of course, dangerously misguided even if it leads to accurate conclusions concerning the use of ענה. However, if Weinfeld means that the author of the biblical text himself cannot conceive the application of the category of rape to a husband's sexual aggression vis-à-vis his wife, then Weinfeld is right. As stated above, the law is not "self-aware" with respect to the category of rape in this scenario.

61.   Frymer-Kensky, "Law and Philosophy," 100 n. 9, notes that ענה signifies rape in the following passages: Judg 19–20; 2 Sam 13:12–13; Lam 5:11. See also Keefe, "Rapes of Women," 81; Mayes, *Deuteronomy*, 304; Pressler, *View of Women*, 12 n. 6.

62.   Pressler, *View of Women*, 12 n. 6, writes: "The *piel* of ענה often is used of forcible violation, but can refer to sexual intercourse with a consenting woman (Deut 22:24; Ezra 22:10)." See also Frymer-Kensky, "Sex in the Bible," 192, especially n. 34; idem, "Law and Philosophy," 93, especially n. 9. Keefe, "Rapes of Women," 81 n. 1, cites Deut 21:14 along with 22:24 as two of three instances where ענה "is used in legal discussions of rape." The third instance is Deut 24:29. However, Deut 22:24 clearly is not recognized by the author of the law as a case of rape. Neither are we, as readers, compelled by extra-textual or intra-textual information to read ענה of Deut 21:14 as "rape." See also Weinfeld, *Deuteronomy*, 286.

63.   Frymer-Kensky, "Deuteronomy," 55; idem, "Law and Philosophy," 100 n. 9; idem, "Sex in the Bible," 192. See Gen 16:6; Exod 1:11.

64.   Frymer-Kensky, "Deuteronomy," 55; idem, "Law and Philosophy," 100 n. 9; idem, "Sex in the Bible," 192; idem, "Sex and Sexuality," *ABD* 5:1145a: Frymer-Kensky notes that when ענה signifies "rape" it refers to "'statutory' rather than forcible rape. A man who has sex with a woman without proper arrangements is said to 'rape' (*ʿnh*; cf. BDB, 776) the woman *even if she consents*" (5:1145, italics are mine). This definition points to the issue of status, which I take to be the core of violence connoted by ענה. However, while the connotation of negative alteration of status is applicable to Deut 21, the connotation of statutory rape is not. See the continuing discussion below.

65.   Frymer-Kensky, "Deuteronomy," 55; idem, "Law and Philosophy," 100 n. 9; idem, "Sex in the Bible," Frymer-Kensky understands this law as providing for a situation in which the man changes his mind before he has sex with the woman. She states, therefore, that ענה in Deut 21 "seems to imply, not only an absence of force, but a failure of sex" (274 n. 34). By "absence of

Whether or not the subcase applies if the ritual ends with the actions described in the clauses of v. 13a is a question which the law itself fails to address explicitly. If the subcase applies in this way, then Frymer-Kensky's explanation fits the motive clause.

However, if the subcase applies only when the actions of v. 13a–b, including sex and marriage, occur, then perhaps a broader issue is at stake in the law. A more succinct statement from Frymer-Kensky targets the broader issue:

> The basic meaning is to treat someone improperly in a way that degrades or disgraces them by disregarding the proper treatment due people in each status.[66]

Bechtel's explanation, akin to Frymer-Kensky's, is even more pointed. She notes that in the Piel ענה means "to humiliate intensely." She states:

> The verb ענה ("to put down") reflects the process of status manipulation inherent in shaming. Given the meaning of "shame" connoted by the verb ʿnh, I will contend that within a sexual context the verb ʿnh in the Piel indicates the "humiliation" or "shaming" of a woman through certain kinds of sexual intercourse including rape, though not necessarily.[67]

The question is: What constitutes the shaming in this act? Bechtel states that sexual intercourse shames "(1) when it violates existing marital, family or community bonding and obligation or (2) when there is no prospect of its leading to marital or family bonding and obligation."[68] Where these conditions are present,

---

force," she is referring narrowly to that part of the procedure where sex is involved. She states that not only is it not rape but it is not sex. This reading depends upon her understanding of the structure of the text. See Pamela Gordon and Harold C. Washington, "Rape as a Military Metaphor in the Hebrew Bible," in Brenner, ed., *A Feminist Companion to the Latter Prophets*, 313 n. 2. If Gordon and Washington had taken into consideration Frymer-Kensky's understanding of the structure of the text, perhaps they would not have found her reading so "incredible." Frymer-Kensky is attempting to walk the world of the text as she exegetes it. An attempt to understand the world of the text *on its own terms* as much as possible facilitates the delivery of a sound reading *and critique* from the walk in our twenty-first century world. The latter, of course, is a necessary enterprise. It is the one that Gordon and Washington engage and insist upon with good reason. See also Washington, '"Lest He Die,'" 209, who states: "By describing rape, like gender, as a discursive formation, I do not mean to de-emphasize the physical reality of sexual violence against women in patriarchal cultures. Rather I adopt this critical perspective to describe how texts like Deuteronomy 22 generate cultural meanings of rape that simultaneously silence women's experience of violence and authorize male force. The fact that the biblical laws do not recognize rape as a crime against women indicates the centrality of violence for the construction of gender in the Hebrew Bible." See Magdalene, "Ancient Near Eastern Treaty-Curses," 336 n. 1. See also Gravett ("Reading 'Rape,'" 279–99) who wrestles with the cultural differences between the two worlds in her discussion of "rape" in the Hebrew Bible. Craigie (*Deuteronomy*, 282) states the following concerning alterations in the woman's status: "The man was not free to sell her as a slave for money, or to *treat her as merchandise*; that is, she could not be given in exchange for some other person or goods. The rights given to the woman seem to be designed as some sort of compensation for the losses incurred by the marriage and subsequent divorce." Compare Cairns, *Deuteronomy*, 190; von Rad, *Deuteronomy*, 137.

66. Frymer-Kensky, "Virginity," 87.
67. Lyn M. Bechtel, "What if Dinah Is Not Raped? (Genesis 34)," *JSOT* 62 (1994): 25.
68. Ibid., 24.

she suggests that the verb ענה references the shaming and she translates it "to humiliate."

If the "violation" which constitutes a violent sexual act in ancient Israel is either the wrong done to the husband, or the negative alteration of female status, then in Deut 21 the first has not occurred because the men are dead. The second, however, has occurred. This means, interestingly, that the text in this instance looks to a wrong done *against the woman* rather than to a wrong *against the man through the woman.*[69] Nevertheless, the "violent act," which we call rape, does not constitute that wrong. The negative alteration of her status, which has been effected "positively"[70] *through the sex act,* is the issue.

Even though the law looks to a wrong done to the woman, "fallen expectations," an emotional concern, are not the issue. שלח is used in Deut 22:19, 29 and 24:1, 3 to signify separative action in the context of marriage.[71] That is its connotation here as well.[72] This means that the subcase applies only when the actions of clauses v. 13a–b transpire. In this case, the actual granting and removal of the wife-status, rather than "fallen expectations," is the humiliation (ענה).[73] This is an entitlement concern. Such entitlements belong to wives. The concern has to do with social position rather than emotion. And it has nothing to do with violent sex, beyond its instrumentation.

Property or entitlement has been given to the woman in the form of wife-status and can be removed because the prerogative of the man to divorce takes precedent. However, beyond solving the man's problem—that is, getting rid of a wife he does not want—the property or entitlement of "freedom," as it occurs in connection with being a wife, cannot be removed. In this respect, the man's prerogatives are limited.[74] The woman's status is raised from enemy female captive—bereft not only of family but of men to whom she belongs—to Israelite wife belonging to a man who has helped to slaughter her family.[75] Because the woman's status has been raised, the law places a limitation on the degree to which it can be lowered. It cannot be lowered to the lowest possible degree, that of a slave who can be sold.[76] It can be lowered only to the degree that transpires when the status of "married woman" is removed from her and she becomes a "divorced woman."[77] She therefore goes away free.[78] Rape, as the twenty-first

---

69. See n. 101 below for discussion of this same issue with respect to Deut 22:28–29.

70. "Positively" refers to the probable assessment of the empowered discourse-constructors of that world.

71. F. Hossfeld, F. van der Velder and U. Dahmen, "שָׁלַח," *ThWAT* 8:49.

72. Westbrook, "Female Slave," 235.

73. See the further discussion of ענה below under Deut 22. See also E. S. Gersternberger, "ענה," *ThWAT* 6:254: "…Ehrverletzung und damit der status verlust gemeint ist…"

74. Pressler, *View of Women,* 9, 15.

75. Niditch, "War," 50.

76. Millar Burrows, *The Basis of Israelite Marriage* (New Haven: American Oriental Society, 1938), 32. See also: Cairns, *Deuteronomy,* 190; Clifford, *Deuteronomy,* 113; Driver, *Deuteronomy,* 244; Tigay, *Deuteronomy,* 195 n. 35; von Rad, *Deuteronomy,* 137.

77. Westbrook, "Female Slave," 235, states: "In my analysis the captive woman is initially a slave, marriage makes her a free person, but subsequent termination of the marriage revives her

century defines it, is insignificant in the eyes of the law of Deut 21:10–14. However, in the eyes of that same law, giving status to the woman, as defined by her connection to men, and then removing that status is significant.[79] Sex is merely the instrument by means of which that status is given, for the sake of the production of progeny, and does not constitute the abuse of the law. Whether the "humiliation" (ענה) is "fallen expectations" or "fallen status," sex per se is not the issue.

c. *Summary.* Thus, the law facilitates the marriage of woman[80] under circumstances in which the normal procedures for effecting marriage are non-existent.[81] Men arrange marriages by contract among themselves. However, the men who can make a contract for the exchange of the female captive have been killed. Their absence removes the usual channels by which the marriage is legitimated.[82]

---

previous status: her husband becomes her master again, and therefore can in principle sell her as a slave. The law forbids him to do so; instead, he must divorce her 'to herself' (*lᵉnapšâh*). This curious and seemingly redundant expression is another facet of splitting the juridical personality. The woman is reunited with herself, that is, she receives back the ownership of herself that was ceded to her captor when she became a slave, regained during marriage, but lost again to him following her divorce."

78.   In Exod 21:7–11, the rejected slavewoman does not go out free. But she may be redeemed and, as in Deut 21, she cannot be sold. By contrast, in Deut 14, the slavewoman goes out free in the seventh year. No comment is made about the master's prerogative, or lack thereof, to sell her. Countryman, *Dirt*, 154; Driver, *Deuteronomy*, 245; Mace, *Hebrew Marriage*, 186; Phillips, *Deuteronomy*, 141. See also Calum M. Carmichael's comments on these matters, in his *The Laws of Deuteronomy* (Ithaca, N.Y.: Cornell University Press, 1974), 57. See n. 41 under discussion of Deut 25:5–10, for a brief treatment of the difficulties of widowhood in ancient Israel. Presumably, the difficulties for a divorced, non-Israelite woman would be more severe than those for a widowed Israelite woman.

79.   Gravett, "Reading 'Rape,'" 285, 287, takes this as one of the passages that confirms the meaning of ענה as "rape." Gordon and Washington, "Rape as a Military Metaphor," 313, state: "The technical term for rape in biblical Hebrew derives from the verbal root ענה II (Deut 21.14; 22.24, 29; Gen 34.2; Judg 19.24; 20.4; 2 Sam 13.12, 14, 22, 32; Lam 5.11)." They observe that it does occur in some contexts where the sexual sense is unlikely. Furthermore they note its use in the context of military assault. While they admit that these military contexts cannot translate ענה as "rape," Gordon and Washington state that these instances nevertheless inscribe "a pattern of domination and submission more extensively than is generally recognized." And that, I would say, constitutes the meaning of ענה. The military examples, as well as the other examples they cite, support the meaning of ענה as "negative status manipulation." This connotation holds within sexual and non-sexual conxts alike. *That* in the ancient conceptuality is the crux of the violence where ענה is used.

80.   Many scholars take the woman to be a non-Canaanite, resolving a presumed conflict between Deut 21:10–14 and 7:3. See the following: Cairns, *Deuteronomy*, 189; Clifford, *Deuteronomy*, 112; Craigie, *Deuteronomy*, 281; Driver, *Deuteronomy*, 244; Mayes, *Deuteronomy*, 303; Phillips, *Deuteronomy*, 140; Tigay, *Deuteronomy*, 194. See von Rad, *Deuteronomy*, 137, for a diachronic explanation. See also Jacob Milgrom, *Numbers* (Philadelphia: Jewish Publication Society of America, 1990), 259.

81.   Pressler, *View of Women*, 11.

82.   Ibid., 11, states: "…this law provides a means for the man to marry a woman in a case where the normal procedures for marriage are not possible, and provides a way for the foreign woman to be assimilated into an Israelite household."

Additionally, the law facilitates the woman's disposal should the man desire to dissolve the marriage arrangement. The law also places minor limitations on the man with respect to his ability to reduce her status.[83]

The primary concern of the law is to provide, on behalf of the man, a means to procure a wife from among the captives and a means to dispose of her if he desires. As part of the procedure for fulfilling that end, the law stipulates a process that includes sex, and which aids the assimilation of the woman and her transformation from "woman belonging to the enemy" to "wife in Israel."

C. *Conclusion*

The primary concern of Deut 21:10–14 is thus a property concern. It is a concern to facilitate the acquisition of a wife under difficult circumstances. A primary component in the process, which effects this end, is sexual intercourse.

The Israelite warrior has exclusive right to her sexuality which is an instrument and a property. It is the means by which the process of her transformation is concluded. And it is that to which the Israelite warrior has exclusive right, not only vis-à-vis other men, but vis-à-vis the woman herself.

While woman retains the rights of "freedom" associated with a wife in Israel, she is marginalized and objectified, although her marginalization is somewhat ameliorated. In addition, she is focalized as property. Thus, Deut 21:10–14 supports the thesis that, in Deuteronomy, where sexuality and women intersect, the primary focus and concern is the woman's sexuality as the property of the man.

83.   Ibid., 9, 15.

Chapter 10

DEUTERONOMY 22:13–23:1

A. *Introduction*

Deuteronomy 22:13–23:1 has been, for a number of scholars, a source of evidence that, with the Deuteronomic reform, adultery became a crime rather than a tort in ancient Israel. These scholars would posit that the sex laws of Deut 22 are concerned with something other than protection of the woman's sexuality as the property of the man. Phillips believes that the Deuteronomic reform made women "equal members of the covenant community with men."[1] Although he recognizes that the property rights of a father remained in place with respect to his virgin daughter,[2] he states the following concerning wives:

> It is too simple a view of the law of adultery to regard the wife as merely part of her husband's property, for, in distinction from a daughter, by virtue of the marriage, she became an extension of the husband himself (Gen. 2:24), and it was through her that his name was continued.[3]

This, according to Phillips, is why the "crime" of adultery was extended "to include lack of virginity on marriage" in cases such as Deut 22:20–21, where Phillips believes the woman's infraction is a crime against a fellow member of the covenant community rather than a tort against his property.[4] Similarly, Weinfeld, who characterizes the primary concern of the author of Deuteronomy as "protection of man" rather than regulation of "offenses relating to property,"[5] concludes that the author of Deut 22:13–19, 28–29 "is concerned with rectifying the moral and personal wrong committed against the maiden and not with the financial interests of the father."[6] He uses this and other examples to argue that "Deuteronomy shows a particularly humanistic attitude towards women."[7]

---

1. Phillips, *Ancient Israel's Criminal Law*, 110; idem, "Another Look," 6.
2. Phillips, "Another Look," 9.
3. Phillips, *Ancient Israel's Criminal Law*, 117.
4. Ibid., 117; idem, "Another Look," 10–11. See my "Introduction" for critique of crime/tort theory.
5. Weinfeld, "Origin of the Humanism," 243; idem, *Deuteronomy*, 283–84.
6. Weinfeld, *Deuteronomy*, 291; Pressler, *View of Women*, 105.
7. Weinfeld, *Deuteronomy*, 291; Pressler, *View of Women*, 105, has adequately replied to these kinds of assertion on the part of Weinfeld and others.

Stulman, who refers to Deut 22 in support of similar conclusions, states: "In D, however, *women are no longer regarded as the personal property of the pater familias*."[8]

These lines of argument ignore important signals in the text of Deut 22:13–23:1 concerning women. As was the case in the previous texts, point-of-view and language-depicting-the-sex-act construct woman's textual marginalization and her objectification, clearly demonstrating her circumscribed and *unequal* position within the author's conceptualization of men and women. However, despite her circumscription, point-of-view also reveals that woman as well as man is subject to the laws. Nevertheless, although she is bound by the laws, her marginalization extends beyond the biases of point-of-view and language-depicting-the-sex-act to actual legal subjugation to the man. The intricacies of this legal subjugation is the topic of the laws. Language-depicting-the-sex-act, identification-of-women, selection-of-laws, reiteration-of-the-man-to-whom-the-woman-belongs and structure all evidence that this legal subjugation assigns her sexuality the status of property. In fact, the primary concern of the series is the protection of this property.

Thus, woman is marginalized and objectified. At places in the text she appears as agent because of her active participation in the infraction. She accrues an implied agency as implicit addressee. But she is focalized as property.

B. *Discussion*

1. *Point-of-View and Language-Depicting-the-Sex-Act*
a. *Point-of-View*. Point-of-view is revealed in this text by the use-of-second-and-third-person and the application-of-taboo which demonstrate that the author explicitly addresses a male collective. Additional signals derived from the logic of the text, as in the sex series of Lev 18 and 20, indicate that the author also implicitly addresses women. The "named-addressee" feature, however, apparent in previous texts, is absent in the present text.

1) *Explicit Addressee*.
a) *Use-of-Second-and-Third-Person*. The specific addressee of Deut 22.13–23:1 remains unnamed both in the sex-law series itself and in the immediately surrounding laws. Without explicitly revealing the addressee, the laws refer to all perpetrators and victims in the third person.

In three of the laws (vv. 21, 22, 24) the author addresses his audience by second masculine singular verbs of a purge formula, directing them to "burn the evil from your midst." The two stoning penalties of the series, which are to be executed collectively, accompany two of the instances of the purge formula, which is to be executed "individually," at least if we read the singulars of the purge-formula verbs in the simplest fashion. This switch in number from the plural verbs of the penalties to the singular verbs of the purge formula, as well

---

8.   Stulman, "Sex and Familial Crimes," 62 (emphasis in original).

as the switch from third to second person, is rhetorical. By means of the purge formula, the author seems to take a momentary, intimate stance with his audience in which he counsels each and every member of the collective rather than the collective as a whole. This intimate stance suggests, perhaps, that the application of the purge formula extends beyond the realm of legal proscription to the legally ungovernable habits of one's personal life, which can and sometimes do lead finally to infractions requiring the death penalty. Whereas the command to "stone" is a prescription against infractions, the command to "burn the evil" is an instruction accompanying motive clauses in two instances and functioning itself as a motive clause in all three instances.[9] The purge formula, however, fails to reveal with whom the author is taking his intimate stance and whom he is attempting to instruct or motivate.

The clues for identification of the addressee from the stoning prescriptions are stronger, although hardly more decisive than the clues from the purge formulas. The change in person from the stoning clause of v. 21 to the stoning clause of v. 24 is more difficult to explain than the change in number from third plural verbs preceding the purge formula to the second singular verbs of that formula.[10] However, perhaps the appearance of the second person in the purge formula of v. 21 triggers the use of second person in subsequent verses in somewhat the same way that keywords trigger certain textual moves in other passages.[11]

Whereas v. 24 prescribes stoning by means of two second masculine plural verbs (וּסְקַלְתֶּם, וְהוֹצֵאתֶם) without naming the executioners, v. 21 explicitly names the executioners whom it otherwise refers to with third common plural verbs (וּסְקָלוּהָ, וְהוֹצִיאוּ). The executioners are the אַנְשֵׁי עִירָהּ. The explicit identification of the executioners as exclusively male in v. 21 means that the representation of both genders by the plural verbs of v. 24 is unlikely. Women are excluded from the group of executioners to whom the stoning commands are addressed.

If this inference is correct, then the "men of the city" are the addressees of at least v. 24a.[12] We might surmise, then, that men are also the addressees of the remaining second person verbs and pronouns of the passage, including v. 21. If this latter inference is correct, then in all probability the series itself is addressed to a male community.

b) *Application-of-Taboo*. The application-of-taboo, another indicator for point-of-view, signals woman's marginalization in the text, as does the use-of-second-and-third-person.

---

9. Mayes, *Deuteronomy*, 233, states: "It is clearly not a legal formula; with its direct form of address it points to a situation of instruction or teaching of the law."

10. For comments on the redaction history of the passage, see the following: Locher, *Ehre einer Frau in Israel*, 39; Yoshihide Suzuki, "The 'Numeruswechsel' in Deuteronomy" (Ph.D. diss., Claremont Graduate School, 1982), 233–34; Merendino, *Deuteronomische*, 262.

11. See the treatment of keywords and triggers under the discussion of Lev 20. See also Locher, *Ehre einer Frau in Israel*, 61.

12. Pressler, *View of Women*, 35.

In Lev 20, initial focus is placed on the man by means of relative clauses, a function of the fact that the taboo is applied against the woman for the sake of the man. Deuteronomy 22:13–23:1, which, by contrast, uses conjunctive particles to construct its conditionals, places initial focus on the man in three out of the six laws:[13] in the newly-wed law (v. 13a), in the unbetrothed-virgin law (v. 28) and in the incest law (23:1). In the adultery law (v. 22), the witnesses have initial focus. In the second betrothed-virgin law (v. 25), the man is the first human to appear, but the locale has initial focus. While the series fails to place initial focus on the man with the consistency of Lev 20, it demonstrates a numerical preponderance for an initial focus on men over an initial focus on women. Although the individual upon whom the taboo is placed can and does appear in initial position, the preponderance of men in that position corresponds to the fact that, as in Lev 20, whereas married women are off limits to men, married men are not off limits to women.

For instance, the text leaves undescribed the scenario in which a woman accuses her husband of lack of virginity. In fact, the virginity of any man, including betrothed and un-betrothed men, is a complete non-issue. No *husband* is described as off-limits for any woman. The rape of no man by a woman is regulated. The laws explicitly restrict the man with respect to particular women. However, even though the laws restrict, by implication, the activity of these same particular women, they do not explicitly restrict women in general with respect to any particular man. This gender asymmetry demonstrates that the taboo is applied to women and not to men.

Thus, application-of-taboo, like the use-of-second-and-third-person, signals woman's marginalization in the text. Men are the explicit addressees.

2) *Implicit Addressee*. Despite these overt signals from the use-of-second-and-third-person and from the application-of-taboo, indicating that the conversation of the text is between the author and a male community, and despite woman's marginalization in the text, the logic of the text reveals that women as well as men are bound by the laws. The illicit sex acts of women as well as men constitute a breach of the laws of Deut 22:13–23:1.[14]

Two exceptions to this assertion occur. In vv. 25–29, women are raped.[15] The two laws of these verses restrict the sexual activity of men alone. These laws

13.   I understand vv. 13–21 to be one law consisting of two "subcases." See structure below.
14.   Frymer-Kensky, "Deuteronomy," 56.
15.   See the discussion, under Deut 21:10–14 above, concerning the use of "rape" to refer to scenarios in the laws of the Hebrew Bible. For the sake of convenience I will continue to use that word in the present discussion to designate forced sex. I ask the reader to keep in mind that the word, when used to describe a phenomenon in the Hebrew Bible, consists of a different conceptuality than the same word in twenty-first-century context. Pressler, "Sexual Violence," 102–3, states: "These laws do deal with forcible sexual intercourse. It is clear, however, that they are not concerned with 'rape' as modern legislation would define the offense." Note also Washington, '"Lest He Die,'" 208, who states: "The statutes of Deut 22.23–29 are not 'rape laws'; they are not designed to protect persons from sexual violence. Most observers today would recognize the two instances of force in the text (החזיק, v. 25; תפש, v. 28) as rape, that is, the violent crime of forcing another person to

regulate women only where their rights or destiny are concerned, upon being raped. Nevertheless, in the remaining four laws, the illicit actions of both men and women are necessary for the breaches which the laws regulate. These four laws restrict the sexual activity of both men and women.

Furthermore, the implementation of penalties against the infraction of at least one of the sex laws, vv. 20–21, can be avoided only if women are also apprised of and follow its implied prohibition. In addition, women would certainly be expected to take note of the in-the-city/in-the-field distinction for the sake of their own welfare. Finally, women as well as men in three of the laws are the subject of the death penalty. The laws state: "she shall die" (v. 21), "they shall die" (vv. 22, 24), "he shall die" (v. 25).

The series as a whole thus addresses men and women. Women are the implicit addressees.

3) *Conclusion.* The laws of Deut 22:13–23:1 are addressed explicitly to a male community at the impersonal as well as at the personal level, demonstrating woman's marginalization in the text as implicit addressee.

b. *Language-Depicting-the-Sex-Act.* Language-depicting-the-sex-act, objectifying woman, corroborates her marginalization in the text as revealed by point-of-view. In addition, it demonstrates that her sexuality is the property of the man and that the intent of the laws is to protect that property.

1) *The Verbs.*
a) לקח, בוא, קרב *and* גלה. Both the law which begins the sex-law series and the law which concludes that series use לקח in a clause accompanying a second clause depicting the sex act. לקח denotes marriage. Its connotations, however, reach the sexual domain, especially in the last law of the series (23:1).[16] Even in the first law (v. 13), intimations of the sexual domain are called forth by לקח. This is because the act of לקח is incomplete until the acts of בוא (v. 13) and גלה (23:1) are committed. In v. 13, לקח partially describes the basic condition of the casuistic law which must be satisfied for both "sub-cases"[17] of vv. 13–21 to apply. The accompanying clause, depicting the sex act in the first subcase, וּבָא אֵלֶיהָ, completes the description of the basic condition for that case. The man must "take" or marry the woman and then he must perform a sexual act; he must "go into her" (בוא). He "takes her" in order to "go into her."[18] לקח and בוא work together to describe the process of marriage which gives the man exclusive rights to her sexuality.[19] The rights extend retroactively[20] into the past as well as

---

submit to sexual intercourse. Biblical law, however, has no category of sexual assault, nor does biblical Hebrew have a word for rape as such."

16.   For use of לקח with an exclusively sexual connotation in narrative, see Gen 34:2.
17.   See the structure below.
18.   The comments made concerning בוא in the discussion of Deut 21 are applicable for the use of בוא in this context as well. See also the comments on לקח in the "Introduction."
19.   Landsberger, "Jungfräulichkeit," 42; Driver and Miles, *Babylonian Laws*, 322.

into the future. The בוא clause and the phrase of 14bβ₂ describe the only act of licit sex in the series. In 14bβ₂ the author uses לקח in conjunction with קרב to depict the sex act. Pressler rightly states that "the plain reading of v. 14 is to assume that the husband's 'drawing near' to his bride refers to sexual inter-course."[21] Thus, sexual connotations permeate the marriage denotation of לקח in 14bβ₂ as well as in v. 13.

In the second law which uses לקח, 23:1, the sexual connotation of לקח is heightened. The accompanying clause describing the sex act uses גלה and refers to an illicit act. The law prohibits marriage with a special emphasis upon prohi-bition of the sex which marriage entails. The sexual relationship is the primary issue. Another way of stating this is to say that motivation for the prohibition of marriage is prevention of the incestuous sexual relationship which necessarily follows.[22] The juxtaposition of the two clauses of the apodictic law—the second of which resembles the language of the incest laws of Lev 18 and Deut 27—demonstrates that the incest prohibition, in turn, places special emphasis on the fact that the woman is the sexual property of the father. The implication of Wegner's statement "that Scripture uses the same verb *l-q-ḥ* (to take) for taking a wife as for buying goods" is, therefore, particularly evident in this law.[23]

Examination of the second clause of 23:1, which uses גלה, is instructive. The object of גלה is כנף, whereas in the first clause the object is the woman. This second clause is either appositional to the first clause or it is a motive clause.[24] With either understanding it has an explanatory function which gains part of its force from the fact that the woman and the skirt occupy the same grammatical position. This latter fact and the juxtaposition of the two clauses multiplies the metaphorical power of the phrase יְגַלֶּה כְּנַף, which is, on the one hand, a general sexual euphemism representing the sex act itself, and, on the other hand, a more specific depiction of sex with the wife of the father.[25] In other words, within this context, the metaphor, derived from the sexual euphemism, is tweaked so as to step down the euphemism to a more literal depiction. The woman becomes the skirt. Carmichael, commenting on Ruth 3:9 and Ezek 16:8, which he considers helpful for understanding the expression, writes:

> The meaning surely is that the male's removal of his garment and placing it upon the woman is for the symbolic purpose that he will obtain a new use for it. She now becomes his skirt, to be put on by him, that is, as a wife.[26]

20.   Pressler, *View of Women*, 30.

21.   Ibid., 27.

22.   I am using "incest" as broadly described by Bigger, "Family Laws," 193, who suggests that the definition of incest can include sex with affines.

23.   Wegner, *Chattel*, 227 n. 84.

24.   Phillips, "Uncovering the Father's Skirt." Contrary to Phillips, I understand the relationship between these two clauses to be similar to the relationship of the two clauses in Deut 27:20. For a critique of Phillips' theory, see the discussion of Lev 18 above and Deut 27 below.

25.   Carmichael, *Women*, 49–50; idem, "A Ceremonial Crux: Removing a Man's Sandal as a Female Gesture of Contempt," *JBL* 96 (1977): 332–33; Clifford, *Deuteronomy*, 122; Driver, *Deuteronomy*, 259.

26.   Carmichael, *Women*, 49–50; idem, "Ceremonial Crux," 332–33.

Just as the כָּנָף which a man acquires and uses might be stolen and misused by another, so also the woman, whom a man acquires and uses, might be stolen and misused by another. If this conclusion is correct, then the language-depicting-the-sex-act of this incest prohibition mirrors the concern to protect the woman as the sexual property of the father.

The issue of blood-incest in general is by nature more of a classificatory rather than a property issue. Incest broadly defined to include affines and others,[27] however, begins to include property concerns, but at heart it is still a classificatory issue. Deuteronomy 23:1 demonstrates, however, that the classificatory issues of incest can be used in the service of property concerns. The syntax and vocabulary evidence this fact. Even so, the strongest argument for this fact is the placement of this incest law at the end of this particular series, as the analysis of the structure below will demonstrate.

In summary, the woman is the object of all four verbs: קרב, בוא, לקח and גלה. The man is the subject. Where the author of the first subcase, in which the woman is guilty, has the opportunity to position the woman as subject, he fails to do so. Instead of depicting the sex act, which she is presumed to have performed, he restricts the depiction to the evidence: lack of בְּתוּלִים. In the second subcase, where the woman is guilty, she is the subject of זנה.[28] However, a male object, prepositional or accusative is lacking. The male perpetrator, as subject, is lacking as well, since he is unknown.[29]

b) שכב. The remaining four laws all use שכב at some point to depict the sex act. In every instance, including the law which clearly describes rape (v. 25), שכב is used with the preposition עִם.[30] This rape law serves as an antidote to the idea that the preposition connotes cooperation or reciprocity on the part of the woman. In each case the man is the subject of שכב and the woman is the object of the preposition.

c) ענה. Two of these four laws (vv. 24 and 29) have motive clauses which explain the prescribed penalties by stating that the male perpetrator committed

27. Bigger, "Family Laws," 193.

28. See the comments on זנה in the discussion above of Lev 19:29 and 21:9, and below in the discussion of Deut 23:18–19. Tigay (*Deuteronomy*, 206) states that the use of זנה in Deut 22:21 is an indication that the infraction occurs before marriage. See also Bird, "To Play the Harlot," 78. Wenham ("*Bᵉtûlāh*," 332), who sees the woman's infraction as a case of adultery, suggests that it occurs after her marriage. Pressler's critique is apt (*View of Women*, 25 n. 11): "If Wenham's interpretation were correct, the case in Deut 22:20–21 would be a specific instance of adultery committed by a betrothed girl (Deut 22:23–24)… By that interpretation, Deut 22:20–21 would not add anything new to the definition of adultery found in Deut 22:22–27." See also pp. 27–28. The accusation itself occurs after marriage according to Craigie, *Deuteronomy*, 292; Angelo Tosato, "Joseph, Being a Just Man: (Matt 1:19)," *CBQ* 41 (1979): 548 n. 4.

29. Rofé, "Family and Sex Laws," 137. Contrary to Rofé, who suggests that the fact that woman alone is punished indicates "legal inconsistency" with vv. 23–24, the woman alone is punished simply because the perpetrator is unknown.

30. For an accounting of the prepositions used with שכב in P and D, see W. Beuken, "שָׁכַב," *ThWAT* 7:1310.

an act represented by עָנָה, of which the man is the subject and the woman the object.

The use of עָנָה in 22:24 is the clearest example of the fact that עָנָה does not necessarily mean rape.[31] Its context, vv. 23–27, indicates that the sex act referred to by עָנָה in v. 24 is consensual.[32] However, two laws later, עָנָה describes a transgression which is not consensual, one which is, in fact, rape (vv. 28–29).[33] Furthermore, עָנָה is absent in the law of vv. 25–27, an even more definitive example of rape.[34] These examples from Deut 22 demonstrate a multivalence for עָנָה. The multivalence suggests that, in those instances where עָנָה does refer to rape, its denotation is broader than the denotation of the English word "rape." Deuteronomy 21:14, as previously argued, supports this observation as well. Other examples throughout the Hebrew corpus contribute to the multivalence or broad denotation of עָנָה.[35]

In the narratives of both Dinah and Tamar, עָנָה, in conjunction with שכב clauses, represents rape scenarios.[36] The narrator describes Shechem's actions in Gen 34:2 with respect to Dinah as follows: "He saw her and he took her and he lay with her and he humiliated her" (וַיַּרְא אֹתָהּ...וַיִּקַּח אֹתָהּ וַיִּשְׁכַּב אֹתָהּ וַיְעַנֶּהָ). Amnon's actions in 2 Sam 13:14 with respect to Tamar are described as follows:

---

31. See the discussion of עָנָה by the following commentators: Frymer-Kensky, "Law and Philosophy," 93, 100 n. 9; Pressler, *View of Women*, 11 n. 6, 37–38 n. 48; Thistlethwaite, "You May Enjoy," 65. See also the notes and observations above in discussion of Deut 21:10–14.

32. Bechtel, "What if Dinah Is Not Raped?," 25.

33. Ibid., 25. Bechtel understands these verses to be about consensual sex in which no violence is present. She states: "Note that in this case the word *ʿnh* follows *škb*, which seems to be the case when rape is not involved." However, it is doubtful that תפש has a non-violent connotation in this pericope, as she suggests. This does not affect, however, the definition she finally offers for עָנָה, which is a sound definition. Concerning תפש, see Pressler, "Sexual Violence," 104.

34. Bechtel, "What if Dinah Is Not Raped?," 26, proposes that עָנָה is absent here because there is no shame for the woman: "The text states that the woman has acted correctly; she has cried out for help, so this sexual intercourse is not voluntary and is not considered a violation by her of her existing bonding and obligation. Consequently, there is no shame for her, and the verb *ʿnh* is not used to describe the rape. It is simply a hostile, exploitative crime against a woman and the community, for which the man deserves to die. There is rape, but no shame, the verb *ʿnh* is not used." However, shame as well as "rape" does not depend upon the disposition of the woman, if shame is a lowering of status, as I would contend that it is. That lowering of status depends upon the sanctity of her womb, not on whether she consented or not. Gravett ("Reading 'Rape,'" 286) proposes that עָנָה is absent "because v. 25 simply continues the thought of vv. 23–24, slightly altering the scenario as indicated grammatically with the conjunction 'but' at the outset."

35. עָנָה occurs in sexual context in the following places: Gen 34:2; Deut 21:14; 22:24, 29; Judg 19:24; 20:5; 2 Sam 13:12, 14, 22, 23; Ezek 22:10, 11; Lam 5:11. For non-sexual contexts in which עָנָה occurs, see Frymer-Kensky, "Law," 100 n. 9. Although multivalence exists in the single chapter of Deut 22, we ought not to assume *prima facie* that the contributions to the multivalence of עָנָה by the other examples throughout the Hebrew corpus belong to a single conceptuality concerning the act which we call "rape."

36. Ita Sheres, *Dinah's Rebellion: A Biblical Parable for Our Time* (New York: Crossroad, 1990), 59, 68–75, 86. If Sheres' intriguing assessment is correct, then the Dinah narrative has within it signals which seem to suggest ambivalence about the idea that Shechem's act was an act of violence or that it was perpetrated without Dinah's consent. Frymer-Kensky, "Virginity," 87, states that Shechem did not rape Dinah. So also Bechtel, "What if Dinah Is Not Raped?," 19–36.

"He was stronger than her and he humiliated her and he lay with her" (יֶּחֱזַק מִמֶּנָּה וַיְעַנֶּהָ וַיִּשְׁכַּב אֹתָהּ). In both narratives the sex act is depicted by שכב. ענה describes the import of that act. ענה thus adds something to the description designated by שכב.[37] It most certainly adds the idea of violence and non-consent underscored by each to the narratives as a whole. The question is: What is the import of the violence and non-consent conjured by ענה? In both narratives male siblings of the violated woman take blood vengeance against the rapist. No explicit indicator in either narrative tells whether they take vengeance on behalf of only the woman's interests or on behalf of only their own interests, or on behalf of both interests. Subtle signals in both narratives, however, suggest their own interests are at stake. The extreme nature of the vengeance of the Genesis narrative suggests that political dynamics which extend beyond the woman's personal humiliation and distress are involved. Certainly, killing Shechem would have been enough to address the latter issue. Nevertheless, the entire community of men to which Shechem belonged was slaughtered. The shape of the vengeance act demonstrates that the ענה act is a violation of the honor and rights of the family of brothers to whom Dinah belongs.[38]

In the Tamar narrative, the consent, as Tamar herself explains, must be obtained from the father. Anything less than this makes the act a נבלה. In other words, even if Tamar consented and the father were not asked, the act would be a misdeed. The idea of consent by the woman as a way of legitimating the act and perhaps taking it from the realm of ענה is absent from the conceptuality of the text. The father's consent constitutes the daughter's consent and not vice versa. This state of affairs suggests that the wrong of ענה has to do with what harms the father and perhaps the larger male contingent of Tamar's family. Again, blood vengeance is taken by the brother Absalom, a male member of the household to which Tamar belongs.

In these instances the import of ענה is multifaceted. The "security" of the woman's womb, which assures a husband, fiancé or potential marriage candidate that the children she delivers are or would be his own, is forever compromised. Even if months pass since the incident and no child from the rape results, the security of her womb never again has the surety of a virgin or the surety of a chaste wife. In addition, unless the woman marries the male perpetrator, her sexuality can never belong to only one man the way a virgin's sexuality or the sexuality of a chaste wife does. The father, therefore, cannot receive the bride-price he might otherwise have expected. Her chances for marriage are diminished.[39] If anthropological studies in the last several decades are correct, then the

---

37. Frymer-Kensky, "Virginity," 87, notes the connection of ענה and שכב, suggesting that the word order determines that this was not rape. So also Bechtel, "What if Dinah Is Not Raped?," 25: "Note that in this case the word ʿnh follows škb, which seems to be the case when rape is not involved."

38. Matthews and Benjamin, *Social World*, 178, state: "Likewise, rape in the world of the Bible was not simply an act of sexual violence, but a political challenge to the father of a household." See the discussion under Deut 21:10–14 above.

39. Pressler, "Sexual Violence," 105, states: "There are some indications in the Hebrew Bible that a woman who had been defiled by illicit sexual relations may not have been eligible for

act represented by ענה is a challenge to the very status of the household to which the woman belongs.[40]

The consequences of ענה, therefore, deprive the man, husband, father or male sibling of his rights to her sexuality—in the case of the father, rights to a bride-price and knowledge concerning extended progeny; in the case of the husband, rights to exclusive entry and to knowledge concerning immediate as well as extended progeny;[41] in the case of the male sibling, honor which translates into power and potential viability as a household or as a political entity in the larger environment. The violence of ענה, cloaked as violence against the woman, is, in fact, violence against the man or men to whom she belongs.

As a result of the threat or damage to the status of the household, the status of the woman herself is irrevocably altered.[42] When the act of ענה is committed against a woman, she becomes a different "kind of woman" than she was before the act. She becomes irrevocably the "kind of woman" whose sexual boundaries are no longer secure. She becomes the "kind of woman" through whom one man does violence to another. This is lowered status. It is effected by ענה.

The use of ענה in Judg 19–20 reveals additional information concerning this "lowering of status." Just as Deut 22:24 demonstrates that the "lowering of status" which occurs as a result of ענה is independent of the woman's intent, so also Judg 19–20 demonstrates that the "lowering of status" is independent of the intent of the man to whom the woman belongs. In the case of the concubine of Judg 19–20, the husband, under duress, hands over his woman's sexuality to a mob. Although the host-father uses the word ענה when he first offers the daughters and the concubine to the mob (Judg 19:24), the husband of the concubine calls the act ענה only after she is dead (Judg 20:5).[43] Whether the husband hands her to the Benjamite mob willingly or under duress, the act of that mob is ענה.

---

marriage... Even if that were not the case, her chances of a good marriage would surely have been greatly reduced."

　40.　Bechtel, "What if Dinah Is Not Raped?," 25, comments accordingly on Deut 22:23–24: "Despite the fact that there is no rape, the sexual intercourse is shameful because it threatens the social bonding of the community." See also Matthews and Benjamin, *Social World*, 176–86; Julian Pitt-Rivers, *The Fate of Shechem* (Cambridge: Cambridge University Press, 1977), 165, states: "The connection between masculine honour and the purity of women which makes a man vulnerable not only through his wife but through his mother, sister, or daughter, is common to all the traditional peoples of the Mediterranean and it poses a problem to the men of the nuclear family." See also the following: David D. Gilmore, ed. *Honor and Shame and the Unity of the Mediterranean* (Washington, D.C.: American Anthropological Association, 1987); Kirsten Hastrup, "The Sexual Boundary—Purity: Heterosexuality and Virginity," *JASO* 5 (1994): 137–47; Matthews, "Honor and Shame"; Sherry B. Ortner, "The Virgin and the State," *Feminist Studies* 4 (1978): 19–35; Alice Schlegel, "Status, Property, and the Value on Virginity," *American Ethnologist* 18 (1991): 719–34; Jane Schneider, "Of Vigilance and Virgins: Honor, Shame and Access to Resources in the Mediterranean Societies," *Ethnology* 10 (1971): 1–24.

　41.　Sheres, *Dinah's Rebellion*, 111.

　42.　See the discussion above under Deut 21:10–14. See also Joseph Blenkinsopp, "The Family in First Temple Israel," in *Families in Ancient Israel* (ed. Don S. Browning and Ian S. Evison; Louisville, Ky.: Westminster John Knox, 1997), 76; Gerstenberger, "ענה," 254.

　43.　Whether the mob or the husband kills her is an open question.

The mob entered where only the husband had the right to enter. The Benjamites lower her status by treating her, a woman who belongs to one man, as if she were a woman whom anyone can access. The husband participates, albeit under duress, in the lowering of her status, which is, in fact, an assault on himself.

Ezekiel 22:10 suggests a classificatory dimension to the use of ענה in addition to the property dimension just described.[44] In that verse ענה represents sex with a menstruant. Pressler is probably right when she suggests that the woman is consenting, although presumably the law applies to non-consenting menstruants as well.[45] In this instance, the lowering of status derives from the woman's capacity to spread her natural blood-impurity during the act. During menstruation a woman's status of sexual integrity continues uncompromised if she maintains her blood impurity within the strict confines of the law. Her sexual integrity is compromised if the boundaries of her blood impurity are breached. She becomes the "kind of woman" who spreads the blood impurity of her discharge. This "kind of woman" in Lev 15 must, along with the man, cleanse ritually. In Lev 18 and 20, she, along with the man, irrevocably risks the כרת penalty.

Thus, in all instances but Ezek 22:10, the use of ענה is closely tied to a lowering of the woman's status which is itself constructed as a function of the loss a man suffers with respect to his sexual property.[46] In Ezek 22:10, it is tied to the loss of purity the man perpetrating the act suffers because of the woman's natural impurity. In all cases the woman becomes the "kind of woman" whose existence in some way harms a man.

d) מצא.[47] Three of the laws, vv. 23, 24, 28, use מצא in conjunction with the language-depicting-the-sex-act. מצא in each case precedes a שכב-clause. This use of מצא attributes a certain amount of chance or happenstance to the illicit act. The infraction is a "crime of opportunity." In each case, the man is the subject and the woman the object.

e) חזק and תפש. Just as לקח accompanies the verbs depicting the sex act in the first and last laws, and just as מצא accompanies the שכב-clause in vv. 24, 25 and 28, so also verbs of seizure accompany the language-depicting-the-sex-act in the laws of vv. 25–27 and vv. 28–29. Again, the man is the subject and the woman is the object of these verbs. These attending verbs in vv. 25 and 28 describe acts of violence preceding the consummation of the sex act. One concerns the betrothed virgin who is raped and the other the unbetrothed virgin who is raped.

Weinfeld argues that תפש in v. 28 does not refer to an act of violence, as does חזק, and that the case is not a case of rape. Rather like Exod 22:15–16, Deut

---

44. The classificatory dimension may also be ascribed to the act which Shechem commits in Gen 34 since he is said to have defiled (טמא) Dinah (vv. 5, 13, 27).

45. Pressler, *View of Women*, 11 n. 6.

46. Lam 5:11 and Ezek 22:11 also fit this pattern.

47. Anthony R. Ceresko, "The Function of *Antanaclasis* (*mṣ'* 'to find'//*mṣ'* 'to reach, overtake, grasp') in Hebrew Poetry, Especially in the Book of Qoheleth," *CBQ* 44 (1982): 557–58. Ceresko notes wide valence in the use of the מצא root in Deut 22.

22:28–29 is a case of seduction.[48] The two laws are essentially the same law revised to fit different authors' intentions.[49]

Weinfeld structures his argument under three points.[50] His first point consists of two assertions. The first is that ונמצאו implies that both the woman and the man committed the infraction willingly. The second is that תפש means "held" rather than "seized." He states that when the author of Deuteronomy wants to refer to rape he uses חזק. תפש, therefore, refers to something other than rape.[51]

However, ונמצאו can just as easily mean that hard evidence, in this instance in the form of testimony from eye witnesses, is necessary for the case to be prosecuted, whether it is a case of rape or of consent. Dempster states the following:

> …the verb, *mṣ*ʾ, particularly in the N stem, is a *terminus technicus* in juridical contexts for the discovery of evidence of crime, whether eye-witness or otherwise.[52]

Pressler's arguments concerning the meaning of תפש are enough to put to rest Weinfeld's contention that vv. 28–29 are a case of seduction rather than rape. She writes:

> Weinfeld overlooks the fact that the meaning of the verb when its object is inanimate differs from its meaning with a human object. תפש ("lay hold of") may be used to refer to "holding" or even "handling skillfully" inanimate objects or cities. When the object of the verb is a human being, however, תפש has to do with involuntary seizure.[53]

תפש occurs in three places in Deuteronomy outside of Deut 22:28: Deut 9:17; 20:19; 21:19. Deuteronomy 20:19 refers to taking a city in war. Deuteronomy 21:19 refers to a mother and father taking hold of a rebellious son to drag him before the elders. Deuteronomy 9:17 refers to Moses' action when he "seized" the tablets and threw them down in fury. The first two citations refer to actions taken against the will of a "victim." The last example refers to the precursor to an act of rage—demolition of the tables. Thus, all three examples refer to acts in the context of violence. תפש as "hold" in the mild sense, which suggests collusion on the part of both man and woman, is not indicated by these three uses in Deuteronomy.

---

48. Weinfeld, *Deuteronomy*, 286. The following commentators are among those who read Exod 22:15–16 as a case of seduction and Deut 22:28–29 as a case of rape: Driver, *Deuteronomy*, 258; Rofé, "Family and Sex Laws," 133–34; Tigay, *Deuteronomy*, 208; David Halivni Weiss, "A Note on אשר לא ארשה," *JBL* 8 (1962): 67. Von Rad, *Deuteronomy*, 142–43, considers vv. 28–29 to be a case of rape. He does not draw a contrast to this case with Exod 22:15–16.

49. Weinfeld, *Deuteronomy*, 285.

50. See the comments on Weinfeld's argument by Yair Zakovitch, "The Woman's Rights in the Biblical Law of Divorce," *The Jewish Law Annual*, vol. 4 (ed. Bernard S. Jackson; Leiden: Brill, 1981), 30–31.

51. Mayes, *Deuteronomy*, 312–13, follows Weinfeld with respect to both assertions. Phillips, "Another Look," 13, also makes the latter assertion.

52. Stephen Dempster, "The Deuteronomic Formula *kî yimmāṣēʾ* in the Light of Biblical and Ancient Near Eastern Law," *RB* 2 (1984): 198.

53. Pressler, *View of Women*, 37–38. F. Hesse ("חזק," *TDOT* 4:304) writes concerning the Hiphil form: "When a living creature or one of its members is 'seized' or 'grasped,' we are often dealing with an act of violence." See also Rofé, "Family and Sex Laws," 134.

Weinfeld's assertion that חזק is the singular verb of choice in Deuteronomy for referring to rape is also untenable.[54] Only one of nine occurrences of חזק in Deuteronomy exists in the context of a sexual act. That occurrence is the present text, Deut 22:25. The one other instance in Deuteronomy of the verb in the Hiphil refers to a woman grabbing the genitals of a man in defense of her husband. All other uses, which occur in the Qal or the Piel, refer to non-sexual acts. Thus, Weinfeld's conclusion that when Deuteronomy refers to rape it uses חזק is based on one example only, precisely the one for which he is arguing.

Weinfeld phrases his second point as follows:

> If we assume that the law of the BC deals with seduction and the book of Deuteronomy with sexual attack, it is difficult to understand why the father's right to refuse his daughter in marriage is mentioned particularly in the law of seduction and not in the law of rape. It is certainly more plausible to assume that the father would refuse to marry his daughter to a rapist but would consent to marry her to her seducer.[55]

This argument, however, assumes that the conceptuality, including intent and motivation of the author, is of one piece for the two texts. Such an assumption is uncertain at best. Even Weinfeld does not hold to it.[56] While it may or may not be true that the sociological reality of the two authors is the same, it is uncertain that the conceptuality of the two texts is the same.[57]

Weinfeld's third point is that if the author of Deuteronomy was referring only to rape, he would have cited the presupposed "legislation for cases of seduction" as he cited the alternative cases in vv. 23–27.[58] But why should we make such an assumption? That such a citation is absent may simply be evidence of the fact that the woman's intent is immaterial to the case. Pressler, who makes a point similar to Weinfeld's third point[59] herself, nevertheless, asserts that the consent is immaterial.[60]

---

54. Weinfeld, *Deuteronomy*, 286; Phillips, "Another Look," 13.

55. Weinfeld, *Deuteronomy*, 286–87. Pressler, *View of Women*, 38–39, agrees with Weinfeld on this point. This point is one of two reasons she gives for concluding that the woman's consent is immaterial. However, all that is necessary for that conclusion is the use of "they were found" as explained above, in conjunction with the fact that compensation is paid to the father.

56. Weinfeld, *Deuteronomy*, 285.

57. Frymer-Kensky and Phillips offer statements that serve as an example of the kinds of theories that might explain the difference between the two texts. Frymer-Kensky, "Deuteronomy," 59, states: "In Exodus, the marriage is at the discretion of the father; in Deuteronomy, it is obligatory. The reason for this difference *may* be that in Exodus the act is consensual whereas the act in Deuteronomy could be considered forcible. More likely this is not the issue, and Deuteronomy is once again limiting the authority of the father to determine his children's fate." Phillips, *Deuteronomy*, 152, suggests that in Deuteronomy the father's right of refusal is "abandoned, perhaps to ensure that the father would not be tempted at a later date to try and pass off his daughter as a virgin (cp. 22:13–21)."

58. Weinfeld, *Deuteronomy*, 287. Pressler, *View of Women*, 38–39, agrees with Weinfeld on this point also. She uses it for the same purpose as the previous reason.

59. Pressler, *View of Women*, 39, states: "First if the redactor of this passage had wanted to distinguish between the case of an unbetrothed girl who consents to sexual relationships and an unbetrothed girl who resists, he would have included the alternate case as he did in v. 23–27, and as

However, if consent is immaterial, then the question arises as to why the author specified תפש. Pressler states the following:

> The language of Deuteronomic law seems to indicate that the girl has not consented to the sexual act. The man's action is described in v. 23 with the verbs מצא ושׁכב, and in v. 25 with the verbs מצא, חזק, and שׁכב. The man's action in v. 28 is described by the verbs מצא, תפש, and שׁכב. The similarity of the phrasing indicates that differences in wording are significant. The drafters want to distinguish the man's action in v. 28 from both forcible rape of a resisting girl in v. 25 and from the seduction of a consenting girl in v. 23.[61]

On the one hand, Pressler says vv. 28–29 are a case of coercion. On the other hand, she says the coercion is somehow different from the coercion of vv. 25–27. On the one hand, she says the case of vv. 28–29 is somehow similar to the seduction of Exod 22:15–16. On the other hand, it is somehow different from the "seduction" of vv. 23–24. Pressler fails to explain what precisely constitutes the differences between the law of vv. 28–29 and the laws of both rape and "seduction" in Deut 22, such that room is left for it to be similar to Exod 22:15–16.

If the case of vv. 28–29 is different from the case of vv. 25–27, as well as the case of vv. 23–24, and similar to the case of Exod 22:15–16, then the alignment of differences and similarities posited by Pressler corresponds precisely to the difference between the betrothed and unbetrothed status of the woman. Pressler's observations concerning the vocabulary in vv. 23, 25 and 28 cannot be easily dismissed. If the conclusion she draws from those observations is correct, then the author conceptualizes "force" against a betrothed maiden as necessarily different from "force" against an unbetrothed maiden.

Finkelstein's conclusions drawn from Mesopotamian law are suggestive.

> It will be noted that there is some sort of correlation between the two axes: married–unmarried, coercion–consent. Thus consent and unmarried women rarely occur together, the only totally unambiguous instance being MAL 56... Unmarried women, even when betrothed, were usually minors, sexually speaking, since with the advent of their nobility they would soon have been married or, if already betrothed, have their marriage consummated. On strictly physiological grounds, therefore, it would have been unusual for a girl in this age group to seek sexual experience on her own initiative. In other words the combination of unmarried woman and the elements of consent was a most unlikely one purely as an empirical matter. Young girls in this age-group, however, were

---

the drafters of the Middle Assyrian laws did in paragraphs 55 (concerning an unconsenting girl) and 56 (concerning a girl who consents)."

60. Ibid., 37, states: "This position holds that פתה denotes seduction, while תפש implies the man's use of force. We accept that the two verbs do have the different meanings of seduction and coercion, but will argue that the difference is legally immaterial. The girl's consent or lack of consent is not a factor which defines the case." See also Pressler, "Sexual Violence," 107. Frymer-Kensky, "Deuteronomy," 58, states: "It is irrelevant to Deuteronomy whether the young woman was actually raped: the issue is not crime and punishment, but wrong and compensation." Phillips, *Ancient Israel's Criminal Law*, 113, states that emphasis is on the distinction between the betrothed and unbetrothed rather than on force or consent.

61. Pressler, *View of Women*, 38 n. 49.

not immune to rape or seduction by strange men, especially under circumstances where men may have mistaken innocent coquetry for an invitation.

With married women, on the other hand, a consentive situation is more readily envisaged, whatever the safeguards established by the society to prevent its occurrence, as, e.g., veiling. Rape plays a lesser role, therefore, in such a situation, although it is by no means ruled out as a possible occurrence.[62]

The betrothed woman of vv. 25–27 and the unbetrothed woman of vv. 28–29 both fall into the first class of women Finkelstein describes, the unmarried women. Such women, he suggests, are "not immune to rape or seduction." Perhaps, however, even finer distinctions than "coercion-consent," as described by Finkelstein, align with the betrothedwoman–unbetrothedwoman axis. In other words, perhaps תפש reflects the fact that every deflowered, unbetrothed woman is presumed to have been raped because of her young age, inexperience and "unsecured" status.[63] Nevertheless, perhaps use of תפש, as opposed to חזק, also attests to the author's perception that these same circumstances can possibly contribute to an unbetrothed woman's "participation" ("coquetry") in the act, such that her "coercion" is generically different from the "coercion" of the betrothed woman of vv. 25–27 and generically similar to the seduction of Exod 22:15–16. The use of פתה, "seduce," in Exod 22:15–16 may simply attest more pointedly than תפש to the latter perception concerning unbetrothed women.

The woman of vv. 28–29 is unmarried, unbetrothed and deflowered. She is, therefore, by legal definition, forced or "raped." To what degree she willingly participated is immaterial to the case. If the infraction comes to light after she is married, as in vv. 20–21, the consequences, akin to the consequences of adultery, are dire. By contrast, in vv. 28–29 the wrong is easily rectified. And this is what the case is about: compensation to the father.[64] That compensation includes

---

62. J. J. Finkelstein, "Sex Offenses in Sumerian Laws," *JAOS* 86 (1966): 368. See the following scholars who make related or similar comments: Biale, *Women*, 241–42; Tigay, *Deuteronomy*, 207–8.

63. Yadin, *Temple*, 369, notes that the author of the *Temple Scroll* "created a smooth text, most of it taken from Deuteronomy, though its 'legal situation' is based on Exodus. In other words, he rules that the seized woman and the seduced woman are identical in circumstance and in law." Yadin contends that the author viewed both the Exodus law and the Deuteronomy law as treating situations in which the woman acts against her will, "for since it is necessary to seduce her, she is not acting of her own free will from the start" (p. 371). See also Pressler, *View of Women*, 37–38.

64. Pressler, *View of Women*, 40. Weinfeld, *Deuteronomy*, 285, sees the monetary penalty (מהר) of Exodus as compensation to the father. He sees the monetary penalty of Deuteronomy (חמשים כסף) as a fine "for violating the maiden and not as compensation for the father's loss of marriage-price." But Pressler has argued rightly that absence of the word מהר in Deuteronomy cannot be taken as evidence that the monetary penalty is a fine rather than compensation. She states (*View of Women*, 40): "In both Deuteronomy and Exodus, the father receives compensation for the economic injury which his daughter's loss of virginity could cause him." Rofé, "Family and Sex Laws," 152, calls the penalties in both vv. 13–19 and vv. 28–29 "symbolic *talio*." Wegner's comments (*Chattel*, 26) with respect to the Mishnah are relevant: "True, the sages distinguish between a seduced girl and a rape victim by awarding pain and suffering to the latter; and they force the rapist to marry his victim (Deut 22:29)—unlike a seducer, who may do so only at the father's option (Exod 22:16)… But these measures do not necessarily reflect a concern with the victim's *personal* rights. All scheduled payments, including pain and suffering for rape, go to the victim's father (*m. Ket.* 4:1),

monetary remuneration and placement of his daughter, which otherwise would be an impossibility.[65]

In summary, חזק, the meaning of which is undisputed, and תפש, the meaning of which is argued, both convey the idea of seizure, perhaps against the will of the woman,[66] but more certainly against the rights of the man.

2) *The Purge Formula.* In addition to the verbs just described, a phrase recurring throughout the series reveals the gender asymmetry of the language-depicting-the-sex-act because of the manner in which the author uses it to qualify the sex act itself. This recurring phrase is the purge formula in vv. 21, 22 and 24.

The purge formula, at first glance, might be read as an injunction focusing on a primary concern to cleanse impurity from the midst of the people, as Thistle-thwaite suggests:

> This crime is so serious a disruptive evil that "you shall purge the evil from Israel" (Deut 22:22b) by killing the evildoers; the language of purging is a clear indication that the purity of Israel is at stake in this violation.[67]

However, the way in which the purge formula is used suggests that a concern for the property rights of the man constitutes whatever concern for purity may be invoked by the formula. The purge formula is instructional advice[68] warning the addressee to rid himself (and implicitly herself) and the community of behavior that undermines such property rights.

The purge formula occurs only with cases in which the *woman* is guilty.[69] It occurs in vv. 21, 22 and 24. It does not occur with the companion case to vv. 20–21 in which the woman is wrongly slandered (vv. 13–19). Nor does it occur in the cases where the women are raped (vv. 25–29), including the case in which the man marries the unbetrothed virgin as a remedy. Finally, it does not occur in 23:1. This is the only law with guilty women from which the formula is absent.

The significance of this singularity becomes apparent only when another singularity of 23:1 is examined. Indeed, within this series, 23:1 is a cornucopia of singularities. 23:1 is the only apodictic law in the series. It is the only law from which penalties are absent. It is the only law with guilty women that lacks a purge formula. It is the only law that treats incest.[70] But most significantly, it is

thus identifying *the father* (not the girl) as the injured party; the requirements that the rapist marry the victim probably stems more from a wish to spare the father the trouble of finding her another husband than from any concern with the girl herself."

65.   Pressler, "Sexual Violence," 109. "The violation also creates a social problem. What is to be done with such defiled maidens? The forced marriage protects the young woman, her father and society" (p. 105). But a social problem is, first of all, a problem for the father. Placement of a "damaged" daughter serves his welfare, removing the crux of *his* social problem.

66.   See the discussion of "intent of the woman" in vv. 23–27 below.

67.   Thistlethwaite, "You May Enjoy," 63.

68.   Mayes, *Deuteronomy*, 233–34, 312.

69.   This, rather than redactional issues, is why it fails to appear with 22:13–19. See Otto, "False Weights," 141.

70.   I am referring to incest broadly defined as described by Bigger, "Family Laws," 193.

the one law in which the victim is dead or divorced.[71] This latter singularity is telling.

Although the primary concern of 23:1 is to protect the dead father's property-interests, the misdeed which it regulates is a *kind of* "victimless" infraction.[72] The offense of the situation is less dire than if the victim were alive. In other words, the bond tying the widow to the father, although strong enough to prevent the son from marrying her, is less "actual" than the bonds tying the other guilty women to their men. It might be thought of as a *virtual* bond, whereas the others are *real* bonds.

One might argue that the apodictic form itself is responsible for the absence of the purge formula and the penalty. However, if the misdeed of 23:1 is a kind of victimless infraction, one might just as easily argue that the infraction itself is responsible for their absence. Perhaps marriage to and ensuing sex with the father's wife is the kind of crime that does not warrant a penalty in the mind of the author. In this case, the infraction *allows* the apodictic form.

Nevertheless, the purge formula is present in all laws where the woman is tied to the man by a *real* bond, marriage or betrothal, and where she is guilty. If the presence of the purge formula is due to the guilt of the woman, in the context of some kind of "real bond," then here is a telling gender asymmetry. A sexual infraction would seem to be especially insidious when the woman cooperates.

Within Deuteronomy, every instance of the purge formula outside of Deut 22 is one in which the infraction strikes at fundamentals.[73] Several of the infractions—false witness (Deut 19:19), rebellion against parents (21:21) and disobedience to priest or judge (17:12)—put at risk the capacity of society to deal with wrongs by defying the very governing bodies, including parents, which are guardians against perpetuation of such wrongs. Related to the three types of infractions just named is the kidnapping infraction in Deut 24:7, with which the purge formula also occurs. While this infraction does not defy a governing body, it does undermine a man's capacity to seek redress for his own rights or to defend those rights. The formula also occurs with the "worship-of-other-gods"

---

71.   Scholars understand this law as applying to only stepmothers who have become widows or divorcees. See Cairns, *Deuteronomy*, 200; Craigie, *Deuteronomy*, 295; Driver, *Deuteronomy*, 259; Frymer-Kensky, "Deuteronomy," 59; Kalland, "Deuteronomy," 139; Mayes, *Deuteronomy*, 313; Phillips, *Deuteronomy*, 153; idem, "Uncovering the Father's Skirt," 38; Tigay, *Deuteronomy*, 209. The strongest argument for this conclusion consists of two points. First, the "wife of the father" rather than the "mother of the addressee" is specified. Second, the law forbids the man to *marry* (לקח) the wife of the father. Such an act on the part of the son would be an impossibility were the father alive. Who in the community would help to formalize and recognize such a legal arrangement? The impossibility is ameliorated, however, if the father is dead. Phillips suggests the law is evidence that inheritance of a dead father's wives was practiced. See Phillips, *Deuteronomy*, 153; idem, "Uncovering the Father's Skirt," 38.

72.   See p. 229 below under the discussion of structure.

73.   Mayes, *Deuteronomy*, 233, writes the following concerning the formula: "So you shall purge the evil from the midst of you: this formula is found also in 17:7; 19:19; 21:21; 22:21, 24; 24:7, and, with 'from Israel' instead of 'from the midst of you', in 17:12; 22:22. In all cases (except 19:19) it follows on the death penalty and describes the consequences of its being carried out. It is not found outside Deuteronomy, but its existence is apparently presupposed in Jg. 20:13."

infraction in Deut 17:7, an infraction which undermines the relationship of Israel to Yhwh and thereby cripples her capacity to follow Yhwh's commands.[74] The admonition not to pity the murderer but to "burn the guilt of innocent blood from Israel" in Deut 21:1–9 is a similar phrase. The infraction of murder, of course, is the ultimate usurpation of a man's capacity to seek redress or defend his rights and is therefore an extreme threat to the power of individuals and society to guard against the perpetuation of such wrongs. These infractions strike at fundamentals. They strike at the very tools that enable Israel to follow the commands laid down by Yhwh.

If the infractions of Deut 22 which bear the purge formula also strike at fundamentals, then the fact that the formula occurs only with those illicit acts in which women are guilty in the context of a "real bond" is significant. Something about the guilt of the woman strikes at fundamentals: her co-participation is a special threat. She is, as it were, a "trojan horse."

3) *Conclusion.* Language-depicting-the-sex-act demonstrates woman's marginalization in the text as well as her implicit responsibility to the laws. In addition, it harbors several clear indicators that woman's sexuality is the property of the male and that the intent of the laws is to protect that property.

2. Selection-of-Laws, Identification-of-Women, Reiteration-of-the-Man-to-Whom-the-Woman-Belongs and Structure-of-the-Text

Four features in the text demonstrate, as does the language-depicting-the-sex-act that the concern of the laws is to protect the woman's sexuality as the property of the man. The four features are selection-of-laws, identification-of-women, reiteration-of-the-man-to-whom-the-woman-belongs and structure-of-the-text.

a. *Selection-of-Laws.* For this series, the author has selected only laws restricting sexual activity with respect to women who belong to men. Sexual activity with respect to the prostitute and spinster are absent. The only widow or divorcee whose sexual activity is regulated is the father's wife. This latter, single incest law, which the author has chosen, is one in which the woman belongs to a man, the father.[75] The woman is off-limits to the son, even if she is not off-limits to other males, because of the "virtual" bond tying her to the father. Laws restricting other affines and consanguines who may or may not belong to men are also absent from the series. Thus, the series, including 23:1, is preoccupied with the protection of the sexuality of women who belong to men.

The series shows special interest in those women most vulnerable in their ties to men, the betrothed women. Furthermore, in four out of the six laws virginity is a central issue (vv. 13–21, 23–29). It is a central issue especially with respect to the liminal scenario of betrothal or the pre-liminal scenario in which woman

---

74. George E. Mendenhall and Gary A. Herion, "Covenant," *ABD* 1:1187.

75. Carmichael, "Ceremonial Crux," 326. See Carmichael's comments for an interesting theory concerning the rationale for the selection within Deuteronomy of this one affinity law from among the possible affinity laws.

has yet to be betrothed. Even the virginity of the woman of the first law, who is married, is a concern only with respect to the period of the time before the consummation of her marriage, either during betrothal or before betrothal.

The fact that the sexuality of only women who belong to men is protected evidences that ultimately the concern is to protect the man. The fact that special interest focuses on women yet to be secured by marriage illustrates that women in transfer or women yet to be transferred are the loci where a man is most vulnerable with respect to his sexual property. The selection-of-laws in this series, therefore, indicates that the primary concern of the series is protection of the woman's sexuality as the property of the man.

b. *Identification-of-Women.* The identification of the women who are central to each of the laws also demonstrates that the primary concern of these laws is to protect the man's sexual property.

1) בתולים/בתולה. Before examining the identification of women in this series, however, a brief note concerning the ongoing discussion of בתולים/בתולה is necessary.

A number of scholars have argued that בתולה, in Deut 22:13–23:1 and other places, means "girl of marriageable age" rather than "virgin."[76] Among these scholars, Wenham makes the most thorough argument. However, Locher, Pressler and others have challenged this notion and Wenham's arguments in particular.[77]

Locher, contrary to the view argued by Wenham, concludes that both Akkadian *batultu* and Hebrew בתולה seem to represent a stage of life,[78] but both can also mean "virgin."[79] Furthermore, in the biblical *legal* texts, the meaning of בתולה is restricted to "virginity." Regarding Deut 22:13–19 he writes:

> Die alternativen Deutungshypothesen von WENHAM haben sich demgegenüber als unwahrscheinlich erwiesen. Das hebr. Wort bᵉtûlā bedeutet in diesem Text und in anderen atl. Rechtstexten „Jungfrau", das Abstraktum bᵉtûlîm „(Zeichen der) Jungfräulichkeit".[80]

---

76. Frymer-Kensky, "Virginity," 79, states: "As is now generally well known, the term normally translated 'virgin', *betûlâ*, means a girl of marriageable age… The term *betûlâ* can also sometimes mean 'virgin.'" She cites Lev 21:14 in support. See also Peggy L. Day, "From the Child is Born the Woman: The Story of Jephthah's Daughter," in Day, ed., *Gender and Difference*, 59; Finkelstein, "Sex Offenses," 356–57; Cyrus H. Gordon, "The Patriarchal Age," *JBR* 21, no. 4 (1953): 240–41; idem, "Glossary," in *Ugaritic Textbook* (Rome: Pontifical Biblical Institute, 1965), 377–78; Landsberger, "Jungfräulichkeit," 57–59; Matthews and Benjamin, *Social World*, 177; Mayes, *Deuteronomy*, 311–12; John J. Schmitt, "Virgin," *ABD* 6:853–54; Wenham "*Bᵉtûlāh.*"

77. Locher, *Ehre einer Frau in Israel*, 192; Pressler, *View of Women*, 25–28. See also Engelken, *Frauen im alten Israel*, 5–43; Frymer-Kensky, "Deuteronomy," 57; H. M. Orlinsky, "Virgin," *IDBSup* 939; M. Tsevat, "בְּתוּלָה," *TDOT* 8:342; Zipor, "Restrictions," 260 n. 10.

78. Locher, *Ehre einer Frau in Israel*, 177–79.

79. Ibid., 173–76, 180.

80. Ibid., 192.

Pressler concurs:[81]

> Words often acquire technical meanings when they are used in a legal context. Wenham's argument no longer holds when one considers the use of the term בְּתוּלָה within the laws. Several of the laws require understanding בְּתוּלָה with the more specialized meaning, "virgin."[82]

The arguments of both Locher and Pressler, regarding בתולים as well as בתולה, particularly with respect to Deut 22:13–23:1, are cogent and convincing.[83] They need not be reviewed here.

However, one observation in addition to their arguments, related to the use of בתולה in Deut 22:13–23:1, is worth mentioning. Wenham writes the following:

> The word *bᵉtûlāh* is only mentioned once in this law, in v. 19, where it seems unlikely to mean 'virgin'. For in the general preamble setting out the background to the case the girl has been described as a wife, to which 'he has gone in'… In this case it would be totally inappropriate to call the wife a 'virgin' but 'teenager' might still be applicable.[84]

In other words, since the woman is described as being married in v. 13, calling her a בתולה in v. 19 would be contradictory if בתולה means "virgin" rather than "girl of marriageable age." The same kind of problem exists with the use of בתולה in Joel 1:8.[85] In short, the problem is that a married woman who is obviously not a virgin is called בתולה. Pressler agrees with Wenham that בתולה cannot mean "virgin" in Joel 1:8.[86] She ignores the same *problem* in Deut 22:19.

---

81.   A number of scholars come to the same conclusion. Engelken, *Frauen im alten Israel*, 10, states: "Aus den Rechtstexten geht die Beurteilung der Virginität am eindrücklichsten hervor." See also Frymer-Kensky, "Deuteronomy," 57. Regarding Deut 22:13–21, she writes: "Normally the Hebrew term *betulah* refers to a young adolescent girl; it does not necessarily connote virginity. When sexual virginity is meant, a phrase such as 'who has not known a man' is sometimes added (e.g. Gen 24:16)… It seems much more probable that *betulim* means 'marks of virginity' despite the fact that *betulah* simply means an adolescent girl." See also Frymer-Kensky, "Virginity," 79–96. Orlinsky, "Virgin," 939, states: "Although the term בתולה basically means 'maiden', it is often used in contexts whose intent is to specify virginity." Tsevat, "בְּתוּלָה," 340–42, states: "Then very gradually this word assumed the meaning 'virgo intacta' in Hebrew and Aramaic, a development that ended in Middle Hebrew, to which the German 'Jungfrau' offers an instructive parallel. It is not surprising that this process of narrowing the meaning and of making it more precise is discernible in legal language… As has already been mentioned, the three passages in which *bethulah* clearly means 'virgin' are found in the law… The third passage has to do with the husband's assertion that his wife was not a virgin when she married him (Dt. 22:13–21)." Zipor, "Restrictions," 260 n. 10, states: "Though I agree that in certain biblical and other Near Eastern passages, especially within poetry, *betûlāh* may signify 'a young woman,' this is not the case in biblical legal texts."

82.   Pressler, *View of Women*, 26.

83.   For a brief overview of scholarly discussion concerning בתולה in connection with the biblical text, see Locher, *Ehre einer Frau in Israel*, 177.

84.   Wenham, "*Bᵉtûlāh*," 331.

85.   Ibid., 345. Wenham writes: "*baˤal* literally means 'lord' and is a regular word for husband. *Prima facie* then *betûlāh* should not be translated 'virgin,' as this text presupposes she has been married… The imagery is the more powerful and plausible if Joel is describing a young girl widowed shortly after her marriage. She has lost a husband and her prospects of finding another are not great."

86.   Pressler, *View of Women*, 26; Frymer-Kensky, "Deuteronomy," 57; idem, "Virginity," 79.

However, the seeming contradiction resolves itself in both examples if בתולה in these instances is understood to denote "virgin at the time of marriage." In other words, a בתולה ("virgin") includes the non-married woman who has never had sex as well as the married woman who, at the time of marriage, had never had sex. It is thus a technical term for status at the time of marriage or prior to marriage. A married woman who is called a בתולה is the "kind of woman" who was *virgo intacta* when she got married. With this understanding the contradiction is resolved.[87]

בתולים/בתולה means "virgin"/"tokens of virginity"[88] in Deut 22:13–21.

2) *Identifying References.* בתולה is only one among several references identifying women in the laws. In every law except the first law, the author makes initial reference to the woman with respect to her legal relationship to men. In other words, what man the woman belongs to and the strength of the bond is central to the concern of these laws. In the course of each law, with minor exceptions, she is identified either with respect to her legal relationship to men or with respect to her sexual history, as it pertains to men. This is true of female victims as well as female perpetrators. Only the male victims, by contrast, are identified with respect to their legal relationship to a woman—as, for example, "the father of the maiden" and "the wife of his neighbor." They are so identified because their legal connection to these women is the source of their victimization. In almost every case this identification of the male victim is repeated.[89] The male perpetrators, on the other hand, are identified simply as "a man," "the man" or "the man who committed X." Their legal relationship to any woman other than the one with whom they commit the illicit act is irrelevant. This gender asymmetry is consistent throughout the text.

In the first law (vv. 13–21) the author initially identifies the woman in the course of the narrative as the אִשָּׁה whom the man takes and goes into. He also identifies her throughout the law as בְּתוּלַת יִשְׂרָאֵל, בַּת, בְּתוּלֵי הַנַּעַר, הַנַּעַר/הַנַּעֲרָה. Every identification of the central woman of this law except for הַנַּעַר/הַנַּעֲרָה specifies the relation of that woman to a man. Age, sexual status and legal relationship to a man are all catalogued by her identifications. In addition, in this law a woman, the mother, is identified only with reference to her daughter. Verse 15 makes reference to the "father of the girl and her mother." This is the only instance in which a woman is identified with reference to another woman. While the mother is mentioned as participating in the complaint by bringing the

---

87. See Locher, *Ehre einer Frau in Israel*, 179–80, and Tsevat, "בְּתוּלָה," 341, for another suggestion resolving this contradiction in Joel 1:8. See also Day, "From the Child," 59, especially n. 13; Engelken, *Frauen im alten Israel*, 14.

88. Frymer-Kensky, "Virginity," 79, takes בתולים to be the "blood of defloration." Many scholars, including the following, take בתולים to be tokens of virginity: Don C. Benjamin, *Deuteronomy and City Life* (Lanham, Md.: University Press of America, 1983), 227; Clifford, *Deuteronomy*, 120; Craigie, *Deuteronomy*, 292; Driver, *Deuteronomy*, 255; Kalland, "Deuteronomy," 138; Phillips, *Deuteronomy*, 148; von Rad, *Deuteronomy*, 142.

89. See the discussion of reiteration-of-the-male-victim below.

בתולים before the elders along with the father, the father's position is central. In fact, he "takes" (לקח) the daughter and the mother (v. 15). Once the complaint begins, the mother disappears. Perhaps, her brief appearance occurs because mothers keep or find בתולים when necessary.

In the second law (v. 22) the woman is identified as אִשָּׁה בְעֻלַת־בַּעַל, "a woman, the lady of a lord," as well as הָאִשָּׁה, "the woman." "A woman, the lady of a lord," catalogues with specificity her legal relationship to the man to whom she belongs. She is the one belonging to the one who owns. Pressler notes that this phrase occurs only here and in Gen. 20:3 and that "in both contexts, the wording emphasizes the husband's claims over his wife. It clearly specifies her marital status."[90] In the third law (vv. 23–24) the woman is referred to as a נַעֲרָ בְתוּלָה מְאֹרָשָׂה לְאִישׁ, "a maiden, a betrothed virgin belonging to a man." She is identified also as simply הַנַּעֲרָ and finally as אֵשֶׁת רֵעֵהוּ. The first and last iden- tifications, as in the second law, explicate the fact that the woman belongs to a man. Age, sexual status and legal relationship to a man are each catalogued. Connection to men is thus central to her identification.

The fourth law (vv. 25–27) describes the woman as הַנַּעֲרָ הַמְאֹרָשָׂה, a "betrothed maiden" and also simply as נַעֲרָ. Legal status and age are catalogued.

The fifth law (vv. 28–29) refers to the woman as a נַעֲרָ בְתוּלָה אֲשֶׁר לֹא־אֹרָשָׂה, "a virgin maiden who is not betrothed," as well as הַנַּעֲרָ. It also identifies her with respect to her future relationship to the man as לְאִשָּׁה, "as a wife." Age, sexual status and legal status are catalogued. Again connection to the man is prominent.

The sixth law (23:1) refers to the woman as אֵשֶׁת אָבִיו, "the wife of his father." She is also represented as כָּנָף. Legal status and sexual status are thus catalogued. The second phrase in 23:1b, or the motive clause, indicates that the ego's relationship to the man to whom the woman belongs is also central. Connection to men is again the central concern for identification of the woman.

Thus, woman is identified in most instances of the text with respect to her connection to men. Her sexual status and/or legal status are catalogued in each case. Her general age is also catalogued in the cases where she is not fully married. Conversely, the law is unconcerned about the male perpetrator's and male victim's sexual status and age. Thus, a relationship to women is catalogued only so as to define the sexual property rights the law intends to protect.

The woman's sexuality is protected precisely because it belongs to the man. Thus, the identification of the woman, which is of central concern to the law, demonstrates that the primary concern of the law is to protect the sexual prop- erty of the man.

c. *Reiteration-of-the-Man-to-Whom-the-Woman-Belongs.* Reiteration-of-the- man-to-whom-the-woman-belongs demonstrates that this man is of central concern to the laws of Deut 22:13–23:1. This, in turn, lends support to the conclusion that protection of his rights and property is the intent of the laws.

90. Pressler, *View of Women*, 31.

Since each woman is initially identified with respect to her relationship to the man to whom she belongs, the author brings these men to the attention of the reader at the beginning of each law, either implicitly or explicitly. The husband, for example, is explicitly called forth by the expression "the lady of a lord" in v. 22. The father is implicitly called to the attention of the reader by the expression "virgin who is not betrothed," since the reader knows unbetrothed virgins belong to their fathers. These initial collocations are necessary because they inform the reader of the context and import of the infractions.

However, in the description of the consequences of every law, except the law of v. 22, this man is mentioned a second time. Since the reader has already been informed of the context and import of the infraction by the first mention, this second mention is unnecessary, at least for understanding the scenario that the law addresses. This second mention recalls, as well, the fact that the woman legally belongs to this man. The author makes this second mention, the "reiteration," explicit in every case except v. 22 and vv. 25–27. In vv. 25–27, the second mention is arguably present, but it is oblique. In v. 22, the author mentions this man only once as part of the woman's identification. No second mention is made.

Verse 22 also differs from the remaining laws in at least one other way and therein lies the explanation for the absence of the reiteration in it as well as the presence of the reiteration in the other laws. In 22:13–21, 23–27 and 23:1, the bonds tying the woman in marriage at the time of the infraction are less secure than the bond of v. 22. In the context of less security, therefore, the author reiterates his presentation of "the man to whom the woman belongs" in 22:20–21, 23–27 and 23:1 so as to demonstrate that this man is of central concern to the law. The same central concern is demonstrated in vv. 13–19 and 28–29 by the fact that the father receives the monetary compensation from the male perpetrator. This stipulation for monetary compensation itself serves as the reiteration in these two laws. Thus, reiteration is absent in the case of v. 22 because the bonds tying the woman to the man at the time of the infraction are so secure as to make reiteration unnecessary.

1) *Verses 22:13–19 and 22:28–29.* In the cases of 22:13–19 and 22:28–29 the reiterations occur, as mentioned, within the narrative description of the compensation to the victims. These are the only two laws in all of LST and DST in which such monetary compensation occurs.[91] The two reiterations, while unnecessary for understanding the scenarios which the laws address, are nevertheless integral to the consequences which the laws dictate. In this way, they differ from the reiterations of the remaining laws.

---

91. See the following scholars for explanation of the nature of the compensation: Cairns, *Deuteronomy*, 198; Mace, *Hebrew Marriage*, 2525; Phillips, *Deuteronomy*, 149; Tigay, *Deuteronomy*, 205–6.

Compensation to the father indicates, in these cases, that the real victim is the man not the woman.[92] In v. 19, the father is recompensed because his daughter's sexual integrity is slandered.[93] In v. 29, the father is recompensed because his daughter's sexual integrity is violated.[94]

In both laws, marriage is stipulated and divorce forbidden. Several scholars, including Pressler, have suggested that this indicates that the laws intend also to protect the woman.[95] The presumption is that a violated woman has no chance of marriage unless her rapist marries her, as Tamar's fate demonstrates.[96] However, a "violated" woman's inability to marry is a function of the rights of men— fathers as well as husbands. The presumption that the father's rights are served, at least as much as the woman's, by the marriage provision is equally as reasonable as the presumption that the law protects the woman. Marriage to the rapist relieves the father of the burden to support a violated daughter for the rest of his life. It may also bring some semblance of repair to the damage done to the honor of the family, of which the father is the head.[97] Furthermore, the assumption that a woman in ancient Israel would prefer to marry her rapist than to go without marriage is by no means self-evident.[98] Sympathy for the psychological, emotional and physical damage done to the woman personally is absent from the law. The marriage provision fails to fill the void of such an absence.

However, the marriage portion of the penalty of vv. 28–29 has a motive clause which states that the reason that the man must marry the woman is because he "humiliated" (ענה) *her*. Concern for the father in this motive clause is unmentioned. Nevertheless, as stated above, implicit within the connotation of ענה as "lowered status" is the damage done to the father and any potential man who becomes a husband to the woman.[99]

---

92. However, the absence of compensation does not indicate, contrary to crime/tort proponents, the converse: that where the death penalty is given, the man to whom the woman belongs is not the real victim.

93. Pressler, *View of Women*, 29, states: "Who does the law consider to have been wronged by the husband's accusations? The father receives the damages even though the motive clause cites the evil name brought upon the girl as the basis for that penalty. Indeed, the father is compensated at the girl's expense; the damages paid to her father are taken from the household to which she is now permanently attached. The law apparently views the father and his household as an injured party." See Matthews, "Honor and Shame," 108, for the way in which this text illustrates the role that maintaining honor plays "in the village setting."

94. Weiss, "A Note," 67; Pressler, *View of Women*, 36 n. 43. See also Mayes, *Deuteronomy*, 312.

95. Pressler, *View of Women*, 29, 40–41. See also Benjamin, *Deuteronomy*, 226; Biale, *Women*, 242; Cairns, *Deuteronomy*, 200; Craigie, *Deuteronomy*, 293 n. 17, 295; Frymer-Kensky, "Deuteronomy," 59; Mayes, *Deuteronomy*, 313; Stulman, "Sex and Familial Crimes," 61; Tigay, *Deuteronomy*, 208.

96. Biale, *Women*, 242–43.

97. Matthews and Benjamin, *Social World*, 178–81.

98. See the discussion below of Deut 25. See also David Werner Amram, *Jewish Law of Divorce* (New York: Hermon, 1968; reprint 1975), 45.

99. This is the case, even though Deut 21:10–14 suggests that the "lawgiver" is *capable* of looking at the harm done to a woman by ענה, lowering her status. Lowering of status has to do with a

A man has rights to the exclusive use of the sexuality of his wife. It belongs only to him. A father has rights to the money and honor the virginity of his daughter brings him. While the money and honor from her virginity is preserved if she marries the rapist, the "exclusivity" of the adulteress has been forever damaged because another man has entered where only one man may go. One man has irrevocably stolen from another man. He cannot ever give back or compensate for what he took. Since the situations of vv. 19–27 cannot be "fixed," death is the penalty. Mace describes the situation as follows:

> From the point of view of property, adultery is clearly a much more serious fault than fornication. Intercourse with an unbetrothed virgin was taking goods which were on the market without fulfilling the necessary conditions; which could be put right by insisting that they be fulfilled. Adultery, however, was taking goods which were no longer on the market, but were already owned by another. No corresponding course could put this right. It was the difference between pilfering from an open stall and committing a burglary by breaking into a private house.[100]

A man's right to exclusive use of his wife's sexuality or his right to the money and honor from his daughter's virginity is the primary concern of the law. When those rights are abrogated such that no "fix" can occur—death is the penalty.

Thus, the reiteration of the male victim in the compensatory clauses of vv. 13–19 and vv. 28–29 clearly emphasize that the law is concerned with the damage done to the father. The damage is property damage in the form of brideprice and honor. The law intends to prevent such scenarios and to mediate rectification when they transpire.

2) *Verses 22:20–21 and 22:23–27.* In the laws of vv. 20–21 and vv. 23–27 the reiteration occurs in clauses explaining the motivation for the penalties.

Verse 21 states that the woman shall die because she committed a נְבָלָה in Israel, by harloting in the house *of her father*.[101] The father is the victim.[102] Verse 24 states that the male perpetrator shall die because he "lowered the status" (עִנָּה) of the woman belonging to *his neighbor*. The male neighbor is the victim.

The reiteration in v. 26 is oblique. The law states: "For like a man rising against his neighbor and killing him, a living being, so is this matter."[103] This

---

shift in possibilities with respect to her connections to men. Her status depends upon the harm or honor done to the men.

100. Mace, *Hebrew Marriage*, 245.

101. Some Scholars conclude that the fact that the woman is stoned at the door of the house of her father indicates that the father is thereby shamed for not guarding his property. See Craigie, *Deuteronomy*, 293; Mayes, *Deuteronomy*, 311. Phillips takes the locale of the punishment to be a "punitive measure directed against the father" (*Ancient Israel's Criminal Law*, 116) "whether or not he was aware of the facts" (*Deuteronomy*, 149).

102. See Countryman, *Dirt*, 164; Frymer-Kensky, *Deuteronomy*, 57; Neufeld, *Ancient Hebrew Marriage Laws*, 164.

103. Mayes, Pressler and Fishbane note that this phrase recalls Deut 19:11. Mayes, *Deuteronomy*, 312, suggests that it has the purpose of "emphasizing the connection between these marriage laws and the earlier complex by showing that in these marriage laws it is also a question of life and

phrase explains the sexual infraction in the field with a betrothed woman. The woman's sexuality is analogous to the "man's life," the ultimate form of property.[104] Taking her sexuality is, therefore, a property offense against him.[105] This is the accepted and most sensible and plain reading. It is the only attribution by DST of "ownership" of female sexuality to the woman herself.

Nevertheless, the analogy simultaneously evokes an additional set of correspondences. In this set of correspondences the fiancé is analogous to "his neighbor" and the fiancé's sexual property is analogous to "the neighbor's life." In other words, rape of the woman is like taking the fiancé's sexual property. Part of the power of this latter evocation derives from the fact that all the characters of the chosen analogy are male. Another portion of its power derives from the alignment of penalties, as Biale's comment suggests:

> The man who meets a betrothed virgin in the country where her crying out cannot be heard, seizes her, and rapes her, is stoned to death. His offense is twofold: like a murderer, he has attacked his victim and he violated the prohibition of adultery. Yet, the essence of the offence is having sexual relations with another man's wife. How do we know that the major offense is having sex with another man's wife rather than the assault entailed in "violating" her? Because the punishment for raping a virgin who does not belong to another man is so much less severe.[106]

The analogy, in the context of the alignment of penalties in Deut 22:13–23:1, thus conjures both readings. As such, it is the reiteration-of-the-man-to-whom-the-woman-belongs. The victim is the woman. The victim is also, however, the fiancé.

3) *Verse 23:1.* Finally, in 23:1 the apodictic law states: "A man shall not take the wife of his father, for he shall not uncover the skirt of *his father*." Reiteration occurs in the second clause.[107] The victim is the father.

4) *Conclusion.* The two reiterations that occur as a result of narration of compensation (22:20–21, 28–29) to the male victim are a necessary part of the narratives of the laws. The remaining reiterations are less necessary to the laws since the woman in each case is initially identified as a betrothed (22:23–27) or a wife (22:13; 23:1). The reiteration is arguably present in v. 26b. Furthermore, this latter reiteration also attributes "ownership" of female sexuality to the woman herself, the only law in all of DST which does so. Its absence in 22:22 fits a reasonable pattern. Thus, six out of the seven cases have reiteration-of-the-man-to-whom-the-woman-belongs. By the inclusion of such reiterations, the author

death." Pressler, *View of Women*, 33 n. 33, considers it secondary and notes that the reference underscores the "innocence of the victim." See also Fishbane, *Biblical Interpretation*, 219.

104. Pressler, "Sexual," 108.

105. Fishbane, *Biblical Interpretation*, 219.

106. Biale, *Women*, 242.

107. See the discussion of the relationship of these clauses in analysis of Lev 18 above and Deut 27 below.

achieves an emphasis upon the victims of concern in each case. The author intends to leave no doubt about that identity.

Thus, reiteration-of-the-men-to-whom-the-women-belong supports the conclusion that the primary concern of the law is to protect the sexual property of the man.[108]

d. *Structure-of-the-Text.* The structure of Deut 22:13–23:1 also demonstrates that the intent of the laws is to protect the woman's sexuality as the property of the man.

1) *Macrostructure.* Deuteronomy 22:13–23:1 occurs within a context in which "use of property" in general is the primary concern. Deuteronomy 22 divides into a three-part structure based on thematic signals. All three parts deal with the use of property. The structure is as follows:

I.	Non-Sexual Property	22:1–11
	A. Brother's Property	1–4
	B. One's Own Property	5–11
	1. body: garments	5
	2. extended environment: birds	6–7
	3. house: parapet	8
	4. immediate environment: vineyard, field, ox, ass	9–10
	5. body: garments	11
II.	Property as Reminder	22:12
III.	Sexual Property	22:13–23:1

Braulik has observed that Deut 21:1–23 and 22:13–29 cohere as separate units thematically, structurally and linguistically.[109] Their coherence isolates Deut 22:1–12, as "a compositionally independent intermediate text."[110] For this "independent intermediate" unit he suggests an "interleaved" pattern that alternates themes concerning forbidden mixtures with themes concerning preservation of life.[111] However, a pattern more fundamental and more comprehensive than the "interleaved" pattern exists within and beyond this unit. This more fundamental pattern reveals that "use of property" is the primary concern not only of vv. 1–12 but also of the chapter as a whole. In fact, the pattern isolates the following three units within the sex-series pericope: vv. 1–11, 12 and 13–23:1.

Verses 1–11, the first part of ch. 22, deal with the use of non-sexual property. Verses 22:13–23:1, the third part, deal with the use of sexual property. Verse 22:12, the second part, also deals with the use of property, in the form of one's garment.[112] This last law is distinguished from the preceding and following laws

---

108. Washington, '"Lest He Die,'" 210.
109. Braulik, "Sequence of the Laws," 328.
110. Ibid., 328.
111. Ibid., 328–29.
112. Tigay, *Deuteronomy*, 455, suggests that the law of v. 12 is triggered by the mention of the garment in v. 11. In addition, he notes that the law following v. 12 also deals with a garment, the בתולים. Tigay also notes that the last law in 23:1 deals with a garment, the כנף.

because it does not protect a specific property in its treatment of "use" as do the other laws. Rather, its prescription concerns the use of the garment for the sake of protecting all other laws, including those that protect property. Carmichael notes that, unlike the surrounding laws, it is a positive injunction rather than prohibition.[113] It commands that tassels be fixed to the four corners of one's cloak so as to remind oneself to keep the other commandments.[114] This law, which prescribes the use of property to protect the use of property, stands between the laws regulating non-sexual property and the laws regulating sexual property.

The first part of Deut 22:1–23:1, which treats non-sexual property, divides into two sections. The first section begins with provisions protecting the properties of one's brother in vv. 1–4. Immediately following this section comes a section dealing with use of one's own property. This latter section, consisting of five parts, is structured chiastically according to a spatial motif. It covers the use of properties within the following three spatial spheres: the body; the house; and the environment around the house, both extended and immediate. The house is the center of the chiasm. The body is the frame.[115] Preceding the house law (v. 8) is a law (vv. 6–7) concerning management of the larger environment in vicinity of the house. Following the house law is a law (vv. 9–10) concerning management of the immediate environment in vicinity of the house. If "vicinity of the house" presumes too much, then the defining signal of the units preceding and following the house law might be described alternatively as "use of environment which is cultivated" (vv. 6–7) and "use of environment which is not cultivated" (vv. 9–10).

"Use of property" is, thus, the primary concern of the larger context in which 22:13–23:1 stand.

2) *Microstructure.* The microstructure of Deut 22:13–23:1 also demonstrates that use of property, sexual property in particular, is the primary concern.

At least four converging patterns reveal that the unit is a list of six laws progressively ordered. The gradation which these converging patterns reveal is itself a function of the concern to protect the woman's sexuality as the property of the man.

The structure is as follows:

| III. | Sexual Property | 22:13–23:1 |
| | A. Bride | 22:13–21 |

---

113. Carmichael, "Forbidden Mixtures," 412.

114. Ibid., 412–13; Jacob Milgrom, "Of Hems and Tassels," *BAR* 9, no. 3 (1983): 65.

115. Carmichael, "Forbidden Mixtures," 412; idem, *The Laws*, 165. Whether or not Carmichael's suggestion concerning the "figurative" meaning of שעטנז and the import of the use of זנה are correct; he has pointed to some intriguing associations suggested by the use of ציצת in Num 15:37–41 and the placement of שעטנז immediately before the sex laws in Deut 22:11 and a sex law in Lev 19:19. See also C. Houtman, "Another Look at Forbidden Mixtures," *VT* 34 (1984): 226–28, who offers a classificatory explanation of the prohibition against שעטנז.

a) *Preliminary Statements.* Deuteronomy 22:13–23:1 consists of six independent laws, two of which, 22:23–24 and 22:25–27, are closely related. These latter two laws might conceivably be grouped together. In fact, to be fully understood they must be read together. Syntax requires it.

All main clause disjunctives[116] occur within an apodosis, except for the two disjunctives which occur after וְאִם, one of which is the clause beginning 22:20, the other of which begins v. 25. These two disjunctives, breaking the usual pattern of disjunctives in the sex series, occur in protases. The disjunctives occurring within the apodoses prescribe that the status quo continue into the future. Both of these disjunctives emphasize a break, a contrast with what precedes. They and the cases to which they belong can be understood only within the context of the immediately preceding cases. Thus, vv. 20–21 go with vv. 13–19. So also vv. 25–27 go with vv. 23–24. However, a significant difference exists between the relationships of these pairs of texts. In the first pair the companion cases are one law subject to the same condition as stated in the clause of

---

116. Thomas O. Lambden, *Introduction to Biblical Hebrew* (New York: Charles Scribner's Sons, 1971), 162.

v. 13a–bα.[117] The second pair, by contrast, are two independent but nevertheless related laws.

Furthermore, the six laws, including the laws of vv. 23–24 and vv. 25–27, exhibit a progression with respect to several features which argues for the structure of the unit as a graded list, ruling out any grouping of any of the laws. The gradation "travels" through each of the laws, including vv. 23–24 and vv. 25–27, with the same force as it travels through all the other laws. That is to say, the laws of vv. 23–24 and vv. 25–27 contribute at the same level as each of the other laws to the gradation which constitutes the structure of the entire unit as a list.

In addition, the motivation for grouping vv. 23–24 and vv. 25–27 together is the fact that the women of these verses have the same kind of bond to the man. Both are betrothed. Pressler, who notes that the betrothed bond is essentially the same as the marriage bond,[118] also groups these two laws with v. 22.[119] She divides ch. 22 as follows: vv. 13–21, 22–27, 28–29.[120] However, the woman of vv. 13–21 is also married, albeit newly married. If the marriage bond is used consistently as a structuring signal and if the betrothed woman is the same as a married woman, then 22:13–23:1 divide as follows: 22:13–27; vv. 28–29; 23:1. Or if the betrothed women are taken to be different from married women the division is as follows: vv. 13–22, 23–27; 23:1. However, although the final law deals with a widow, the *marriage bond* (between father and wife), which in this law is a thing of the past, reaches proactively into the future to prevent the relationship prohibited by the law of 23:1. Therefore, this last law might also be seen as belonging to the "marriage bond" laws. Nevertheless, it is separated from those laws by vv. 28–29. These inconsistencies argue against grouping the laws and structuring the chapter exclusively according to the "marriage bond."

Furthermore, the assumption that betrothed women are like married women needs further study before the marriage bond is full-heartedly accepted as the only structuring device of the chapter. The three laws concerning the guilty betrothed woman (v. 23), the non-guilty betrothed woman (v. 25) and the unbetrothed woman (v. 28) each have a clause using מצא which precedes the שכב-clause depicting the sex act. In short, only the laws concerning inchoate

---

117. See below.

118. Pressler, *View of Women*, 21 n. 1, 39 n. 51; Cairns, *Deuteronomy*, 199; Clifford, *Deuteronomy*, 121; Craigie, *Deuteronomy*, 294; Driver, *Deuteronomy*, 257; Frymer-Kensky, "Deuteronomy," 58; Phillips, "Another Look," 11; Tigay, *Deuteronomy*, 207.

119. Pressler, *View of Women*, 21.

120. Ibid., 21 n. 1. Pressler leaves aside 23:1 on redactional grounds. See also Pressler, "Sexual Violence," 106. Washington ("'Lest He Die,'" 208) follows Pressler with his suggestion that vv. 23–29 "are best classified as a subset of the general law of adultery preceding them in Deut 22.22." See also Gravett ("Reading 'Rape,'" 286) who follows Washington. Otto ("False Weights," 133–34) also considers vv. 23–27 to belong in some way to v. 22. He posits that v. 22a functions as a principal provision. An adultery law (v. 22) and a rape law (vv. 28–29) frame vv. 23–27, which are a redactional extension, "incorporating the inchoate marriage and differentiating between adultery and rape." See my analysis of the structure above for a critique of this position and a counter solution.

or unmarried women use this מצא clause. The laws concerning married women do not.

This phrase attributes a certain amount of chance or happenstance to the illicit act. It suggests that these infractions are a "crime of opportunity." The fact that this connotation occurs only with inchoate and unmarried women demonstrates some nervousness about these women. The author perceives them to be more vulnerable. Either their sexuality is more easily compromised than the others, or the compromise of their sexuality has greater or special import with more dire consequences. Or both options are the case. If the general direction of the honor/shame discussion by anthropologists is correct, then the latter is a more probable explanation.[121]

In fact, the issue at stake in every law using מצא with שכב is virginity. Each of the women, in contradistinction to the married woman, can be assumed to be a virgin even though the word בתולה is absent from the law of vv. 25–27. While virginity is also an issue in vv. 13–21, the woman in that law is "secured" by the bond of marriage so that the virginity issue is slightly different. Thus, the author is especially nervous about virgins. It seems that special dangers apply to women in the process of transfer or to women for whom the process of transfer has not yet begun.

One of the implications, if these observations are correct, is that, in spite of the warrantable conclusion on the part of many scholars that betrothed women are essentially the same as married women, such women are, in fact, conceptualized, at least by the author of Deut 22, as "unsecured" in a way similar to the unbetrothed woman. However, they are not quite like the unbetrothed women either, as previous discussion of the author's conceptualization of the nature of "force" against betrothed and unbetrothed women demonstrates.[122] Betrothed women are in a liminal state unlike both married and unbetrothed women. Biale writes as follows:

> A betrothed virgin is in a particularly vulnerable position: while she is legally committed to a certain man through betrothal, she is still a virgin living with her own family as if she were single and available. She is not yet under the protection of her husband.[123]

Conceptually, these women are between two abodes of safety—the house of their husband and the house of their father; as such, they themselves as well as their fathers are particularly vulnerable. As a result of this, provision is made for the case in which they are guilty and the case in which they are not guilty.[124] Such provision is not made with respect to married women who are secured in marriage conceptually and physically, nor is it made with respect to unbetrothed

121. Matthews and Benjamin, *Social World*, 180; Gilmore, ed., *Honor and Shame*; Hastrup, "Purity," 137–47; Pitt-Rivers, *Fate*, 165; Ortner, "Virgin," 19–35; Schlegel, "Status," 719–34; Schneider, "Vigilance," 1–24.

122. See above.

123. Biale, *Women*, 241. See also the comments by Matthews and Benjamin on rape in Matthews and Benjamin, *Social World*, 178.

124. Frymer-Kensky, "Deuteronomy," 58.

women who are not yet secured in marriage but are secured to their father's house, physically and conceptually. Two different extremes of "security" (married and unbetrothed) surround the liminal (betrothed). Conceptually speaking, the betrothed woman can no more be grouped with married women than she can with unbetrothed women.

Finally, Wenham and McConville note two patterns within the text which argue against structural proposals such as Pressler's.[125] The first is a pattern of "two parallel panels," which they present as follows:

vv. 13–22	Offences of married woman	
13–19	Offence in father's house	(*kî*, gate of the city)
20–21	Offence in father's house	(*wᵉʾim*)
22	Adultery	(*kî*, caught in the act)
vv. 23–28	Offences by unmarried girls	
23–24	Betrothed girl in city	(*kî*, gate of city)
25–27	Betrothed girl in field	(*wᵉʾim*)
28–29	Unbetrothed girl	(*kî*, caught in the act)[126]

The parallel panels separate the married women from the betrothed women. Wenham and McConville also notice the following chiastic pattern.

A	v. 19 damages of 100 shekels paid to girl's father, no divorce
B	v. 21 woman executed
C	v. 22 man and woman executed
C¹	v. 24 man and woman executed
B²	v. 25 man executed
C³	v. 29 damages of 50 shekels paid to girl's father, no divorce[127]

This chiasm might also be thought of as having two panels. The split between the panels comes between the married women and the betrothed women. Pressler critiques the pattern described by Wenham and McConville on the basis of the distribution of the death penalty and the distribution of אשה/נערה.[128] However, the distribution of the death penalty as well as אשה/נערה, as a structuring signal, is problematic even for Pressler's own structure. Verses 20–21 use the death penalty. Both אשה and נערה appear in vv. 13–21. Nevertheless, Pressler separates vv. 13–21 from vv. 22–27, ignoring the very signals she is claiming are constitutive for grouping v. 22 with vv. 23–27. Pressler's critique, therefore, fails and the Wenham–McConville pattern succeeds.

Thus, the ubiquity of the marriage bond throughout the list, including its presence in the last law, the use of the מצא-clauses in conjunction with the שכב-clauses and the two patterns noted by Wenham and McConville, argue against groupings such as those suggested by Pressler. However, perhaps the strongest argument against Pressler's structure and others like it is the fact that such

125. Wenham and McConville, "Drafting," 250.
126. Ibid., 250.
127. Ibid., 250.
128. Pressler, *View of Women*, 21 n. 1.

structures miss another pattern apparent in the laws. This pattern is the gradation of the laws and is actually constituted by four converging patterns.

b) *Two Challenges*. Before a full explanation of the converging patterns and the structure they constitute can be given, two challenges to the proposed structure must be met. The first challenge has to do with the relationship of 22:13–19 to 22:20–21. The second has to do with the relationship of 23:1 to the rest of the sex-law series. Both challenges are related to redactional problems.

(1) *Verses 22:13–21*. Locher divides into two groups the arguments typically marshaled by scholars to support the conclusion that 22:20–21 are a redactional addition to vv. 13–19. These two groups of arguments depend on formal evidence ("*formal*") and content evidence ("*inhaltlich*").[129] Few scholars have gone beyond a redactional explanation to solve the structural problems created by the formal and content features which these arguments assess.[130] Even such scholars as Locher and Pressler, who posit the unity of vv. 13–21,[131] fail to provide a structural solution that entirely satisfies. Locher's comparative study comes closest to such an attempt.[132] While Pressler states that vv. 13–21 are a unit, she considers and treats vv. 13–19 and vv. 20–21 as if they are two independent laws, in effect, ignoring the structural problem created by the introductions to each law.[133] Nevertheless, the extant form of the text presents a structurally coherent, single law.

Although Locher and Pressler have failed satisfactorily to solve the structural problem, they have aptly solved several problems related to it. For example, Locher's comments and comparative analyses are convincing statements against arguments from style for the disunity of vv. 13–21. He writes:

> Aber es könnte doch sein, dass die Unterschiede zwischen den beiden Teilen gattungs-mässig bedingt sind: sie ergeben sich von den Eigenheiten eines „Doppelgesetzes" her. Was im Fall VV. 13–19 ausfürlich dargelegt wurde, braucht im Gegenfall VV. 20–21 nicht ebenso ausfürlich wiederholt zu werden. Hier wären altorientalishe Parallelen zu berücksichtigen, bes. CH §142/43 und MAG A §55/56.[134]

In addition, Pressler has convincingly argued that the parents are the plaintiffs in the case and that the husband's action is slander in the community rather than false witness given in court.[135] With this understanding, the apodosis begins at

---

129. Clemens Locher, "Deuteronomium 22, 13–21 von Prozeßprotocoll zum Kasuistischen Gesetz," in Lohfink, ed., *Das Deuteronomium*, 299. See also idem, *Ehre einer Frau in Israel*, 60–64.

130. Mayes, *Deuteronomy*, 309; Phillips, *Deuteronomy*, 148; Rofé, "Family and Sex Laws," 135–37.

131. Locher, "Deuteronomium," 299–303. See also idem, *Ehre einer Frau in Israel*, 61, 110–16.

132. Locher, "Deuteronomium," 303. See also idem, *Ehre einer Frau in Israel*, 67.

133. Pressler, *View of Women*, 22.

134. Locher, *Ehre einer Frau in Israel*, 61, 110–16. See also dem, "Deuteronomium," 299–303.

135. Pressler, *View of Women*, 23–25.

v. 18.[136] Furthermore, both Locher and Pressler argue successfully against Wenham that in Deut 22 בתולה means "virgin" and בתולים means "tokens of virginity."[137] Verses 13–21 cannot, therefore, be grouped with v. 22 as a case of simple adultery.

Each of these several arguments from Pressler and Locher are related to the structural problem of vv. 13–21. Their solutions support the structural unity of that pericope. Nevertheless, the primary structural obstacle to the unity of vv. 13–21 remains when Locher and Pressler are done.

This obstacle is the perception that whereas the protasis of the second case presupposes information which must be surmised from the first case, in particular but not exclusively from the protasis of the first case, the introduction at the beginning of the protasis to the first case seems to fit only the case of vv. 13–19 and not vv. 20–21.[138] Rofé states it as follows:

> Furthermore, the opening formula (vv 13–14) does not allow for the possibility that there may be truth in the husband's claim: "Then he takes an aversion to her…and defames her." (New JPS). This is no neutrally-worded preamble introducing a discussion of two opposing instances. We must conclude that whoever formulated the opening verses and the rest of the first section (vv 15–19) did not write the second (vv 20–21).[139]

Pressler calls the two cases a "main case" and a "sub-case."[140] Such a characterization, however, ignores the problem which Rofé describes and of which Pressler is well aware.[141] Locher calls vv. 13–21 a "*Doppelgesetz*" consisting of a "*Fall*" and a "*Gegenfall*."[142] He examines comparative ancient Near Eastern *Doppelgesetze* and finds similar inconsistencies.[143] He explains the "*Spannungen zwischen*" vv. 13–19 and vv. 20–21 as follows:

> Aus einer dem sum. Modell entsprechenden Vorlage ergibt sich, daß die "Einleitung" vv. 13–14a nur im Hinblick auf den bis v. 19 reichenden "Fall" formuliert ist, nicht für einen alternativen Prozeßausgang. Die Spannungen zwischen 22, 13–19 und 22,20f. erklären sich ohne weiteres, wenn der erste Teil von einer solchen Vorlage abhängig, der zweite Teil dagegen nachträglicher Zusatz des "Gesetzgebers" ist, der das Prozeßprotokoll zu einem kasuistischen Gesetz umformte.[144]

---

136. Locher, "Deuteronomium," 299, 303. See also idem, *Ehre einer Frau in Israel*, 64–66. Locher also begins the apodosis at v. 18.

137. Pressler, *View of Women*, 23–28; Locher, *Ehre einer Frau in Israel*, 176–92. See the brief comments above under "Identification-of-Women." See also Matthews, "Honor and Shame," 109.

138. Locher, *Ehre einer Frau in Israel*, 62; Mayes, *Deuteronomy*, 310.

139. Rofé, "Family and Sex Laws," 136.

140. Pressler, *View of Women*, 22. Benjamin, *Deuteronomy*, 222–23. Benjamin's structure is similar to Pressler's.

141. Pressler, *View of Women*, 22.

142. Locher, "Deuteronomium," 299.

143. Ibid., 299.

144. Ibid., 303.

However, Locher does not go beyond this description of the writing process to solve the structural problem which remains in the final text even after applying his nomenclature.[145]

The solution to this problem requires flexibility concerning the possibilities for the structure of casuistic law. Verses 13–21 are, in fact, not simply a "main case" and a "sub-case." Nor are they simply a "*Fall*" and a "*Gegenfall*." Rather, they are a single law consisting of an introductory partial-protasis and two related cases, both of which are dependent on and share that introductory partial-protasis. Intuitively we know that the two laws share the following situation: "A man takes a woman and goes into her." Structurally, however, we are unaccustomed to reading separate but related laws as sharing a portion of their protases and extending that shared-protasis separately. Furthermore, the Masoretes are as unaccustomed as are we.

The Masoretes understood v. 13, including וּשְׂנֵאָהּ, to be a complete unit, obviously describing part of the conditions for the first case. How they understood the relationship of the two cases structurally is less clear, even though their pointing assures us that they did not understand it the way I am reading it.

Nevertheless both laws have in common the circumstances described in v. 13a–bα. If Westbrook's understanding of שׂנא as denoting "divorce without grounds" is correct,[146] then clause 13bβ, by contrast, is not shared by both cases.[147] Pressler notes that the first case is a case of slander impugning the woman's virgin status at marriage. If שׂנא, in this case, does not mean "divorce without grounds" then the husband's slander is inexplicable, since he has an absolute right to divorce if he wants to,[148] irrespective of the presence or absence of בתולים.[149] Furthermore, by engaging in slander he risks not only a fine and discipline but also the right to divorce. If שׂנא means "divorce without grounds," then his slander makes sense.[150] His slander is an attempt to manufacture grounds for divorce so as to gain, or at least not to lose, financially from the divorce. Phillips states the following:

---

145. Ibid., 301, 303. See his form-critical discussion of the text: idem, *Ehre einer Frau in Israel*, 68.

146. See my argument supporting Westbrook's understanding in the discussion of Deut 24 below, and Raymond Westbrook, "The Prohibition on Restoration of Marriage in Deuteronomy 24:1–4," in Japhet, ed., *Scripta Hierosolymitana*, 387–405.

147. Locher, *Ehre einer Frau in Israel*, 62.

148. However, see Blenkinsopp, "Family," 65.

149. David Daube, "The Culture of Deuteronomy," *Orita* 3 (1960): 32; Reuven Yaron, "On Divorce in Old Testament Times," *RIDA* 4 (1957): 127. See also Mace, *Hebrew Marriage*, 252–53, and Patai, *Sex and Family*, 118–19.

150. Yaron, "On Divorce," 119, states that שׂנא meaning "to divorce" is not probable in Deut 22 since v. 19 forbids "divorce altogether if the accusation is proved false." However, if שׂנא means "divorce without grounds" then the prohibition against divorce in v. 19 makes sense. The man's attempt to divorce is successful if the surrounding community accepts it. In this case, however, where fraud is involved, they do not accept it. Furthermore, they thwart and penalize his attempt by forbidding divorce altogether.

The situation envisaged here is not a petition for divorce which the husband could obtain without recourse to the courts (cp. on 24:1–4), but an action by the husband to recover from his father-in-law the bride-price paid on marriage.[151]

Although the husband's slander may not be a petition for divorce, שׂנא, in fact, refers to the *act* of divorce.

The first case is, thus, a case of slander for the sake of financial gain in the context of divorce.[152] Since the husband in the second case has unequivocal grounds for divorce, שׂנא cannot refer to this case. Thus, the shared protasis of the two laws ends at phrase 13bα, excluding וּשְׂנֵאָהּ and what follows.

Each of the laws adds its own details to the shared protasis. The first case extends the protasis in vv. 13bβ–17. The second case extends it in v. 20. In the first case, the added details indicate that the husband divorces without grounds but attempts to manufacture grounds by publicly slandering his wife. In the second case the added details simply indicate that the בתולים are lacking.

This second case, beyond the shared protasis, requires no information from the first case in order to be understood. Although, הַדָּבָר הַזֶּה (v. 20a) seems to refer obliquely to the husband's accusations described in the first case (vv. 14–19), the author clarifies this phrase sufficiently in the second case by clause 20b, which straight-forwardly describes "this matter" as the absence of בְּתוּלִים. Neither the husband's attempt to divorce without grounds not his attempt publicly to accuse is a condition necessary to the second case. We might surmise that the most logical and perhaps only way for such information to come under juridical authority is by means of the husband's accusation. And our logic might be supported by the circumstances of the first case. However, the second case is, in fact, unconcerned about the way this information comes to light. The only condition necessary for the consequences of vv. 20–21 to take effect is that the man "take" the woman and go into her and that the בְּתוּלִים be lacking. Nevertheless, הַדָּבָר הַזֶּה may serve as a linking device between the two cases functioning *both* as an oblique reference to the scenario that precedes and a straight-forward reference to the description that follows.

Thus, although vv. 13–19 and vv. 20–21 are not separate cases, contrary to Pressler and others, with the information provided by the "partial-protasis" of vv. 13a–bα and the information of their separate extended protases, they are independently complete.

As unaccustomed as we are to such a structure, it is not entirely unfamiliar. The law of levirate marriage, for example, uses a similar construction.[153] The only difference is that the second case (Deut 25:7–10) alone continues the shared protasis (25:5aα) with ancillary information. For the first case (25:5aβ–10), the shared protasis (25:5aα) is the entire protasis. Deuteronomy 21:10–14 has a similar structure. Like 25:5–10, the second case (21:14) continues the

---

151. Phillips, *Deuteronomy*, 148.
152. This is not, as Dempster ("Deuteronomic," 201) suggests, a case of suspicion like the case in Num 5. See Matthews, "Honor and Shame," 103.
153. See the discussion of Deut 25 below.

shared protasis (21:10–11) while the shared protasis is the full protasis for the first case (21:12–13). These two texts strengthen the plausibility of the proposed structure for 22:13–21.

Verses 22:13–21 are, thus, a single law consisting of a shared partial-protasis and two cases which are dependent on that shared partial-protasis.

(2) *Verse 23:1.* The relationship of 23:1 to the rest of the sex-law series is the second challenge. Pressler leaves 23:1 out of her discussion because of its redactional status.[154]

The apodictic form of 23:1 contrasts with the preceding casuistic laws of the series. In form, it resembles the laws that follow it.[155] Furthermore, thematically, it seems more to closely resemble the incest series of Lev 18, Lev 20 and Deut 27, in contrast to the sex laws of Deut 22:13–29.[156] These differences are the source of the conclusion by scholars that this law is an addition.[157] The conclusion is logical and seems warranted.

However, in 23:1 the use of כָּנָף, as argued above, demonstrates that this is an incest law with a property emphasis. The incest concern serves the property concern. In this respect, as will be demonstrated below, 23:1 is more akin to the incest curses of Deut 27 than it is to the incest prohibitions of Lev 18 and Lev 20.[158] The central concern of 23:1 is protection of the man's sexual property, as is the case in Deut 27:20–23, rather than protection of classificatory concerns, as is the case in Lev 18 and 20.

In addition, 23:1 is a fitting conclusion to the progression of laws to which it has been added, as the description of the gradation pattern below demonstrates.

c) *The Gradation Pattern.*[159] As in Lev 20, several converging patterns within the text reveal that the structure is a graded list of six laws.[160] The converging patterns are four in number. They themselves constitute gradations with respect to (1) nature-of-the-bond, (2) penalties, (3) time-of-infraction-and-its-discovery and (4) guilt-of-the-woman/harm-done-to-the-man.

(1) *Nature-of-the-Bond.* Several aspects define the first converging pattern. The most prominent aspect is the presence or absence of the marriage bond.[161] In the

---

154. Pressler, *View of Women*, 21 n. 1.

155. Mayes, *Deuteronomy*, 313, calls it a "connecting link between what precedes and what follows."

156. Carmichael, *The Laws*, 169–70, states: "Unlike the priestly legislation's extensive lists of forbidden degrees of affinity (Lev xviii, 6ff., xx. 11ff.), this is the only law of its kind in the D code (although the list of curses in xxvii. 15ff. mentions two other forbidden degrees)."

157. Merendino, *Deuteronomische*, 271.

158. See the discussion of Deut 27 below.

159. See Chart 4 in the Appendix.

160. See the methodological comments concerning discernment of gradation in discussion of Lev 20 above.

161. Thistlethwaite, "You May Enjoy," 63, notes this pattern: "Sexual crimes relate to the female as sexual property. The penalties for rape committed against a betrothed woman (one whose

first two laws (22:13–21 and 22) the marriage bond is present. With respect to marriage, these women are the most *securely* situated of all the women of the text. The women of the next two laws (vv. 23–24 and 25–27) are less securely situated because the marriage bond is in the process of being formed. In the fifth law (vv. 28–29) the process which establishes a marriage bond has not yet begun. While this woman is securely situated in her father's house, she is not securely situated with respect to marriage. In the last law (23:1) the marriage bond has been lived through and ended. Although it has ended, it has retained a residue of force and has the power to prevent a son from marrying the widow. Nevertheless, the woman has passed through the security of the marriage bond to the "insecurity" of widowhood.

Thus, from the first to the sixth law, the bonds which tie women to men are decreasingly secure or present with respect to marriage. The gradation of the list moves from women who enjoy the status of marriage in decreasing degrees, to women who have yet to enjoy it, to women who no longer enjoy it. The degrees to which a woman belongs to a man, with marriage as the highest degree, is significant for the list.

(2) *Penalties*. The penalties for the sexual infractions also exhibit a gradation. They go from most severe to least severe.[162] The first four sexual infractions are punishable by death. Frymer-Kensky posits some semblance of a gradation for the crimes of this series on the basis of the penalties which she takes as an indicator of the seriousness of the crime. Nevertheless, she writes:

> Because the girl, although still a virgin, is legally considered married to the man to whom she has been betrothed, both partners are therefore guilty of adultery and are deserving of death. Their offense is even more serious than adultery: in normal instances of adultery, the couple is to be killed, but not stoned. But in this case, the adultery is compounded; the couple has both violated the rights of the future husband and offended against the girl's obligation to her father.[163]

However, that "stoning" is a more severe penalty than "death" is unclear. In any case, for the gradation, the method of execution is irrelevant. "Execution" itself is the constitutive factor.

In the fourth law the man alone dies since the woman is not guilty. In vv. 28–29, her guilt is irrelevant because the problem caused to the father can be remedied by a fine, marriage and revocation of the right to divorce. This infraction therefore receives a less severe penalty than death.[164] The final law fails to mention a penalty at all.[165]

---

sexual property has been claimed) are more severe than against an unmarried virgin. Adultery is by far the most serious crime; the law prescribes death by stoning for both parties (Deut 22:22)."

162.   See the methodological comments on penalties in the discussion of Lev 20 above.

163.   Frymer-Kensky, "Sex in the Bible," 192. See also Thistlethwaite, "You May Enjoy," 63.

164.   Craigie, *Deuteronomy*, 295, states that the penalty is less severe in this case because the "crime does not involve a breach in a relationship in the sense that it does with adultery." While this

Obviously the penalties beginning the list deprive the perpetrator of the greatest value—life. Thus, the penalties go from most severe to least severe. Furthermore, the most severe penalties correlate with the strongest bonds.

(3) *Time-of-Infraction-and-Its-Discovery*. The time-of-infraction-and-its-discovery is the third converging pattern.

In the first law (vv. 13–21) the infraction occurs prior to marriage but is discovered during marriage. In the second (v. 22), third (vv. 23–24) and fourth (vv. 25–27) laws the infractions occur during marriage or during the process which culminates finally in marriage. In the fifth law (vv. 28–29) the infraction occurs before marriage. In the last law (23:1) it occurs after marriage.

Thus, in law #1 the infraction is discovered during marriage having occurred prior to marriage. From laws #2 and #6 the discovery of the infraction and its occurrence moves gradually from the confines outside of marriage, with both the confines before and after marriage represented.

This pattern demonstrates a clear concern on the part of the author with the timing of the infraction in connection to "degrees of marriage." Occurrence of the infraction within the context of marriage correlates with the strongest bonds and the most severe penalties.

(4) *Guilt-of-Women/Harm-Done-to-the-Man*. The guilt-of-the-women also reveals a gradation.[166] In the first two laws (vv. 13–21 and v. 22) the women are guilty. Furthermore, in the law beginning the series two wrongs are compounded. Not only has illicit sex taken place; the husband has also been deceived. The harm done to the man in the first law is, thus, the most serious harm done in all the laws.[167] Since the woman is guilty of compound infractions against the man,

---

is the case, it does involve a violation of a father's rights. That violation, different from the violation of adultery, can be remedied.

165.   See the discussion above concerning the possibility that absence of a penalty may be due to the fact that this particular infraction does not require such a penalty.

166.   Tigay, *Deuteronomy*, 456. Tigay states the following: "Verses 13–29 deal with types of sexual misconduct: accusations of premarital unchastity, adultery and rape. Accusations of premarital unchastity appear first (vv. 13–21)... The remaining cases appear in decreasing order of gravity: clear-cut consensual adultery, cases in which the woman's consent is uncertain, and non-adulterous rape (vv. 22–29)" (p. 204). Tigay thus grades vv. 22–29 on the basis of the intent of the woman. He leaves vv. 13–21 and 23:1 out of the gradation. Careful scrutiny, however, demonstrates that a gradation encompasses the entire sex series of the final form of the text. The rationale for this latter gradation, of course, goes beyond the single feature of "consent/non-consent" of the woman.

167.   Thistlethwaite, "You May Enjoy," 64, notes the following: "In the Hebrew Bible the offended party is the one who is the sexual property holder: in the case of the betrothed woman, her husband; in the case of the unmarried virgin, her father... The husband of a betrothed woman is by far the most offended person in this system, since what has been stolen from him is his right to legitimate offspring...a right that is central to the way the society was organized." However, the husband of a married woman has rights similar to the husband of the betrothed woman. Furthermore, his rights have been "locked down" by the bond of marriage, a stronger bond than betrothal. He, in fact, is the more offended person.

she has the highest degree of guilt of women in the laws. The law with the most guilty woman, coincidentally, thus, heads the list.

In addition, absent from the list is the idea of forced sex with a married woman. The married woman is presumed guilty. The "generous" contingencies offered betrothed women do not apply to her. According to the list, she is guilty in every instance of illicit sex, regardless of the circumstances.[168]

In the third law (vv. 23–24) the woman is also guilty. As mentioned above, the purge formula occurs in these first three laws where the woman is guilty.[169] In the fourth law (vv. 25–27) she is not guilty. In the fifth law (vv. 28–29) she is also not guilty. Up to the fifth law, the gradation moves from guilty to not guilty.

However, in the last law (23:1) the woman willingly cooperates and must be considered guilty. This last law seems to break the progression. Nonetheless, if for a moment we *assume* the gradation for heuristic purposes, then something conceptually interesting reveals itself.

If 23:1 is a *kind of* "victimless crime," as suggested above, then even though the father's property is at stake, the infraction does not harm him in the way that it harms the men of the preceding laws. Neither the raped women (vv. 25–27), nor the "raped/seduced" woman (vv. 28–29), nor the wife of the father (23:1) are punished. *Legally*, the guilt of one is not more than the guilt of any of the others. Nevertheless, of all the men harmed by the infractions of the series a dead man is harmed least. This is the very law placed last. Does the author in some way perceive the guilt of this last woman conceptually to be less than the guilt of the preceding women, including the rape victim?

Certain entitlements with respect to sexual property remain after a man dies. When that property is harmed or misused, the dead man becomes a *virtual* victim. The men of the preceding laws, on the other hand, are *real* victims, living victims. As a result, the infraction of marriage to and sex with a father's wife is perhaps somehow less severe than the rape of a man's daughter or betrothed. The woman of 23:1 is guilty, as are the women of vv. 13–24. Conceptually, however, her opprobrium is the least of all the women, even the rape victims.

This means that the "guilt" of the woman depends to some extent on the harm done to the man. The law with the least guilty woman is the law in which the least harm is done to the man. This law concludes the list.

The nature of the evidence required throughout the laws suggests another intriguing piece of information concerning the author's conceptualization of the guilt of women in connection with sexual infractions. It suggests that guilt and intent in the laws are not coterminous and that the intent of the woman is irrelevant.[170]

---

168. Pressler, "Sexual Violence," 107. However, Pressler contends that one who follows this list of laws would "be expected to reason from the case of an inchoately married woman to the case of a woman whose marriage had been consummated." My understanding of the structure suggests a strong enough division between v. 22 and vv. 23–27, such that the move Pressler is suggesting would be unwarranted.

169. See the discussion above under "Purge Formula."

170. Washington, ' "Lest He Die," ' 210; Anderson, *Women, Ideology, and Violence*, 41, 86.

The Niphal form of מצא in vv. 22 and 28–29 indicates that evidence in the form of witnesses are required as part of the stated conditions of these two laws.[171] Since v. 22 describes a situation in which the woman presumably colludes and vv. 28–29 describe a situation in which she does not, the presence of witnesses is not an indicator of the intent of the woman in the commission of these infractions.[172]

Verses 22 and 28–29 are the only two laws which require such witnesses. In the first law of the series (vv. 13–20) witnesses are unmentioned because the infraction comes to light by virtue of the husband's accusations. Although the apodictic form of 23:1 precludes the mention of witnesses, a substantive reason also exists for their absence in this law. Marriage to one's father's wife, or to any woman for that matter, is a public affair. It is not hidden and therefore witnesses need not be stipulated. The evidence is the public marriage itself.

In vv. 23–27, locale, rather than the testimony of witnesses, serves as evidence. Witnesses are unmentioned. If illicit sex with a betrothed woman occurs in the city she is guilty and put to death along with her co-perpetrator. If illicit sex with a betrothed woman occurs in the field she is innocent and only the guilty man is put to death. The evidence required to convict is less than in the other cases. The evidence required to exonerate is also weaker. The less stringent requirements in the case of guilt and innocence demonstrate that the author perceives betrothed women to be exceedingly vulnerable.[173] Vulnerability requires special provisions both for guilt and innocence.

Everyone who reads this text knows innocent women can be raped in the city and guilty women can carry out their assignations in the field. We ought not to assume that the author is somehow exempt from such knowledge or even that the cultural/historical divide between us is so vast that he would not know that women who resist can be raped in the city and women who collude can rendezvous in the field. Frymer-Kensky writes:

> Biblical law realizes that forcible rape is a crime of violence and that the girl is a victim: it explicitly compares forcible rape to murder.[174]

However, vv. 23-27 also demonstrate that the destinctions that matter to the author are different from the distinction codified by the word "rape" in the twenty-first-century Western world.[175]

The law understands that whether a woman is raped in the city or whether she cooperates in the city, *she is guilty*. Whether she is raped in the field or whether she cooperates in the field, *she is innocent*. Benjamin states that the woman is "executed not because she had or did not have intercourse with her assailant, but

---

171.   Daube, "Culture," 43, especially 46; Dempster, "Deuteronomic," 188–211, especially 189; Mace, *Hebrew Marriage*, 247; Merendino, *Deuteronomische*, 261.
172.   See the comments above.
173.   Biale, *Women*, 241.
174.   Frymer-Kensky, "Sex in the Bible," 192.
175.   See the discussion under Deut 21:10–14 above.

because she failed *to cry out* (*ṣāʿaq*)."[176] But even her cry is not determinative. The locale alone is determinative. It is evidence for the cry. The author is unconcerned whether the woman cooperated or not. Her guilt is relevant. Her intent is not. The parameters for guilt depend only on locale.

These parameters make sense if we surmise that several assumptions are packed within them. The first assumption is that in the city a woman is necessarily safe. That is, the men and the community to which she belongs will protect her from being sexually forced against her will. She, herself, has a responsibility to follow the conventions, customs and laws which support this protection. If she is raped or if sex occurs in the city, then she is presumed guilty regardless of her intent with respect to the specific sex act. *At the very least*, she is guilty because she failed to follow the conventions and customs which "necessarily" support the system of protection that is in place in the city. Only in this way can a non-consenting woman reasonably be guilty. *At the very most*, she is guilty because she willingly participated. Her failure to follow convention and her willing participation are the two places where a man is most vulnerable with respect to his sexual property. The author has absolute faith in the security of women when two factors intersect: (1) when she is within the confines of her city-community and (2) when she follows the conventions, customs and laws which support the protection that community affords. Thus, a woman who intends to engage in sex in the city is guilty for the same reason a woman who is forced in the city is guilty. Protection is present. Her intent with respect to the sex act per se is irrelevant.

However, sometimes women who fastidiously follow the conventions and customs which are part of the protective system must leave the physical boundaries of the community. They must go into the field. *The text presumes that innocent women may do this.* When a woman leaves the physical boundaries of the community the issue shifts. Whether or not she follows custom, convention and law, and whether or not she willingly participates is irrelevant. The issue in the field is that the protective community is absent. The presumption is that under such circumstances even the most fastidious woman may be overcome. She has stepped outside of the place of safety such that no amount of conscientious behavior on her part can save her.

Surely, however, the author knows that some women may rendezvous in the country. Either the author is willing to let such women go for the benefit of the innocent ones, or he perceives even the women who intentionally rendezvous in the country to be somehow "not responsible" for their actions. That he is willing to let the guilty pass for the sake of the innocent is unlikely since he is unwilling to do the same within the confines of the city. Thus, we must conclude that the author perceives even women who intentionally rendezvous in the country to be somehow "not responsible" for their actions. Only in this way can a consenting woman be innocent. Thus, a woman who intends to engage in sex in the field is

176. Benjamin, *Deuteronomy*, 241–42.

innocent for the same reason a woman who is forced is innocent. Protection is absent. Intent is irrelevant.

It seems that in the field no degree of wrongdoing can overcome the absence of the safety net of the community, so as to make the woman guilty by doing wrong. From this we might infer that the safety net of the city protects women from their own errant behavior to some degree, such that when it is absent, as in the field, it becomes apparent that women are "not responsible" for their behavior. On the other hand, in the city the safety net will never fail a woman who is doing good. From this we might infer that some women are so errant that they subvert the safety-net, such that it becomes apparent that women have the capacity for extreme "irresponsibility."

Thus, the author perceives that if an illicit sexual experience transpires in the life of a betrothed woman, either it happened in the city and she cooperated or it happened in the field and she was victimized. If she cooperated she is guilty. If she was victimized she could not save herself. The first option perceives her as "irresponsible" and the second perceives her as "not responsible." Behind both options is the assumption that a betrothed woman, in whose life illicit sex transpires, is somehow "morally defective";[177] that is, she lacks the kind of moral maturity that would make her guilty if she rendezvoused in the field, or she lacks the kind of moral integrity that would make her innocent if she was forced in the city. Furthermore, she has a potential capacity for evil such that she can subvert the safety-net of the city in which the author places such faith that its absence, in his view, absolves guilt.

The betrothed woman's guilt, therefore, is shaped by four factors. The first is the occurrence of an illicit act which involves herself. The second factor is the presence of the protection of the community. The third is her failure to follow the conventions, customs and laws, irrespective of her intent concerning the specific sex act, which support the protection of her community. The fourth factor is conceptualization of woman's moral constitution as weak, ranging from mildly to grossly defective.

For the most part, the author is consistent throughout in his lack of concern for intent. The law is as much a warning to women to guard their virginity as it is a protocol for what happens when the betrothed is overtaken in the city and the field. Whereas intent is irrelevant, guilt is not. Just as intent is irrelevant in vv. 28–29[178] and vv. 23–27, so also it is irrelevant in v. 22 which, as stated, implies that both married women who are forced and those who cooperate in an act of illicit sex are guilty. We may infer the same conclusion for vv. 20–21.

---

177. Washington, ' "Lest He Die," ' 210, states: "Thus Deuteronomic law refuses to recognize that rape can take place in town or in the home (a notion of collective male honor may be at stake here). This creates an impossible contradiction in a woman's standing under the law: the culture defines masculine gender in terms of strength and domination, while the feminine is seen as intrinsically weak and dependent. A woman is not generally positioned as one with the capacity to consent (or not), yet here she is presumptively blamed (and in v. 24 executed), for having consented to imposed illicit intercourse."

178. See the discussion above.

Thus, no gradation pattern exists with respect to intent. However, a pro-nounced gradation pattern exists with respect to the guilt of the woman. The greatest guilt corresponds to the strongest bonds, to the most severe penalties and to the occurrence and/or discovery of the infraction during marriage rather than outside marriage.

(5) *Summary.* The list moves from the superlative to the diminutive. A logical inference based on all four converging patterns just described is that the strong-est bonds, the most severe penalties, the greatest guilt accruing to the woman and the most harm done to the man correspond to the most serious infractions.[179] These most serious infractions correspond to those illicit acts which occur within the context of marriage or are finally discovered within the context of marriage. The least serious infractions occur outside the context of marriage.

These correspondences indicate, in turn, that the boundaries, which securely tie a woman to a man and give him exclusive rights to use of her sexuality, pro-tect what is most valued by the law. The concern, rather than protection of boundaries per se or boundaries in general, is the protection of only one class of boundaries, those that guard sexual property which has been secured in varying degrees. The lawgiver, in fact, is concerned to protect what this narrow spectrum of boundaries encompasses. In other words, the concern is to protect that which the boundaries demarcate as belonging to the man—the woman's sexuality.

The gradation of the list thus demonstrates the law's concern to protect woman's sexuality as the property of the man.

C. *Conclusion*

Thus, point-of-view and language-depicting-the-sex-act demonstrate woman's marginalization and objectification. Language-depicting-the-sex-act, selection-of-laws, identification-of-women, reiteration-of-the-man-to-whom-the-woman-belongs and structure-of-the-text all indicate that, contrary to crime–tort proponents, the primary concern of Deut 22:13–23:1 is to protect the woman's sexuality as the property of the man.

In Deut 22:13–19, 22–24, woman, like the man, is responsible for protecting this sexual property, which is coterminous with herself. She is an implied addressee and she is pictured in the law as actively responsible for the infractions described. In Deut 22:20–21, 25–23:1, the rape laws, woman is not pictured as actively responsible in the same way as the other laws, and her responsibility is apparent only if she is implied addressee. In Deut 22:20–21 and 25–29 she is a helpless victim. Nevertheless, since she is considered guilty in vv. 13–29 and v. 24, we can infer that she is also expected to know the parameters that define the guilt and innocence of the scenarios of vv. 20–21 and vv. 25–27.

---

179. See the methodological comments concerning discernment of value from converging patterns above in the discussion of Lev 20.

For all of the laws of this series, including the remaining laws (22:28–29 and 23:1), she is an implied addressee. She is therefore accorded responsibility from which comes her appearance as implied character agent. In 23:1, the father's wife is implicitly warned against the father's son. In vv. 28–29, an unbetrothed daughter, as implicit addressee, is also expected to be know about the kind of scenario that can marry her to a man who will force her sexually. This last law is second only to the war-captive-bride law in its curtailment of agency to the woman. Out of the series she is accorded the least responsibility. The author does not equivocate about her guilt or innocence, as with the betrothed women. It is a total non-issue.

In conclusion, woman is focalized as property, even while accruing agency through the addressee feature and through her active participation in some of the laws.

Chapter 11

DEUTERONOMY 24:1–4

A. *Introduction*

Westbrook concludes that the primary concern of Deut 24:1–4 is to regulate property with respect to special circumstances relating to divorce.[1] He writes:

> it is the unspoken property aspect which runs like a thread through the whole protasis and accounts for its attention to detail and the distinctions that those details contain; it must therefore be the key to the law's rationale.[2]

Furthermore, according to Westbrook, עֶרְוַת דָּבָר has a broader referent than the referent of sexual promiscuity and הַטַּמָּאָה denotes something other than sexual impurity. Thus, according to Westbrook, the law of Deut 24:1–4 does not regulate or otherwise pertain to sexual intercourse. If Westbrook is correct, the law of Deut 24:1–4 is outside the defined text-base of this study.

However, recently Pressler has critiqued Westbrook's understanding and drawn conclusions of her own as follows:

> The significance of the law…is that it suggests the Deuteronomic view of proper or improper sexual conduct was not defined exclusively in terms of men's legal rights… [T]he relationship prohibited by the law should be seen as analogous to adultery, and understood in terms of sexual purity and pollution… The prohibition against a woman's involvement with first one man, then a second, then again with the first, cannot be explained in terms of claims over her by either man. Indeed, here the threat of pollution and concern for purity actually limit the first husband's prerogatives in relationship to his former wife. Deuteronomy seems to view such intermixed relationships as in and of themselves polluting.[3]

If Pressler's conclusions are accurate, then not only does Deut 24:1–4 regulate sexual intercourse, but its primary concern with respect to sexual intercourse and women is to guard classificatory boundaries rather than sexual property. Her conclusion is, thus, diametrically opposed to my thesis. For this reason, Pressler's argument requires a detailed review and analysis. A close look at her argument demonstrates, in fact, that her critique of Westbrook fails.

---

1. Westbrook, "Prohibition."
2. Westbrook, "Prohibition," 404.
3. Pressler, *View of Women*, 46, 61. Countryman, *Dirt*, 29, 37, also reads this law as having to do with purity issues.

B. *Discussion*

1. *Background*

Pressler, Westbrook, Wenham, Yaron and Instone-Brewer have summarized and critiqued the scholarly proposals which have preceded their own concerning the rationale of the law of Deut 24:1-4.[4]

Before reviewing their proposals, two prior proposals pertaining to this discussion must be cited. The first, represented by Philo, asserts that the wife of Deut 24:1-4 has committed adultery. This proposal has at least two variations.[5] The first variation assumes that, by definition, the woman commits adultery when she remarries.[6] The second assumes that עֶרְוַת דָּבָר refers to adultery she committed during her first marriage. In either case, the law forbids the first husband from remarrying an adulterous woman.[7] Scholars critique this proposal by noting that disapproval of divorce is entirely absent from Deut 24:1-4,[8] and that other laws in the Pentateuch prescribe death rather than divorce as the penalty for adultery.[9]

The second proposal, represented by Driver, assumes that Deut 24:1-4 guards against hasty divorce on the part of the first husband.[10] Scholars critique this

---

4. David Instone-Brewer, "Deuteronomy 24:1–4 and the Origin of the Jewish Divorce Certificate," *JJS* 49 (1998): 231–38; G.J. Wenham, "The Restoration of Marriage Reconsidered," *JJS* 30 (1979): 36–38; Westbrook, "Prohibition," 388–93; G. R. Yaron, "The Restoration of Marriage," *JJS* 17 (1966): 5–8. See also Carmichael's critique in *The Laws*, 203–7, and Myrna Kysar and Robert Kysar, *The Asundered* (Atlanta: John Knox, 1978), 24–25.

5. Which of these variations Philo has in mind is unclear. See Westbrook "Prohibition," 389.

6. Some scholars make a connection between this law and Jesus' comments on adultery in Matt 5:32; either basing their argument on Jesus' comments or drawing on his comments to support their position. See Amram, *Jewish Law*, 84; Gordon Wenham, "The Biblical View of Marriage and Divorce: 2—Old Testament Teaching," *Third Way* 1, no. 21 (1977): 8–9; Yaron, "Restoration," 7–8; Zakovitch, "Woman's Rights," 33.

7. Philo, *De Specialibus Legibus* (trans. André Mosès; Paris: Cerf, 1970), 3:30–31; Craigie, *Deuteronomy*, 305; Miller, *Deuteronomy*, 164; Rofé, "Family and Sex Laws," 154; Tigay, *Deuteronomy*, 220–21; Zakovitch, "Woman's Rights," 32.

8. A. Toeg, "Does Deuteronomy XXIV, 1–4 Incorporate a General Law on Divorce?," *Dine Israel* 2 (1970): xiii; Wenham, "Restoration," 36; Westbrook, "Prohibition," 388–89; Yaron, "Restoration," 6–8.

9. Cairns, *Deuteronomy*, 210; Mayes, *Deuteronomy*, 322; Phillips, *Deuteronomy*, 159; Pressler, *View of Women*, 57 n. 44; Yaron, "On Divorce," 127. The question concerning the application of the death penalty in actual cases of adultery in ancient Israel is open. See the following: Greenberg, "Postulates," 5–28; idem, "More Reflections," 1–17; Goodfriend, "Adultery," 83; Jackson, *Essays*, 43, 60–62; Kornfeld, "L'adultère," 92–109; Samuel E. Loewenstamm, *Comparative Studies in Biblical and Ancient Oriental Literatures* (Neukirchen–Vluyn: Neukirchener, 1980), 146–72; Mace, *Hebrew Marriage*, 249–50; McKeating, "Response," 25–26; idem, "Sanctions," 57–72; Neufeld, *Ancient Hebrew Marriage Laws*, 163–67; Phillips, "Another Look," 3–25; idem, "A Response," 142–43; Pressler, *View of Women*, 34 n. 41; Rofé, "Family and Sex Laws," 147; Stulman, "Sex and Familial Crimes," 59; Tigay, *Deuteronomy*, 71, 206, 221, especially 71 n. 112. Toeg, "Deuteronomy," vii–viii; Westbrook, "Adultery," 542–80; idem, "Prohibition," 396; idem, *Studies*, 97 n. 36; Yaron, "On Divorce," 127.

10. Driver, *Deuteronomy*, 272–73.

view by asserting that a husband who wants to divorce is unlikely to give considered reflection to circumstances which might transpire after the divorce.[11]

Yaron's suggestion, a third proposal, states that the law protects the second marriage from a first husband's attempts to take back the wife.[12] He reasons that the impulses driving an ex-husband to such intrigue are analogous to impulses that drive family members to commit incest.[13] Just as incest laws are required to curb such impulses, so also is the law of Deut 24:1–4 required to curb the impulses of an ex-husband and wife. Scholars reject this proposal by noting that it fails to account for the provision concerning the death of the second husband.[14]

Wenham offers a related, fourth proposal. He suggests that marriage "creates both vertical blood-relationships in the form of children and horizontal 'blood'-relationships between the spouses.[15] Deuteronomy 24:1–4 thus "uses the logic of the incest laws" to forbid remarriage.[16] Both Westbrook and Pressler reject this proposal, indicating that it fails to account for the intervening marriage.[17]

The dismissal of these four proposals leaves the two remaining proposals of Westbrook and Pressler as explanations of the rationale for the law of Deut 24:1–4.[18]

2. *Westbrook and Pressler*

a. *Westbrook.*

1) *The Proposal.* Westbrook's proposal originates in the difference between the dissolution of the first marriage and the dissolution of the second marriage. He writes:

> In the former, the husband finds "some indecency" in his wife and divorces her; in the latter he "dislikes" her and divorces her, or in the alternative, dies. There must therefore exist some underlying factor which is on the one hand common to divorce for "dislike" and death, and on the other distinguishes these two types of dissolution from divorce for "indecency." That factor, we submit, lies in the property aspect of marriage—more exactly, in the financial consequences of its dissolution.[19]

---

11.   Pressler, *View of Women*, 51–52; Wenham, "Restoration," 36; Westbrook, "Prohibition," 389; Yaron, "Restoration," 5.

12.   Yaron, "Restoration," 1–11; Wenham, "Divorce: 2," 9.

13.   Yaron, "Restoration," 8.

14.   Wenham, "Restoration," 37; Westbrook, "Prohibition," 389–90; Pressler, *View of Women*, 52–53. Carmichael, *The Laws*, 204–5, alternatively, suggests that the stories in Gen 12:10 and 20 concerning Abraham and Sarah furnish the model for Deut 24:1–4. Both Wenham and Westbrook rightly consider Carmichael's solution to be a reinstatement of Philo's view. See Wenham, "Restoration," 37; Westbrook, "Prohibition," 391.

15.   Wenham, "Restoration," 39. See also Miller, *Deuteronomy*, 164.

16.   Wenham, "Restoration," 40.

17.   Westbrook, "Prohibition," 390–91; Pressler, *View of Women*, 52.

18.   David Instone-Brewer, *Divorce and Remarriage in the Bible: The Social and Literary Context* (Grand Rapids: Eerdmans, 2002), 31. See Instone-Brewer's discussion of the ancient Near Eastern context, in which "a woman could be reclaimed by her first husband, even if she had remarried, since she had been left by him. The Middle Assyrian law #36…put a limit of five years on this right."

19.   Westbrook, "Prohibition," 393.

Westbrook admits that, aside from Deut 24:1–4, the Bible lacks supporting evidence for the significance and meaning of the distinction between the first dissolution and the second.

Nevertheless, he notes that the fact that the first husband has *found* עֶרְוַת דָּבָר suggests that the first husband has grounds for divorce.[20] Furthermore, he establishes the idea that שִׁנְאָה connotes divorce without grounds, by means of circumstantial evidence from cuneiform and post-biblical Jewish sources.[21] In addition, again by means of extra-biblical evidence, he demonstrates that when a marriage ends by death or divorce, the wife receives a financial settlement,[22] except, that is, in cases of divorce with grounds, where she has committed some wrong.

Westbrook concludes that the rationale of the law of Deut 24:1–4 derives from the difference between the two instances of dissolution in connection with the corresponding financial settlements:

> The effect would be that the first husband profits twice: firstly by rejecting his wife and then by accepting her. It is a flagrant case of unjust enrichment which the law intervenes to prevent. The prohibition on remarriage is based on what in modern law would be called estoppel. This is the rule whereby a person who has profited by asserting a particular set of facts cannot profit a second time by conceding that the facts were otherwise. He is bound by his original assertion, whether it is objectively the truth or not.[23]

In the first instance, the man has grounds for divorce (עֶרְוַת דָּבָר) and the wife receives no settlement. In the second instance, the man lacks grounds for divorce (שִׁנְאָה) and the wife receives a settlement. The woman, who the first man divorced, is now financially secure and therefore more attractive. The first man is therefore motivated to remarry her. The intent of the law based on the principle of estoppel is to forbid him to do so because such an act ignores the grounds upon which he first divorced her.[24]

---

20. Ibid., 399. Westbrook argues that עֶרְוַת דָּבָר broadly references the grounds for divorce by signifying "the type of misconduct referred to in CH 141–142 and in *m. Ketub.* 7:6," rather than narrowly signifying adultery. He cites the only other occurrence of the phrase in Deut 23:15, where it clearly signifies something other than sexual misconduct. See also Daube, "Culture," 32–33; Greenberg, "Female Sexuality," 34; Neufeld, *Ancient Hebrew Marriage Laws*, 178–79; Tigay *Deuteronomy*, 221. The following scholars are among those who disagree with Westbrook: Amram, *Jewish Law*, 32–40; Toeg, "Deuteronomy," x; Zakovitch, "Woman's Rights," 32. See also Countryman, *Dirt*, 173–76; Driver, *Deuteronomy*, 27–271; Jacob Neusner, ed. and trans., *Gittin, The Talmud of the Land of Israel*, vol 25 (Chicago: University of Chicago Press, 1982), 9:11.

21. Westbrook, "Prohibition," 399–402.

22. Ibid., 396.

23. Ibid., 404.

24. The occurrence of two analogous post-biblical examples in the *Talmud* lend credibility to Westbrook's theory. Amram, *Jewish Law*, 86, notes that, in addition to the case of remarriage after and intervening marriage by the wife, five other cases occur in the *Talmud* in which the husband may not marry his wife after divorcing her. Of the five cases Amram discusses, two guard against scenarios analogous to the scenario which Westbrook describes as operative in Deut 24:1–4. The first of the two cases occurs in *Baba Batra* of the *Palestinian Talmud* where a man divorces his wife; the wife claims her *ketubah* which has been secured by a third party; the man then remarries the ex-wife and benefits from the *ketubah*. See Jacob Neusner, ed. and trans., *Baba Batra, The Talmud of*

At first glance the motive clauses seem to belie Westbrook's explanation of the rationale of the law. The verbal root טמא and the word תּוֹעֵבָה, potential signals to a primary concern for sexual impurity,[25] occur within these motive clauses. Westbrook, however, analyzes הֻטַּמָּאָה as a Hophal,[26] which means "she has been caused to be unclean."[27] The connotation is that the woman's first husband has declared her unclean. Furthermore, his grounds for doing so may have nothing to do with sexual impurity. Westbrook understands the infraction of Deut 24:1–4, a case of estoppel, as a precise example of the hypocrisy which Weinfeld suggests that תּוֹעֵבָה signifies.[28] If Westbrook's conclusions are accurate, the motive clauses refer to something other than sexual impurity, and offer no threat to his property theory. Walton, however, convincingly parses the verb as a *hutqaṭṭēl* in which the *taw* has assimilated to the following consonant,[29] suggesting the translation: "she had been made to declare herself to be unclean."[30]

---

the Land of Israel, vol. 30 (Chicago: University of Chicago Press, 1984), 190–91. Amram, *Jewish Law*, 87, writes: "The husband cannot remarry her after he had divorced her, because it is possible that he might divorce her in order that she may claim her Ketubah from the guarantor, and then by marrying her again he would enjoy the benefit of the Kethubah which she had collected." The second example occurs in *Tractate Arakhin* of the *Babylonian Talmud* where a man, who has sanctified his property subject to a potential *ketubah* claim, divorces his wife; the wife claims the *ketubah*; the man remarries her and benefits from the *ketubah*. See Jacob Neusner, ed. and trans., *The Talmud of Babylonia, An American Translation*. Vol. 32, *Tractate Arakhin* (Chico, Calif.: Scholars Press, 1984), 176–77. Amram, *Jewish Law*, 87, writes: "Where one has consecrated all of his property to religious uses, subject to the wife's Kethubah, he must, according to Rabbi Eleazar, on divorcing her, renounce his right to remarry her, lest the divorce and remarriage be used as a scheme to re-possess himself of his property through her..." In the *Talmudic* cases, the divorce and remarriage are a scheme worked out by the husband and presumably the wife from the beginning. In the Deuteronomic case, on the other hand, the wife has grown more attractive because of her financial gain through the second marriage, subsequently motivating the husband to remarry her. Nevertheless, all three examples guard against remarriage undertaken so as to profit by property, which the wife receives through a second marriage subsequent to the initial divorce.

25.   G. André and H. Ringgren, "טמא," *TDOT* 5:330–42 (337).

26.   Pressler, *View of Women*, 48 n. 9, agrees with his grammatical rendering.

27.   Westbrook, "Prohibition," 404. See also Pressler, *View of Women*, 48 n. 9; E. Kautzsch, *Gesenius' Hebrew Grammar* (trans. A. E. Cowley; Oxford: Clarendon, 1910, second English edn reprinted from corrected sheets of the second edition) §54h.

28.   Westbrook, "Prohibition," 405; Weinfeld, *Deuteronomy*, 267–69.

29.   John H. Walton, "The Place of the *hutqaṭṭēl* within the D-Stem Group and Its Implications in Deuteronomy 24:4," *HS* 32 (1991): 9–10. He states (p. 11): "Working from the hypothetical profile constructed above, we would expect the *hutqaṭṭēl* of טמא to be reflected by a passive subject and undersubject while also featuring the factitive/estimative or declarative elements of the D group as well as the reflexive element common to the corresponding *hutqaṭṭēl*." The respective meanings based on his analysis for Qittel, Qittal, Hitqattel and Hutqattel are as follows (p. 12): declare/consider someone to be unclean; declared/considered to be unclean; declare/consider oneself to be unclean; be made to declare/consider oneself to be unclean.

30.   Walton, "Place of the *hutqaṭṭēl*," 12, states: "The nature of the *hutqaṭṭēl* suggests to us that this uncleanness is not because of an immoral act by the woman. Rather, as Waltke and O'Connor's description maintains, her passivity is substantiated grammatically: 'With the *Piel*, the object is transposed passively into a new state or condition. Philosophers would refer to this transposition as "accidental" because the object makes no contribution to the verbal notion...' This concept would

He suggests that the estimative sense, as opposed the declarative sense, would also work.[31] This translation, however, also works with Westbrook's theory.[32]

2) *The Critique.* Pressler gives three reasons why Westbrook's "argument is not finally persuasive."[33]

a) *First Reason.* Her first reason consists of two points.

(1) *First Point.* The first point critiques Westbrook's analysis of *zêru* in the cuneiform texts. By means of this analysis, Westbrook draws a correspondence between the verb "to hate" and groundless action. Subsequently he contrasts the phrases לֹא תִמְצָא־חֵן בְּעֵינָיו כִּי־מָצָא בָהּ עֶרְוַת דָּבָר and שָׂנֵאה to conclude that the first phrase signifies divorce with grounds and the second divorce without grounds.[34]

Pressler states, in a footnote, that Westbrook is unable "to cite any cases which clearly uses *zêru* to indicate that the party initiating the divorce was at fault."[35] Although Westbrook's evidence for *zêru*, and therefore for שָׂנֵאה, from the cuneiform sources is admittedly circumstantial, his evidence for the עֶרְוַת דָּבָר phrase, as described above, is from the deuteronomic text itself, requiring no substantiation from the extra-biblical evidence. The עֶרְוַת דָּבָר phrase within the deuteronomic text thus removes some of the burden of proof from the evidence pertaining to שָׂנֵאה. Since one half of the equation (i.e. עֶרְוַת דָּבָר) is in place within the deuteronomic text itself, even circumstantial evidence for the other half of the equation (i.e. שָׂנֵאה) lends plausibility to Westbrook's theory.

---

extend to all of the stems in the D group. As both subject and undersubject her role is passive. It is because of the discovered ערות דבר that she would have been forced to declare herself unclean."

31. Ibid., 11.

32. Instone-Brewer, "Deuteronomy," 233, states: "Walton strengthened Westbrook's case by arguing that the verb is an example of the rare *hutqattel* form…" However, Walton ("Place of the *hutqaṭṭēl*," 14–15) objects to Westbrook's theory because the "protasis does not mention any financial arrangement that the woman may have benefited from as a result of the second marriage." He suggests that ערות דבר refers to menstrual irregularities: "Such a condition would certainly not be the fault of the woman, but it could be legitimate grounds for divorce. The laws concerning uncleanness would make it difficult for such a woman to conceive a child for she could be perpetually unclean and prohibited from participating in intercourse (Lev 15:14). Her condition would create a very convenient situation for a husband who saw it as an opportunity to either get out of the marriage that was not to his liking, or following Westbrook, dismiss the woman and keep her dowry." Does the woman then deceive the second man about her condition? Walton admits that her condition is a matter of public record, in so far as it is reported to the priests; and it "would have been public knowledge" when the second man married her. That a second man would accept her as his wife out of the goodness of his heart ("ostensibly more charitable than the first husband") when reproduction of progeny is at such a premium, is not credible, Jesus' exegesis notwithstanding. But, perhaps her condition has been verified to have ceased, after her first divorce. If that is the case, then Walton's suggestion is plausible. But why does the law not mention the contingency of the disappearance of the ערות דבר which opens the way to a second marriage? It is, after all, not a minor detail to be forgotten by the law.

33. Pressler, *View of Women*, 56.

34. Ibid., 56. Westbrook, "Prohibition," 393–400.

35. Pressler, *View of Women*, 57 n. 43.

Westbrook builds his case concerning *zêru* as follows. He examines the use of terms and phrases for "hate" and "divorce" in the context of dissolution of marriage and concludes that their individual use is only a shortened form of their formulaic use together.[36] Pressler accepts this portion of Westbrook's argument.[37] In addition, Westbrook concludes that the two terms/phrases are not appositional or in other ways redundant. Rather, they are exclusive. He writes:

> The term "hate" is therefore an addition to the divorce formula which expresses not the divorce itself (for which there is another technical term) but some extra dimension thereof.[38]

Having concluded this exclusivity, Westbrook cites cases unrelated to dissolution of marriage in which "hate" occurs.[39] From these cases he concludes that "the verb invariably appears in combination with a verb of action, providing the motivation for that action.[40] In three cases which Westbrook cites, the individual "hates" and then flees or leaves. Westbrook suggests that the action of the "hater" in these cases implies guilt.[41] Accordingly, "the verb 'hate' is used to show that the action arose from a subjective motive and without objective grounds to justify it—and for this reason is blameworthy."[42] Therefore, if "hate" signifies scenarios of separation without grounds, and if "divorce" and "hate" are exclusive, then "divorce" signifies separation with grounds.[43]

Thus, while Westbrook has found no cuneiform text which explicitly indicates that "hate" signifies dissolution without grounds, he has found direct evidence that the distinction between divorce with and without grounds was addressed in the law.[44] Furthermore, he has found indirect evidence suggesting that the verb "hate" signifies guilt with respect to the individual who takes separative action. In conjunction with the first divorce of Deut 24:1–4, which is self-evidently a case with grounds, the circumstantial and other evidence which Westbrook gathers builds a strong case for the plausibility of his theory, contrary to the implications of Pressler's assertions concerning *zêru* in her footnote.[45]

(2) *Second Point*. However, Pressler continues her critique with an example from Hammurabi's Code, which she considers to be problematic for Westbrook's theory. She writes:

---

36. Westbrook, "Prohibition," 400–401.
37. Pressler, *View of Women*, 54 n. 35, writes: "Westbrook convincingly argues that the terms are used in these documents as abbreviations of the fuller phrase 'hate and divorce'..."
38. Westbrook, "Prohibition," 401.
39. Ibid.
40. Ibid.
41. Ibid.
42. Ibid., 401–2.
43. Ibid., 403–4.
44. See above.
45. See above.

The one time the Code of Hammurabi uses the verb *zêru* in connection with divorce, however, is found in a case where an inchoately married woman who "hated" her betrothed husband and refused to marry him was determined by the local court to be blameless (CH 142). The companion case, where the woman is found to be a gadabout and suffers the death penalty, does not use the term *zêru*[46]

This portion of Pressler's critique also consists of two points. One concerns CH 142 and the other concerns CH143 ("the companion case").

Before addressing Pressler's critique, the following observation concerning CH 142–43 must be made. The unit is exceptional in at least two ways. Westbrook determines that this is a law concerning the dissolution of an inchoate marriage arrangement rather than a marriage arrangement.[47] Pressler agrees.[48] Second, this is a dissolution initiated by the woman not the man. For these two reasons, irregularities with respect to what constitutes "grounds or lack of grounds" as well as irregularities with respect to financial settlement should not *prima facie* be taken as exceptions to rules that apply when men initiate dissolution of either a choate or inchoate marriage.

In fact, Westbrook asserts that the apparent exception of CH 142 to the rule is a function of the higher standard to which women, and in particular inchoately married women, are held.[49] He writes:

The one example that does not seem to fit into this argument is CH 142, where the woman does in fact have grounds for her conduct. But the use of the verb "to hate" even there is, we submit, an indication of the hostile attitude to the wife's action taken by the law…CH is a ruling on a case where the presumption of lack of justification was much stronger for a woman than for a man."[50]

In CH142, an inchoately married woman divorces without grounds. Although this woman divorces without grounds, she receives a marriage settlement, taking her dowry with her.[51] Since the woman is held to a higher standard, her husband's slander fails to constitute legal grounds for her divorce. Therefore, the writer uses *zêru*. However, presumably, according to Westbrook's reasoning, since the woman's behavior, up to the point of her "hating," is flawless, she is permitted the financial settlement. Such irregularities are a function of the fact that a woman initiates the separation in this case.

Having made this observation, Pressler's critique can be addressed. Concerning CH 142, Pressler notes that not only does the woman have grounds, but the law explicitly states that the woman is "blameless."[52] Pressler's point is that *zêru* is used to signify separation with grounds, contrary to Westbrook's theory.

46. Pressler, *View of Women*, 56–57.
47. Westbrook, "Prohibition," 397; idem, "Old Babylonian Marriage Law," vol. 2 (Ph.D. diss., Yale University, 1982), 100–104, 198.
48. Pressler, *View of Women*, 56.
49. Westbrook, "Old Babylonian," 228; idem, "Prohibition," 397.
50. Westbrook, "Old Babylonian," 228.
51. See the discussions by both Pressler and Westbrook on dowry and marriage price: Pressler, *View of Women*, 54–55 n. 36; Westbrook, "Prohibition," 394–96.
52. Pressler, *View of Women*, 56.

However, Pressler has confused the guilt of the "*mens rea*"[53] with the guilt of other actions. If Westbrook's theory holds, then the woman is blameless with respect to the rumors her husband is spreading. Whether or not she is blameless with respect to the grounds for her separative action is another question. Westbrook deduces the *mens rea* from verbs accompanying the "hate" verb in Codex Eshnunna 30, CH 136, 142 and 193. He writes:

> The verb invariably appears in combination with a verb of action, providing the motivation for that action. The motivation appears to turn what might otherwise be an innocent act into a guilty one, and we therefore feel justified in applying the terminology of modern criminal law: it is the *mens rea*, the "guilty mind", which is a necessary constituent of the offense. The verb "hate" is used to show that the action arose from a subjective motive and without objective grounds to justify it—and for this reason is blameworthy.[54]

Thus, Westbrook offers the *mens rea* as evidence that the separative action taken is groundless. The person committing the separative act flees or goes or says "You shall not marry me" precisely because his or her "hating" is groundless. Since slander by a husband does not constitute the improper behavior which would justify separative action on the part of the woman, the woman is blameworthy with respect to her separative action. But she is blameless with respect to the unspecified rumors the husband spreads. Therefore, she takes the dowry.

Pressler's second point is that in CH 143, where the woman is blameworthy with respect to her general behavior, *zêru* is unmentioned altogether.[55] However, *zêru* is unmentioned in CH 143 because CH 143 is framed as a subcase of CH 142. CH 143 does not begin with a phrase such as *šumma awilum, šumma sinništum,* or *šumma wardum,* which signal separate cases by identifying at least one of the principal individuals targeted by the law. Rather, it begins with *šumma la nasratma,* indicating that this case is a subcase of that which precedes.[56] In other words, the phrase *šumma sinništum musà izerma,* which begins CH 142, applies to CH 143 as well.[57]

Finally it must be noted that Westbrook does not rely on this single example to establish the alignment of "hate" with groundless dissolution. As stated above, he builds his case, circumstantially, on the basis of several laws including some which are unrelated to dissolution of marriage.

b) *Second Reason.* Pressler's second reason that Westbrook's argument is unpersuasive is that he fails to give due consideration to the relationship between Jer 3:1–5 and Deut 24:1–4.[58] Indeed, Westbrook mentions Jer 3:1 only in the last

---

53. Westbrook, "Prohibition," 401.

54. Ibid., 401–2.

55. Pressler, *View of Women,* 56–57.

56. Rykle Borger, *Babylonisch-Assyrische Lesetücke,* vol. 1 (AnOr 54; Rome: Pontificium Institutum Biblicum, 1979), 29.

57. Borger, *Babylonisch,* 1:29; Locher, "Deuteronomium," 300. Locher has already made this point while drawing comparisons among Deut 22:13–21, CH 142/143 and MAL55/56.

58. Pressler, *View of Women,* 58. See the discussion of this relationship by the following: T. R. Hobbs, "Jeremiah 3:1–5 and Deuteronomy 24:1–4," *ZAW* 86 (1974): 23–29; J. D. Martin, "The Forensic Background to Jeremiah III 1," *VT* 19 (1969): 82–92.

footnote of his study where he doubts the connection between the two pericopes (on the basis that the second marriage is unmentioned and the husband rather than the wife "returns").[59] He describes the scenario of Jer 3:1 and the following verse as "an illicit liaison between the man and his former wife."[60]

Pressler states that Westbrook fails to account for "the freedom of the poet/ prophet."[61] This freedom, presumably, is why the author fails to mention the dissolution of the second marriage.[62] But Westbrook's explanation for the absence of the dissolution of the second marriage is at least as persuasive as Pressler's.

Jeremiah 3:1–5 is about a man who has divorced a woman for unspecified reasons. The woman marries a second man. The woman then has many lovers. The dissolution of the second marriage is absent from the text. However, the woman returns to the first man and asks if he will always be angry, if he will always "be careful" with respect to her. Contrary to Pressler's assertion, the text does not tell us that the woman attempts to return for remarriage.[63] The point is that the woman acts as if her illicit deeds have not occurred at all, as if her life is "normal" and nothing wrong has been done. Perhaps, as part of her agenda, she returns to make the first husband "another one of her harloting escapades." In any case, she attempts to co-opt the first husband to participate in or bless the state of affairs she has created. The first husband, Yhwh, is incredulous at her nonchalance and brazenness. He is incredulous at not only the wrongs she has committed, but at her attempts to act as if nothing wrong has been done. He himself refuses to agree to act as if nothing wrong has been done. Remarriage is not the issue. The issue is denial of her sins.[64]

In this way, Westbrook's suggestion that "the reference may therefore be to an illicit liaison between the man and his former wife" is believable.[65]

c) *Third Reason.* Pressler's third reason that Westbrook's argument is unpersuasive has to do with the motive clauses of the law, v. 4aβ–b. She writes:

> The third reason that Westbrook's interpretation cannot be sustained is because it is not supported by the motive clauses in Deut 24:4. The first motive clause could be made to fit Westbrook's interpretation by translating it "she has been declared defiled." As argued above, however, the second and third motive clauses indicate that the prohibition is concerned with purity and pollution rather than with rconomic [*sic*] justice.[66]

Pressler agrees with Westbrook's grammatical rendering of הֻטַּמָּאָה.[67] Furthermore, she admits the plausibility of his understanding of the meaning of the

59.   Westbrook, "Prohibition," 405 n. 66.
60.   Ibid.
61.   Ibid., 59.
62.   Ibid., 58–59.
63.   Ibid., 59.
64.   See Jer 3:9–10, 13–14 where the issue is such denial. Prov 30:20 reads: "This is the way of the adulterous woman. She eats; and she wipes her mouth; and she says, 'I have not done wrong.'"
65.   Westbrook, "Prohibition," 405 n. 66.
66.   Pressler, *View of Women*, 59.
67.   Ibid., 48 n. 9.

words as well as the fact that the difference between her choice in meaning and his choice is exegetical. This means that she can draw support for her reading of the law from only the last two of the three motive clauses, which she presents as follows:

1. She has defiled herself/been declared defiled.
2. It is an abomination before Yaweh.
3. You shall not cause the land which Yahweh your God is giving you as an inheritance to incur guilt.[68]

The second of the three motive clauses uses the word תּוֹעֵבָה. Pressler states that "the theme common to all of the laws using תּוֹעֵבָה is the concept of purity."[69] She ignores Weinfeld's suggestions concerning תּוֹעֵבָה,[70] from which Westbrook derives[71] his own understanding. All the examples which Pressler cites, including Deut 14:3,[72] which Weinfeld leaves out of his discussion, can be explained as "hypocrisy," or, as Mary Douglas puts it, "contradictions between what seems and what is."[73] Pressler fails to mention Deut 25:13–16 where false weights and measures are called an abomination. This is the key example with which Weinfeld launches his hypocrisy theory. It is the one example difficult to explain as a matter of purity in the way that Pressler describes.

Westbrook, following Weinfeld's lead, posits that the word, rather than connoting sexual impurity, connotes hypocrisy.[74] However, his understanding of its use in Deut 24:1–4 is slightly different from Weinfeld's understanding.[75] Weinfeld proposes that תּוֹעֵבָה signifies the hypocrisy of remarrying a woman whom one had initially divorced after finding some sexual indecency in her.[76] Westbrook, on the other hand, proposes that it signifies the hypocrisy which "estoppel" bars.[77] Therefore, if תּוֹעֵבָה signifies impurity, as Pressler suggests, then the locus of the impurity is the hypocrisy of the act.

This leaves only the final motive clause. Pressler states that this final clause "categorizes the prohibited remarriage as polluting."[78] Citing Frymer-Kensky, she argues that "the kinds of sin which are said to pollute the land consistently fall into three categories."[79] These three kinds of sin are apostasy, bloodguilt and sexual defilement. Since the kinds of sin which pollute the land fall into these

---

68. Ibid., 48.
69. Ibid., 50.
70. Weinfeld, *Deuteronomy*, 267–69.
71. Westbrook, "Prohibition," 405.
72. The permitted animals part the hoof and chew the cud. Those animals which have only one of the qualifications, that is, those animals which masquerade as belonging to the two-qualification category but in fact do not, are not permitted. They are an abomination or hypocrisy.
73. Douglas, *Purity*, 53–54.
74. Instone-Brewer, "Deuteronomy," 233–35. See Instone-Brewer's critique of Westbrook's explanation of "abomination" as a possible strengthening amendment to Westbrook's argument.
75. Westbrook, "Prohibition," 405; Weinfeld, *Deuteronomy*, 269–70.
76. Weinfeld, *Deuteronomy*, 269, especially n. 4.
77. Westbrook, "Prohibition," 404–5.
78. Pressler, *View of Women*, 50.
79. Ibid., 51. See also Frymer-Kensky, "Pollution," 406–9.

three categories, Pressler concludes that the consequence of the last motive clause must follow an act which falls into one of the three categories. Sexual defilement is the obvious choice.

However, the relationship between crimes and the land is more complex than Pressler's description would lead us to believe. Even Frymer-Kensky leaves room for more acts than those that comprise only the three categories as pollutants. She states:

> General misdeeds and sins are also categorized as polluting the people (Ps 106:39; Ezek 14:11; 20:43), though this may be a late extension of the pollution concept as it refers to the people… The crimes of the people are considered to pollute the very earth of Israel (Jer 2:7; Ezek 36:17), and certain acts are explicitly termed contaminants. Bloodshed… Idolatry…wrongful sex acts… These three classes of pollutants—murder, sexual abominations, and idolatry—pollute both the people and the land.[80]

The interpreter is not thus necessarily compelled to conclude that the acts which lead to the consequences of v. 4b must fall into one of the three categories: apostasy, bloodguilt and sexual defilement.

The connection of defilement with the land (ארץ or אדמה) signified by טמא occurs only three times in all of Leviticus, Numbers and Deuteronomy: Lev 18:24ff; Num 35:34; Deut 21:23. All three citations account for two of the categories, sexual defilement and bloodshed. Deuteronomy 24:4, by contrast, uses the verb חטא. Weinfeld states the following:

> The concept of the pollution of the land by murder and sexual aberrations is most explicitly expressed in the Priestly code, by means of three idioms: טמא (Lev. 18:25, 27, 28; Num. 35:34, cf. Ezek. 23:17, 36:17–18), זנה (Lev. 19:29, cf. Hos. 1:2, 5:3, Ezek. 23:17), חנף (Num. 35:33, cf. Isa. 24:5, Jer. 3:1, 2, 9, Ps. 106:38). In contrast to this D speaks about blood guilt *amidst the people* or *on the people* (19:10, 13, 21:8, 9), and about *bringing sin* upon the land in connection with sexual aberrations.[5] Of the three idioms used in P in connection with defiling the land, Deut preserved only one and only once, טמא in 21:23. One might say, though only on the basis of a single attestation, that side by side with the notion of sin lying on the people D also preserved the idea of contamination of the land.

---

[5]The analogy from Jer. 3:1 f. does not hold since in Jeremiah we often find combinations of Priestly and Deuteronomic phraseology, cf. e.g. in 34:8, 15, 17: קרא דרור, which is Priestly (comp. Lev. 25:10), and 34:14 which is a quotation from Deut. 15:12; 44:23: ובחקתי...לא הלכתם which is to be compared with Lev 26:3 אם בחקתי תלכו.[81]

80. Frymer-Kensky, "Pollution," 407–8.

81. M. Weinfeld, "On 'Demythologization and Secularization' in Deuteronomy," *IEJ* 23 (1973): 232. The footnote within this quote is a response to the following statement by Milgrom in his "The Alleged 'Demythologization and Secularization' in Deuteronomy," *IEJ* 23 (1973): 157, where he states: "According to Weinfeld, D is free of P's notions that impurity is a miasmic, palpable substance (pp. 225–26) because in P bloodshed contaminates the land (Num 35:33–34) whereas in D it falls upon the people (19:10; 21:8). This distinction is illusory: P's concept of the contamination of the land also informs D. Remarriage with a divorced woman who meanwhile has been contaminated (הטמאה) by another man is forbidden 'that you may not bring sin (תחטיא) upon the land' (24:4). The exact meaning of תחטיא is clarified by Jer 3:1, a passage influenced by D, which employs the synonym תחניף 'pollute' (see Num 35:33)." See also Martin, "Forensic Background," 83–84: "The idea of a land being defiled or polluted is fairly common in the Old

Repeatedly throughout Deuteronomy the people are urged to keep Yhwh's laws so that their days might be long in the land which he has given them.[82] While in Leviticus illicit acts such as sexual promiscuity result in the land vomiting the inhabitants, in Deuteronomy social injustices such as unjust weights and measures lead to shortened days in the land.[83] Whether or not we decide that pollution is always a factor, the deeds affecting an inhabitant's connection to the land can fall outside the three categories.

Thus, while Rabbinic and other later sources may classify the sins which pollute the land according to the three categories,[84] Pressler's assertion that the third motive clause of Deut 24:1–4 *compels* us to conclude that the infraction of the law belongs to the category of sexual defilement is unfounded.

b. *Pressler.* Pressler herself understands the law of Deut 24:1–4 as regulating relationships which are analogous to adultery.[85] She analyzes the relationships of adultery in general as follows: "Adultery involves a woman having sexual relations with man A, then man B, then again man A."[86] ABA, she suggests, is precisely the pattern of relationships in Deut 24:1–4. Thus, Deut 24:1–4 is analogous to adultery.[87] The adultery proposal, represented by Philo, is, in fact,

---

Testament. Most of the instances, however, bear the idea that a land is polluted as a result of the collective sins of the totality of its inhabitants, and nearly all of these instances are found in Jeremiah, cf. ii 7; iii 2, 9; xvi 18. This is also the idea behind Deut xxix 27 where the anger of Yahweh is said to be kindled against the land because of the idolatry of the people. The only legal contexts in which this concept occurs, apart from Deut xxiv, are three in number. In Num xxxv 33–4 the land is said to be polluted (*ḥnp*) by the shedding of innocent blood and by letting that innocent blood go unexpiated… The second legal context is that of Deut xxi 22 f., where the context is that of a hanging for a crime punishable by death… The third context is that of Lev xviii where we find a series of sexual offences… The root is again *ṭmʾ*. But the occurrence of the idea in Deut xxiv is unique. The context of Lev xviii could also be brought under the heading of defilement as a result of the collective sins of the totality of the inhabitants, but Deut xxiv is referring only to one particular enactment, not to a series of offences. Num xxxv and Deut xxi also refer to one single enactment, but in neither of these cases has the verb used quite the force and significance of the one in Deut xxiv 4, the Hiph'il of *ḥṭʾ* with the meaning of 'cause to sin.' This form of *ḥṭʾ* is often used of the kings of Israel (and, to a lesser extent, those of Judah) who are condemned in the books of Kings for having 'caused Israel to sin,' but there, of course, the idea is that they have led the *people* astray, not that they have brought guilt upon the *land* as such."

82. Deut 4:40; 5:33; 25:15. Tigay, *Deuteronomy*, xvi.

83. Deut 25:13–16.

84. Frymer-Kensky, "Pollution," 408.

85. Otto, "False Weights," 138, states that restoration of divorced marriage is "not only a provision analogous to those against adultery but deals with adultery."

86. Pressler, *View of Women*, 60–61.

87. Amram, *Jewish Law*, 30, 83, 102. Amram's position is similar to Pressler's (p. 80): "The law intimates that even after her divorce, the wife had still clinging unto her some of the duties of wifehood; for the marriage of the divorced woman, although entirely legal, was deemed improper, a *quasi*-adultery. There seems to have been some analogy between the case of the divorced woman who had married another and the case of the adulteress; and even as the law would not permit a man to live with an adulterous wife, so he was forbidden to live in a second marriage with his divorced wife, if she had in the meantime been the wife of another." However, Amram concedes the following (p. 80): "Adultery was punished by death, and if the analogy between the two cases is a true one,

the one interpretation of the law which Pressler fails to review and critique. Nevertheless, she seems to be aware of the dismissal of this view by Yaron and others because she avoids Philo's simple proposal that the law is a case of adultery. Her explanation is more complex.

> Partly by a process of elimination, we are pushed to interpret the relationships prohibited by the law as analogous to adultery. Adultery involves a woman having sexual relations with man A, then man B, then again man A. Deut 24:1–4 prohibits just such a pattern of sexual relations, even when the first and second relationships were legally contracted and legally dissolved.[88]

Several points can be made with respect to Pressler's understanding. The first is that more is significant concerning the relationships in Deut 24:1–4 than the simple ABA pattern. The *kind* of bonds and boundaries that bind and demarcate the relationships of Deut 24:1–4 is as significant as the pattern. In fact, the pattern cannot be understood without them. An unattached woman can participate in the ABA pattern without reprisal. The difference between the unattached woman and the adulterous woman is the nature of the bond that binds them and the boundaries that separate them. Furthermore, the relationships of Deut 24:1–4 differ from the relationships of simple adultery precisely with respect to these bonds and boundaries. Pressler's dismissal of the significance of the *kinds* of bonds that bind, on the basis of her proposed significance of the ABA pattern, is thus unwarranted.

Furthermore, Pressler seems to be aware of the fact that selection of the classificatory idea as a primary concern can come only as a last resort when she states "Partly by a process of elimination, we are pushed to interpret the relationships prohibited by the law as analogous to adultery."[89] Pressler makes this statement with the classificatory explanation in view. However, as demonstrated above, Westbrook's understanding is plausible and survives Pressler's critique. The classificatory explanation is unwarranted.[90] In fact, Westbrook's understanding rules it out as an option.

C. *Conclusion*

Pressler's critique of Westbrook fails as does her own explanation of the law.

Westbrook's interpretation stands. The law of Deut 24:1–4 concerns property issues related to special circumstances of divorce. The law is not about sexual impurity and does not regulate sexual intercourse.

Thus, the text does not belong in the text-base of this study.

---

the offence of remarriage with the divorced woman should also be punished by death. On this point Deuteronomy is silent."

88. Pressler, *View of Women*, 60–61.
89. Ibid., 60.
90. Frymer-Kensky, "Deuteronomy," 60. Frymer-Kensky, without reference to Westbrook and Pressler, is nevertheless unable to choose between the two positions which these scholars represent. She suggests that two factors, closely resembling the factors proposed by *both* Westbrook and Pressler, may be operative in the law.

Chapter 12

DEUTERONOMY 25:5–10[*]

A. *Introduction*

The primary concern of Deut 25:5–10 is to "establish the name" of a dead man. "Establishment of the name" is his entitlement. The legal intersection of what functions as the dead man's progeny and what would have been the dead man's landed inheritance guarantees this entitlement. The vehicle for this intersection is the sexuality of the widow, which the law treats as property, and the sexuality of the dead man's brother. The woman's welfare is entirely incidental to the law. The primary concern of Deut 25:5–10 is, thus, protection of a dead man's entitlement, requiring protection of woman's sexuality as property.

Outside of the masculine pronouns in some of the laws proximal to Deut 25:5–10,[1] no clue exists that the levirate law is explicitly addressed to men rather than women. The masculine pronouns occurring outside the law, by themselves, are ambiguous signals for the point-of-view of the law itself. The law itself seems to be addressed equally to men and women. Thus, with respect to the addressee of the levirate law, woman's marginalization in the text is not apparent. Nevertheless, fulfillment of the man's destiny is written and codified by this law, while the fulfillment of the woman's destiny is only implied. In this respect, she is marginalized in the text. Moreover, the language-depicting-the-sex-act clearly objectifies her. In addition, her relationship to the author's primary concern focalizes her as property.

B. *Discussion*

1. *Background*
Scholars have offered a variety of suggestions concerning the purpose of the levirate law of Deut 25:5–10.[2] The suggestions fall into at least four groups:

---

[*] Some of my thoughts concerning Deut 25:5–10 were stimulated by a lively discussion with Rafael Chodos, Junko Chodos and Harold Ellens.

1. Deut 25:4, 13–16.

2. Deut 25:5–10 is one of three pericopes in the Hebrew Bible associated with levirate practice. The other two, Gen 38 and the book of Ruth, are narratives. The relationship of these three texts has been the subject of much discussion among biblical scholars. See the following for a review and analysis: Raymond Westbrook, "The Law of the Biblical Levirate," *RIDA* 24 (1977): 66–68, 76; idem, *Property and the Family in Biblical Law* (JSOTSup 113; Sheffield: JSOT Press, 1991), 70–79. See also the following: D. R. G. Beattie, "The Book of Ruth as Evidence for Israelite Legal

(1) those having to do with progeny;[3] (2) those having to do with inheritance of landed property[4] and sometimes with inheritance of sexual property;[5] (3) those having to do with the welfare of the widow;[6] and, finally, (4) those having to do with the perpetuation of the deceased's name.[7] Scholars take a variety of stances within the four groups. For example, Neufeld seems to suggest that the widow's welfare (group three) is the sole or main concern of levirate law.[8] Some have suggested that it is one among several competing concerns.[9] Others have suggested that the welfare is entirely incidental to the concern of the law.[10]

Practice," *VT* 24 (1974): 264–65; Samuel Belkin, "Levirate and Agnate Marriage in Rabbinic and Cognate Literature," *JQR* 60 (1970): 275–329; Millar Burrows, "The Marriage of Boaz and Ruth," *JBL* 59 (1940): 453; Cairns, *Deuteronomy*, 216–17; Eryl W. Davies, "Inheritance Rights and the Hebrew Levirate Marriage: Part 2," *VT* 31 (1981): 267; de Vaux, *Ancient Israel*, 37–38; Richard Kalmin, "Levirate Law," *ABD* 4:296–97; E. Kutsch, "יבם," *TDOT* 5:367–79; Donald A. Leggett, *The Levirate and Goel Institutions in the Old Testament* (Cherry Hill: Mack, 1974), 271–91; Dale W. Manor, "A Brief History of Levirate Marriage as It Relates to the Bible," *RQ* 27 (1984): 131; Mayes, *Deuteronomy*, 328–29; H. H. Rowley, "The Marriage of Ruth," *HTR* 40 (1947): 77–99; Thomas Thompson and Dorothy Thompson, "Some Legal Problems in the Book of Ruth," *VT* 18 (1968): 79–84; Tigay, *Deuteronomy*, 483; von Rad, *Deuteronomy*, 154–55.

3.   Belkin, "Levirate and Agnate Marriage," 280; George W. Coats, "Widow's Rights: A Crux in the Structure of Genesis 38," *CBQ* 34 (1972): 462; Craigie, *Deuteronomy*, 314; Eryl W. Davies, "Inheritance Rights and the Hebrew Levirate Marriage: Part 1," *VT* 31 (1981): 139; de Vaux, *Ancient Israel*, 38; Epstein, *Marriage Laws*, 79; Frymer-Kensky, "Deuteronomy," 61; Kalmin, "Levirate Law," 296–97; Leggett, *Levirate and Goel*, 49–51; Mace, *Hebrew Marriage*, 97; Manor, "Brief History," 131; Pedersen, *Israel*, 78; Phillips, *Deuteronomy*, 168; Pressler, *View of Women*, 73; Thompson and Thompson, "Legal Problems," 88, 96; Tigay, *Deuteronomy*, 482; Westbrook, *Property*, 74.

4.   Belkin, "Levirate and Agnate Marriage," 280; Millar Burrows, "Levirate Marriage in Israel," *JBL* 59 (1940): 28; Cairns, *Deuteronomy*, 216; Craigie, "*Deuteronomy*," 314; Davies, "Inheritance: 1," 142; de Vaux, *Ancient Israel*, 38; Frymer-Kensky, "Deuteronomy," 328; Miller, *Deuteronomy*, 165; Phillips, *Deuteronomy*, 168; Pressler, *View of Women*, 69 (for a summary and critique of this suggestion); Thompson and Thompson, "Legal Problems," 88, 96; Tigay, *Deuteronomy*, 482; von Rad, *Deuteronomy*, 154; Westbrook, *Property*, 74.

5.   Epstein, *Marriage Laws*, 79; Burrows, "Levirate Marriage," 28; Wegner, *Chattel*, 99.

6.   Belkin, "Levirate and Agnate Marriage," 293; Cairns, *Deuteronomy*, 216; Coats, "Widow's Rights," 462; Davies, "Inheritance: 1," 139, 142, 144; Epstein, *Marriage Laws*, 79; Frymer-Kensky, "Deuteronomy," 61; Kalmin, "Levirate Law," 296–97; Leggett, *Levirate and Goel*, 40–41, 57–61; Miller, *Deuteronomy*, 165; Neufeld, *Ancient Hebrew Marriage Laws*, 29–30, 40; Pressler, *View of Women*, 73; Thompson and Thompson, "Legal Problems," 96; Tigay, *Deuteronomy*, 482.

7.   Burrows, "Levirate Marriage," 293; Cairns, *Deuteronomy*, 216; Coats, "Widow's Rights," 462; Davies, "Inheritance: 1," 139, 142, 144; Epstein, *Marriage Laws*, 79; Frymer-Kensky, "Deuteronomy," 61; Kalmin, "Levirate Law," 296–97; Leggett, *Levirate and Goel*, 40–41, 57–61; Miller, *Deuteronomy*, 165; Neufeld, *Ancient Hebrew Marriage Laws*, 29–30, 40; Pressler, *View of Women*, 73; Thompson and Thompson, "Legal Problems," 96; Tigay, *Deuteronomy*, 482.

8.   Neufeld, *Ancient Hebrew Marriage Laws*, 30; Thompson and Thompson, "Legal Problems," 85.

9.   Blenkinsopp, "Family," 64; Frank S. Frick, "Widows in the Hebrew Bible: A Transactional Approach," in Brenner, ed., *A Feminist Companion to Exodus to Deuteronomy*, 147; Pressler, *View of Women*, 63–64, 73; Davies, "Inheritance: 1," 142–43; idem, "Inheritance: 2," 267–68; Epstein, *Marriage Laws*, 79; Thompson and Thompson, "Legal Problems," 85, 96.

10.   Leggett, *Levirate and Goel*, 54 n. 60; Mace, *Hebrew Marriage*, 108, 113; Westbrook, *Property*, 72.

Furthermore, many scholars offer a combination of the four groups as explanation of the purpose of the text. In particular, group four usually consists of a variety of combinations of the first three groups, sometimes in addition to other proposed factors such as ancestor worship[11] or vague notions concerning a man's "continued existence"[12] in this world after his death.

2. *Purpose of the Law*
However, any solution to the problem of the purpose of the levirate law in Deut 25 must account for at least four factors: (1) the phrase יֵשְׁבוּ אַחִים יַחְדָּו; (2) the group of references related to establishing the brother's name in vv. 6, 7 and 9; (3) the requirements to enter, to marry and יבם; and (4) the function of חֲלִצָה. An accounting of all four factors indicates that the primary concern of the text is the protection of a dead man's entitlement, which requires the protection of woman's sexuality as property.

a. *Structure.* Awareness of the placement and function of these factors in the structure of the text is helpful for understanding their significance and thereby answering the question of purpose or primary concern.

A collapsed version of the structure of Deut 25 follows:

I.	Beating a man	25:1–3
II.	Muzzling an Ox	25:4
III.	Wives	25:5–12
	A. Levirate Law	5–10
	1. protasis	5aα
	2. apodosis	5aβ–10
	a. basic stipulation	5aβ–6
	1) negatively stated	5aβ
	2) positively stated	5b–6
	a) re: the woman	5b
	(1) יבא	5bα
	(2) לקחה	5bβ
	(3) יבמה (be levir)	5bγ
	b) re: the name	6
	(1) positive (establish name)	6a
	(2) negative (name not wiped out)	6b
	b. contingent stipulation	7–10
	1) protasis	7a
	2) apodosis	7b–10

11. Burrows, "Ancient Oriental Background," 2; Pressler, *View of Women*, 67 n. 18; Tigay, *Deuteronomy*, 482–83.

12. Pressler, *View of Women*, 73; Thompson and Thompson, "Legal Problems," 86–87. Tigay's description of the way this "continued existence" worked is more specific and therefore more believable than the descriptions of Pressler and Thompson. Tigay, *Deuteronomy*, 482, states: "Many of these methods involved keeping a deceased man's name present on earth, thus perpetuating his spirit's contact with the living. Perhaps the reasoning was that just as the mention of a person's name can conjure up a very real mental picture of him, wherever a person's name was present his spirit was present. In this respect, a name functioned more or less as an image was thought to function."

The law consists of two parts, a protasis and an apodosis. The protasis states the conditions which must hold for the law to take affect. The conditions are three: (1) two brothers dwell together; (2) one brother dies; and (3) the dead brother has no sons.[13]

The apodosis, on the other hand, sets out the consequences of the conditions. The apodosis has two parts. The first part is the basic consequence. The second part is the consequence that applies should a particular contingency arise, that is, the refusal of the levir to perform his duty. Both parts are subject to the conditions of the protasis in v. 5aα. The contingent portion of the consequence itself

---

13. Since בכור in v. 6 is "first born son," בן in v. 5 must refer to male progeny. Westbrook, *Property*, 82, states: "The term used for the issue of the levirate in Deut 25.6 should be conclusive, since it is supposed to replace the missing offspring. The term is *bkwr* meaning 'first-born', but the Septuagint translates differently: παιδίον meaning 'little child.' So far is this from the Hebrew, not even expressing the element of primogeniture (even conceding that the first-born could be a girl) that it is an obvious sign of an attempt to alter the meaning of the law. We therefore consider, with Neufeld, that the most likely hypothesis is that until late biblical times at least, the existence of a daughter did not affect the imposition of the levirate, nor was the birth of a daughter considered fulfillment of the duty." See also J. Derby, "The Problem of the Levirate Marriage," *JBQ* 19 (1990): 12; Leggett, *Levirate and Goel*, 49 n. 51, 50 n. 52; Mayes, *Deuteronomy*, 328–29; Neufeld, *Ancient Hebrew Marriage Laws*, 45; Pressler, *View of Women*, 64–65, especially n. 5; Wegner, *Chattel*, 234 n. 161.

consists of a protasis and an apodosis. This protasis (clause 7a) names the contingent condition which applies in addition to the basic conditions listed in v. 5aα.

The protasis and the apodosis of the contingent portion are subject to the basic protasis in phrase 5aα in different ways. The conditions of the protasis in clause 7a are subject to those of phrase 5aα since the conditions of v. 5aα are necessarily prior. Similarly, the apodosis of vv. 7b–10 is subject to both the protasis of phrase 5aα and the protasis of clause 7a because the conditions of *both* protases must hold for the apodosis of vv. 7b–10 to take place. Both protasis and apodosis of the contingent portion are thus subject to the basic protasis in phrase 5aα.[14]

Within the apodosis of the contingent portion, a two-part procedure is described. This procedure is the consequence of the full set of conditions named in both protases. Three parties appear in the first half of the procedure: the woman, the elders and the levir. Two parties appear in the second half: the woman and the community. The actual procedure ends with the woman's speech. Furthermore, her freedom comes with the completion of her speech since that is the end of the procedure. But the law does not end with the woman's freedom. It goes beyond the actual procedure to a final description of the outcome of that procedure for the levir (v. 10). This final outcome completes the consequences which derive from the formative conditions.

b. *Four Factors.*

1) *"And Brothers Dwell Together."* The first factor necessary for understanding the levirate law of Deut 25 occurs within the initial element of the structure of the law. It is the first conditional of the basic protasis: יֵשְׁבוּ אַחִים יַחְדָּו. This phrase ties the levirate law of Deut 25:5–10 to issues concerning inheritance of landed property.[15]

---

14. Pressler, *View of Women*, 64. For this reason, Pressler is wrong when she states that the law consists of two parts: vv. 5–6 and vv. 7–10. Her division fails to account for the fact that vv. 5aβ–6 are as much subject to the conditions of v. 5aα as vv. 7–10.

15. Malul, *Knowledge, Control and Sex*, 356–57. See Malul's discussion of "ownership" of landed property: "As I have demonstrated elsewhere (Malul 1996: 194ff.), the very idea of ownership in ancient times has to be construed in a completely different sense than is expected by an average modern person. Following the Hohfeldian philosophy of law, ownership is defined in sociological terms, and property is characterized as a social entity. A person could not have any legal relationships with a piece of property, for legal relationships can exist only between persons. That is: a person's relations vis-à-vis a piece of property are predicated upon his position within the social matrix and his relationships with the other members of the social group. In these terms, it is only as a full and legitimate member that one can have access to the group's property, to an extent which depends upon his hierarchical location within the social matrix. The conclusion of the foregoing is that no person can own immovable property, and the 'ownership' of the latter is vested with the social group as a whole." If Malul is right, then issues of landed property in this law have to do fundamentally with issues of the dead man's "standing" in the group. That "standing" is preserved through his progeny. In the above quote Malul is making reference to the following work, which should also be consulted: M. Malul, "*ʿĀqēb* 'Heel' and *ʿĀqab* 'to Supplant' and the Concept of Succession in the Jacob–Esau Narratives," *VT* 46 (1996): 190–212 (194).

Daube's explanation for this conditional is the best offered to date. He concludes that the father has died[16] and that the phrase signifies the fact that the brothers have yet to divide the property.[17] Their relationship to the estate under these circumstances is, therefore, similar to their relationship to it when the father was alive. Westbrook states that Deut 25:5–10 is one of three different scenarios in the Hebrew Bible in which the levirate practice is represented at different stages.[18] In Gen 38, the father is alive and the brothers have yet to divide the estate. In Deut 25:5–10, the father is dead and the brothers have yet to divide the estate. In Ruth, the fathers and brothers are dead and the land is alienated. In each of these three cases the brothers are not holding or have not held their own division of the inheritance. The phrase "when two brothers live together" applies to the second scenario.[19]

Its presence in the law of Deut 25:5–10 establishes a condition which necessarily ties the levirate practice of that law to issues concerning inheritance of landed property.

2) *Establishing the Brother's Name; Building Up the Brother's House.*
a) *"Title."* The nature of this tie between the levirate practice of Deut 25:5–10 and landed inheritance is partially clarified by Westbrook's explanation of the absence of a possible fourth scenario from the Hebrew Bible. The implications of its absence reveal the second factor. In the fourth scenario, the brothers have already divided the land when one of them dies. Westbrook suggests that the reason for the absence of this scenario is that when brothers divide the land, "title" is established by each brother.[20] Thus, the problem which levirate practice

16. David Daube, "Consortium in Roman and Hebrew Law," *JR* 62 (1950): 72–74. See also Leggett, *Levirate and Goel*, 45, citing Driver and Miles, *Assyrian Laws*, 243 n. 18; and von Rad, *Deuteronomy*, 155.

17. David Daube, *Ancient Jewish Law* (Leiden: Brill, 1981), 38, calls the law in Deut 25:5–10 an "extended application" of the more general "Biblical levirate." "There is one extended application: if, after the father's death, his sons stay together on the undivided estate and one of them, married, dies childless, again, the widow is taken over by a brother and the first son ranks as the deceased's." See also Carmichael, *Women*, 65–66; Daube, "Consortium," esp. 74, 76, 90; Westbrook, "Law," 76. Leggett, *Levirate and Goel*, 45–48, accepts Daube's explanation. However, he states that כי ישבו אחים יחדו refers to the typical situation rather than the exclusive conditions under which levirate law operates. The specificity of the several conditions under which this law operates argue against Leggett. The author is precise in his statement of those conditions, excluding the other several ways in which the levirate arrangement transpires. Thompson and Thompson ("Legal Problems," 90), whom Leggett cites, themselves describe the specificity of the conditions of the law. They make a distinction between "levirate law" in general and the levirate law of Deut 25:5–10, which answers a "specific need," even while claiming that this specificity is "typical."

18. Westbrook, *Property*, 78.

19. Otto, "False Weights," 139, states: "In the case of undivided property there was no such economic stimulus to fulfill the levirate obligation because the property of the deceased fell automatically to his brother's share. Normally the local courts had nothing to do with the institution of levirate marriage, but in this special case their help was needed."

20. Westbrook, *Property*, 75, states: "Apparently, therefore, it was a man's landed estate which gave him his 'name.' Neufeld considers that in this text 'name' actually means a man's property. Perhaps a sense closer to the meaning in this context is given by the English legal term 'title,' which refers not to the property itself but to a man's right to a particular piece of landed property."

addresses fails to transpire in this scenario and the scenario is therefore absent as an example of levirate practice. If Westbrook is right, then establishment of a *proper connection* between the dead man and the landed inheritance is the core of the levirate law of Deut 25:5–10.

Westbrook's use of the word "title" is an attempt to clarify this "proper connection" as a component of "establishing the name." Pressler has critiqued Westbrook for his use of "title" as follows:

> First, while Westbrook seems on safe ground when he connects שֵׁם with possessing and passing on the land, his definition of the term as "title" seems overly precise. Westbrook understands the clause "when brothers dwell together" to indicate that the law would not apply when brothers had already divided the property. In that case, the title of the deceased man would have been established during his lifetime and would be perpetuated when his brothers inherited his estate. It is more likely that the perpetuation of the man's name has to do not with the establishment of his title to land, but with his descendant's continuing possession of his ancestral land. In the story of Zelophehad the rationale for allowing daughters to inherit if their father died without sons implies that the father's name would not be preserved if the land were inherited by the deceased's brothers or other more distant male kin. Yet, according to Westbrook, the man's title to the property would be established by the brother's inheriting the land.[21]

While "title" may be "overly precise" to Pressler, it aptly serves the purpose for which Westbrook intends it. It serves this purpose despite the fact that "title" is a "modern" term which carries within its total conceptual matrix constructs that are probably inapplicable to the ancient scenario. The purpose for which Westbrook intends it is simply to point to "proper connection" between the dead man and the landed property which is essential for "establishing the name." Pressler's aim in her critique is not the denial of a connection.[22] Rather, her critique aims at Westbrook's fourth scenario, against which she argues by means of the Zelophehad story.

However, the Zelophehad story, contrary to Pressler's understanding, in fact, supports Westbrook's theory. This story is not about inheritance. It is about an apportionment which stands at the beginning of a line of inheritance. The story describes the initial division that begins the generational practice of holding "title."

By the time the process of apportionment begins Zelophehad is a dead man. Furthermore, he is a dead man who has failed to effect a proper connection to the land whereby his name is established. His story, therefore, parallels the levirate scenario of Deut 25:5–10. Following Westbrook's logic, Zelophehad's brothers cannot inherit his portion so as to establish his name because Zelophehad himself never had "title" to it. Westbrook's assumption is that if a man has established the proper connection to the land, then his name can continue in either a descendent who inherits or in a collateral who inherits. If the man has

21.   Pressler, *View of Women*, 67 n. 17. See also Thompson and Thompson, "Legal Problems," 87–88.

22.   Pressler, *View of Women*, 63–64, and 67 n. 17, also affirms this as an aim of law: "Its principal aim is the provision of male heirs to men who die without sons. This aim includes and ensures the orderly succession of property from father to son."

not established the proper connection, that is, if he has not inherited his portion, then his name can continue only through his descendents or a son, who by a "legal fiction" becomes his descendent.

Some legal fictions are more believable than others. The legal fiction that the dead man's name is established through the brother when the dead man has never inherited his divided portion is evidently unbelievable. The legal fiction that a child, engendered by widow and brother, is the dead man's own and can continue his name is, on the other hand, evidently believable. Only conjecture can answer the question as to why one option works and the other does not.

Conjecture might take the following line of reasoning. A *true* division on behalf of the man who dies or is dead is necessary for establishment of his name. Only a true division on his behalf can keep his portion from melding with his brother's and "his name" from vanishing when the brother inherits. If the dead man inherits before he dies, as in the fourth scenario, then a true division has occurred and the property does not meld, even though it is managed and owned by one person, the living brother. If a descendent, separate from the descendents of the dead man's collaterals, inherits after he is dead and before he himself has inherited, then a true division has occurred as well—and his name continues. Property must pass through a *true* division on behalf of the man who dies in order to establish the name. That is, it must divide among separate *living* entities. Two divisions are not two divisions if the living entity which initially receives those two divisions is one entity. Under such circumstances those two divisions are necessarily one division. This is Westbrook's point and it is, indeed, plausible.

Pressler cites 2 Sam 18:18 and Isa 56:4–5[23] as two examples of "establishment of the name" by means other than inheritance of the land.[24] These examples also support Westbrook's understanding. In these examples the name is fixed to a memorial object. Just as attachment of the name to an object establishes the name, so also does attachment of the name to the land. The latter attachment is known in modern parlance as having title to the land.

Thus, if two brothers share the estate under "common ownership" such that "each partner theoretically owns the whole,"[25] and one of them dies, then a proper connection, for which a true division is necessary, has failed to occur. Levirate practice establishes the necessary true division posthumously.

b) *Progeny.* The usage of the phrase "establish the name" as well as the phrase "build the house" in Deut 25 and in other passages reveals the mechanism by means of which the proper connection between the dead man and the land takes place. The mechanism is progeny. Furthermore, the placement of these phrases in the structure demonstrates that production of progeny for the sake of establishing the name is the primary concern of the law.

23. Thompson and Thompson, "Legal Problems," 87.
24. Pressler, *View of Women*, 68 n. 19.
25. Westbrook, *Property*, 78–79.

"Building up the house," in the Hebrew corpus, refers to the production of progeny. In Gen 16:2, Sarai says that perhaps she herself will be built up (בנה) through her maid. In Ruth 4:11, Rachel and Leah together build up (בנה) the house of Israel, bridging the present and past representations of the lineage with future representations. In both these cases, בנה clearly refers to the production of offspring. In Deut 25:5–10, the בְּכוֹר of the widow and the levir suffices to "build the house of the brother."

"Establishing the name," within the Hebrew corpus is likewise associated with production of progeny.[26] Pressler notes rightly that "the phrases וְהָקֵם זֶרַע לְאָחִיךָ (Gen 38:8) and לְהָקִים לְאָחִיו שֵׁם (Deut 25:7) seem equivalent."[27] In 1 Sam 24:22, Saul asks David to promise that he will not cut off Saul's seed after him and will not destroy his name from the house of his father. In 2 Sam 14:7 the woman of Tekoa makes her fictional complaint indicating that killing her only surviving son would leave her husband without a name and a remnant upon the earth. Absolom says, in 2 Sam 18:18, "There is no son to me to cause remembrance of my name." Zelophehad's daughters ask, in Num 27:4, why their father's name should be taken from his family (מִשְׁפַּחְתּוֹ) because he has no sons. They seek land to prevent the disappearance of their father's name. Another example which associates name and land is Ruth 4:5 and 10, which speaks of establishing the name of the dead man upon his inheritance. Deuteronomy 25:6 explicitly associates the בְכוֹר of the union between widow and levir with establishment of the name. Verse 6b also indicates that the name has a presence which can be "wiped out." Lack of progeny constitutes this "wipe-out."

Thus, "building the house" and "establishing the name" are clearly associated with production of progeny. On occasion within the Hebrew corpus their association intersects with such things as remembrance and, as in Deut 25:5–10, with landed inheritance.

Furthermore, the phrases referring to name and house occur at the conclusion of the basic portion of the apodosis and at the conclusion of the contingent portion of the apodosis, strategic positions for anchoring the idea of production of progeny as at least one component of the primary concern of the law.

3) *Enter, Marry, יבם.*
a) *Refusal and Requirement.*
(1) *Levir's Refusal.* Just as phrases concerning the name and the house point to the primary concern of the text, so also do clauses depicting the levir's refusal: לֹא חָפַצְתִּי לְקַחְתָּהּ (7b) and לֹא אָבָה יַבְּמִי (8b).

The clauses, depicting the levir's refusal, reference three acts which the levir is required to perform. בוא, לקח and יבם are the three acts. בוא, referenced implicitly by the two clauses, denotes sexual intercourse and is the initial of the three acts in v. 5, as if לקח and יבם are somehow subordinate to it. It depicts the sex act graphically. Woman is object and man is subject. The result of entering, taking and יבם is the production of progeny which establishes the name. All

26. Ibid., 75.
27. Pressler, *View of Women*, 66 n. 14.

three acts are the levir's stated responsibility, as their association in vv. 5 and 6 indicate. They are what he refuses. Deuteronomy 25:5–10, regardless of other representations of levirate practice in the Hebrew corpus, thus requires sex with and marriage to the יָבָם for the sake of production of progeny and establishment of the name.

However, within the first half of the procedure, the woman's description of the levir's refusal in 7bβ$_{2b}$ and the express refusal of the levir in 8bβ seem to focus on what the levir does to the woman instead of on what he does to the dead man. This impression, in turn, seems to indicate that the concern of the law is to protect the widow's welfare rather than the dead man's entitlements. Such impressions are mistaken.[28]

The first clause, which is the widow's description of the levir's refusal to perform the duty of a יָבָם for her in 7bβ$_{2b}$, is immediately preceded by a statement concerning the levir's refusal to establish the name of his brother in 7bβ$_{2a}$. These two statements by the widow are the sole content of her complaint to the elders. They are complementary statements, both of which point to the responsibility which the levir refuses. The first statement concerning establishment of the name targets the levir's unwillingness to achieve the goal of the law. The second statement concerning his failure to perform the duty of a יָבָם targets his unwillingness to construct the mechanism by which the goal is achieved. Both statements serve the single goal of the law: establishment of the name. In neither of the statements is the widow's welfare a concern.

The second clause is the levir's refusal, in 8bβ. All the levir says is "I do not want to take her," as if the point of the law and his sole responsibility are simply to marry the widow. However, the ritualistic response by the widow to these words indicates otherwise. She removes the levir's sandal, spits in his face and says: "Thus shall it be done to the man who does not build up the house of his brother" (9b). The levir's express refusal must be understood in conjunction with her reply. Her reply indicates that he has refused to construct the vehicle by means of which the dead man's name is established. Pressler rightly states the following:

> She appears to act before the elders in a representative capacity. Her complaint and her solemn declaration to the brother-in-law are couched in terms of the interests of her dead husband, not in terms of her own interests. Or, rather, her interests appear to coincide with and be subsumed under the interests of the deceased.[29]

28. Weisberg has made an interesting observation that I have not seen elsewhere. See Dvora E. Weisberg, "The Widow of Our Discontent: Levirate Marriage in the Bible and Ancient Israel," *JSOT* 28 (2004): 403–29, who notes that within the Hebrew corpus the male characters consistently show reluctance or discomfort with levirate marriage, while the women are willing, "even eager." She writes: "Both Deuteronomy and Genesis indicate a resistance, on the part of men, to levirate marriage... Women are portrayed as the strongest advocates of levirate marriage. These patterns make sense if we suppose that, rhetoric notwithstanding, providing for widows rather than securing offspring for the deceased had come to be seen as the primary benefit of levirate marriage." However, this willingness, even eagerness, on the part of the woman is a function of her desire to fulfill her duty/destiny (see below). That "duty/destiny" is the use to which her sexuality as property is put. It is the purpose for which the levirate law secures her sexuality as property.

29. Pressler, *View of Women*, 74.

The clauses depicting the levir's refusal during the procedure thus serve the phrases concerning name and house which point to the dead man's entitlement as the primary concern. Thus, the clauses depicting the levir's refusal, rather than establishing the widow's welfare as the primary concern, are drawstrings which, along with phrases concerning name and house, securely fasten to the text, as its primary concern, "protection of a dead man's entitlement."

(2) *Requirement to Marry*. However, contrary to these signals, scholars have taken one of the three required acts, "to marry," as evidence that the law is concerned primarily or secondarily with the widow's welfare.[30]

Although the law of Deut 25:5–10 requires the levir to marry the widow and expressly forbids the widow to go outside the family to become the wife of a stranger, some scholars have noted that marriage seems unnecessary to levirate practice in general. This would suggest that the marriage requirement of Deut 25:5–10 is optional, which, in turn, suggests that the author included it to serve the welfare of the widow rather than the entitlement of a dead man.

The idea that marriage is unnecessary to levirate law comes from Gen 38 where Tamar seems to fulfill levirate requirements without marriage. Westbrook, however, states the following concerning the three instances of levirate practice in the Hebrew Bible:

> But in all three sources the terminology of marriage is expressly used. In Gen 38,14 Tamar sees that she was not "given as a wife" to Shelah (*ntnh lw l' šh*), in Deut 25,5 the levir must take his sister-in-law to him "as a wife" (*wlqhh lw l' šh*). The only doubtful case is Judah... If we return to our earlier suggestion that in the case of the levirate, marriage was by consummation, then it is quite possible for Judah to have been considered to be married to Tamar, even though it was achieved by a trick... Again, the narrative states that once Judah realized what Tamar had done, he did not have intercourse with her again. That could mean that he was entitled to and chose not to do so. There is also no suggestion that Tamar subsequently married a third person, or even Shelah. The question whether Tamar's unorthodox procedure was regarded as marriage must, therefore, remain open.[31]

---

30.   Scholars are divided on whether the widow or the levir retains the husband's/brother's property upon the levir's refusal. See Davies, "Inheritance: 2," 262. Matthews ("Honor and Shame," 102) believes the levir retains it, and Matthews takes this as providing a plausible reason for refusal in the face of public humiliation. Otto ("False Weights," 140) believes the widow retains it, and Otto takes this as an indication that the woman is "installed by this provision as a legal subject in her own right." Anderson's (*Women, Ideology, and Violence*, 55, 99) critique of Otto's assessment of Deut 25:5–10 has to do with this point. Westbrook's (*Property*, 83) reasoning is plausible. Referring to the possibility that the widow retains the property, he writes: "To assume that right here would be to reverse the roles of the parties. The widow would be more eager to avoid the levirate, while the brother would be more eager to perform it: yet it is the widow who disgraces her brother-in-law in the ceremony. Morgenstern's suggestion that she thereby receives her personal freedom receives no mention in the text, which indeed ends with a statement of the brother's status, not of the widow's."

31.   Westbrook, *Property*, 85; idem, "Law," 82–83. See also Pressler, *View of Women*, 65 n. 7. Regarding the Tamar/Judah story, she writes: "It cannot serve as evidence for the marriage or non-marriage between a brother-in-law and sister-in-law in the typical levirate situation. Tamar's observation in Gen 38:14 that she had not yet been given to Shelah as a wife is better evidence for the nature of the levirate relationship between a sister-in-law and brother-in-law. The language in

Westbrook's observations suggest the possibility that the marriage requirement of Deut 25:5–10 is, perhaps, not optional.[32] If he is right, then this requirement cannot be seen as a special endeavor on the part of the author of Deut 25:5–10 to provide for the widow, in contradistinction to other levirate scenarios. Nevertheless, Westbrook's observations raise the question as to whether the marriage requirement within levirate practice in general intends to provide for the widow.

However, at least one other plausible explanation for the marriage requirement exists. This explanation fits the theory that protection of a dead man's entitlement is the exclusive and primary concern. The author of the law may have required marriage for the sake of the progeny alone. He may have considered children who grow up in stable, secure, protected environments *more able* to "continue the name" than those that do not. A stable, secure, protected environment would have been one with a living father and mother. Thus, the landed inheritance, the name and the house would be most secure if the levir married the woman. In the process, naturally, the woman's security, as defined by the standards and values of that time, would have been inadvertently established as well.[33]

Lending support to this explanation as rationale for required marriage is the fact that the law "provides" for exclusively widows who are childless. Other widows must presumably fend for themselves, as must their children.[34] Under these circumstances, the children must grow up in the "insecure environment" of a family without a father, which means that the most that can be said about the "presence of a father" for "continuing the name" is that it is desirable as opposed to necessary. The levirate law reaches for that desirability. The widow's welfare per se, as a concern of the law, is incidental to the establishment of progeny in connection with landed inheritance. Her welfare is not at stake.

Furthermore, not only is the widow's welfare incidental; but, if Wegner is right, then the widow's sexuality is property as well.[35] Wegner writes:

> Following Scripture, the levirate widow is transferred to her husband's brother in the hope that he may engender a son to perpetuate the dead man's name. But the levir consummates the union, or releases the widow, at his option; the woman has no say in the matter. In this context the man is a person and the woman is his sexual property, to be retained or discarded at will, as in the law of divorce.[36]

Deut 25:5–10, וּלְקָחָהּ לוֹ לְאִשָּׁה, moreover, is the standard language for marriage. Marriage is explicitly mentioned in Ruth."

32. See also Kutsch, "יבם," 371.

33. Ibid., 372.

34. Blenkinsopp, "Family," 72, states: "Contrary to the common practice in the ancient Near East, there seems to have been no legal provision for a widow to succeed to her husband's estate other than recourse to levirate marriage (Deut 25:5–10), discussed earlier, though we have noted that some nevertheless did so. It is therefore hardly surprising that widows and their children are mentioned so often as in need of protection and charity."

35. Wegner, *Chattel*, 99.

36. Ibid., 99. See Westbrook's critique of the idea that the woman is inherited in Westbrook, *Property*, 72–73.

As Wegner suggests, this law places the widow's sexuality at the disposal of the levir. Levirate marriage protects a levir's sexual property and a dead man's entitlement. The former, however, serves the latter. The *opportunity* for disposal protects the right of the levir to choose. The *placement* of the widow's sexuality at the levir's disposal protects the dead man's entitlement. In short, the woman is focalized as property.

Pressler uses the "socially anomalous"[37] status of a widow to support the idea that the marriage requirement provides for her welfare. But childless widows may have more options than her socially anomalous status might suggest.[38] After all, in the event of a levirate refusal, she might marry someone else and have children.[39] Westbrook states:

> Tamar in Genesis 38 appears to be in no material distress. The widow in Deuteronomy 25 claims that her brother-in-law has failed to perpetuate her brother's name, not that he has failed to support her. She is even contemplated as being able to re-marry in the absence of the levirate, whereby she would solve any material problems. Support of the widow may well have been a motive behind the introduction or retention of the institution, but it is unlikely to have been the main purpose of the law.[40]

Are we to presume that remarriage as an option to establishing the name was so difficult for a fertile widow that this was the reason levirate practice was required? When the question is posed in this manner the fact that levirate law does not provide for the welfare of the widow becomes clear.[41] That marriage to

37. Pressler, *View of Women*, 74. See also Kalmin, "Levirate Law," 297; Niditch, "Wronged," 145–46.

38. Wegner, *Chattel*, 97–99. Furthermore, Wegner's comments on women in the Mishnah, although slightly afield from our corpus, nevertheless must give us pause concerning this matter. She writes (pp. 97–99): "The levirate widow's position is anomalous: Most widows enjoy autonomy and a considerable degree of personhood, but the husband's death without heirs turns the widow into a sexual chattel inherited by the levir along with the deceased's estate. In the Mishnah an interplay of conflicting factors is reflected in rules that treat the levirate widow sometimes as chattel and sometimes as person, depending on context... That the levir actually *inherits* his brother's widow is clear from the automatic formation of the bond on the brother's death. Unlike marriage, this bond requires no act of betrothal or espousal by the levir; and should he reject the union, his mere refusal to consummate it does not suffice to free the widow. She must be released by *ḥaliṣah*—in effect a form of divorce."

39. In fact, the eventual decline of levirate practice and the shift from insistence on marriage to insistence on חליצה in the later history of the practice might also suggest that in the earlier period such options existed, even if they were not preferred as they were in later history. See Belkin, "Levirate and Agnate Marriage," 328; Mace, *Hebrew Marriage*, 110.

40. Westbrook, *Property*, 72.

41. This does not gainsay the extreme difficulties of widowhood in ancient Israel. See Anderson (*Women, Ideology, and Violence*, 29–31) and Paula S. Hiebert ("'Whence Shall Help Come to Me?': The Biblical Widow," in Day, ed., *Gender and Difference*, 130–31) for a discussion of those difficulties. Hiebert writes (p. 130): "The Hebrew ʾalmānâ, like the gēr, existed on the fringes of society... Not only was she bereft of kin, but she was also without a male who ordinarily provided a woman with access to the public sphere." Anderson writes (p. 29): "Therefore, the widow and the gēr share a common plight because they are without kinship ties in a society where such ties provided identity." However, see also Frick ("Widows," 148–49) who observes that Judith, "a young, apparently childless widow, wealthy and well respected [is] the very antithesis of the traditional

the levir would establish for the widow a connection with men, boosting her economic security and a social status, is undeniable. That it was the only avenue available for her wellbeing as defined by these two factors is less than self-evident.[42]

However, an additional factor exists which is as essential to one's survival as economic security and social status. Concluding that avenues other than levirate law were available for meeting the need of this additional factor is more difficult. This factor is the need to fulfill one's destiny, however one perceives it. Whereas the man's destiny is written and codified with explicit protection in Deut 25:5–10, the woman's destiny is written, codified and protected only implicitly and only with respect to the man's destiny. In this respect woman is marginalized in the text.

Woman's destiny serves the man's destiny. Her destiny is to bear children who will succeed to her husband's inheritance. The desire to fulfill this destiny drives the actions of Tamar, Ruth, Sarai, Hanna and others. It explains the willing initiative of the woman implied by Deut 25:7–10.

If production of progeny for every husband the woman has had, including the first one, is her destiny, then levirate law is necessary for meeting this need. In this case, the law necessarily provides for the widow. The likelihood that the law intends to provide for the widow is then greater. But the possibility that a woman might fulfill her destiny by providing children to a second husband, even though she failed to provide children for the first husband, seems too reasonable to dismiss. If a widow can remarry and fulfill her destiny with a second husband, then the levirate arrangement loses the necessity which compels the reader to surmise that the law intends to provide for the widow's welfare.

While fulfillment of her *duty* may require providing children for each husband, fulfillment of her *destiny* requires providing children for at least one of her husbands. Fulfillment of her destiny has to do with her welfare. Fulfillment of her duty has to do with a man's entitlement. Thus, neither social status, nor economic security, nor fulfillment of perceived destiny compel us to conclude that Deut 25:5–10 intends to provide for the welfare of the widow.

Some final observations, admittedly concerning the silence of the text with respect to the marriage requirement, support the conclusion that this requirement

---

picture of a biblical widow... Here then is a picture of an ancient Israelite woman who is *not* 'inherited' by one of her husband's kinsmen, is *not* pitied as an object of charity as the childless widow often is, and who *does not*, out of either desperation or duty, return to her father's house."

42.   Amram, *Jewish Law*, 101–2, 105. While Amram notes that the widow of Lev 21:14 is classed with "the divorced woman, and the less respectable members of society" (p. 103), he nevertheless describes the freedom of both the widow and the divorcee as follows (pp. 101–2): "The divorced woman, like the widow, was *sui juris*. Before her marriage the woman was subject to the authority of her father (*patria potestas*); during the marriage her husband was her master; if widowed or divorced, she did not again become subject to her father's *potestas*, but became her own mistress. She then had the right to give herself in marriage, whereas as a maiden, before her maturity, she was given in marriage by her father; and unlike an unmarried woman or a wife, she could bind herself by her vows. The only absolute disadvantage that a bill of divorce wrought for the woman was the denial of her right to marry a Kohen, or Priest."

fails as evidence that the law's primary concern is the welfare of the widow. If the welfare of the widow were even a secondary concern, then one might expect a corresponding statement concerning provision for her welfare in the contingency of a levir's refusal. One might also expect a statement affirming her freedom. Such statements are nowhere to be found in Deut 25:5–10. Furthermore, Westbrook notes that if the purpose of the law is to protect the widow then it has done so in a "roundabout" way.[43] He asks, "Why should the brother not simply be obliged to support the widow?"[44]

(3) *Conclusion*. Both "the clauses depicting the levir's refusal" and the "the requirement to marry" support the assertion that the primary and exclusive concern of the text is the establishment of a dead man's entitlement. This involves production of progeny and requires the protection of a woman's sexuality as property in the form of marriage to the levir.

b) *The* חֲלִיצָה *Procedure*. In addition to the clauses depicting the levir's refusal and the requirement to marry, scholars find evidence in the חֲלִיצָה procedure that the primary or secondary concern of the law is the welfare of the widow.

The חֲלִיצָה procedure, in which the phrases depicting the levir's refusal occur, gives remarkable initiative to the woman. Some scholars have understood this initiative to be evidence that the law aims at the widow's welfare.[45] Furthermore, several scholars have understood the חֲלִיצָה procedure itself as intending to benefit the widow by freeing her, upon the levir's refusal from levirate obligations, enabling her to remarry.[46] However, close scrutiny indicates otherwise. The חֲלִיצָה procedure is, in fact, concerned exclusively with the entitlements of the dead man.[47]

The חֲלִיצָה procedure, which begins with a statement concerning the refusal to establish the brother's name and concludes with a statement concerning the refusal to build up the brother's house, is punitive to the levir. It humiliates and curses him.[48] Moreover, this is its aim. Carmichael states that "the puzzle is: in what way does the removal of the sandal constitute a humiliation of him and in what way does this action tie in with spitting in his face?"[49] Whether or not we agree with Carmichael's theory as to the origin of this Deuteronomic law,[50] his suggestions concerning the meaning of חֲלִיצָה procedure are intriguing. He writes:

43. Westbrook, *Property*, 72.
44. Ibid., 72.
45. Robert Gordis, "Love, Marriage, and Business in the Book of Ruth: A Chapter in Hebrew Customary Law," in *A Light Unto My Path* (ed. Howard N. Bream, Ralph D. Heim and Carey A. Moore; Philadelphia: Temple University Press, 1974), 248; Leggett, *Levirate and Goel*, 57, 60–62; Westbrook, *Property*, 84.
46. Frymer-Kensky, "Deuteronomy," 61; Leggett, *Levirate and Goel*, 57, 60–62.
47. Pressler, *View of Women*, 74; Westbrook, *Property*, 83–84.
48. Cairns, *Deuteronomy*, 217, states: "In ancient belief, spittle and other bodily fluids contained a person's life potential, and were therefore powerful vehicles for imparting blessing or curse."
49. Carmichael, "Ceremonial Crux," 321.
50. Ibid., 327.

Thus the drawing off of the sandal (as in the Arab divorce ceremony the sandal sym-
bolizes a woman or woman's genitals) from the man's foot (in Hebrew the foot can
allude to the male sexual organ) signifies, by a process of transference, the man's
withholding conception. Moreover, when after removing his sandal she spits in his face
this action is a symbolic reminder of Onan's spilling of the semen on the ground. The
man's passive role in the ceremony corresponds to his reprehensible passiveness in
regard to his duty to her. Her doing the action, removing the sandal, spitting in his face,
is by way of transferring Onan's action with Tamar to him because of the view that his
non-action amounts to the same thing as Onan's quasi-one. In each case conception was
denied the woman.[51]

In addition, Carmichael suggests that the procedure publicly disgraces the levir
who refuses to perform his duty.[52] Carmichael posits only the disgracing power
of the ceremony. But if the removal of the sandal represents the sexual non-
compliance of the levir, the failure to conceive and the subsequent disappearance of the name of his brother from Israel, then the woman's last statement in
the procedure, indeed the very last statement made by anyone in the procedure,
amounts to no less than a curse.

It curses the refusing levir with the same thing he has done to his brother: the
disappearance of his name.[53] The widow aims the curse against the establishment of the refusing levir's name, stating that his name will be "house of the
unsandalled one" (v. 10). His house will be known as the one in which the male
genitals have been removed from the woman's genitals. His house will be one in
which conception is withheld. The woman's actions are a ritual of public dis-
grace.[54] Her words are a public curse.[55]

The חֲלִצָה procedure itself ends with the curse. But the levirate law continues.
The final statement of the law describes the consequence of the procedure which
extends into the future. That consequence concerns only the levir.[56] If the welfare
of the widow is the primary concern, this final statement in v. 10 is unnecessary.

---

51. Ibid., 329, 331. See also Calum M. Carmichael, " 'Treading' in the Book of Ruth," *ZAW* 92
(1980): 248–66. Other scholars have suggested that the removal of the sandal is a symbol for transfer
of property. See Manor, "Brief History," 133.

52. Carmichael, "Ceremonial Crux," 335–36; Daube, "Culture," 35–36, discusses (p. 36) the
shame aspect of this ceremony and writes: "In a certain kind of society—the society of which
Deuteronomy is a product—to be branded in this fashion can be a severe sanction."

53. Rofé, "Family and Sex Laws," 151–52, calls the name which the refusing levir's house will
carry subsequent to חלצה a "symbolic *talio*." He writes (p. 151): "In this case, the punishment fits
the crime in that it reflects its character in some way, sometimes even to the extent that the crime
itself becomes the punishment." See also Manor, "Brief History," 134.

54. Leggett, *Levirate and Goel*, 58, notes that this is the only law in the Pentateuch which
contains a punishment consisting of public degradation.

55. Matthews suggests that the status of the levir is altered, and ("Honor and Shame," 101–2)
states: "While not all the ritual aspects of this ceremony are fully understood, it is clear that what has
occurred transforms the status and applies a new label to the levir. This may have actually been the
lesser of two evils for the levir, if the law, as E. W. Davies suggests, is designed to give him the
opportunity to refuse the widow while retaining inheritance rights to the land of the deceased
kinsman. To bear public humiliation and a pejorative title, while undesirable, may thus be balanced
by the desire to keep one's inheritance rights intact."

56. Westbrook, *Property*, 83–84.

Both the punitive nature of the procedure and the consequence that extends into the future demonstrate that the primary concern of Deut 25:5–10 is establishment of the dead man's name, rather than the welfare of the widow.

c. *Conclusion.* The following four factors are significant for understanding the levirate law of Deut 25:5–10: (1) the phrase יֵשְׁבוּ אַחִים יַחְדָּו; (2) the group of references related to establishing the brother's name in vv. 6, 7 and 9; (3) the requirements to enter, to marry and יבם; and (4) the function of חֲלִצָה. An accounting of these four factors demonstrates that the primary concern of the levirate law of Deut 25:5–10 is establishment of a dead man's entitlement, involving inheritance of landed property by the dead man's progeny and, thus, requiring the protection and use of the widow's sexuality as property. The woman is thus focalized as property.

3. *Point-of-View*

These four factors thus reveal the gender asymmetry of the text's point-of-view. The point-of-view of this text is a male author protecting male concerns. While the male author requires the service of both male and female sexuality for his program of protection, he requires it asymmetrically with respect to gender.

The four factors above demonstrate that the law has been written in order to protect a dead man's entitlement. Both the sexuality of the levir and the sexuality of the widow are required to serve this purpose. However, this requirement distributes unevenly between the widow and the levir. Until the levirate objective is accomplished or rejected, the widow's sexuality serves the dead man's entitlement exclusively. The levir's sexuality, on the other hand, serves this purpose non-exclusively. Only the levir has sexual access to the widow, whereas another wife or other wives or unattached women have access to the levir's sexuality. The widow must serve.[57] The levir may refuse to serve at the expense of a penalty. No penalty, lenient or otherwise, is described for a widow's refusal to serve.

Thus, the point-of-view, as revealed by the four above factors, is consonant with the law's treatment of the woman's sexuality as property. Furthermore, its asymmetry with respect to gender underscores the woman's circumscribed status.

4. *"Single Legal Object"*

One final issue remains concerning Pressler's critique of Westbrook's suggestion that the levirate law aims at a "single legal object." Referring to Gen 38, Deut 25:5–10 and Ruth, Westbrook writes:

> In summary, we are of the opinion that all three biblical sources reflect an institution with a single legal object: to prevent extinction of the deceased's title to his landed inheritance.[58]

57. Pressler, *View of Women*, 74.
58. Westbrook, *Property*, 76.

Pressler has critiqued Westbrook's statement and asserted that Deut 25:5–10 has more than one aim. She writes:

> Second, Westbrook holds that the law of the levirate had only one goal. There seems to be no reason to assume that ancient laws had one and only one aim. I will argue that Deut 25:5–10 was also intended to protect the deceased man's widow. It is even more unlikely that the levirate institution had only one aim; social institutions arise out of complex factors and tend to serve multiple purposes. Westbrook overstates his case.[59]

As Pressler implies, a single law regulating a particular practice and the actual practice as it occurs in a particular culture or society are two different things. While a practice like the "levirate institution," as Pressler calls it, may conceivably, in its several permutations, exhibit several aims, and while it may even in one instance of its occurrence exhibit several aims, laws can and do often intend to regulate a single phenomenon. They can regulate a single phenomenon broadly or narrowly. The law of Deut 25:5–10 regulates the single phenomenon of its concern narrowly.[60] The specificity of its formulation, in fact, is notable. That specificity, as revealed in the discussion above, aims at the protection of a dead man's entitlement.

Another useful distinction clarifies the issue. The intent or primary concern of a law and the accomplishments of the law are two different things. Often these two features are not co-terminus. For example, the primary concern of a law requiring a driver's license intends to ensure that only people who know how to drive are the drivers of cars. One accomplishment of this law is the provision of a picture ID that is universally accepted for purposes of identification. The primary concern of the law requiring licenses, however, is not to provide citizens with a picture ID per se. It intends to regulate the competence of the drivers of cars.[61] The same "mechanism," the driver's license, serves the intent of the law and an ancillary accomplishment of the law.

This distinction between the primary concern and the ancillary accomplishments of a law is not trivial. For example, sorting what is intended and what is accomplished by a law such as Deut 25:5–10 is essential to understanding the place of women in the conceptual matrix that underpins the law. A failure to discern precisely this distinction is the source of Pressler's critique of Westbrook on this point.[62] Indeed, much of the variety of suggestions concerning the purpose of the law in Deut 25:5–10 is a function of the fact that, while the intention or primary concern of the law is narrow and specific, its accomplishments

---

59.   Pressler, *View of Women*, 67 n. 17.

60.   Carmichael, *Women*, 65. Concerning Deut 25:5–10, he writes (pp. 65–66): "It is commonly thought that the first part of this law is a general statement of the levirate custom, a description of the ordinary circumstances in which it is invoked. We have seen, however, that such general statements of law are quite *un*characteristic of this lawgiver; rather the tendency is invariably in the direction of a limiting set of circumstances. This law is no different. Closer scrutiny reveals that it is prompted by a need to legislate for the particular circumstances in which the head of the family, the father, is dead." See also Westbrook, *Property*, 71.

61.   I am indebted to Harold Ellens for this example.

62.   Pressler, *View of Women*, 67 n. 17.

are broad. Westbrook maintains that the purpose of levirate law is to provide the deceased with a successor to his estate, that is, to establish the dead brother's title to his inheritance. Pressler, on the other hand, maintains that the purpose of the law is the perpetuation of the name of the dead man, orderly succession of property and, finally, protection of the widow. Westbrook has named the primary concern or intent of the law and Pressler has named at least one of its accomplishments in addition to the primary concern.

C. *Conclusion*

The assumption by several scholars that protection of the widow's welfare is either additionally or exclusively a primary or secondary concern of the law fails to consider the function of her sexuality with respect to the production of progeny for the sake of passing the dead man's landed inheritance to descendents. In fact, protection of her welfare is an incidental, perhaps even coincidental, result of the execution of this law. The primary concern is exclusively the establishment of a dead man's entitlement. The levirate law of Deut 25:5–10 protects the woman's sexuality as the property of the levir. The levir has the right to dispose of her sexuality as he wishes. Unless and until he disposes of it, her sexuality, as his property, serves the dead man's entitlement. Thus, although the woman shows remarkable initiative in the חֲלִיצָה procedure, the four factors detailed above, as well as the point-of-view revealed by those four factors, demonstrate that her status is circumscribed by men.

The woman is thus objectified. With respect to fulfillment of destiny, she is marginalized. She appears as character-agent through her active participation in the remedy and through the addressee feature. However she is focalized as property in a law, the primary concern of which is to protect and preserve a dead man's entitlements.

The law of Deut 25:5–10 supports the thesis that Deuteronomy focuses on the woman's sexuality as property.

Chapter 13

DEUTERONOMY 27:20–23

A. *Introduction*

The sex curses of Deut 27:20–23 occur within a larger series of curses, the primary concern of which is to guard against crimes committed in secret. All four curses of the sex series fit this primary concern. However, within the sex series itself, that primary concern, while an essential component, is insufficient to explain the particular selection of curses represented. Property concerns, instead, explain the selection. Restriction of sexual activity with respect to certain properties is, in fact, their primary concern. This primary concern is the key to the author's conceptualization of women in the sex series. She is focalized as the sexual property of the *pater familias*. In addition, point-of-view marginalizes women in the text and language-depicting-the-sex-act objectifies her.

B. *Discussion*

1. *Structure*

While the structure itself is incidental for discernment of the primary concern; it, nevertheless, provides clarity concerning features that shape the primary concern.

A partially collapsed version of the structure follows:

I.	Ritual and Comment #1			27:1–10
	A.	Ritual		1–8
		1.	introduction: Moses and elders to the people	1a
		2.	speech	1b–8
	B.	Comment		9–10
		1.	introduction: Moses and priests to all Israel	9a
		2.	speech	9b–10
II.	Ritual and Comment #2			27:11–28:68
	A.	Introduction		27:11
	B.	Speech		27:12–28:68
		1.	ritual	27:12–26
			a. the ones standing	12–13
			1) blessings	12
			2) cursings	13
			b. the ones answering	14–26
			1) introduction	14

The unit within which the sex series occurs extends from Deut 27:1 to 28:68.[1] This unit is part of what scholars consider to be the frame of Deuteronomy.[2] It is outside that group of laws which form the central core of the book (Deut 12:1– 26:15).

Chapters 27 and 28 consist of two sets of "Ritual and Comment." In the first "Ritual and Comment," the "Ritual" concerns the construction of an altar. The "Comment," directed by Moses and the levitical priests to the people, is a statement about the significance of the particular day on which the altar is constructed and the import that day carries for the people. Within the second "Ritual and Comment" the "Ritual" is a description of the tribes standing for the blessings and the tribes standing for the curses as well as a listing of the curses presented by the levitical priests.[3] The "Comment" details the blessings and curses that will transpire for those who keep and those who fail to keep the law of Yhwh.

The sex curses, which occur together, are four among the twelve curses presented in this second "Ritual." The twelve curses begin with the familiar association of acts that dishonor God and parents in vv. 15–16. The three curses (vv. 17–19), which follow, concern either an area of special vulnerability within the domain defining the properties of an individual, or they concern individuals who are themselves especially vulnerable. Following the "vulnerability curses" is the series of sex curses (vv. 20–23). The sex series, along with the two curses (vv. 24–25) which follow it, concern either improper crossing of bodily bounda- ries, which are sexual, or they concern physical injury itself to the body. The final curse, v. 26, is a general summary.

2. Conceptualization of Women

Although the context of the sex series, as described above, contributes to the discernment of the primary concern of that series, the features shaping that pri- mary concern come from within the sex series itself. In addition, a preliminary examination of point-of-view and language-depicting-the-sex-act reveals a con- ceptuality with respect to women, which is consonant with the conceptuality reflected in the primary concern.

a. *Point-of-View and Language-Depicting-the-Sex-Act.*
1) *Point-of-View.* The content of the speeches of chs. 27 and 28 are addressed to "the people" and to "all Israel." Furthermore, in the curse series, "all the people"

---

1.   This unit is generally considered to be part of the larger unit Deut 26:16–28:68. Alexander Rofé, "The Covenant in the Land of Moab (Dt 28, 69–30, 20)," in Lohfink, ed., *Das Deuter- onomium*, 310–20, proposes that v. 69 goes with what follows instead of what precedes. According to him, it begins the unit Deut 28:69–30:20. See also Mayes, *Deuteronomy*, 358–59.

2.   R. E. Clements, *Deuteronomy* (OTG; Sheffield: JSOT Press, 1989), 13–22; Moshe Weinfeld, "Deuteronomy, Book of," *ABD* 2:171–73.

3.   See Mayes, *Deuteronomy*, 344–46, for a brief overview and bibliographic listing concerning redactional issues related to this text. See also M. Weinfeld, "The Emergence of the Deuteronomic Movement: The Historical Antecedents," in Lohfink, ed., *Das Deuteronomium*, 79–80, for the relationship of Deut 27:11–13 to 28:3–6, 16–19.

respond. Nevertheless, the author directs the curses of the sex series against the *man* who commits the infraction. Except for v. 21, in each case the curse begins "Cursed is the one who…" using a masculine participle, qualified by a phrase concerning the woman with whom the action of the participle is committed. These masculine participles therefore denote only men. In v. 21, however, the qualifying phrase, unlike the other curses, leaves open the possibility that the author intends to represent both genders with the participle.[4]

All the curses except the first and last share this initial masculine participle. The first and last curses, which scholars have taken to be redactional insertions because of their divergence, use the relative.[5] Verse 15 uses אִישׁ in conjunction with the relative, explicitly directing the curse to men. Verse 26, on the other hand, a general summary for the list of curses, uses the relative alone without gender distinction. For the most part, the illicit act is explicitly pictured as the responsibility of the man. The representations of the curses are thus gender-polarized.

However, since the man cannot commit at least three of the sex acts listed without women, and given the addressee "all Israel" in the larger frame, the prohibitions seem also to apply to women. We might surmise that the author, in a time and place where the concept of female consent/non-consent is non-existent, implicitly directs his curses to women as well. Nevertheless, the wording of the curses demonstrates extreme marginalization of woman's representation in the text.

2) *Language-Depicting-the-Sex-Act.* The language-depicting-the-sex-act supports the signals given by point-of-view. In each case the man is subject of the clause and the woman is the object of a preposition. The verb depicting the sex act in each case is שָׁכַב. Thus, the series lacks the kinds of verbs denoting "seizing," "humbling," "holding" and "capturing" which occur in the latter half of Deut 22. "Lie with" seems to imply a certain amount of reciprocity. However, as in Lev 20, Deut 27:20 has an accompanying *Urteil* from which reciprocity is clearly lacking. The *Urteil* in this one curse, like the *Urteile* of Lev 20, indicates that, whatever reciprocity is connoted by the phrase "lie with," that reciprocity is in all probability highly qualified in favor of the man.

b. *Primary Concern.* The signals of point-of-view and language-depicting-the-sex-act complement the signals reflected in the primary concern. An analysis of the curse series as a whole and in the sex series by itself reveals the primary concern.

4. See the discussion below.
5. Elizabeth Bellefontaine, "The Curses of Deuteronomy 27: Their Relationship to the Prohibitive," in *No Famine in the Land* (ed. James W. Flanagan and Anita Weisbrod Robinson; Missoula, Mont.: Scholars Press, 1975), 51; Hans Jochen Boecker, *Law and the Administration of Justice* (Minneapolis: Augsburg, 1976), 198; Mayes, *Deuteronomy*, 346–48; von Rad, *Deuteronomy*, 167; Willy Schottroff, *Der altisraelitische Fluchspruch* (Neukirchen–Vluyn: Neukirchener, 1969), 57; Volker Wegner, *Rechtssätze in gebundener Sprache und Rechtssätzreihen im israelitischen Recht* (BZAW 127; New York: de Gruyter, 1972), 33.

1) *Verses 15–26: The Curse Series.* A near-consensus exists among scholars that all curses within the series of vv. 15–26 regulate crimes for which the usual judicial process fails because the infractions are committed in secret.[6] Weinfeld notes that "the medieval scholars Abraham ibn Ezra and Samuel ben Meir pointed out long ago that this is the common denominator of these verses."[7] However, the nomenclature "in secret" is slightly inaccurate. Nevertheless, the distinction in the text to which it points is real. For this reason, and because it has gained common parlance among scholars, I will continue to use it. Weinfeld, who also uses the designation "in secret," more accurately describes the distinction represented by this phrase as follows:

> The sins here enumerated are usually committed by stealth, or in such a manner that it is difficult to prove them.[8]

This characterization of the curse series is accurate.

The phrase "in secret" is explicitly appended to two of the curses. These two curses out of the twelve are least likely to be qualified as acts which by nature are committed in secret.[9] Idols are displayed usually in a place of worship for the veneration of more than one person. Striking someone can leave visible signs and more often than not transpires with commotion that draws attention from others. But bribes, by their nature, are taken without witnesses other than the perpetrators themselves. Moving a boundary marker is successful only if done secretly. This latter infraction depends upon a scenario in which the owner's testimony that the boundary marker has been moved is not credible. This is possible only if the boundary stands in a new place as if it has stood there all along. This, in turn, requires secrecy. The wrongs against blind men, widows, orphans and sojourners are wrongs against individuals who lack the power to establish their own credibility. Wrongs against such individuals are successful precisely because these individuals are unable credibly to bring before the public or the court the wrongs done to them. Sex, of course, customarily occurs in private. Thus, Weinfeld's characterization of the curse series as targeting "acts committed by stealth" or acts "difficult to prove" is accurate.

"Committed by stealth" and "difficult to prove" share the common denominator of being difficult to regulate by the usual legal processes. This, in fact, is what the scholars, who posit the "in secret" qualification, notice. Bellefontaine writes:

> The curse ritual as such does not necessarily promulgate new demands. The deeds mentioned were already known to the community as liable to the wrath of God. It was the possibility of their secret commission, of the criminal's eluding of justice and the

---

6.   Albrecht Alt, *Essays on Old Testament History and Religion* (trans. R. A. Wilson; Oxford: Blackwell, 1966), 115; Bellefontaine, "Curses," 58; Boecker, *Law*, 199; Craigie, *Deuteronomy*, 331; Phillips, *Deuteronomy*, 181; Weinfeld, "Uniqueness," 15; idem, *Deuteronomy*, 276–77. The following commentators dissent from this view: Cairns, *Deuteronomy*, 237; Mayes, *Deuteronomy*, 345.

7.   Weinfeld, "Uniqueness," 15. See also idem, "Decalogue," 21; Craigie, *Deuteronomy*, 331.

8.   Weinfeld, "Uniqueness," 15; idem, "Decalogue," 22.

9.   Weinfeld, "Decalogue," 22.

consequent fearful results for the people, that prompted the community's solemn invocation of divine retribution upon the criminal... The death law, as we have seen, makes
its corresponding prohibitive legal by defining the act more precisely and by providing
a definite legal penalty: death. In like manner, the curse brings into the legal sphere
certain prohibitives whose violation in secret would escape the ordinary legal process.[10]

Thus, the infractions of the curses of vv. 15–26 share the qualification of being
difficult to regulate by the usual legal processes. In this respect, they are
committed "in secret."

The primary concern of the curse series is thus to regulate acts committed "in
secret."

2) *Verses 20–23: The Sex Series.*

a) *Discussion.* The "in-secret" qualification, however, is inadequate to explain
the *selection* of curses within the short sex series. All sex prohibitions regulate
acts which are customarily committed in private. The "in-secret" qualification,
therefore, fails to explain why these sex prohibitions among all possible sex
prohibitions were chosen. It cannot qualify as the primary concern.

Analysis of the distinctions among the four curses is helpful for determining a
common denominator and a corresponding primary concern. The sex curses
treat relationships which fall into two groups. The first group is relationships
between humans. More specifically, this group consists of human relationships
constituted by affines or consanguines. The second group consists of relationships between humans and animals.

The two groups are intermixed. However, a "paradigmatic" curse representing each of the two groups begins the sex series.[11] Curses belonging to the first

---

10. Bellefontaine, "The Curses," 58. The existence of prohibitions prescribing the death penalty
in conjunction with correlative curses, the acts of which by nature are committed "in secret," is
possible for the following reasons. First, secrets do become known. Second, when they do, the
domain of the prohibitive has been entered and the death penalty applies. For the power of אָרַר to
regulate, see Herbert Chanan Brichto, *The Problem of "Curse" in the Hebrew Bible* (Philadelphia:
Society of Biblical Literature and Exegesis, 1963), 216, who writes: "Distinct from the sense of
"pronouncement" in *ʾālā* is the force of the verb *ʾrr* and its corresponding noun *məʾērā*. The force
underlying this stem is the curse from the operational point of view. Whether by means of an
incantation or other procedure this stem has the sense of to impose a ban or barrier, a paralysis on
movement or other capabilities." See also the following: Schottroff, *Fluchspruch*, 27, and especially
32; von Rad, *Deuteronomy*, 167–68.

11. Schulz, *Todesrecht*, 64–65, conceives the paradigmatic nature of these two curses more
broadly than I do. He writes (p. 65): "Mit den beiden repräsentativen Tatbeständen Dtn 27:20f.
sollten beiden durch die Reihen Lev 20:11f.17.(19).20f. und Lev 20:13–16.18 (Ex 22:17–19)
angegebenen Kategorien von Sexualvergehen umfaßt sein." These two curses, according to Schulz,
are representative of the prohibitions from the two categories of laws present in Lev 20. The same
two categories, of course, are also present in Lev 18. However, while I take Deut 27:20 to be
paradigmatic for consanguine/affine relations as described in previous discussion, I do not take Deut
27:21 to be paradigmatic of the group which includes the following relations: homosexuality, relations with menstruant, cult of Molek and neighbor's wife. I take it as paradigmatic for bestiality
relations alone. While my thesis that the primary concern for selecting this curse for inclusion is the
property concern forces this conclusion, the conclusion itself is not unreasonable. See also Mayes,
Deuteronomy, 347.

group and specifying more detail follow these two paradigmatic curses. The second group is represented by its paradigmatic curse alone (v. 21). The paradigmatic curse (v. 20) of the first group concerns women belonging to the father.[12] The paradigmatic curse of the second group concerns bestiality. Unlike the bestiality laws of Leviticus, this curse fails to specify with respect to gender. If its masculine participle applies to both men and women, then it is the only sex curse within Deut 27:20–23 in which such application occurs. This singularity alone argues against such application.

All three women in the curses of the first group share one qualification, which is the key to the selection of the curses and their primary concern. The sexuality of all three women in each of the affine/consanguine curses belong the *pater familias*. The primary concern represented by the selection of these three curses is thus to protect the sexual "property" of the father.

However, the "identification of women" in these curses fails to support this conclusion in the way that "identification of women" supports such conclusions in Leviticus. While the "wife of the father" (v. 20) is explicitly identified so as to make clear her relationship to the man to whom she belongs, the "mother-in-law" is less so identified and the sister even less. The mother-in-law is identified with respect to her relation to the ego alone. Nevertheless, the fact that she is the ego's wife's mother means that her sexuality does belong to the father of the ego's wife. This is understood in the text. The sister, in one instance, is identified as belonging to the father, in which case the "keeper" or "owner" of her sexuality is explicitly brought into the text. But she is also identified as belonging to the mother, in which case the male "owner" of her sexuality is entirely absent from the text.

In previous sex texts, this kind of waffling with respect to "identification of women" was used to support the claim that women's sexuality as property is not the primary concern. However, in these previous texts, "identification of women" was corroborating evidence, supporting a multitude of additional signals which, in this instance, are lacking.

"Selection of curses" is one important signal that fails to corroborate, although at first glance the opposite might seem true. The sexuality of every woman present in the sex series of Deut 27 belongs necessarily to the *pater familias*. In fact, no consanguine/affine relation in which sexuality belongs to the *pater familias* is absent from the list. Furthermore, the qualifier "women whose sexuality necessarily belongs to the father" explains the presence of a curse representing a prohibition which is found nowhere else in all of LST and DST. Deuteronomy 27:23 is the only occurrence of a prohibition against sex with the mother-in-law, who, more than likely, lives in a household separate from the ego.[13] She is present here because the author's primary concern is to prohibit

---

12.   See the discussion of this paradigmatic relationship under Lev 18 and 20 and Deut 22.

13.   However, see Porter, *Extended Family*, 20–21, who states: "We may think of a situation in which a mother accompanies her daughter to join the husband's family because her own husband has died, or even of the man going to live with his wife's family with which her mother would also be living…and we may note the somewhat analogous state of the widowed Naomi in the book of *Ruth*,

sexual relations with all consanguines and affines whose sexuality belongs to fathers. Thus, while the author has failed to make this belonging explicit by "identification of women," he has made it explicit by the "selection of texts."

In conclusion, "women-who-are-one's-consanguine-or-affine-relations-and-whose-sexuality-necessarily-belongs-to-the-father" is the constitutive qualifier for the selection of the curses regulating consanguine/affine relations. These laws focalize the woman as property. Protection of her sexuality as the property of the *pater familias* is the primary concern.

This same concern, however, fails to explain the presence of the bestiality curse. Furthermore, this mix—consanguine/affine and bestiality—seems to mimic the combinations of laws in Lev 18 and 20 where such combinations were used to support the classificatory concern as primary.

The author selected the bestiality relation of Deut 27:21 from a set of relations whose participants include men, Molek, menstruants and neighbor's wives.[14] When compared with these relations, two qualifications concerning the bestiality relation are apparent. First, bestiality is qualified by the greatest amount of "secrecy" possible in sexual relations. While sex between humans always has at least two "eyewitnesses," that is, the "perpetrators" themselves, the act of bestiality has only one "eyewitness," the human.[15] In this respect, the bestiality act is qualified by the greatest amount of "secrecy" of all sex acts represented in the Hebrew Bible.

But while this latter qualification, "extreme secrecy," might, by itself, explain the inclusion of the bestiality in the larger curse series, it fails to explain its inclusion in combination with the three affine/consanguine curses. In order to explain its inclusion in conjunction with these three latter relations, a second qualification is necessary. This qualification concerns the status of the animal.[16] Out of all possible sex relations the human–animal relation is the only one, aside from the slave–master relation,[17] in which the sex partner is *legal* property.[18] We cannot presume that the beast referred to is the *father's* beast and that all four curses thus refer to the property of the *pater familias* alone. All we can surmise is that three curses guard against misuse of the sexual property of the *pater familias* and one curse guards against the sexual misuse of anyone's property in the form of an animal. Furthermore, the "property qualification" is only implicit in the bestiality curse, just as it is only implicit in the affine/consanguine curses.

Undeniably, the author, by including the bestiality curse, has included a curse which guards against mixing of categories, a classificatory idea. However, the

---

who returns to her own family group with her widowed daughters-in-law..." See also Mayes, *Deuteronomy*, 347; Phillips, *Deuteronomy*, 183.

14. See n. 12 above.

15. This conclusion presumes the animal does not count as an eyewitness.

16. I assume that sex with an undomesticated animal is unlikely, unless it is dead.

17. In certain instances, the client–prostitute relation might be included as an exception as well.

18. The slave–master relation may be included under the father–wife curse. By "legal property" I mean property which can be bought, sold and used in the same manner as material property. See Wegner's distinctions regarding chattel and person in *Chattel*, 6–12.

fact that property concerns characterize all four curses argues against "mixing of categories" as the primary concern. Deduction of the classificatory idea, from the "mix" as a primary concern, is possible only if the total mix warrants it and only if no other narrower concerns explain the mix. In Deut 27:20–23, a narrower concern explains the mix.

b) *Conclusion.* The primary concern of the sex series is, thus, to regulate the sexual property of the *pater familias* and to regulate sexual activity with respect to animal property.

The consanguine/affine curses and the bestiality curse of Deut 27, in contrast to the laws of Lev 18 and 20, fail to bring the constitutive factor to the surface of the text by means of the "identification" signal. The constitutive factor, property, is nevertheless operative. Thus, although the sex curses of Deut 27 and their combination are similar to the laws of Lev 18 and 20 and their combinations, the sex curses of Deut 27 demonstrate a differing conceptuality.

Bellefontaine's comments concerning the bestiality relation underscore this latter difference:

> The act of bestiality accursed by Deut 27:21 has a prohibitive correlative in Lev 18:23 and is placed under the sentence of death by Exod 22:18 and Lev 20:15. The verb used to describe the action is *škb* (to lie with) and designates sexual intercourse. It is questionable, however, that the prohibitive of Lev 18:23 forms the basis for the curse. It belongs to a short rather loosely unified list (Lev 18:18–23) dealing with unnatural sexual acts. It seems to have been composed expressly as an appendix to the preceding series of prohibitions on sexual relations within the family (Lev 18:7–17). It bears the stamp of the priestly tradition and is more concerned with ritual cleanness than with the actual crime.[19]

Thus, the laws of Lev 18 and 20 regulate classificatory issues. The curses of Deuteronomy regulate property issues.

C. *Summary*

The primary concern of the sex curses of Deut 27 is regulation of property in the form of female sexuality and animals. The woman is focalized as property. The gender polarizations of point-of-view and language-depicting-the-sex-act complement the gender polarization of the primary concern, marginalizing and objectifying the woman.

Deuteronomy 27:20–23, therefore, supports the thesis that DST is concerned with property issues, in particular with woman's sexuality as property.

---

19.   Bellefontaine, "Curses," 55.

Chapter 14

DEUTERONOMY 28:30

A. *Introduction*

Deuteronomy 28:30 occurs within the "Comment" portion of the second "Ritual and Comment" of the unit 27:1–28:68.[1] The series of curses within which it occurs differs generically from the series of curses in ch. 27.[2] Each curse of ch. 27 reflects its own prohibition.[3] The curses of ch. 28, however are future, conditional punishments for failure to keep Yhwh's laws in general.

Deuteronomy 28:30 is the only curse within the series associated with sexual intercourse. It applies to the man who betroths a woman. The curse states that the man will betroth a woman and another man will ravish her. The curse intends to harm the sexuality of the woman belonging to the newly betrothed man who fails to keep Yhwh's law.

Woman is thus focalized as the sexual property of the man. Woman's marginalization and objectification complement her focalization.

B. *Discussion*

Three features pertaining to Deut 28:30 reveal the above intention and the conceptualization of woman it entails: point-of-view, language-depicting-the-sex-act and structure.

1. *Point-of-View*
Deuteronomy 28:30 belongs to the same unit as the previously discussed text, Deut 27:20–23. Thus, it is also part of a unit addressed to "all Israel" and "the people." However, just as 27:20–23 belies the inclusiveness of this address with a point-of-view favoring the man, so also does 28:30.

Second person masculine verbs occur throughout the curse series in Deut 28, including v. 30. The man is addressed directly as "you." However, the woman, the betrothed who is ravished, is referred to by third person. The conversation of

---

1. See the discussion of Deut 27.
2. Pierre Buis, "Deuteronome XXVII 15–26: Maledictions ou exigencies de l'alliance?," *VT* 17 (1967), 478–79; Andrew E. Hill, "The Ebal Ceremony as Hebrew Land Grant?," *JETS* 31 (1988): 399–400; Miller, *Deuteronomy*, 194; Weinfeld, "Emergence," 81; idem, *Deuteronomy*, 147.
3. See Bellefontaine, "Curses," 49–61 (50), for a summary and brief review of the scholarly discussion pertaining to this subject.

the text is thus between Moses and the male addressee. The author, through the mouth of Moses, refers to the woman as if she is absent from the conversation. This arrangement indicates that the tragedy invoked by the curse is a tragedy, first of all, for the man. His sexual property is used by another. The woman is merely the instrument through which the tragedy comes to the man.

The tragedy for the woman, while obvious, is nevertheless only implied. Furthermore, the converse situation is absent from the text: the woman is not warned that if she fails to keep the law her husband will be sexually ravished. Nevertheless, the law may also be an implicit warning to her that she will become the instrument of the curse if she does not follow Yhwh's commands. In this respect, she may also be addressed implicitly. In this respect, her marginalization may be slightly ameliorated.

The curse overtly intends to harm the man who fails to keep the law. While the woman is also harmed, point-of-view marginalizes the woman and suggests her focalization as the sexual property of the man.

2. *Language-Depicting-the-Sex-Act*
Language-depicting-the-sex-act, objectifying the woman, supports this conclusion.

a. *Syntax.* Verse 30 consists of three curses. Each curse consists of two clauses. The two clauses pertaining to the betrothed occur in 30aα. In each clause of 30aα, man is subject and woman is direct object. In the first clause, initial focus is on the woman in the same way it is on each of the properties named in subsequent curses.

b. שגל. The sex act is depicted in the second clause of 30aα by means of the verb שגל. All four occurrences of this verb in the Hebrew Bible, including 30aα, are designated by the Masoretes as *Ketib–Qere*.[4] The sensitivity of the Masoretes to this verb derives, perhaps, from the conjunction of violence and sexual intercourse within the conceptual matrix of the verb.

In two out of the three other occurrences of שגל, Isa 13:16 and Zech 14:2, שגל describes the rape of one's wife as punishment for sins on the Day of the Lord. Each pericope describes a scenario of violence in which a man's properties are taken from him. The woman is one among a list of property items plundered. שגל depicts the plunder of the woman. Deuteronomy 28:30 describes the same kind of scenario. Again, the converse scenario in all three instances is absent from the text. שגל, therefore, describes an act of violence against a man. More specifically, it describes the plunder of his sexual property.

---

4.   Emanuel Tov, *Textual Criticism of the Hebrew Bible* (Minneapolis: Fortress, 1992), 63, 272. The Masoretes considered שגל to be "indelicate" and consistently replaced it with שכב. For the most part, the textual witnesses reflect this same sensibility. The Samaritan Pentateuch, Samaritan Targum, Syriac, Onkelos and Neofiti all have verbs which mean "to lie" or "to recline." The Vulgate has *dormiat*, "to sleep." Aquila has συγκοιτασθησεται, "to sleep with" with sexual connotations. LXX, on the other hand, has ἕξει, "to take"; and PJ has שמש, "to couple."

In the fourth occurrence, Jer 3:2, שׁגל describes the unfaithfulness of Israel. In this context the verb signifies illicit sexual partners. The "female sexual companion," Israel, has cooperated in doing violence to the "man," Yhwh, by seeking other "male sexual companions."[5] The verb שׁגל in this context is a metaphor connoting illicit sexual behavior, in which the male plunderer and the woman (Israel) who belongs to the male victim (Yhwh) both willingly participate. It does not refer to rape or ravishing. Therefore, it signifies only the wrong done to the "male" victim (Yhwh). It does not signify the wrong done to the woman. Its use in Jer 3:2 thus differs from its use in Isa 13:6, Zech 14:2 and Deut 28:30.

Despite this difference the usage in Jer 3:2 suggests an operative nuance for שׁגל in Isa 13:6, Zech 14:2 and Deut 28:30. Even if the female's cooperation is absent in these latter texts, שׁגל within these passages may connote primarily the violence against the male victim as it does in Jer 3:2. The syntax of all four examples supports this understanding. If this understanding is plausible, then שׁגל connotes sexual violence against a man through the woman who belongs to him, either with or without her cooperation. שׁגל depicts the violation of a man's sexual property. Language-depicting-the-sex-act thus objectifies the woman. The word field of שׁגל suggests her focalization as sexual property—a suggestion supported by the structure.

3. *Structure*
A collapsed version of the structure is as follows:[6]

II.	Ritual and Comment #2	27:11–28:68
A.	Introduction	27:11
B.	Speech: Moses to the People	27:12–28:68
1.	ritual	27:12–26
2.	comment	28:1–68
a.	blessings	1–14
b.	curses	15–68
1)	group #1: misfortune	15–57
a)	basic conditional	15
b)	amplifying consequences	16–57
(1)	1st amplification: general	16–46
(a)	alteration of daily concerns	16–19
(b)	alteration of larger concerns	20–46
α.	curses	20–44
aa.	personal and ecological health ative	20–24
bb.	military defeat	25–26
cc.	personal health	27–29
dd.	property	30–33
ee.	personal health	34–35
ff.	military defeat	36–37
gg.	property	38–44
β.	conclusion	45–46

---

5. Gravett, "Reading 'Rape,'" 289, states: "In only one instance, Jer 3.2, does this word not raise the spectre of sexual violence."

6. See the structure in the discussion of Deut 27.

(2) 2nd amplification: military defeat	47–57
(a) introduction	47
(b) curses	48–57
2) group #2: ultimate destruction	58–68

a. *Verses 1–69.* The "Comment" portion of this text divides into "Blessings" and "Curses."[7] The curses consist of two groups (vv. 15–57 and vv. 58–68). The first group begins with a basic conditional (v. 15). The apodosis of this basic conditional is more specifically qualified by additional consequences which I call "amplifications" and which themselves divide into two parts. Verse 30 occurs within the first set of "amplifications" (vv. 16–46). This first set, in turn, divides into two parts, the first of which concerns the normal activities of an average person's life, such as working the field, making bread and giving birth. The curses state that these activities will alter negatively if Yhwh's law is abandoned. McCarthy has noted that these curses are impersonally formulated in contradistinction to most, but not all, of the curses that follow.[8]

b. *Verses 20–46.* The second portion of the "First Amplification" (vv. 20–46) consists of the curses proper and a conclusion. The curses fall into seven divisions which themselves comprise three groups. The three groups are: failure of health (personal and ecological), military defeat and loss of property. The seven divisions in conjunction with these three groups form the following literary pattern: ABACABC. The "BACAB" portion of the pattern is an obvious chiasm. The "B" member forms its outermost frame. The outermost frame to the *total* pattern, within which the chaism stands, consists of the other two members of the chiasm (A and C). This means that the two outermost frames of the total pattern utilize all three elements of the pattern. Thus, even though the outermost frame consists of mismatched elements, the mismatching itself is a deliberate pattern.

The pattern has several emphases. First, "failure of health" (A) is emphasized by the number of times it occurs. It occurs three times while the other two elements occur only twice.[9] Second, "loss of property" (C) is emphasized as the center of the chiasm. In fact, the central element is the unit in which v. 30 occurs, highlighting the importance of the security of a man's property as an indicator of his wellbeing. The remaining element, "military loss" (B), which lacks the special emphasis given to "A" and "C," is precisely the element that the author pulls out and expands in the "Second Amplification" (vv. 47–57) which follows.

---

7. I leave aside the redactional problems connected with this text so as to focus on the treatment of women in the extant form of the text. For the redactional problems, see the following: Craigie, *Deuteronomy*, 339; Mayes, *Deuteronomy*, 348; Dennis J. McCarthy, *Treaty and Covenant* (Rome: Biblical Institute Press, 1978), 174, especially n. 32; von Rad, *Deuteronomy*, 175; Weinfeld, *Deuteronomy*, 122.

8. McCarthy, *Treaty and Covenant*, 177–79. See pp. 178–80 for McCarthy's suggestions regarding structure.

9. However, the first occurrence of "(A)" is slightly different than the two subsequent occurrences because the first occurrence consists of ecological health as well as personal health.

c. *Verses 30–33.*

1) *Sexuality of the Woman as Property.* The unit vv. 30–33, the central element of the chiasm, lists the removal by plunder of certain properties from the one who fails to keep Yhwh's law. These properties include house, vineyard, bull, ass, sheep, sons and daughters, and produce.[10] The initial item of this list in 30aα is the betrothed, as if she herself is one among these several properties owned by the man.[11] Von Rad writes:

> The curse will fall upon Israel in the shape of diseases of the body (v. 27) and the mind (v. 28) and damage to property (vv. 30–33).[12]

For most of the property items the loss invoked by the curse is qualified by the strategic time at which it occurs. The man builds a house but cannot live in it. He plants a vineyard but cannot ripen the fruit of it. He cares for a bull but another slaughters and eats it. He grows produce and another people consumes it. He betroths a woman and another man ravishes her. The loss occurs after the man has invested the work, care or planning to acquire the item and before he is able to enjoy the fruit of his efforts.

Verse 30 consists of the first three curses of this unit. These three particular curses correspond to the three exemptions from war in Deut 20:5–7.[13] The three exemptions, by way of military deferment, confer three blessings upon the man who otherwise meets the requirements for military service. Verse 30 deprives the man of those same three blessings should he fail to keep the law. In both chapters, the three blessings and three curses apply to the betrothed, the vineyard and the house, a short list of properties.

The contexts of both Deut 20 and Deut 28 suggest that the sexuality of the betrothed is perceived as a form of property.

2) *Violence against the Man.* In ch. 28 this short list of three is expanded. Furthermore, the concern for what might be taken from a man is heightened.

The contrast between Deut 20 and Deut 28 highlights the special emphasis of Deut 28:30aα, underscoring the primary concern of the verse. In ch. 20, the man is exempt from war so that he might "take" or marry the woman he has betrothed, lest another man complete this duty, right or privilege in the event of the first man's death.[14] In ch. 28, the man is warned that if he fails to keep the laws of Yhwh, another man will sexually violate his betrothed. Chapter 20 concerns marriage. Chapter 28 concerns sexual violation. Although one is a blessing and one is a curse, and although both concern the betrothed, they do not treat

---

10.   Women are part of another triad of properties within the blessings section. In vv. 4, 11 and 18, a blessing applies to the "fruit of your womb and the fruit of your ground and the fruit of your animals." The context suggests that the womb of the woman is the property of the man, as are his plants and his animals. All three produce for the man.

11.   Mace, *Hebrew Marriage*, 245.

12.   Von Rad, *Deuteronomy*, 175.

13.   Craigie, *Deuteronomy*, 345; Mayes, *Deuteronomy*, 355.

14.   Washington, " 'Lest He Die,' " 202, states: "The man's participation in war is checked, but only to preclude another Israelite male's encroachment upon his unrealized right of ownership."

opposite concerns. That is, the curse of ch. 28 does not state that the man will be unable to "take" or marry his betrothed. Rather, it states that another man will use her sexually. The blessing of ch. 20 does not aim at protecting the woman against sexual violation. It aims at enabling the man to bring the marriage process to completion. In Deut 20, a man, unable to complete his tasks with respect to his "properties," is replaced by another man. The concern is marriage. In Deut 28, what belongs to a man is taken from him. The concern is sex. The contrast between these two pericopes emphasizes the aspect of violence and plundering present in the curse of Deut 28:30aα. Furthermore, it highlights the fact that the violence, at the hand of "another" man, is aimed through the woman at the man who fails to keep Yhwh's law.[15]

Additionally, in Deut 20 the tragedies, which each exemption attempts to avoid, occur by means of *another man* completing the task that the addressee should by rights have completed himself. In Deut 28:30, on the other hand, only the curse concerning the betrothed (30aα) mentions *another* man. The other two curses, concerning the house and the vineyard, simply state that the man will not live in the house he builds and he will not pierce the vineyard he plants. However, *another man* will ravish his betrothed. The curse emphasizes the fact that the tragedy with respect to sex, in contradistinction to the other properties, is that *another* man takes what rightfully belongs to the man who fails to keep Yhwh's law.

Thus, the concern in Deut 28:30aα, with respect to women and sexual intercourse, is the same as the concern throughout DST. It is a property concern. It has to do with what one man takes from another. Concern for either the gender converse of this scenario or for the loss that the woman herself experiences, in the scenario depicted, is absent from the text.

The primary concern of v. 30 is the removal of the woman as sexual property of the man. Woman is focalized as property.

C. *Conclusion*

Thus, woman, marginalized and objectified, is also focalized as the sexual property of the man in Deut 28:30aα. The curse places upon the lawbreaker the catastrophe of the "loss" of this property. The primary concern is to guard the law of Yhwh by threatening such disasters as the loss by one man of his sexual property, in the form of the woman who belongs to him, at the hands of *another* man.

---

15.   Gravett, "Reading 'Rape,'" 289. Nevertheless, Gravett, referring to the modern category of rape, states: "Deuteronomy 28.30 raises some interpretive difficulties, but the understanding of rape still applies." Whether or not the author of the text, or the world which generated the text, understands this act as a violation against the woman is an open question. However, I am inclined to agree with Gravett that, in this context, the author would have understood the conceptuality of female nonconsent and its violation. This understanding would have been facilitated by the fact that the men in the community (to whom the woman belongs) are themselves violated, not through their women only, but through direct, violent subjugation of their own bodies, to another people. Nevertheless, the principal violence of this text is against the man, through the woman.

Part IV

COMPARATIVE ANALYSIS

Chapter 15

COMPARATIVE ANALYSIS

A. *Introduction*

Many comparisons can be made of the laws in LST and DST, within and between the two groups. However, the only comparisons of interest to this study are those pertaining to the conceptualization of women.

The following comparative analyses proceed with respect to three classes of rubrics: (1) nine topics occurring in the sex laws,[1] (2) genre features and (3) the three rhetorical components of marginalization, objectification and focalization.[2] Comparisons under the "nine topics" reveal gender symmetry or asymmetry with respect to specific concerns such as menstruation, adultery, incest and virginity, for example. Comparisons under the "genre features" reveal symmetry or asymmetry in the representation of gender with respect to three "structures." The first is the "structure" of the series, a generic form. The second is the "structure" of boundaries or of properties, a social form. The third is the "structure" of the sources, a literary-critical form. Comparisons under the "three components" reveal gender symmetry or asymmetry in the author's relationship to his audience and in the male and female characters' relationship to one another in the depiction of coitus.

A final caveat is required at this point. Comparisons under the last class of rubrics constitute the thesis of this study. Since this is so, the question concerning the relationship of the first two classes to the last class must be raised. Comparisons under the first two classes of rubrics consider, at close range, issues which apply to comparisons under the last class of rubrics. However, I have listed the three classes of rubrics as if they are separate and on the same level because the same issues, looked at from different angles, can reveal different information. Thus, posing the last class of rubrics as merely one among three questions concerning comparisons is useful, even if finally it becomes the operative rubric for the thesis.

The results of the comparative analyses, for which the last class of rubrics becomes finally operative, demonstrate that LST and DST share a conceptualization of women as circumscribed by and subordinate to men. In all laws of both groups, women are marginalized and objectified. To varying degrees, the

---

1. See Chart 5 in Appendix.
2. See Chart 6 in Appendix.

marginalization is ameliorated and on occasion the objectification is ameliorated as well. LST and DST, however, differ in their focalization of women. In LST she is, for the most part, focalized as agent responsible to the law. Two exceptions occur. In Lev 19:20–22 the woman's status is legal property. She is focalized as "forgotten." She never accrues agency. However, beyond serving as the occasion of the infraction, the woman as sexual property is irrelevant. In Lev 19:29 the woman is the father's property. This text also fails to manifest agency for her. Nevertheless, her status as property serves the purity rather than the property concern. She is focalized as "valued." In DST, on the other hand, woman is, for the most part, focalized as property, even while manifesting an accrual to agency by way of implied addressee and active participation in the infraction. Deuteronomy 21:10–14 is singular among the laws of both LST and DST because it is the only instance in which amelioration of her marginalization does not imply her focalization as agent.

The primary concern of the laws of LST is, thus, to protect a classificatory order, an ontology. Woman, for the most part, focalized as agent and not as property, has a duty to protect that order, as does the man of her community. The primary concern of the laws of DST, on the other hand, is to protect the proprietary interests of the man, that is, woman's sexuality. Woman is focalized as property. Her appearance as character-agent in the text serves the purpose of protecting those interests, which are coterminous with her own body.

B. *Discussion*[3]

1. *LST*

With the exception of Lev 15:18, 24, 33b and 19:20–22, the laws of LST all prohibit certain sexual behaviors. They are framed apodictically or casuistically. The sex laws of 15:18, 24, 33b and 19:20–22, both of which are casuistic, do not regulate sexual intercourse by prohibiting sexual behavior. Leviticus 20:10–21 and 21:9 might also be thought of as mediating the effects of sexual behavior for the community by limiting or altogether removing the perpetrators from the community. However, the force of the penalties of these laws suggest that even if they intend to mediate impurity within the community, they also intend to prohibit certain sexual behaviors.

Thus, the laws of LST fall into two classes with respect to their intent to regulate sexual intercourse. Either they intend to prohibit sexual intercourse under certain circumstances or they intend to mediate impurities as well as prohibit sexual intercourse. In all cases, the primary concern is regulation of a variety of classificatory matters with respect to sexual intercourse.

---

3. I beg the reader's forgiveness for repetition that occurs in the following discussion. Since I methodologically discuss comparisons under the topics of LST, DST, and LST and DST with the same rubrics for each, I repeat myself in some instances. For systematic reasons I have not excised this repetition. Because of the number of texts involved, the charts in the appendix may facilitate navigation of the ensuing discussion.

a. *Nine Topics Occurring in the Sex Laws.*
1) *Menstruation.* Perhaps nowhere is the significance of this difference of intent more apparent than in the laws concerned with menstruants. In Lev 15:18, 24, 33b, intercourse with a menstruant is not forbidden. As menstruant, her condition is only one among several kinds of genital-discharge impurities presented with pronounced gender symmetry between men and women. No special aversion accrues to her, either because she is a woman or because she has genital discharge.

By contrast, intercourse with a menstruant in Lev 18:19 and 20:18 is forbidden.[4] Accordingly, in 15:18, 24, 33b, the consequences of intercourse with a menstruant are mediated by non-punitive cleansing rituals. In both 18:19 and 20:18, the consequences are כרת. Thus, although all three texts consider sex with a menstruant to contaminate the man, the woman alone is the contaminator in Lev 18 and 20 whereas both men and women are contaminators in Lev 15.

The gender symmetry of the context of Lev 15:18, 24, 33b is, thus, absent from the contexts of both 18:19 and 20:18. The infractions are conceived differently. Accordingly, woman is also conceived differently. Women in the latter two texts are inferiorized on account of their genital discharge. They have the negative, non-legal power to harm a man. Unlike the woman in Lev 15, they pose a special danger to the man. In Lev 15, the man and the woman are both agents who must protect the purity of one another, themselves and thereby the larger social arena, as well as the land itself. In Lev 18:19 and 20:18, the man and the woman are also agents. The man, however, must protect *himself* and thereby the social arena, whereas the woman must protect the *man* and thereby the social arena. Thus, although woman is agent in all three texts, her *duties* as agent are qualified by gender asymmetry in Lev 18:19 and 20:18, whereas in Lev 15 they are qualified by gender symmetry.

The language-depicting-the-sex-act in Lev 18:19 and 20:18 also contrasts with Lev 15. The former texts use the נלה phrase, the same vocabulary as the incest laws. Leviticus 15 uses a שכב phrase. The sense of the נלה phrase is that the woman has something or is qualified by something which the man ought not to expose. More precisely, he ought not to expose himself to the impurity of the woman. This language underscores, in contrast to Lev 15, the idea that the woman alone is impure.

2) *Incest.* Incest is treated in two texts: Lev 18:6–18 and 20:11–12, 14, 17–21. In Lev 18, incest laws begin the sex series. The incest laws are grouped together. In Lev 20, the incest laws are preceded by an adultery law. Laws on bestiality and homosexuality interrupt them.

---

4. Countryman, *Dirt*, 23, compares the treatment of menstruation in Lev 15 and the Holiness Code as follows: "The first code [Lev 15] thus shows its [i.e. sex with a menstruant] relatively mundane character; it recognizes dirt as an inevitable aspect of daily existence, however much the society may seek to avoid it, and offers remedies to restore those polluted to the normal state of cleanness. The Holiness Code holds up the ideal of an absolute separation between Israel and all that is unclean and utters a 'No' to uncleanness so absolute that it is often enforced through the execution or the 'cutting off' of the polluted."

In both series, sex with women connected to men as well as sex with women unconnected to men is regulated. Nevertheless, Lev 20 lacks prohibitions against four incestuous relations which are present in Lev 18. These relations are with: (1) granddaughters, (2) stepsisters, (3) a woman and her sister and (4) mothers, unless the mother is covered by the father's-wife prohibition. In addition, the father–daughter prohibition is implied by Lev 18:6 but is missing entirely from 20:10–21. The brother's wife, sanctioned by levirate law, is forbidden in both series (18:16; 20:21).

As a result of these absences in Lev 20, the ratio of affinal to consanguinal boundaries protected by the incest laws of Lev 18 and 20 differs. Their comparative ratios are suggestive. Eight consanguines and four affines are forbidden in Lev 18, including four kinds of sisters. Leviticus 20, on the other hand, forbids three consanguines and four affines. If the "father's wife" of Lev 20 covers both a consanguine and an affine, then the same number of prohibitions pertaining to affines occur as prohibitions pertaining to consanguines. If this tally is accurate, then the "incest" emphasis in Lev 20 distributes more evenly between consanguines and affines than in Lev 18. This means that more relationships guarded by marriage are of concern in Lev 20 than in Lev 18. This difference in emphasis suggests that Lev 20 has a slightly greater concern for boundaries in which the property or "belonging" component figures than Lev 18.

In addition, Lev 20 begins its series with the neighbor's-wife prohibition, a law in which property is a necessary component because of the marriage boundary. Furthermore, both the wife of the father and the mother of the ego are forbidden in Lev 18 whereas only the wife of the father is explicitly mentioned in Lev 20. Again, the relationship emphasizing the property component as opposed to the classificatory component of blood incest is chosen by the author of Lev 20.

The mother–daughter relation, with respect to marriage and sex, is forbidden in both chapters. However, instead of forbidding a man to marry a *woman* and her *daughter*, as in Lev 18:17, 20:14 forbids a man to marry a *woman* and her *mother*.[5] In Lev 20, the man is thus warned against women of his own generation (sister), against women of a higher generation (aunts, father's wife) and against only *mature* women of a lower generation (daughter-in-law, woman and mother). In Lev 18, he is warned against women of his own generation (sisters), women of a higher generation (aunts, father's wife, mother) and against *immature* as well as *mature* women of a lower generation (granddaughter, woman and daughter, daughter-in-law). Thus, the author of Lev 20 has again selected a configuration with a heightened property component, since property concerns become more acute as a girl approaches puberty.

Despite this greater emphasis on the property component in Lev 20, the penalties which encircle both men and women, are an indicator of woman's

---

5.   The actual proximity in age of the male ego to the women against whom he is warned is uncertain since ages of a single generation can diverge as much as ages from one generation to the next.

responsibility to the law. Although the penalty indicator is absent from Lev 18, other more subtle indicators, in both Lev 18 and 20, also demonstrate her responsibility to the law.

The heightened emphasis on the property component in Lev 20 is not enough to neutralize the primary concern for classificatory issues which 20:10–21 shares with Lev 18. The property component serves the classificatory concern. Thus, in both texts woman is agent, like the man, who must protect the classificatory system which constitutes their world.

3) *Adultery*. The adultery law of Lev 18:20 uses the verb נתן in the language-depicting-the-sex-act. Leviticus 20:10, by contrast, uses the term נאף. As explained in the exegesis portion of this study, נתן implies reciprocity. Whatever is given must be received. Otherwise, the act of giving is incomplete. נאף has a different connotation. The notion of crossing property boundaries, as defined by marriage, is a necessary component of its word field, a component which is absent from the word field of נתן. The classificatory component connected with adultery, made explicit in 18:20 by use of טמא, is absent in 20:10 since the connotations of נאף narrow the classificatory component to a property compo-nent. The context in which 20:10 rests recontextualizes that narrow property component so that it signifies the broader classificatory concern.

Nevertheless, again, in Lev 20 a heightening of the property component occurs when compared with Lev 18. Even so, woman is an implied agent responsible for protecting the classificatory concern of the laws in both texts.

4) *Homosexuality*. Both laws concerning homosexuality, Lev 18:22 and 20:13, describe the act by reference to a phrase suggesting penetration of a woman. The import is that penetration is at issue in both laws, a classificatory concern. Male to male anal sex is the extent of the prohibition against male eroticism. *Penetra-tive* licit sex is presumed to take place with women only. Male to male penetra-tive sex is a categorical violation. Female to female eroticism is not. Therefore, prohibition against lesbianism is absent. It is a non-issue.

Protection of classificatory boundaries is the primary concern.

5) *Bestiality*. In both bestiality laws, Lev 18:23 and 20:15–16, woman is mar-ginalized by use of second masculine verbs or pronouns. However, in both chapters men and woman are separately and relatively equally regulated with respect to bestiality. In both texts she is subject vis-à-vis the animal. The verbs used to depict the sex act in both texts suggest similar conceptualizations in Lev 18 and 20 with respect to women. Her role as producer of offspring is high-lighted by the vocabulary of these laws. In both texts she is conceived as cir-cumscribed by and subordinate to the man.

Protection of classificatory boundaries is the primary concern.

6) *Prostitution*. LST do not regulate the practice of harlotry as a profession. Their regulation has to do with fathers and daughters.

Leviticus 19:29 concerns the possibility of a father causing his daughter to practice harlotry. This law restricts his right to do so, stating that such practice would fill the land with infamy. Leviticus 21:9 concerns the possibility of the daughter of a priest engaging in harlotry, defiling her father as a result. The law is a prohibitive against such behavior. It also provides a remedy in the event that such behavior transpires.

The difference in the concerns of these two laws is obvious. In Lev 19:29, the father is the agent responsible for committing the infraction. The land and the daughter suffer the results. In 21:9, the daughter is the agent responsible for committing the infraction. The father suffers the results. She is burned to death.

In both cases, defilement or purity issues are the primary concern. The daughter's relationship to those issues is different in the two chapters. In both texts she has the status of property as a daughter. In Lev 19:29, her status as property gives her father the power to defile her. Her focalization as the property serves to protect the *purity* of that property and the land. In 21:9, she is focalized as agent. The property component, again, enters in by way of the father–daughter relationship. Nevertheless, as agent, she has power that no other woman in LST and DST has. She has the negative power to harm a man without his cooperation by altering his state of purity.

In both cases, the property component, although necessarily present because of the father–daughter relationship, and although essential to the infraction, is relevant only insofar as it contributes to the author's primary concern to protect purity. Otherwise it is a non-issue. The law limits the father's power in Lev 19:29 and the daughter's power in 21:9 in the interests of purity.

7) *Rape*. LST has no law concerned with the issue of "rape." That is, no law in LST explicitly intends to regulate a situation in which a woman's sexuality is perceived as being taken from its owner, that is, the man to whom she belongs.

8) *Virginity*. Virginity in LST is also a non-issue. Although prohibition against harlotry, that is, prohibition of sex outside the context of marriage, may imply a valuation for virginity, virginity per se is not the issue. In Lev 19:29, the issue is the father's initiative to cause his daughter to harlot. Her status as virgin is ignored by the law. In Lev 21:9, the issue is compromise of the priest's sanctity by means of his daughter's illicit sexual acts. LST know what virginity is. Within the book of Leviticus, however, virginity is an issue *only* in the context of the marriage of the high priest or in the context of the death of his virgin sister.[6]

No laws of LST regulate virginity.

9) *Slaves and Captives*. None of the laws of LST regulate sex with respect to female captives of war. One law, does, however, regulate sex with a slave, that is, a שׁפחה. Such a woman is legal property. Exchanges can be made for certain rights of access to her, with respect to her labor or to her sexuality. In the case of

---

6.   Engelken, *Frauen im alten Israel*, 27.

Lev 19:20–22, however, rights to her sexuality are ambiguously limited. Breach of those rights gives rise to the author's primary concern, the impurity of the perpetrator. Beyond that concern, breach of her sexuality is forgotten.

The שפחה of Lev 19:20–22, unlike the daughters of 19:29 and 20:9, is *legal* property. Like 19:29, she is not focalized as agent. Her status as property is the source of the perpetrator's capacity to transgress the "property" boundaries of "assignment." It is the source of the infraction which creates the impurity that is the concern of the law. Nevertheless, the impurity itself of the perpetrator rather than the woman's status as property is, in fact, the primary concern of the law. She is focalized as "forgotten."

Her relationship as property to the primary concern is finally irrelevant to that primary concern. The property component serves the classificatory concern.

10) *Summary*. Comparisons with respect to the nine topics demonstrate that the property and purity components configure differently in the texts, constructing slight nuances in the conceptualization of women. Nevertheless, in every law of LST, both the purity and the property components serve the classificatory concern.

In all three menstruation texts woman is agent who must uphold the law. However, only in Lev 15 are her duties as agent characterized by extensive gender symmetry. Furthermore, her agency is more explicit in Lev 15 than in Lev 18 and 20. Nevertheless, all three texts expect her to uphold the laws concerning sex with a menstruant. Within Lev 18 the incest and adultery laws demonstrate a heightened emphasis on the property component when compared to Lev 20. Nevertheless, that property component fails to supercede the classificatory concern of the text as a whole. In 19:20–22, 29 and 21:29, woman's status as property is essential to commission of the infraction. However, again, that status recedes before the classificatory concerns of the text.

The bestiality texts are similar in their treatment of women, highlighting her role as producer of offspring. She is to be bred. Both laws prohibiting homosexuality forbid only male-to-male anal sex. No law prohibits lesbianism. No law prohibits rape. And no law regulates virginity.

Thus, nuances in the conceptualization of women exist among the laws of LST with respect to purity and property components. Nevertheless, the classificatory concern is primary. With the exception of Lev 19:29 and 19:20–22, woman is focalized as agent. In all texts, including 19:29 and 19:20–22, her status as property or agent serves the classificatory concern.

b. *Genre Features*.
1) *Series*. LST contain two series of laws, Lev 18 and 20:10–21. The two series regulate relations with women who belong to men as well as with women who are not designated as belonging to men. In addition, both series regulate infractions that have nothing to do with women or have nothing to do with the sexual combinations of men and women. Thus, both lists are interested in the same kind of variety of infractions.

The lists in these two series, however, are organized differently, indicating differences in understanding and intent. The first part of the series of laws in Lev 18 (vv. 6–18) guards against sexual relations with consanguinals and affinals. The second part of the series of laws in Lev 18 (vv. 19–23) guards against sexual relations which fail to result in progeny for the male ego. Two different intents characterize these two sections. Furthermore, two different conceptualizations concerning what is problematic about sex shape these two sections. Naturally, placing the two sections in juxtaposition recontextualizes their separate intents and their conceptualizations concerning what is problematic. Nevertheless, the two units are discrete, as if the final redactor understands the original intent and conceptualization of each of the individual sections.

In Lev 20, however, this same understanding concerning knowledge of intent and conceptualization of the problematics of sex is lacking. The two sets of laws are not discrete. They are interspersed. This interspersing is a function of priority judgments concerning the severity of the infractions in relation to one another, as well as a function of the writing process. The most heinous infractions come first. The least severe infractions come last. This same organization is lacking in Lev 18.

With respect to women, the gradation in Lev 20 places an emphasis on the property component. The three laws that begin the series pertain to married women, the first of which—the neighbor's wife—is outside the family. Although the entire series concludes with a married woman—the brother's wife—this relation is precisely the one sanctioned by levirate law. Its placement last along with the other non-propertied relations is, thus, not accidental.

In conclusion, a comparison of the organization of Lev 18 and 20:10–21, as series, demonstrates differing taxonomies for the problematics of sex. Leviticus 20:10–21 demonstrates a taxonomy which depends on a gradation that is in large part, but not exclusively, a function of the property component. Leviticus 18, on the other hand, demonstrates a taxonomy that separates relations with affinals and consanguinals from relations with non-affinals and non-consanguinals, which fail to result in progeny. These differences construct slight nuances in the conceptualization of woman.

2) *Boundaries of Primary Concern.* A primary concern to regulate purity, that is, a primary concern to protect classificatory boundaries with respect to sexual intercourse, characterizes every law in LST. Nevertheless, different laws in LST defend different kinds of classificatory boundaries. Although this feature is not a "form" in the same way that a "series" is a form, it may nevertheless also be considered a generic difference among the laws.

Two texts of LST forbid nothing. Lev 15:18, 24, 33b mediates contagion transpiring in the body from anomalous and non-anomalous genital discharges without forbidding the acts which cause the impurity. This text is concerned with natural impurity while all other texts are concerned with moral impurity.[7]

---

7. For this distinction and a variety of ways of assessing it, see the following: Frymer-Kensky, "Pollution," 399–414 (404); Neusner, "Uncleanness"; Wright, "Two Types," 180–93; idem,

The manner in which this text treats the woman is equal to the manner in which it treats the man. Like 15:18, 24, 33b, Lev 19:20–22 forbids nothing, although the opprobrium attached to the sexual act is obvious. Rather, like 15:18, 24, 33b, it mediates impurity. In this case, it mediates the impurity that accrues to the perpetrator.

Three texts of LST explicitly state their concern for defilement of the land. Each, with greater or lesser specification, describes or prescribes a solution that rids the community of the problem. Leviticus 18 guards against defilement of the land by forbidding certain consanguinal and affinal relations as well as sexual relations which cannot result in progeny. Leviticus 19:29 guards against defilement of the land and defilement of daughters by restricting the prerogatives of fathers. Leviticus 20:10–21 guards against defilement of the land[8] by forbidding a gradation of sexual infractions with respect to the following: consanguinals, affinals, men with men, animals and menstruants.

One text of LST expressly protects a man from a woman. Leviticus 21:9 protects against the profanation and defilement[9] of a father-priest by prohibiting the harlotry of his daughter. In addition, it mediates the problem by prescribing the burning penalty.

In Lev 15:18, 24, 33b; 18; and 20:10–21 no single, particular victim is in the mind of the author when he regulates his infractions. In 19:20–22 the perpetrator is protected. In 19:29, the daughter is protected from her father. In Lev 21:9, the father is protected from his daughter. These differences are responsible for differing focalizations of women. In Lev 15, she is focalized as agent equal to the man with respect to the primary concern. In Lev 18, she is focalized as agent and treated with less equity than in Lev 15. The same is the case in 20:10–21, however, with a slightly greater emphasis on the property component than in Lev 18. In Lev 19:20–22 and 19:29, her status is as property, but that component is not the concern of the law. She is focalized as "valued." In 21:9, she has the status of "daughter-property" and is focalized as agent who, unlike all the other women of LST, has the capacity to harm the relevant man without his cooperation.

In all these laws, classificatory issues, figured in various ways, are the primary concern. The boundaries protected vary in kind. Nevertheless, in every case, the property components and the purity components serve the classificatory concern.

3) *Holiness Code/Priestly Writing.* The one group of laws concerned with natural impurity is also the only group of laws in LST that occurs outside the Holiness Code. These laws, Lev 15:18, 24, 33b, are precisely the ones that are unrivaled in LST with respect to gender equity. Thus, a shift from the Priestly Writings outside the Holiness Code to the Priestly Writings within the Holiness

"Unclean and Clean (Old Testament)," *ABD* 6:729–30. For a suggestion concerning the relationship of the two kinds of impurity, see Jenson, *Graded Holiness*, 53–54; Kiuchi, *Purification*, 62–64.

8. Its concern for the defilement of the land is evidenced by the immediate larger context, specifically v. 22.

9. For the distinction between profanation and defilement, see Jenson *Graded*, 43–55.

Code corresponds to a shift in concern from the "natural" realm to the moral realm of impurity. These two shifts, interestingly, correspond to a shift from gender symmetry to gender asymmetry in the treatment of woman.

c. *Marginalization, Objectification and Focalization.*
1) *Marginalization.* In all texts of LST woman is marginalized. The men are addressed directly. In all but two of the texts of LST woman's marginalization is slightly ameliorated by the fact that she too is implicitly addressed. In one of the two texts, in which her marginalization is not ameliorated (Lev 19:20–22), her status as property is lower than that of an Israelite wife. She is a שפחה. In the second (19:29), her status as property is constituted by the father–daughter relationship. Again, that status is lower than an Israelite wife. Nevertheless, woman's marginalization is present throughout LST.

2) *Objectification.* In every instance of LST where the sex act is depicted, except in the female bestiality laws, woman is objectified. She is object and man is subject.

Two texts refer to sexual behavior without expressly depicting the sex act. Both these texts treat the topic of harlotry: Lev 19:29 and 21:9. In 19:29, woman is objectified by verbs qualifying the effects of illicit sexual behavior. In 21:9, by contrast, she is the subject of the verbs of the law. Leviticus 21:9 is, coincidentally, the only law in LST and DST in which the woman has the power to harm a man without his cooperation. The man is a priest and the harm is his loss of sanctity. Priests thus have a special vulnerability with respect to women.

Nevertheless, woman's objectification is present throughout LST.

3) *Focalization.*
a) *Agent.* Three texts in LST, Lev 15:18, 24, 33b; 18; and 20:10–21 focalize woman exclusively as agent. She is not focalized as property. However, Lev 18 and 20:10–21 each contain an adultery law in which the property component is necessarily present because of the marriage bond. In Lev 15, the equal focalization of man and woman is made explicit by the structure of the text and other features. Although the man's status as agent in Lev 18 and 20:10–21 is explicit, the woman's status as agent must be inferred. Furthermore, in Lev 18 and 20:10–21, woman, as agent, is somewhat inferiorized or circumscribed, as compared to Lev 15. Nevertheless, within the context of Lev 18 and 20:10–21, the property component becomes entirely incidental with respect to the primary concern. It is simply one among several kinds of boundaries which are defended by the two series. Furthermore, the inferiorization fails to neutralize the implied responsibility to the law which constitutes woman's status as agent.

All three texts presume woman's responsibility, explicitly or implicitly, to the law.

b) *Property.* The two texts in which woman's marginalization is not ameliorated (Lev 19:20–22, 29) are also the two texts of LST in which her status as property is prominent. In these two texts she is respectively a שפחה and a daughter.

Neither the שפחה nor the daughter is focalized as agent. Furthermore, their portrayal accords them less power than any of the other women of LST. The status of each of these women gives the men, to whom they are connected, the power to commit the infraction which the law forbids. Their property status is, thus, significant with respect to the primary concern. However, in both cases the primary concern leaves aside the property component to focus on something else. In the case of the infraction with the שפחה, it focuses on remediation of the male perpetrator. In the case of the infraction with the daughter, it focuses on the defilement of the daughter and the land. The primary concern in each case is, thus, classificatory. The women are focalized respectively as "forgotten" and "valued."

c) *Agent and Property.* The woman of Lev 21:9 is also a daughter. She, unlike the daughter of 19:29, acts. Her responsibility to the law is obvious. She is, thus, agent even while her status is "daughter-property." The property component, present because of the father–daughter relationship, is significant because it is essential for understanding the nature of the infraction that transpires. Nevertheless, that property component is not the primary concern. Furthermore, it fades in significance in its service to the primary concern. As agent she has the power to harm her father. This harm constitutes the primary concern. Thus, although the woman is focalized as property and as agent, once the nature of the infraction is understood, only her status as agent matters with respect to the primary concern. Even her status as property of the father cannot save her from the penalty of burning.

In both Lev 18:20 and 20:10, in which the woman is a non-blood relative and is married to a non-blood relative, the woman's status is as property. The property component recedes, however, in the context of the primary concern. And the woman as implied addressee is agent, responsible to the law.

d. *Synthesis.* Comparisons with respect to the "nine topics" and "genre features" demonstrate that purity and property components are both present in various configurations throughout the laws. The primary concern of each law in LST is, nevertheless, to protect a classificatory system. In every case the property component as well as the purity component serves this classificatory concern. However, no laws regulate "rape" or virginity, in which the property component generally dominates.

In all texts except Lev 21:9 woman is objectified. In this law, which concerns the sanctity of the priest, she is subject who has the power to harm the man. In all texts she is also marginalized. However, her marginalization and objectification are ameliorated to varying degrees by contraindicating factors, some subtle, some overt, in various texts.

Sometimes the woman's status as property is essential to the commission of the infraction. However, that property component beyond "setting the scene" is irrelevant to the primary concern. Thus, the property status as a concern "fades." Its irrelevance takes one of two forms. The first is the situation in which woman is focalized as agent with a status as property and only her implied agency is relevant *to the primary concern*,[10] as in the adultery laws and in Lev 21:9. The second is the situation in which a woman is not focalized as agent and has property status, as in 19:20–22 and 19:29. In this latter case, her property status becomes irrelevant because the primary concern has nothing to do with its protection, which is ignored. No mention is made of virginity in 19:29. In 19:20–22, woman is forgotten altogether in the concern to remediate the perpetrator. In both laws, woman is relevant only as the initiating locus of the problem. As such, however, she is not the problem the author wishes to solve. In 19:20–22, the problem is harm done to the man in the form of defilement. In 19:29, the problem is the harm done to the land, through the daughter, by the father, in the form of defilement.

With the exception of the latter two examples, woman is always focalized as agent. This focalization must be inferred in every text except Lev 15 where that focalization is explicitly brought to the surface by the structure and other features.

In every case, except Lev 19:29 and 19:20–22, the primary concern is for the woman and the man to protect a *third entity*—the boundaries constituting the classificatory system which constitutes their world. This is an ontological concern. In 19:29 and 19:20–22, the primary concern is for the man to protect the same "third entity," but the woman, as object and as property, is never pictured as acting as agent. The agency accrues, therefore, only within particular configurations of status.

While woman is circumscribed and subordinate to the man, she and the man are, for the most part, both agents who must act vis-à-vis a third entity, that is, an entity which is not exclusively coterminous with themselves. The property component always serves that end. Protection of woman's sexuality as property or protection of woman herself as property is never the concern of the laws of LST.

2. DST

All the laws of DST are casuistic except Deut 5:18; 27:20–23 and 28:30. The latter two texts are curses. The curses of 27:20–23 are directed against the one who commits the named infraction, explicitly anyone from the men of the community. The curses of 28:30 are directed against whoever fails to keep Yhwh's commands in general; again, explicitly anyone from the men of the community. The initial text, 5:18, is an apodictic law. It prohibits the infraction of adultery.

The remaining laws of DST may be described as follows. Deuteronomy 21:10–14 mediates at least two problematic situations for a male Israelite. Deuteronomy 25:5–10 mediates a problematic situation concerning a dead man's entitlements. Deuteronomy 22:13–23:1 prohibits a variety of sexual infractions with an emphasis on those related to virginity. In addition, it mediates the problem caused by the infractions it regulates.

---

10. Her status as property is relevant, of course, in the sense that it is the initiating locus of the infraction. However, the law is not attempting to defend this property vis-à-vis other males per se. It is attempting to protect a classificatory sphere, which is one among many spheres it protects.

In two of these laws, the infraction, in contradistinction to all other laws of LST and DST, is the failure to perform sex. Deuteronomy 25:5–10 prescribes sex between a widow and her brother-in-law. It also mediates the failures of the brother-in-law to complete this duty. Deuteronomy 21:10–14 mediates the failure of a man to continue the marriage that he forced upon a woman. Since sex is necessary to marriage, his failure to continue the marriage is a failure to continue the context which legitimates sex for the woman. It is also a failure to continue the sex which itself initially legitimated the marriage.[11]

Thus, the laws of DST fall into four groups: (1) laws which prohibit certain sexual relations (Deut 5:18; 23:18–19); (2) laws which prohibit certain sexual relations and mediate the problems that occur when those relations transpire (22:13–23:1); (3) laws which mediate the problem that failure to perform sex creates (21:10–14; 25:5–10); and (4) laws which either place victimization, by way of harm to sexual property, upon men who fail to keep Yhwh's commands (Deut 28), or which simply curse the men who commit certain sexual infractions (27:20–23).

Thus, while the primary concern, with respect to sex, in all these laws is to regulate property, their interests in that property are varied.

a. *Nine Topics Occurring in the Sex Laws.*

1) *Menstruation.* No law in DST concerns the regulation of sex with a menstruant. Interest in this matter is entirely lacking in DST. It is a non-issue.

2) *Incest.* Two texts treat the subject of incest: Deut 23:1 and 27:20, 22–23. In addition, 25:5–10 regulates the brother/sister-in-law relationship, which in LST is considered to be incestuous.

The laws of 27:20, 22–23 curse men who commit the incestuous acts listed. The infractions with a father's wife, a sister and a mother-in-law are thus forbidden. Deuteronomy 23:1 differs from 27:20 because it also forbids *marriage* to the father's wife. As such, we must conclude that the father is dead. The same conclusion cannot be made for 27:20.

The only place the brother's wife is mentioned is in the levirate law of Deut 25:5–10. She is not forbidden. In fact, sex with her is a responsibility the law expects the brother-in-law to fulfill.

In every case of incest represented in DST the women are connected to men by the marriage bond or by the father–daughter bond. Even the woman of the levirate law is compelled by the marriage bond she had with the husband, who is now dead, in order to pursue his entitlements.

Thus, the property component is operative in every case including the levirate law. Nevertheless, women as well as men are expected to uphold the law. In Deut 25:5–10 her status as agent in the חֲלִיצָה ritual is pronounced.

---

11. Both, of course, constitute rape in our twenty-first-century world.

3) *Adultery*. Two texts in DST treat adultery: Deut 5:18 and 22:22, 23–24. Although betrothed women and married women are conceptualized differently by the author of 22:13–23:1, they are both connected to men other than their fathers by a bond which gives either present or future sexual access to only those men. The breaking of that exclusivity incurs the death penalty. Thus, for *comparative purposes*, I group Deut 22:23–24 with the adultery laws.[12]

The property component is explicit in Deut 5:18, which provides no details outside the simple prohibition of וְלֹא תִּנְאָף, because נאף necessarily carries in its word field the property component. This is so even though the woman makes no appearance in the law and the man makes appearance only by way of the masculine form of the verb. Deuteronomy 22:22, 23–24, on the other hand, uses שכב and delineates several nuances with respect to "adultery," by treating situations in which the woman is married and in which the woman is betrothed. Specifications regarding the bonds that tie these women to their men are explicit. Therefore, the property component in these laws is also explicit.

Not only is the property component explicit in every adultery law, that component is the central concern of each law as well. In every case, both women and men are expected to protect the sexuality of the woman as the property of the man.

4) *Homosexuality*. No law among DST regulates homosexuality, male or female. The subject is a total non-issue.

5) *Bestiality*. Only one law in DST, a curse, regulates bestiality: Deut 27:21. This curse does not specify with respect to gender, aside from using a masculine participle. The surrounding incest curses are all unquestionably aimed at men. This state of affairs suggests strongly that 27:21 is also aimed at men. Men, rather than both men and women, are the perpetrators.

6) *Prostitution*. As I define the text-base, one law treats harlotry in DST: Deut 22:20–21. It refers to the illicit sexual activity of a married woman, occurring prior to marriage, as זנה. The woman is discovered after her marriage to be a non-virgin. She is designated as having committed harlotry in her father's house. She is guilty of illicit sex as well as fraud against her husband and her father. The sex act is not depicted explicitly. Virginity is an issue in this law since its loss victimizes both men. The woman is the grammatical subject of the verb describing the activity constituting her infraction. Her male partner(s) is/are absent from the law. She alone is the vehicle for the infraction and she alone is stoned to death. The law thus prohibits and mediates with considerable gender asymmetry.

Woman's sexuality as property is the primary concern.

---

12. See the discussion above under Deut 22 where the *difference* between married and betrothed women rather than the *similarity* between them is constitutive for the structure of the text.

7) *Rape*. Two texts treat "rape." The first is Deut 22:25–27, 28–29. The second is 28:30.

The first text treats rape of a betrothed virgin woman and a non-betrothed virgin. Virginity is an issue. The second threatens a lawbreaker with loss of his sexual property. Violence to the woman is only one aspect of the denotation of שׁגל. Violence done to the man through violence done to the woman is a more complete description of its denotation. Violence is also depicted in 22:25–27 and 22:28–29. The woman's lack of cooperation is most evident in 22:25–27. As argued in the above exegesis, the woman's intent with respect to the infraction is irrelevant. Deuteronomy 28:30 does not disabuse the exegete of this view.

Thus, "rape" is violence done to a man by means of sexual misuse of his betrothed wife-to-be or his unbetrothed daughter. Rape of a wife is non-existent in DST. This is because rape in DST is an act of violence by one man against another man, through harm done to the latter's most vulnerable sexual property: daughters and betrotheds. With respect to "adultery," wives and betrothed women are similar (22:22–24). With respect to "rape," they are not. Wives cannot be raped while betrothed women can. "Adultery" is the category of default for a wife, regardless of her intent.

The violence associated with שׁגל indicates that Deut 28:30, like 22:25–27 and 28–29, is rape rather than adultery. In all three cases, the degree of cooperation from the woman is irrelevant in the articulation of the law. In all three cases, the victim is the man to whom she belongs. In all three cases she is the sexual property which is wrested from the man.

8) *Virginity*. In Deut 22:13–23:1 four laws are devoted to issues pertaining to virginity. Virginity is a commodity which belongs to a man, husband or father, and to which he has rights. In DST, concern for virginity materializes as a sexuality problem where "liminal" women are present. That is, it is an issue with respect to betrothed and non-betrothed women, both of whom are of marriageable age.[13]

Liminal women are a place of special vulnerability for the man, with respect to his sexual property. Deuteronomy 22:13–21 is different from 22:23–29 because its infraction, which occurred before marriage, is discovered only after marriage. The law demonstrates that the husband's rights to this virginity are retroactive.

In all four laws, however, virginity before marriage is a prized value. It is a "state" to which the father and husband have rights. The woman's status as sexual property of the man is especially apparent in these laws. Protection of that property is the primary concern.

---

13.   This is evidenced by the fact that the women are betrothed or by the fact that the non-betrothed woman becomes betrothed as part of the remedy for rape.

9) *Slaves and Captives*. No laws concerning regulation of sex with a שפחה occur in DST. However, one law (Deut 21:10–14) regulating sex with captive women of war does occur. Sex is the final part of the process which transforms the female captive into an Israelite wife. This sex is not considered "rape," even by ancient conceptuality. It is not considered a violation of any kind. As consummation of the marriage process, it accords certain minimal rights to the woman which cannot be taken from her. While the man does not have the right to sell such a woman or her sexuality after completing the marriage process, he does have the right to end the marriage.

The issue of primary concern is to facilitate, on behalf of the man, the acquisition and disposal of female sexual property under unusual circumstances.

10) *Summary*. With respect to the above nine topics, the configuration of property and purity components in the laws of DST varies. The slight nuances in the conceptualization of women constructed by these variations are less than in LST. In every law of DST, protection of woman's sexuality as property is the primary concern. She is focalized as property with an implied status as agent who must protect that property. In every law of DST, both the purity components and the property components serve the property concern.

In every incest case, for example (Deut 23:1; 27:20, 22–23; 25:5–10), the property component is operative. Protection of woman's sexuality as property is the primary concern even though incest per se is largely a classificatory issue. All the texts (5:18; 22:22, 23–24) treating adultery also protect woman's sexuality as property. In both the rape and virginity laws (22:13–23:1; 28:30) emphasis is on the man as the party injured by the illicit sex act. Woman's sexuality is the property of the father, husband or husband-to-be. The primary interest of the war-bride law (21:10–14) is to facilitate acquisition and disposal of woman as sexual property, even though this law accords the woman certain minimal rights. In 22:20–21, the harlotry of the woman is an offense against both her father and her husband, since her sexuality belongs to them.

No law regulates menstruation. No law regulates homosexuality. And no law regulates female bestiality.

In every law of DST, including Deut 23:18–19 and the male bestiality law (27:21), proprietary issues are the primary concern.

b. *Genre Features*.
1) *Series*. Only two series occur in DST, one of which consists of casuistic laws as well as a single apodictic law (Deut 22:13–23:1); and the other of which consists of curses (27:20–23).

The series of curses, Deut 27:20–23, pertain to incestuous relations with respect to women who are the property of the *pater familias* and with respect to animals who are the property of the some man. The series of casuistic laws, 22:13–23:1, are concerned, largely but not exclusively, with infractions disturbing virginity. All the women of both laws are connected to men by marriage, betrothal or the father–daughter bond. The sexuality of each is thus the property of some man.

However, Deut 22:13–23:1 grades the infractions, thus revealing a conceptuality which values property within a range of property arrangements. Deuteronomy 27:20–23, on the other hand, has chosen only one class of property arrangements with respect to women: those belonging to the *pater familias*. A gradation might be surmised with respect to the laws regulating women in this list. However, in the series as a whole the prohibition concerning the animal is problematic for a gradation.

Both series share the value of woman as property of the man. Protection of that property is the primary concern.

2) *Properties of Primary Concern.* The laws of DST have varied interests in property connected with sexual intercourse.

Deuteronomy 5:18 is interested in the infraction that breaches the sexual property demarcated by the bonds of marriage. Deuteronomy 22:13–23:1 is interested in the same kind of infraction. It expands this interest to include a variety of degrees of bonds with respect to marriage, as well as the situation in which no marriage bond exists. In addition, it includes laws treating an infraction before marriage (22:13–21) and an infraction after marriage (23:1), each of which abrogate respectively the retroactive and proactive rights which these marriages have established for the husbands. Deuteronomy 21:10–14 provides for the rights to establish and dissolve the marriage bond as well as the sexual rights which go along with it. Deuteronomy 25:5–10 seeks to establish a sexual bond on the basis of a prior marriage bond for the purpose of establishing the progeny of the man of the prior marriage unit. The curses of 27:20, 23 treat "incestuous adultery." Deuteronomy 28:30 treats breach of a betrothal bond. In every one of these cases, varying degrees of bonds, which give men rights to use of a woman's sexuality, are at issue.

One other kind of bond is represented in DST. It is the father–daughter bond in Deut 22:20–21, 22:28–29 and 27:22. While the incest component is undoubtedly present in the latter, as exhibited by use of the identifying reference "his sister, daughter of his father and daughter of his mother," that incest component serves the author's property concern. In 22:20–21 and 22:28–29 the incest component is absent. Deuteronomy 22:28–29 is about forced sex, a non-issue in 27:22. Deuteronomy 22:20–21 is about a daughter's loss of virginity prior to marriage and her attempt at deception, non-issues as well in 27:22. Nevertheless, all three laws concern abrogation of the father–daughter bond. This bond gives the father different rights of access to sexuality than the marriage bond gives to the husband. Specifically, it gives rights to remuneration in exchange for the daughter's sexuality at marriage and it gives honor.

The bestiality law, Deut 27:21, is also an exception because its interest is in something other than the bond which ties a woman to a man. Nevertheless, selection-of-laws and structure demonstrate that the classificatory component serves the property component in this law as well.

Thus, in every law of DST except 27:21, interest is in the woman's sexuality as property, defined by either the marriage/betrothal bond or the father–daughter bond. In 27:21, other property concerns related to sexuality are paramount.

3) *Deuteronomic/Deuteronomistic.* All but three texts fall within the Deuteronomic Writings. The three texts which fall outside it are Deut 5:18; 27:20–23 and 28:30. This demarcation corresponds to other generic demarcations. All laws within the Deuteronomic Writings are casuistic except 23:1. The deuteronomistic laws are either apodictic or they are curses. They also contain the incest series and the bestiality law. They are thus dissimilar from the deuteronomic laws in several ways.

Both the deuteronomic and the deuteronomistic laws, however, concern a variety of bonds tying women to men and giving the men varying rights to their sexuality.

c. *Marginalization, Objectification and Focalization.*
1) *Marginalization.* In each of the DST woman is marginalized. Her marginalization is, to some extent, ameliorated in each text by the fact that she is also addressed by the lawgiver, albeit implicitly.

This statement needs to be explained with respect to two of the more difficult texts. First, the amelioration of woman's marginalization is apparent in Deut 21:10–14 since the female captive has some forced "minimal responsibility" in the mourning ritual, but more importantly because her rights are protected once she becomes a wife. She is implicitly addressed since the law accords her those "minimal rights." For who will ensure that her minimal rights are protected if she herself is not apprised of them? However, her forced "minimal responsibility" is not a *real* responsibility since the law does not presume she will act of her own accord to accomplish it. The law, instead, presumes her captor will compel her to accomplish this "responsibility." She has no choice. Second, woman's marginalization in 25:5–10 becomes apparent only when the codification of provisions for the fulfillment of the destinies of the man and the woman are examined. The codification for the man is explicit. For the woman it is implicit.

Thus, in each of the DST woman is marginalized.

2) *Objectification.* In every case of DST where the sex act is depicted, woman is objectified. In one instance the sex act is not depicted: Deut 22:21. It refers to harlotry. Woman is placed in the grammatical subject slot of this law. The man with whom she performs the illicit sex is absent from the text. In at least two other laws she is the subject with respect to non-sexual acts: Deut 25:5–10 and 21:10–14.

3) *Focalization.*
a) *Agent.* In no law of DST is the woman focalized as agent.

b) *Property.* In Deut 21:10–14, woman is focalized as property. She has no status as agent, except under one possible contingency of the law: divorce. The primary concern of the law is to facilitate the acquisition and disposal of the woman as wife and sexual property. This legislation enables the man to do what he needs to do to get what he wants to get. The actions prescribed by the law, ensuring the success of the primary concern, are all done to the woman. She is not expected to act as agent with respect to this primary concern. That is, she is not expected to follow the law. The captor *causes* her to follow the law. She is expected to follow his instructions and directives. She is reasonably expected to follow these instructions because her survival, as something more than a captive, requires it. In this way she is both "implicitly addressed by the law" and "not focalized as agent by the law." In this respect, 21:10–14 is singular among the laws of DST and LST.

In 27:20–23 and 28:30, woman is also focalized as property with a *possible* attribution of presumed agency by way of her possible implication as addressee.

c) *Agent and Property*. The remaining laws focalize woman as property, with implied agency: Deut 5:18; 22:13–23:1; 25:5–10. Her property status is explicit. Her agency in each case is implied. In the rape laws of 22:25–29, a minimal agency is inferred through her implication as addressee. Her responsibility to uphold the laws of 22:25–29 is apparent in the implied warning against placing herself in a position leading to rape.

As property, the woman or her sexuality is the thing each of the laws is concerned to protect. As agent, the woman is responsible to protect that property which is coterminous with herself, specifically her body.

d. *Synthesis*. Property and purity components are present in varying degrees in the laws of DST. Woman is focalized as property, most often with a status of implied agent. Nevertheless, the primary concern is always protection of properties related to sexual intercourse. Furthermore, no laws regulate menstruation, homosexuality or female bestiality, in which the classificatory component is generally dominant.

In all the laws that property is the sexuality of the woman. In Deut 28:30 her agent status is *possibly* implied. The same can be said for the incest laws of 27:20–23. In the laws of 22:25–29, where rape is violence against the man to whom the violated woman belongs, her agency is implied by the addressee signal. In 21:10–14, which facilitates the acquisition and disposal of sexual property under unusual circumstances, the woman is focalized exclusively as property. In this last law, woman is not responsible for obeying the prohibitions in the usual way. She is *forced* to obey them. Everywhere else, however (5:18; 22:13–24; 23:1; 25:5–10), woman is focalized as property with implied agency. She is both the one who must protect and that which is protected.

Deuteronomy 25:5–10 is singular because it has to do with the rights of a dead man exercised through his brother. Woman's agency is heightened in this law by her role in the חֲלִצָה ceremony. Outside this ceremony, her status as non-agent and property is prominent.

In Deut 21:10–14 and 25:5–10, failure to perform sex is the infraction. In 25:5–10, the victim of such failure is the dead husband. In 21:10–14, the victim is the woman herself. The laws allow these victimizations with minimal limitations.

In all texts of DST, woman is, to varying degrees, marginalized and objecti-fied. The concern is always regulation of property in connection with sexual intercourse. As such, woman is focalized as property, with implied agency. The interest that DST have in property connected with sexual intercourse is varied among the laws. Nevertheless, the *presence* of such interest as a primary con-cern is constant. Woman, as agent, must protect the proprietary interest, which is coterminous with herself.

3. *LST and DST*

The laws of DST divide into a greater number of groups than those of LST with respect to the items they intend to regulate in connection with sexual intercourse.

Both LST and DST have laws which intend only to prohibit illicit sexual intercourse. Both groups have laws which intend both to prohibit sexual inter-course and to mediate the effects of illicit sexual intercourse. However, DST also has laws that mediate the problem of failure to perform sexual intercourse. In addition, it has one law that wishes the victimization, by way of harm to sexual property, on the man who fails to keep Yhwh's commands (28:30).

The *effects* of illicit intercourse, which LST and DST mediate, also differ. LST mediate impurity. DST mediate social problems, often by removing the sources of the property "dispute," including the property itself, from the com-munity.

In short, the concern in all groups of DST laws is proprietary while the concern in all groups of LST laws is classificatory. Woman is agent who must protect the classificatory concern in LST. In DST her implied agency must protect the property of the man. She is the property itself.

a. *Nine Topics Occurring in the Sex Laws.*

1) *Menstruation*. DST and LST differ in their concerns for menstruation. Whereas the concern for menstruation in LST is exhibited in no less than three texts (Lev 15:18, 24, 33b; 18:19; 20:18), with at least one-half of a chapter devoted to the subject, the concern in DST is non-existent. Not even in Deut 27:20–23, where bestiality appears, is menstruation visible. Thus, the significant variations in the treatment of menstruants with respect to sexual intercourse all occur in LST.

If DST's concern is primarily for regulation of property, then the absence of menstruation is unsurprising.

2) *Incest*. Both DST and LST have laws regulating incest. The range of incest relations regulated in LST is much wider than the range in DST. This is unsurprising since incest, in general, has enfolded within it a necessary and pronounced classificatory component, unconnected to the property component.

In DST (Deut 23:1; 27:20, 22–23; 28:5–10), incestuous relations exclusively with women connected to men are regulated. In LST (Lev 18:6–18; 20:11–12, 14, 17–21), relations with both women connected to men and women uncon-nected to men are regulated. Furthermore, only incestuous relationships involv-ing exclusively women connected to the *pater familias* are regulated in DST. In

LST incestuous relations with women belonging to brothers, sons and uncles are also of concern.

In addition, the brother's wife is treated as an incestuous relation in LST with no explicit specification concerning the husband's status as dead or alive. In DST it is treated as a non-incestuous relation if the husband is dead. In fact, that relation in DST is treated as an obligation, establishing the dead husband's property rights. The brother/sister-in-law relation thus illustrates graphically the difference in intent between LST and DST. Where proprietary concerns are foremost, the incestuous nature of the relation is forgotten. Where classificatory concerns are foremost, the property obligations are forgotten.

In every case in DST the classificatory issues, necessarily connected to incest, recede in their service to the property concern which is the primary concern of DST. In LST, the property component, which is necessary to relations with women connected to men, recedes in service to the classificatory concern, which is the primary concern of LST.

3) *Adultery*. The range of laws dealing with adultery is wider in DST than in LST. This is unsurprising since adultery has enfolded within it a necessary property component.

A divergence between the two groups of laws shows up in vocabulary. Leviticus 20:10 shares the word נאף with Deut 5:18. This is all that is shared. The "incestuous adultery"[14] laws of Lev 18 use the גלה phrase while the adultery law of Lev 18:20 uses נתן. Deuteronomy 22:22, 23–24 and the "incestuous adultery" laws of Deut 27:20, 23, by contrast, use שכב.

Adultery is explicitly addressed in LST only in Lev 18:20 and 20:10, both laws which regulate sex with the neighbor's wife. The adultery component is necessarily implied in any relationship with any woman who belongs to a man. However, in LST, that component, even in laws regulating relations with a neighbor's wife, recedes in its service to the classificatory concern, which is its primary concern.

DST, by contrast, regulate a *variety* of kinds of relationships in which women belong to men. Not only is their interest in this matter explicit, they are also more sophisticated with respect to the distinction, they draw between married women (Deut 22:22) and betrothed women (22:23–24) who engage in illicit sex. The group of laws which have primary interest in property concerns, DST, thus delineates an extra distinction concerning the *degree* to which a woman belongs to a man. The group of laws which have a primary interest in classificatory issues, LST, leaves such distinctions aside.

4) *Homosexuality*. DST lack any law regulating homosexuality. LST, on the other hand, have two such laws (Lev 18:22; 20:13). Since homosexuality does not involve women's sexual property, its absence in DST, is unsurprising. Its presence in LST is equally unsurprising.

---

14. By "incestuous adultery" I mean merely incest in which a marriage bond is abrogated as well as the "blood" bond.

5) *Bestiality*. Both LST and DST contain laws regulating bestiality. The laws of LST (Lev 18:23; 20:15–16) are careful to distinguish between female and male bestiality. Such careful distinctions are entirely absent from DST. In fact, the law of DST (Deut 27:21) is aimed at the man *alone*. The proprietary interests of DST fail to motivate the author to make the gender distinctions which interest the classificatory aficionado who wrote LST.

If the property component within the bestiality law is significant, as argued in the above exegesis, then this state of affairs suggests that foremost in the mind of the writer of DST is the harm that one man can do to another man through the latter's property. This emphasis, of course, is lacking in LST.

6) *Prostitution*. One law in DST and two in LST refer to prostitution or harlotry. The three laws are similar in that they all concern sex outside the context of marriage and none of them explicitly depict the sex act. In all three laws, prostitution pertains to daughters.

In all three laws the male sexual partner(s) of the woman is/are absent. The infraction, although requiring both men and women for its consummation, is conceptualized primarily in Lev 21:9 and Deut 22:21 as an infraction by the woman against her father. In Lev 19:29, it is an infraction forced on the *woman* by her father. Thus, of those individuals participating in the sex act, the woman alone is the significant vehicle of the infraction.

Leviticus 21:9 concerns the harm that a prostituting daughter does to her priest-father's sanctity. In Deut 22:21, no reference is made to compromise of the father's sanctity or even purity. נבלה is used to emphasize the deceptive nature of the daughter's behavior. From the context, the reader can infer that the victims are actually two, the father and the husband. But the father may also in some way be responsible. It happened in his house. He married off a non-virgin to another Israelite male. The stoning takes place at his door. The wrong done to the husband is loss of virginity to which he has retroactive rights. The wrong done to the father, likewise, has to do with rights to virginity. Her virginity at marriage brings him property in the form of brideprice. Furthermore, his honor, and to some degree the future security and success of his family, depends upon her virginity. Thus, the difference between these two laws with respect to women is precisely the difference between the classificatory and property concerns which constitute the differing primary concerns of LST and DST.

The final law, Lev 19:29, concerns a father's use of his daughter's sexuality for prostitution. The issue, explicitly stated in the law, is her defilement and the defilement of the land. Although the law intends to limit the father's rights to use of her sexuality, that limitation serves the primary concern which is classificatory.

The difference with respect to treatment of women in laws regulating prostitution in LST and DST is, therefore, the difference between classificatory concerns and property concerns.

7) *Rape*. No law in LST regulates rape or issues related to rape. The absence of rape in LST is a function of the way rape is conceived in ancient Israel. Rape is an abrogation of the rights of a father, fiancé or husband. It is violence by one man against another man through harm to the latter's sexual property. Therefore, its absence in LST and its presence in DST (Deut 22:25–29; 28:30) is consistent with their primary concern.

8) *Virginity*. Virginity is also absent from LST as a concern, while nearly an entire chapter is devoted to it in DST (Deut 22:13–21, 23–29). In all of Leviticus, virginity is an issue only with respect to the marriage of priests and the death of their virgin sisters. Whereas the father–daughter relationship is of interest in LST with respect to prostitution, in DST it is of interest with respect to virginity.

Although virginity would seem to be an implied component of the two harloting laws of Leviticus (Lev 19:24; 21:9), virginity per se is not highlighted or designated as an issue even in these laws. However, in Deut 22:13–21, the relationship of harlotry and virginity is explicit. Moreover, their relationship is made explicit in this text with respect to daughters. The author has stated that the loss of the woman's virginity before marriage is harlotry (זנה). The *behavior* is harlotry; the *result* is loss of virginity. Loss of virginity, although related, is an issue different from harlotry even when the harlotry addressed is the harlotry of a daughter. In DST, *loss of virginity* as a result of harlotry is the issue.

The vulnerability that virginity represents to a man who has a daughter, wife or fiancé in DST is of no concern to LST.

9) *Slaves and Captives*. LST and DST each have a law regulating sex with a woman whose status as property is lower than the average Israelite wife's status. In LST (Lev 19:20–22), that woman is a שפחה. In DST (Deut 21:10–14), that woman is a female captive of war.

The interests in these two women are, of course, different. DST is interested in facilitating the acquisition and disposal of the war captive by a man. In the process of facilitating her acquisition, the law also raises her status, a status which, to some degree, the law protects. The acquisition of the woman as a wife involves an act which would be defined as rape by modern standards. By the standards of DST, it is an entirely legitimate act.

In LST, on the other hand, the sexual property is more ambiguously defined. The possibility that the woman's status might be raised creates the ambiguity which justifies the absence of the death penalty. In short, one man takes sexual property ambiguously defined as belonging to another man. However, the primary concern of LST leaves aside the property issue and focuses on remediation of the perpetrator who has contracted impurity as a result of his act. The woman is, in fact, forgotten.

Thus, the difference in treatment of and interest in the women of these two laws is a graphic illustration of the influence of the differing primary concerns of LST and DST.

10) *Summary*. In summary, LST and DST differ in their emphasis on the purity and property components of the sexual infractions connected with the nine topics. As a result, they differ, with respect to these nine topics, in their treatment of women as well.

LST, which de-emphasize the property component, lack laws regulating rape and virginity in which the property component is necessarily pronounced. DST, which de-emphasize the purity component, lack laws regulating menstruation, homosexuality and female bestiality in which the purity component is necessarily pronounced. LST, with their emphasis on purity, regulate a wider range of incest infractions. DST, with their emphasis on property, regulate a wider range of adultery infractions. The emphasis in the prostitution laws of LST (Lev 19:29; 21:9) is classificatory. By contrast, the emphasis in the "prostitution" law of DST (Deut 22:21) is proprietary.

LST and DST each have a law regulating sex with a woman whose status as property is lower than the average Israelite wife's status. In LST, the woman is a שפחה. Her status as property recedes in importance before the author's concern for the welfare of the male perpetrator, a classificatory concern. In DST the woman is a war bride. Sex is the consummation of the process that facilitates acquisition and use of the woman as the sexual property of the man. It transforms her from captive to wife and accords her minimal rights. However, the law also establishes the man's right to dispose of her. The primary concern is proprietary.

Thus, with respect to the nine topics, a clear pattern establishes itself in LST and DST concerning the purity components and the property components constituting the infractions. LST emphasize the purity component. DST emphasize the property component. The differing emphases give rise to differing treatments of woman. In DST, she is the property of primary concern. The agency she accrues must protect that coterminus property. In LST, her status as property is not of primary concern. As agent, she must protect the classificatory system which constitutes her world.

b. *Genre Features.*
1) *Series*. DST and LST each have two series of laws: Lev 18; 20:10–21 and Deut 22:13–23:1; 27:20–23.

The laws of Lev 18 as well as the law of Deut 23:1 are apodictic, whereas the laws of Lev 20:10–21 and Deut 22:13–29 are casuistic. The laws of Deut 27:20–23 are curses.

These curses treat incestuous relations and bestiality as do the laws of Lev 18; 20:10–21 and Deut 23:1. Unlike the Leviticus series, however, Deut 27:20–23 and 23:1 lack laws regulating homosexuality, acts with respect to Molek, sex with a menstruant and sex with the neighbor's wife. The only incestuous relations they regulate are those with women connected to men. In fact, every woman of both DST series belongs to a man either as daughter or as wife or as fiancée. Both LST series, in contrast to the DST series, regulate a variety of sexual relations including sexual relations which do not involve combinations of men and women and sexual relations which do not involve women. Further-more, in the bestiality curse of Deut 27:21, the property component is para-mount, whereas the purity component is paramount in the bestiality laws (Lev 18:23; 20:15–16) of the LST series.

In addition, only the laws of the DST series are careful to regulate the point of greatest vulnerability to a man with respect to sexual property: virginity. The LST series leaves this issue aside.

Both Lev 20:10–21 and Deut 22:13–29 have penalties which encompass both men and women. Furthermore, these two series also grade their infractions. The gradation of Deut 22:13–23:1, however, is strictly a function of a valuation based on the marriage bond, a property issue. By contrast, this valuation is only one of multiple factors structuring the gradation of Lev 20:10–21, including a factor depending on the writing process itself.

These configurations reveal the influence of the differing primary concerns of LST and DST and the differing conceptualizations of women which they shape.

2) *Property and Boundaries of Primary Concern.* A comparison between the primary concern of LST and the primary concern of DST is facilitated if we "translate" the property concerns of DST and the purity concerns of LST to the same genre of concerns. If we understand the property concern as a subset of the wider range of classificatory concerns, this is possible.[15]

When the concerns of the two groups are compared as subsets of classifica-tory concerns, then a significant difference in focus appears. Moving from LST to DST, a "shift"[16] becomes apparent from the boundary per se to what the boundary demarcates. DST look away from the boundary, forget the boundary as it were, and become obsessed with what happens to the "thing" inside the boundary, in this case the woman's sexuality.

DST are concerned to protect this "thing," which belongs to one man, from other men. Thus, DST value a man's security vis-à-vis other men by the sex infractions it regulates. The system which DST picture is a system consisting of men and their property in relation to one another, governed by rules which protect the discreteness or security of these individuals vis-à-vis one another.[17] Within this system, woman as sexual property is an extension of the man. As such, her sexuality is never protected from him. That conceptuality has no reference in this system. However, her sexuality is protected from other men. With this focus, she *becomes* exclusively her sexuality. With respect to the system as a whole, she becomes invisible. Although she is invisible, she never-theless has an active part to play in the system. She is like the fence on any man's property guarding the "thing" which might be stolen. In this case the "thing" she guards is coterminous with herself. It is not a third entity. She is at once agent and property. Her agency, with respect to sexuality, however, cannot

15. See the "Introduction" to this study.
16. I am not implying that LST is prior by use of this word; rather, I am simply signifying the difference between the two groups of texts.
17. Houston, *Purity*, 226–27.

go beyond that program which serves the man and makes her invisible. She becomes visible when one man threatens another man's sexual property.

The system LST protect, on the other hand, is a system consisting of many entities, including men and women, all of which must be maintained in a certain order and arrangement of discreteness. The laws govern and maintain this order. Both man and woman, whose relationship is asymmetrical, are agents responsible for maintaining this order, consisting of a particular configuration of human and other relationships. The exception is the שפחה and, in certain circumstances, the daughter. Many of these relationships belong together in certain spheres called marriage or families or clans. The order of the system configures these spheres in a variety of overlapping arrangements. Within these spheres, both the man and the woman are visible. She is not primarily an extension of him. She is not her sexuality any more than he is his sexuality. I believe that this is the phenomenon Biale notices when she states that whereas the laws of adultery do not apply equally to men and women, the laws of incest do.[18] The woman, as agent, must, along with the man, guard a third entity which is not coterminous with herself: the order of the classificatory system. The classificatory "distraction" prevails even when agency is absent as in the "story" of the שפחה.

c. *Marginalization, Objectification and Focalization.*

1) *Marginalization.* Woman is marginalized in all the laws of LST and DST. The author addresses the man explicitly. For the most part only subtle indicators, including the logic of the text, suggest that woman is also implicitly addressed.

Since ameliorated marginalization means that, whereas the man is explicitly addressed by the author, the woman is implicitly addressed, it also means that she is an implied agent. Thus, in every case but Deut 21:10–14, which is an exception to the rule, amelioration of her marginalization means her accrual to agency in her focalization. In Deut 21, under the contingency of rejection by her warrior rapist/husband, she gains the agency of a free woman.[19]

2) *Objectification.* Woman's objectification is also fairly constant throughout LST and DST. With two exceptions, wherever the sex act is explicitly depicted she is objectified. These two exceptions are the bestiality laws of Lev 18:23 and 20:16, where she is *subject* in contradistinction to an animal. However, she does occasionally appear as subject in other places in the sex texts where the sex act is not explicitly depicted. And in one instance she is the subject of a sexual gesture preceding the sex act (Lev 20:17).

In three texts she is both subject and object. In Deut 21:10–14, woman is the subject of some of the actions constituting her mourning ritual. Otherwise she is the object in this law. In Deut 22:13–21, the newly married wife is portrayed as the grammatical object of various acts including the sex act. In addition,

---

18.   Biale, *Women*, 183.
19.   See n. 41 above under discussion of Deut 25:5–10 (Chapter 12). This may have been a tough role to live in ancient Israel.

however, in v. 21 she is the subject of an act described as נְבָלָה. This law, which refers to harlotry, does not depict the sex act. The male sex partner(s) is absent. In Lev 21:9, again, the sex act is not depicted and the male sex partner(s) is/are absent. The woman is the grammatical subject in this law, which is the only law that portrays her as having the power to harm a man without his cooperation. In Deut 25:5–10, she is *subject* in the חֲלִצָה ritual.

Nevertheless, throughout LST and DST, with the exception of the bestiality laws, wherever the sex act is depicted, woman is the object.

3) *Focalization.*

a) *Agent.* Three texts focalize woman as agent: Lev 15:18, 24, 33b; 18; 20:10–21. This qualifying arrangement is absent from DST.

In the first text, pronounced (Lev 15:18, 24, 33b) gender equity with respect to her focalization as agent is supported by the structure of the text. Her accrual to agency, in the form of responsibility to the primary concern, fails to neutralize her subordination and circumscription as demonstrated by point-of-view and language-depicting-the-sex-act. Nevertheless, she exhibits a radical form of agency. Leviticus 15 concerns the natural impurity of men and women. Woman's relationship to this concern is as agent responsible for guarding against discharge impurity. Leviticus 15:18, 24, 33b is singular among all the laws of LST in its equal attribution of this form of agency to the man and woman.

In Lev 18 and 20:10–21, the remaining two texts, the primary concern is also classificatory. The laws guard an order defined by a variety of factors. Woman's relationship to this primary concern is as agent responsible for maintaining this order. Two laws in these series, Lev 18:20 and 20:10, which regulate adultery, necessarily have within them a property component. However, within the context of their series, the property component of these adultery laws recedes in its service to the classificatory concern. The same may be said for any of the incest laws in which a marriage bond is operative. The agency qualification can be inferred from the addressee and other signals.

Thus, in three laws of LST, woman is focalized as agent. She is responsible for maintaining the purity system which constitutes the text's primary concern.

b) *Property.* In one law, Deut 21:10–14, woman is focalized as property with no implied agency. In two laws, Lev 19:20–22 and 19:29, where her property status is essential to commission of the infraction, she also lacks implied agency. In these latter two laws she is focalized respectively as "forgotten" and "valued."

In the first law woman is a captive of war. The law accords her no responsibility to the rules it establishes. All action is done to her. She is even *caused* to do the mourning ritual.

In Lev 19:20–22 woman is a שִׁפְחָה. Again the law accords her no responsibility to the rules it establishes. The absence of the death penalty, in fact, underscores this point. Her status as property, like the war captive, is lower than a wife in Israel. Her status gives the man the power to commit the infraction. It is not, however, the primary concern. Remediation of the impurity of the male perpetrator is the issue. The woman is forgotten, along with her "owner(s)."

In Lev 19:29, the property component is present because of the father–daughter relationship. It also contributes to the infraction. However, although it gives the man the power to commit the infraction, as in Lev 19:20–22, it is not the primary concern of the law. The primary concern is the defilement of the land and the defilement of the daughter caused by the infraction.

Thus, in the laws of DST where woman is property lacking implied agency, she is a *war captive* with a status lower than an Israelite wife. In LST she is a *daughter* with a status lower than an Israelite wife. However, in LST, although her status contributes to the infraction, which is of primary concern because it gives the man the power to commit it, it is not the primary concern. In both laws of LST, in which woman is only property, the primary concern is classificatory.

Thus, woman's *status* as property in Lev 19:20–22 and 19:29 receives a different focus from the *status* of woman in Deut 21:10–14 and other laws of DST, in which the woman's sexuality as property is the primary concern. In Lev 19:20–22 she is "forgotten." In Lev 19:29 she is "valued" vis-à-vis her "owner." In Deut 21:10–14, her status is the lowest possible for all women in ancient Israel. The law alters that status and under certain contingencies grants her a form of legal agency.

c) *Agent and Property.* Five laws from DST focalize woman as property with a form of implied agency: Deut 5:18; 22:13–23:1; 25:5–10; 27:20–23; 28:30. Three laws from LST focalize woman as agent with property status essential to commission of infraction: Lev 18:20; 20:10; 21:9.

In the two laws from DST, woman's implied agency is only suggested by her possible implied addressee status: Deut 27:20–23 and 28:30. Her focalization as property is overt. In Deut 5:18 and 22:20–21, 25–26; 23:1, her agency is implicit, but it is made certain by her implied addressee status. In Deut 25:5–10, her focalization as agent in the חֲלִצָה ritual is overt because of her participation in the remedy. In Deut 22:13–19, 22–24, it is overt because of her participation in the infraction. In all five laws woman's sexuality as property is protected from other men. Deuteronomy 28:30, which does not protect her sexuality, nevertheless demonstrates a valuation of such protection by wishing its abrogation upon the breaker of Yhwh's commands.

The conceptuality of the protection of woman's sexuality from the man to whom she belongs is non-existent in all of LST and DST with the exception of Lev 19:29. In DST, the concept is unknown. In LST, even if the concept were known, it would be irrelevant except for the kind of scenario that Lev 19:29 represents.

In DST, woman must protect property coterminous with her body: her sexuality. In the three laws from LST the property component deriving from the wife or father–daughter relationship recedes in service to the purity concern. The sanctity of the priest-father whom the daughter, as agent, has the power to harm without his cooperation is protected. Marriage, one of the categorical spheres of the ontology of P, is also protected. Woman's sexuality as property is a non-issue.

d. *Synthesis.* Property and purity components are present in varying degrees in the laws of LST and DST. They configure differently throughout the two groups. In LST, the primary concern is always classificatory. In DST, the primary concern is always proprietary. LST and DST share a conceptualization of women as circumscribed by and subordinate to men. While marginalization and objectification of woman remain fairly constant throughout LST and DST, her focalization differs dramatically. That is, the expectation the author/text has for the woman with respect to its primary concern is significantly different between the two groups of texts.

Three out of six texts in LST focalize the woman as agent, who must protect the purity system of her world: (1) Lev 15:18, 24, 33b; (2)18:6–19, 21–23; (3) 20:11–21. Two of the laws of LST, in which woman's status is respectively legal property and "daughter-property," focalize her as "forgotten" and "valued": 19:20–22 and 19:29. Three texts in LST focalize woman as agent with status essential to the commission of the infraction: 18:20; 20:10; 21:9. The property component here is important for the same reason it is important in Lev 19:20–22 and 19:29. It recedes in significance in service to the purity concern. In LST, the woman's status as property is important only because it is one of the contributing factors to the infraction. It is not the primary concern, which is classificatory.

By contrast, in six out of the seven DST laws in which the woman is focalized as property with implied agency, the property component is both a contributing factor to the infraction and the primary concern. Woman's sexuality is protected vis-à-vis other men. She is expected to protect this "thing" that is coterminous with her own body from other men. It is never protected from the man to whom she belongs and no law prescribes that she stand guard over it vis-à-vis him. Agency appears in the text in one of three ways: as *possible* implied addressee, as implied addressee, as active participant in the infraction or remedy. In Deut 22:23–29 it would appear that the woman lacks implied agency, but in these laws, where "true" consent/non-consent is a non-issue, she is an implied addressee and expected, at the most, to uphold the law and, at the least, to pay attention. In Deut 21:10–14 she lacks real agency, except under one contingency of the law.

Where woman's sexuality is the primary issue in DST she is always focalized as property. In all cases in DST where her status is above that of a female captive of war, her focalization as agent is also implied. In LST, woman's sexuality as property is a *contributing* factor to the infraction which is the primary concern in three laws: Lev 19:20–22, 29; 21:9. However, that aspect of her sexuality is never the primary concern. In the two adultery laws within the series, 18:20 and 20:10, the property component is even less a contributing factor. The expectation of woman in all laws of LST is to serve as agent to protect the purity system.

In LST, laws concerning rape and virginity are absent. They are non-issues. In DST, laws concerning menstruation, homosexuality and female bestiality are absent. They are non-issues. LST regulate more variety with respect to incest. DST regulate more variety with respect to adultery.

These distributions correspond to the difference in the primary concerns of LST and DST.

Part V

CONCLUSION

Chapter 16

CONCLUSION

A. *Woman*

1. Personhood

Several feminist scholars have observed that the biblical text may accord to women rights and responsibilities that vanish when the focus moves to reproductive issues.[1] Shreds and aspects of agency, manifesting in other arenas, shut down in the presence of sexuality. This study finds that a divide exists even within the realm of sexuality when the focus is "distracted" from property to ontology.

Across the social field of the world of the ancient text a mix of agencies, subordinations and conscriptions plays out depending upon class, status and gender. That mix is the presented construction of those who had the power to write the text and to cause it to endure. Anderson calls the construction violence. She states: "In the legal corpus, violence against women has been seen to result either from a law's act of omission or commission."[2] Hens-Piazza states: "Law is a discourse of male power. Moreover, the legal system as objective process rendering just judgment and punishment shows itself to be a cover for a violence that maintains male domination."[3] Pressler states: "These texts do what rape does. They eliminate women's will from consideration and erase women's right to sexual integrity."[4] Washington states: "The laws might be called 'rape laws,' not because they provide sanction against sexual assault, but because they institute and regulate rape so that men's proprietary sexual access to women is compromised as little as possible."[5]

Washington's judgments apply easily to DST. Rape *as we conceive it in the twenty-first century* is a non-issue in that body of texts. The conceptuality is "unknown." For the same reason, in LST rape as violence done to the woman is absent as well. "Rape," as violence done to the male owner of female sexuality, is as close as DST are capable of getting to the conceptuality of sex forced upon

---

1. Frymer-Kensky, "Deuteronomy," 59a; Pressler, *View of Women*, 91; Wegner, *Chattel*, 19
2. Anderson, *Women, Ideology, and Violence*, 9.
3. Hens-Piazza, "Terrorization, Sexualization, Maternalization," 167.
4. Pressler, "Sexual Violence," 103
5. Washington, "'Lest He Die,'" 211.

a woman. As such, DST have no concept of female consent/non-consent.[6] But in LST, even DST's "truncated" conceptuality of "rape" cannot be found because of a distraction to other concerns. While the issue of "rape," an assault upon the male owner of female sexuality, lacking the conceptuality of female consent or non-consent, is absent from LST, "violence"[7] through the vehicle of point-of-view and language-depicting-the-sex-act marginalizes and objectifies woman in that body of texts. LST like DST present a text exhibiting the gendered constructions of class, an institutionalized vehicle of violence against woman. In LST the vehicle is the שפחה and in DST the female war-captive. The adultery laws of both groups of texts exhibit the violence of "ownership" which gives the female sexuality exclusively to him and none of him to her, granting to him protection for *his* female sexuality and no protection to her for *her* sexuality from him. The latter conceptuality is, again, "unknown." Neither LST nor DST can escape judgments akin to these. Such judgments are an essential part of a responsible hermeneutic applied to texts, the use of which is as much a construction of power, and more often than not—violence, as was their composition.

This study, however, is exegetical and interested in all the many nuanced conceptualities that bear upon women in the text. It, therefore, calls attention to the *mix* of agencies and conscriptions that play out within the text through its presentation of powers, duties, rights and other factors, some of which must be mined below the surface of the text and which may appear, perhaps, minor or even trivial. They are not. As the mix is present in the social body of the text across divides such as class, status and nationality, so also it is present in the individual body, or "character" of the text. That is to say, the individual character *herself* manifests a mix. A divide in the presentation of that manifestation exists between LST and DST. Woman's focalization, that is, the female character's relationship to the author's primary concern, a mined feature of the text, demonstrates a difference in conceptuality with respect to the woman. An accrual to agency, a function of focalization, is patent in LST and latent in DST, where the property concern predominates.

Agency appears in one of three ways in the text: (1) as implied addressee; (2) as initiating/active participant in the infraction; (3) as responsible actor for the text's primary concern. In combination with the property attribution, that agency may recede or dominate depending upon the character's placement with respect to focalization. If the primary concern is classificatory, the woman may be focalized as agent, "forgotten" or "valued." Her status as property may or may not be essential to the commission of the infraction. If the primary concern is property, the woman is focalized as property with a variety of agency qualifications.

6.   This is the case, even if the author may have understood some semblance of such a concept, as suggested by Deut 22:24–27. If he had such a concept he did not incorporate it in these laws, the difference between v. 24 and vv. 25–27 notwithstanding. See the discussion above under Deut 22:24–27.

7.   See Anderson (*Women, Ideology, and Violence*, 3–10) for a discussion of this use of the word violence.

In the presence of the above-described violences of the text, the accrual to agency represented by focalization may seem minor or trivial. It is nevertheless present. The "distraction" that gives rise to it has the power to produce a text such as Lev 15, where incredible equity defies the gender constructions of the world from which it must have come.[8] It has the power to forget not only the female victim (Lev 19:20–22), which is no surprise, but also the male victim who is her owner. It brings to the surface of the text the power a woman has to harm a man without his cooperation (Lev 21:9). And while this is a demonization of her agency, that demonization is a pointer to male desires, exchanges, demands and fears in the deepest layers of the texts from which it is constructed.[9] LST, not DST, bring such a clue to the surface. The same power appears in the conceptual shift from Lev 15 to 18:19 and 20:18, where the woman has the power to defile the man with her discharge and the obverse is absent. In Lev 15 she has an agency equal to the man. In Lev 18:19 and 20:18 her agency is radicalized and demonized in its power.

In DST, focused on the protection of property, woman whose body is coterminous with that property is invisible. Her implied agency serves this invisibility. In LST, where attention is distracted to protection of an ontology, woman whose body is not coterminous with that ontology stands *with the man* in her responsibilities to the security of that ontology. She is *not* her sexuality with respect to the primary concern, any more than the man is his. In this respect, she becomes visible. This is the case, even though, at the same time, the adultery laws, point-of-view and the language-depicting-the-sex-act in LST all demonstrate that most of the considerable gender asymmetries of DST's conceptuality are not absent from LST. In the presence of distraction, however, they recede. Woman's objectification and marginalization are supratextual concepts common to all texts of LST and DST, testifying to her subordination and circumscription in the worlds of the text. Her focalization, with variation, is an intertextual concept, a function of the differing interest and concerns of the texts.

If we borrow from Wegner's model, which tracks *legal* powers, duties and rights, can we say in LST we are seeing a woman who appears to have more personhood than the woman in DST? In that moment where the "distraction" occurs, I believe we can. But to say this does not abrogate the ever-present circumscription and subordination, and particularly not the violence. Rather, it posits a mix of agencies and subordinations to the woman character of the text.

Woman has two related *duties* which appear in both groups of texts. These duties, however, receive different treatment within the two groups. First, the woman like the man, in both LST and DST, has a duty to uphold the law. In LST, however, the primary concern of the law is that the woman and the man protect a third entity—the classificatory system which constitutes their world. In DST, the concern is that the woman and the man protect the woman herself as the sexual property of the man. The concern is to protect something coterminous

---

8. Ellens, "Menstrual Impurity and Innovation," 29–44.
9. This project is outside the bounds of this study and must remain for future work.

with her body, belonging to the man. The gender asymmetry which characterizes this duty in DST is absent in LST.

Second, the woman in both LST and DST has a duty to reserve exclusive
sexual access for one man. The man does not have the reciprocal duty. The
writer of DST is obsessed with this exclusive access whereas the writer of LST
is not. Again, the gender asymmetry which characterizes the duty in DST is
absent in LST.

According to Wegner's model, duties are only one of three factors by which
an individual's personhood can be measured. *Powers* and *rights* are the other
two factors. Whereas in DST man's legal power to appropriate, exchange and
use woman's sexuality is prominent, in LST the legal power of either man or
woman to use the other receives no emphasis. Furthermore, whereas the rights
of men to exclusive use of female sexuality is prominent in DST, in LST,
although apparent in laws where the marriage bond or the father–daughter bond
is operative, such rights, again, receive little or no emphasis. In both groups of
texts woman receives no protection from her owner. This is so in DST because
the conceptuality is unknown. It is so in LST because of the "distraction."

Thus, examination of the legal categories of power, duties and rights, as
described by Wegner, and borrowed for literary study, suggests a higher level of
personhood for the woman-character in LST than in DST. In LST, her
focalization demonstrates an accrual of agency that does not occur in DST.

2. *Conceptualizations*

Since both purity and property *components* are present in both groups of texts,
the differing classificatory and proprietary *concerns* within LST and DST are a
result of different emphases on the purity and property components. These
different emphases bring to the fore different conceptualizations of women.

This does not mean that LST have reconceptualized the view of women in
DST or vice-versa. Rather, the evidence seems to suggest that two different conceptualizations of woman exist and that both authors of LST and DST know
both conceptualizations. The seed of each is in the other. However, in each group
of texts one of the conceptualizations is prominent. Thus, LST know about
woman as sexual property and DST know about woman as agent. Nevertheless,
in LST woman is focalized as agent and in DST woman is focalized as property.

That both authors know both conceptualizations and that one or the other of
the conceptualizations is prominent in each group of texts is an oblique demon-
stration of the fact that, just as the lives of actual women are multifaceted,
circumscribed though they may be, so also the lives of the women of ancient
Israel, as the writers perceived them, were multifaceted. Although woman's
circumscription and subordination, as demonstrated by her marginalization and
objectification, is a constant in the text, with respect to certain aspects of the
female character's life, a male writer assumes she had responsibilities, presumes
her capacity to act with initiative and perceives her as a moral agent with
independent duties.

Thus, LST manifest narrow spaces in which the woman was expected to "breathe." These narrow spaces in LST are particularly astonishing since the property component could theoretically have played a greater part in the construction of its purity concern than it did. The purity component pertaining to sexuality could have been conceived primarily or even exclusively as a property issue. It was not. Are these narrow spaces—barely grasped in LST and DST—akin to the genre of spaces that allow a woman to command her husband for the sake of securing progeny, to consider her own spiritual prowess equal to someone like Moses, to save a city, to judge a people, to lead an army in war, to kill the enemy, to conjure the dead for a frightened king, to prophecy concerning the fate of Israel?

In short, although woman's position as demonstrated by her marginalization and objectification in both LST and DST is undeniable, remarkable nuances also suggest that, with respect to different aspects of her life, she experienced different levels of personhood known to the authors of both LST and DST. Furthermore, even with respect to the narrow and confining subject area of sexual intercourse, such spaces exist.

We are all a complex of agencies and subordinations, legal and non-legal. Depending upon the "distraction" to which we are called, we "breathe" more or less easily. Constructions such as slavery, forced prostitution, capture and rape in war and male ownership of female sexuality narrow the distractions and suppress the breath. They limit the complex of agencies and squeeze a life to agonizing circumscriptions.

Nevertheless, where these constructions are absent and the distraction to ontology is present agency accrues to woman in the form of responsibility and duty to protect that distraction on a par with the man. She becomes visible for a moment in a man's world.

B. *Writers*

The very least one can conclude concerning the source of the differing conceptualizations of woman in LST and DST is that the difference is a function of the interests and concerns of the writers. Both groups of laws share the picture of woman as circumscribed and subordinate, indicated by her marginalization and objectification. They share the presence of both purity and property components to varying degrees. They also share, to varying degrees, the presence of woman as agent and as property. These supratextual components suggest continuity in the worlds of the writers. Thus, LST and DST may share the same world. The text suggests that they share similar experiences with respect to women. Nevertheless, both groups of texts demonstrate decidedly different interests in and concerns about women and sex.

To put it another way, they differ in what they understand to be problematic concerning women and sexual intercourse. The author of LST is interested in woman's capacity to maintain the classificatory system of his world. The author of DST is interested in the protection of woman as the property of the man.

Thus, DST shows pronounced concern for what one man might do to another through harm to his sexual property. LST show pronounced concern for what both men and women might do to the order and harmony of his world, through the illicit crossing of a variety of sexual boundaries, only some of which are property boundaries. These intertextual concerns suggest that the subject of sex and woman is approached by LST and DST for different reasons. This, in turn, suggests that the social pressures which DST and LST face are different. This is the very most one can conclude on the basis of the sex texts alone.

The sex texts themselves do not require the conclusion that the difference between LST and DST is due to the differing cultural, historical or even socio-logical circumstances in which the authors stand, although this is certainly a possibility. A fourth possibility is that the authors may simply have held different social positions in the same cultural-historical-sociological milieu. Nevertheless, a decision concerning these four possibilities as the source of the differing conceptualizations of women in LST and DST is more than can be made on the basis of the sex texts alone. Such a decision is, needless to say, outside the parameters of this study.

C. *Method*

1. *Immediate Implication*

The differences between LST and DST, demonstrated in the above exegesis and comparative analysis, suggest that the treatment of women in these two groups of texts cannot be viewed monolithically. Nor can woman's status as property in DST be denied. Furthermore, one cannot simply assume woman's conceptu-alization from the presence of purity components or property components alone in the text.

Methodologically, consideration must be given to a variety of factors, includ-ing the interests and concerns of the author, when considering woman's concep-tualization with respect to sexuality. These factors may suggest competing or conflicting impulses with respect to the conceptualization of women. Examina-tion of at least two sets of related factors is essential for understanding the treatment of women in the biblical laws regulating sexual intercourse. The first set of factors is woman's marginalization, objectification and focalization in the text. The second set of factors is the purity and property components and concerns constituting respectively the infractions and the laws.

A study of women in the sex laws which fails to examine these factors will invariably miss signals essential to understanding her treatment in those laws.

a. *First Set of Factors*. Woman's marginalization and her focalization are rele-vant for biblical law, while they might be less relevant or irrelevant for narrative because of the prescriptive nature of "law."[10] That is, the author expects the content of his text to bind the audience he addresses, *either by instructional*

---

10. See n. 123 of the "Introduction" above.

force or by jurisprudential force. He expects it to compel the behavior of his audience in accordance with his specific directives. Since this expectation is a significant component of the text, any variance in this expectation with respect to different members of his audience is also significant.

In other words, since the author considers his prescriptions to be binding, the choices he makes concerning whom he binds and to what he binds them is significant. Thus, in the exegesis of biblical law, the author's relationship to the audience he addresses is of particular importance in an investigation of the treatment of women. His relationship to the audience is revealed in two ways. First, it is revealed by the *choice* the author makes concerning whom he addresses. Second, it is revealed by the *expectations* the author has concerning those whom he addresses. The author's *choice* concerning whom he addresses reveals woman's level of marginalization. The author's *expectations* concerning those whom he addresses reveals woman's focalization. These two features are thus essential for investigation of the treatment of women in biblical law, especially laws regulating sexuality.

The third feature within the first set of factors, woman's objectification, is also significant. It is revealed by the author's presentation of the man and the woman in relationship to one another within the laws he articulates.

These three features within this set of factors may compete or conflict in the conceptualizations of woman they suggest, as they do in LST and DST.

b. *Second Set of Factors.* A second set of factors—the configuration of the purity/property components of sexual infractions and the purity/property concerns of the laws regulating those infractions—is also essential for understanding the treatment of women in the biblical laws regulating sexual intercourse. Again these features may compete or conflict in the conceptualizations of women they suggest, as they do in LST and DST.

Differing configurations within these two sets of factors reveal a complexity in the conceptualization of women in the text that otherwise remains unnoticed. This complexity is not trivial since it suggests a range of "personhood"/"chattel" or agency/subordination distinctions qualifying woman's experience.

2. *Extended Implications*

An investigation which tracks the treatment of women by examining the above three features in conjunction with the property/purity components and concerns has implications, of course, for other scholarly investigations, including those related to women. I will offer only one minor example to illustrate the point, since digression concerning these implications constitutes another study.

The treatment of woman with respect to sexual intercourse serves as a dye by which one might trace the author's interests in the issue concerning the "purity" of progeny and by implication inheritance of the land.

In LST, secure progeny are progeny which come from pure lines of descent. Such lines are constituted not merely by a man's exclusive access to his wife but by a variety of other right combinations that must also be observed. For example, if one marries a woman and her daughter so that both are one's wife, even though the "exclusive access" rule is followed, the rule against the improper combination of a woman and her daughter is not. Therefore, the progeny will be impure and the inheritance of the land threatened. In DST, by contrast, the *only* issue that is relevant for "purity" of descent is the "exclusive access" issue. If a man's sexual property is protected from access by other men, then the progeny will be pure and the land secure.

In this instance the different conceptualizations of women in LST and DST also imply different preoccupations with progeny and, by extension, with inheritance of the land.

APPENDIX

Chart 1. *Text List*

Lev 15:18, 24, 33b	Genital Discharges
Lev 18	Illicit Sex Series without Penalties
Lev 19:20–22	שפחה
Lev 19:29	Harlotry of Daughter
Lev 20:10–21	Illicit Sex Series with Penalties
Lev 21:9	Daughter of Priest
Deut 5:18	Seventh Commandment
Deut 21:10–14	Captive War-Bride
Deut 22:13–23:1	Illicit Sex Series with Penalties
Deut 24:1–4	Divorce
Deut 25:5–10	Levirate Marriage
Deut 27:20–23	Illicit Sex Series: Curses
Deut 28:30	Betrothed: Curse

Chart 2. *Leviticus 18: Forbidden Relations*

Primary Consanguinity

v. 6	mother, daughter, maiden sister	primary consanguinity
v. 7	mother	primary consanguinity
v. 8	wife of father	primary consanguinity + affinity
v. 9	sister who shares ego's mother or father	primary consanguinity

Secondary Consanguinity

v. 10	granddaughter	secondary consanguinity
v. 11	daughter of father's wife by male relative relative of father	secondary consanguinity + primary consanguinity (**also:** secondary consanguinity + affinity + primary Consanguinity (**also:** affinity + primary consanguinity)
v. 12	sister of father	secondary consanguinity
v. 13	sister of mother	secondary consanguinity
v. 14	wife of brother of father	secondary consanguinity + affinity

Primary Consanguinity

v. 15	daughter-in-law	primary consanguinity + affinity
v. 16	wife of brother	primary consanguinity + affinity

Affinity + Consanguinity

v. 17a	woman and daughter	affinity + primary consanguinity
v. 17b	woman and granddaughter	affinity + secondary consanguinity
v. 18	woman and sister	affinity + primary consanguinity

Chart 3. *Leviticus 20:10–21: Forbidden Relations and Penalties*

Verse	Forbidden Party	Penalty
10	neighbor's wife	put to death
11	father's wife	put to death
		blood upon them
12	daughter-in-law	put to death
		blood upon them
13	another man	put to death
		blood upon them
14	woman and mother	burn
15	animal and man	put to death (man), kill (animal)
16	animal and woman	kill (woman and animal), put to death (woman and animal)
		blood upon them
17	sister	be cut off (brother & sister), sin carry (brother)
18	menstruant	be cut off
19	sister of mother or sister of father	sin (עון) carry
20	father's brother's wife	sin (חטא) carry, die childless
21	brother's wife	be childless

Chart 4. *Deuteronomy 22:13–23:1: Penalties*

vv. 13–21	**Slandered Bride/Harloting Daughter**
v. 19	fine the slanderer, woman must remain his wife; cannot divorce
v. 21	stone her (cause to go out); she shall die; burn the evil

v. 22	**Adultery**
	they shall die; burn the evil

vv. 23–24	**Betrothed Virgin: Guilty**
v. 24	stone them (cause to go out); they shall die; burn the evil

vv. 25–27	**Betrothed Virgin: Not Guilty**
	the man shall die; nothing done to girl

vv. 28–29	**Unbetrothed Virgin**
	the man gives father money; woman must become his wife; cannot divorce

Chart 5. *Texts According to the Nine Topics*

1. Menstruation
LST: Lev 15:18, 24, 33b; 18:19; 20:18   DST: —

2. Incest
LST: Lev 18:6–18; 20:11–12, 14, 17–21   DST: Deut 23:1; 27:20, 22–23; 25:5–10

3. Adultery
LST: Lev 18:20; 20:10   DST: Deut 5:18; 22:22, 23–24

4. Homosexuality
LST: Lev 18:22; 20:13   DST: —

5. Bestiality
LST: Lev 18:23; 20:15–16   DST: Deut 27:21

6. Prostitution
LST: Lev 19:29; 21:9   DST: Deut 22:21

7. Rape
LST: —   DST: Deut 22:25–27, 28–29; 28:30

8. Virginity
LST: —   DST: Deut 22:13–21, 23–29

9. Slaves and Captives
LST: Lev 19:20–22   DST: Deut 21:10–14

Chart 6. *Texts According to Focalization*

Appearing as Agent
Focalized as Agent *implied by a variety of textual features*
(1) Lev 15; (2) Lev 18:6–19, 21–23; (3) Lev 20:11–21

Appearing as Property
Focalized as "Forgotten," with legal property status
Lev 19:20–22
Focalized a "Valued," with "daughter property" status
Lev 19:29
Focalized as Property
Deut 21:10–14 (under a contingency law she is granted a higher level of agency)

Appearing as Agent and Property
Focalized as Agent, with property status *essential to commission of infraction*
(1) Lev 18:20; (2) Lev 20:10
All incest laws in which the affine relationship is essential to commission of infraction
Lev 21:9
Focalized as Property, with *possible* agency *via implied addressee status*
(1) Deut 27:20–23; (2) Deut 28:30
Focalized as Property, with agency *via implied addressee status*
(1) Deut 5:18; (2) Deut 22:20–21, 25–26; 23:1
Focalized as Property, with agency *via active participation in infraction or remedy and implied addressee status*
(1) Deut 22:13–19, 22–24; (2) Deut 25:5–10

BIBLIOGRAPHY

Alt, Albrecht. *Essays on Old Testament History and Religion.* Translated by R.A. Wilson. Oxford: Blackwell, 1966.

_____. *Kleine Schriften zur Geschichte des Volkes Israel.* 3 vols. Munich: Beck, 1959.

_____. "Zu HIT'AMMĒR." *VT* 2, no. 2 (1952): 153–49.

Amorin, N. D. "Desecration and Defilement in the Old Testament." Ph.D. diss., Andrews University, 1986.

Amram, David Werner. *Jewish Law of Divorce.* New York: Hermon Press, 1968. Reprint 1975.

Anderson, Arnold A. "Law in Old Israel: Laws Concerning Adultery." Pages 13–19 in *Law and Religion.* Edited by Barnabas Lindars. Cambridge: James Clark & Co., 1988.

Anderson, Cheryl B. *Women, Ideology, and Violence: Critical Theory and the Construction of Gender in the Book of the Covenant and the Deuteronomic Law.* London: T&T Clark International, 2004.

Anderson, Gary A. "Sacrifice and Sacrificial Offerings (Old Testament)." *ABD* 5:870–86.

André, G., and H. Ringgren. "טָמֵא." *TDOT* 5:330–42.

Archer, Leonie J. "Bound by Blood: Circumcision and Menstrual Taboo in Post-Exilic Judaism." Pages 38–61 in *After Eve: Women, Theology and the Christian Traditions.* Edited by Janet Martin Soskice. London: Marshall Pickering, 1990.

_____. *Her Price is Beyond Rubies: The Jewish Woman in Graeco-Roman Palestine.* JSOTSup 60. Sheffield: JSOT Press, 1990.

_____. "The Role of Jewish Women in the Religion, Ritual and Cult of Graeco-Roman Palestine." Pages 273–87 in *Images of Women in Antiquity.* Edited by Averil Cameron and Amélie Kuhrt. Detroit: Wayne State, 1983.

_____. "The Virgin and the Harlot in the Writings of Formative Judaism." *HWJ* 24 (1987): 1–16.

Baab, O.J. "Sex." *IDB*: 817–20.

Bach, Alice, ed. *Women in the Hebrew Bible.* New York: Routledge, 1999.

Bal, Mieke. *Narratology: Introduction to the Theory of Narrative.* 2d ed. Toronto: University of Toronto Press, 1997.

Bamberger, Bernard J. *Leviticus.* New York: The Union of American Hebrew Congregations, 1979.

Barthélemy, Dominique et al. *Preliminary and Interim Report on the Hebrew Old Testament Text Project,* vol. 1. Stuttgart: United Bible Societies, 1976.

Bassett, Frederick W. "Short Notes—Noah's Nakedness and the Curse of Canaan: A Case of Incest?" *VT* 21 (1971): 332–37.

Beattie, D. R. G. "The Book of Ruth as Evidence for Israelite Legal Practice." *VT* 24 (1974): 251–67.

Becher, Jeanne, ed. *Women, Religion and Sexuality.* Philadelphia: Trinity, 1990.

Bechtel, Lyn M. "What if Dinah Is Not Raped? (Genesis 34)." *JSOT* 62 (1994): 19–36.

Belkin, Samuel. "Levirate and Agnate Marriage in Rabbinic and Cognate Literature." *JQR* 60 (1970): 275–329.

Bellefontaine, Elizabeth. "The Curses of Deuteronomy 27: Their Relationship to the Pro-hibitives." Pages 49–61 in *No Famine in the Land*. Edited by James W. Flanagan and Anita Weisbrod Robinson. Missoula, Mont.: Scholars Press, 1975.

Benjamin, Don C. *Deuteronomy and City Life*. Lanham, Md.: University Press of America, 1983.

Beuken, W. "שָׁכַב." *ThWAT* 7:1306–18.

Biale, Rachel. *Women and Jewish Law*. New York: Schocken, 1984.

Bigger, Stephen F. "The Family Laws of Leviticus 18 in Their Setting." *JBL* 98 (1979): 187–203.

Bird, Phyllis A. "The End of the Male Cult Prostitute: A Literary-Historical and Sociological Analysis of Hebrew QĀDĒŠ-QĚDĒŠÎM." Pages 37–80 in *Congress Volume: Cambridge 1996*. Edited by J. A. Emerton. VTSup 66. Leiden: Brill, 1997.

_____. "The Harlot as Heroine: Narrative Art and Social Presupposition in Three Old Testament Texts." *Semeia* 46 (1989): 119–39.

_____. "To Play the Harlot: An Inquiry into an Old Testament Metaphor." Pages 75–94 in Day, ed., *Gender and Difference*.

Blenkinsopp, Joseph. "The Family in First Temple Israel." Pages 48–103 in *Families in Ancient Israel*. Edited by Don S. Browning and Ian S. Evison. Louisville, Ky.: West-minster John Knox, 1997.

Blidstein, Gerald. *Honor Thy Father and Mother*. New York: Ktav, 1975.

Boecker, Hans Jochen. *Law and the Administration of Justice in the Old Testament and Ancient East*. Minneapolis: Augsburg, 1976.

Borger, Rykle, *Babylonisch-Assyrische Lesestücke*, vol. 1. AnOr 54. Rome: Pontificium Institutum Biblicum, 1979.

Boyarin, Daniel. "Are There Any Jews in 'The History of Sexuality'?" *JHS* 5, no. 3 (1995): 333–55.

_____. *Carnal Israel: Reading Sex in Talmudic Culture*. Los Angeles: University of California Press, 1993.

Braulik, Georg. "The Sequence of the Laws in Deuteronomy 12–26 and in the Decalogue." Pages 313–35 in Christensen, ed., *A Song of Power*.

Brekelmans, C., "Deuteronomy 5: Its Place and Function." Pages 164–73 in Lohfink, ed., *Das Deuteronomium*.

Brenner, Athalya. *The Intercourse of Knowledge: On Gendering Desire and "Sexuality" in the Hebrew Bible*. Leiden: Brill, 1997.

_____. "On Incest." Pages 113–38 in Brenner, ed., *A Feminist Companion to Exodus to Deuteronomy*.

——, ed. *A Feminist Companion to Exodus to Deuteronomy*. FCB 6. Sheffield: Sheffield Academic Press, 1994.

——, ed. *A Feminist Companion to the Latter Prophets*. FCB 8. Sheffield: Sheffield Academic Press, 1995.

Brenner, Athalya, and Carol Fontaine, eds. *A Feminist Companion to Reading the Bible: Approaches, Methods and Strategies*. FCB 11. Sheffield: Sheffield Academic Press, 1997.

Brett, Mark G. "Motives and Intentions in Genesis 1." *JTS* 42 (1991): 1–16.

Brichto, Herbert Chanan. *The Problem of "Curse" in the Hebrew Bible*. Philadelphia: Society of Biblical Literature and Exegesis, 1963.

Brooten, Bernadette J. *Love Between Women: Early Christian Responses to Female Homo-eroticism*. Chicago: University of Chicago Press, 1996.

Brundage, James A. *Law, Sex and Christian Society in Medieval Europe*. Chicago: University of Chicago Press, 1987.

Buis, Pierre. "Deuteronome XXVII 15–26: Maledictions ou exigences de l'alliance?" *VT* 17 (1967): 478–79.

Burrows, Millar. "The Ancient Oriental Background of Hebrew Levirate Marriage." *BASOR* 77 (1940): 2–15.

_____. *The Basis of Israelite Marriage*. New Haven: American Oriental Society, 1938.

_____. "Levirate Marriage in Israel." *JBL* 59 (1940): 23–33.

_____. "The Marriage of Boaz and Ruth." *JBL* 59 (1940): 445–54.

Buss, Martin J. "The Distinction Between Civil and Criminal Law in Ancient Israel." Pages 51–62 in *Proceedings of the Sixth World Congress of Jewish Studies*. Edited by Avigdor Shinan. Jerusalem: Jerusalem Academic Press, 1977.

Butler, J. *Gender Trouble: Feminism and the Subversion of Identity*. London: Routledge, 1990.

Cairns, Ian. *Deuteronomy: Word and Presence*. Grand Rapids: Eerdmans, 1992.

Carmichael, Calum M. "A Ceremonial Crux: Removing a Man's Sandal as a Female Gesture of Contempt." *JBL* 96 (1977): 321–36.

_____. "Forbidden Mixtures." *VT* 32 (1982): 394–415.

_____. *The Laws of Deuteronomy*. Ithaca, N.Y.: Cornell University Press, 1974.

_____. *Law, Legend, and Incest in the Bible: Leviticus 18–20* (Ithaca, N.Y.: Cornell University Press, 1997).

_____. "'Treading' in the Book of Ruth." *ZAW* 92 (1980): 248–66.

_____. *Women, Law and the Genesis Tradition*. Edinburgh: Edinburgh University Press, 1979.

Carr, David. *The Erotic Word: Sexuality, Spirituality and the Bible*. Oxford: Oxford University Press, 2003.

Carroll, Michael P. "One More Time: Leviticus Revisited." Pages 117–26 in Lang, ed., *Anthropological Approaches to the Old Testament*.

Ceresko, Anthony R. "The Function of *Antanaclasis (mṣ'* 'to find'// *mṣ'* "to reach, overtake, grasp') in Hebrew Poetry, Especially in the Book of Qoheleth." *CBQ* 44 (1982): 551–69.

Chia, Mantak. *Taoist Secrets of Love: Cultivating Male Sexual Energy*. Santa Fe: Aurora, 1984.

Cholewinski, Alfred. *Heiligkeitsgesetz und Deuteronomium*. Rome: Biblical Institute Press, 1976.

Christensen, Duane L., ed. *A Song of Power and the Power of Song*. Winona Lake, Ind.: Eisenbrauns, 1993.

Clements, R. E. *Deuteronomy*. OTG. Sheffield: JSOT Press, 1989.

Clifford, Richard. *Deuteronomy*. Wilmington, Del.: Michael Glazier, 1982.

Coats, George W. "Widow's Rights: A Crux in the Structure of Genesis 38." *CBQ* 34 (1972): 461–66.

Cohen, Shaye J. D. "Menstruants and the Sacred, in Judaism and Christianity." Pages 273–99 in *Women's History and Ancient History*. Edited by Sarah B. Pomeroy. Chapel Hill: The University of North Caroline Press, 1991.

Cole, William Graham. *Sex and Love in the Bible*. New York: Association Press, 1959.

Cosby, Michael R. *Sex in the Bible*. Englewood Cliffs: Prentice–Hall, 1984.

Countryman, L. William. *Dirt, Greed and Sex*. Philadelphia: Fortress, 1988.

Cover, Robin. "Sin, Sinners (Old Testament)." *ABD* 6:31–40.

Craigie, Peter C. *The Book of Deuteronomy*. Grand Rapids; Eerdmans, 1976.

Daube, David. *Ancient Jewish Law*. Leiden: Brill, 1981.

_____. "Biblical Landmarks in the Struggle for Women's Rights." *JR* 23 (1978): 177–97.

_____. "Consortium in Roman and Hebrew Law." *JR* 62 (1950): 71–91.

_____. "The Culture of Deuteronomy." *Orita* 3 (1960): 27–52.

David, M. "*ḤITʿĀMĒR* (Deut. xxi 14; xxiv 7)." *VT* 1 (1951): 219–21.

Davies, Eryl W. "Inheritance Rights and the Hebrew Levirate Marriage: Part 1." *VT* 31 (1981): 138–44.

_____. "Inheritance Rights and the Hebrew Levirate Marriage: Part 2." *VT* 31 (1981): 257–68.

Day, John. *Molech*. Cambridge: Cambridge University Press, 1989.

Day, Peggy L. "From the Child Is Born the Woman: The Story of Jephthah's Daughter." Pages 58–74 in Day, ed., *Gender and Difference*.

———, ed. *Gender and Difference in Ancient Israel*. Minneapolis: Fortress, 1989.

Dempster, Stephen. "The Deuteronomic Formula *kî yimmāṣēʾ* in the Light of Biblical and Ancient Near Eastern Law." *RB* 2 (1984): 188–211.

Derby, J. "The Problem of the Levirate Marriage." *JBQ* 19 (1990): 11–17.

DeYoung, James B. *Homosexuality: Contemporary Claims Examined in Light of the Bible and Other Ancient Literature and Law*. Grand Rapids: Kregel, 2000.

Dommershausen, W. "חלל." *TDOT* 4:409–17.

Douglas, Mary, "The Abominations of Leviticus." Pages 100–16 in Lang, ed., *Approaches to the Old Testament*.

———. *Implicit Meanings*. London: Routledge & Kegan Paul, 1975.

———. *Purity and Danger*. London: Routledge & Kegan Paul, 1966.

Driver, G. R., and John C. Miles. *The Babylonian Laws*, vol. 2. Oxford: Clarendon, 1952. Reprint Oxford: Oxford University Press, 1960.

Driver, S. R. *The Book of Leviticus*. London: James Clarke & Co., 1898.

———. *Deuteronomy*. New York: Charles Scribner's Sons, 1906.

Dupont, Joanne M. "Women and the Concept of Holiness in the 'Holiness Code' (Leviticus 17–26): Literary, Theological and Historical Context." Ph.D. diss., Marquette University, 1989.

Eilberg-Schwartz, Howard. *The Savage in Judaism*. Bloomington: Indiana University Press, 1990.

Ellens, Deborah. "A Comparison of the Conceptualization of the Women in the Sex Laws of Leviticus and in the Sex Laws of Deuteronomy." Ph.D. diss. Claremont Graduate University, 1998.

———. "Leviticus 15: Contrasting Conceptual Associations Regarding Women." Pages 124–51 in *Reading the Hebrew Bible for a New Millennium: Form, Concept, and Theological Perspective*. Vol. 2, *Exegetical and Theological Studies*. Edited by Wonil Kim, Deborah Ellens, Michael Floyd and Marvin A. Sweeney. Harrisburg, Pa.: Trinity, 2000.

———. "Menstrual Impurity and Innovation in Leviticus 15." Pages 29–43 in De Troyer et al. eds., *Wholly Woman Holy Blood*.

Elliger, Karl. "Das Gesetz Leviticus 18." *ZAW* 67 (1955): 1–25.

———. *Leviticus*. Tübingen: J. C. B. Mohr, 1966.

Emmerson, Grace I. "Women in Ancient Israel." Pages 371–94 in *The World of Ancient Israel*. Edited by R. E. Clements. Cambridge: Cambridge University Press, 1989.

Engelken, Karen. *Frauen im alten Israel*. Stuttgart: Kohlhammer, 1990.

Epstein, Louis M. *Marriage Laws in the Bible and the Talmud*. Cambridge, Mass.: Harvard University Press, 1942.

———. *Sex, Laws and Customs in Judaism*. New York: Ktav, 1968.

Erlandsson, S. "זנה." *TDOT* 4:99–104.

Even-Shoshan, Abraham. *A New Concordance of the Old Testament*. 2d ed. Jerusalem: Kiryat-Sefer, 1989.

Falk, Ze'ev W. "Spirituality and Jewish Law." Pages 127–38 in Firmage, Weiss and Welch, eds., *Religion and Law*.

Fearer, Tim. "Wars in the Wilderness: Textual Cohesion and Conceptual Coherence in Pentateuchal Battle Traditions." Ph.D. diss., Claremont Graduate University, 1993.

Feldman, Emanuel. *Biblical and Post-Biblical Defilement and Mourning: Law as Theology*. New York: Ktav, 1977.

Fensham, F. C. "Liability of Animals in Biblical and Ancient Near Eastern Law." *JNSL* 14 (1988): 85–90.

Feucht, Christian. *Untersuchungen zum Heiligkeitsgesetz*. Berlin: Evangelische, 1964.

Fewell, Danna Nolan, and David M. Gunn. "The Subject of the Law." Pages 94–116 in *Gender, Power, and Promise: The Subject of the Bible's First Story.* Nashville: Abingdon, 1993.

Finkelstein, J.J. *The Ox That Gored.* Transactions of the American Philosophical Society 71/2. Philadelphia: The American Philosophical Society, 1981.

_____. "Sex Offenses in Sumerian Laws." *JAOS* 86 (1966): 355–72.

Firmage, Edwin B., Bernard G. Weiss and John W. Welch, eds. *Religion and Law.* Winona Lake, Ind.: Eisenbrauns, 1990.

Fishbane, Michael. *Biblical Interpretation in Ancient Israel.* Oxford: Clarendon, 1985.

Fisher, Eugene J. "Cultic Prostitution in the Ancient Near East: A Reassessment." *BTB* 6 (1976): 225–36.

Freedman, D. N., and B. E. Willoughby. "נָאַף." *ThWAT* 5:123–30.

Freund, Richard A. "Murder, Adultery and Theft." *SJOT* 2 (1989): 72–80.

Frick, Frank S. "Widows in the Hebrew Bible: A Transactional Approach." Pages 139–51 in Brenner, ed., *A Feminist Companion to Exodus to Deuteronomy.*

Friedman, Richard Elliott. *Who Wrote the Bible?* New York: Harper & Row, 1987.

Frymer-Kensky, Tikva. "Deuteronomy." Pages 52–66 in Newsom and Ringe, eds., *The Women's Bible Commentary.*

_____. "Law and Philosophy: The Case of Sex in the Bible." *Semeia* 45 (1989): 89–102.

_____. "Pollution, Purification, and Purgation in Biblical Israel." Pages 399–414 in *The Word of the Lord Shall Go Forth.* Edited by Carl L. Meyers and M. O'Connor. Winona Lake, Ind.: Eisenbrauns, 1983.

_____. "Sex and Sexuality." *ABD* 5:1144–46.

_____. "Sex in the Bible." Pages 187–98 in *In the Wake of the Goddesses.* New York: Fawcett Columbine, 1992.

_____. "Virginity in the Bible." Pages 79–96 in Matthews, Levinson and Frymer-Kensky, eds., *Gender and Law in the Hebrew Bible.*

Gagnon, Robert A. J. *The Bible and Homosexual Practice: Text and Hermeneutics.* Nashville: Abingdon, 2001.

Garrett, Duane A. "Votive Prostitution Again: A Comparison of Proverbs 7:13–14 and 23:28–29." *JBL* 109 (1990): 681–82.

Gerstenberger, E.S. "עָנָה." *ThWAT* 6:234–70.

Gilmore, David D., ed. *Honor and Shame and the Unity of the Mediterranean.* Washington, D.C.: American Anthropological Association, 1987.

Goodfriend, Elaine Adler. "Adultery." *ABD* 1:82–86.

_____. "Prostitution (Old Testament)." *ABD* 5:505–10.

Gordis, Robert. "Love, Marriage, and Business in the Book of Ruth: A Chapter in Hebrew Customary Law." Pages 241–264 in *A Light Unto My Path.* Edited by Howard N. Bream, Ralph D. Heim and Carey A. Moore. Philadelphia: Temple University Press, 1974.

_____. "On Adultery in Biblical and Babylonian Law—A Note." *Judaism* 33 (1989): 210–11.

Gordon, Cyrus H. "Glossary." Pages 347–507 in *Ugaritic Textbook.* Rome: Pontifical Biblical Institute, 1965.

_____. "The Patriarchal Age." *JBR* 21, no. 4 (1953): 238–43.

Gordon, Pamela, and Harold C. Washington. "Rape as a Military Metaphor in the Hebrew Bible." Pages 308–25 in Brenner, ed., *A Feminist Companion to the Latter Prophets.*

Gravett, Sandie. "Reading 'Rape' in the Hebrew Bible: A Consideration of Language." *JSOT* 28 (2004): 279–99.

Greenberg, Blu. "Female Sexuality and Bodily Functions in the Jewish Tradition." Pages in 1–44 Becher, ed., *Women, Religion and Sexuality.*

Greenberg, Moshe. "The Decalogue Tradition Critically Examined." Pages 83–119 in Levi, ed., *The Ten Commandments.*

_____. "The Etymology of נִדָּה '(Menstrual) Impurity.'" Pages 69–77 in *Solving Riddles and Untying Knots: Biblical, Epigraphic, and Semitic Studies in Honor of Jonas C. Greenfield*. Edited by Ziony Zevit, Seymour Gitin and Michael Sokoloff. Winona Lake, Ind.: Eisenbrauns, 1995.

_____. "More Reflections on Biblical Criminal Law." Pages 1–17 in Japhet, ed., *Scripta Hierosolymitana*.

_____. "Some Postulates of Biblical Criminal Law." Pages 5–18 in Haran, ed., *Yehezkel Kaufmann Jubilee Volume*.

Haag, H. "מוֹלֶדֶת." *TDOT* 8:162–67.

Halperin, David M. *How to Do the History of Homosexuality*. Chicago: University of Chicago Press, 2002.

_____. *One Hundred Years of Homosexuality and Other Essays*. New York: Routledge, 1990.

Halpern, Baruch. "Jerusalem and the Lineages in the Seventh Century BCE: Kinship and the Rise of Individual Moral Liability." Pages 11–107 in *Law and Ideology in Monarchic Israel*. Edited by Baruch Halpern and Deborah W. Hobson. JSOTSup 124. Sheffield: Sheffield Academic Press, 1991.

Hamp, V. "נֶגֶב." *TDOT* 3:39–45.

Haney, Randy. "'And All Nations Shall Serve Him': Text and Concept Analysis in Royal Psalms." Ph.D. diss., Claremont Graduate University, 1999.

_____. *Text and Concept Analysis in Royal Psalms*. Studies in Biblical Literature. New York: Peter Lang, 2002.

Haran, M., ed. *Yehezkel Kaufmann Jubilee Volume*. Jerusalem: Magnes, 1960.

Harris, Kevin. *Sex, Ideology and Religion: The Representation of Women in the Bible*. Brighton, UK: Wheatsheaf; Totowa, N.J.: Barnes & Noble, 1984.

Hasel, G. F. "כָּרַת." *TDOT* 7:339–52.

Hastrup, Kirsten. "The Sexual Boundary—Danger: Transvestism and Homosexuality." *JASO* 6 (1975): 42–56.

_____. "The Sexual Boundary—Purity: Heterosexuality and Virginity." *JASO* 5 (1994): 137–47.

Hayes, Christine E. "Parallelism and Inversion in Lev 21:1b-15." Pages 1834–36 in Milgrom, *Leviticus 17–22*.

Heider, George C. *The Cult of Molek*. JSOTSup 43. Sheffield: JSOT Press, 1985.

_____. "Molech." *ABD* 4:895–98.

Hens-Piazza, Gina. "Terrorization, Sexualization, Maternalization: Women's Bodies on Trial." Pages 163–77 in Kirk-Duggan, ed., *Pregnant Passion*.

Hesse, F. "חָזַק." *TDOT* 4:301–308.

Hiebert, Paula S. "'Whence Shall Help Come to Me?': The Biblical Widow." Pages 125–41 in Day, ed., *Gender and Difference*.

Hill, Andrew E. "The Ebal Ceremony as Hebrew Land Grant?" *JETS* 31 (1988): 399–406.

Hobbs, T. R. "Jeremiah 3:1–5 and Deuteronomy 42:1–4." *ZAW* 86 (1974): 23–29.

Hoffman, Lawrence A. *Covenant of Blood*. Chicago: University of Chicago Press, 1996.

Holladay, William I. *A Concise Hebrew and Aramaic Lexicon of the Old Testament*. Grand Rapids: Eerdmans, 1971.

Hooks, Stephen A. "Sacred Prostitution in Israel and the Ancient Near East." Ph.D. diss., Hebrew Union College, 1985.

Horner, Tom. *Sex in the Bible*. Rutland: Charles E. Tuttle, 1974.

Horton, Fred L. "Form and Structure in Laws Relating to Women: Leviticus 18:6–18." Pages 20–33 in *SBL 1973 Seminar Papers*. SBLSP 1. Cambridge, Mass.: Society of Biblical Literature, 1973.

Hossfeld, F., F. van der Velder and U. Dahmen. "שָׁלַח." *ThWAT* 8:46–70.

Houston, Walter J. *Purity and Monotheism: Clean and Unclean Animals in Biblical Law*. JSOTSup 140. Sheffield: JSOT Press, 1993.

_____. "Towards an Integrated Reading of the Dietary Laws of Leviticus." Pages 142–61 in Rendtorff and Kugler, eds., *The Book of Leviticus.*

Houtman, C. "Another Look at Forbidden Mixtures." *VT* 34, no. 2 (1984): 226–28.

Hulst, A. R. *Old Testament Translation Problems.* Leiden: Brill, 1960.

Hutton, Rodney Ray. "Declaratory Formula: Forms of Authoritative Pronouncement in Ancient Israel." Ph.D. diss., Claremont Graduate School, 1983.

Instone-Brewer, David. "Deuteronomy 24:1–4 and the Origin of the Jewish Divorce Certificate." *JJS* 49 (1998): 230–43.

_____. *Divorce and Remarriage in the Bible: The Social and Literary Context.* Grand Rapids: Eerdmans, 2002.

Jackson, Bernard S. *Essays in Jewish and Comparative Legal History.* Leiden: Brill, 1975.

_____. "Travels and Travails of the Goring Ox." Pages 41–56 in *Studies in Bible and the Ancient Near East.* Edited by Yitschak Avishu and Joseph Blau. Jerusalem: E. Rubenstein, 1978.

Jacobs, Mignon. "Conceptual Coherence of the Book of Micah." Ph.D. diss., Claremont Graduate University, 1998.

_____. *The Conceptual Coherence of the Book of Micah.* JSOTSup 332. Sheffield: Sheffield Academic Press, 2001.

Japhet, Sarah, ed. *Scripta Hierosolymitana.* Jerusalem: Magnes, 1986.

Jenson, Philip Peter. *Graded Holiness.* JSOTSup 106. Sheffield: JSOT Press, 1992.

Jepsen, A. "Ama[H] and Schiphcha[H]." *VT* 8 (1958): 293–97.

Johnstone, William. "The 'Ten Commandments': Some Recent Interpretations." *ExpTim* 100 (1988–89): 453–61.

Kalland, Earl S. "Deuteronomy." Pages 3–235 in vol. 3 of *The Expositor's Bible Commentary.* Edited by Frank E. Gaebelein et al. Grand Rapids: Zondervan, 1992.

Kalmin, Richard. "Levirate Law." *ABD* 4:296–97.

Kautzsch, E. *Gesenius' Hebrew Grammar.* Translated by A. E. Cowley. Oxford: Clarendon, 1910. Second English edn reprinted from corrected sheets of the second edition, Oxford: Oxford University Press, 1985.

Keefe, Alice A. "Rapes of Women/Wars of Men." Pages 79–97 in *Women, War, and Metaphor: Language and Society in the Study of the Hebrew Bible.* Edited by Claudia V. Camp and Carole F. Fontaine. Semeia 61. Atlanta: Society of Biblical Literature, 1993.

_____. "Women, Sex and Society." Pages 162–89 in *Woman's Body and the Social Body in Hosea.* Gender, Culture, Theory 10. Sheffield: Sheffield Academic Press, 2001.

Kikawada, Isaac M. "The Shape of Genesis 11:1–9." Pages 18–32 in *Rhetorical Criticism.* Edited by Jared J. Jackson and Martin Kessler. Pittsburg: Pickwick, 1974.

Kim, Hyun Chul Paul. *Ambiguity, Tension, and Multiplicity in Deutero-Isaiah.* New York: Peter Lang, 2003.

_____. "Salvation of Israel and the Nations in Isaiah 40–55: A Study in Texts and Concepts." Ph.D. diss., Claremont Graduate University, 1998.

Kim, Wonil. "Toward a Substance-Critical Task of Old Testament Theology." Ph.D. diss., Claremont Graduate University, 1996.

Kirk-Duggan, Cheryl A., ed. *Pregnant Passion: Gender, Sex, and Violence in the Bible.* SBLSS 44. Atlanta: Society of Biblical Literature, 2003.

Kiuchi, N. *The Purification Offering in the Priestly Literature.* JSOTSup 56. Sheffield: JSOT Press, 1987.

Klawans, Jonathan. *Impurity and Sin in Ancient Judaism.* Oxford: Oxford University Press, 2000.

_____. "The Impurity of Immorality in Ancient Judaism." *JJS* 48 (1997): 1–16.

Knierim, Rolf P. "אשׁם." *THAT* 1:251–57.

_____. "שׁגג." *THAT* 2:869–72.

_____. "Criticism of Literary Features, Form, Tradition, and Reaction." Pages 123–65 in *The Hebrew Bible and Its Modern Interpreters*. Edited by Douglas A. Knight and Gene M. Tucker. Philadelphia: Fortress, 1985.

_____. "Custom, Judges, and Legislators in Ancient Israel." Pages 3–15 in *Early Jewish and Christian Exegesis*. Edited by C. A. Evans and W. F. Stinespring. Atlanta: Scholars Press, 1987.

_____. "Old Testament Form Criticism Reconsidered." *Interpretation* 27 (1973): 435–68.

_____. "The Problem of Ancient Israel's Prescriptive Legal Traditions." *Semeia* 45 (1989): 9–11.

_____. *The Task of Old Testament Theology: Substance, Method, and Cases*. Grand Rapids: Eerdmans, 1995.

_____. *Text and Concept in Leviticus 1:1–9*. Tübingen: J. C. B. Mohr, 1992.

_____. "The Problems of Ancient Israel's Prescriptive Legal Traditions." *Semeia* 45 (1989): 7–25.

Kornfeld, Walter. "L'adultere dans l'orient antique." *RB* 57 (1950): 92–109.

_____. "Ein unpublizierter Levitikustext." *ZAW* 87 (1975): 211–13.

_____. *Levitikus*. Würzberg: Echter, 1983.

_____. *Studien zum Heiligkeitsgesetz*. Vienna: Herder, 1952.

Kunin, Daniel Seth. *The Logic of Incest: A Structuralist Analysis of Hebrew Mythology*. JSOTSup 185. Sheffield: Sheffield Academic Press, 1995.

Kutsch, E. "יבם." *TDOT* 5:367–79.

Kysar, Myrna, and Robert Kysar. *The Asundered*. Atlanta: John Knox, 1978.

Lambden, Thomas O. *Introduction to Biblical Hebrew*. New York: Charles Scribner's Sons, 1971.

Landsberger, Benno. "Jungfräulichkeit: Ein Beitrag zum Thema 'Beilager und Eheschliessung.'" Pages 41–105 in *Symbolae Iuridicae et Historicae*, vol. 2. Edited by J. A. Ankum, R. Feenstra and W. F. Leemans. Leiden: Brill, 1968.

Lang, Bernhard, ed. *Anthropological Approaches to the Old Testament*. Philadelphia: Fortress, 1985.

Larue, Gerald. *Sex and the Bible*. Buffalo: Prometheus, 1983.

Lee, Won W. "Punishment and Forgiveness in Israel's Migratory Campaign: The Macrostructure of Numbers 10:11–36:13." Ph.D. diss., Claremont Graduate University, 1998.

_____. *Punishment and Forgiveness in Israel's Migratory Campaign*. Grand Rapids: Eerdmans, 2003.

Leggett, Donald A. *The Levirate and Goel Institutions in the Old Testament*. Cherry Hill: Mack, 1974.

Levi, Gershon, ed. *The Ten Commandments*. English edn. Jerusalem: Magnes, 1990.

Levine, Baruch A. *Leviticus*. Philadelphia: Jewish Publication Society of America, 1989.

Lips, Hilary M. *Sex and Gender: An Introduction*. Mountain View: Mayfield, 1988.

Locher, Clemens. "Deuteronomium 22, 13–21 vom Prozeß-Protocoll zum kasuistischen Gesetz." Pages 298–303 in Lohfink, ed., *Das Deuteronomium*.

_____. *Die Ehre einer Frau in Israel*. Göttingen: Vandenhoeck & Ruprecht, 1986.

Loewenstamm, Samuel E. *Comparative Studies in Biblical and Ancient Oriental Literatures*. Neukirchen–Vluyn: Neukirchener, 1980.

_____. "The Laws of Adultery and Murder in Biblical and Mesopotamian Law." Pages 146–72 in his *Comparative Studies in Biblical and Ancient Oriental Literatures*.

Lohfink, Norbert, ed. *Das Deuteronomium*. Leuven: Leuven University Press, 1985.

Lowe, E. J. *A Survey of Metaphysics*. Oxford: Oxford University Press, 2002.

Maccoby, Hyam. *Ritual and Morality: The Ritual Purity System and Its Place in Judaism*. Cambridge: Cambridge University Press, 1999.

Mace, David R. *Hebrew Marriage*. New York: Philosophical Library, 1953.

Magdalene, F. Rachel. "Ancient Near Eastern Treaty-Curses and the Ultimate Texts of Terror: A Study of the Language of Divine Sexual Abuse in the Prophetic Corpus." Pages 326–52 in Brenner, ed., *A Feminist Companion to the Latter Prophets.*

Magonet, Jonathan. "'But if It Is A Girl She Is Unclean for Twice Seven Days...' The Riddle of Leviticus 12.5." Pages 144–52 in *Reading Leviticus: A Conversation with Mary Douglas.* Edited by John F. Sawyer. JSOTSup 227. Sheffield: Sheffield Academic Press, 1996.

_____. "The Structure and Meaning of Leviticus 19." *HAR* 7 (1983): 151–67.

Malul, Meir. "*ʿĀqēb* "Heel" and *ʿĀqab* 'to Supplant' and the Concept of Succession in the Jacob–Esau Narratives." *VT* 46 (1996): 190–212.

_____. *Knowledge, Control and Sex: Studies in Biblical Thought, Culture and Worldview.* Tel Aviv–Jaffa: Archaeological Center, 2002.

_____. "The Laws of the Goring Ox in the Old Testament and the Ancient Near East." Pages 113–52 in *The Comparative Method in Ancient Near Eastern and Biblical Legal Studies.* Neukirchen–Vluyn: Neukirchener, 1990.

Manor, Dale W. "A Brief History of Levirate Marriage as It Relates to the Bible." *RQ* 27 (1984): 129–42.

Martin, J. D. "The Forensic Background to Jeremiah III 1." *VT* 19 (1969): 82–92.

Matthews, Victor H. "Honor and Shame in Gender-Related Legal Situations in the Hebrew Bible." Pages 97–112 in Matthews, Levinson and Frymer-Kensky, eds., *Gender and Law in the Hebrew Bible.*

Matthews, Victor H., and Don C. Benjamin. *Social World of Ancient Israel: 1250–587 BCE.* Peabody, Mass.: Hendrickson, 1993.

Matthews, Victor H., Bernard M. Levinson and Tikva Frymer-Kensky, eds. *Gender and Law in the Hebrew Bible and the Ancient Near East.* JSOTSup 262. Sheffield: Sheffield Academic Press, 1998.

Mayer, Günter. "אוה." *TDOT* 1:134–37.

Mayes, A. D. H. *Deuteronomy.* Greenwood: Attic, 1979.

_____. "Deuteronomy 5 and the Decalogue." *Proceedings of the Irish Biblical Association* 4 (1980): 68–83.

McCarthy, Dennis J. *Treaty and Covenant.* Rome: Biblical Institute Press, 1978.

McKeating, Henry. "A Response to Dr. Phillips by Henry McKeating." *JSOT* 20 (1981): 25–26.

_____. "Sanctions against Adultery in Ancient Israelite Society, with Some Reflections on Methodology in the Study of Old Testament Ethics." *JSOT* 11 (1979): 57–72.

Melcher, Sarah J. "The Holiness Code and Human Sexuality." Pages 87–102 in *Biblical Ethics and Homosexuality: Listening to Scripture.* Edited by Robert L. Brawley. Louisville, Ky.: Westminster John Knox, 1996.

Mendenhall, George E., and Gary A. Herion. "Covenant." *ABD* 1:1179–202.

Merendino, Rosario Pius. *Das Deuteronomische Gesetz.* Bonn: Peter Hanstein, 1969.

Milgrom, Jacob. "The Alleged 'Demythologization and Secularization' in Deuteronomy." *IEJ* 23 (1973): 156–61.

_____. "The Betrothed Slave-girl, Lev. 19:20–22." *ZAW* 89 (1977): 43–50.

_____. *Cult and Conscience.* Leiden: Brill, 1976.

_____. "The Dynamics of Purity in the Priestly System." Pages 29–45 in *Purity and Holiness: The Heritage of Leviticus.* Edited by M. J. H. M. Poorthuis and J. Schwartz. Leiden: Brill, 2000.

_____. *Leviticus 1–16: A New Translation with Introduction and Commentary.* New York: Doubleday, 1991.

_____. *Leviticus 17–22: A New Translation with Introduction and Commentary.* New York: Doubleday, 2000.

_____. *Numbers.* Philadelphia: Jewish Publication Society of America, 1990.

_____. "Of Hems and Tassels." *BAR* 9, no. 3 (1983): 61–65.

_____. "Rationale for Cultic Law: The Case of Impurity." Pages 103–9 in *Thinking Biblical Law*. Edited by Dale Patrick. Semeia 45. Atlanta: Scholars Press, 1989.

_____. "Sacrifices and Offerings (OT)." *IDBSup* 763–71.

Milgrom, J., D. P. Wright and H. Fabry. "נָדָה." *ThWAT* 5:250–54.

Miller, Patrick D. *Deuteronomy*. Louisville, Ky.: John Knox, 1990.

Morgenstern, Julian. "The Decalogue of the Holiness Code." *HUCA* 26 (1955): 1–27.

Mosca, Paul G. "Child Sacrifice in Canaanite and Israelite Religion." Ph.D. Diss., Harvard University, 1975.

Neufeld, E. *Ancient Hebrew Marriage Laws*. New York: Longmans, Green & Co., 1944.

Neusner, Jacob, ed. and trans. *Baba Batra: The Talmud of the Land of Israel*, vol. 30. Chicago: University of Chicago Press, 1984.

_____. *Gittin: The Talmud of the Land of Israel*, vol. 25. Chicago: University of Chicago Press, 1982.

_____. *The Idea of Purity in Ancient Judaism*. Leiden: Brill, 1973.

_____. *The Talmud of Babylonia: An American Translation, XXXII, Tractate Arakhin*. Chico, Calif.: Scholars Press, 1984.

_____. "Uncleanness: A Moral or an Ontological Category in the Early Centuries A.D." *BBR* 1 (1991): 63–88.

Newsom Carol A., and Sharon H. Ringe, eds. *The Women's Bible Commentary*. Louisville, Ky.: Westminster John Knox, 1992.

——. *Women's Bible Commentary, Expanded Edition with Apocrypha*. Louisville, Ky.: Westminster John Knox, 1998.

Niditch, Susan. "War, Women, and Defilement in Numbers 31." *Semeia* 61 (1993): 39–57.

_____. "The Wrong Woman Righted: An Analysis of Genesis 38." *HTR* 72 (1979): 143–49.

Nielsen, Eduard. *The Ten Commandments in New Perspective*. London: SCM Press, 1968.

Nissinen, Martti. *Homoeroticism in the Biblical World: A Historical Perspective*. Translated by Kirsi Stjerna. Minneapolis: Fortress, 1998.

Noordtzij, A. *Leviticus*. Grand Rapids: Zondervan, 1982.

Noth, Martin. *Leviticus*. Philadelphia: Westminster, 1977.

Oden, Robert A. *The Bible without Theology: The Theological Tradition and Alternatives to It*. New York: Harper & Row, 1987.

Olyan, Saul M. " 'And with a Male You Shall Not Lie the Lying Down of a Woman': On the Meaning and Significance of Leviticus 18:22 and 20:13." *JHS* 5 (1994): 179–206.

Orlinsky, H. M. "Virgin." *IDBSup* 939–40.

Ortner, Sherry B. "The Virgin and the State." *Feminist Studies* 4 (1978): 18–35.

Otto, Eckart. "False Weights in the Scales of Biblical Justice? Different Views of Women from Patriarchal Hierarchy to Religious Equality in the Book of Deuteronomy." Pages 128–46 in Matthews, Levinson and Frymer-Kensky, eds., *Gender and Law in the Hebrew Bible*.

Paige, Karen E. "Women Learn to Sing the Menstrual Blues." *Psychology Today* (September 1973): 41–46.

Palmer, David B. "Text and Concept in Exodus 1:1–2:25: A Case Study in Exegetical Method." Ph.D. diss., Claremont Graduate University, 1998.

Parunak, H. Van Dyke. "Transitional Techniques in the Bible." *JBL* 102 (1983): 525–48.

Patai, Raphael. *Sex and Family in the Bible and the Middle East*. Garden City, N.Y.: Doubleday, 1959.

Patrick, Dale. *Old Testament Law*. Atlanta: John Knox, 1984.

Paul, Shalom M. *Studies in the Book of the Covenant in the Light of Cuneiform and Biblical Law*. Leiden: Brill, 1970.

Pedersen, Johs. *Israel: Its Life and Culture*. London: Oxford University Press, 1926.

Perry, Frank L. *Sex and the Bible*. Atlanta: Christian Education Research Institute, 1982.

Philo. *De Specialibus Legibus.* Translated by André Mosès. Paris: Cerf, 1970.

Phillips, Anthony. *Ancient Israel's Criminal Law.* New York: Schocken, 1970.

_____. "Another Look at Adultery." *JSOT* 20 (1981): 3–25.

_____. "The Decalogue—Ancient Israel's Criminal Law." *JJS* 34 (1983): 1–20.

_____. *Deuteronomy.* Cambridge: Cambridge University Press, 1973.

_____. "A Response to Dr. McKeating." *JSOT* 22 (1982): 142–43.

_____. "Some Aspects of Family Law in Pre-Exilic Israel." *VT* 23 (1973): 349–61.

_____. "Uncovering the Father's Skirt." *VT* 30 (1980): 32–43.

Phipps, William. "The Menstrual Taboo in the Judeo-Christian Tradition." *Journal of Religion and Health* 19 (1980): 298–303.

Pitt-Rivers, Julian. *The Fate of Shechem.* Cambridge: Cambridge University Press, 1977.

Plaskow, Judith, *Standing Again at Sinai.* San Francisco: Harper, 1990.

Porter, J. R. *The Extended Family in the Old Testament.* London: Edutext, 1967.

_____. *Leviticus.* Cambridge: Cambridge University Press, 1976.

Pressler, Carolyn. "Sexual Violence and Deuteronomic Law." Pages 102–22 in Brenner, ed., *A Feminist Companion to Exodus to Deuteronomy.*

_____. *The View of Women Found in the Deuteronomic Family Laws.* Berlin: de Gruyter, 1993.

_____. "Wives and Daughters, Bond and Free: Views of Women in the Slave Laws of Exodus 21.2–11." Pages 147–72 in Matthews, Levinson and Frymer-Kensky, eds., *Gender and Law in the Hebrew Bible.*

Preuss, Horst Dietrich. "בוא." *TDOT* 2:20-49.

Preuss, Julius. *Biblical and Talmudic Medicine.* Translated and edited by Fred Rosner. New York: Sanhedrin, 1978.

Rad, Gerhard von. *Deuteronomy.* Philadelphia: Westminster, 1966.

_____. *Studies in Deuteronomy.* Translated by David Stalker. Göttingen: Vandenhoeck & Ruprecht, 1948. Reprint London: SCM Press, 1953.

Rashkow, Ilona. *Taboo or Not Taboo: Sexuality and Family in the Hebrew Bible.* Minneapolis: Augsburg, 2000.

Rattray, Susan. "Marriage Rules, Kinship Terms and Family Structure in the Bible." Pages 537–44 in *SBL 1987 Seminar Papers.* SBLSP 26. Missoula, Mont.: Society of Biblical Literature, 1987.

Rendtorff, Rolf, and Robert A Kugler, eds. *The Book of Leviticus: Composition and Reception.* Leiden: Brill, 2003.

Reventlow, Henning Graf. *Das Heiligkeitsgesetz.* Neukirchen–Vluyn: Neukirchener Verlag, 1961.

Ringgren, H., and W. Kornfeld. "קדש." *ThWAT* 6:1188–201.

Rofé, A. "The Covenant in the Land of Moab (Dt 28,69–30,20)." Pages 310–20 in Lohfink, ed., *Das Deuteronomium.*

_____. "Family and Sex Laws in Deuteronomy and the Book of the Covenant." *Henoch* 9 (1987): 131–59.

_____. "The Laws of Warfare in the Book of Deuteronomy: Their Origins, Intent and Positivity," *JSOT* 32 (1985): 23–44.

_____. "Tenth Commandment in the Light of Four Deuteronomic Laws." Pages 45–65 in Levi, ed., *The Ten Commandments.*

Rowley, H. H. "The Marriage of Ruth." *HTR* 40 (1947): 77–99.

Sarah, Elizabeth. "Judaism and Lesbianism." Pages 95–101 in *Jewish Explorations of Sexuality.* Edited by Jonathan Magonet. Providence, R.I.: Berghahn, 1995.

Satlow, Michael L. " 'They Abused Him Like a Woman': Homoeroticism, Gender Blurring, and the Rabbis in Late Antiquity." *JHS* 5 (1994): 1–25.

Sawyer, Deborah F. *God, Gender and the Bible.* London: Routledge, 2002.

Schenker, Adrian. "What Connects the Incest Prohibitions with the Other Prohibitions Listed in Leviticus 18 and 20?" Pages 162–85 in Rendtorff and Kugler, eds., *The Book of Leviticus.*

Schlegel, Alice. "Status, Property, and the Value on Virginity." *American Ethnologist* 18 (1991): 719–34.

Schmitt, John J. "Virgin." *ABD* 6:853–54.

Schneider, Jane. "Of Vigilance and Virgins: Honor, Shame and Access to Resources in the Mediterranean Societies." *Ethnology* 10 (1971): 1–24.

Schottroff, Willy. *Der altisraelitische Fluchspruch.* Neukirchen–Vluyn: Neukirchener, 1969.

Schulz, Hermann. *Das Todesrecht im Alten Testament.* Berlin: A. Töpelmann, 1969.

Schwartz, Baruch J. "A Literary Study of the Slave-girl Pericope—Leviticus 19:20–22." Pages 1241–55 in Japhet, ed., *Scripta Hierosolymitana.*

Schweiker, William. "Power and the Agency of God." *Theology Today* 52 (July 1995): 204–24.

Seebass, H. "לָקַח." *TDOT* 8:16–21.

Sheres, Ita. *Dinah's Rebellion: A Biblical Parable for Our Time.* New York: Crossroad, 1990.

Shuttle, Penelope, and Peter Redgrove. *The Wise Wound.* New York: Grove, 1978.

Skinner, Quentin. "Motives, Intentions and the Interpretation of Texts." *New Literary History* 3 (1972): 393–408.

Snaith, N. A. *Leviticus.* London: Thomas Nelson, 1967.

Speiser, E. A. "Leviticus and the Critics." Pages 123–42 in *Oriental and Biblical Studies.* Edited by J. J. Finkelstein and Moshe Greenberg. Philadelphia: University of Pennsylvania Press, 1967.

Stamm, J. J., and M. E. Andrew. *The Ten Commandments in Recent Research.* Translated by M. E. Andrew. London: SCM Press, 1967.

Stone, Ken. "Gender and Homosexuality in Judges 19: Subject–Honor, Object–Shame?" *JSOT* 67 (1995): 87–107.

_____. ed., *Queer Commentary and the Hebrew Bible.* JSOTSup 334. Sheffield: Sheffield Academic Press, 2001.

_____. *Sex, Honor and Power in the Deuteronomistic History.* JSOTSup 234. Sheffield: Sheffield Academic Press, 1996.

Stulman, Louis. "Sex and Familial Crimes in the D Code: A Witness to Mores in Transition." *JSOT* 53 (1992): 47–63.

Sun, Henry. "An Investigation into the Compositional Integrity of the So-Called Holiness Code (Leviticus 17–26)." Ph.D. diss., Claremont Graduate School, 1982.

Suzuki, Yoshihide. "The 'Numeruswechsel' in Deuteronomy." Ph.D. diss., Claremont Graduate School, 1982.

Swidler, Leonard. *Biblical Affirmations of Woman.* Philadelphia: Westminster. 1979.

_____. *Women in Judaism.* Metuchen: Scarecrow, 1976.

Taber, C. R. "Sex, Sexual Behavior." *IDBSup* 817–20.

Taylor, Charles. *Sources of the Self.* Cambridge, Mass.: Harvard University Press, 1989.

Thistlethwaite, Susan Brooks. "'You May Enjoy the Spoil of Your Enemies': Rape as a Biblical Metaphor for War." *Semeia* 61 (1993): 59–75.

Thompson, Thomas, and Dorothy Thompson. "Some Legal Problems in the Book of Ruth." *VT* 18 (1968): 79–99.

Thomson, William A. R. *Black's Medical Dictionary.* 33rd ed. Totowa: Barnes & Noble, 1981.

Tigay, Jeffrey H. *Deuteronomy.* Philadelphia: The Jewish Publication Society of America, 1996.

_____. "Some Principles of Arrangement in the Laws of Deuteronomy." Paper presented as part of Biblical Law Group at the Annual Society of Biblical Literature Meeting, November 1994.

Toeg, A. "Does Deuteronomy XXIV, 1–4 Incorporate a General Law on Divorce?" *Dine Israel* 2 (1970): v–xxiv.

Tov, Emanuel. *Textual Criticism of the Hebrew Bible.* Minneapolis: Fortress, 1992.

Tosato, Angelo. "Joseph, Being a Just Man (Matt 1:19)." *CBQ* 41 (1979): 547–51.

_____. "The Law of Leviticus 18:18: A Reexamination." *CBQ* 46 (1984): 199–214.

Troyer, Kristen de. "Blood: A Threat to Holiness or toward (Another Holiness)?" Pages 45–64 in De Troyer et al. eds., *Wholly Woman Holy Blood.*

Troyer, Kristin de, Judith A. Herbert, Judith Ann Johnson and Anne-Marie Korte, eds. *Wholly Woman Holy Blood: A Feminist Critique of Purity and Impurity.* New York: Trinity, 2003.

Tsevat, M. "בְּתוּלָה." *TDOT* 2:338–43.

Van der Toorn, K. "Female Prostitution in Payment of Vows in Ancient Israel." *JBL* 108 (1989): 193–205.

_____. "Prostitution (Cultic)." *ABD* 5:510–13.

_____. *Sin and Sanction in Israel and Mesopotamia.* Assen: Van Gorcum, 1985.

Van Selms, A. "The Goring Ox in Babylonian and Biblical Law." *Archiv Orientálni* 18 (1950): 321–30.

Vaux, Roland de. *Ancient Israel*, vol. 1. New York: McGraw–Hill, 1965.

Wallis, G. "חָמַד." *TDOT* 4:452–61.

Walsh, Jerome T. "Leviticus 18:22 and 20:13: Who Is Doing What to Whom?" *JBL* 120 (2001): 201–9.

Waltke, Bruce K., and M. O'Conner. *Biblical Hebrew Syntax.* Winona Lake, Ind.: Eisenbrauns, 1990.

Walton, John H. "The Place of the *hutqaṭṭēl* within the D-Stem Group and Its Implications in Deuteronomy 24:4." *HS* 32 (1991): 7–17.

Walzer, Michael. *Just and Unjust Wars.* New York: Basic, 1977.

Washington, Harold. "'Lest He Die in the Battle and Another Man Take Her': Violence and the Construction of Gender in the Laws of Deuteronomy 20–22." Pages 185–213 in Matthews, Levinson and Frymer-Kensky, eds., *Gender and Law in the Hebrew Bible.*

Wegner, Judith Romney. *Chattel or Person?* New York: Oxford University Press, 1988.

_____. "'Coming Before the Lord': The Exclusion of Women from the Public Domain of the Israelite Priestly Cult." Pages 451–65 in Rendtorff and Kugler, eds., *The Book of Leviticus.*

_____. "Leviticus." Pages 36–44 in Newsom and Ringe, eds., *The Women's Bible Commentary.*

Wegner, Volker. *Rechtssätze in gebundener Sprache und Rechtssatzreihen im israelitischen Recht.* Vandenhoeck & Ruprecht. Reprint London: SCM Press, 1963.

Weinfeld, Moshe.

_____. "The Decalogue: Its Significance, Uniqueness, and Place in Israel's Tradition." Pages 3–47 in Firmage, Weiss and Welch, eds., *Religion and Law.*

_____. *Deuteronomy 1–11.* New York: Doubleday, 1991.

_____. *Deuteronomy and the Deuteronomic School.* Winona Lake, Ind.: Eisenbrauns, 1992.

_____. "Deuteronomy, Book of." *ABD* 2:168–83.

_____. "Deuteronomy: The Present State of Inquiry." Pages 21–35 in Christensen, ed., *A Song of Power.*

_____. "The Emergence of the Deuteronomic Movement, The Historical Antecedents." Pages 76–98 in Lohfink, ed., *Das Deuteronomium.*

_____. "On 'Demythologization and Secularization' in Deuteronomy." *IEJ* 23 (1973): 230–33.

_____. "The Origin of the Humanism in Deuteronomy." *JBL* 80 (1961): 241–47.

_____. "The Uniqueness of the Decalogue and Its Place in Jewish Tradition." Pages 1–44 in Levi, ed., *The Ten Commandments.*

_____. "The Worship of Molech and of the Queen of Heaven and Its Background." *UF* 4 (1972): 133–54.

Weisberg, Dvora E. "The Widow of Our Discontent: Levirate Marriage in the Bible and Ancient Israel." *JSOT* 28 (2004): 403–29.

Weiss, David Halivni. "A Note on אשר לא ארשה." *JBL* 8 (1962): 67–69.

Wenham, Gordon J. "*Bᵉtûlāh* 'A Girl of Marriageable Age.'" *VT* 22 (1972): 326–48.

_____. "The Biblical View of Marriage and Divorce: 2—Old Testament Teaching." *Third Way* 1, no. 21 (1977): 7–9.

_____. *Leviticus*. Grand Rapids: Eerdmans, 1979.

_____. "The Restoration of Marriage Reconsidered." *JJS* 17 (1966): 36–40.

_____. "Why Does Sexual Intercourse Defile (Lev 15:18)?" *ZAW* 95 (1983): 432–35.

Wenham, Gordon J., and J. G. McConville. "Drafting Techniques in Some Deuteronomic Laws." *VT* 30 (1979): 248–51.

Westbrook, Raymond. "Adultery in Ancient Near Eastern Law." *RB* 97 (1990): 543–44.

_____. "The Female Slave." Pages 214–38 in Matthews, Levinson and Frymer-Kensky, eds., *Gender and Law in the Hebrew Bible*.

_____. "The Law of the Biblical Levirate." *RIDA* 24 (1977): 65–87.

_____. "Old Babylonian Marriage Law," vol. 2. Ph.D. diss., Yale University, 1982.

_____. "The Prohibition on Restoration of Marriage in Deuteronomy 24:1–4." Pages 387–405 in Japhet, ed., *Scripta Hierosolymitana*.

_____. *Property and the Family in Biblical Law*. JSOTSup 113. Sheffield: JSOT Press, 1991.

_____. "Punishments and Crimes." *ABD* 5:546–56.

_____. *Studies in Biblical and Cuneiform Law*. Paris: J. Gabalda et Cie, 1988.

Whitekettle, Richard. "Leviticus 12 and the Israelite Woman: Ritual Process Liminality and the Womb." *ZAW* 107 (1995): 393–408.

_____. "Leviticus 15.18: Reconstructed Chiasm, Spatial Structure and the Body." *JSOT* 49 (1991): 31–45.

_____. "Levitical Thought and the Female Reproductive Cycle: Wombs, Wellsprings, and the Primeval World." *VT* 46 (1996): 376–91.

Wold, Donald J. "The *Kareth* Penalty in P: Rationale and Cases." Pages 1–45 in vol. 1 of *SBL 1979 Seminar Papers*. 2 vols. SBLSP 16–17. Missoula, Mont.: Scholars Press, 1979.

Wright, David P. *The Disposal of Impurity*. Atlanta: Scholars Press, 1987.

_____. "The Spectrum of Priestly Impurity." Pages 151–81 in *Priesthood and Cult in Ancient Israel*. Edited by Gary A. Anderson and Saul M. Olyan. JSOTSup 125. Sheffield: Sheffield Academic Press, 1991.

_____. "Two Types of Impurity in the Priestly Writings of the Bible." *Koroth* 9 (1988): 180–93.

_____. "Unclean and Clean (Old Testament)." *ABD* 6:729–30.

Wright, David P., and Richard N. Jones. "Discharge." *ABD* 2:205.

Yadin, Yigael, ed. *The Temple Scroll*. Jerusalem: Israel Exploration Society, 1983.

Yaron, G. R. "On Divorce in Old Testament Times." *RIDA* 4 (1957): 117–28.

_____. "The Restoration of Marriage." *JJS* 17 (1966): 1–11.

Zakovitch, Yair. "The Woman's Rights in the Biblical Law of Divorce." Pages 28–46 in *The Jewish Law Annual*, vol. 4. Edited by Bernard S. Jackson. Leiden: Brill, 1981.

Zipor, M. "Restrictions on Marriage for Priests (Lev. 21,7.13–14)." *Biblica* 68 (1987): 259–67.

Ziskind, Jonathan R. "The Missing Daughter in Leviticus XVIII." *VT* 46 (1996): 125–30.

INDEXES

INDEX OF REFERENCES

INDEX OF AUTHORS